THE MYTH OF THE
WELFARE STATE

THE MYTH OF THE WELFARE STATE

Jack D. Douglas

Transaction Publishers
New Brunswick (U.S.A.) and London (U.K.)

First paperback reprint 1991

Copyright © 1989 by Transaction Publishers
New Brunswick, New Jersey 08903

Library of Congress Catalog Number: 88-16861
ISBN 0-88738-246-0 (cloth); 0-88738-874-4 (paper)
Printed in the United States of America

Library of Congress Cataloging-in-Publication Data

Douglas, Jack D.
    The myth of the welfare state.

    Includes index.
    1. Individualism.   2. Liberty.   3. Collectivism.   4. Welfare state.
I. Title.
    JC571.D76 1988   320.5'12--dc 19   88-16861
    ISBN 0-88738-246-0

Contents

Modern man is lost in the mass in a way which is without precedent in history. . . . In a thousand different ways mankind has been persuaded to give up its natural relations with reality and to seek its welfare in the magic formulas of some kind of economic and social witchcraft, by which the possibility of freeing itself from the economic and social misery is only still further removed. And the tragic meaning of these magic formulas, to whatever kind of economic and social witchcraft they may belong, is always just this, that the individual must give up his own material and spiritual personality and must live only as one of the spiritually restless and materialistic multitude which claims control over him. . . .The great conflict of our times is personality versus collectivism. In our times the spirit of Hegal and the spirit of Goethe are fighting everywhere. Collectivism in its various forms has deprived the individual of his individuality. All the troubles of the world come from this. The task immediately before us is to safeguard the integrity of the individual within the modern state. I have great confidence in the individual forces of the spirit. The future depends on them. If these spiritual forces are brought into play, the world's future will be improved. . . .The final decision as to what the future of a society shall be depends not on how near its organization is to perfection, but on the degree of worthiness in its individual members.

Albert Schweitzer

It is beyond the power of philosophy to destroy the political myths. A myth is in a sense invulnerable. It is impervious to rational arguments; it cannot be refuted by syllogisms. But philosophy can do us another important service. It can make us understand the adversary. In order to fight an enemy you must know him. That is one of the first principles of a sound strategy. To know him means not only to know his defects and weaknesses; it means to know his strength. All of us have been liable to underrate this strength. When we first heard of the political myths we found them so absurd and incongruous, so fantastic and ludicrous that we could hardly be prevailed upon to take them seriously. By now it has become clear to all of us that this was a great mistake. We should not commit the same error a second time. We should carefully study the origins, the structure, the methods, and the technique of the political myths. We should see the adversary face to face in order to know how to combat him.

Ernst Cassirer

Acknowledgments

I have planned to write a book explaining the great tidal drifts of imperial state powers since my high school years, when I discovered the scholarly joys of reading Pitirim Sorokin, Arnold Toynbee, Joseph Spengler, and so many other exciting explorers of these awesome mysteries of human life. Though I came eventually to see some fundamental flaws in their macro-perspective on human life, and have had to take very different approaches to explain the great tidal drifts of the waxings and wanings of statist powers, this work began with them and is still grounded in many of their brilliant insights.

They were crucial in my decision as a freshman at Harvard to avoid all the professional careerism and blinders that have long afflicted social scientists and humanists. I set out to study human beings from all perspectives that offered any hope of throwing light upon the great mysteries that envelop us in darkness (if I may indulge in an emanationist point of enlightenment—see appendix IV). I obviously had to choose a profession to get one of the Ph.D. licenses prerequisite in our bureaucratized world to an academic job that would allow me the leisure to pursue this quest. I chose sociology, the official moniker of Pitirim Sorokin, who had just been forced into emeritus exile at Harvard, because it seemed to bridge the ever-widening cultural gaps between commonsense wisdom, the other social sciences, and the humanities better than any of the other professions. Though the "sociological imagination" has been starved and greatly distorted in recent decades by the government-financed and -regulated academic bureaucracies of scientism, this decision was probably wise. We still manage to live and find leisure enough for such works as this in the many niches not yet completely controlled by the bureaucrats.

Most of my published work for the past twenty years has been concerned with the fundamental problems of discovering the truth about the details of everyday life and then explaining them. As I explained in *Investigative Social Research* many years ago, I had come to realize with a shock that most of the work in the social sciences was built on misinformation and disinformation, including the carefully constructed theodicies and propaganda of some statist bureaucratic information. Though their commonsense wisdom and clear-eyed scholarship, unblinded by professional blinkers, saved Sorokin and the other theorists of cultural drift from most of these pitfalls and snares, they did not realize how fundamental the problems were. It will be obvious to anyone who knows about these great epistemological issues in the social sciences, and knows my own earlier works on those, that this work is built firmly on the foundations of the so called "everyday life" perspective. That is, it begins with the raw realities of individuals doing real things in real life, undistorted by bureaucratic or academic preconceptions, and builds upward to more general ideas. I obviously owe an immense amount to all of the many people who have toiled with me over the decades in the trenches of everyday life—uncovering, preserving, honing, grasping, understanding and explaining the raw facts of all human life.

I began this work over ten years ago while on a sabbatical from the University of California and a fellowship from the Guggenheim Foundation which provided the leisure to study British socialism firsthand, down in the labyrinthine coils of one of the socialist megastates that bureaucratizes life even more than our American megastate. I have given early drafts of pieces of this work at conferences sponsored by many foundations and academic groups. This has allowed me to present the facts and ideas to small groups of hundreds of scholars and scientists from all the major disciplines. This work was truly forged in the fiery crucibles of intellectual teamwork and combat. Though I cannot name all the individuals who have helped so much, I owe special thanks to the Liberty Fund, the Institute for Humane Studies, the Reason Foundation, the Center for Libertarian Studies, and, very recently, the Rockford Foundation.

It will be apparent to all scholars that all of the points in this work could be buttressed and attacked by clouds of footnotes. I have chosen not to engage in such pedantic battles. I have cited only the ones most important to my important points. I am quite aware of thousands of other works that have contributed to my argument and certainly of the many thousands of statist works that disagree. I expect most readers are as well. Since I have no desire to obscure the important with the obvious, I keep them to a minimum and get on with it.

I have also tried to avoid all the pitfalls of official statistics. I warn here and repeatedly in the work that all official information is highly problematic. I have chosen statistics carefully, use them only after due consideration of pros and cons, and use even the best such information only as guesstimates of orders of magnitude. There are endless debates among the denizens of the pulp industry over decimals, such as the exact percentage of the real gross national product the Reagan administration spent last year. Everyone with any experience knows that we now have a massive and growing underground economy, but no one knows anything precise about its magnitude. Official statistical data on our economy do not take that fact into consideration. Thus, they are only *very* rough guesstimates of reality, and arguments over decipoints are much less worthwhile than arguments over how many angels can dance on the head of a pin.

My wife has worked assiduously over the years as managing editor and librarian for this far-flung work. She has certainly done more than anyone else to bring it to fruition, often under difficult circumstances. Sue Sullivan has worked for us under the great stress of deadlines, doing brilliant computer work and word processing. John Hillebrand did yeoman library assistance on some of the early drafts. The Academic Senate of the University of California at San Diego helped greatly with grants for this research.

Finally, the indomitable Irving Louis Horowitz and his colleagues at Transaction have been most supportive during our massive and painful labors over the final, final draft.

Introduction

It has been frequently remarked that it seems to have been reserved to the people of this country, by their conduct and example, to decide the important question, whether societies of men are really capable or not of establishing good government from reflection and choice, or whether they are forever destined to depend for their political constitutions on accident and force. If there be any truth in the remark, the crisis at which we are arrived may with propriety be regarded as the era in which that decision is to be made; and a wrong election of the part we shall act may, in this view, be considered as the general misfortune of mankind.

The Federalist, No. 1

The ten years during which I have worked on this book have been years of tumultuous political changes, though, as usual, far more in rhetoric than in actions. When I began the Chinese had barely recovered from the era of the Maoist Empire and the Great Cultural Revolution that were intended to catapult them into Mao's ninth heaven of millennial bliss, but had cast them instead into mass starvation and civil war. The Soviets were still mired in the Brezhnev era's smug conviction that the central planning of the communist bureaucracy was going to usher in utopia on the Volga and bury Western economies. The Japanese were busily making automobiles and electronic equipment, but had barely emerged on the scene of international finance and were little noted nor much feared there by Western competitors. Western bankers and government officials had gone on an orgy of recycling petrodollars to Third World bureaucrats and were heartily congratulating themselves on this miraculous scheme for making the deserts bloom. American intellectuals were still half-convinced the communists were right and were issuing grand proclamations, similar to those of the ill-fated Club of Rome, proclaiming our freer economy was doomed to massive shortages of oil, food, and everything else. French intellectuals, as usual, were dreaming of socialist glories just beyond the next election, and when it brought the beatification of Mitterrand's neo-Keynesian socialism they danced in the streets—heaven

1

had arrived on earth at last. In Britain the intellectuals were striving valiantly to prove to themselves that Britain's century-long drift into the status of "sickman of Europe" did not matter because genteel poverty and good intentions are more important, while James Callahan's socialists were beating the drum for welfare-statism and were well ahead of Margaret Thatcher's hearty band of reformationists in the polls.

In these ten years we have seen many striking reversals of these political skits of gloom and doom, hope and euphoria, decay and bright renewal. The Chinese and the Soviets have admitted that their earlier rulers lied in their official histories and statistics, have proclaimed "near revolutions" against the orthodox collectivism of their own parties, and have vowed to soar onward and upward with economic "restructuring" and democratic "openness." Zhao Ziyang has just proclaimed to the Thirteenth National Congress of the Chinese Communist Party that "whatever is conducive [to China's economic growth] is in keeping with the fundamental interests of the people and is therefore needed and allowed to exist by socialism." He has also redefined such capitalistic measures as free markets to be the "primary stage" of socialism itself, so that capitalism is no longer merely a predecessor of socialism, as Marx proclaimed, but is actually part of socialism. Mikhail Gorbachev has proclaimed, both officially and in a best-selling book reaping capitalistic profits in America, that the future utopia on the Volga no longer works and has actually entered a "precrisis stage," which is a euphemism for the official Marxist category of "pre-revolutionary stage." He is striving mightily to create capitalistic communism, in the name of Marxist orthodoxy, and democracy without freedom, in the name of total freedom.

The Japanese are still busily making automobiles and electronic equipment, though increasingly in Korea and other nations, but they have also exploded into the international financial markets and Western journalists, awestruck by the "yen tide," now publish daily headlines about the "dollar crisis." The "American Challenge" so much ballyhooed in the 1970s has been transliterated into the "Japanese Challenge." Vast cadres of American intellectuals have become neo-Marxists and are rabidly "deconstructing" all thinking, while the American people have undergone a "Reagan Revolution" widely believed to have "gotten the government off the backs of the people," but which in fact has increased the federal government's spending of the gross national product at a faster pace than that of any other peacetime administration and increased the national debt by 100 percent in a dramatic display of neo-Keynesianism in the name of fiscal conservatism. American journalists have forgotten all about the Club of Rome and gone back to denouncing rampant consumerism, capitalistic greed, and our failure to solve all the problems of hunger created by socialists around the world. The French people have discovered that dancing in the streets for socialism leaves a nation with a bad economic hangover, and have launched de-socializing schemes under Mitterrand's socialist government, while legions of "creative" French intellectuals have discovered that the ideas about economic freedom created by the physiocrats in the eighteenth century may have something worth considering after all. The British people have elected "Iron Maggie" to a record third term by a landslide, thereby proclaiming their disgust with sinking happily into the demoralized embrace of poverty and decline, while many British intellectual Marxists have emigrated to the United States to get higher salaries.

None of this neorealistic rhetoric means that we are witnessing a turning of the tides of political ideas and practices. As much as I would dearly love to think so, and however confident I am that we shall some day do so, I am not hereby proclaiming a rebirth of freedom. As I shall argue throughout this book, reality is inherently quite uncertain and we can predict neither precise events nor the timing of catastrophic changes in trends. All of the history of civilizations shows that great increases in statist bureaucratic powers eventually produce stagnation, often greatly exacerbated by rampant inflation, and this in turn eventually produces wanings of statist powers. But history also shows that these great waxings and wanings follow various paths that are not predictable in their details or timings, and that the wanings are normally accompanied by the catastrophes of rebellions, revolutions, or foreign conquests—"times of troubles," as they have been called for many centuries. We have not yet entered a great "time of troubles." We could do so any day, as, perhaps, the great rows of "dominoes" of highly risky debts run up by our monstrous states in pursuit of their modernist illusions collapse. But this is not a fate to which we are doomed, as many gloom and doom experts now proclaim. With a modicum of common sense and economic technology, the politicians could turn back from the bankruptcy precipice toward which we are now headed, just as they turned back from the hyperinflation escalator we were approaching in the 1970s. It takes uncommon stupidity and bad luck to instantaneously precipitate a great systemic crisis. There are normally many reforms that overcome short-run crises, but do not reverse the long-run drift, before a society enters a period of self-reinforcing crises (see chapters 7 and 8) that culminate in a great crisis. There are also normally many "false turnings of the tides," periods of temporary pauses and even slight reversals in the great drift process, that hide the long-run trend at the time. The 1950s were such a period of temporary reversal of modernism and statism in the United States, which many people at the time mistook for a turning of the tides of history, until the great ratchets-up came in the 1960s. Many others thought the "Reagan Revolution" marked the sure turning of the tides in the early 1980s. Then his administration presided over an explosion in deficit spending and a 10 percent increase in the federal government's expenditure of the gross national product. The great turning back turned out to be a symbolically concealed gallop into statism.

The convoluted political permutations, combinations, and transformations that we have witnessed in the past ten years are partly real, but they are far more examples of the vast unpredictability and changability of political rhetoric in our world of mass-mediated politics. They are examples above all of the immense self-deceptions suffered today, of the omnipresent deceits perpetrated by rulers marching under polychromatic and blinking neon banners, of the great successes of deceits in our age of "agitprop," and of the multifarious fads and foibles that so often pass for serious thinking in an age of mass-mediated rationalism, scientism, technologism, credentialism, and expertism. They are excellent examples of the tremendous problems we face in our attempts to truthfully analyze social trends, no matter how cautious and objective the attempt, and of the even-greater problems we face in communicating those analyses in a world in which the most important words are routinely used as political weapons in a manner that would shock even Lewis Carol's Humpty-Dumpty.

Politics in the vast and complex societies called civilizations have always been ruled by the iron law of political deceit, which assures us that deceit tends on average to drive truth out of the political marketplace to the degree that the constituents have little direct experience with the objects of deceit (such as those portrayed in official economic statistics and press releases about international affairs). But the immense complexity and collectivization of worldwide civilization today has made political deceit more effective than at any previous time in human history. The average intelligence quotient has probably not budged since tiny civilizations were first created roughly five thousand years ago, but the average ignorance quotient about relevant economics and politics has soared in this century.

Early rulers from Egypt to China made state secrets of astronomical predictions that gave them the appearance of controlling the heavens and the life-giving waters, they systematically controlled and corrupted the historical accounts of intellectuals and bureaucrats to glorify their powers, they trained the young intellectuals in state schools to become servile singers of praise for the states and rulers, and they used the pseudoscientists of astrology and other esoterica to mystify the people. Yet their powers were inherently limited by the simplicity and small scale of their world. Astronomers and their pharaoh masters could awe the people by their simple knowledge of the annual movements of Sirius and the correlation of this with the overflow of the Nile, which made them remarkably more effective economic predictors than computerized econometric models make our politicians, but everyone shared the same basic cultural experience of peasant life and it was undoubtedly hard to mislead a small nation of several million people about conditions of farming or village life. How totally different it is today even in something as relatively simple as farming. The average American now has almost no knowledge of farming and is easily led down endless and labyrinthine primrose paths by the myriad government programs pronounced in esoteric tomes by government "experts" to be solutions to problems in the international grain markets. Anyone who proposes anything commonsensical to reverse the plumeting share of American agricultural exports in the world markets, such as "get the bureaucrats off the backs of the farmers," is easily buried in an avalanche of political statistics of factoids, commodity epicycles, regression misanalyses, microanalyses of indifference curves, and macro-econometric simulations. Since, as David Stockman has borne testimony from inside the great labyrinthe, the "experts" themselves almost never know what these numbers really mean, and since no one knows much with certainty about anything as inherently uncertain and rapidly changing as international markets, it is easy to mystify most of the public most of the time and paralyze them with political agitprop.

Indeed, it is central to my argument that most of the mistakes and mythifications being perpetrated politically are not even intentional. The politicians themselves are normally quite ignorant of the overall facts and quite mystified by it all. They present carefully coiffed images of themselves to the world as the founts of knowledge and wisdom, but the private realities reveal that they are commonly ignorant of the most basic facts of the most important apparatuses of their own huge governments. For example, James Tobin, one of the foremost economists advising John Kennedy on how to project his profiles of economic omniscience, has revealed that on Inauguration Day the newly elected president needed tutoring on the working of the Federal Reserve, presumably so that he could better plan our vastly complex world economy.

Such "cram sessions," combined with ghostwritten speeches of sonorous wisdom, ear-plugs, and teleprompters, now allow our politicians to flash bright images around the world of their presiding confidently over the vast realms of their bureaucracies wisely planning the lives of us all. These pretensions and deceits are eventually unmasked but are always replaced by similar Machiavellian contrivances, so they succeed in fooling most of the voters most of the time. Our politics have been turned into sleazy confidence games that rob the people not only of their fortunes, and some times of their lives, but of truth itself, on which the success of everything ultimately depends. As Edward Tufte and many others have shown in detail, and as I have argued in general in earlier works, our "welfare states" are now literally gigantic political machines in which everything, even life itself, is bought and sold for money, votes, and power.

In view of this soaring average ignorance quotient and political corruption, it should not be surprising to find that the language and ideas for discussing politics and political economics is a total muddle to most people. This verbal muddying of political discourse is vitally important in deceiving them into supporting the growth of the modernist megastates. Most revealing of all is the fact that our mass-media, mass-education, and mass-political rhetoric are now almost always based on the assumption that political views and actions divide nicely along a continuum from "leftist liberal" to "rightist conservative." No one who knows the ABC's of politics believes this, but it is an item of faith in public discourse. It is little wonder, then, that even most ostensibly serious discussions of politics are little more than a verbal hash.

In America today "liberal" generally means "collectivist" in economics, the exact opposite of what it meant until recent decades and still means in most of the world; but it also generally means "anti-police power" for some forms of erstwhile "crime," such as drugs and abortion, and totally "pro-police power" for some new forms of "economic crime." (In appendix I, I have tried to present the clearest possible American meanings of the political labels most commonly used today.) Educated Americans today are genuinely perplexed to learn that Adolph Hitler was a self-proclaimed "socialist," since they do not know that "Nazi" was his acronym for his Party, the National Socialist Workers' Party, are almost completely ignorant of the Nazis' economic planning, and assume the Nazis were "conservative right-wingers" because they fought their fellow collectivists, the communists, for power. (Nazism and communism were in fact two distinct but closely related brands of collectivism, among many, which competed for support under various names, guises, and realities. Hitler learned immensely from the Bolsheviks, and later communist statist engineers learned from him.) They are equally astounded to learn that Teddy Kennedy is far more "socialist" in the normal sense of that term today than many Swedish or West German "socialists." When the certified "expert" in politics does not know the difference between a "Burkean conservative" and a "Tory conservative," and believes that Nazism was in fact, and not merely in political rhetoric, a "conservative" reaction against "communism, it is not surprising to find that political thinking in the mass media is a rank stew indeed.

Twenty years ago the term "welfare state" was rarely used to refer to the American megastate, probably because its historical association with British socialism still offended too many Americans. Today "welfare state" is a hot term in the American mass media. It should not be surprising, in view of the verbal muddle and mass deceit in our popular political terminology, to find that such a hot label is one of the most misleading, mythifying, and deceitful of all political terms today. The ostensible meaning of the term is simple. A welfare state is a state asserted by its rulers and other supporters to be dedicated to the welfare of the citizens. But this obvious meaning is absurd to anyone who examines it the least bit critically. *What state has ever been presented by its rulers and other supporters as a "dyswelfare state"?* Is it conceivable to anyone with common sense that a ruler who wants to remain a ruler would announce to his subjects, "I rule not to increase your welfare, but to bring you dyswelfare—poverty, misery, suffering, and a great knashing of teeth"? Such a skit might be a very funny scene in a postmodernist spoof on the absurdities of today's political rhetoric, but it is obvious that sane rulers make such proclamations only to potential enemies, not to the subjects whose support they must have to rule. Though it is not so obvious, it also seems likely that almost all rulers have also believed their powers were necessary for the welfare of the whole state.

The use of the term welfare state implicitly assumes that the traditional—ancient or premodernist—governments in our Western nations were in fact dyswelfare states that brought misery to the people or, at least, did not care what happened to them. Since our traditional, constitutional System of Natural Liberty (as it was called) and the comparable democracies elsewhere presided over the greatest explosion of freedom, philanthropy, creativity, economic production, happiness, patriotism, and optimism in history, and since these are all elements of welfare alluded to in the term welfare state, it is preposterous to assert that our traditional leaders produced dyswelfare in general *and* to imply that they intended to do so. Since our American constitutionalists also believed firmly and announced to all the world that "that government governs best which governs least," it is equally preposterous to assert that they opposed Big Government of the sort we now have because they were against the welfare of the people. The leading founders of the American system of strictly limited government proclaimed that all forms of Big Government are inherently evil—that they are repressive by their very nature and are, therefore, the most awful form of dyswelfare state, in modernist terms. With the partial exception of Theodore Roosevelt, all U.S. presidents and the great majority of other leaders have pronounced Big Government to be necessarily a dyswelfare state, even when most of them have energetically built our present megastate. Their denunciations of Big Government have echoed in all eras and all corners of our land:

> He has erected a multitude of New offices, and sent hither swarms of Officers to harass our People, and eat out their substance. . .
>
> Declaration of Independence

> Those who would give up essential liberty to purchase a little temporary safety deserve neither liberty nor safety.
>
> Benjamin Franklin

Beware of energetic governments. They are always oppressive. . . .If we can prevent government from wresting the labors of the people under the pretense of caring for them, we shall be happy.

Thomas Jefferson

Those who won our independence believed that the final end of the State was to make men free to develop their faculties. . .they valued liberty both as an end and as a means. They believed liberty to be the secret of happiness and courage to be the secret of liberty. . .Experience should teach us to be most on our guard to protect liberty when the Government's purposes are beneficent. Men born to freedom are naturally alert to repel invasion of their liberty by evil-minded rulers. The greatest dangers to liberty lurk in insidious encroachment by men of zeal, well-meaning but without understanding.

Louis D. Brandeis

A history of liberty is the history of the limitations of government powers, not the increase of it.

Woodrow Wilson

These, of course, are merely examples of the vast number of denunciations of Big Government by American leaders. I need hardly remind any reader that all of our recent presidents—Richard Nixon, Gerald Ford, Jimmy Carter, and Ronald Reagan—have been far more extreme than most earlier presidents in these denunciations of "caring" Big Government and in their arguments that it is a matter of life and death for our freedoms and our faltering prosperity to "get government off the backs of the people."

The fact is that rulers always threaten dyswelfare (the stick) to those who threaten their rule, but they normally are even more profuse in promising welfare (the carrot cake) to anyone who will submit to their rule or support it. All sane statist rulers have been welfare statists, just as all our sane republican leaders were welfare federationists. All mentally competent children understand the same iron rule of threats-and-inveiglements that rulers use to govern states, and the children use it in their dealings with pets, other children, and adults. As we shall see, the earliest recorded proclamations of statist rulers either take it for granted, when dealing with their more-contented subjects, or strenuously insist on it, when dealing with people who obviously doubted their good intentions.

The core meaning of welfare state is, then, completely absurd. The term is a weapon of political agitation and propaganda—agitprop. It would be immediately seen as such were the great mass of people not firmly in the grip of some dimensions of the myths of the modernist welfare states. It is these myths that make the absurd appear rational and taken for granted as sacred truth. The great myth of modernism in its fully developed form is made up of the passionate convictions that human nature is either nonexistent or inherently good and inherently extremely plastic, hence overwhelmingly determined by cultural conditioning; that the earliest human beings were noble savages who hunted and gathered in the pristine (unpolluted) innocence of peaceful and cooperative hordes ("The Good Life"), who inhabited a heaven on earth (Nature) in which freedom, equality, prosperity with no meaningless toil, and casual sex reigned; that the noble savages were conquered and repressed (chained) by the ancient regime of historical traditions (superstitions) enforced by the bourgeois church and state; that reason and science broke or will break these chains of conservative repressions; and that the good community of (pure and poor) scientists is creating in their own image a world of rationality, freedom, and happiness that transcends (revolutionizes) all of the historical conservativeness of the ancient regime. Modernists, then, assume themselves and the parts of the world they control to be vastly superior to all previous civilizations and their miserable, repressed denizens; and they assume they are marching resolutely toward the new heaven on earth, the secular millennium just around the corner. The realm of the history of civilizations is the realm of evil and should be studied, if at all, only to show what satanic pollution is like, what must be transcended in a great burst of purifying light—revolution.

Renaissance scholars saw themselves as pygmies standing on the shoulders of intellectual giants, in the same way that almost all previous human beings had seen themselves as standing upon the immense bodies of accumulated commonsense wisdom, laws, and customs. Complete modernists see themselves as gods soaring on the wings of their own unchained, annihilating, burning reason and on the purity of their good intentions. It is this myth of their own purity and rationality which leads them to scoff at the dread our constitutionalists had of all great concentrations of power and most of all of government power, of the awful Leviathan. The founding fathers believed with the ancients that great power eventually produces self-righteous arrogance or hubris which in turn produces corruption of reason and terrible abuses of all the rights of the weak. The modernist sweeps all such ancient wisdom aside with scorn and denial. For the modernist political hubris has become the supreme virtue and the guarantor of universal equality.

The great myth of modernism is what mythologists call a *monomyth*, though it might better be called a monomaniacal myth. In its weaker variations it pervades, underlies, and overarches our dominant public culture, though it obviously coexists with many other myths in our still pluralistic civilization and is quite shunned by millions in some of our subcultures. Few Americans outside of our ivy-covered institutions of pure rationalism are complete modernists. Most true believers vary in their emphases on its many dimensions, and the more millennial strains of the myth are normally found only in situations of extremely ambivalent conflict between hope and despair which trigger extreme millennialism (see chapter 6). Indeed, complete modernists, such as the godly Lenin or Stalin, would see the modernism of most of our democratic welfare-statists as pale stuff indeed. American modernists have generally been more pragmatic than their European and British coreligionists, and far more so than the communist modernists. (Some of the most abstract intellectuals have now admitted the need for revisionism, but most of these "new-modernists" and "post-modernists," like their allies the neo-Marxists, are revising more of the rhetoric and public image than the heart of the faith.) More orthodox modernists, such as John Kenneth Galbraith or Teddy Kennedy, see our present welfare-statism as merely a compromise, a halfway house or Purgatory, one small step on the long journey to the New Heaven on Earth. (Anyone who doubts this need only consider how greatly our society would be transformed if these true believers were made Social Scientist Central Planners for a day.) The record also shows that every small ratchet-up leads them to call for bigger ratchets-up.

It is this dominant myth of modernism which makes the idea of the modern welfare state seem reasonable, even obviously true and taken for granted in most of what passes for serious political analysis in this golden age. Modernist society is vastly superior to all earlier civilization; modernist society is made up of welfare states; therefore, all earlier civilized states were made up of dyswelfare states. One can put this mythical syllogism in various ways, but the crucial point is that the ancient regimes were evil states dedicated to the dyswelfare of their subjects, because only our modernist states can be truly dedicated to the welfare of their "citizens." (Modernist states do not have "rulers" who exercise power. They have "leaders" who build consensuses by "reasoning." Hence, they have "citizens," not "subjects." Our vast police forces and gigantic military machines are merely embarrassing anachronisms of the ancient regime which will be transcended, no doubt as soon as the last unrepentant conservative is "regulated.") Most American welfare-statists are like pygmy modernists standing on the giant shoulders of Robespierre and quailing before the absolute purity of his motives, but we do have our Pure Scientists who are every bit as dedicated as the master of the guillotine was to purifying the whole world of the pollution of the ancient regime.

As is true of all great monomyths, the myth of the modernist welfare state is actually hybridized with or grafted onto the earlier convictions of the people, especially that of Judeo-Christianity in America. (That is why I noted above the earlier forms of the dimensions of the new myth.) Human beings are so inherently conserving of what has worked for them over the eons that they never completely give up the old, and any new great myth must absorb the most vital earlier convictions to be accepted. (In this standard format Mao Tse-tung consciously modeled his public image on that of the First Great Emperor of China from the third century B.C., and the Soviets modeled the giant icons of Lenin on those of the earlier saints, the apostleship of the politburo on that of the Church, and the nomenklatura of the Soviet bureaucracy on the bureaucracy of the czars.) Because of this, the welfare states in the most Christian Western states have strongly emphasized their supposed enactments of the Christian virtues—compassion, charity, forgiveness, kindliness, and so on, even when they have simultaneously been rabidly pursuing the seven deadly sins. (The Kennedy clan went one up on the Christian modernist welfare statists by purposefully identifying their reign with the realm of Camelot and singing of the Second Coming while mourning the murder of the Hero.) And in the United States the modernist welfare state has also had to be grafted onto that most intensely American value—freedom.

Thus it came to pass that the modernists attacking the ancient regimes did so most passionately in the very names of the sacred virtues of those ancient regimes. This is the only "good" nonreason why such a huge part of both the most mass-mediated and the most scientistic literature about our welfare states is concerned with questions of poverty, equality, and fraternity (community caring) and with individual freedom in the United States, even though it is at the same time anathema to those who most passionately embrace "community caring." The truth is that only a miniscule part of the modernist welfare state is concerned with the poor, or equality, or communal caring, and the whole idea of making people more free by giving greater political power over them all to politicians and millions of bureaucrats is bizarre in the extreme. The roughly one-tenth of the people politically labeled as poor are rich by any standards that have ever prevailed before in any society, they can never conceivably be made equal by building an immense hierarchy of politicians and bureaucrats upon their bent backs, and no one believes that bureaucrats will ever become as communally caring for the poor as nuns, priests, ministers, rabbis, maternalistic volunteers, and paternalistic gentries were in their immense charitable activities over the centuries of Western civilization. Moreover, anyone with experience of our "poverty programs" knows that much of the money goes to the welfare bureaucrats, the researchers who study and plead in the name of "the poor" from the pulpits of the universities and foundations, and other affluent welfare-state big brigades, such as the corporate farmers who get paid for the food that is dispensed through food stamp programs.

Any significant studies "discover" these facts, in spite of the many ways in which bureaucratic costs are hidden in official information. Nevertheless, almost all serious scholars and scientists fighting desperately to slow the growth of the modernist megastates long ago realized that they were falling into a political poverty trap built around the rhetorical shibboleth of the welfare state. Anyone who opposed the growth of the megastate and its necessary erosion of freedom was attacked as an enemy of the welfare both of the general public and of the poor—and, thus, were stigmatized as anti-Christs. They started insisting that they were not against caring for the poor, showing compassion for the old, helping handicapped children, or doing anything else Christian, fair, and decent. Many of them, notably Milton Friedman and his co-workers, strongly proposed being compassionate *and* really preserving everyone's freedom by giving the poor "negative income taxes," thereby doing away with the bureaucrats and quasi-scientists who profit directly from administering and studying the poor and helpless. This idea, which would greatly increase the flow of funds to the victims without increasing taxes, has been resoundingly defeated by the coalition of their helpers, largely through media silence.

The serious issues of the modernist welfare state have little or nothing directly to do with poverty, compassion, caring, or equality. The poor have become a symbolic shibboleth used by modernists in their fervent quest for power, very much as "urban mobs" and "rabble" have been used by demagogues for thousands of years. The many wars on poverty and crusades for communal bureaucratic caring have progressively chained the poor who were their central target, the poorest urban blacks in the United States, to the bureaucrats. Systematic economic studies have shown that the massive programs such as union monopoly powers, minimum wages, rent control, public housing, and socialized medicine sold as "help" for the poor have helped some in the short run but have hurt far more over the long run. Union monopoly powers and minimum wages, for example, are cynical forms of corruption by which relatively rich unions "milk" consumers and force the poor out of the work force so they cannot compete with them. Unionized big businesses also commonly support both to increase the costs of their nonunionized, small competitors. Any effective rent control in an age of statist inflation is obviously a transfer of property rights to those granted the controls and a catastrophe to both the previous owners and to all future generations who must inhabit deteriorating housing or have none at all because investing in guaranteed losses is not a rational business practice. All of the massive income redistribution programs have failed to budge the real distributions in any nation. When all of the direct and indirect, official and unofficial, publicly visible and undergound "perks" of power are considered, it is most likely that the biggest of the megastates have greatly redistributed almost all assets upward to those with the most political power. While "going on the dole" may not produce lifelong dependency for most, it does obviously fail to solve long-run problems, and greatly increases the most awful problem of all social life, the repression of the less powerful by the most powerful.

All knowledgeable people know these facts in general. We know that only the very ignorant but very caring can be deceived by such rhetoric, and we know that no amount of rational argument will stop the modernists from eulogizing themselves for saintly caring as long as there is this political or economic incentive for doing so. Since I am obviously not writing this book for true-believing modernists or for the ignorant, I shall have nothing much to say about poverty, compassion, caring and so on, except as they bear on the crucial issues of statist powers and our freedoms. Like anyone else with common sense, it is obvious to me that there is always a small percentage of people who cannot care for themselves, including a tiny percentage who have no families to care for them; and that local, caring groups can do an immensely better job of caring for them than huge federal bureaucracies of burned out "helping professionals." It will be clear once my argument is fully developed that I believe the continued growth of the modernist megastate is the one sure path to eventual poverty in real terms for the vast majority of us, but that is not my primary concern here. If these monstrous state bureaucracies continue to grow over the next century at the pace they have grown over the past century, the poverty of the great mass of people will be among the least painful of their immiserizations. My concern is with the central arena of the modernist welfare states, not with the sideshows. The focus of this work is on freedom and its opposite, power—dominance and submission; on the methods used to create power and exercise it; and on the long-run consequences of vast statist and bureaucratic concentrations of power.

I am concerned with the big picture, the great tidal drifts of modern history. The big picture can only be seen and understood truthfully by understanding the major current flows making up the tidal drifts, but at the same time the currents can only be seen as parts of the drift, or as running against or independently of the drift, in the context of the whole drift process. Almost all works of real social science today are concerned only with tiny waves upon the many crosscurrents and cannot begin to see the tidal drifts truthfully. The analyses that do focus on the big picture, such as the neo-Marxist ones, are almost all mythopoetic proclamations rather than empirical analyses. We are confronted with a situation in which almost all empirical works in themselves are largely meaningless or greatly distorting because they are torn out of the real contexts of everyday life. For example, the great outpourings of professional works recently on the American poor or the homeless are overwhelmingly concerned with convoluted methodological issues over whether there have been changes of a few percentage points in the official statistics on income distributions, female-headed households, mental health-care budgets, and on and on endlessly. These are internecine disputes among different factions of our megastatists. They give no significant consideration to the basic questions of freedom and statist power, pathologies of bureaucratic (official) information, or any of the other big issues. These factional civil wars are remarkably like those between the Guelfs and Ghibellines over the doctrinal claims to political powers, this tax benefice or that, and so on, which enflamed Italian politics during the early centuries of the late-medieval and early-renaissance welfare states. (See chapters 3 and 4.)

Given the vast scope of this work, I have necessarily relied on a very great many detailed analyses by many scholars. I have had to develop the general picture to give them context and, once this big picture was clear, it allowed me to see the problems with most of these sources. Because of the great space constraints such a sweeping work faces, I cannot include much consideration of the immense details. I refer to the best sources so the reader can pursue the details, but I try to limit these. I am concerned here with the most clear patterns, with those that are obvious to any objective observer of the great tidal drifts of human history. Here too I have drawn upon a number of excellent predecessors who have analyzed many of the patterns of crucial importance to my own analyses. Some economists, notably Robert Higgs, have provided analyses of the vastly complex data on the ratchets-up of our megastates. Milton Friedman has given us some beautifully clear analyses of what has happened, and William Simon's anguished accounts of how even the political champions of freedom have unwittingly supported the drift into megastatism have been of invaluable help. I have, however, found it necessary to develop a more general model to understand how all of this happened to us.

I have found it necessary to develop both a general model of human nature and its involvement in the waxing and waning of statist powers. I have not tried to develop a grand theory of everything human, or even to develop a general theory of human nature involved in the waxing and waning of statist powers. Any valid general theory is quite beyond our capabilities as social scientists today, and will probably always be so. Grand theories—mythological ideologies—were the affliction of the would-be sciences of human beings for one hundred and fifty years. They are still the symbolic shibboleths of the collectivizers of human life, most obvious today in the extreme form of Marxism. What I have developed is a general model of the dimensions of human life that concern us here. A model tries to show as truthfully as present information allows the basic dimensions (or variables) involved and their most important interdependencies. It does not try to create a closed system of absolutely defined variables that allow precise predictions—such as Marxists delight in making about the inevitable trends of historical determinism, in spite of all the hilarious failures of their prophecies.

Probably the most important "discovery" of the social sciences and biological sciences has been the *partial freedom* of human life resulting from our genetic programming to be partially open to situational inputs. (The exact meanings of all this will be made clear later. See, especially, chapters 7 and 8.) Western common sense, and especially the American variant of that, has always assumed that we have free will. (Even materialistic and cultural determinists act in accord with this common sense most of the time.) The grand theorists of man and biology asserted that the opposite is true, that either society or biology determines what we do. This is most obvious in the iron determinism of Marxism and Social Darwinism, but almost all the general theories of social structure, culture, and so on assumed it in some form. The failures of all such positivistic and structuralistic theories, as they are called within the disciplines of social science, is now obvious to anyone not under the sway of their great myths. Any truthful understanding of human beings is based on the idea that we are both free and constrained by biological, physical, and social situations. The only questions of interest scientifically are how more specifically we are free and constrained in different situations by genes, personality, culture, and social situations. (Economic situations are generally among the most important social situations.)

Because of this necessary partial freedom, specific human actions cannot be predicted with high reliability even in the mass dealt with by statistical analysts. It has always been obvious that knowledge of the motives and intentions of individuals in routine situations allows us to correctly guesstimate their actions in new occurrences of those situations. That is another commonsense assumption that underlies all of everyday life. That is one basis of my whole argument in this book. I am showing the general patterns of action that generally occur when human nature (genetic programming) encounters some common situations. Over the long run, those are by far the most reliably guesstimable forms of human action. It is very clear, for example, that protracted (decades long) bureaucratic collectivization of decision making will produce increasingly unadaptive or inefficient patterns of action. This general knowledge of the general patterns of human-nature-guided actions is the most important knowledge we can gain about human action, as intelligent people have realized for eons and have clearly said since Thucydides did so 2300 years ago. But we must not confuse this wisdom with the phony precise predictions of economic wizards and political gurus who infest our world of modernist rationalism and agitprop. No one can reliably predict when stock markets or whole economies will soar or collapse. A very knowledgeable person with the wisdom of the ages (that is, with knowledge of the human-nature-guided patterns), and with great knowledge of the immediate situations, can make good guesstimates of drifts over the long run, but not of specific turnings of the tides or of the magnitudes of the specific social or personal patterns that will develop. Those involve irreducible uncertainties—freedoms—that increase rapidly as we go from the level of general patterns guided by human nature, to cultural patterns, and to any instances of these in concrete situations. These inherent uncertainties are greatly multiplied by problems in the information about human beings normally used in political and economic analyses.

One of the greatest problems of anyone trying to understand human beings scientifically is that almost all of the information about us is problematic, though to wildly varying degrees. The most basic mistakes in understanding human beings have come from a failure to even realize that the information is problematic, so that the problems certainly cannot be solved and the analyst easily becomes an unintentional perpetrator of political deceits. These problems are worst and their consequences most disastrous with official statistical information, precisely the form still used uncritically by almost all journalists, politicians, and bureaucrats and by many would-be scientists. Official information is constructed by officials for the purposes of controlling people in the ways they wish to do. Moreover, the subjects of this information are generally aware of this, so they often have vastly complex strategies for hiding and subverting such information. The statistical processing of vast amounts of data then makes it nearly impossible even for those who construct it to know the details of the particulars sufficiently to see the problems in the information. When this official statistical information is then used to test preconceived theories, as is done in the "testing of hypotheses," the data is often chosen in biased ways that lead to confirmations of the preconceived theories. This biasing is most common in the historical comparisons of whole societies and eras for which there are a great many forms of official statistical data from which the hypothesizers can pick and choose. The result is that the theory is used to select the data by which the theory is confirmed, so the whole work tends to become a "verification" of preconceptions. While the best hypothetical and statistical studies use methods to try to control such biases, the problem is inherent in the method and is all too rarely completely controlled. I make use of many of the best of these studies, since they can be invaluable in revealing crucial patterns. I have always tried to evaluate how effectively they control the informational problems. Still, we must always keep this problem in mind when using the sources on which a general model such as this is necessarily based.

Each particular form of official information, and nonofficial information, has its own problems and the degrees of the problems vary vastly. (I have dealt with these problems in many earlier works, notably *American Social Order* and *Investigative Social Research*.) Some official statistics, such as those on felonious drug use or theft, are wildly wrong. Some, such as those on the number of people in federal prisons at a give time, are probably generally accurate within several percentage points. Most of the kind we shall be concerned with in this book, economic statistics, are probably wrong by anywhere from several percentage points, as in the case of most annual changes in gross national product data, to scores of percentage points, as in the case of export data. Statist bureaucracies often, but by no means always, systematically manipulate such data. China's rulers, for example, wildly overestimated their gross national product data during the Great Leap Forward, then denounced the frauds after the Gang was thrown out. (But did the new regime overestimate the wildness of the discrepancies to discredit the old regime?) I shall deal with some of these problems as I develop the argument, but for the most part it must simply be taken for granted that they are very important. I have dealt with them in a great number of earlier works and have tried to keep them constantly in mind here, correcting for them as best I can. When I use numbers, they are used predominantly as the best guesstimates of the orders of magnitude and must not be taken as absolutes.

In many instances official statistics are totally misleading. All of the good (directly observed) unofficial information, for example, indicates that a high proportion of the real economies are now underground in all societies with really powerful bureaucratic regulators. Consequently, the *nominal*, or officially visible, economies are only very problematic guesstimates of part of the *real* economies. The proportions underground vary widely, and are known only very problematically, sometimes by running the risk of imprisonment, and even the best guesstimates of real economic activity remain problematic. Analysts who believe that communist bureaucrats plan the whole real economies of their subjects completely misunderstand how the world really works. Those megastatist bureaucracies stagnated and eroded the official (nominal) economies long ago. Only the relatively free markets underground have prevented the communized peoples from starving or revolting, which is why all of these regimes have come increasingly to tolerate underground capitalism as a kind of officially unofficial economy— or planned nonplanning. Informational pathologies and labeling absurdities of this sort are rampant. One of the major goals of this work is to uncover and analyze informational pathologies and labeling absurdities—agitprop—so I have tried assiduously *not* to become their victim. (See, especially, chapter 9.)

In our megastate democracies today, almost all of the most important social factors at work are *mass-mediated*, and this fact pervades every aspect of my argument. I do not mean that the mass media create images or myths, as many who have studied them argue. Nor do I mean that they *are* the message of reality, as a few extreme analysts contend. Almost all of these general criticisms of our mass media seize one real part of the vast pluralism of media messages and treat it as the whole, just as the more totalitarian theorists have seized upon the values most common in our media and asserted they prove the media are part of the *bourgeois conspiracy*. Our mass media range from the sublime to the satanic, from the creative to the humdrum, from the profoundly serious to the ludicrous. Almost anything might show up in them and eventually does. I find the most valid material in the best of them to be of great value in helping to understand the world beyond my own immediate experience. But it is also the case that the media in general operate in certain crucial ways that mass-mediate the realities they are trying to convey. They severely decontextualize reality, reconstruct it in ways to fit their own operational needs, and sell it in information packages intended to grab attention, sell the media, and have political impact. Each medium does these in widely varying ways, but the overall effect is to greatly distort realities, in rough proportion to their complexity and uncertainty, for viewers who do not understand the mass-mediation processes and do not know enough about the realities to recontextualize the media messages validly. The mass media are not the primary force producing our drift into statism, but most of them greatly amplify this tendency today, far more by sincerely and instantly purveying and amplifying mistakes, myths, and political deceits than by creating them or attempting to be part of the deceits. Most of the media people are caught up and swept away by the great myths that are the most important forces inspiring our drift into megastatism. But they are the broadcasters, the high-powered loudspeakers and the great screens for these forces, not their conspiratorial creators.

Even some readers who agree with my findings about politics and the media may at first feel piqued by some of the terms or tones I use. For example, my use of agitprop to refer to the political agitation and media propaganda of our own politicians may arouse suspicions that I am a right-wing extremist trying to insinuate communist sympathies among our left-wing politicians and journalists. This is not so. I use terms like agitprop only because they are the best available terms for analyzing realities. The Soviets who invented the term to refer to their vast armory of creative strategies and tactics of political and military deceit were and are among the most brilliant scientists and engineers of statist power in history. Yes, they are our mortal enemies, but I respect their brilliance and courage in precisely the way soldiers respect their most deadly enemies. In the same way, I respect the wondrously creative agitprop of "FDR," "Tricky Dick," "Teddie," and "Ronnie." Sometimes without knowing it, sometimes very consciously, they have learned greatly from their Soviet enemies, just as their Soviet enemies are now learning from them. All of our megastates, whether nominally "total" or "democratic," have vast cadres of scientific experts and engineers engaged in the dedicated manipulation of publics and elites around the world. ("Gorbymania" in 1987 was an excellent Soviet campaign of mass media agitprop—of political warfare by mass media means. It appears to owe much to a careful study of the agitprop of "JFK" and "Ronnie.") I do sometimes feel exasperated, and once in a while even frightened, by the oceans of agitprop that now wash over us and so often deceive most people. I make that clear in some of the tones of my analysis. My tone complements my analysis. These are monstrous evils that threaten all of us over the long run. But these emotions must not be allowed to mythify our thinking or color our analyses. Today agitprop is a vital part of the worldwide business of power—of politics and war. I am analyzing it, not moralizing. I am also not an extremist in favor of freedom. As will become apparent, I see both freedom and constraint as necessary realities of the many vastly complex dimensions of life. Old-fashioned socialist values like cooperation and consensus are far more old-fashioned than socialism, which is one reason they were seized as rhetorical weapons in the socialist agitprop to increase their own power. Everybody with common sense is partly cooperative and consensual with friends and friendly teams—and the opposite with enemies, to appropriate degrees. Nobody with common sense believes in *baby power*—that is, freedom from the vast power parents must have for the baby's own welfare. And no rationally prudent person today who really wants freedom from statist powers is in favor of doing away with our powerful bureaucracies of military force while the totalitarians are building theirs. This work is not advocating any abstract ideals or other utopian plans for our world. It is also not a detailed political policy for anything. It is an analysis of the great tidal drift into megastatism and the most important effects of this—stagnation, Caesarist warfare, and eventually catastrophic changes (if the drift long continues).

Our goal here is practical wisdom and understanding. Any attempt to explain everything, or even much, of human life by some simple determinants is scientism—pseudoscience, not social science. Modes of production, social class, rates of investment, income distribution, and hundreds of other factors are important in human life, but anyone who seizes upon them to explain everything important produces monstrous misunderstandings such as have led over and over into catastrophes. All of these modernist theories deny or assume away the fundamental factors—human nature and the human condition, which include partial free choice by individuals and situational accidents—"fortuna." They begin with the more superficial and, thus, are able at best to provide only correlational analyses that hold for some situations (where the parameters are the same, as they say). Almost all of the recent analyses fail completely to see the vast importance of the specific properties of the dominance drive—the lust for power—and of statism, and bureaucracies. If you exclude from your analysis the lust for power, statism, and bureaucracies, you easily conclude that the collectivization of power in statist bureaucracies ruled by the best and brightest will be the most rational, efficient, and benevolent of all social orders. That is precisely what most social "scientists" have concluded, from the Marxist-Leninists to our current "industrial policy" central planners. Since they have denied or never seen the

crucial factors, they can only produce monstrous misunderstandings and catastrophes, if their rationalistic plans are long followed. Our goal here is to
deal with first things first, to understand the crucial factors at work. Everything else is secondary and must build on that.

If people come to see how the mistaken modernist ideas about human
beings, especially about economics and politics, have brought us to these
brinks—that we are not the victims of mere accidents, nor of the wages of
economic freedom, as the megastatists of all stripes insist, then I feel sure
they will find ways to turn the great tidal drift. Until they have that general
understanding, the great myths of the modernist welfare state will reign
supreme and no effective policy proposals for deratcheting megastatist
powers will be adopted. Once the people rediscover that most American of
all ideas—that "Freedom works!" and, consequently, "Statist repression
fails!" we shall see a new birth of freedom, philanthropy, prosperity, and
peace—no utopia, but the New World, a shining land of hope—America.

1

The American Megastate

The overriding fact of human life in the twentieth century has been the systemic drift of our great world civilization into gigantic webs of bureaucratic statism and the stagnation and ferocious struggles for power inspired by this drift. All serious analysts agree that our Western economies have been wracked by growing inflation and decreasing investment, productivity, and real-income growth in recent decades. Most fail to realize that these problems of the official, publicly visible economies are vast by comparison with America's experience in the last century, when economic freedom was still a dominant reality and not a rhetorical shibboleth, as it increasingly is today. In fact, many of them still believe our growing stagnation is produced by our having too many remnants of economic freedom and are anxious to install more centralized planning in the new guise of "industrial policy."

All serious analysts also recognize that this century has seen an explosion of totalitarianism and warfare more vast than ever before experienced.[1] But they normally see this growth of totalitarian statism and warfare as separate from the more general growth of megastatism and stagnation in our Western democracies.[2] Nazism, communism, all the other brands of extreme statism and "their" wars are seen as merely accidents, the whims of a few evil men or parties, not the natural extremes of the drift into megastatism that afflicts all of our societies to widely varying degrees and in different cultural forms.

21

They fail almost completely to see that the lust for power is unleashed in all our societies, that all of us have been drifting into megastatist oppression, stagnation, and warfare at different speeds and in various cultural forms. Because of the myths of modernism and rationalism, they have lost touch with the simplest truths about human nature and are blinded to what has been obvious to intelligent observers since the ancient world.

Some analysts have shown in excellent detail that militaristic expansion or imperialism in the very long run erodes a nation's economy severely, even though it may increase it in the short run. Paul Kennedy has shown this correlation at work in Western states over the last five hundred years,[3] but it has been true over the whole five thousand years of "civilized" bureaucratic states. Pitirim Sorokin and the others who have studied the whole history of "civilized" warfare have shown that the correlations are quite complex.[4] What they have generally failed to see, because they have forgotten or deny the vast importance of both human nature and bureaucracy, is that these are the crucial factors interacting with all the others. When the ever-present lust for power is combined with vast statist bureaucracies, the militarism erodes the economies terribly. The United States was able to expend 10 percent of its gross national product on the military in the 1950s while still expanding economically, though much less than it would have without that burden. Today the expenditure of a mere 7 percent is eroding the economy because our statist bureaucracies exploded in their regulatory powers in the 1960s. The vast powers of huge bureaucracies erode the efficiency of military machines and whole economies, at the same time they attract the most power hungry and then trigger their power hunger into bureaucratic and military expansion.[5] (Of course, once the people or other elites, or foreign powers, check their power hunger, this process stops, but normally through rebellions, revolutions, civil wars, and foreign defeats.) As Polybius saw over two thousand years ago, great concentrations of statist power eventually trigger ferocious struggles for power at home and imperial wars abroad, regardless of the benevolent slogans and political banners under which the would-be rulers march.[6]

As the ancients also knew from their own awful experience, the great concentrations of statist power generally grow under the banners of the most noble ideals shared at the time. Aristotle concluded from his careful comparative study of the history of states that the most repressive rulers—the tyrants—build their vast new powers deceitfully in the names of freedom, equality, prosperity, justice, and whatever will be popular.[7] The people will only begin the surrender of their precious freedoms and self-integrity to the rulers of the state to the degree they believe this sacrifice is necessary for their common welfare and only to the degree they trust the analyses and promises of the politician and his supporters. Once they have allowed him to build his infrastructure of tyranny, it is exceedingly difficult to stop the drift into ever greater tyranny. The Athenians were acutely aware of these basic facts of statism because the first famous Greek tyrant, Peisistratus, revealed the basic pattern of successful tyrannization from within which prevails everywhere, with cultural and situational variations. (See appendix I for a brief presentation of this process.) Until modernism inspired a growing devaluation of all historical knowledge, educated Westerners for almost two thousand years were keenly aware of the dangers of Caesarism and of the corruptions of great power which were so obvious in Imperial Rome.[8] John Acton summed up this knowledge in his still famous law of power: "Power tends to corrupt and absolute power corrupts absolutely."[9] Our terrifying experience in the twentieth century has confirmed this historical law with tens of millions of human corpses and hundreds of millions of broken lives.

Statist powers can exist for long only when they are seen as *necessary* for the common welfare—as welfare states—in whatever terms seem most moral and fashionable at the time; and they normally grow slowly, in fits and starts, ups and downs that only later can be seen to be ratchets-up in a great systemic drift into statist bureaucratization. As Michael Rostovtzeff said of the Romans,[10] most of their leaders did not even realize at the time that they were building a huge empire; and certainly, failing to heed Polybius's warning, they had no idea that by doing so they were marching toward an age of terrible civil wars that would destroy their republic and install the Augustan tyranny disguised as an ideal republic serving the common welfare. They drifted blindly into empire, civil war, and a huge bureaucratic regimentation of life that eventually snuffed out the earlier creativity of the Mediterranean peoples.

Though there have been many vast imperial states in the last five eons, none have been as vast in their scope or as minute in their regimentations of everyday life as our twentieth-century megastates have been. All of the earlier empires were presented by their rulers as welfare states and the vaster ones have produced Caesarism and stagnation, but none before this century—not even the dreaded Assyrians or Mongols—ever produced the colossal regulations of everyday life minutiae now taken for granted, nor the total warfare against defenseless civilian populations which is already the standard operating plan of the gigantic war machines of our superstates. Though many earlier rulers aspired to rule totally, none before our century came near the real totalitarian regulations over all life which have been the goal of our most enflamed modernists. We know of no earlier rulers who even dreamed of building a "new man" through cradle-to-grave statist education, or of redefining the status of human being through court proclamations, but all of this is standard fare in our age of megastatism.

The megastate ratchets up slowly, always in the guise of "serving the common welfare" and generally in the pretense of meeting a crisis.[11] Once the bureaucratic regimentation of everyday life has become pervasive, it begins to trigger the very real crises of ferocious domestic and foreign struggles for power, alienation and outrage over the injustices inevitably perpetrated by bureaucrats using their necessarily distorted information about the world (see chapter 9), and economic stagnation and decline (for reasons we shall examine in detail thoughout this book). These crises triggered by the higher levels of statist bureaucratization then become the enabling crises of further ratchets-up in statist powers—it becomes a vital necessity for "the common welfare" to "solve" the problems being caused by the drift into statist collectivization by increasing the bureaucratic regulations, which in turn produce new crises that must be solved by further ratchets-up.

The drift into statist regimentation of life is, thus, an *autocatalytic process*—it reinforces itself, or feeds upon itself. The drift upward into greater regimentation accelerates because the new statist attempts at solutions to problems destroy the old ways of dealing with them, and build ratchets under the dependencies on the new statist "solutions" as people restructure their life commitments in expectation of continuing those statist dependencies. At the extreme, statist bureaucracies first breed a generalized dependency in individual personalities and then in whole subcultures, whose members transmit this dependency to new generations. Each increase, then, tends to produce a ratchet (which accounts for the obvious *downward rigidity*). Beyond a *critical range* (the tipping or take-off in the drift into statist regulation), the acceleration is so great and the ratchet dependencies so generalized that it is extremely rare for the process to be reversed by any means other than civil wars or foreign conquests that destroy the ratchets and produce sudden restructuring.

The drift into the massive regulation of life by statist bureaucracies is partially hidden from its victims by massive self-deceits and by massive political deceits, agitprop, which are purveyed by politicians and, far more importantly, by the intellectuals and publicists who depend for their support on the state (but pretend to be independent and objectively scientific) and by the bureaucracies of mass education. The fits and starts of the upward-drift process (one step backward and two steps foreward, as Lenin put it) confuse even objective and careful observers. The slowness of the drift allows the people to adjust to each step into submission, hardly noticing it and easily excusing it as merely a small encroachment. It also allows those who remember what life was really like before the drift into the "iron cage" of bureaucratic regimentation to die off before the contrast is stark, thereby preventing their effective challenges to the agitprop indoctrination of the young. Our modernist megastates in the democratic nations have grown very slowly over this century and only behind ever-more massive agitprop in support of them by our ever-more massive cadres of intellectual *grantsmen*, journalists, and bureaucrats of the ministries of official education.

Who now even remembers that a mere seventy-five years ago, one human life span, our Western world had lived for a century, that of the now-stigmatized bourgeois era, in greater peace and harmony than ever before?[12] Who now remembers that the statist powers even in the remaining monarchies were so weak, and the internationalism of our religions and our cultures were so great, that passports were not required for crossing the almost invisible national boundaries? Who now remembers that our nations were not then pervaded by hundreds of thousands of secret agents and counterspies tapping our everyday communications? That "little old ladies" strolled the streets of our great cities at night without fear? That businesses were not mummified in vast reams of millions of laws and untold legal precedents? That the poor fleeing from the corrupt statist bureaucracies around the world were welcomed to our American shores by the tens of millions and rose steadily in wealth and status (so that today the once desperately poor and stigmatized Japanese, Chinese, and Jews have the highest incomes in our nation)?[13] That real per capita economic growth was many times more rapid than now?[14] That the now-despised gold standard protected all citizens, the richest and the poorest, from statist expropriation by inflation of the centrally planned currency?[15] That the states exercised little power over marriage contracts and no woman could imagine the politicians expropriating her contractual rights by passing no-fault divorce laws and casting her and her children into poverty? That official divorce rates were one-seventh what they are today and family life on average far more certain and happy than in our day, when most marriages end in misery and divorce? That no one could imagine the horrors of superpowers waging "total war," wantonly firebombing great cities and pushing mankind toward the brink of nuclear annihilation with pacts of Mutual Assured Destruction? That the rich and affluent were inspired by community spirit and altruism, as well as by the natural human vanity, to create worldwide webs of philanthropic organizations on a scale never before seen? And that almost everyone assumed that the excitement and fulfillment of Providential Progress, the secular god of that bygone era of the bourgeoisie, was their natural and inalienable right?

The drift into our megastates has now gone on so long and their police powers are now so omnipresent that most young people assume them to be their inalienable reality. So many generations have now been subjected to an ever-increasing number of years of official education that they now take for granted the exact opposite of all these simple facts and assume that anyone who challenges their ignorance is an ideologist trying to repress their bureaucratically guaranteed statist rights. Most of these miseducated young people assume the ancient regime of our traditional System of Natural Liberty, a term that they have rarely even heard, was an unending "grapes of wrath" for the poor ruled over by evil robber barons who stole from the poor and created thousands of philanthropic institutions only to escape income taxes.[16] Even as they rage against the awful impersonal destructiveness of the bureaucratic juggernauts that stifle their lives, many of them fight desperately to increase the bureaucratic powers, because they assume these powers are necessary to build the welfare state, and, indeed, that all welfare in life *must* flow from the official forms of the bureaucracies because they *are* reality. They have no idea that their ignorance puts them firmly in the grip of the core enabling myth of the welfare state and that, consequently, their every twist and turn to escape one bureaucracy by building a more powerful one only compounds their growing misery. Only a tiny fraction of Americans now even remembers that the once-sacred name for opponents of statist powers— liberals—has been transformed by political-historical amnesia and deceit to mean the opposite, those who support the collectivization of all of life. When our own best and brightest young people, who have been "educated" for two decades at the greatest cost per head in the world, have no understanding of the simplest facts about political labels, who can be surprised to find many ignorant peasants around the world seeking salvation and total freedom in the iron tyranny of the totalitarian communist regimes?

The modernist megastates are presented in vastly diverse guises and march under the polychromatic banners of many rationalistic-scientistic myths of legitimacy. Democratic socialism, communism, fascism, nazism, Maoism, Peronismo, shining-pathism, liberalism, democratic welfare statism, Square Dealism, New Dealism, Fair Dealism, Great Societism, and many other brand names have been used and will be invented by the new masters of agitprop, who know in minute and scientific detail how important deceitful political labels are in selling their common product of subservience to the rulers of the state apparatuses.

Certainly there are important differences in the realities of the various nominal brands of statist collectivism, both in their degrees of real (effective) collectivization and in the dimensions of life they collectivize. The cadres of Western intellectuals who now blindly assume or pretend to believe that there is no significant difference between the "democratic centralism" of the one-party megastates, now popularly called "communist states," and the still less centralized and more factionalized democratic states have built their case on the important fact, noted decades ago by Pitirim Sorokin, that these two camps of modernist megastates are built largely on the same myths and are rapidly approaching each other in their degrees of the collectivization of life.[17] It is an important part of the argument presented here that the communist rulers and bureaucrats have never been nearly as "totalitarian" in their "central planning for freedom" as they themselves pretended to be and as their enemies feared them to be. (We shall see that such a degree of totalitarianism is impossible except during brief periods of dread in human life.) It is an even more important part of my argument that the "free" nations have not been very free during most of this century. In fact, they have now put in place most of Marx's ten demands in *The Communist Manifesto* and are considerably more collectivist than Soviet communism was in the 1920s. But these facts must never be construed as proof that our differences are insignificant.

Communist political systems have been the most extreme form of mass slavery yet invented, one in which much of the cultures and self-identities of the slaves have been stolen from them by the parties and replaced with monstrous systems of statist myths, mistakes, and lies. It is true that the communist parties now seem to be drifting toward more indirect means of executing their central planning of life and toward less intrusion into the souls of their slaves, but they have done so only because more indirect slavery is far more effective, especially when the slaves are revolting against direct slavery. They have not forsaken their claims to absolute sovereignty over everything, nor have they yet relinquished the democratic centralism that allows the few rulers of the parties indirectly to control most of the lives even of the party members. Some of our democracies are still far from that degree of political collectivization rightly called slavery. While they now use a huge mix of direct and, increasingly, indirect, means of regulating almost every realm of life of every subject, especially the economic realms that are a matter of life and death, we may still retain sufficient freedoms to reverse by democratic means this great systemic drift into slavery.

Regardless of these vital differences, all of these brands of modernist statism march under their own renditions of the common banner of the welfare state, which they proclaim to be the necessary and rightful scientific liberator from the chains, slavery, inequality, injustice, corruption, and chaos of the ancient bourgeois regime. Some of them, notably the communist regimes, are more extreme in denouncing the supposed evils of the ancient regime and lump monarchy, church, and capitalism together as *the* great satan that they promise will be transcended in the posthistorical secular heaven just around the corner from party totalitarianism. Others, notably our less total Western democratic states, content themselves with more moderate denunciations of the ancient regime of monarchy, unbridled (unregulated) capitalistic greed, and puritanical church and promise only peace, prosperity, sexual bliss, and just equality for all in our time. But they are united in their denunciations of the ancient regime as purposefully and obviously oppressive, while at the same time they suffer from the mythical delusions of the ancient religions and cultural prejudices. All of them proclaim their vast statist powers to be necessary for the common welfare. They differ only over what state powers or what degrees of the various powers they believe are crucial to achieving the common welfare. The planners of the Soviet central planning agency, Gosplan, might insist that everything should in theory be planned and enforced by the state, while Western Keynesian economists would insist that the common welfare or the "public utility function" demands a more moderate planning and enforcement of public goods, but in fact they are converging toward a huge bureaucratic system in which the state rulers regiment as much of life as they can through ever more indirect means.

All long-lasting states throughout history have been built partly on the bureaucratic regimentation of life necessary to building the real power of their rulers, and the statists have always praised these regimentations in their rhythms of song and their rotes of mass agitprop as necessary for the common welfare, as welfare states by whatever labels and in whatever terms would be believed by their subjects.[18] The pharaohs' claims to be the necessary interceders with the Gods to get their subjects into heaven, or even the Popes' claims to be the only holders of Saint Peter's keys to heaven, are obviously not popular in our secular age, just as the claims of Soviet general secretaries of the party or of American presidential candidates that they are the way to eternal prosperity and peace would not have been popular in those less-credulous eras. The verbal forms, tones, and rituals of the agitprop change; the basic realities live after them. Some of the hymns to statist dependency have, however, remained remarkably unchanged throughout the millennia. Always, for example, we hear the sonorous recitations of the multifarious benefits, entitlements, mercies, and acts of rightousness granted by the rulers. While more restrained, Hammurabi's welfare-state rhetoric in the second millennium B.C. sounds remarkably like the proclamations of American senators and the bureaucracts manning our ziggurats of health and human services when he promises "to pronounce judgements for the land, to render decisions for the land, to give justice to the oppressed. . . .Let any oppressed man who has a cause come before the image of me, the king of righteousness. Let him give heed to my weighty words!"[19]

Augustus, the first emperor of Rome, was presented by his bureaucrats and intellectual grantsmen as the good shepherd, the protector of the peace and harmony of the realm, of its good fortune and well-being, especially of personal security (maintaining law and order), and of food, because of his valour, clemency, liberality, humanity, justice, devotion to duty, and wise forethought for his subjects' welfare. (He even changed his name to Augustus because this resonated with ancient religious undertones of godliness, in the same way Hitler's "Thousand Year Empire" resonated with the undertones of Christian Millennialism.) These paeons to the ruler's virtues and to the necessity of welfare statism are remarkably similar to popular biographies by our modern Virgils, as we see in the court biographies by Arthur Schlesinger, Jr.[20] and by Kenneth Davis[21] of "FDR" (whose initials stand as a symbol of his public divinity separating him from those of us with mere private names) and the many hymns to "JFK" and the Second Coming of Camelot. In an age of secular millenialism in which presidential candidates not only promise pie in the sky in the by-and-by, but actually lay claim to having already produced an "economic miracle" in Italy or Massachussetts, Augustus's advance men, public relations experts, media experts, and intellectual hagiographers sound oddly humble, but this is only because his powers were in fact so great that he had to use more massive agitprop to feign even greater freedoms and humility, very much as today's more totalitarian rulers must wrap themselves in more layers of public humility as "secretaries" of the parties of the peoples' unions of democratic, republican, liberationist, egalitarian, freedom-loving nonstates. (Tiberius, Augustus's heir to the hidden throne, became severe in opposing those who publicly proclaimed his divinity or vast powers. Displays of humility are one of the most potent weapons of the tyrant.)

The principle of the imperial Roman welfare state, "Salus populi suprema lex" ("The welfare of the people is the highest law"), gave the same license to unbridled regimentation of life as that given by the principle of the National Socialist Workers' Party ("Anything is good if it serves the people") and as that given by the unwritten principle of "liberal interpretation" which now dominates our American courts. But the greatest difference between the traditional welfare states, even those stigmatized as oriental despotisms by their Western rivals, and our modernist welfare states is that none of the earlier states came remotely close to encompassing the entire world, nor, since they were greatly constrained by the traditional legitimacy of sacred customs, did any of them dare to aspire to the reconstruction of human nature, nor, since they had no idea of the technologies necessary, did any of them try to impose the minute police controls over everyday life which are taken for granted in the iron cages of our modernist totalitarian societies and which have become widespread intellectual ideals, if not yet realities, in our modernist democracies. As Albert Schweitzer saw so clearly, decades before our democratic megastates had begun to impose the minute police controls that now prevail, "Modern man is lost in the mass in a way which is without precedent in history. . . .Collectivism in its various forms has deprived the individual of his individuality. All the troubles of the world come from this."[22]

This great transformation is most striking and most tragic in the United States. Most Americans are now all but blind to this brute fact. Their attention is so riveted upon the awful tyrannies of the totalitarian welfare states, and even our educated citizens are now so ignorant of all history except the revisionist version of radical modernists increasingly enforced by our official education bureaucracies, that they fail to see what has happened to us in this century.[23] Almost all of the totalitarian societies were already regimented by state and church bureaucracies for centuries before they succumbed to the millennialist myths and millennialist promises of the more totalitarian modernist versions. The average Russian peasant is certainly far more immiserated today than he was under the czar's regime because his cultural self-identification and his religious identification with all of Being have been partly expunged and replaced by the lies of the party, but his ancestors lived for centuries under a bureaucratic regime that otherwise did not differ greatly from this modernist slavery. The fourteen-rank officialdom of Peter the Great has merely been expanded into the megastatist nomenklatura of the communists. The nine ranks of the imperial Chinese mandarinate have been expanded into the vast phallanxes of twenty-five grades in "The People's Republic." The northern German people also lived under the less-oppressive police powers of the "Prussian Welfare State"[24] for two centuries before subjecting themselves to the democratic socialism of the Weimar Republic, then to the socialist regime of Nazism and then to post-Nazi democratic socialism. The oppressive bureaucratization of French life made its first start in medieval statism, waned after the Caesarism of the Hundred Years War, and was built into the massive Colbertisme of the seventeenth century. As one executive of St. Gobain said knowingly when Mitterrand's neo-Colbertisme nationalized his company, "After all, this company was started by Louis XIV, and this is the fourth time we've been nationalized."

But America before this century was the heartland of individual freedom and of an effective balance of powers and constitutional constraints upon the unlimited claims of statist sovereignty. America did not even have a significant state power at the federal level. Until the Civil War, our federal government was predominantly a federation, not a statist power. We shall see how vitally important this distinction is and how the myths of statism have become the cornerstones of our modernist welfare state. Commensurate with its nonstatist nature, our federal government was almost invisible to the average citizen until it began in the Civil War to take on the mythical legitimizations and the immense powers of the ancient welfare states. "Nothing is more striking to the European traveler in the United States than the absence of what we term. . .government. . . . We have seen that in the United States there was no administrative [bureaucratic] centralization. There is scarcely a trace of a hierarchy."[25] When Alexis de Tocqueville wrote these words in the nineteenth century, the American federal government controlled roughly two and one-half percent of the gross national product, almost entirely through customs duties and by selling federal lands. There was not a single federal regulatory agency. The federal government had no control of the money supply and did away with the short-lived United States Bank in 1832. While there were short-run gyrations due to situational factors, most especially inflation in the 1830s fueled by the earlier policies of the U.S. Bank, followed by depression when the bank was done away with, over the long run consumer prices were either constant or declined as the gold standard kept the value of money nearly constant and new technology increased productivity. America was famous throughout the world and infamous among the ruling classes of Europe, as the land of economic freedom and, thus, of economic opportunity and achievement for the huddled masses fleeing the vast bureaucratic powers of the European states. Over the century roughly forty million people fled to these shores in the greatest migration in human history. Most of them came in poverty, approximately half as indentured servants and ignorant even of the common language. Unregulated by federal planners, unaided by federal welfare, they built the first new nation, a nation of greater political and economic freedom than the world had yet seen and, thus, a nation of bounding energy, of soaring wealth, and of community caring and philanthropy. As Tocqueville said, "I know of no other people who have founded so many schools or such efficient ones, or churches more in touch with the religious needs of the inhabitants, or municipal roads better maintained."[26] The economy grew by great leaps and bounds, soaring over the long run 5 to 6 percent a year, and catapulting the nation from lowly status to the pinnacle of wealth and power in one century. This was done in spite of the myriad attempts of state and local governments to plan life, for citizens could always migrate to the greater freedom of other states anxious to compete in freedoms and to the frontiers beyond the reach of almost all bureaucrats, and did so by the tens of millions.

No rational observer of the facts would think of our nation today as one characterized by an "absence of government." Government at all levels now controls roughly 35 to 40 percent of our gross national product through direct expenditures and through the hidden indirect expenditures of off-budget subsidies, moral responsibility guarantees of bond issues, and under many other guises.[27] The indirect taxation and controls mandated by the myriad government regulations are also huge and have far greater impacts on all our lives, but they are so complex and their effects are so intertwined and undefinable that no valid quantitative measure of them can be made. Since the establishment of the Interstate Commerce Commission in 1887, approximately 91 other independent federal regulatory agencies have been added (depending on how you count them) and untold thousands of new state and local agencies have mushroomed.

For the first one hundred twenty-six years of our nation's existence, until the establishment of the Federal Reserve System in 1913, the federal government had few direct controls over our money supply. As noted already, over the long run prices were stable or declined slightly as productivity increased and the long-run value of our hard, gold-based currency remained roughly constant. (Even inflation of the federal paper currency during the Civil War was eliminated by a slow return to the gold standard.) In the seventy-five years—roughly one average life span—since the federal government seized control of our money supply, we have had inflation of roughly 800 percent. (I suspect it has been much more, but measurements are highly problematic.) In the first twenty years alone of the Federal Reserve's control of the money supply, the nation had one of its worst bouts of inflation, the crash of 1921–1922 that cut industrial production in half and caused unemployment of about one-fourth of the labor force, the hyperinflation in the stock market of the late 1920s, the Great Depression following the burst of that inflationary bubble, and the great inflation of World War II through the Korean War. In the last twenty-five years, the Federal Reserve's inflation has raised prices roughly 300% and destroyed roughly one-half the value of all savings, a hidden taxation of monstrous proportions which has done more than anything else to destroy the incentive to save and invest and to turn us into spendthrift consumers and borrowers. During this fourth great bout of Federal Reserve inflation, we have plummeted from the position of the world's greatest creditor to that of its greatest debtor (though the official statistics on this are quite unreliable). Far more importantly, the inflation, erosion of savings, and general uncertainty resulting from massive and erratic government actions have reduced our investment rate, while the explosion in new technology demands great increases in investment to retain world competitiveness. The result has been a great decline in our international competiveness, which is now used by statists as proof that we need far more government intervention in the economy—even massive central planning in the guise of industrial policy.

Contrary to mass-mediated myths and political rhetoric, this general trend has not been reversed by the Reagan administration. When the first Reagan administration came to office, the federal government spent roughly 23 percent of our official gross national product. In 1987 it spent roughly 25 percent, the greatest peacetime acceleration of federal expenditures in our history. Our national debt has more than doubled in eight years, turning us into a debtor nation at the erratic mercy of the great swings in international currency and credit markets. No single regulatory agency has been dismantled. Inflation is now running at a "mere 5 percent" a year, but that was bought at the price of the second most severe recession in our history, and the administration has made no hint of imposing anything to restrain it in the future beyond the promises of the central planners of our money, who operate in secrecy and are well documented in their lies to the public.[28] As William Niskanen, a former member of the president's council of economic advisors, summed it up, "In the end, there was no Reagan revolution."[29]

America today is a government-dominated society in which all of us are controlled in innumerable ways directly and, far more, indirectly by vast and still-proliferating regulatory agencies issuing a torrent of administrative laws, by untold thousands of planning commissions and committees, by soaring police powers, by a tidal wave of legislative laws and activities, and by a tumultuous sea of injudicious court decisions in which revolutionary ukasi are masked in the rhetoric of constitutional precedents, rational interpretation, and due process. Interlocking layers of our huge government bureaucracies now dictate minute details of our lives and enforce these dictates with vast police powers. There is literally no realm of life that is still free from massive intrusions by government legislative, regulatory, and judicial fiat.

Even the meanings of "human life" and "death" are now minutely defined and administered by political and judicial fiat. For untold thousands of years unborn human beings were taken for granted in our Western communities as exactly that, unborn human beings, and as such were protected by the morals of common sense and by the common laws of the land. Overnight, and with no significant political debate or legislation, unborn human beings were redefined by the United States Supreme Court as nonhumans—"fetuses"— and the meaning of "fetuses" has since been defined in more technical ways by court and regulatory fiats. The nation that fought a terrible Civil War that ended the legal definition of black slaves as "inferior human beings" outside the law and that reviles the Nazi "supermen" who secretly (but never in open court) redefined Jews as "nonhumans" (*Untermenschen*) and administratively "exterminated" them, then proceeded to legalize openly and even fund the "termination" of three times more "nonhumans" than the Nazis did. Each year one million three hundred thousand "non-human beings" are officially "terminated" by doctors sworn to protect human lives. These "Untermenschen" have no rights because the megastate has redefined life itself. "Fetus tissue" is already being used in medical experiments to advance the "common welfare." Nazi doctors would envy such totalitarian powers.

It is one of the great myths of our age that at least "sexual" matters are now more free from state domination than in earlier centuries. The exact opposite is true. Our education boards and our government bureaucrats known as teachers now "educate" almost all of our children in the minutiae of sexual modernist ideas and regulations, all approved and certified in the official government textbooks and all censored more effectively than in any earlier state or church society.[30] Because most sexual modernists are adamantly opposed to the forms of marriage and family life which have been the foundation of all human life, our American textbooks now include almost no reference to such forbidden roles as "husband" or "wife." Because our modernists in general are revolting against the religion of the ancient regime, our textbooks now rarely mention the fact that American society was founded by

Christian Protestants, so the Pilgrims are defined in the modernist-speak of our textbooks as "people who travel long distances."[31] This modernist agitprop is mandated by the state governments and courts. Parents who refuse to surrender their children for approximately eight hours a day to the ministries of public education or to regulated private proxies may be imprisoned.

Until the last century most Western states had almost no direct control over marriage contracts, since they were religious contracts. Today the government not only mandates and regulates these contracts, but also freely abrogates the property rights agreed to in them by *consenting adults*, without due process and *ex post facto*, by passing no fault divorce laws. Even the supposed modernist freedoms to indulge in noncontracted alliances and prostitution are myths protected by historical ignorance. Common-law marriages and prostitution were rampant and normally uncontrolled by state powers throughout Western history until the rise of the modernist welfare states in the past century. Prostitutes were subject to little formal police intervention even in the United States early in this century. Today prostitutes and customers alike are routinely processed and secretly administered by the police and the news media.

Regardless of how we might feel individually about drugs (and I myself feel strongly that mind-altering "recreation" is highly irrational), no one who knows the historical facts can doubt we now live in a police state as far as drugs are concerned. Until World War I there was not a single federal drug law or regulator in this nation. Today drugs are subject to massive investigation, minute legislation, and extreme police powers. The immense police powers of our government today are obvious not only in the deployment of our police agencies and armed forces to interdict drugs in other nations and in international airspace, in the many thousands of people imprisoned for drug uses, and in the other untold thousands who must go abroad to get the drugs they believe will cure them or alleviate their sufferings, but also in the routine heliocopter surveillances of the millions of us who are gardeners and the searches of the luggage and persons of tens of millions of us at our borders.

America today is ruled by an immense imperial state bureaucracy headed by an imperial president, imperial legislators, and imperial courts, all of which strive mightily every day to extend their powers over our lives. We have drifted blindly, in the quest for the deceitful lures of utopian ideals and greed, into the tyranny of the majority which the founding fathers saw as the greatest danger to the System of Natural Liberty. The tyranny of the majority is the rule by the majority unconstrained by anything but their own momentary political definitions of the common welfare. In a society in which the mass, counted by one man, one vote, can liberally reinterpret everything, including life itself, the logic of totalitarian collectivism is unconstrained and infinite. As *The Federalist* said,

> If a faction consists of less than a majority, relief is supplied by the republican principle, which enables the majority to defeat its sinister views by regular vote. It may clog the administration, it may convulse the society; but it will be unable to execute and mask its violence under the forms of the Constitution. When a majority is included in a faction, the form of popular government, on the other hand, enables it to sacrifice to its ruling passion or interest both the public good and the rights of other citizens. . . .

> . . .a pure democracy, by which I mean a society consisting of a small number of citizens, who assemble and administer the government in person, can admit of no cure for the mischiefs of faction. A common passion or interest will, in almost every case, be felt by a majority of the whole; a communication and concert result from the form of a government itself; and there is nothing to check the inducements to sacrifice the weaker party or an obnoxious individual. Hence it is that such democracies have ever been spectacles of turbulence and contention; have ever been found incompatible with personal security or the rights of property; and have in general been as short in their lives as they have been violent in their deaths. Theoretic politicians, who have patronized this species of government, have erroneously supposed that by reducing mankind to a perfect equality in their political rights, they would, at the same time, be perfectly equalized and assimilated in their possessions, their opinions, and their passions.

> A republic, by which I mean a government in which the scheme of representation takes place, opens a different prospect and promises the cure for which we are seeking.[32]

The Constitution denied almost all powers to the republican federal government, carefully enumerated those few it was to have, and severely limited it in all powers by checks, balances, the ancient morality embodied in the common law and natural rights, conscience, and the universal morality of Christianity. Now those bulwarks against the totalitarian logic of the statist common welfare have been so severely eroded by historical revisionism, judicial liberal interpretations, legislation, and regulatory fiats that most of our rulers see them as shams or even a conspiracy of selfish interests. How many, even of our Supreme Court justices sworn to uphold the Constitution, would deny that "the welfare of the people is the supreme law," or that "anything is good if it serves the people"? If they remembered that these were the official slogans of the tyrants of the Imperial Roman welfare state and of the National Socialist Workers' Party (the Nazis), they would surely demure. But their actions have shown that many of them, and often a majority, reason in the same way.

The American people and the Constitutionalists intended the courts to be grounded in the invariant morality of conscience and natural law and in the ancient tradition of the common law. The courts were to be the strongest bulwark within republican democracy against the encroachments of government powers upon the inalienable and invariant rights of the people. They believed that the judges could perform this vital duty only if they could be as isolated from the ferocious passions of political struggle as possible. No one with common sense expected that society or the Constitution could be unchanging, which is precisely why the provisions for revising the most fundamental laws of the land were spelled out meticulously. No one with practical political experience could doubt that political factionalism would erupt at some time concerning everything, which is precisely why it was seen as so vitally important to build bulwarks against the passions of politics which would inevitably be aimed at the Supreme Court. Modernist Constitutional revisionists who insist that the Constitution and the Supreme Court cannot really be completely isolated from politics and must, therefore, be embroiled in politics, even violated in spirit to preserve them, as the progressive Walter Lippmann put it, have used the obvious to jump to an absurd conclusion.[33] It is precisely because we human beings are attacked by viruses and by other enemies that we must defend *against* them, not encourage them. And it is precisely because political passions eventually attack all laws and legal institutions that we must strenuously defend them *against* politics. The Constitutionalists knew well from their great knowledge of history that these passions are very powerful, but they believed it possible to devise a system of checks and balances in which men of good will who understood the dangers of such political passions, and who made their decisions within the constraints shown by the precedents of experience to be wise, would be able to transcend them sufficiently to prevent a tyranny by mobs or by one faction becoming a tyranny of the majority. They saw law as the accumulation of the wisdom of commonsense experience and judges as the people of reason and scholarship who could interpret those historical precedents to fit emerging situations and, thereby, constrain the animal passions, especially the most powerful of all the ferocious lust for power unleashed by all political factionalism. They believed, however, that judges could do this *only* if they decided within the constraints of reason and scholarship and, thus, *only* if they were chosen outside of the vortex of political passions and then buffered from such passions by such devices as lifetime tenure and privacy in their deliberations.

It soon became apparent in the great controversies over federal powers that erupted over decisions by the Marshall court that the constitutionalists had underestimated the degree to which the political forces of our teeming and rambunctuously changing democracy would impinge on the decisions of the Supreme Court. Judges in the early decades were more swayed by personal and political partisanship than expected, so that, in a few instances at least, even major decisions by earlier courts were overturned by later ones—a fact that violated the ideal of judicial decisions made in the full wisdom of the accumulated commonsense wisdom of legal precedents.

Nevertheless, on the whole the justices did seem to be buffered from political passions and those in the later nineteenth century were much more scholarly and constrained in their decisions—a development that owed much to the increased scholarly standards of American law in general. Their decisions were generally made in the ancient tradition of the common law, as analyzed by Frederich Maitland and Friedrich Hayek.[34] That is, they made their decisions "at the margin," cautiously adapting the ancient commonsense wisdom of the whole body of laws and precedents to the emerging, most lasting, and seemingly most wise social trends. While few of the justices attained the universality of Solomonic wisdom, few, if any, sought to change the whole course of society by creating radically new interpretations of the accumulated wisdom. Right up to the New Deal, the vast majority of attacks on the Court were for supposed crimes of conservatism—"dragging their feet" against popular passions by grounding their decisions in the whole centuries-long body of laws and precedents. Regardless of how we feel individually about their decisions, that is certainly a crucial indication that they were acting within the intended constraints and that they were not often swept by the political passions of the day. The whole idea of law and judiciousness, as understood by the constitutionalists and by the majority of Americans today, has always been to *conserve* the wisdom of the ages, to conciliate and compromise sincere differences, and to be a bulwark against the evil passions that so easily sweep us all away—and thus threaten to sweep away *all* rights—in political warfare.

Today there is still a minority of legal scholars, judges, and lawyers who hold firmly to this classical liberal and moderate (Whig) conservative idea of law and judicial decisions, and there is a much smaller minority of politicians (most of whom are also lawyers) who agree with them, if less firmly. But the dominant majority of the legal professors and politicians now takes it for granted that the constitutionalists were wrong. They assume, without examining the vast evidence from all civilizations, that law and judicial decisions are predominantly determined—*caused*—by political interests and passions and that, consequently, judicial decisions cannot to any significant degree be buffered from and transcend the political passions. (They share a kind of watered-down version of the economic determinism of Marxist theory that is now firmly embedded in the positivist, structuralist, and critical theories of the social sciences and history that are dominant in our law schools and "elite" universities in general, but the explanation of their views is not our purpose here.)

This revolution in legal philosophy is not a figment of conservative dread. It is a fact both admitted and hailed by honest liberal jurists. In his biography of *Earl Warren*, G. Edward White,[35] who served as a law clerk to the chief justice, is very explicit in showing that Warren was driven by his "mission to do justice" and had little concern for the Constitution or precedents. In *How Courts Govern America* Richard Neely,[36] a member of the West Virginia Supreme Court, argued that courts do, must, and should govern the nation by exceedingly liberal interpretations, and he provided practical guidlelines for doing so. As he concluded:

> Once we are willing to admit that courts have political roles which are dictated by the nature of other institutions, we can begin to speak to those roles directly and not in the slave language of constitutional interpretations, statutory construction, or result-oriented standards of review dressed up as neutral principles. . . .Many of the framers dimly perceived that the judiciary would serve some type of balancing function, but of course they could never have envisaged the functions which are currently undertaken by courts. The proper role of courts is still evolving. Dean Rusk once told me that after Earl Warren's retirement from the court, he went to speak at the University of Georgia, where Secretary Rusk was teaching, and met with a small group of law professors. At that meeting the former chief justice said that the primary political function of the courts was to break the impasses which are inherent in any structure of balanced powers—a function which I doubt even John Adams anticipated. If the courts are going to break impasses, only the courts can define 'impasse.' So the limits on court power in government are not set by either constitutional theory or discoverable law, but rather by the tolerance of the counter-vailing powers. What happens when Plato's millennium of the philosopher kings actually arrives, I am not sure.[37]

The basic principle is obvious enough: Power makes right, as Thrasymachus put it, or, as America's liberal judges put it today when they are as honest as Warren and Neely, the meaning of the law is what judges say it is, until someone exerts greater political force to constrain them. (Judge Neely is a graduate of Yale Law School and is quite conservative compared to some of the critical legal theorists ensconced at Harvard Law School and other law schools. Critical theorists believe the traditional idea of law, as defined by the constitutionalists, is both absurd and a weapon of class oppression.)

In recent decades the U.S. Supreme Court has so obviously become a fount of radical revisions of the Constitution, and thence of radical changes in our whole lives, that even some liberal interpreters have sounded the tocsin of alarm. In 1987 the U.S. Senate held hearings on the president's nomination of Judge Robert Bork to the Supreme Court which erupted on network television into fiery political factionalism.[38] When the nation's legislators perpetrate such travesties of the Constitution, in the very name of upholding the Constitution, it is hardly surprising to find physicists asserting their right to elect politicians to deny the constitutional rights of everyone else.

In America today the nuclear physicist who would laugh uproariously at the thought that the average businessperson should have a vote on whether to allow physicists to study the atom would immediately turn around and insist that he or she, as a citizen and nothing more, should have the right to elect politicians whose votes determine whether the owners of Texas gas wells should have the right to set their own prices in a competitive market for their gas, whether the Federal Reserve should increase the money supply at a faster rate, or whether the federal government should stimulate the economy by running budget deficits and talking down the dollar in exchange markets. The same sociologist who asserts with contempt that the average politician knows nothing about the realities of drug use and their effects would assert with aplomb, and without thinking to consult a single empirical study or economic theory, that the government should solve the problem of inflation by imposing wage and price controls or income policies upon all those businesspeople who "set their prices to rip off obscene profits." And many of our average voters assert blandly that their votes do and should justify the politicians' and judges' use of police powers to dictate to doctors the standards of medical care, the maximum charges they can ask for their services, and their "termination" of millions of "nonhuman" lives. How many of our citizens now doubt that politically appointed judges have the right to redefine life and to allow the "termination" of millions of them to protect the newly proclaimed "right to privacy"?

Why? Why does the physicist think he should have a vote to determine what price Texas gas owners can ask for their gas, while it is ludicrous for the Texan to vote on whether the physicist be allowed to investigate the atom? Because, says the physicist and his liberal political philosophers, the price of gas is a *political question* that affects the common welfare. The price of gas, therefore, is a political issue that should be controlled by the state for the common welfare, to keep prices down. But our physicist has forgotten that there are few forms of basic knowledge or action in our interdependent world that do not potentially affect almost everyone in some way. What could be more important in determining the future—or lack of future—of all officially defined human beings than nuclear research? By our physicists's own standards, then, what could be more "political," and thus more subject to decision by mass vote, than nuclear physics? And, if our political philosopher can use his vote to dictate the asking price for gas in Texas, why cannot the gas owner use his vote to dictate the admission and grading standards of the political philosopher, or his hiring standards, or his subject of research? And is it not totally logical for the same politician who dictates the medical standards and prices of doctors to dictate for our Mr. and Mrs. Everyperson the standards of their most intimate acts and thoughts? When, for example, a government is granted authority to plan controls on the population growth of a nation, where is there any logical constraint on its authority to plan abortions for unplanned "fetuses?" Or to systematically monitor the sex practices and menstrual cycles of its "bearing population?" All of this and far more have followed logically from the collectivist logic of communist China. And what logical constraint now exists in their planning "euthanasia" for the unplanned? Should our welfare-statist planners assert logical constraints by illogical fiat, what evidence have they to show that rationalistic state planners will be constrained by their illogical fiats? Have we victims of the twentieth century not seen the extremes to which the relentlessly logical pursuit of state planning has carried such well-meaning, benevolent, and otherwise decent technocrats as Lenin?

The logic of totalitarian collectivism is simple, brutal, and entirely consistent. Once a people has decided—whether actively or, more commonly, by default, by not actively stopping them—to allow politicians to decide by legislation, and without severe constraints of custom, moral principle and constitutional law, what is right and wrong in such basic realms of life as economic property rights, then there is no longer any logical constraint upon their exercise of power in all other realms of life. As classical liberals saw, even in the vastly more simple and self-contained society of the eighteenth century, without inviolate property rights no other rights can long be sustained. The government that controls our property rights must ultimately control our right to the pursuit of happiness, our right to free speech and to the publication of that speech, our right to take a spouse or have children, our right to work and choose an occupation, our right to life itself—for all things of life are ultimately dependent upon material goods and, thus, upon the controls of those goods we call property rights.[39]

The government that has the right to legislate gas prices in Texas, or income redistribution nationwide, has every logical right to dictate research standards in physics, hiring standards in sociology, wage rates for black teenagers in New York, parental care standards for all parents, the right to bear children, the right to redefine life, and—the right to everything. When the American people, tempted by the ancient enabling myth of the welfare state, used the power of their votes to give the politicians and, by inaction, the courts the power to legislate away and rule away our ancient economic rights—our freedoms from unconstrained government control of our property for the common welfare—they unknowingly gave them power to legislate away and rule away all our ancient rights. Almost a hundred years ago Theodore Roosevelt, one of the first heroes of the rationalistic state planning of American progressivism, proclaimed, "Every man holds his property subject to the general right of the community to regulate its use to whatever degree the public welfare may require it." The insidious implications of that "to whatever degree" for the counterrevolution against the System of Natural Liberty became clear only slowly, but for almost a century now the American state has been pursuing that relentless logic of totalitarian collectivism at an accelerating rate.

The most extreme and fearsome exercises of power are logically contained in any grant of authority to government to plan and regulate society for the common welfare. If government is once entrusted with authority to plan for the common welfare—not for a specific purpose, such as defense against oppression, bounded by specific and absolute injunctions against further encroachments upon private rights, but a general, all-encompassing goal, such as caring for the common welfare—there is no logical constraint upon its exercise of the most total oppressions of individual and minority rights in pursuit of that common goal. The government that has the authority to redistribute anyone's property to this minority or that obviously has the logical authority to redistribute the property of those minorities to the majority, or to the representative of that majority, the government itself. The revolutions launched in the modern world in pursuit of a rational plan for the common welfare, and most of all those launched in pursuit of an ideal society in pursuit of an ideal common welfare, have always discovered this inner totalitarian logic of statist planning. In the first of these revolutions, the Jacobins started as the ardent defenders of private property against the rapacious usurpations of the king's bureaucracy, but their pursuit of the worldly millennium led ineluctably to Robespierre and to Babeuf's communism. Saint Guillotine became the symbol of rationalistic perfection, a veritable diadem of the Goddess of Reason in pursuit of Rousseau's *common will*. Saint Guillotine is the logical perfection of all state planning for the common welfare.

All of this has been obvious since the rationally planned atrocities of the "benevolent" tyrannies of the ancient world—and who could doubt this inner logic would prevail after the fiery evidence given by the Dominican bureaucrats of the Inquisition? If the most holy of the pure did not flinch in burning little old ladies and schoolgirls in pursuit of the common welfare and in the name of the victims' own eternal welfare, what sane person could ever doubt that more worldly bureaucrats would pursue this inner logic of the state planning of the common welfare? Certainly this fact has been crystal clear for many generations to any scholars unblinded by myths. Well over a century ago, Herbert Spencer saw this inner logic at work in the idealistic democratic socialism of his day and predicted what has already come to pass in communist nations:

> The fanatical adherents of a social theory are capable of taking any measures, no matter how extreme, for carrying out their views: holding, like the merciless priesthoods of past times, that the end justifies the means. And when a general socialistic organisation has been established, the vast, ramified, and consolidated body of those who direct its activities, using without check whatever coercion seems to them needful in the interests of the system (which will practically become their own interests) will have no hesitation in imposing their rigorous rule over the entire

lives of the actual workers; until, eventually, there is developed an official oligarchy, with its various grades, exercising a tyranny more gigantic and more terrible
than any which the world has seen.[40]

As Hilaire Belloc saw in *The Servile State*, a book that in 1912 prophesied
the totalitarianism that would grow out of the benevolent intentions of socialism, "The control of the production of wealth is the control of human life
itself."[41] By the 1950s, even Roscoe Pound, overly famous for often siding
with the proponents of state controls in his theory of social interests, was
calling for constitutional constraint on the power of majorities and warning,

> Growth of a feeling of divine right of majorities, akin to that of divine right of
> kings, has led to an assumption that concern about oppression by government is
> something we have outgrown. Yet distrust of absolute majority or absolute plural-
> ity is as justified in reason and in experience as distrust of the absolute personal
> ruler. Indeed, the latter may be given pause by fear of an uprising which an
> intrenched majority need not fear. . . .The service state, taking over all functions of
> public service, operating through bureaus with wide powers and little practical re-
> striction on their powers, through government positions for a large and increasing
> proportion of the population, and through systematic official propaganda and a sys-
> tem of subsidies to education, science, and research, can easily be taking strides
> toward an absolute government, although under forms of democracy. Indeed, the
> extreme advocates of the service state insist that constitutional democracy is a con-
> tradiction in terms. A democracy must be an unrestricted rule of the ruler in all
> things as was the French king of the old regime in France or the Czar in the old
> regime in Russia. As the seventeenth century argued that a monarchy must in the
> nature of things be an absolute not a constitutional monarchy, on the same logical
> grounds it is argued that a democracy must be an absolute not a constitutional
> democracy.[42]

The modernist welfare state is ultimately, if unknowingly, built on the
logic of totalitarian collectivism: when the goal of the state becomes that of
pursuing the common welfare, without basic constraints of custom, moral
principle, or constitutional law, then the welfare of any individual or sub-
group rapidly approaches zero. Thus, we eventually arrive at the logical conclusion of the egalitarian welfare state, the conclusion Rousseau and socialist
revolutionaries in Europe reached two centuries ago: the equal welfare of all
demands that the individual welfares of everyone be totally sacrificed to the
state that is rhetorically committed to the common welfare. And so the Juggernaut of the modernist welfare state trundles onward, slowly but relentlessly crushing beneath its bureaucratic powers our ancient freedoms one
after another—to serve the common welfare of all, of course. Today the
businesspeople, the gas producers, and the steel makers; tomorrow the doctors; then the parents; and someday the whole world.

The opposite of the logic of totalitarian collectivism is the logic of individual freedom within the System of Natural Liberty. The logic of collectivism

computes the individual welfare, if at all, in terms of the collective welfare, that is, in terms of *aggregates* like gross national product, income distribution, relative poverty, and, above all distributive justice—equality. The logic of individualist freedom does the opposite, that is, it computes the *general welfare* in terms of all the individuals' welfare as defined and experienced by the individuals. Certainly the individuals define their welfare in good part in terms derived from their family and community lives, in communion with their own consciences and with the embodiments of their consciences in the Constitution; for we human beings are profoundly loving beings who identify with our ancestors, our communities, and our posterity. But it is we alone, acting as individuals, who can know in our hearts what is right and good for us and our loved ones. It is we alone who can most truthfully define our own welfare.

The American Constitution was built upon the logic of individual freedom. The American government was founded to promote the general welfare, but to the eighteenth-century classical liberals that meant the exact opposite of what the common welfare means to the American statists today. Because they assumed that welfare could only be defined individually, most Americans intended the government to promote the general welfare by remaining as small and weak as it could while serving the two obvious, specific, and explicitly bounded forms of general welfare: that of defense against foreign powers that wanted to impose absolutist tyranny on Americans and that against the domestic oppression of crime and rebellion. Thus it was that they discovered that revolutionary idea of individual freedom: minimizing the power of government will optimize the welfare of all. Liberty was both the greatest blessing in itself and the fount from which would spring all others by enabling individuals to use all their potentially vast spiritual energy and creativity. Thus it was that when Tocqueville visited America in the early 1830s, he found a remarkable "absence" of government and an equally remarkable high level of general welfare—a land of freedom and, thus, of peace and plenty.

> Experience should teach us to be most on our guard to protect liberty when the Government's purposes are beneficent. Men born to freedom are naturally alert to repel invasion of their liberty by evil-minded rulers. The greatest dangers to liberty lurk in insidious encroachment by men of zeal, well-meaning but without understanding.
>
> Louis D. Brandeis

> Dictatorship is also usually achieved without *disturbing the forms of free government*, forms which may linger on for many years after dictatorship has been firmly established. An attack on those forms would sound a tocsin of public alarm, while their astute retention makes it difficult to perceive clearly the emerging substance of dictatorship. . . .A leader must emerge championing the economic misery of the

people and promising them relief. The friend of the people then makes the people docile to his will through government spending which gives them jobs. Under this soothing treatment, the democratic process is then used to destroy democracy.

Willis J. Ballinger

Notes

1. The explosion of warfare and totalitarianism in our century was already obvious in all the major studies *before* the immense devastation of World War II and the endemic warfare and totalitarianism since. See, especially, Pitirim A. Sorokin, *Social and Cultural Dynamics* (New York: Bedminster Press, 1937, rpt. 1962), especially vol. 3, pp. 259–380.
2. Fortunately, there are some very valuable exceptions to this rule to which I shall refer throughout this book. Three excellent sources that I discovered after writing this book are Robert G. Wesson's books: *The Imperial Order* (Berkeley: University of California Press, 1967); *The Russian Dilemma* (New Brunswick, NJ: Rutgers University Press, 1974); and *State Systems* (New York: The Free Press of Macmillan, 1978).
3. Paul Kennedy, *The Rise and Fall of the Great Powers* (New York: Random House, 1988).
4. Sorokin, *Social and Cultural Dynamics.*
5. The catastrophic explosion of bureaucracy in the American military machine is documented in detail by Edward Luttwak, *The Pentagon and the Art of War* (New York: Simon and Schuster, 1984).
6. Polybius, *The Burden of Rome*, especially book VI.
7. *Politics* (New York: Viking Press, 1957). Aristotle distinguished between early Greek tyranny, in which military power was more important, and the demagogic tyrannies of his own day, in which deceit was more important and their power less total. His discussion of the means the tyrant must employ (book 5, ch. 11, pp. 151–56) shows that deceit is always crucial, the point Machiavelli elaborated in *The Prince.* The arts of political deceit were highly developed by the early Roman emperors. See David Stockton, "The Founding of the Empire," in John Boardman et al., eds., *The Oxford History of the Classical World* (New York: Oxford University Press, 1956), pp. 531–59.
8. Michael Grant, *The Twelve Caesars* (New York: Charles Scribner's Sons, 1975). Grant argues that the emperors were generally lustful for power and oppressive before they became emperors. The vast power of the emperorship lured them, triggered their lust, and corrupted (mythified) their thinking (Ibid., pp. 256–66). These are vital parts of my argument.
9. See Gertrude Himmelfarb, *Lord Acton* (London: Routledge & Paul, 1952). M. Rostovtzeff (*Rome* [New York: Oxford University Press, 1960]) notes that this corruption of power was already apparent in the senate a century earlier and that the reforms of Cato and others failed to curtail it (pp. 95–97).

10. Rostovtzeff, p. 77. Roman historians today argue that Romans were partly deceitful about their militarism and imperial motives. (See Elizabeth Rawson, "The Expansion of Rome," in *The Oxford History of the Classical World*, pp. 417–37.) This so-called "modern interpretation" is based on the same evidence as the traditional ones are. It is pervaded by neo-Marxist revisionism and fails to see how people can deceive themselves and how important noneconomic motives and "luck" are.

11. The general nature of the drift process, especially its "small steps" aspect, has been understood since Aristotle presented it. See *Politics*, book 5, chaps. 4 and 8. Thomas MacKay gave an excellent statement of it almost a hundred years ago. See his *A Plea for Liberty* (rpt. Indianapolis: Liberty Classics, 1981).

12. Certainly there were wars launched by the bureaucratic states, especially by Bismarck in building the German megastate, which also launched the great ratchets-up in statist powers soon sacralized as "the welfare state" (see chapter 4). And even in the United States the first massive ratchet-up in central statism led to the Civil War. But these were rare by comparison with the almost continuous warfare of the "prebourgeois" era and very rare by comparison with the "postbourgeois" era.

13. See Thomas Sowell, *Ethnic America* (New York: Basic Books, 1981).

14. There is little disagreement, even among revisionists, about the vast growth of American wealth in the last century. The growth was awesome to Americans at the time. There are few reliable bits of statistical data on it, but it is well captured in standard sources such as Page Smith, *A People's History of the Ante-Bellum Years* (New York: McGraw-Hill, 1981).

15. The great increase in statism during the Civil War was accompanied by the usual paper currency and inflation, but the gold standard was "resumed" after the war.

16. Terms such as "The Gilded Age," "robber barons," and "grapes of wrath" were all created by intellectuals to stigmatize American economic freedom. Other intellectuals, especially historians, then made the stigmas standard parts of rote memory in public education.

17. William McNeill (*The Pursuit of Power* [Chicago: University of Chicago Press, 1984]), has given a good statement of this convergence of Soviet and American collectivism.

18. By far the best comparative study of the bureaucratic states throughout history is that by S. N. Eisenstadt, *The Political Systems of Empires* (New York: Macmillan, 1963).

19. There are now a vast number of works on the rhetorics and practices of all of the most powerful rulers of history about whom we know much. Long bibliographies can be found in the general works referred to already and those referred to below. On Hammurabi (or Hammurapi) see Joyce Hertzler, *The Social Thought of Ancient Civilizations* (New York: Russell and Russell, 1961) especially p. 89; and Joan Oates, *Babylon* (London: Thomas and Hudson, 1979), pp. 60–82.

20. Arthur Schlesinger, Jr., *The Crisis of the Old Order* (Boston: Houghton Mifflin, 1957), and *The Coming of the New Deal* (Boston: Houghton Mifflin, 1958).

21. Kenneth S. Davis, *FDR, The New Deal Years, 1933–1937* (New York: Random House, 1986).

22. See my fuller quote from Schweitzer in the frontispiece to this book.

23. The revisionist historians have succeeded so completely in imposing their "reconstructed" myths of American history that Robert Middlekauf begins his history of the American revolution, *The Glorious Cause* (New York: Oxford University Press, 1982) with the sad statement, "The title that I have given this book may be understood in this day—when all is suspect—as irony. I do not intend that it should be."

24. See Reinhold August Dorwart, *The Prussian Welfare State Before 1740* (Cambridge, MA: Harvard University Press, 1971). There is a vast literature on "the coming of the welfare state." Most of this is concerned with the British and continental welfare states. The best of these, such as Dorwart's work, will be dealt with throughout this book. These are quite opposed to the vastly more common, accepted escatology that sees the "social problems" as the direct causes, aided by supplementary factors such as Christian socialism and radical utilitarian-rationalism. Among the most factual and stimulating of these are Karl de Schweinitz, *England's Road to Social Security* (New York: A. S. Barnes, 1943); David Roberts, *Victorian Origins of the British Welfare State* (New Haven: Yale University Press, 1960); Pauline Gregg, *The Welfare State* (London: George G. Harrap and Co., Ltd., 1967); D. C. Marsh, *The Welfare State* (London: Longman, 1970); Maurice Bruce, ed., *The Rise of the Welfare State* (London: Weidenfeld and Nicolson, 1973); Ursula R. Q. Henriques, *Before the Welfare State* (New York: Longman, 1979); and Peter Flora and A. Heidenheimer, *The Development of Welfare States in Europe and America* (New Brunswick, NJ: Transaction, Inc., 1984).

25. Alexis de Tocqueville, *Democracy in America* (Garden City, NY: Anchor Books, 1969), p. 89, and see pp. 262–76.

26. Ibid., p. 92.

27. In addition to current government information, the standard works on the growth of the American federal government are Solomon Fabricant, *The Trend of Government Activity in the United States Since 1900* (New York: National Bureau of Economic Research, 1952); M. Slade Kendrick, *A Century and a Half of Federal Expenditures* (New York: National Bureau of Economic Research, 1955); Roger A. Freeman, *The Growth of American Government: A Morphology of the Welfare State* (Stanford: Stanford University Press, 1975); and Robert Higgs, *Crisis and Leviathan* (New York: Oxford University Press, 1987).

28. See William Greider, *Secrets of the Temple: How the Federal Reserve Runs the Country* (New York: Simon and Schuster, 1987). Greider's policy position supports the great political movement underway to make the money supply a direct form of statist bureaucratic power, rather than the indirect form of oligarchic state capitalism it now is. But his evidence about Federal Reserve deceit is sound.

29. For the basic facts and Niskanen's quote, see "Mixed Report," *The Wall Street Journal*, Nov. 17, 1987.

30. See my essay on "The Sexual Modernists," in *The Family in America*, Rockford Institute, vol. 1, no. 3, May 1987; and my work with Freda Cruse Atwell, *Love, Intimacy and Sex* (Beverly Hills, CA: Sage Publications, 1988).

31. Paul Vitz, "Textbook Bias Isn't of a Fundamentalist Nature," *The Wall Street Journal*, Dec. 26, 1985.

32. James Madison, *The Federalist*, no. 10 (New York: The Modern Library, no date), pp. 53–62. I shall deal with totalitarian democracy in many parts of the book. The classical analysis is Alexis de Tocqueville, *Democracy in America*,

and Jacob Talmon, *The Origins of Totalitarian Democracy* (London: Secker and Warburg, 1955).

33. The most effective works of "Constitutional revisionism" are those that adopt a "moderate" tone to justify the revolution that has occurred in this century. See, for example, Michael Kammen, *A Machine That Would Go of Itself* (New York: Vintage Books, 1987). On p. 399 he names the Woodrow Wilson–Walter Lippmann progressive view "constitutional revisionism" and quotes approvingly Lippmann's defense of "violating the very spirit of the constitution...to preserve the very letter of it." See W. Lippmann, *A Preface to Politics* (New York: Mitchell Kinnerley, 1913), pp. 17–18). The most immoderate—slashing—attacks on our entire ideas of law and legal practice are launched by "critical theorists" from our preeminent law schools. See, for example, Mark Kelman, *A Guide to Critical Legal Studies* (Cambridge, MA: Harvard University Press, 1988).

34. Friedrich Hayek has systematized the ideas of Burke and Maitland in *Law, Legislation and Liberty* (Chicago: University of Chicago Press, 1973).

35. G. Edward White, *Earl Warren*, (New York: Oxford University Press, 1982).

36. Richard Neely, *How Courts Govern America* (New Haven: Yale University Press, 1981).

37. Ibid., pp. 216–17. Neely himself proposes that judges use their powers to break the "impasses" and sees this as critical for the "reindustrialization of this country" (p. 216). The way is being prepared for the great leap forward (that is, ratchet-up) to direct central planning of the economy.

38. See my essay, "The Supreme Court is too Important to be Left to the Politicians," *Chronicles*, March 1988.

39. Though Marx was wrong about the "bourgeoisie" controlling all the means of production, and thence everything else, his economic determinism showed the communist regimes the way to the most total power possible in life—the control of as much of the means of production, that is, "property," as possible through the monopoly power of the party. See J. D. Douglas, "The Road to Modernist Slavery," in Kurt Leube and A. Zlabinger, eds., *The Political Economy of Freedom* (Munich: Philosophia Verlag, 1984).

40. Herbert Spencer, "Introduction: From Freedom to Bondage," rpt. in Thomas MacKay, *A Plea For Liberty*, p. 29. See also Herbert Spencer, *The Man versus The State* (Indianapolis: The Liberty Fund, 1981). Spencer's predictions grew out of the long tradition of warnings of the evils of collectivized (concentrated, unchecked) powers. Montesquieu, Burke, *The Federalist*, and Tocqueville are obvious predecessors.

41. Quoted in F. Hayek, *The Road to Serfdom* (Chicago: University of Chicago Press, [1944] 1972), p. 13.

42. Roscoe Pound, "The Rise of the Service State and Its Consequences," quoted in S. Glueck, ed., *The Welfare State and the National Welfare* (Cambridge, MA: Addison-Wesley, 1952), pp. 215, 218–19.

2

The Essential Roots of Welfare Statism

Above all things our royalty is to be reverenced, and if you begin to poke about it you cannot reverence it. . . .Its mystery is its life. We must not let in daylight upon magic.

Walter Bagehot

Most accounts of the rise of the modernist welfare states are built on the implicit assumption that they are necessary for the common welfare, but they rarely attempt to portray the immense powers of these megastates as good in themselves. Their authors are well aware of the ever-growing alienation and rage against *big government*, a phrase which has become a political stigma. Anyone today who studies politics even casually knows that the protest voters are now the most powerful voting bloc in national elections. In the United States about half the eligible voters now refuse to vote even in presidential elections, and our three recently elected presidents have been outsiders who sternly attacked Babylon on the Potomac and vowed to "get big government off the backs of the people." Many of the confidants of our recent rulers have later revealed the pervasive usurpations of power, lies, and corruption festering even in the inner sanctum of the Oval office, and some have been imprisoned for such crimes.

Numerous former bureaucrats who ruled the pyramids of power in this New Babylon have published anguished confessions full of dismay and outrage. David Stockman has shown how the people are deceived and how the rulers who pretend to be planning all our lives for the common welfare do not even know "what these numbers mean."[1] Joseph Califano, one of the most experienced of all liberal democratic bureaucrats, has decried the massive usurpations of powers by the federal judges and has painted a horrifying picture of a nation being devoured by "vultures" posing as the champions of the common welfare: "the eagle that once symbolized our nation—powerful, protective, armed with both sword and olive branch, head held proudly, ready to soar, is perilously close to being pushed off its perch by the vulture—also powerful, but self-interested, armed only with vicious talons, head down, poised for its carnivorous descent."[2] Even in once-great Britain, the cradle of Fabian socialism, Iron Maggie sternly denounces the massive oppressions of individual freedoms by our megastates. Almost no one argues that our mega-states are good governments, nor denies that they are immensely corrupting and oppressive.

John F. Kennedy, now the apotheosized torchbearer of American welfare statism, is most famous for denouncing selfish interests in his inaugural plea, "Ask not what your country can do for you, ask what you can do for your country." He also proclaimed sweepingly, "Every time that we try to lift a problem from our own shoulders, and shift that problem to the hands of the government, to the same extent we are sacrificing the liberties of our people." He echoed the awful forebodings of the titular Father of the American Welfare State, Franklin Delano Roosevelt, who denounced Herbert Hoover's deficit spending and proclaimed, "The lessons of history. . .show conclusively. . .that continued dependence upon relief induces a spiritual and moral disintegration fundamentally destructive to the national fibre. To dole out relief is to administer a narcotic, a subtle destroyer of the human spirit."

All of the founders of American megastatism, with the exception of Theodore Roosevelt, denounced it at the very time they were building it. It is not at all surprising, then, that the casuists of megastatism rarely praise it in itself, and, indeed, call endlessly for "Reforms, Reforms" to cleanse it of the "bad apples" and absurd "unintended consequences." Rather, they claim only that it is a necessary evil to overcome the greater evils of "unfettered capitalism." Most of these casuists do not even know the history and economics that they insist proves this necessity. Those who do almost always rest their arguments solidly on the absurd testament of the nineteenth-century Marxist or socialist faith in the inevitable immiserization of the proletariat by the capitalists and argue that the welfare state is necessary both to prevent this immiserization through oppression and inequality and to save capitalism from the political fate of this immiserization. For example, Lester Thurow, probably the most popular liberal American economist today, argued in December, 1987, that the "Welfare State Keeps Capitalism Working":

An understanding of the welfare state begins with the vision of the 19th-Century economists. The most famous, Marx, thought that capitalism would produce such sharply rising income inequalities that it would ultimately end up destroying itself in a revolution.

Marx was not alone in his prediction; almost all 19th-Century economists had a similar vision of rising inequality.....the 19th-Century economists also misidentified the role of the state. Instead of being an instrument of oppression, it would transform itself into the welfare state to prevent inequality from forever rising.

The welfare state was initially an invention of the right, Bismarck in Germany; and later an invention of the left, the Swedist and English socialists. In America, it was the invention of the man who saved capitalism from the crisis earlier predicted by Marx—Franklin D. Roosevelt in the Great Depression.

But those early economists were not wrong about the inherent tendency of the unfettered capitalism to move toward inequality.....The welfare state is an essential ingredient in capitalism. Without it, capitalism cannot long survive. This does not mean that the welfare state doesn't need reforms or that it cannot grow too large. But it does mean that the welfare state hardly is a foreign virus in the body of capitalism.

Quite the opposite, the welfare state is the immune system of capitalism that prevents it from becoming infected with the germs of too much inequality.

The key goal is to make the welfare state more efficient. This is a task that capitalists should willingly undertake since a wise capitalist knows that, without the welfare state, there will in the long run, be no capitalism.[3]

Even the more empirical accounts of college textbooks try to show that sincere and heroic politicians built these megastates in direct response to the growing "injustices" and "critical social problems" produced by our traditional System of Natural Liberty, which they stigmatize as an evil social system labeled "Capitalism," the very meaning of which now implicitly *assumes* that those who had capital oppressed the poor workers through the iron tyranny of economic necessity and the police powers of their bourgeois state. But the whole idea of economic freedom being saved from itself—its "internal contradictions"—by statist powers progressively destroying those freedoms, and administered by the avowed enemies of economic freedom, is patently absurd to anyone not caught in the great web of modernist statist myths who has any knowledge of history over the last few centuries. It is obvious that the economic growth rates of all of the Western capitalist societies in the last century were at least twice as high as they are now, and that all of the megastates today are rapidly "immiserating" the mass of their populations, roughly in direct proportion to their massive powers. Many of our social "scientists" may believe that Marx's theory of immiserization was true, but almost everyone in the gargantuan Marxist megastates are certain that statist bureaucracies do so and growing majorities in the democracies believe so. The casuists of megastatism are wrong on all counts about the origins of our modernist welfare states. The casuists assume that massive central planning by bureaucrats—but not "too much"—works, but the evidence that it does not work is writ large in the blood and immiserization of billions of people in our century, as well as in uncounted thousands of economic studies of them. I shall present many of these facts in this work, but not to prove the obvious. My focus will be on explaining how the obvious comes about.

Even historians who are well aware of the deceitful machinations of politicians such as Franklin Delano Roosevelt and who seem to sense the absurdities of the sacrosanct myth of the origin of our welfare state, desperately affirm the Panglossian faith that what the rulers have done is necessary for the common welfare—in spite of the evils they enumerate. Albert Romasco, for example, has given a vivid portrayal of Roosevelt's political machinations, his early confusion, his refusal to help Hoover stop the falling dominoes of the banking system, the vast uncertainty and anxiety this caused in the minds of all knowledgeable investors and businessmen, and his creation of the massive political system of payoffs. He also clearly laments the loss of freedom all growth of state powers necessarily entails. Yet at every major point he turns back from confronting the obvious alternative interpretations of the haloed Great Depression. He begins his analysis of the depression two decades after the federal government had seized control of the money supply and after the years of hyperinflation in the stock market prices fueled by the Federal Reserve's low discount rate. He even quotes some economists of the era who warned of the grave dangers of economic collapse posed by all of this, yet he refuses to consider the obvious possibility that they were responding to hard realities of statist central planning. He notes the remarkable fact that Roosevelt's silence during the many months between his election and his inauguration fueled uncertainties and dreads about what he was going to do about credit, and the more remarkable fact that the approaching inauguration of this dreaded Sphinx was exactly correlated with the growing bank panic, and the most remarkable fact of all that the panic erupted precisely at the time of the inauguration, yet he never considers the obvious possibility that Roosevelt was an inspiration of the panic and not merely marching in perfect correlation with it—that, rather than being the savior of the banks, he was their foremost destroyer and then used their failure politically to become their regulator and milker.[4] "The Ancient Regime had become corrupt and thereby fell into Primordial Chaos. And the Lord saw that it was evil and smote it with the Great Depression. And he spoke the Word of Reason and the Light of the New Order spread upon the land and all the waters. And the people rejoiced in the benevolence of the Lord." The realities of both the Depression and FDR were vastly more complex, yet it is remarkable how the theodicies recounting the glorious origins of our modernist welfare states fall routinely into this basic structure of the ancient creation myths. (We shall see much more of this in chapter 5.)

Most prominent social scientists and humanistic scholars subscribe to less extreme forms of these metaphysical theories, yet embrace blatantly political statements as objective historical analyses, and appear ignorant of the explanations of the Great Depression which try to show that the predominant factor among the many important ones was the central planning of money supplies and the many government programs that greatly exacerbated, extended, and protracted the fluctuations found in all economic systems, including the sometimes-severe business cycles of our fractional credit system.[5] The versions of this myth of the capitalistic Götterdämmerung written by Arthur Schlesinger, Jr., and John Kenneth Galbraith are probably the best known of these modernist epics and are firmly embedded in all of the usual political programs for building the modernist megastate.[6] But even more scholarly works, such as historian John Garraty's recent book *The Great Depression*, show the same absolute unwillingness—or inability—to consider the massive evidence that government already *was* the problem rather than the solution. Garraty's story begins with the usual scenario of the Great Depression but provides "flashbacks" to the historical context of disruptions of trade by the war, credit imbalances due to reparations, deflationary policies such as Britain's return to the gold standard in 1926 at prewar values, and massive rigidities caused by government subsidies and trade barriers. But he can never squarely face the unthinkable fact that these huge governments were the prime movers in producing the severity and protractedness of the deflation. He refers to Lionel Robbins's classic analysis, *The Great Depression*, published in 1934, and declares, "Robbins was an excellent economist; his reasoning was logically impeccable, though based on premises that were quite unreasonable."[7] He never says what these "unreasonable" premises were, perhaps because they are now almost unpublishable, but in the context he appears to mean that Robbins believed the economic problems would be solved over the long run only by largely eliminating the massive monopolies and oligopolies of business and labor unions, subsidies, trade barriers, credit controls, central planning of money, and the massive array of other rigidities mandated by government which prevent effective adaptations to the great changes inevitable in the massively complex world economy. The very idea of reducing these massive government regimentations of life are still so "unreasonable" that they are unmentionable for almost all scholars and scientists.

The grapes-of-wrath stories and bowdlerized accounts of the Great Depression are "histories" only in Herodotus's original sense of "stories." They involve the same hodgepodge of fact, rumor, self-presentations, lies, political fables, and myths that his work did twenty-five hundred years ago. Unlike his great work, however, they involve almost no objective analysis— or even mention—of alternative explanations considering the "unreasonable" possibility that impeccable logic may be true. They are done within the political assumptions of the modernist welfare states and are really rationalizations of the ways of the new secular gods—the politicians and their social scientist planners and regulators—to their subjects. They are secular eschatologies and play vital roles in the new secular religions of statist powers.

These hero-worshipping eschatologies of New Federalists, Square Dealers, New Dealers, Fair Dealers, Great Socialists, and others deserve no more credence than the ancient Chinese historians' assertions that their emperors fulfilled the "mandate of heaven" by maintaining the "innate unity of the Chinese realm" (t'ien-hsia), or Virgil's cheerleading for the vast new, but hidden imperial powers of Augustus's welfare state in ancient Rome. Indeed, many of these modern adulatory eschatologies of imperial powers have been written for the same corrupt reasons the Mandarins "proved" the necessity of the emperors' omnipotence and Virgil wrote the *Aeneid*. Just as Mandarins often lived or died at the word of the emperors and Virgil secretly received grants from Augustus's friends to support his "historical" research showing the inevitability of Augustus's new imperial welfare state, so our modern grantspeople are generally supported, both directly and indirectly, by the very powers they are supposedly trying to analyze objectively. Some of them were important personae in the courtly and sacred sagas they have written. Their stories of happy warriors besmiting the evil capitalists and of the wonders of the second coming of Camelot sometimes even have the delightful ring of the stories about divine kings, such as the court historian Callisthenes' breathless account of the sea parting and bowing before the august Alexander. To anyone whose mind is unblinkered by the vast presumptions of our modernist states, what could be more delighting than the accounts of FDR saving the nation by banning uncertainty and fear from the realm, saving capitalism from itself by imposing an immense array of bureaucratic regulations to prevent too much economic freedom, denouncing deficits and the dole and then causing them to soar, slaying the dragon of depression which refused to die, saving the world from tyranny by uniting with Stalin to free Eastern Europe, and declaring an end to poverty and injustice for all time in the charter of the United Utopias?

Even if these acts of the hero are all divine, are they not still divine comedy? No objective observer today who has carefully followed the factual revelations about the political machinations of our presidents, and least of all those of most lesser politicians, takes seriously the stories about selfless and caring politicians chaining the fiery dragon of capitalism. Our politicians are not entirely cynical manipulators of the voters, seeking to maximize their own interests, as journalists who work closely with them every day would have us believe, but neither are they heroes of purity who have transcended the human passion for dominance, as these hagiographers would have us believe. Nor can any objective analyst with a modicum of historical knowledge believe that our modernist welfare states began as simple responses to economic inequalities, since inequalities have been far greater in all other civilizations, or that they began in response to the Great Depression, which, as we shall see, happened long after the foundations of these modernist megastates were firmly in place. It is, in fact, one small part of the argument presented here that these "enabling crises" were normally produced by the growing regulatory powers of the state bureaucracies and that even the most famous of them all, the Great Depression, was initially a severe form of the systemic fluctuations found in all civilizations which was magnified into a protracted systemic crisis primarily by the massive new state powers intended to make them impossible. The modernist welfare states have grown explosively in recent decades primarily because they are self-reinforcing, or autocatalytic. Once they have grown beyond a *critical range*, any increases in their real centralized bureaucratic powers inspire more problems than they solve. (The critical range of *bureaucratic degradation* varies with the *cultural homogenization* and *cultural morale*. In general, the more homogeneous a culture and the higher its members' morale—that is, their optimistic commitment to shared goals—the higher the range of bureaucratic degradation. Thus, a highly homogeneous culture with high morale, such as Japan or Sweden, can endure relatively high levels of central bureaucratization before it erodes the economy and political consensus.[8] The basic reasons for this are presented in chapter 9.) Beyond this critical range of bureaucratic degradation, each new solution to problems in the short run (proximate problems) winds up on average inspiring more problems over the longer run than it solves, which must in turn be "solved" by new bureaucratic powers. At the same time, each "solution" leads masses of people to rearrange their lives in ways that commit them—or "lock them in"—to the "solutions," thereby building a political floor or ratchet under the "solution." The whole system ratchets up by this autocatalytic process toward economic and political catastrophes that can no longer be temporarily alleviated by new state powers. At that point, the megastate is radically restructured by revolutions or foreign conquests.

Most unfortunately, the many serious scholars who have opposed these welfare state eschatologies have normally done so from the fortresses of narrow professional disciplines, especially from those of specializations within neoclassical economics and economic history. (The historians, anthropologists, and political scientists who analyze the origins of state powers, as examined below, rarely mention our modernist welfare states and when they do they almost invariably assume their growth is necessary for the common welfare). The best earlier works have provided most of the bricks of fact and some of the theoretical mortar of my general argument here, but they are inherently incapable of explaining or helping us to reverse the tidal drift of our entire civilization into what Max Weber early in this century called the "iron cage" of modern bureaucratic regimentation. Most of them seize upon a few obvious mistakes in rational calculations of earlier economic theorists, and of interest groups in their grip, as the only important factors producing the ratchets-up in state powers (see appendix III). The revolution against the centuries-long progress of classical liberal philosophy and science, the betrayal of our most basic and most cherished political ideas and institutions integrated with those, and the sweeping tidal drift of this most worldwide and most wondrous of all civilizations into these megastates can hardly be explained as the result merely of mistakes in arcane economic theories.

Certainly there have been many mistakes in fact and theory which have played important supporting roles in this great drift process. John Maynard Keynes's ideas, which are by far the best known of these, certainly had major impacts. That they were built on foundations of false economic *factoids*, statistical *numeroids*, and misanalyses is now admitted even by most of their former supporters. (The even more famous ideas of Karl Marx proved so completely wrong that they are now infamous for their distortions even among Marxists. There are almost no serious Marxist scholars left, since erstwhile serious Marxists, including those in the Kremlin, now generally suppress the many errors of their master's ways and have become neo-Marxists and socialist free marketers.) But Keynesianism and most other enabling economic theories were only one important part of the great tidal drift.

Such economic theories were mainly important in providing the sacred mantle of scientific legitimacy for the new forms of statist ideas hidden in their macro-concepts (see below) and for the ratchets-up after the drift was well under way. They were themselves inspired by the more basic factors of impassioned myths, government programs and the autocatalytic drift that had long been at work. The basic ideas of Keynesian policies and most of those of the American New Deal were proposed by many people in the nineteenth century, but they were firmly repudiated at that time. (Thomas Malthus's famous *Principles of Political Economy Considered with a View to their Practical Application*, published in 1820, presented a theory of "effective demand" and public-works policies for achieving it which were remarkably Keynesian—and Malthusian.) Moreover, the progressive intellectuals of Roosevelt's administration and the fascist planners of Italy and Germany had already put those policies firmly in place before they knew of Keynes's new scientistic mantle for what they had done. Keynes himself was a Labourite socialist many years before he "discovered" the necessity of collectivist economic policies and presented his revelations to a profession already anxious to be converted (just as Marx hated capitalism long before he "discovered" the rationale for his political passions in the musty tomes of the British Museum).[9] A whole generation of Western economists were enthralled and thrown into the full-blown conversion experience at their first hearing of the arcane ideas of Keynesianism, not because his speculations, which were supported only by the flimsiest empirical evidence, were scientifically powerful, but because there were deeper, more passionate, more mythical powers at work inspiring distortions in their thinking. (See chapter 5.[10]) The economic policymakers did not carefully and systematically analyze the validity of such theories in the light of the vast evidence available from all of human history, as one would hope any scientist would do before unleashing extremely speculative ideas upon the world that were intended to transform and even destroy centuries of development of economic ideas, political practices, and institutions. On the contrary, they fell in love with earlier theories and then with Keynes's theory passionately and blindly, in exactly the same passionate conversion experience that seized Albert Speer upon his first hearing of Hitler's messianic program of deliverance for Germany. In the same way, they fell into hatred of classical liberal theory. The converts to economic collectivism did not debate the classical theorists; they heaped scorn and villification upon them. They scourged them and scorched them at academic stakes as if they were witches conspiring with capitalistic Satans. To this day, even after the catastrophic failures of all such collectivist policies, and the vast success of most free-market policies—notably those of Hong Kong, Switzerland, and Japan—it is still routine practice for economic journalists and politically activated economists to blindly attribute ideas to conservative economists which are the exact opposite of what they have clearly and simply stated. These stigmatizing inversions of the enemies' ideas, and even their physical appearances, are found wherever the blind passions of mythical convictions are at work, as any educated American today is aware from reading the latest villifications of the warmongering and totalitarian Americans by Soviet democratic, republican welfare statists.

Since almost all serious scholarship done on the actual workings of our modernist welfare states is done by economists, it is not surprising to find little consideration in this mountain of work given to the great passions and myths, which come before, lie behind, set the goals for, and continually shape the powers of reason, roughly in direct proportion to the arousal of the passions and mythical preconceptions (beyond a critical range, see chapter 5). Almost all economists today work within the paradigm of rationalism created by the ancients, by the French philosophes of the Enlightenment, by the positivist sociologists, and by the so-called neoclassical logicians and mathematicians who progressively replaced the empirical foundations of classical liberal economics with the rationalistic preconceptions of "homo economicus" now enshrined in structural-functional analysis, neoclassical economics, and macro-econometric models. As Wassily Leontief has shown by his analysis of the *American Economic Review*, only a tiny part of what passes for science in economics today is based on direct observations of the real world. A great majority of articles (66 percent) were mathematical models or analyses with no empirical evidence and only 1.4 percent were based on data researched by the author. This former president of the American Economics Association concludes that the professional journals "were filled with mathematical formulas leading the reader from sets of more or less plausible but entirely arbitrary assumptions to precisely stated but irrelevant conclusions."[11] Most of these economists are aware of this and justify their work by arguing that it is prescriptive and proscriptive, rather than inductive in the normal way of the sciences. What they commonly fail to see is that their rationalistic model building and quasi-research is built on the same rationalistic foundations that led to the building of all the welfare-state policies they commonly oppose in the name of efficiency (see chapters 7 and 8). Their arguments are overwhelmingly merely disagreements with the socialistic rationalists over the more efficient means to achieve the same ends. As we shall see, this economic rationalism is a crucial part of the problem, not the solution to the immense, long-run problems of our modern welfare states.

Some economists, including the most empirical of the neoclassical theorists, have always opposed these rationalists and have provided many of the empirical building blocks of my own analysis. Some of these, notably Milton Friedman and most of the so-called "Austrian" and "public choice" economists, have strongly criticized and gone beyond the simplistic theories regarding the rise of our megastates. Robert Higgs's recent work on *Crisis And Leviathan* has made major contributions in analyzing the drift process at work and in concluding that political ideologies (myths) are the crucial factor in the rise of the American welfare state in this century.[12] Their work and that of many other economists have revealed many of the fundamental mistakes of the dominant neoclassical paradigm in economics. Most of them have, however, unknowingly continued to suffer from some of the fundamental mistakes of the rationalistic paradigm they criticize and from the narrow approach that paradigm inspired, especially its focus on the few important variables involved for which there is quantitative official information. While some of them, notably Friedman and Higgs, have concluded that changes in ideological, or mythical, preconceptions were the ultimate causes of the changes they document in the official figures (state control of the gross national product and so on), they have rarely attempted to systematically describe and analyze these ultimate factors. They have also generally failed to see the extreme importance of the myth of the welfare state which is the cornerstone of all long-successful statism and, by failing to look at the basic dimensions of human nature through the eons of the history of the great drifts in the waxing and waning of state powers, have failed to see that state powers do not simply continue to soar onward and upward into ever more steely cages of enslavement. (Welfare statism, as we shall see, was obvious in the first imperial states five thousand years ago and has been the cornerstone of all state powers. Human beings caught up in the great drifts into state bureaucratic regimentation do often wind up being enslaved, as has happened on the most massive scale in history in the communist nations, but, just as there are autocatalytic processes at work in the waxing of state powers, so are there obviously downward-autocatalytic processes that come into play at the higher levels of bureaucratic regimentations. The informational pathologies of bureaucracies themselves produce unintended consequences rejected by human nature, so that these iron cages eventually produce their own denouements, usually by producing political catastrophes that lead to an escape from statist regimentation.) Equally importantly, they have failed to see that the great myths sweeping our modern world interacted with the ancient enabling myths, apparatuses, and operations of the state and the normal striving for political power to inspire acceptance of the new ideologies of welfare statism which have been the focus of their attention.

Early Theories of the State

Considering the immense impacts the huge bureaucratic states have on human life, it is remarkable how little serious thought has been devoted to analyzing statism. Certainly there have been some major contributions made in several eras in which great crises of statist powers erupted. The works of Aristotle, Thucydides, the Legalists of ancient China, the *Artha–śāstra* of ancient India, Machiavelli, Hobbes, Bodin, Locke, Montesquieu, the authors of *The Federalist*, and roughly a few score of modern analysts remain fresh and relevant to statism today. But these are only a handful of works. A random sample of books published today, when everyone knows a nuclear war between the super states could kill most of us in half an hour, would reveal whole libraries of anguished analyses of dieting and cosmetizing, but few analyses of statism that go beyond summaries of Aristotle, Machiavelli, Hobbes, and others. Today the literature concerning the practical issues of government policies is immense. There are small mountains of works arguing that they are evil or wonderful, the cause of warfare and poverty, or the savior from strife and all of life's erstwhile ills (or eventually the savior, since no sane person believes anything has yet banned nuclear holocaust or many other great evils such as poverty from our world). There are great mountain ranges of works presenting the labyrinthine complexities of the cost-benefit analyses of these myriad programs. But recent creative analyses of the fundamental nature and origins of the states enforcing these policies is little more than a molehill.[13]

The reasons for this deafening silence seem clear. In almost all of the ancient civilizations and in almost all of the more recent ones, state powers are so pervasive that they have been almost completely taken for granted and are thus not visible enough for rational analysis. Moreover, any serious questioning of them has commonly been seen as secular heresy—treason, in modern terms—warranting censorship and ostracism by the mass media and excommunication by professional groups in our democratic realms. Meddling with the taken-for-granted assumptions, the deep backgrounds of everyday life, is normally a dangerous enterprise until a great crisis is recognized, as Socrates demonstrated so graphically and as any social scientist out of step with today's fashionable *Zeitgeist* can well attest.

The vast majority of social theorists have been saved from the testing of their courage by the self-imposed blessing of cognitive blindness. They have not even realized that their analyses were built on the invisible foundation of the core enabling myths and operations of state powers. Even the classical liberal economists took for granted the existence of the state as the protector, the umpire, and the guarantor of contracts. The neoclassical economists today do the same, with an occasional nod toward Adam Smith's assertion about public goods and the "invisible hand," and the assertion that the legislative and regulatory "umpire" (Hobbes's "sovereign" in a sporty disguise) reduces transaction costs. Adam Smith's invisible hand may be only a metaphor, but it encourages the myth that the market is a mechanistic, separate level of existence operating at a distance on the individuals, rather than all the unseen individuals making their trillions of decisions that in aggregate *are* the market. Economic analysts today routinely reify markets when they say, "The markets did X, Y, and Z."

Structuralist sociologists, tracing their roots back to the totalitarian ideas of Rousseau, Fourier, Saint-Simon, and Comte, so completely take it for granted that "society is a separate level of reality," as the professional founding father Emile Durkheim put it, that they rarely even know there is a theoretical argument. (The sociologists of everyday life, so-called micro-sociologists, believe society is an aggregate of the individuals who make it up, but they rarely discuss larger orderings or patterns seen as relevant to social policy today.[14]) Political scientists are more diverse and some still show a lively interest in some of the basic questions raised many centuries ago by political theorists, but the vast majority of them are now blinded to those questions by the many problems involved in calculating the latest blips in opinion surveys about one of the many thousands of government programs. Almost all historians and historical political scientists are now so completely lost in the minutiae of searching for the twists and turns in former rulers' rationales for state powers that even most of the rare comparativists must concentrate on the minutiae of a few disparate threads of the history of state powers or fear excommunication.[15] Though one might expect that political scientists in the most freedom-loving of major nations would be deeply concerned with analyzing the nature of statism, the opposite has been true. American political scientists in the late nineteenth century were extremely important in importing and grafting onto the traditional American ideas of national federationism the ancient ideas of statism and legalism, in their modernist forms of positivistic structuralism or macro-analysis. (See chapter 4.) With some important exceptions, especially conservative analyses of nationalism, political scientists have become even more blind in taking for granted the self-professed benevolence and happy consequences of the modernist politicians. For every social scientist seriously analyzing the nature of statism and its consequences, there are scores passionately dedicated to writing the hagiographies of benevolent welfare-statists, polling voters to help politicians and bureaucrats increase their statist powers, lobbying for public interest causes, and milking our welfare states through academic grantsmanship and bureaucratic politicing.

Most social scientists, journalists, and other public figures today also show a growing schizophrenic fissure between their analyses of politics in the narrow sense (elections, votes by representatives, etc.) and public policy in an even broader sense. Since all of our ideas and institutions of democracy were created (or, actually, basically reformulated) by classical liberals who believed individuals are the primary reality (or the only reality for the most consistent), our political symbols still show this sediment of individualism.[16] Our courts proclaim more sternly than ever, "One adult, one vote," now with no restrictions of responsibility (property or taxation), knowledge, or even much mental competence. Only children and convicted felons remain outside of the mass aggregate of lever pullers.

But this residue of the classical liberal symbolism of individualism and aggregate federalism is completely misleading. In fact, these external nominal forms of Jeffersonian individualism now vary inversely with the inner realities of statism and statist powers. We see this most obviously in all of the totalitarian communist realms, where voting is a statist duty obeyed by almost 100 percent of the repressed individualists and where some of the most statist societies in history are proclaimed to be People's Democratic Republics. The symbolic forms of classical liberalism have obviously become the clothing for extreme statist tyranny in those nations. In our still-real democracies they have the similar effect of promoting our self-deceptions. Precisely at the same time mass and direct individualist forms have advanced, the inner and real meanings of all the basic ideas, and, thus, of the practices, have been eroded and replaced by statist ideas and practices.

This schizophrenia is still most extreme in the economic realm. For example, in the nineteenth century when consumer sovereignty (the freedom to buy) was at its zenith, little was heard of capitalism or even the free market. Today capitalism and free-market names are broadcast shrilly by all the mass media, but the reality is a vast explosion of statist bureaucracies of regulations to "protect the (common) consumer welfare." The same thing is happening in all other realms of life—air, water, excretion, and so on. The common welfare defined and enforced by the statist executives, legislators, judges, and bureaucrats is rapidly eliminating all real individualistic ideas and practices in the still-sacred name of our traditional System of Natural Liberty.

Most serious and creative work in recent decades on the origins of state powers has been done by anthropologists. The values of this work, as of the rare works in other fields, will be obvious throughout this book, but there are two serious problems with it that must be kept in mind. Because anthropological education is concerned overwhelmingly with stateless (primitive or simple) societies, most of the anthropologists analyzing the origins and nature of statism know relatively little about the vast history of statism which has accumulated in the five thousand years of written records. These records are the only ones that, however incompletely, give us any direct access to the vastly complex political feelings, values, ideas, and strategies involved in the struggles over statism and individualism. Unfortunately, anthropologists have maximized this problem by focusing increasingly on the area of expertise over which they have academic sovereignty—archaeology. Since archaeologists concentrate overwhelmingly on nonwritten cultural artifacts and on highly decontextualized early written records, they wind up building their theories largely on records that by their very nature give no direct access to what the actors were thinking or feeling. Thus, their analyses wind up being extremely general and highly problematic inferences about what the actors felt, thought, and did. Since physical artifacts are so "thing-like," they easily mislead their analysts into believing they have "hard" evidence, even the "thing in itself" that alone gives hard, scientific knowledge. This is the illusion of mechanistic materialism that led centuries of would-be social thinkers down the primrose path to scientism and to complete irrelevance in scientifically understanding human beings. Anyone with the slightest acquaintance with the complex strategic thinking and action of Shih Huang-Ti, Pericles, Phillip, Alexander, Thucydides, Caesar, Augustus, or thousands of other politicians and military rulers we know from written records is aware that the ancients were every bit as complex, sophisticated, wily, and deceitful as their modernist cultural heirs. Such a person also knows how adept the ancients were even at using material artifacts to mislead their enemies and awe their subjects. The best anthropological theorists certainly know about these problems and try to avoid them. They also rightly argue that the written records are far more easily falsified—a major point I shall make especially about all statist records—and need to be checked against unwritten ones. Unfortunately, they still put far too much trust in their inferences of vastly complex meanings from tiny and scattered physical droppings and greatly underestimate how much history must be understood backward from our understanding of human nature today and how vital the vastly complex assumptions of situational contexts are in truthfully inferring meanings.

The anthropologists also argue that this great reliance on archaeological evidence is necessary because the processes involved in the origins of the first states, the *primary states*, in any cultural tradition can be fundamentally different from the processes involved in creations of the later *secondary states*. Since the earliest roots of the states grew before there were any written records, we necessarily rely on material artifacts to study them. This is obviously true and it is obviously important to know as much as we can about origins that did not involve imitation or, more important, responses to the threats posed by the far-larger military machines of the primary states. Knowing the origins of the primary states would give us a baseline of information about human nature in relation to statism. They would show us how statist powers originate when there are no statist powers to copy or pose a threat. If nothing else, these studies of the earliest human artifacts make it quite clear that states are very recent in human history, that they are not in any way the result of direct genetic programming (see chapter 3) and that, once bureaucratic military machines are able to concentrate far-greater military power than can nonstatist societies, the nonstatist societies must organize themselves as federations or states, or become the tax-exploited or enslaved subjects of the state rulers.[17] These studies are vital in leading us to expect that state powers necessarily breed discontent or alienation which are endured once they get going primarily because of the real threats of subjugation by other states and because of mistaken and mythical thinking. (Freud's argument that civilization necessarily breeds discontent was largely a result of the early archaeological arguments, which fascinated him, that the earliest states created civilization and, thus, that state repressions are coterminous with civilization. This idea is now discredited by the archaeological findings of the prestatist roots of civilization.)

In spite of the importance of these studies of the first origins, they also pose a great danger of misunderstanding. The very nature of the material artifacts precludes their containing any direct communications of such nonmaterial phenomena as identifications of the self with abstract essences of being, membership, and rulership. As soon as we have written records or can directly observe the processes of state formation, we can see the vast importance of divine kingship, of the mythical identification of the rulers with the gods and the essences of being.[18] None of this can be directly observed in the early artifacts, but can easily be inferred backward from our understanding of sacred kingship in the ancient world and in later states, from more than the artifacts themselves.

Consider, for example, how totally anyone could be misled by the artifacts—or non-artifacts—of our own Western societies in recent decades.

Anyone studying Europe in the early 1940s could easily infer from the twisted weapons remaining that there were great battles. But what would they know about the motives for these battles? Considering how many more of the weapons could be traced to the United States, they might well infer that this was a great imperialistic invasion from the new world. How would they know that it had anything to do with democratic and totalitarian political systems, with the Versailles Treaty, with French and German nationalism, or with Hitler's religio-statist myths of the Thousand Year Reich (with its passionate resonances of both Christian and modernist millennialism) and Leadership (with its passionate resonances of sacred kingship and sacred warriorship). In fact, since the allies destroyed so many of the massive artifacts of Nazi statism, while leaving their own in place, it might easily look as if the Nazis were fighting against the monstrous statism of the democracies, especially when the monstrous artifacts of Stalinist statism were discovered and Stalin was found to be allied with the democracies. Not only did the allies destroy the material Hitlerian monuments to Caesarism built by Albert Speer, but his most awe-inspiring sacraments of Nazism were the cathedrals of light and the immense gatherings of worshippers before the host, which leave no material droppings.

Again, consider how easy it would be to observe the colossal stone and earth monuments to American nationalism built early in this century and conclude that the American rulers were the pharaohs of the modern world who forced their slaves to build huge monuments to worship their images. These are indeed colossal monuments of American statism, but it would be a great mistake to infer that they show that most Americans submitted to these nationalist myths and the rulers identified with them. It would be a complete inversion of the truth to infer that the absence of colossal Hitler statues means that he had no pharaonic aspirations and that the colossal Washington, Lincoln, and Jefferson monuments show they did. It is also almost certainly an inversion of the truth to infer from their colossal mausoleums, as modernist Hollywood movies have done, that the pharaohs were cruel totalitarians forcing a dyswelfare state upon enslaved subjects. Though totalitarian aspirations and some quite-modern totalitarian methods existed in the ancient world, as we find from the written records concerning the Assyrian empire, the extreme totalitarian statism we have seen so commonly in our century has become possible only because of the new technologies of immense firepower, mass-education indoctrination, and mass-mediated mythification—agitprop.

The informational biases resulting from the emphases on archaeological information have led recent anthropologists to concentrate on two simple factors as sources of powers in the primary states, both of which can be plausibly inferred from the skimpy material records. (I shall deal with these in chapter 3.) The *conflict theorists*, following the lead of classical scholars and nineteenth century theorists such as Herbert Spencer, argue that statist powers were first built on the physical force of military power. The ferocious struggles for empire throughout all written history provide a rich source of support for such theories when the interpretations are done backward from written records. Since the earliest known sites of civilized habitation were commonly assumed to be coterminous with statism, especially when theorists such as Karl Wittfogel[19] argued that the statists created civilization, the evidence that they were generally built on easily defended mounds or surrounded by walls seemed to lend strong support to the theory. The *integrative theorists*, who interpreted their archaeological evidence backward from studies of primitive big men and chiefs directly observed by anthropologists around the world, argued that the first state rulers performed core welfare functions for their societies which integrated the subjects into far more efficient systems of trade and law (peace and order). Their archaeological evidence is more complex and tenuous, since official records of trade and the material evidence of production and trade are not as directly attributable to creation by the rulers.

These theorists have faced many other problems in addition to those inherent in all theories based on archaeological evidence. Most importantly, it has become increasingly clear that it is not generally possible to disentangle military power from trade and law, or to establish that one came before the other. Much evidence has been marshaled by each side to prove that its factor was the prime mover or first cause of statist powers, but each new bit of evidence is soon countered by another. Also, the more complete records, such as those of the Aztecs, now seem clearly to show vastly more complexity in the power relations than was first thought. It used to seem obvious that the central powers subjugated the provincial elites through the use of raw military power, or the plausible threat to do so. More detailed evidence reveals that the provincial elites received various benefits from the redistribution efforts of the emperors which encouraged them to submit, or to conspire with their subjugators to subjugate the provincial populations, while appearing to be unhappy with imperial subjugation in order to placate their own unhappy subjects.[20] We are well aware today of how mixed such motives are of the various East European communist rulers and of how inherently problematic it is to infer such motives even when we have massive direct observations of the rulers. We are also well aware that the leaders of the PRI in Mexico today talk like Marxist planners and redistributors at home, talk like capitalists to Western leaders and journalists, and pursue Byzantine strategies in action that deceive or befuddle almost everyone. It is not surprising to find the brilliant Mexican politicians several centuries ago behaved in similar ways, nor will it be at all surprising to find the earliest statists from all cultures did such things, if we ever get good enough records to trust such inferences.

Recently the most comprehensive anthropological analysts of the origins of states have recognized more of these problems inherent in the nature of the records and have guided their interpretations of the skimpy findings of archaeology by their understandings of how rulers today behave, though they still are more apt to bootleg this understanding than to admit it. (The sophisticated hypotheses of Jonathan Haas,[21] for example, are obviously derived from observations of more contemporary political thought and action.) This has led them very quickly to see that there is no clear evidence for any single path to state powers. The most comprehensive analyses now recognize that there are a number of basic factors involved in state powers and that rulers may accumulate those different power bases over time in almost any combination. Their analyses are rapidly approaching the complexity and sophistication achieved by S.N. Eisenstadt[22] in his work twenty-five years ago on the "rise and fall of historical bureaucratic societies"—the great imperial states that have ruled most civilized human beings for the past five thousand years. (For some nonreason, presumably having far more to do with professional turf struggles and fashions in respectability than scientific truth, they have rarely discovered his massive work, or that of the great general theorists in history of the last three centuries.)

These analysts have come increasingly to recognize that a distinctive ideology used by the would-be rulers to justify their power to the people is crucial to their long-run success. As Eisenstadt noted, for example, the two most glaring examples of empires that declined very quickly, the Carolingian and Mongol, failed to develop ideologies that were distinct to the rulers and that legitimized their rule sufficiently to the people.[23] Both relied on earlier, more traditional forms of ideological legitimacy, rather than developing ideologies that legitimized their own exclusive exercise of power. (They tried to *graft* their power onto traditional ideologies, groups, and states without creating anything sufficiently distinctive to legitimize their power over that of traditional competitors, which would produce a real *hybrid state*. Hybrid states tend by far to be the most successful forms of statism. Both *grafted states* and their opposite, the relatively *upstart states* such as the Soviet communist state, are inherently very unstable and tend not to last long. As we shall see, situational factors always play a big part in such drift processes. The existence of external threats, for example, can lead people to cling to the military power of statists they abhor, as was obvious when Russians who first welcomed the Nazi invaders turned against them because they discovered the Nazis came as worse enslavers rather than liberators.)

Unfortunately, these analysts have tended to limp along on the popular conception of ideology as any system of ideas. Most systems of statist ideas eventually prove highly illegitimate to most people, even when they have welcomed the ideas at first as a possible salvation from a failed ideology. And no matter how legitimate ideas are nominally—in the abstract, generally because they fit some traditional ideals—the failure of rulers to operate them in such a way as to deliver some minimally acceptable basket of welfare quickly erodes the legitimacy of the ideology and of the rulers using it. (The Weimar Republic may have had legitimacy only with a minority of Germans from the beginning, and much of that was eroded in a few years by catastrophic government operations, especially hyperinflation. The communist parties around the world are now facing great crises because their communist ideologies, immense central planning, and colossal bureaucratic administration have failed to deliver the minimal welfare goods. The Soviets, being upstart rulers who sternly attacked traditional Christian values and practices that still have great legitimacy among the people, face a far greater crisis than the Chinese communist party, which retained far more of the traditional Mandarin legitimacy.)

More importantly, they have failed to see the categorical difference between all other ideologies and a system of *statist myths* which convince the people that the state is a separate and higher level of reality from the people who make it up. Almost all very successful and powerful states in these first five thousand years of statism have relied predominantly on some variants (grafts and hybrids) of the sacred kingship myths which encourage the faithful to believe that the ruler of the state is directly identified with, descended from, or otherwise linked to the essence of all being and all power.[24] The more anthropologists have made use of more detailed and full records, the more they have come to recognize that the most successful statist rulers, like the monarchists, have always tried mightily through their massive agitprop to identify themselves with the gods, with the essence of all being and all magico-religious power. The direct descent from the gods claimed by the sacred kings is only the most extreme form of this essential identification. The Lenins and Stalins who claim to be the ineluctable wave of the historical process, and the Hitlers who claim to be the voices of providence and of the sacred essence of the blood of the people are making the same kind of mythical identification of themselves with all being and all power. The American president who claims to speak for a "nation" that is outside of the individual Americans, and that demands the obedience of the individuals to this greater and transcendent good, or who claims to be acting in accord with the iron truths of absolute economic science or of an absolute moral vision is making a claim to identification with the sacred essence of being, only weaker and in more secular garb (see chapter 4). What varies are the degrees and the cultural forms of expression, not the essential identification of the ruler with the state and the state with sacred being.

The rulers of ancient Egypt and Sumeria, at least one of which is recognized by all the archaeologists to be the first state, were at the extreme in sacredness. It was long thought that the priests of the ziggurats (pyramidal temples) in Sumeria ruled by their sacred myths alone, but this is now disputed. The pharaohs of Egypt were not only seen by the faithful as descended from the gods but as the necessary intermediaries between the gods and the people, hence as the necessary interceders between the people and eternal afterlife. When everything in this world and in eternity in the other world is believed to depend ultimately on the will of the ruler, the ruler's power is vast indeed. Since we know little from the early centuries except what was recorded in official records, especially in the royal tombs, we can have no good idea of just who believed these myths or how strong their faith was; but the general guesstimate is that the faith was widespread and deep. The very fragmentary records and folk legends about the earliest rulers in the primary states of China, India, and the Americas indicates that they were roughly as sacred. Some fragments of these mythical convictions can still be directly observed in peasant convictions about reigning monarchs, even the rather scientific emperor of Japan.

In the Western nations the earliest known states in Greece and Rome seem to have had sacred kings. However, by the time written records were common enough to give much of an idea about political ideas, the kings had been overthrown by foreign conquerors or by aristocrats and remained only as legendary memories. In the sixth and fifth centuries B.C. the people of the city-states of Greece and Rome differed considerably in their ideas about their states. The non-Asian Greek political ideas involved consideration of the individual and family perspectives as well as the statist perspective of the common welfare of the city. The statist perspective seems clearly to have eroded the individual and family perspective, but the nominalist view of the political body of the city—that the body is made up of all its individual members—probably remained the dominant one, in spite of Plato's assertion that all reality is derived from the abstract symbols of the particulars and his totalitarian organic view of the state. The nominalism of Aristotle, however, was not entirely consistent. He and other Greeks of his day also partially reified abstract ideas, such as that of the state, arguing that they are the essences or substances that lie behind, live in, and animate (as formal causes and teleological causes) the world of particulars or individuals. The Aristotelian Greeks were remarkably similar in this basic respect to Americans in this century, including the neoclassical economists with their extensive ideas of public goods. In Macedonia, by contrast, the myths of sacred kingship were still far more accepted and became the ideological foundation for Alexander's grandiose plans to rule the world. His conquests and the subsequent Hellenistic regimes led to a resurgence of sacred kingship which probably greatly influenced Roman ideas of the state and ruler.[25]

The Romans were generally statist in their political ideas even during the republican period. The primal concept of Roman political thought in this area was the *res publica*, which literally meant the "thing" or "being" of the Roman Republic. This Romanness was clearly believed to be a separate, higher, and ultimately sacred reality to which individuals should and must subordinate their lives, even to the point of giving up their lives for this essence of Roman statism. This Roman idea of the state became the common coin of Western political thought (see chapter 4) and to this day remains the ideal of Western thinkers who share the conviction that identification with the essence of the state is necessary for the common welfare, though they are now commonly unaware of the ancient origins of their idea. While it acted initially to constrain tyranny (*regnum*), the *res publica* provided the emperors from Augustus onward with the conceptual foundation for the principate. Once the principle of the superiority of the public welfare over private welfare ("Utilitas publica prefertur utilitati privatae")[26] was wedded to *res publica*, the princes exercised *regnum* in the name of freedom. Thomas Macaulay, though a founder of Whig historical interpretation, presented a shining image of this ideal almost two centuries ago which captures the Roman ideal, if not the inevitably more complex realities.

> Then none was for a party—
> Then all were for the state;
> Then the great man helped the poor,
> And the poor man loved the great;
> Then lands were fairly portioned;
> Then spoils were fairly sold:
> The Romans were like brothers
> In the brave days of old.

Though their explanations differ greatly these days, historians generally agree that this identification with the *res publica* waned rapidly in the second and first century B.C. For centuries historians saw the Gracchi Revolt, beginning in 133 B.C., as a catastrophic break in the commitment to the Republican spirit which led to a century of terrible civil wars and eventually the Augustan tyranny. Their basic argument was that the noble Gracchi brothers betrayed the spirit of the *res publica* by turning the landless and urban mobs against the senators, the rulers who embodied this spirit of the republic. Once broken by factional conflicts, the rulers' claim to sovereignty was denied or quickly eroded and the "war of all against all" necessarily followed. Augustus then supposedly enforced order by the use of illegitmate, tyrannical power, which is the only substitute for the legitimacy derived from the conviction that all citizens are identified with each other and through their common commitment to the conviction that the rulers of the state represent the common interest.

Historians now recognize that this is much too simple, and most seem to despair of explaining what happened. It is clear, for one thing, that the traditional ideas never completely waned. Whereas Caesar had openly defied the republican traditions, and thus made it apparent that "The state *is* Caesar," as Ovid said, Augustus went to the opposite extreme of presenting himself as the humble servant of the people and the spirit of the republic. He hid his tyrannical powers behind massive fronts and extreme rhetoric of republicanism. As Rostovtzeff said, "Augustus avoided all appearances of unconstitutional action."[27] Moreover, his rule was a tyranny primarily from the perspective of the senators, not that of the businessmen or plebeians who supported him. But the senators apparently so deeply dreaded a return of the slaughter of senators that they acquiesced in not living by their own ideal, much as the Soviet elites today acquiesce in bureaucratic tyranny rather than court a return to the dreaded years of terror. Regardless of his public protestations of humility and any senatorial disquiet, the plebeians of the city grasped the essential reality of his awesome powers and duely identified him and his powers with the sacred essences of being. As is true of all godly powers, Augustus's awesome person and powers were believed to pervade being itself and, thus, to permeate the physical objects and places with which he made any contact. Suetonius, thus, reported that the people were actually afraid to enter the room in Velitrae where he had been born and insisted that strange things happened to those who did. By his mere presence, his holy personhood could excite the ecstasy that comes from the feeling of merging with the godhead, the awesome excitement seen in the presence of all powerful state rulers. (*Ex-stasis* literally meant the losing or transcendence of the individuated sense of self, as seen in the mystical communions with gods such as Dionysus.) Though succeeding emperors became increasingly open in their claims to identification with the gods, they maintained the outer formalities of Augustan humility, presumably because they knew well from Caesar's example that the most vital tactic in building tyrannical powers is precisely the front of humility and public submission to the will of the people.[28] As they humbly proclaimed, "Salus populi suprema lex" ("The welfare of the people is the highest law"). But, of course, the people came in time to see the brute, if veiled, realities of awesome statist powers: when the common welfare of the people is checked by nothing but the will of the people who support the statist ruler, he is absolute until the people revolt against his power. As the Greek historian Appian of Alexandria wrote in the second century A.D., "And the government has remained in the hands of one ruler up till now. They do not speak of them as kings, out of respect, I believe, for the ancient oath, but call them Imperatores, which used to be the title of those who held command for limited periods. But they are in fact in every respect kings." We shall see in the next chapter that these basic ideas of the essence of statehood have been transmitted down through the centuries and that once again we may be witnessing the rebirth of sacred kingships in the humble garbs of our modernist welfare statists who proclaim the welfare of the majority of voters to be the highest law.

These ancient roots of statism in the reification of sacred essences have been recognized in bits and pieces for many centuries. In the last century a number of brilliant analysts analyzed what Leonard Hobhouse called *The Metaphysical Theory Of The State.*[29] In this century some historical analysts—especially Robert MacIver,[30] Ernst Cassirer,[31] Ernst Kantorowicz,[32] and Reinhard Bendix[33]—have made major contributions to the understanding of these mythical ideologies that lie behind the most important of the more proximate ideas and practices of our modernist welfare states. (This whole tradition of thought must be distinguished from the far more famous tradition of the Machiavellian theory of *statist engineering*. In the beginning of *The Prince*, Machiavelli notes that he is concerned with power that is *not* based on what we now call legitimacy. He was concerned, then, with *tyrannical government* powers, not the far more important *statism* that is crucial to the rise of tyrannies *from within* and their continuance through the use of agitprop to engineer new legitimacies.[34])

I have had to develop these basic ideas further to take into consideration the major differences in the drift processes followed in our different societies. Even the most developed of these theories place far too much emphasis on the earlier myths and not enough on the newer ones of modernism, rationalism-scientism, and secular millennialism. (Ernst Cassirer, for example, did so in part because he focused on Nazi Germany where these were not nearly so important as in more rationalistic and scientistic France. Reinhard Bendix sees the conflict between modernists and traditionalists as crucial, but has little consideration of the rationalism-scientism and secular millennialism-utopianism of the modernists in the West, China, and elsewhere.) Very importantly, I have had to develop a general model of the drift processes at work which shows the major importance of economic and political factors in our modernist societies. It will be a very great help in understanding this complex theory to present its major outlines in the beginning. This model, however, is a system of conclusions, not of hypotheses derived *ex cathedra*.

The Core Myths, Operations, and Bureaucratic Apparatuses of State Rulers

Because most analysts have taken the foundations of our welfare states for granted as necessary and right, they have rarely looked at those foundations.

Our modernist welfare states are *states* first and foremost. *Statism* is the necessary foundation of all of the most enduring of them, especially in the West, Russia, and China. Statism is a set of impassioned beliefs, or convictions, that are hybridized with and built upon the natural human identifications with loved ones, especially in the extreme form of parent-child identification in which children at first so greatly identify with the father and mother that they barely have a separate sense of self and must slowly drift away from their parents to do so. (All would-be powerful rulers to this day encourage the people to fall in love with them and identify them as "fathers" of their nations and states.) These basic convictions of statism have existed and been transmitted from the first successful states of the ancient world, roughly five thousand years ago. Our modernist welfare states have added vitally important dimensions to those ancient foundations, especially rationalist-scientism, the futuristic legitimacy of modernism, and the secularization of millennialism (see chapter 6). But our megastates are grafted on or hybridized with the same ancient foundations.

Government apparatuses that are not built on these ancient foundations of statism *mimic* welfare states in some respects. Most of the roughly 150 sovereign governments in the world today are not states; they are merely governments and some are little more than shells making claims to nominal powers they do not exercise effectively. They often rely heavily on infusions of foreign aid and foreign loans to payoff so called interest groups and individuals for their subservience or acquiescence. But these welfare payoff systems without a foundation of statism are really what Americans call political machines and are run very much the way gangsters and politicians ran Chicago, Boston, and other American cities. When the payoffs end, there is normally little foundation except bureaucratic military suppression left and the system comes unraveled in domestic strife. Governments can combine any degree of statism with any degree of such bribery systems and military suppression. The Mexican government is a very complex combination of both, while most African governments are little more than a core-state of one minority tribal nation with a payoff system or *machine empire* built around it,[35] and largely financed by foreign aid and unrepayable loans.

Certainly our modernist welfare states show wide variations on the earlier forms of statism, and certainly they have their unique characteristics hybridized with or grafted onto the earlier roots, just as all successors to the original states have had. The vast scope of their bureaucratization of life makes minnows of all previous Leviathans, and this bureaucratic gigantism alone adds new dimensions to all earlier forms (see chapter 9). But these variations on the ancient centralized powers have been possible only because the impassioned beliefs, the myths, that the elites and masses of people assume as the background of all of their thinking about the bigger social world changed in integral dependency with the explosion of these powers. Most importantly, the ancient impassioned beliefs in statism have progressively swept aside the impassioned beliefs and the rational thinking that formed the foundation of our traditional System of Natural Liberty, commonly referred to in the United States as our constitutional form of republican federalism. If there had been no foundations of statist myths on which to build these variations, or if they had not been reinvented, there would be no modern welfare states, by any accepted definition. We might well have monstrous political machines, but these quickly run their greedy course as the payoffs bankrupt the political coffers.

No matter how rational the arguments of neoclassical economists might be, it is exceedingly unlikely that they could convince a group of hunters and gatherers to submit themselves to statist powers. Thomas Hobbes's rationalistic argument in favor of the totally centralized powers of the state ruler (sovereignty) did not convince the classical liberal thinkers, including the American constitutionalists, that they should submit to the one-and-only word of any totalitarian (as we would now call his monarch). On the contrary, his rationalistic proof of the origins and the necessity of totalitarian power, which he couched in the scientistic rhetoric of the classical mechanics of his day, was almost universally rejected and condemned by the most empirically rational philosophers of the English-speaking world, almost universally adored by the grantsmen of the would-be absolute monarchs of Britain and Europe, and revived by rationalists building the foundations of our modernist megastates in the nineteenth century. The vast powers of the state, and most obviously the theoretically unlimited powers of the absolute (completely sovereign) state, are never built on reason alone, though rulers of the states are always anxious to claim they are, especially in our age of rationalism-scientism, and always pay intellectual wordsmiths to prove they are.

A rationally agreed upon set of decisions and actions in which the identities of the individuals remain separate and aggregated realities is a *federation*, not a state. Federations are probably as old as the human mind and were fully developed in ancient Greece, in the form of *synoecism*. Acting by federated cooperation is a very rational and vastly productive human enterprise, as we see in the teamwork of our most successful neighborhood projects, scientific work, and business corporations. (These are not "corporations" in the ancient Roman sense of the "sole corporation"—which is a concretized essence of the group—except in certain legal fictions. In Japan the traditional corporations do partake of the statist essence; thus individuals identify with their corporations to a high degree. American businesspeople sometimes are swept away by megalomania and try to induce Fordism or something similar by mass agitprop, but American workers remain cool to corporatism.) Statism is not mere federationism. A federation may be a small group, which is what so-called voluntary organizations are, or a huge aggregation of individuals or nations in which there are no elements of statism, as we see in the famous league, or federation, of the Iroquois Indian nations. Normally, however, large federations with governmental bureaucratic apparatuses are built out of subunit states. The common form of this is what is known as an *empire*, most obvious in the ancient forms of the Roman Empire, the Aztec Empire, the Inca Empire, the Hapsburg Empire, the British Empire, and the Soviet Empire today. Empires in the beginning are normally largely involuntary groups in which the imperial power uses military force and payoffs to subunit state rulers to gain subservience or acquiescence, but emperors from the very beginning of the dual empire of ancient Egypt (under Narmer or Menes) have used every means, especially those of mass agitprop, to foster the myths of statism. Though their success has varied greatly, successful empires tend over the very long run to drift from indirect controls to the more direct controls of statism, in direct proportion to their direct and central bureaucratic regimentation of life, especially of education, throughout the subunit states. Nevertheless, states are quite distinct from empires.[36]

Statism involves a belief, whether implicit or explicit, that the *identities* of the individuals involved in collective decisions and actions (beyond the family and love partnerships) are to some degree *fused*, so that the individuals to that degree become less real while the collectivity becomes more real— *reified* abstractions. States are not mere "nations," though the most successful state rulers begin with nationhood and build their creations of statehood into nation-states. A *nation* is a group of people who have a *sense of community* which is the recognition of common *identifications* made up of common morals, common territory, common language, and common interests symbolized by common names, flags, and so on. The national sense of community is any degree and type of common *identification of selves* beyond those based on family and loving partnerships (friendships, romantic loves, etc.[37]). They range from the intense common identifications of *tribalism* to the looser ones of *federalism* such as we see in "Americanism" or "Swissness." Family, loving, and national (community) identifications of selves are normally *partial* and recognized as *symbolic* (moral). They are intended to increase the individual self and to make the individual more whole in the partial union. (When they are not, they are seen to be dependent, repressive, and so on.[38]) They add to the individuals' sense of selves, without submerging the identities of the individuals who make up the nation and share the sense of community. Nations may exist and even be spread around the world without constituting a state. The Jews from the time of the Roman expulsion until the founding of Zionism were a highly united people in this sense of sharing a sense of community, without having any idea of being a state, of having their individual identities submerged in a whole greater than their individual parts and subordinate to rulers representing that statehood.

A state exists only when individual identities and rational decision making and action based on aggregating the decisions of those individuals is superceded by what is believed to be a separate, greater, and unitary reality. Statism is a mythical reification or concretization of supra-individual identification which is always partly based on extra-rational, impassioned beliefs, or myths. This crucial fact was well recognized and analyzed by Western political thinkers over several centuries, but it was increasingly excluded from serious analysis as Western scholars became increasingly swept up in the impassioned beliefs of statism and devoted to building the foundations and the powers of modernist megastates.[39]

There are variations in the degree of separateness conceived to exist between the state and its members; and there are variations in the degree of separateness believed to exist in the calculations of state (common) welfare and the aggregated individual welfares, which is probably what most American constitutionalists had in mind when they spoke of the general welfare (a practice I shall continue here). But the distinction between individual welfares and *the* common welfare supposedly represented by the state and interpreted by the rulers has been important in Western societies since the ancient world. Almost all rulers have insisted, at least when rebellious opposition arises, that there is not only a great difference between the two, but that there are some inherent contradictions between the common welfare and the general welfare. These supposedly inherent contradictions have been called "reasons of state" by Western statists for centuries and are vitally important assumptions, rarely verbalized in our pseudo-egalitarian age, in all arguments that state budgets and their consequences are inherently different from those of aggregated individual budgets and their consequences, and so on. (Thus states can supposedly run perpetual deficits financed by printing more money, yet thereby produce net increases in real wealth—the exact opposite of what happens to individuals who try this bit of levitation.)

The direct implication of this myth of the "reasons of state" is that only those who represent the state reasons—the rulers or their bureaucratic representatives—can provide for the common welfare; and they must do this by using a plethora of police or regulatory powers that constrain individuals to act in ways they would not choose to do on the basis of calculations of individual welfares, but which are supposedly necessary to allow them to pursue their individual welfares effectively at all. Neoclassical economists have contributed mightily to this argument for the "reasons of state" by arguing that some individual actions have consequences (costs) that are external (exogenous) to aggregated market considerations. The argument has the appearance of plausibility even to federationists who deny the existence of a common welfare and reasons of state, because there are always individuals who violate rules (deviants) and hurt others. Indeed there are, and they have always been dealt with individually in all stateless societies, in which deviance is by almost all accounts far less than in statist societies.

The whole idea of the common welfare and reasons of state is a violation of the *logical law of composition*, which tells us that the sum of the parts is equal to the whole, and that the whole cannot be more than the sum of the parts. Synergy and dyssynergy can certainly exist in systems, as we see in the greater efficiency of a federated system of free trade, but this is true because the individual units—the members—of the system increase or decrease their efficiency, not because the system becomes more or less efficient by operating at a separate level of reality from the members. According to Plato, Socrates struggled with precisely this trap of the common welfare and, having decided to serve the common welfare, submitted to the will of his evil executioners and lost his life, out of which presumably came a greater common welfare. (There is, indeed, a *transformational myth* involved in this myth of the common welfare and we shall see how it operates in radical social thought today.) The true believers in Marxist-Leninism are trapped in the same way by their statist (party) myths and may even sincerely denounce themselves before their statist executioners. Of course, there have probably been few true believers when it comes to the moment of execution, but it is clear that violating the law of composition, or any other basic law of nature, can be dangerous to your health—an externality of statist rationalism.

The extreme assumption of the common welfare and reasons of state becomes the totalitarian assertion that only through total subjection of all individuals to an absolute sovereign, the only representative of the common welfare, and common will can all of them be made free. In the West, especially in the United States, we commonly see the common welfare or common interest used in the less extreme form of socialists arguing that the state must plan the best future for those who elect them.[40] At the extreme of statist absolutism the ruler proclaims with Louis XIV,[41] "The state is me," or in our egalitarian age the rulers act as if everything and everyone in the realm *is* theirs, as we see in the assumptions of liberal economists today that property that is not taken away by the state in taxes is a "tax expenditure," and the assumptions of warring statists that the lives of all young men (and potentially everyone) are rightly and necessarily sacrificeable for the common welfare. When Abraham Lincoln decreed, "A house divided against itself cannot stand," he assumed unthinkingly that the state is a common identity in the same way a family is (only more so, since some conflicts and divisions are inevitable in family households), that all the ideas of the classical liberals and Burkean conservatives about the pluralism inherent in society were totally wrong, and that the state has a right and duty to command the lives of all the individuals for the common welfare of the monolithic house-state. The Confederacy agreed completely, but relegated this absolutist authority to the individual states, and then to the increasingly totalitarian Confederacy state. Robespierre had preempted all of their claims to originality by proclaiming, "The revolutionary government is the despotism of liberty against tyranny."

The opposite extreme from the absolutist statist position is one that argues there is no such thing as a common welfare *or* a valid general welfare. This position of *absolute anarchism* denies even the existence of a valid general welfare, that is, of situations in which the aggregated interests of the individuals are advanced by cooperating and compromising differences. This argument appears plausible when it is looked at only in the extreme case, that of so-called perfect democracy in which there is assumed to be no right of the majority at all. As everyone knows commonsensically, there are always some deviants who are a threat to others. All societies place constraints on deviants, very roughly in proportion to the sense of threat about them. The basic idea of the American constitutionalists that there is a right of the majority to protection from such threats embodies this commonsensical idea. The question for the vast majority of people who deny the common welfare idea of the statists is how much sacrifice of the interests of tiny minorities is necessary to prevent harming the aggregate interests, the general welfare. Absolute anarchists are rare (almost nonexistent among serious thinkers) and are rightly called *libertinists*. Most anarchists today would call themselves *limited state libertarians* (see appendix II) and merely agree with Jeremy Bentham's radical utilitarian argument that ". . .the community [state and common welfare] is a fictious *body*. . .The interest of the community then is, what?—the sum of the interests of the several members who compose it."[42]

Almost all statist rulers and their subjects have forced each other to compromise somewhere between the extremes of absolutist statism and anarchism, generally far to the left of center toward absolutist statism. But these compromises are inherently problematic, conflictful, and changing with the situations faced and with the individuals involved.[43] There are many dimensions of individual freedom and constraint (see the next section). There are great conflicts within individuals, so that someone who is absolutely anarchic about sexual matters can be a totalitarian statist about economic matters—something that is a very common combination today among American liberals—and someone who is absolutely anarchic about economic matters can be a totalitarian statist about sexual matters—a combination not uncommon among American conservatives today. All such thinking and action is profoundly affected by great and sudden crises both individually and in the aggregate. When greatly threatened, almost all of us feel dread and automatically switch to a program of absolutist stigmatization and either panicky escape or hate-filled attack, depending on our interpretations of the situation.

Americans are normally very tolerant about the differences of "foreigners," but they can be absolutely murderous in total wars, as we saw in the strategic bombing of Germany and Japan.

Summary of the Model of Statist Powers

All state powers have been built ultimately on complex foundations of passions, moral legitimacies, and reasons. These complex foundations have been created and recreated by political actors in various ways to fit, or appear to their would-be subjects to fit, the ever-changing situations they faced. They have always included at least five impassioned beliefs that have been shared by most of the dominant subjects and many of the others: (1) the impassioned belief that the state is a separate, concrete, and yet transcendent level of reality from that of its members; (2) the impassioned belief that there is a common welfare (common interest, common good, common spirit, etc.) of the state that is unitary (homogeneous), separate from, and more important than the aggregated individual welfares of the members; (3) the impassioned belief that the individual welfares of the members are inherently, necessarily dependent on the common welfare in some way(s); (4) the impassioned belief that the ruler(s) to some degree embody and administer the unitary essence of the state (they have "executive sovereignty") and, consequently, the subjects are inherently dependent on the rulers for their common and, thus, individual welfares; (5) the impassioned belief that this necessary dependency also gives moral force (legitimacy) to the decisions and actions of the rulers.

Our modern word "state" is derived from the ancient Roman word "status." The word state can still be used rightly to mean most of what the word status still means—condition, ordered circumstances, positions, or attributes. But, while status now has *only* the meanings of abstract ordering or relatedness, state means both those and their concrete (physical) reification. The statuses of the state are conceived of as existing to some degree independently of the minds of individuals who think of "it." Moreover, the concreteness of the word state is at its extreme when it refers to the real persons who represent it (government) and to the physical territory they claim as their domain. These impassioned beliefs are myths in the classical sense (see chapter 5). The five myths are what I shall call the *core enabling myths* of all state powers. I shall refer to them collectively as the *enabling myth of the welfare state*. The faith in each varies widely in degree from one state to another, and among individuals and groups within each one. These core enabling myths are necessary to the long-run existence of the powers of any relatively small elite groups of rulers over much larger groups of subjects. Very roughly, the real powers of rulers, as distinct from their nominal powers (claims), vary directly with the strength of faith in these myths.

The focus of traditional social science theorists on the exclusive claims to legitimate exercise of violence in certain territories is extremely misleading. The most successful rulers make those claims, and the effective enforcement of it is of great importance in perpetuating state powers (see below), but it is the sharing of the core enabling myths by the elite groups and important segments of the nonelites which makes it possible for the rulers to exercise such military powers effectively. (The Catholic Church was a very powerful state in terms of these core enabling myths. It has exercised vast powers for fifteen hundred years because of these myths, without making direct claims to significant direct use of violence or to much territory. It has made massive indirect use of the bureaucratized violence of the secular states sharing nonexclusive sovereignty over their subjects. See chapter 4.) Once the myths wane and the people recognize that they have done so, military power wanes.

Military power, then, is itself largely dependent ultimately on the cognitive and moral forces of the myths. (Pope Gregory VII was able to totally humble Emperor Henry IV at Canossa with a flourish of moral attack, but Henry was able to win with his military forces once he had rallied his imperial moral forces.) This is true primarily because the state rulers are always greatly outnumbered by their subjects, because the statist myths are vital to the cohesion and morale of the military forces from within the society, because the internally recruited forces are both subjects and elites (hence ambivalent), and even highly rewarded outsider imperial guards become extremely dangerous when they do not share the myths, as approximately half of the would-be divine emperors of the late Roman imperium discovered when their non-Roman guards murdered them to seize their power. "Who will guard the guards?" (or police the police?) is a statist cry as old as statism, in spite of all the stern claims to exclusive legitimacy (sovereignty) in the use of force. Napoleon's guesstimate that "the moral is to the physical as three to one" in exercising power seems a wise rule of thumb.[44] Mussolinis may strut and make bombastic claims to totalitarian powers, but when their armies lose faith in the core enabling myths or operations they fade away, as the newly wise Italian armies did in Sicily.

While necessary, these core enabling myths are not self-sufficient. Just as Hobbes failed to convince people of them by his ever-so-rationalistic arguments, so have all would-be rulers failed to convince most of their would-be subjects by merely proclaiming the myths. Indeed, no matter how completely the rulers seem to control mass education and the mass media, they do not ever seem to have been able to long continue to instill these passionate beliefs in their subjects through mass agitprop alone. The core enabling myths are necessary but not sufficient for state powers. The rulers can rule only when the core enabling myths of state powers are systematically integrated with at least six patterns of more or less *effective core enabling state* operations: (1) the waging of peace and war abroad (outside of the state); (2) the waging of peace and war at home—maintaining law and order; (3) distributing justice at home; (4) collecting (and especially taxing) and redistributing valued goods, both at home and abroad; (5) performing rituals that demonstrate the magical and religious powers of the rulers; and (6) controlling the mass media and public performances (agitprop) that constitute the most powerful forms of education of the subjects concerning all of the core enabling myths and all of the core enabling operations of the state.

It is obvious that the "effectiveness" criteria that state operations must face are inherently problematic and vary widely with individuals, cultures, and situations. As any careful observer is aware, the long suffering subjects of more totalitarian states are far more willing to be long suffering, and their cultural criteria help mightily to continue their long-suffering state. However, even they have criteria that specify some range of enough is enough, as seen in the obvious fact that all of the most mighty totalitarian regimes eventually wane and disappear. The most mighty often remain cognitively because their agitprop was so successful that some shreds and tatters are transmitted down the centuries to become symbols grafted onto new states, as we see in Mussolini's flourish of Roman imperium or de Gaulle's whiffs of Bourbon grandeur.

The great power of the myths of statism comes precisely from their prevention, paralysis, or confusion of any thinking about a balance sheet of state government costs and benefits. To the degree the individuals identify themselves with the state-being and the rulers who represent this noumenon, they cannot think of the state and the government operations having costs or benefits for their selves. The rationalists' double-entry model of legitimacy, obedience, and rebellion is absurd to the degree the selves are identified with the state and its rulers, in precisely the same way it is absurd to try to understand why lovers put up with, accept, and even encourage abuse and battering. The person who identifies himself with the loved one, and most of all the person who subsumes himself under the ideal self of the beloved, does not see the beloved as a separate being who has costs or benefits. The more the identification, the more the beloved *is* the self—the more there is a fusion of being—so to that degree the beloved cannot be evaluated separately. Abused children commonly identify so closely with the abusing parent, or even subsume themselves so completely under the idealized parent, that the idea of "abuse" becomes largely absurd. The parent is reality, is necessary being—timeless and universal. All of this "union of souls" is most obvious in the language of romantic lovers. When Dante felt humiliated by Beatrice, he did not hate her. He felt ashamed of himself, contrite toward her, and desperately wanted absolution and forgiveness for his unknown evil. (He was far more childlike in his love—more subsumed under her—than the vast majority of romantic lovers.) In precisely the same way, the true believer in the Church or the Soviet party-state goes ashamedly, humbly, contritely, even lovingly to the stake or the bullet behind the ear. The true believers know the Mother Church or the Fatherland or Papa-Joe executes them for their own good— exactly as Abraham knew that God's will is being, is goodness, and so on. Of course, few people ever succumb so completely to statist agitprop that they lose themselves in the godhead, but most people submerge themselves sufficiently to risk their lives on the battlefields and to render their goods unto Caesar or Pope in taxes or tithes.

It is not possible to say how long a statist apparatus (government) can continue to exist as the faith in the statist myths fades. It is clear that some of the core enabling myths can wane and leave a *shell state* apparatus operating with considerable effective powers for many years. The lag period is probably affected more by the aggregate evaluations of faith in the myths than anything else. In general, to the degree that the subjects estimate that the other subjects still believe in the myths, they will tend to obey externally, while hating internally. For this reason, *public displays* of disobedience, especially "scofflawing," is extremely dangerous to all authority systems and statist terrorism against any such public displays, which drives deviance underground, is very effective in allowing small minorities to rule. However, other factors such as external threats and the nature of the internal opposition (cell structures, burrowing into statist bureaucracies, etc.) are also important.

As the faith in the myths wanes and the state operations become more and more a set of merely nominal, *shell* operations, the probability of explosions—sudden collapses under external pressures (as we see in the collapse of the Romanovs)—and implosions—sudden collapses from internal pressures (as we see in the French Revolution)—becomes very great. Revolutions in highly repressive, terroristic regimes normally look impossible until the day they happen, because even the people who launch the great revolts commonly do not know how much other subjects have come to hate the state operators. In most regimes using little terror, however, there are many growing signs of a "time of troubles," as ancient historians of the dynastic cycles have called it, or of a "prerevolutionary phase," as modernists call it. The communist governments today are increasingly shell states. They show these signs of alienation very clearly among the elites, including the communist parties themselves, but no one can predict when an obscure spark might light the fires of revolution. Our modernist democratic welfare states are also generating rapidly growing alienation, as we see in the growing refusal to vote and the growing fury directed at the politicians, but there is a great difference in degree from the communist states, and revolution seems quite unlikely unless there are great external or internal shocks that erode both the statist myths and the federationist beliefs.

There are many bases of power in human life in addition to the core statist power bases, and we shall consider many of them throughout this work. The obvious *general principle of overall power* tells us that the more consistent bases of power a ruler uses effectively, the greater his power will be. Some bases of power are inconsistent or contradict each other, as can happen in the use of caring love and violence at the same time. (But the meanings of all such things are highly problematic and situational. The parent who uses physical punishment out of caring love to prevent children from doing things that will harm themselves, may have greater power over the children, as long as the children believe this is the case. The same is true of other power relations.) With that important proviso in mind, the general principle tells us that *power is additive or multiplicative*, that power bases supplement and can substitute for each other. This may at first seem obvious, but it has been forgotten by some rulers tempted by the hubris of great power to believe in their own divinity and has almost always been overlooked by theorists. Theorists have been over anxious to study the most distinctive forms of state power bases, those of the rational-legal forms seen in the massive bureaucracies, especially those of the police and military who use violence. In doing so, they have generally relegated the nonbureaucratic bases of power to the wastebasket or residual category of informal powers and paid them little heed, or they have categorized them as "charisma" and assumed them to be too mysterious to analyze.

The fact is that all of the most powerful rulers, those aggrandized by traditional historians with the sobriquet of "Great," have used a wide spectrum of power bases—mystery, charm, paternalism and maternalism, friendliness, caring love, sex appeal, warmth, courage, steadfastness, rhetorical exhortations, dominance stares, and so on—in vastly varying combinations. The most successful democratic and totalitarian welfare statists of our age have used most of these.[45] The warmth, sex appeal, and caring of the Kennedys is obvious to our new statist grantsmen who write their eulogies, but they are commonly blind to the appearances of fatherly caring, warrior courage, and Merlin-wisdom used with dramatic success by our legions of totalitarian rulers. The rhetorics and mystiques of great power tend to produce power-ecstasy that mythifies the thinking of subjects in general. The subjects then easily read great benevolence and other noncoercive bases of power into the performances of the totalitarians, but it is also true that our Lenins, Stalins, Hitlers, and many more have been masters at presenting such appearances and acting consistently with them as long as this builds their power. (In the apparently uncensored third volume of his memoirs, Anastas Mikoyan recently reported that Stalin spent many months comporting himself with modesty, tact, and "emphatically humble behavior" to win trust from the Central Committee. Because of this, they trusted him to become ruler and he then executed most of them.[46]) Almost all of the most powerful have been very ascetic, which is vitally important in convincing their subjects that they have "pure" intentions—that is, that they are really driven by the welfare-statist passions of caring and morality rather than by selfish motives such as greed or lust. (Fidel Castro would have been immensely more successful in his quest for power in Latin America if he had presented himself convincingly as a Saint Francis in state robes, rather than as a seedy barfly. The "saintly" Che Guevara lit revolutionary fires in the minds of men and women far more often than Fidelio.) The very murderousness of such "moral fanatics" becomes evidence of the purity of their commitment to their awed, adoring, and obsessed fans, for he who will murder for his love and morality must surely have the greatest love and morality of all. (Of course, those of us who are not fans see this purity as proof of fiery hatred and evil, but then, power is inherently double-edged.)

Great rulers are never powerful because they are bureaucrats, though they generally are masters at creating bureaucratic power and always are masters at using it. Stalin was probably the greatest master of bureaucracy of our modernist Greats, but it was not his adherence to the formal, legalized rules that constituted the core of bureaucracy that made him powerful. It was his misuse of the bureaucratic rules—his deviance—that allowed him to usurp and vastly concentrate the power bases in his persona, which Lenin realized and warned his deaf friends about. The party rulers who created the Soviet bureaucracy with him intended it to be free of factionalism. Stalin was the master at creating and using intraparty factionalism, dividing one faction from others, building a coalition of the center and right to destroy the left (Trotskyites), and then turning the center against the right (the Bukharin forces) to destroy it.

But, while these are vitally important truths about statist powers, it is also true that all rulers who are very successful over the long run have relied upon the bureaucratic state apparatus now called *government* as the *core apparatus of statist powers*. A *state bureaucracy apparatus* (*government*) is an integrated system of formally, legally defined operations planned to extend, preserve, and carry out the powers ("rules") of the state rulers. It is only such explicitly, formalized, legalized operations that allow rulers to apply their wills with enough certainty, to recruit operators of their powers (functionaries) with maximum dependency on the rulers' wills, and to get sufficient feedback on the operations of the functionaries to be able to check the inherent tendencies of human beings to increase their own powers until a greater or equal power stops them. (See chapter 8 for a discussion of this *Clausewitz principle*.) It has been apparent to the most successful rulers since the ancient world that any other extension of their powers through the actions of others produces far more deviance or subversion of their powers by the

operators than bureaucracies do. Not being social theorists, the most successful rulers have not understood why in explicit and symbolic form, but they
have always grasped this general truth and they have drifted toward reliance
on the bureaucrats. The tremendous reliance of statist rulers on bureaucratic
operations is well symbolized by the very name "ruler"—that is, one who
issues and enforces formal rules.

Of course, even the most bureaucratic (that is, formalistic and legalistic)
bureaucrats are still human beings, so they do in fact drift toward exercising
their own wills independently of what the rulers will. This is precisely the
reason why successful rulers do not rely merely upon bureaucratic means of
controlling the bureaucracies. They must be eternally vigilant, divide factions
among the bureaucrats to foster dependency on themselves and conquer
them, develop friendships up and down the lines of the bureaucracies, use
end runs around the formal reporting procedures (official information), play
both ends against the middle, and so on. (Mikhail Gorbachev is now providing us with dazzling displays of all these ancient strategies.) As we shall see
in chapter 9, over the decades bureaucrats always devise standard and
situated means of hiding and protecting themselves from the ruler's observations and controls—they "enfeudate" the bureaucracy with their own subcultures, including claims to sovereignty; and the rulers always drift toward
creating further extrabureaucratic, extralegal means of getting feedback on
and controlling the bureaucrats (such as fostering factions, creating parallel
bureaucracies of censorates, ombudsmen, plumbers, and eventually using
outright terroristic methods); but over the long run the bureaucrats always
win in this struggle. (This enfeudation combines with the other accelerating
sources of informational pathologies inherent in gigantic bureaucracies to
become the fatal flaw of statism. See chapter 9.) Nevertheless, no one has yet
devised any means that give more effective, more extended, or more long-
lasting operations of state powers than bureaucracy does. Statist bureaucracy,
then, is the core operating apparatus of all long-lasting states. The powerful
rulers who do not understand this or fail for whatever reason to create these
effective core apparatuses are doomed to be the shooting stars of statism. The
charismatic leaders of social movements that rise on waves of mass passion
and community feeling soon fall into internal strife and disappear if they do
not normalize their charisma through bureaucratization, as we see in the
Students for a Democratic Society.

The statist ruler is normally so dependent on his bureaucrats, and they are
so ultimately dependent on his statist myths, that the two are commonly
identified by the same name, even in our highly federationist tradition. While
the "state" is a set of abstractions, the state also commonly refers to the concrete individuals and operations—government—supposedly representing

those abstractions (and to the physical territory they claim). Thus, the state not only *is*, but *does*, and lives in a territory. This nominal identification is a crucial support for the rulers' efforts to concretize their myths of statism and at the extreme the statist absolutist may openly proclaim, "I am the state." (It ill behooves us in our attempts to be objective in analyzing statism and government to fall into this misidentification, but the words are so commonly used interchangeably these days that I cannot guarantee my own linguistic purity. Reader beware, and please check the context.)

These core enabling myths, operations, and bureaucratic apparatuses of states have been the subjects of immense creativity by rulers and their supporting casts. They have drawn on the myriad cultural forms of the whole world; their incentives have been immense, since they have been driven by the most powerful passions of human beings (especially the fully enflamed lust for power); they have commonly had the immense resources of whole civilizations at their disposal; and the successful rulers and their supporting casts have been the most intelligent practitioners of all the arts of deception and of all the arts of human engineering in general. It is little wonder that this basic structure lying beind all state powers and constituting their foundation has been so obscure to the subjects. The greatest practitioners of *state engineering* have almost always wrapped the knowledge of their arts in layers of secrecy, because any serious failure of secrecy almost instantly tears away the veil of the enabling myths and the state powers soon crumble. There have been millions of brilliantly successful state engineers, but only a few Machiavellis; and they have partially torn away the veils only after their own failures, presumably in bids to recoup their lost fame and power or to get revenge.[47] Many of them have left a few excellent epigrams of their political strategies, such as those of Napoleon and Mao, but these have been mere hints meant to reveal their brilliance and downgrade their enemies. They offer no systematic understanding. A few have written more systematic accounts before their successes, as we see in Lenin's brilliant analyses of professional revolutionary strategies and in Hitler's brilliant analyses of political lies and mythmaking in *Mein Kampf*. But these were neophyte statements meant to gain support so they could get the power to practice state engineering on a massive scale. Once they gained such power and became the world's most successful practitioners of state engineering, they were extreme in their efforts to hide their artistic powers even from their closest supporters (as the young novitiate Albert Speer eventually realized Hitler had done). Even the fact of their having revealed their strategic thinking before gaining power gave more secretive competitors great advantages, as we see in Joseph Stalin's masterful outmaneuvering of the other heirs to Lenin's overt legacy of professional revolution. Fortunately for them, almost everyone who read such early revelations considered them the ravings of lunatics, except their fellow practitioners who were so inspired by their brilliant insights that they rallied around the masters.

Lenin and Hitler were such brilliant statist engineers that they realized that telling Great Truths about their state-engineering strategies was itself one of the most successful of all political ploys of feinting and sandbagging. Just as Hitler knew that the Great Lie is far more believable to most people than little lies, so he and Lenin knew that the Great Truth is far less believable to most people than little truths and, thus, that Great Truth can be used to hide little truths. Millions of European Jews went to the gas chambers believing it impossible that Hitler had meant what he said, the democratic leaders marched lockstep down the path of appeasement for years, and their descendents are now pooh-poohing all of the early communist proclamations of their intentions to achieve world revolution and domination.

The complex patterns of statist engineering have also been greatly obscured by many other factors. Very importantly, none of the enabling myths or operations comes in the glaringly obvious form of either-or. They come not only in myriad cultural variations, and under many brand names, but also in all degrees and many combinations. Unfortunately for rationalists trying to fit such human events to the simple models of the physical sciences or statistics, these foundations of state powers do not come in neatly coded binary boxes. Mussolini pretended to lay claim to total power, and he created the proud label of totalitarian for his government, but no government has really come remotely near this dream of all megalomaniacs, least of all his own fascist muddle.[48] Totalitarian can be useful as an ideal type describing the desires and intentions of the rulers and trends and relative scope of state powers, but it is totally misleading to concretize this ideal type and think that any such government ever has or ever could exist. (As we shall see, any extreme centralization of information creation and decision making would violate what I shall call the law of situational efficiency and, thus, generates informational pathologies—misinformation and disinformation—that erode the effectiveness of the core operations of the bureaucracies. See chapters 7–9).

In any society there are as many continua of freedom and constraint, degrees of individual power and collective power, as there are dimensions of life. Statist collectivists sternly condemn the constraints involved in wage contracts enforced by state powers and thereby gain much of their initial support for building megastatism. The anarcho-syndicalists recognized the absurdity of building totalitarian statist powers over all of life in order to constrain the constraints in the workplace, so they opposed state powers even more adamantly and insisted on a decentralized society of worker teams—"soviets," as Russians called them. The communists recognized the power of this rhetoric, especially in the slavic nations where village teams of peasants had worked for centuries under the distant suzerains. They secretly co-opted the soviets by making their nominally elected heads real appointees of the party. Socialists, communists, and modernist collectivists of all varieties are merely using the ancient political tactic of allying with your enemies' enemies to defeat them both, which is a variation on the general strategy of divide and conquer. Renaissance monarchs, especially the English Tudors, built their absolute powers on the traditional myths of statism, the alliance with the sacred statism of Christians, the myth of the Great Chain of Being, many lesser myths, and complex alliances with local powers against the great lords.[49] The businesspeople, anxious to escape the constraining taxes and regulations of local lords, and anxious to gain monopolies and other subsidies from the crown, worked with the greater power to overcome the lesser, only later discovering that a greater evil is inherently worse than a lesser evil. They were deceived by focusing on the short-run gains of freedom rather than the long-run costs of constraints. The modernist megastatists have all combined in various complex ways with many local powers to erode the countervailing middle-level powers. Montesquieu, the classical liberals, and de Tocqueville were extremely aware of the importance of the middle-level counterweights in checking the growth of absolute powers, and a large group of social scientists have developed this into the "mass society" theory. It is still a wondrously effective political strategy. (Gorbachev is playing both ends against the middle in this way. He is rallying the lowest-end, the masses and de-classed intellectuals, and the top-end of the Party against the middle-level Party aparatchiki, all for the purpose of centralizing power at the top, in his own "benevolent" hands. Stalin, whom Gorbachev denounces, was a master of this strategy.)

Firsthand reports consistently indicate that even in Russia and China today, which probably have the most *overall* totalitarian states in history, most workers have far more freedom to loaf and do shoddy work while still being paid than do most workers in our democratic Western societies, which are still among the freest overall in the history of civilizations. In the same way, dimensions of life normally vary widely within any society. For example, though we do not have firsthand reports, Russian workers in the industries run by the defense ministries seem to work under far more constraining controls over quality, since their products are far more comparable in effectiveness to those of Western industries. Again, the freedom to divorce is far greater in most communist states than in most democratic states, but there are vast variations within the two camps.

In fact, the general trend within communist states has long been toward greater freedom in most realms of life that do not seem to the state engineers to endanger their core enabling myths or operations. These relative totalitarians have apparently concluded that their vast powers can best be preserved by allowing as much freedom as is consistent with vast centralizations of core powers. Freedoms in spheres of life not so relevant to statist myths and operations—such as sex—are ideal bribes, emotional ventings, and diversions encouraging support for, or inattention to, those spheres crucial to the statists. (Sex is the opium of modernist masses in the same way the violence of the circuses was to Romans. In fact, violence today is being sexualized in the modernist circuses of the mass media.) The policy of glasnost (public openness) now being pushed by Mikhail Gorbachev may even indicate that he and his team have decided that the mass media are not as important in determining mass action as the Party rulers used to think, so that they may allow more public freedom of expression in order to distract, vent, and deceive the people, thus reinforcing their more total control of other dimensions of core enabling operations.

As this example also suggests, the core enabling myths and operations vary greatly in their importance from one culture and state to another. Very tight central controls over the public media of information may be the most important core-state operation in a society with little contact with the outside world and few media with mass audiences, as was true in Russia until the 1960s, is still more true in Russia today than in Poland or East Germany, and is most true today in largely illiterate peasant societies in Latin America, Africa, and Asia. Once a society becomes quite literate and the most educated are quite involved in international personal contacts, as Russian elites are today, then the rulers find any visible controls over the media are counterproductive for their state powers, so they must shift to more indirect, less visible media controls and to controlling life more through the other core state operations. There are also situations in which rulers, even supposedly totalitarian ones, accept greatly diminished controls over core enabling myths and operations in order to continue ruling at all. This, after all, is what the royal rulers of Europe did in the past few centuries.

These complex, inherently problematic, and ever-changing realities of politics will be taken for granted throughout the rest of this book. The vast majority of political categories used by social scientists have in fact been forged as symbolic weapons by politicians waging political warfare. They are commonly meant by their political creators to hide as well as reveal, to deceive and injure enemies, and to illuminate and aid allies. I shall use them sparingly, try always to make their meanings clear in the contexts, and never intend them as shibboleths. In addition to all the clarifications I shall make in detail, a few more general ones should be kept in mind.

Most importantly, "freedom" and its many cognates on one hand, and "totalitarianism" and its cognates on the other, are the prime shibboleths of political warfare in our age of modernism. In addition to the argument I made above about the multidimensional continua of freedom-and-constraint, two further points must be kept in mind about "free" societies and "totalitarian" ones. First, totalitarian regimes may in general be more total because of the megastatism of our age and its new technologies, but it is not something new under the sun, as the newness of the category "totalitarian" implies. There were many traditional names for the same basic phenomena, notably "absolutism" and "despotism" in the West.

Many attempts have been made to distinguish modernist totalitarianism from monarchy, even from absolutist monarchy, and from "merely authoritarian" systems today. These attempts are usually based on the assumption that political powers come in either-or (binary), categorically disjunct extremes, rather than in the infinite degrees of continua, and on some mistaken implicit assumptions about modernist totalitarian regimes, such as that they are in principle unconstrained by canons of responsibility to the people or any higher authority, as the monarchs were by God in Christian philosophy and in the great myth of the Great Chain of Being. This is not true, except, possibly, with an Idi Amin or two. Communist totalitarians insist absolutely in public that they are bound by their constitutions and that they speak as the voice of the inevitable historical process. In principle— nominally—they are extreme democracies and absolutely responsible to the people and to God (history). It is equally wrong to argue that modernist totalitarians are in fact always more unconstrained by public opinion than earlier ones were. As Albert Speer noted, even Hitler was excruciatingly sensitive to public opinion, so much so that he never allowed Speer to switch *any* consumer production to military production. The totalitarian power has become less total and more indirect in the Soviet empire, and the rulers of the politburos and their bureaucrats have become ever more responsive—and instantly so—to producer and consumer pressures. Solidarity was a general strike that exploded the myth of total statist power in the communist world. Stalin the Terrible was in fact terrible, but so was Ivan the Terrible, and neither was more terrible in their plans than the kings of ancient Assyria. Nor is it true to say our modernist totalitarians lack all legitimacy, or that they try to control the inner thoughts more than early Inquisitors did. What is true is that there are now and have always been wide variations in the degrees of totalitarianism of regimes, including variations in principle and name (rhetoric), in fact, in legitimacy, and so on. The total view of totalitarianism that afflicts history and all the social sciences today, to varying degrees, is in major part a legacy of the myth of modernism which inspires a too-great willingness to take the political shibboleths of our modernist absolutists at face value. Statists today are different, not so much in their desires for total power as in their greater abilities to get great power resulting from the massive new technologies of agitprop.

Second, the immense politicization of economic life over the past century has resulted in growing confusion of the continua of freedom-and-constraint in the economic realm with those in the political realm. It is a vital part of my argument that there are inherent interdependencies between economic life, which is ultimately always a matter of life-and-death itself, and the forms of government. But these are complex, and often involve lag periods, not simple and direct the way Marxists and most other popular theorists of the age assert. The practices of economic freedom now called capitalism—that is, economic freedom to invest, produce and consume—is not an either-or issue. They come in all degrees of the vital dimensions of economic freedom, as do all freedoms and constraints. To equate our economy today—when federal government constrains almost everything to some degree—with that of a century ago—when federal government constrained little—by calling both capitalism is absurd. Even rulers and state bureaucracies may operate in economic spheres with varying degrees of freedom and constraint from the powers of legal systems (courts and judges) and citizens. In general, the more the rulers or bureaucrats operate free of such constraints, the more they are said to operate by *fiat law*, such as the traditional "ukazi" of Russia's czars and the massive interpretations now given to legislation by American regulators, as distinct from legislative, judicial, and bureaucratic legal systems. The more statists rule by fiat law, the more entrepreneurial they are—that is, free in their decisions. Capitalism—economic freedom—practiced by statists is definitely not very efficient, compared to nonstatist individuals free to pursue their economic goals largely independent of their relations to statist power, but it is still free by comparison with economic activity actually constrained by legal systems. Our central bank, hidden behind its name, the Federal Reserve System, is run in such an entrepreneurial-statist manner that its operations are seen as erratic by many of its closest observers.[50] In the stock market crisis of October 1987, the Fed Chairman, Alan Greenspan, acted like a banking tycoon, very much like J.P. Morgan did in 1907.

As state bureaucracies become more massive, ossified (paralyzed by formal legal procedures and by their informal subcultures), enfeudated, and corrupt, their would-be rulers use more and more fiat-law as a vital part of their complex strategies to shake up their stagnation and regain power over them and their outputs (see chapter 9). As their biographers have argued, Franklin Roosevelt and Adolph Hitler were masters in the use of fiat-law and other strategies for shaking up and ruling their massive bureaucracies.[51] They were both state capitalists, but, as Hitler consolidated his powers behind the front of financial conservatism, he moved to more fascistic and then totalitarian methods.

Once statists operate much of the economy through fiat-laws, they are called *state capitalists* or state *corporatists*.[52] State corporatism is any system in which state power is focused on the external relations of groups, but allows them considerable freedom over their internal activities. State capitalism is often used to refer to a form of state corporatism in which owners or managers are allowed more power than the workers by statists. In these terms, Yugoslavia is a form of corporate statism in which workers have had veto powers, but is now drifting toward state capitalism to overcome the protracted paralysis and deficits produced by these powers. The Soviet communist and Chinese communist societies are drifting rapidly toward state capitalism in which the secret police and party rulers act as fascists. In December of 1987 the Hungarian communist party officially adopted a state capitalist plan for Hungary, but, of course, in the name of "communism."[53]

Once the state rulers and bureaucrats become even more unresponsible to electors and less constrained by preestablished laws, we reach a stage of state power commonly called *fascism* (after the Italian idea of a supposedly synergistic sheathing of the separate strands—fasces—of society by state fiat powers.) Governments by fiats may solve short-run problems, but eventually produce their own accelerating problems, especially because of the soaring uncertainties and anxieties high levels of fiat (arbitrariness) involve, so more and more extralegal and illegal *terror* is used, which constitutes the more extreme forms of *totalitarianism* commonly associated with that name. It is commonly thought that in Nazi Germany the government controlled everything and was totalitarian from the beginning. They could have tried to do so by using their massive entrepreneurial, extraordinary and extralegal forces, but in fact they rarely did. Businesspeople were allowed to run their businesses largely as they saw best, but increasingly to achieve the wartime production of material mandated by the Führer and the party through the wartime planning of Albert Speer. Hitler largely left earlier forms and practices intact and went around them—or over them—by creating personal ties and eventually by Speer's entrepreneurial fiats. When he wanted to build the now-famous system of Autobahnen, he went around the state bureaucracy of roads. When he wanted to maximize wartime production, he gave Albert Speer the power to set up a tightly run, extraordinary or extra-legal team that went around the old state bureaucracies.[54] The extraordinary, extralegal, illegal, and terroristic methods of all advanced (mature) totalitarian states are the final attempt to deal with the soaring problems of stagnation, inflation, escapes into undergrounds, and civil wars that the massive bureaucratic and fiat state controls eventually produce (to varying degrees depending on the specific policies used). (In chapter 9, I shall explain why all collectivist systems of economic control drift—and eventually gallop—toward greater use of fiat and finally terrorism.)

While these many categories, such as "communism," will be useful to us at times, it must never be assumed their meanings can be torn out of their contexts. Just as American capitalism today is far more state-capitalism than the individual-capitalism the term originally meant, so communism varies tremendously from one time to another, from one state to another, and from one area to another within one state. As noted earlier, our capitalist economy is more state controlled today than the Soviet communist economy was until Stalin's ratchets-up in collectivization and the Five Year Plans in the 1930s. Real Soviet economic life was always far more free than its name of communism and the rhetoric of central planning implied, because managers always found it necessary to negotiate far more freely with each other underground to make the nominal, public system work at all, and because other producers, investors, and consumers have always operated an underground, far freer market, making up roughly one-fourth to one-third of the total economy.[55] The same is true to wildly varying degrees in all our megastates today. In the same ways, Soviet communism is very different from Chinese communism. Chinese communism is more total at the center in some realms of life, but is more decentralized (provincialized) in other spheres. Both are wildly different from Yugoslavian communism, which is in fact very sovietized (i.e., influenced by worker councils—soviets) compared to the nominal "soviets" in the Union of Soviet Socialist Republics where the workers' councils are highly coopted and manipulated from the top of the Party. Sometimes it will make sense to speak of the overall collectivism of decision making, but sometimes these differences in patterns and degrees make a big difference. Reader, beware of the context.

Given all of the conceptual problems, the highly problematic nature of all evidence about politics and statism, and many lesser ones that cannot directly concern us in the short space of this book, it would be quite contrary to the spirit of scientific enquiry to try to present here a general theory of the waxing and waning of state powers, and quite absurd to present a general theory of statism. My purpose here is to present what seems to be a very useful model of the most important factors involved in the waxing and waning of state powers, especially those at work in our modernist societies. The purpose of a model is to show what the crucial dimensions are and what their most important interdependencies are. It is meant to give a rough approximation of the Big Picture to show us what important details need to be investigated further, which in turn will reveal weaknesses in the model that must be reconstructed.

The Perilous Futures of Modernist Welfare States

Once many people become aware that the ratchets-up in statist powers are producing more problems than they solve, and at an accelerating rate, they quickly recognize that less government is the only general solution to the drift into catastrophic problems. Since most people today are rationalists to some degree, they easily assume this will be an easy task. They will amass the overwhelming evidence that government is the problem, not the solution, publish it, and then watch the people ratchet-down the bureaucracies and the problems. The people will see the truth and it will make them free. Clearly, these mass of publications showing how Big Government is the problem have complemented real experience to enlighten most voters. As noted above, most leaders elected at the national level today criticize or even denounce Big Government and promise "Reforms, Reforms." Even the communist world is filled with the new agitprop of glasnost and perestroika.[56] But it does not really work that way. Everywhere government operations are merely plateaued, as in much of Europe and the communist world, or still growing, as in the United States. The rationalists are dismayed and resort to rationalist arguments about national interest group politics to explain why—and unintentionally fall into assuming that we are eternally trapped in the iron cage, since their theories purport to explain only how we can go up, not down.

I shall show that the rational interests theory is actually of little value in explaining the *origins* of the modernist welfare state, especially in the United States where the idea of the general welfare and the morality of individual rights (including equal opportunity) were and still are powerful (see chapter 4 and appendix III). But a revised version is very important in helping explain the extreme difficulty any nation faces in reversing the process, that is, in deratcheting the modernist welfare state. Deratcheting statist powers is always very painful because people restructure their lives to deal with the statist programs. For example, they buy houses as hedges against inflation which would have been too expensive for them without inflation or other subsidies, and can only be paid for or sold at a profit *if* inflation or other subsidies continue. The longer the state programs continue and the higher they go, the more people restructure their lives to accommodate the programs, so the more painful deratcheting becomes. (Andrew Jackson's electors wanted hard money, but some of them rioted over the pains of disinflation. American farmers have repeated this ancient scenario in recent years.)

Reversing the modernist welfare state involves all of those pains plus others. The millions who receive the benefits from the state, especially those who receive the legal guarantees known as entitlements, restructure their lives even more than people do for inflation. For example, tens of millions slow their saving for retirement because Social Security "guarantees" them retirement benefits for the rest of their lives, so the personal savings rate shrinks to an abyssmal 5 percent—or even 3 percent, as it did recently—and the people become hostages to government guarantees. Even the hostages of murderous terrorists often come to identify their interests with those of their jailers. Welfare state hostages "rationally" see how much they have to lose in entitlements and overall life structure, present and planned. Their hostage commitments to the state are powerful incentives to identify with it and to oppose deratcheting.

But there is more to their continued demands for their entitlements than reason. After all, even in a zero-sum society it would be rational for almost everyone to sacrifice in the short run to avoid foreseen systemic catastrophes in the long run. The reason they resist doing so for so long is because the millennial myths and historical ignorance of past calamities (which the historical ignorance encouraged by modernism so greatly encourages) combine to greatly discount the catastrophes—until they are at hand, at which time social disorder may already be so great that government operations crumble and any organized policy becomes terribly difficult. Normally, as we have seen in recent years in Uruguay, Argentina, Chile, Turkey, Central America, and many other nations, the mature modernist welfare state produces terrorist civil wars, which then undermine all government institutions.

This, of course, does not mean that there is no way to ratchet-down the modernist welfare state, nor that after this economic Götterdämmerung must follow political Armageddon. (If so, this book would be a mere lamentation—and unwritten by your ever-so-rational author.) The crucial point is to keep in mind how excruciatingly difficult, protracted, and uncertain such processes are—and how crucial it is to stop the ratchet-up process as soon as possible.

As force is always on the side of the governed, the governors have nothing to support them but opinion. It is, therefore, on opinion only that government is founded; and this maxim extends to the most despotic and most military governments, as well as to the most free and the most popular.

David Hume

The state is the great fiction by means of which everyone tries to live at the expense of everyone else.

Frédéric Bastiat

Wherever liberty as we understand it has been destroyed, this has almost always been done in the name of some new freedom promised to the people.

Friedrich Hayek

Notes

1. David Stockman, *The Triumph of Politics* (New York: Harper and Row, 1986).
2. Joseph Califano, *Governing America* (New York: Simon and Schuster, 1981) pp. 451–2.
3. Lester C. Thurow, "Welfare State Keeps Capitalism Working," *Los Angeles Times*, Dec. 20, 1987.
4. Albert Romasco, *The Politics of Recovery* (New York: Oxford University Press, 1983).
5. The best known of these many explanations are those by Lionel Robbins, *The Great Depression* (London: MacMillan, 1934); and Milton Friedman and Anna J. Schwartz, *A Monetary History of the United States* (Princeton: Princeton University Press, 1963).
6. Arthur Schlesinger, Jr., *The Crisis of the Old Order* and *The Coming of the New Deal*; John Kenneth Galbraith, *The Great Crash* (Boston: Houghton Mifflin, 1961). A more balanced, yet "standard," account is C. P. Kindelberger, *The World in Depression* (Berkeley: University of California Press, 1973).
7. John Garraty, *The Great Depression* (San Diego: Harcourt, Brace, Jovanovich, 1986), p. 12.
8. Most comparative analysts of our megastates have been aware that in some way the more homogeneous ones with higher morale remain more efficient than those at the same level of bureaucratization which are more diverse and conflictful and have lower morale. Japan, Sweden, Austria, and, to lesser degrees, France and West Germany are seen as the greatest success stories of homogeneity and morale, while Britain and the United States are among the nations with high heterogeneity and declining morale. The best consideration of these factors so far has been David Marquand, *The Unprincipled Society* (London: Jonathan Cape, 1988). Unfortunately, he does not see the separate dimensions at work and their systematic interdependencies. The spurts of Soviet efficiency during World War II and after show what bursts of morale alone can do. The vast importance of cultural homogenization and morale in producing efficiency in operation are most obvious in military bureaucracies where they are inculcated with a vengence in all "elite" (most effective) units. Of course, one of the crucial facts about bureaucracy is that over the long run it deadens morale. A war or other crisis that is felt to be a shared threat can produce only a short-run burst of morale.
9. Some of Keynes's early works were far more factual and of more lasting value, but he is remembered overwhelmingly for *The General Theory of Employment, Interest and Money* (London: MacMillan, 1936). Perhaps the best postmortem on Keynes's crucial mistakes by a former disciple is John Hicks, *The Crisis of Keynesian Economics* (Oxford: Basil Blackwell, 1974). There are many excellent critiques of Keynesianism, beginning at the first publication of *The General Theory*, by Ludwig Mises, Friedrich Hayek, Murray Rothbart, James Buchanan, and others. See the general critiques in W. H. Hutt, *Keynesianism* (Chicago: Henry Regnary, 1963); and Robert S. Skidelsky, ed., *The End of the Keynesian Era*, (New York: MacMillan, 1977). My inferences about Keynes's motives are obviously problematic. They are based predominantly on the fine biography of Keynes by Donald Winch in *Economics and Policy* (New York: Walker and Company, 1969) and on my general understanding of Western human beings. Similar interpretations of Keynes's motives have been expressed

(and even more often hinted at) by some who knew him, quite independently of Winch's biography. See, for example, Friedrich A. Hayek, *A Tiger by the Tail* (London: The Institute of Economic Affairs, 1972), especially pp. 99–106.

10. I do not have the space in this book to present the mass of evidence from earlier studies showing the mythical, ideological nature of much of the social sciences. I have published many earlier books that do some of that and there are many works by other scholars which do so. See, especially, Friedrich Hayek, *The Counter-Revolution In Science* (Glencoe, IL: The Free Press, 1955); P. A. Sorokin, *Fads and Foibles in Modern Sociology* (Chicago: Henry Regnery, 1956); Stanislav Andreski, *Sociology as Sorcery*. Many such analyses have been done of Keynesianism. For an excellent overview of these, see Joseph J. Spengler, "Social Science and the Collectivization of Hubris," in Harold D. Lasswell, et al., eds., *Propaganda and Communication in World History* (Honolulu: University of Hawaii Press, 1980), vol. III, pp. 461–81.

11. Quoted in *The Economist*, July 17, 1982, p. 67.

12. Robert Higgs, *Crisis and Leviathan*, (New York: Oxford University Press, 1987).

13. I shall be dealing with the most important works on the origins of statist powers throughout the book. The most important recent sources are the following: David Apter, "Government," in David L. Sills, ed., *International Encyclopedia of Social Sciences* (New York: MacMillan and Free Press, 1968); Georges Balandier, *Political Anthropology* (New York: Pantheon Books, 1970); Roderick Bell, David V. Edwards, and R. Harrison Wagner, eds., *Political Power: A Reader in Theory and Research* (New York: Free Press, 1969); Robert L. Carneiro, "A Theory of the Origin of the State," *Science* (1970) vol. 169: pp. 733–38; Henry J. M. Claessen and Peter Skalnik, eds., *The Early State* (The Hague: Mouton, 1978); Robert A. Dahl, "Power," in David L. Sills, ed., *International Encyclopedia of Social Sciences* (New York: MacMillan and Free Press, 1968); "The Concept of Power," in Roderick Bell et al., eds., *Political Power: A Reader in Theory and Research* (New York: Free Press, 1968), pp. 79–93; Raymond D. Fogelson and Richard N. Adams, eds., *The Anthropology of Power* (New York: Academic Press, 1977); Morton H. Fried, *The Evolution of Political Society: An Essay in Political Anthropology* (New York: Random House, 1967); Max Gluckman, "The Kingdom of the Zulu of South Africa," in Meyer Fortes and E. E. Evans-Prichard, eds., *African Political Systems* (New York: Oxford University Press, 1940), pp. 25–55; Jonathan Haas, *The Evolution of the Prehistoric State* (New York: Columbia University Press, 1982); Eva Hunt and Robert C. Hunt, "Irrigation, Conflict and Politics: A Mexican Case," in T. E. Downing and McGuire Gibson, eds., *Irrigation's Impact on Society*, Papers of the University of Arizona 25, 1974, pp. 129–58; Lawrence Krader, *Formation of the State* (Englewood Cliffs, NJ: Prentice-Hall, 1968); Lucy Mair, *Primitive Government* (Harmondsworth: Penguin Books, 1962); Charles L. Redman, *The Rise of Civilization: From Early Farmers to Urban Society in the Ancient Near East* (New York: Freeman, 1978); Elman R. Service, *Origins of the State and Civilization: The Process of Cultural Evolution* (New York: Norton, selections reprinted by permission, 1975); Henry T. Wright, "Toward an Explanation of the Origin of the State," in James N. Hill, ed., *Explanation of Prehistoric Change* (Albuquerque: University of New Mexico Press, 1977), pp. 215–30.

14. I have analyzed these ideas and their histories in many books. See, especially, *American Social Order* (New York: Free Press, 1971); and *Introduction to the Sociologies of Everyday Life* (Boston: Allyn and Bacon, 1980).
15. The few comparative historians have made the argument many times. See, especially, William McNeill, *Mythistory and Other Essays* (Chicago: University of Chicago Press, 1986), including his presidential address to the American Historical Association. (He does, however, use "myth" in a much broader sense than anthropologists and I do.)
16. The classical history of individualistic theories of society is Otto Gierke, *Natural Law and the Theory of Society* (Cambridge: Cambridge University Press, 1958).
17. See William McNeill, *The Pursuit of Power* (Chicago: University of Chicago Press, 1984).
18. The literature on divine kingship is very extensive. See, especially, John N. Figgis, *The Divine Right of Kings*, 2d ed. (Cambridge: Cambridge University Press, 1922); Arthur Hocart, *Kingship* (Oxford: Oxford University Press, 1927); Charles Seligman, *Egypt and Negro Africa: A Study in Divine Kingship* (London: Routledge, 1933); Henri Frankfort, *Kingship and the Gods* (Chicago: University of Chicago Press, 1948); and R. Bendix, *Kings or People* (Berkeley: University of California Press, 1978).
19. Wittfogel's materialistic determinist theory had a profound influence on theorists of the state and civilization. See his *Oriental Despotism* (New Haven: Yale University Press, 1957).
20. Michael E. Smith, "The Role of Social Stratification in the Aztec Empire: A View From the Province," *American Anthropologist* 88 (March 1986): 70–91.
21. Haas, *The Evolution of the Prehistoric State*.
22. S. N. Eisenstadt, *The Political Systems of Empires* (New York: MacMillan, 1963).
23. Ibid, pp. 28–9.
24. See footnote 18 above on sacred kingship.
25. The dominance of ideas of sacred kingship during the Hellenistic period, after Alexander's conquests, is very subject to controversy, in good part because of the flood of official agitprop unleashed by the new regimes. There was, however, clearly some admixture and much variation. See G. J. D. Aalders, *Political Thought in Hellenistic Times* (Amsterdam: 1975); U. Ehrenberg, *The Greek State* (London: Methuen, 1969); and S. R. F. Price, *Rituals and Power* (Cambridge: Cambridge University Press, 1984).
26. Walter Ullmann, *The Individual and Society in the Middle Ages* (Baltimore, MD: John Hopkins University Press, 1966), pp. 36–37.
27. M. Rostovtzeff, *Rome* (New York: Oxford University Press, 1960), p. 178.
28. Augustus's principate is of great importance in understanding the rise of "democratic tyranny" in all republics with strong traditions of checks and balances against powerful rulers. The same tactics of deceitful humility, meticulous respect for constitutional forms, and so on, must always be followed in such societies, as we see our own rulers doing today. The best interpretations of the large literature seem clearly to be those of Michael Grant, *The World of Rome* (New York: New American Library, 1960); and *The Twelve Caesars* (New York: Charles Scribner's Sons, 1975). See also David Stockton, "The Founding of the Empire," John Boardman, et al., eds., in *The Oxford History of the Classical World* (New York: Oxford University Press, 1956), pp. 531–59; M. Rostovtzeff, *Rome*, pp. 162–82; H. H. Scullard, *From the Gracchi to Nero* (New York: Praeger, 1959); and F. Millar and E. Segal, eds., *Caesar Augustus*

(Oxford: Oxford University Press, 1984).
29. Leonard Hobhouse, *The Metaphysical Theory of the State*. The best philosophical, historical analyst who supports the metaphysical theory as transmitted and augmented by Hegel is Bernard Bosanquet, in *The Philosophical Theory of the State* (London: MacMillan, 1958). And see Stefan Collini, "Hobhouse, Bosanquet and the State," *Past and Present* 1976.
30. Robert M. MacIver, *The Modern State* (Oxford: Oxford University Press, 1926). This beautifully clear work examines the history of ideas and practices of the state in Western culture.
31. Ernst Cassirer, *The Myth of the State* (Garden City, NY: Doubleday, 1955).
32. Ernst Kartorowicz, *The King's Two Bodies* (Princeton: Princeton, New Jersey, 1957).
33. Bendix, *Kings or People.*
34. Public, mass education is the most important form of agitprop, but any form of ritual or information can be statized. We shall consider many of these.
35. Bendix, *Kings or People*, is the best earlier source I know of on these issues.
36. The many historical arguments over what empires are, how they arise, the more and less direct (formal and informal) means of control, and so on, are dealt with in Michael Doyle, *Empires* (Ithaca, NY: Cornell University Press, 1986).
37. These symbols of *common identity* are found universally in family, clan and tribal names, but flags, pennants, banners, insignias and so on emerged with statehood in the ancient world, presumably because they are a powerful form of symbolic identification (agitprop) for people having fewer degrees of common identification. On the ancient history of nation-state symbols, see George H. Preble, *The Symbols, Standards, Flags, and Banners of Ancient and Modern Nations* (Winchester, MA: The Flag Research Center, no date).
38. I have discussed these distinctions in *Love, Intimacy and Sex* and in "Cooperative Paternalism Versus Conflictful Paternalism," in Rolf Sartorius, ed., *Paternalism* (Minneapolis: University of Minnesota Press, 1983), pp. 171–200; and in "The Emergence, Security and Growth of the Sense of Self," in J. Kotarba and A. Fontana, eds., *The Existential Self in Society* (Chicago: University of Chicago Press, 1984), pp. 69–99. Such distinctions are discussed in many of the sources on statehood and those concerned with the rise of states (see chapter 3). I have had to change and sharpen some of the distinctions, especially to emphasize their *continuous* nature, rather than the discontinuous, either-or distinctions often made. A valuable traditional discussion is Charlotte Waterlow, *Tribe, State and Community* (London: Methuen, 1967).
39. The Aristotelian conception of the political identification of human beings (in *Politics*) is predominantly, but not entirely, what we now call a *nation* or *community*, but it is commonly translated as *state*. This causes endless confusions. Edmund Burke used "state" in the original Aristotelian sense, but George F. Will has taken his use of "state" more in the Platonic sense of a supra-individual, concrete thing. It is most moral and freedom inspiring for the leader of a family, love partnership, and nation to engage in "soulcraft," and most oppressive for a state ruler to do so. See George F. Will, *Statecraft as Soul Craft* (New York: Simon and Schuster, 1983).
40. One of the most famous socialist arguments of this sort is the "progressive" form given it by Walter Lippmann, *The Public Philosophy* (Boston: Little, Brown, 1955), especially p. 34.

41. See R. Hatton, ed., *Louis XIV and Absolutism* (Columbus: Ohio State University Press, 1976).

42. Jeremy Bentham, *The Utilitarians: An Introduction to the Principles of Morals and Legislation* (Garden City, NY: Anchor/Doubleday, 1973), ch. 1, sec. IV.

43. A classical discussion of the major positions found in American and British politics in the last two centuries is Samuel Beer, *British Politics in the Collectivist Age* (New York: Vintage Books, 1969), especially pp. 3–102.

44. See my essay on "A Grand Moral Strategy," in Robert Poole, ed., *Defending a Free Society* (Lexington, MA: D. C. Heath, 1984), pp. 317–43.

45. John Keegan has considered some of these in his multidimensional view of *The Mask of Command* (New York: Viking, 1987).

46. Reported in the *Los Angeles Times*, Dec. 15, 1987.

47. There are now a number of brilliant works by Americans who held powerful positions and helped to build our megastate until they realized what they were doing, quit, and wrote their "confessions." See, especially, William Simon, *A Time for Truth* (New York: Berkeley Books, 1979).

48. See Dennis Mack Smith, *Mussolini* (New York: Knopf, 1982).

49. These factors will be dealt with in later chapters, especially in Chapter 3. The monomyth of the *Great Chain of Being* was the crucial statist myth in the Western World. The general idea was that all beings are linked *necessarily* in a great chain from the greatest—God—down to the least. This was seen as the natural state—order—of Being and was a hierarchy of good, value, power, and so on. It synthesized the classical Roman ideas, especially of the state and rulership, with Christian religious ideas. See Arthur Lovejoy, *The Great Chain of Being* (New York: Harper Torchbooks, 1960).

50. The extreme view of Federal Reserve fiat power is presented very well by William Greider, *Secrets of the Temple: How the Federal Reserve Runs the Country* (New York: Simon and Schuster, 1987). A normal view of the Fed's entrepreneurial powers is presented by Lindley H. Clark, Jr., "Will Money Keep Economy on the Rise?" *The Wall Street Journal*, Nov. 30, 1987.

51. See James MacGregor Burns, *Roosevelt: The Lion and the Fox* (New York: Harcourt Brace, 1956), pp. 371–375; and Karl Bracher, *The German Dictatorship* (New York: Holt, Rinehart and Winston, 1970), p. 212, ff.

52. Albert Speer, *Inside the Third Reich* (New York: Avon, 1972), is probably the best-known practitioner of state capitalism on the grand scale. Adolf Berle, Franklin Roosevelt's "brain truster," was probably the most explicit proponent in America. (See Jordan A. Schwartz, *Liberal* [New York: The Free Press, 1987].) But most American presidents since Hoover have used *indirect* threat-ukazi extensively to keep business in line and our regulatory bureaucracies now use direct ukazi massively.

53. Barry Newman, "Hungary Plunges into State Capitalism," *The Wall Street Journal*, December 23, 1987.

54. Speer, *Inside the Third Reich*. Speer's accounts of his involvements in Nazi Germany have been challenged effectively, but it remains one of the great works in the Machiavellian tradition of realpolitik.

55. The huge literature on the Soviets certainly includes wide disagreements on how they "really work." There are also disagreements on how much of the economy operates underground as a relatively free market, but all factual accounts with

inside information agree the free activities are massive. The classical scholarly account by Merle Fainsod, *How Russia Is Ruled* (Cambridge: Harvard University Press, 1956) remains invaluable. See also, A. Nove, *An Economic History of the U.S.S.R.* (London: Allen Lane, 1969); A. Nove, *The Soviet Economic System* (London: Allen & Unwin, 1977); and Marshall Goldman, *USSR in Crisis* (New York: W. W. Norton, 1983). Robert G. Kaiser's *Russia* (New York: Pocket Books, 1976) and Hedrick Smith's *The Russians* (New York: Ballantine, 1976) are good examples of more popular accounts. For the general scholarly picture see Archie Brown, et al., eds., *The Cambridge Encyclopedia of Russia and the Soviet Union* (New York: Cambridge University Press, 1982). For comparisons of "communist" economies, see R. W. Campbell, *Soviet-Type Economies* (Boston: Houghton Mifflin, 1974).

56. See the American best seller on these plans for the *new planning* by M. Gorbachev, *Perestroika* (New York: Harper and Row, 1987).

3

The Ancient Dawn of Welfare Statism

. . .here are men, men of education and intelligence, honest and upright men who suddenly give up the highest human privilege. They have ceased to be free and personal agents. Performing the same prescribed rites they begin to feel, to think, and to speak in the same way. Their gestures are lively and violent; yet this is but an artificial, a sham life. In fact they are moved by an external force. They act like marionettes in a puppet show—and they do not even know that the strings of this show and of man's whole individual and social life, are henceforward pulled by the political leaders.

Ernst Cassirer

One of the great controversies between statists and antistatists since the nineteenth century has been over whether human beings are cooperative or conflictful. Statists have asserted passionately that the evidence proves absolutely that human beings are either by nature cooperative or, far more commonly in recent decades, that they can be molded by culture to be cooperative. They have marshaled evidence from around the world to prove their point, ranging from Kropotkin's early sociobiological studies of herds to more recent studies of the Samoans, Zuñi, and Tasaday. The antistatists took the opposite end of the stick and argued that human beings are by nature conflictful—or "selfish" as the argument generally puts it.

This great historical debate obscures the vastly complex human realities, as do most of these ideological either-ors. We are inherently conflictful and cooperative to vastly different degrees in different cultures, individuals, and situations. It is obvious to anyone who surveys human history that we human beings are both predators and prey, both attackers and defenders; that even our most intimate partnerships, those within the family, inevitably involve some major conflicts; and that *all* civilizations have normally been peaceful within and in a state of limited war much of the time with some outside competitors. Consequently, human beings make almost constant use of vastly complex strategies of deceit, attack, and defense in combination with vastly complex strategies of honesty, cooperation, and waging peace.

Secrecy and camouflage are basic strategies of deceit in attack and defense throughout the animal world and much of the plant world. Misinformation and disinformation (purposeful misinformation) are endemic in human life. Even the most loving—cooperative—parents find that by the age of two or three years the normal child is not only thrilled by hide-and-seek, but quite adept at hiding from them and sometimes lying to them. If children were not by nature prone to use strategies of disinformation in some conflict situations, it would hardly be important to teach them by example and incentive that "honesty is the best policy." Though Diogenes may have lived in an especially corrupt age, all competent adults realize that totally honest men and women are nonexistent. After all, if adults were naturally honest, there would be a vast supply of honesty, so it would hardly be one of the most prized characteristics and there would hardly be such a plethora of rules against dishonesty or of methods of investigation to smoke it out. In our world of conflict, anyone who was totally honest would be unbearably tactless.

We are reminded every day of the vast duplicity of our world. We scientists are acutely aware these days that even our own professions, which are dedicated publicly to truth, are extremely vulnerable to carefully planned and systematically-executed fraud. Our scientific professions have been rocked to their foundations by discoveries of monstrous frauds that successfully deceived almost all of the greatest experts for decades. In fact, the thing that has most shocked scientists is that most of these scientific frauds have been so patently obvious once the evidence was looked at with any of the suspicion normal in everyday public life. Medical researchers have created experimental results out of thin air, evolutionists have created Piltdown Man out of orangutan parts and chemicals, historians have created capitalists supporting Hitler by making up footnotes and quotes from nonexistent sources, psychologists have proven theories of genius by using nonexistent case studies and faking statistics, and anthropologists have created whole cultures by discovering them in totally fraudulent accounts. Some of the most studied cases of fraud have revealed that in the "hard sciences" of biomedical research even the supposed "coauthors" of extremely fraudulent reports of experimental results did not know what was going on in their own laboratories where they worked every day.

In the social sciences it has been known for decades that some of the most basic findings were really the result of dishonesty by experimental "subjects" who did not want to be embarrassed, and of the self-deceptive coaxing of professors anxious to prove their theories, but the discovery that some of the most famous and celebrated professionals, such as Cyril Burt in psychology and Margaret Mead in anthropology, were either outright frauds or the dupes of frauds by their "subjects" has raised the specter of mass disinformation.[1] The problems are clearly at their extreme in anthropology because the strangeness of the new people makes it easy for them to deceive the anthropologists. It has been clear to any prudent observer since James Cook's experience with the Tahitians in the eighteenth century that it is very easy to be misled in understanding new cultures, because the outsiders are so ignorant, because these colonial subjects have had great incentives to deceive such whites, and because almost all fieldwork has been done by one person and never retested. It has been obvious for decades that the independent restudy of any culture generally leads to great disagreements among anthropologists about the culture. Now that it appears likely that the most famous anthropologist, Margaret Mead, was systematically misled by her Samoan "subjects," in spite of the existence of many earlier studies contradicting her findings, and that at least one whole people, the famous Tasaday, never existed, the evidence on which much of their recent conclusions about human nature are based has become highly suspect.

But, of course, these are minor problems compared to dishonesty among politicians, even in the West where political corruption is minor compared to that in most states.[2] In American education George Washington and Abraham Lincoln are lauded above all other political leaders for their great honesty. This is mainly because it is easy to prove that almost all of our other presidents were involved in massive disinformation, ranging from dirty tricks and international secrecy to secret adulteries in the White House and felonious conspiracies to obstruct justice. It is, then, most indicative of the nature of politicians to remember that George Washington is also lauded as a great military hero because he so completely deceived the English and Hessians, while "Honest Abe" was not only the master of political dirty tricks who secretly made up the propaganda slogan of Honest Abe, but also delighted in retelling some of his dirty tricks and turned Sherman, the master of military deceit, loose upon the South.

We are reminded of these facts of life every day. It is exceedingly unlikely that a day goes by in which there are no major news stories revealing new political secrecies, lies, feints, ploys, dirty tricks, fraud, theft, and any number of the scores of the specific forms of political deceit we distinguish in American English. A typical example is the news stories in the Western media about China's treatment of Tibet, which was forcefully constituted as an "autonomous republic" of China in 1965. During a trip to China in June 1987, former president Jimmy Carter "lavished praise upon China's treatment of the Tibetan people."[3] On October 1, 1987, violent riots broke out in Tibet against China. On October 6, 1987, the official Chinese communist paper,

China Daily, carried a front-page story that reminded its readers around the world that before the Chinese communist party liberated Tibet its former masters treated the mass of the people as serfs and sometimes gouged out their eyes, split their noses, ripped out their hearts, threw them into pits of scorpions, and raped their daughters. *China Daily* goes on to remind them that the Chinese had ended all of these horrendous evils and had been so benevolent as to give them schools, tractors, new large buildings and, no doubt, the full panoply of the modernist welfare state.[4]

Even the readers of this account who are highly sympathetic to the communist party of China, and eager to believe there must have been some evil landlords and monks who did those things, will almost automatically discount the honesty of such an account, simply because common sense tells us that the unarmed Tibetans would hardly be willing to die attacking the heavily armed Chinese army if their communist welfare state had delivered Tibetans from rape, pits of scorpions, slit noses, gouged-out eyes, and ripped-out hearts. Even modernist gullibility has its limits, especially after the discoveries that the great majorities of intellectuals, journalists, and politicians were almost totally deceived by the early Soviet regime, by Stalin, by Hitler, by Castro, by Mao, and by phalanxes of other politicians who were most profuse in their proclamations of welfare-statist benevolence. After decades of historical revelations about the secret sex lives of FDR in the White House itself and of JFK more peripatetically, only historical amnesiacs were surprised by Gary Hart's sex antics and brazen campaign of news-disinformation in 1987.

In view of all of this, it is astounding to see how totally gullible almost all of the famous archaeologists, historians, and social scientists have been in their interpretations of the records of the most ancient and the most modern civilizations. Though it will be a long time before we can sort out the complexities, it is now shockingly clear that even the most honest of these experts were generally the victims of a great self-deception for almost two centuries. This great self-deception consisted of their relatively uncritical acceptance of the official records of government bureaucrats as representative evidence of the everyday realities of the ancient civilizations. At the very time that Biblical scholars were finding ever more reasons to interpret their texts critically, the scholars studying immensely skimpier and more problematic official records from other civilizations were taking them largely at face value.

Recognizing the Problem of the Origins of States

Since almost all historical, written records came into existence only after state bureaucracies were firmly established, and were created largely to justify or carry out the functions of those statist bureaucracies, the origins of states was not seen as a problem by educated people in these statist civilizations until scientific studies of nonstatist societies began in the sixteenth and seventeenth centuries. Even the ancient Western anthropologists were restricted in their direct observations to human beings within city-states or within huge imperial states. They were aware of the "barbarians" who lived beyond the fringes of statist powers, but they were the objects of stigmatization, outrage, and humor rather than serious study. Assuming that "man is a political animal," and assuming that politics involved some form of state, they saw state powers and their exercise as natural, as part of human nature. It did not occur to them to explain the origins of statism in general. Social theorists in other civilizations apparently made the same basic assumptions. The Confucian mandarins of China were far more aware than other theorists of the fragility of the powers of particular states, since Confucianism had roots in China's era of warring states, but they saw even those small states as unnatural remnants from the decline of the Shang empire and they longed for the natural day of universal state powers. They saw statist ideas and powers as natural extensions of the family and certainly saw statist unity as necessary for natural human life.

Early Western explorers who encountered the huge, highly centralized empires of Mexico and Peru felt quite at home and knew very well how to go about conquering them, by seizing power at the top, and then using their statist convictions and bureaucratic operations to rule the people. But most of the people they discovered were quite stateless. This led the explorers to make countless mistakes in dealing with them, especially when they kept assuming the "Indians" were the outlying subjects of great Indian rulers, as Columbus and his immediate successors did. But some of them, and even more the social thinkers back home, soon came to realize they were dealing with people in raw, savage, nonstatist conditions. Both the noble savages and the ignoble savages were living in Adam and Eve conditions, in which there were no statist gentlemen or ladies. States could not be a simple matter of human nature working itself out, so what produced them?

The dominant answer for centuries was the rationalist theory of the social contract, which now appears as absurd as the ideas of the "primal horde" of barbarians who supposedly did not even have incest rules, first reported (on the basis of rumor) by Herodotus. While their answer was quite fanciful and was apparently understood by some of them to be merely a useful presupposition, they were quite right to conclude from their skimpy factual material that state social order was not a result of human nature. Human beings are obviously not genetically programmed to be statist animals. If they were, states would not be such recent and rare phenomena. The earliest states for which there are any records at all were Egypt and Sumeria, which were built a mere five thousand years ago. While I suspect there were state organizations before those that left no records yet discovered, the great military advantage and staying power given to states by their core myths and operations makes it unlikely there were many before this known cultural horizon of statism. Of all the thousands of human societies for which we have any reliable evidence in this era of statism, only a tiny fraction have been dominated by the core enabling myths of statism, or by major fragments of them. To this day, after thousands of years of massive statist agitprop by these huge bureaucracies, large percentages of the populations of the great empires remain secretly alienated, to widely varying degrees, from the statist myths and bureaucracies. The Soviet Empire has obviously not succeeded in statizing the peoples of their many overtly submissive nations—Ukrainians, Georgians, Armenians, Azerbaijanies, Uzbekis, Kazakhs, Kurdistanis, Mongols, Germans, Jews, Latvians, Lithuanians, Estonians, and many more. Wherever the great religions remain strong in the West and Middle East, large segments of the populations remain secretly wedded more to their other-world kingdom than to the states whose worldly domains they inhabit. The peoples of China and Japan are probably the most homogeneous and statist in the world today, largely because their statism has been so ancient, ferocious and largely unopposed by great religions. But China remains far more heterogeneous and even Taoist than Western admirers of the Middle Kingdom like to admit. As John King Fairbank has noted, this "central myth of the Chinese state," that of "the innate unity of the Chinese realm" (*t'ien-hsia*), was swallowed whole by early Western sinologists and transmitted down to the mass media today.[5] As we shall see, most Americans remain ambivalent about Americanism—the myths of American statism—or consciously oppose them both for Christian reasons and because of their gut-level federationism or outright anarchism. Very few Americans agree with that moral litmus test of statism—"My state (country) right or wrong." Many of us still assume conscience, family, church, the morals of common decency and fair play, community, and nation (the Sacred Constitution) came before the nebulous statist myths of Americanism. Most of us today who are very patriotic are very much against the modernist megastate on the Potomac. Any statist administration that forgets this risks rebellion, as LBJ discovered.

Human Nature and Statist Powers

Some animals, at least some insects, have highly complex forms of social organization with rigid caste systems that totally subordinate lower-caste individuals to the collective welfare embodied in a few upper-caste rulers, such as queen bees. All of these terms the entomologists use to talk about these insects are taken from our human terms for discussing highly monarchical states (though they are more totalitarian than any monarchy that ever existed). The reason is that the analogy is so close (one-to-one in the idealized theory). In the theory of absolute (totalitarian) monarchy, the monarch symbolically represented—embodied—the common welfare through his divine link with God. (The pharaoh of Egypt, an extreme form of divine king, was literally presented as the *only* way anyone else could get to eternal life. In China each new emperor climbed to the peak of Mount Tai'Shan to symbolize that his "mandate of heaven" made him the vital link between heaven and the needs of the people. In the absolute monarchies of Europe's Renaissance welfare states, statists saw the monarchs as the highest human link in the Great Chain of Being that descended from God to the lowliest being.) In a more real sense, the queen bee represents the real interests of all the drones subordinate to her. She has the same genes as the lower-caste bees. The queen alone can lay fertilized eggs to pass on their common genes. So when the drone dies to protect his queen, he dies to protect himself genetically. Biologically, then, there is an identity of interests at the most basic level between this queenly state-ruler and the ruled.

In higher animals only parents, their children, their grandchildren, their siblings, and close cousins have enough mutual genetic investment to make it biologically adaptive ("rational") for individuals to identify their genetic interests with the group. And, of course, they do so to varying degrees roughly in direct proportion to their genetic sharedness (and to some more complex considerations of adaptability). Parents the world over will sacrifice the most for their children. The family is the one group the world over with which individuals tend to strongly identify their interests and, in fact, their very selves.[6] The family group is always conceived of as a separate level of existence from its members, a thing that exists down through the stream of time even as its members die; and the family is conceived to have a common welfare which partly transcends that of each member. These basic ideas of the family spring from the basic genetic realities and the emotional identifications that spring from those. All states are in part mythical extensions of this universal nature of kinship identifications.

As far as we know, the earliest form of all human groups, like other primate groups today, was the small band of hunters and gatherers. These groups consist of subgroups of generally closely related families, and their common identity is overwhelmingly that of extended kinship (which is also identified with a common territory, certain moral rules, rituals, and language). There is leadership within these groups, but it tends strongly to be a very subtle, complex, situated (task-oriented) form of consensus leadership closely related to parental authority.[7] There is a common conception of identity which identifies many of the interests of the individual with those of this kin group. Effective rulers of states must use these kin-identifications to identify the subordinates with themselves by mythical extensions ("Father of His people," "paternalism," etc.), but these real kin-identifications are not state relations.

A state exists only when the members *identify* themselves with each other in non-kin terms (or only fictionalized kinship terms) by believing they share a common essence (German blood, Americanism, etc.), in common submission to rulers who are believed to represent the *collective* (common) *essence* and serve its common welfare (see chapter 2). The state is seen as a (non-kin) *separate* (higher) *level of existence* from the members subordinate to it. The means by which rulers have succeeded in getting people to believe in these statist myths seem vastly complex and at this time we cannot hope to do more than build a general model of their foundations. There appear to be different paths by which they first succeeded and there are no simple evolutionary paths from their origins to our modernist megastates. States wax *and* wane and it is a crucial part of my argument that the very success of states, their ratchet-up process, has thus far always produced accelerating problems that eventually lead to their declines. This model must begin with and be built on a better understanding of the nature of all power or dominance relations in human life. After this analysis of power, I shall try to show that there are certain types of power relations which developed in nonstatist societies that formed crucial breakthroughs and building blocks for the creation states.

The Ultimate Sources of All Power

Political theorists have put vast effort into showing that power, or dominance as ethologists prefer to call it, is not at all as simple as the commonsensical idea of *physical force* assumes. While this is true and vitally important, the theorists have almost always proceeded to greatly obscure power by focusing on the vastly varying social conditions and arrangements, such as statist bureaucracies and social classes, which affect the distributions and exercise of power. All of these analyses then beg the crucial question of what power is, of what all of these social conditions are affecting. We must first look at the subjective meanings that are being communicated and affected when we talk about power.

Theorists agree in general that aggregate power is the relative degree of assymetric influence that one individual or group has on others. This is not a mere tautology. The point is that an individual has power to the degree that he can produce more changes in the internal and external states of others than they can produce in his states. (If there is no assymetry, they are in an aggregate state of no power. Since there are different dimensions of power, one may have more power in some dimensions but be checked overall by the other having greater power in other dimensions.) As classical Western theorists put it, power is what compels others to "fulfill one's will." The materialism of the modernist age then leads easily to the materialistic fallacy of power, the assumption that power is the material force (weapons, objects of wealth) used to change the will of someone else. The classical theory of war did not see it that way at all. As Clausewitz, following his idol, Napolean, saw it, power consisted of material means multiplied by the nonphysical factors of strength of will (morale, determination, and so on). They saw the nonphysical differences as far more important in these differences of willfulness or power. (Napoleon saw the nonphysical as three times more important.) This is obvious in the extremes, as we see when vast hordes melt away before tiny forces because they have no will to fight. Belisarius, for example, was reported to have thrown a huge army into panic by having a lone trumpet blown to their rear.

But I believe this classical analysis also fails to see the crucial point about power. Mercantilists mistook the physical substance of gold for value itself, in the same way Marxists mistake physical labor for value. But gold is merely the proximate (or immediate), material representation of aggregated symbolic values—internal states of comparative evaluations which we call money values. Differences in amounts or weights of gold have differences in value only to the degree they affect or represent internal, symbolic comparisons of values. In the same way, proximate material factors in general affect power relations only to the degree they affect the ultimate internal, meaningful states in human beings. Power differences exist to the degree one individual (or group) has more effect on the internal, meaningful states of others than they have in return. The internal states that ultimately have the crucial effects in life are emotional states—such as pain and dread that can be inflicted by weapons, both physical and nonphysical (such as expressions of contempt and hatred). Power, then, consists in the differences in the ultimate emotional effects one individual can have on others. Since our beliefs about such ultimate effects have some short-run independence from demonstrated effects, they too are important determinants of power. To the degree that we identify ourselves with the self of anyone else, or with any abstract being (noumenon) he is identified with or controls, then to that degree our emotional states—our very selves—are directly dependent on his actions or mere thoughts toward us.

Emotional dependency is the ultimate source of all power and, thus, of all statist powers. The more one individual believes his general emotional welfare depends ultimately on that individual, the more he will be influenced by that individual, or have his will bent by that other even without the actual eliciting of the ultimate emotional state. Dependency is ultimately always emotional. Power, then, is always ultimately based on the belief one individual has about the ability another has to affect his emotions or the actual triggering of that emotion. The more he believes his emotional state ultimately depends on the other, the more power that other has over him.[8]

The nature and the dangers of power can be seen most easily in love partnerships. The more you love someone, the more you identify with them and the more your emotional state is affected by them; thus, the more you are dependent on them; and, thus, the more power they have over you. All of us learn this early in life. And almost all of us become acutely aware of how much we can be hurt by individuals we love when they do not love us. If they love us in return, we have love-power to counteract their love-power. If they do not love us, and our love is a great love, they are in a position to control our lives to an extreme degree—even to the point of suicide. As James McGregor Burns has noted:

> To define power not as a property or entity or possession but as a *relationship* in which two or more persons tap motivational bases in one another and bring varying resources to bear in the process is to perceive power as drawing a vast range of human behavior into its orbit. The arena of power is no longer the exclusive preserve of a power elite or an establishment or persons clothed with legitimacy. Power is ubiquitous; it permeates human relationships. It exists whether or not it is quested for. It is the glory and the burden of most of humanity. A common, highly asymmetric, and sometimes cruel power relation can exist, for example, when one person is in love with another but the other does not reciprocate. The wants and needs and expectations of the persons in love are aroused and engaged by a partner whose resources of attractiveness or desirability are high and whose own cluster of motives is less vulnerable. The person possessed by love can maneuver and struggle but still is a slave to the one loved, as the plight of Philip in Somerset Maugham's marvelously titled *Of Human Bondage* illustrates.[9]

Very importantly, this love-power can be exercised without any control over material goods or physical force. The most powerful and richest men have been humbled and led about like lambs by the tiniest slips of beautiful vixen, and mighty Roman soldiers have been bent to the will of aging mothers.

All wise parents know that children will obey out of fear only as long as the parents are watching and are strong, but will obey out of love regardless. And all wise children know that parents who sincerely love them can be trusted to act for their best welfare, while unloving parents easily become terrible totalitarians. In the same way, every wise ruler knows that subjects who love him and who believe he loves them in return will be the most obedient—especially if they also know punishment for their best welfare will quickly follow disobedience. In small societies like the hunting and gathering ones, the leaders are generally related to everyone else and leadership involves far more loving identification than fearful disidentification. In societies in which there is a strong consensus and sense of communal love, combined with strong checks on the power of the leaders, mutual love, or at least mutual respect, are still vitally important in leadership. (The great reluctance of the King of Prussia to lead his people into potentially disastrous wars was partly inspired by his love of his people and the mutual trust he knew was vital to his power. Bismarck had to deceive the king even more than the people to get the wars for which he lusted.)[10] As conflict and distrust grow, and as power is shorn of restraints, the ruler's love becomes merely a deceitful pose to trick the people into believing it—the mythical love of paternalism, if they fall for it. But it can still be a remarkably powerful force leading the people to love and worship the Leader and to mythically submerge their selves in union with Him.

Americans used to love their greatest leaders moderately, and were thereby tempted to mythically idealize them moderately into benevolent father figures (e.g., Founding Fathers) and mother figures. Even with the coming of the terrible conflicts and distrust of the modernist welfare state, the sex appeal, if not love, of the Kennedys was an important ingredient in their leadership style. But a majority of us has never yet been tempted by terrifying insecurities, soaring greed, and a mythically loving Leader to lose ourselves in a mythical identification—*communion*—with the state (Holy Spirit) through the medium of The Leader (Savior). To see this vast power of the mythical love of a Leader and the identification with him it welds, we must look abroad (or to the thralldom of our religious fanatics or of our fans for their Superstars).[11]

"Infallible" popes who coveted absolute power always presented themselves as the fount of divine and absolute love. Absolutist monarchs presented a solid front of "benevolent despotism" to their people. Albert Speer has shown us how he and most other Germans were swept away by worshipful love for Hitler, the Great Deceiver whom he mistook for a Great Lover:

> I was not choosing the NSDAP [the Nazis], but becoming a follower of Hitler, whose magnetic force had reached out to me the first time I saw him and had not, thereafter, released me. His persuasiveness, the peculiar magic of his by no means pleasant voice, the oddity of his rather banal manner, the seductive simplicity with which he attacked the complexity of our problems—all that bewildered and fascinated me. I knew virtually nothing about his program. He had taken hold of me before I had grasped what was happening.
>
> Now I was completely under Hitler's spell, unreservedly and unthinkingly held by him. I was ready to follow him anywhere. . . . Years later, in Spandau, I read Ernst Cassirer's comment on the men who of their own accord threw away man's highest privilege: to be an autonomous person.
>
> Now I was one of them. . . .
>
> Meanwhile, thousands of people were gathering outside chanting calls for Hitler. . . .
>
> Everywhere in the countryside farmers left their implements, women waved. It was a triumphal procession. As the car rolled along, Hitler leaned back to me and exclaimed: 'Heretofore only one German had been hailed like this: Luther. When

he rode through the country, people gathered from far and wide to cheer him. As they do for me today!'

This enormous popularity was only too easy to understand. The public credited Hitler and no one else with the achievements in economics and foreign policy of the period. They more and more regarded him as the leader who had made a reality of their deeply rooted longing for a powerful, proud, united Germany. Very few were mistrustful at this time. And those who occasionally felt doubts rising reassured themselves with thoughts of the regime's accomplishments and the esteem it enjoyed even in critical foreign countries.[12]

Emotional dependency can be both unmediated and mediated by external means. Even love can be love entirely for yourself or love for you because of the means—wealth, prestige, etc.—that you control—or are believed to control. Anything that you control which in turn affects someone else's emotions (or is believed to do so) can give you power over that person. Hitler achieved mythical power over millions of Germans by appealing directly to their emotions long before he had any mediated means. Albert Speer has described Hitler's hypnotic powers of inducing identification with him:

Hitler's initial shyness soon disappeared; at times now his pitch rose. He spoke urgently and with hypnotic persuasiveness. The mood he cast was much deeper than the speech itself, most of which I did not remember for long.

Moreover, I was carried on the wave of the enthusiasm which, one could almost feel this physically, bore the speaker along from sentence to sentence. It swept away any skepticism, any reservations. Opponents were given no chance to speak. This furthered the illusion, at least momentarily, of unanimity. Finally, Hitler no longer seemed to be speaking to convince; rather, he seemed to feel he was expressing what the audience, by now transformed into a single mass, expected of him. It was as if it were the most natural thing in the world to lead students and part of the faculty of the two greatest academies in Germany submissively by a leash. Yet that evening he was not yet the absolute ruler, immune from all criticism, but was still exposed to attacks from all directions.[13]

If a woman loves a man, he has power over her. If he also controls (or is believed to control) her children, her food, and her home, he has vastly more power. The same works in all realms of life: The more you believe anyone controls something, and the more you believe this thing affects your emotions, the more you believe your emotional welfare depends on this person, so the more power he or she has over you. This is the *iron law of emotional welfare and power*. It is the law all effective rulers have learned to use to maintain or increase their power by encouraging subjects to love and identify with them and the state they represent; and by encouraging them to believe their love will be rewarded with welfare goods controlled by the ruler. The more you identify with anyone else and the more you believe that person controls goods that affect your emotional well-being, the more you believe all of your emotional states depend on that person, so the more power his or her very person exerts over you.

The Original Patterns of Leadership

As I noted earlier, the hunting and gathering societies are very important in understanding all human life because they are one of our best baselines for judging issues of "nature and nurture," that is, for assessing the contributions of human nature (genes) and our situations to our feelings, thoughts, and actions. As far as we know, all human societies were hunting and gathering bands for their first (roughly) two million years, ninety-nine percent of mankind's total existence. Only between ten and fifteen thousand years ago did they begin to give way to herding and agricultural societies. As far as we know, our genes are much the same today as those of the hunters and gatherers because there have not been enough generations for major changes.

Hunting and gathering societies are always overwhelmingly familial. Loosely knit bands of very small numbers up to several hundred roam definite territories hunting and gathering. The bands are always made up of nuclear and extended families that are closely related to each other by real and fictional kin partnerships. Leaders of hunting and gathering societies are almost exactly like leaders of groups of kin or of friends today. They rely overwhelmingly on rational persuasion, first unmediated and only secondly mediated emotional appeal to get power over others.[14]

Since these people have few sources of *stored* value, and since their territory is held in common, it is very difficult for anyone to gain greater control over any external means of affecting others emotionally. Hunting is normally done most efficiently as a group activity, which is necessary in hunting the more valuable large animals, so even the best hunters get little more mediated power. Colin Turnbull notes that sharing is their environmental necessity and that "it would be rare to meet a hunter who did not try to keep the best part of his catch for himself, but it would be far more rare to find a hunter who refused to share with one who had nothing. There is often an acute awareness among hunters that one day they themselves might need assistance, and old age is an ever-present reminder of the dependence of one human being upon another."[15] Food, then, is subject to the basic rule of human social order, *reciprocal altruism*: do unto others today what you want them (and expect them) to do unto you later on. This "silver rule" is explicitly stated, in slightly varying and generally more idealized ("golden") forms, in all the great religions and in developed systems of folk wisdom, but, stated or not, it is the basis for all free (uncoerced) human exchange (and, thus, is the basis for the free market system, as we shall see). Tools, clothing, and so on are all private property and subject to all the feelings and rules we find in our family, friend, and neighbor groups today.

Having little basis for mediated power, power is based overwhelmingly on unmediated personal interaction. Since no individual is likely to be that different from all others in personality, looks, intelligence, and so on, and since these differences wax and wane and apply to different situations, no individual ever becomes much more powerful over everyone else for long. (Even the most beautiful and otherwise lovable would find their power did not extend much to their own sex and was counterbalanced, thus checked, by envious rivalries and soon waned.) What little power is accumulated by anyone for long is almost always situated to tasks (like hunting or defense) or is the result of their mythical mediation with the forces of magic and religion. But even the mythical mediation of these gives little power beyond the rituals. The members do identify themselves as soul-essences with the essences of gods or ancestors, their environment (spiritual territory), and their culture. The magical and religious leaders mediate these forces and, thus, have great power at times of rituals. But the ritual leader does not normally seem to be able for long to get people to identify themselves with these powers in an exclusive way. There is no evidence of divine kings growing directly out of this magical mediation, though it obviously has possibilities on which some religious entrepreneurs might have capitalized. (The great redistributive, judicial, and other powers of the priests of the ziggurats in Sumeria, one of the first known state civilizations, may have been built first on their magico-religious power.)

The prevailing norms of our genetic ancestors were liberty, equality, and fraternity—exactly the norms that are dominant today among groups of siblings in all societies, though to various degrees. (Some societies today prescribe brotherly dominance over sisters or dominance by the older over the younger. But these variations are rarely great, are commonly more ideals than realities, and produce envious countermeasures.) But note that liberty of adults meant only freedom from any great submission to others. They are generally (always?) very dependent on, thus submissive to, absolutist rules. They submit to internal mythical powers that actually help to prevent anyone from gaining much dominance. The most power individuals exercise is found in parent-child relations, but these relations are predominantly love partnerships and have little of the sternness seen in so many religious groups of the nineteenth century in the West. Fighting and warfare occur within and between all the bands, but they are unusual and very limited in scope. They never seem to produce lasting violations of the norms of liberty, equality, and fraternity. Only unusual combinations of individual characteristics lead to Big Man status, that is, to any great dominance for long. A.R. Radcliffe-Brown gave a classic description of these Big Men and their limited powers:

> Besides the respect for seniority there is another important factor in the regulation of the social life, namely the respect for certain personal qualities. These qualities are skill in hunting and in warfare, generosity and kindness, and freedom from bad temper. A man possessing them inevitably acquires a position of influence in the

community. His opinion on any subject carries more weight than another even older man. The younger men attach themselves to him, are anxious to please him by giving him any presents that they can, or by helping him in such work as carving a canoe, and to join him in hunting parties or turtle expeditions. In each local group there was usually to be found one man who thus by his influence could control and direct others. Amongst the chief men of several friendly local groups it would generally happen that one of them, by reason of his personal qualities, would attain to a position of higher rank than the others. Younger men would be desirous of joining the local group to which he belonged. He would find himself popular and respected at the annual meetings of the different groups, and his influence would thus spread beyond the narrow limits of his own community.

There was no special word to denote such men and distinguish them from others. In the languages of the North Andaman they were spoken of as *er-kuro* = *"Big."*[16]

June MacNeish has given a similar summary of the very limited powers of the Big chiefs of the Northern Athabascans.[17] We can speculate that some of these Big Men might have become permanent rulers at some time, but none have ever been observed to do so.

This pattern of relative liberty, equality, and fraternity was apparently remarkably stable, presumably because it was remarkably adaptive in all long-lasting environmental situations human beings inhabited, ranging from the deepest forests of Africa and New Guinea, to the arid lands of the Bushmen of the Kahlahari and the Aborigines of Australia, to the hot plateaus of the Shoshone and the deep freeze of the Eskimo. Some of these societies, such as the Pygmies, developed little technology; others, like the Eskimo, developed some of the most complex technology of precivilized people. Some lived in easy environments and thus had extensive leisure; others had to work much harder. But the basic norms and patterns remained. Why? The most important reason is almost certainly that none of them had developed any means of storing great value. (By some quirk of the academic imagination, this "stored value" explanation has come to be seen as Marxist. Actually, Marx saw the means of production as the crucial causal factor. The means of production varied widely from seal hunting to nut gathering, but the social values and patterns of behavior remained basically similar. As usual, Marx was wrong, but creative deceit—fanciful reinterpretation and relabeling—have hidden this fact.) Their food (except for nuts, especially acorns, and a few other things) was highly perishable, so it had to be eaten soon after gotten or not at all. Only some, such as the Eskimo, could preserve food by freezing and then only until the thaw. They had also all developed cultures that were extremely fitted to their environmental niches and patterns of hunting. (They were extreme environmentalists and are the ideals of modernist naturalists today.) And their intense communal life allowed them to envelop every member in a vastly rich "cake of custom" and enforce those customs unremittingly. Finally, the customs were obviously fitted remarkably well to their environments and their basic human emotions. Though bullies and even murderers popped up now and then, there were few real rebels and certainly few revolutionaries. Very importantly, as long as their situation changed only slowly, they had little incentive to change their customs except by slow cultural drift and they had a full panoply of emotions and patterns of behavior to maintain their basic liberty, equality, and fraternity.

Envy was a basic bulwark protecting liberty and equality. Anyone who has raised a number of children knows how deeply each sibling envies any unequal distribution of goods or dominance by the others. Envy is probably very adaptive biologically because it assures each child will push to get at least an equal share of food and general parental love and care, thus guaranteeing the survival of all, except in a situation of extreme scarcity, in which envy could lead to everyone's death. What actually happens in a family is that each child tries to get as much as he can, but the other children do the same before they're taught not to. The parent soon finds that any unequal treatment for long produces intense envy, resentment, hatred, and conflict. Even the smallest preferential treatment of one can produce a violent explosion of envy-fed hatred. If it is continued for long, and the "injured" child is forced to repress his outbursts of envy, the victim's entire life may be pervaded by envy and much of his adult strivings aimed at getting revenge— "getting even." *The only stable strategy that minimizes envy and conflict is rough equality for those who see themselves as equals.* Each child tries to get more, but each is *willing to put up with* rough equality; and each is totally unwilling to put up with preferential treatment for equals. (Again, this is probably due to genetic programming because it works to keep them all alive in a situation of scarcity.) Note that envy is at a maximum when the victim sees himself as the equal of the other: in general, *the more equal individuals see themselves, the more potentially envious they are over any unequal treatment.* This is what Helmut Schoeck had in mind in his classic work *Envy*: "that our fellow man is always potentially envious—and the probability as well as the degree of his envy increases in ratio to this propinquity. . ."[18] It is the three-year-old who most envies his four-year-old brother, whereas he feels much less envy over what his sixteen-year-old sister gets, and probably none over what his father gets.

Hunting and gathering societies are extended families that evolved in situations of scarcity and little stored food in which equal sharing among equals (more for big adults) produces the maximum preservation of all members. Equal sharing is their iron rule of survival, and that rule springs from the emotion of ferocious envy and fear of that envy. Of course, the sharing within the family also springs from the feelings of love and caring that kin, friends, and lovers feel for each other. So sharing and the equality that results from it spring from both very powerful negative emotions (envy, hatred, and fear of that envy and hatred) and very powerful positive emotions (love and caring); they are explicitly stated in iron rules; and these are sternly enforced, by rejection or even ostracism, both deadly in such a society.

Since most human societies have lived close to the margin of subsistence and almost everyone in them has been equal in poverty, tasks, and roles, they have been pervaded by envy, the fear of envy, and by the iron rules of sharing and equality. Almost everywhere the fear of the evil eye of envy and of black-magic revenge for inequality or pride has been rampant. In some societies, like the Dobu and the Navajo, almost all disease and other misfortune is blamed on some one practicing black magic to get revenge out of envy. Note that feelings of envy are always much harder to observe in others, or even to recognize in yourself. I believe the reason is that admitting envy in yourself normally implies that you think you have a reason to think you're less good or successful than the one you envy, which pride abhors; and that showing your envy might lead to fearful counter action. As Schoeck says, we hide our envy behind outraged denunciations of evil "injustice": that is, we hide the emotion and denounce the supposed violator of the rules of sharing and equality.

Peasant societies, villages, and small towns are normally pervaded by envy, and this can lead to the enactment and enforcement of a mass of specific rules of sharing and equality and of veritable inquisitions by the envious or against them. In the great witch crazes of the late sixteenth and early seventeenth century, one of the reasons poor little old ladies were normally accused of witchcraft (in the early stages of outbreaks) was that they had such real reasons to be envious. Some of them no doubt really did perform revengeful black magic, but most of them were the victims of mythical thoughts springing from paranoid fears (and maybe some guilt). The big witch panics were especially common after famines, wars, or plagues inspired dread in people and their emotion-inspired mythical thoughts merely led them to look for the envious. Of course, envy also inspired the occasional witch's mythical thought that her magic could get revenge on those better off than she. In times of dread, peasants were easily swept away by paranoid myths of persecution by the rich or powerful. In 1774–1776 Turgot tried to deregulate the immense web of laws and enforcements the mercantilistic bureaucracies of France had created to "protect" the people. He believed, quite rightly as all subsequent history was to show, that freeing the people of these regulations and cutting back the massive taxes and other feudal duties would enable the people to work and invest more to increase their crops, thus increasing incentive, efficiency, and wealth for all. But the peasants were close to the margin of subsistence, and when the weather led to poor crops they insisted with fear and outrage that "monopolists" were rigging the market to rob them or starve them. Turgot had protected against this and there was no evidence of it, but there were riots that undermined his position with the king. This enabled the biggest special interests among the clergy and nobles to get him dismissed. The massive regulations were reimposed and the ancient regime plummeted on toward its violent death in 1789.[19]

In more complex and differentiated societies, envy and its hatred are directed primarily at those most similar to the "victim" who are believed to be "lording" it over the victim. Very importantly, as Tocqueville argued, rebellions and, even more, revolutions come after long periods of increasing equality; and they are spearheaded by those who are relatively successful, not by the most oppressed. The growing equality means the subordinates are getting more equal in the means of revolt, but the crucial emotional factor is the envy, resentment, and hatred that grows with every step toward greater equality. It is this growing equality that makes the superior look more similar, thus more an object for comparison, and thus more an object of envy, resentment, and hatred—and of the mythical thoughts about the evil of the oppressor inspired by those powerful emotions. Servants do not revolt against their lords unless driven by near despair and a spark of hope (as in the Jacqueries): they rarely make any comparison between their lowly status and that of the Exalted Lord. The servants take pride in serving The Lord and they insist on the incomparable Highness of The Lord, for they are thus spared the shame of inferiority and the pains of envy and can take pride in their social identification with such a Highness. It is the rich nonaristocrat, the once-rich aristocrat fallen on bad times, and the intellectual near-aristocrat who brood with enormous hatred and wait for the chance to strike. The American colonists did not revolt because they suffered such great increases in oppression by the British crown. On the contrary, they suffered from growing prosperity and power, which made them suffer more the pains of shame and envy from the remaining inequalities. It was not the poor who revolted but the intellectuals, the rich, and the rising bourgeoisie. In France it was the same thing, and they were joined by some lumpen-aristocrats and aristocrats-on-the-make (especially LaFayette and Mirabeau). The peasants were mobilized only once the revolution started. When it did they were already frightened by a crop failure, and their fears and hatreds were turned first against the poor vagabonds seeking food, then in The Great Fear against the local aristocrats whom they were absolutely convinced were launching a Great Conspiracy of vagabond-briggands to seize or destroy their food. They eulogized the distant and exalted king, though, of course, the aristocrats never did any of the things the peasants feared, while the king did conspire against the revolutionaries. In the United States the blacks did not riot and shout revolution when they were impoverished and oppressed in the South. It was only after two decades of steady progress on all fronts that they broke out in moral outrage against the remaining inequalities—and they did this in the North, where they were more equal.

Today in every Western nation, it is the upper and upper-middle class intellectuals, joined at times by a nouveau rich union leader and an ex-aristocrat (even self-exiled ones like Anthony Benn), who are so outraged over inequality. The richer and more powerful they have grown, the more equal to the rich and aristocratic they have become, so the more outraged they have become and the more they have demanded more power and money for themselves (and for their pawns in this war game for dominance, the poor). It is precisely because our Western democracies have become ever more egalitarian politically and (less so) economically over the past two centuries that equality has become such a burning issue. The more equal we are, the more we compare ourselves to each other, and the more the ancient human passions of shame, envy, resentment, and hatred are unleashed; and the more these passions threaten the very values, institutions, and forms of economic exchange which have produced our greater equality.

When we look at the hunters and gatherers, we can also see the rudiments of another fundamental pattern in human society. As we noted, they have powerful emotions and stern rules supporting sharing and equality in general, but these seem to apply more to material goods, and certainly to food, than to authority. The Big Men can at times achieve considerable reputations and followings, thus leading others to depend on or submit to them, but only as long as they are really helpful, show proper humility rather than pride, and live in strict accord with the rules on sharing and equality. In general, we human beings are significantly more willing to accept—and appreciate—unequal dependency in any form of leadership than in the distribution of material goods. (As we shall see more fully in chapter 5, all such genetic tendencies may be reinforced or diminished by the partially independent shared—cultural—and individual experiences.) The biological value of this is obvious in a situation of extreme scarcity where all people live at times under threat of imminent death from starvation. One or two months of extreme scarcity in their average lifetime of thirty or forty years would be enough to make an iron rule of extreme material equality, above all in food, extremely adaptive and, thus, likely to be encoded in both genes and cultural rules. Of course, they could be more relaxed in situations of plenty, but in situations of great scarcity the emotional demands (envy, etc.) would become extreme, especially within the immediate family. At the ultimate extreme of near death, selfish hunger would overcome the other feelings and cause the rule to begin to crumble, as we see in mass starvations. In famines the Eskimo even suspend their stern rule on band sharing—every family for itself becomes the rule when cooperative behavior is no longer adaptive.

At the same time, leadership by the most successful (Aristotle's "natural aristocracy") would be extremely adaptive, for it would lead everyone to act like and be coordinated by the most successful people. This would apply especially to the vital economic activities, particularly to hunting big animals, which is both highly problematic and necessarily cooperative, and to magic, which was a matter of life and death in dealing with disease. The basic meaning of "economic" is "fitting scarce means to alternative goals." Economics, then, is the scientific study of how people choose to fit scarce means to alternative goals. Note that this choosing may be rational, irrational or, what is most common by far, complex mixtures of both. But, of course, the danger of such dependency would always be that if it got too great, the leader could expropriate more food, thus endangering everyone else. So the leader could get prestige (pride) as his reward, but only as long as he did not get more material goods and as long as his power remained quite limited. The consequence is that even the economic leader had no right to more of his own produce, though hunters did get first choice of the pieces of their product. When the best hunters or gatherers produced more, they redistributed it and were rewarded with prestige and gratitude, basic components of dominance. His overriding incentives, like those of other leaders, were the wondrous feelings of pride and general self-security.

I believe this basic pattern has continued throughout human history. Dominance inequalities of any degree have almost always been more acceptable than material or consumption inequalities. Economic leadership is always highly prized, if it is successful, but greater material rewards for it are envied—especially in a peasant society. This is the secret of the Grand Inquisitor in The Brothers Karamazov. In a poor society, the poor have tolerated even the despotic power of rulers and massive bureaucracies living off their toil, as long as the bureaucrats redistributed their produce more or less equally and shared in their poverty, at least symbolically and to all appearances. Once the priests felt secure enough in power they lived in luxury, but because of this they were seen as "corrupt" (polluted). Then the people, especially the better off, envied and hated them—and Reformations erupted. This bias against wealth has often been used by politicians to help legitimize vast increases in their own power. One of Augustus's crucial forms of deceit used to gain popular acquiescence in his creation of a tyranny was his public display of his humility: he hid his vast power behind public presentations of egalitarianism. In American terms, he tried to look like "just another guy." And, as Michael Grant argues, one crucial aspect of this was his pretense that he was not vastly rich:

> ...Augustus, borne along on the wings of an abundant belief that the wars were over, made his absolutism palatable to the majority of westerners by concealing it, just sufficiently, behind the imposing restored front of venerable institutions. 'I am

as much for government by consent as any man,' observed Oliver Cromwell; 'but if you ask me how it is to be done, I confess I do not know.' Augustus, even if there were some who would not accept his solution, more nearly solved the riddle than Cromwell or any other absolute ruler.

His personal habits were simple. Renowned for his frugality, Augustus enjoyed simple foods like green figs; and unlike most of the later emperors of his house he was only a moderate drinker. He frequently gave formal dinner-parties, but was sometimes in the habit of eating alone before or after his dinner, though often what he ate was little more than a snack.

In all his social contacts he was genial and accessible—the very opposite, it would seem, to the traditional tyrant, with the praetorian guard kept as far out of sight as possible. . . .Genuinely preferring simplicity to luxury, he at first lived in an unpretentious part of Rome near the Forum, and then moved to a modest though tastefully decorated house on the Palatine (the excavated "Casa di Livia"), where for forty years he slept in the same bedroom. A later ruler, Marcus Aurelius, said he had been taught by his unostentatious predecessor Antoninus Pius that an emperor could almost live like a private gentleman. The founder of the principate had already been imbued with the same idea.

True, there was a somewhat dismaying contrast between this homeliness and his soaring position, not to speak of the scarcely human designation "Augustus."[20]

The "great" totalitarians of our century have normally been ascetic by our standards and have been Christlike in their sufferings during the years of exile. Hitler enjoyed few worldly pleasures and hid those from the public.

But the merchant, whose work actually brought the people greater wealth (through the law of comparative advantages), has been far more envied and hated in proportion to the degree of his perceived superiority in consumption. The law of comparative advantages merely says that some groups, including nations, are more efficient in producing some products than other groups are, so they have lower costs and can sell them more cheaply; therefore, it is to the advantage of people in the less efficient groups to buy those products from the more efficient group. At the same time, this buyer will be more efficient at producing other products, so the other group will benefit by buying these products from them. At the extreme, Samoans benefit by specializing heavily in the production of coconuts to export to Argentina; and Argentina benefits by importing coconuts, rather than trying to grow them in Tierra del Fuego, and exporting wheat and beef from the Pampas. Free trade among specialized producers and consumers whose products and demands are complementary benefits them all.

It has always been easier for despots and their bureaucrats to mythically convince the people of a myth, that their welfare state was absolutely necessary to their survival, than it has been for businesspeople to convince others of what was true—that, regardless of the merchants' consumption level, the people were better off (as long as the merchants could not rig prices), because of the law of comparative advantages. And so it is that in the *New*

Testament we have the remarkable attacks on the rich and the businessmen, such as the money changers, coupled with an almost obsequious injunction to "Render unto Caesar." The money changers in the temple polluted it, even though they were vitally important to the people and their very multiplicity indicates a competitive price for their services. Caesar had put down an uprising at terrible loss of life, had taken their queen as hostage, and exacted taxes for his war machine, but Caesar was not a social problem.

The consequence of this is that political power and priestly power have always been more accepted and prestigious than economic power. Pitirim Sorokin studied all forms of success throughout Western history. In all ages the political and religious successes were more famous and prestigious; and more of them by far were considered great enough to remember in history.[21] This was in spite of all the deaths and devastation they caused by starting wars. Economic power has almost always implied more possible pollution, and has almost always been the greater potential trigger of envy and hatred. One obvious result has been that religious leaders, who are in charge of depollution rituals, and thus must always be pure, sometimes can be political leaders (as the pharaohs of Egypt and the priests of Sumeria were) and it is almost always the case that religious leaders agree, often under duress, to sanctify the political leaders (as we see in divine kings who are not priests). It is even possible, though uncommon, for military leaders to be sanctified, even, on rare occasions, to be priests. But priests and rulers can almost never be businesspeople at the same time. (As far as I know, priests never can be businesspeople at the same time. Rulers can be businesspeople in plutocracies like Carthage and Venice, but these are rare, and almost always they are allowed only to be investors, not directly engaged in business operations.) Aristocrats normally are military leaders with considerable judicial power and some religious power. And they normally have contempt for the businesspeople, including those who provide much of their wealth through taxes and (sometimes forced) loans. Almost all aristocracies have rules against their being involved in business, but they often make investments secretly even when this is forbidden, as Cicero did. Even in business oligarchies like Venice, the most successful business oligarchs tend in time to become aristocrats and move out of business. Almost everywhere the aristocrats and monarchs have tried to tie the peasants to the land, to drain money into nonproductive adventures, and to exalt their own power through military bureaucracies abroad and regulatory or police bureaucracies at home. When the businesspeople could not join the aristocrats, they have generally done the opposite and have increased everyone's wealth, but almost everywhere they have borne a far heavier burden of envy and hate. Almost everywhere they have had to expiate and palliate by giving money away and by being taxed unequally—both to cleanse themselves and to produce more equality.

This was true even under the Calvinist regime, which did more than other religions to bridge the gap between piety and profit. Recognizing the obvious fact that monarchs, aristocrats, and other rulers have always had the best deal possible, businesspeople have almost always preferred to join them, even at vast financial cost.

The Origin of the Spontaneous Natural Order of Trade

This crucial, envy-born prejudice against economic leadership and in favor of judicial, political and religious leadership has had a profound influence on the development of all human society beyond the hunting and gathering stage. One of the basic forms of this influence on economic life was apparent from the beginning of economic exchange. Economic exchange within the hunting and gathering bands is, of course, the same as found in our families today. *Reciprocal altruism* with little or no time constraint applies: I'll give to you now and, when you can, you give in return. The giving from parents to children is a more pure, one way or asymmetric, form of altruism. Parents give to the very young regardless of considerations about whether they will be alive to receive in return someday. With each step away in genetic relation, the *moral rule of reciprocal equivalence* becomes more strict and the time of return more important. There is only one exception within the band: the more you like or love someone, the more purely altruistic the giving becomes, even if they are not kin. But even in extreme love there is the expectation of the return of love and services. (Unrequited love produces few presents, and spouse support after a divorce produces immense resentment.)

Even within the family the rule of reciprocity is guarded by the passions of envy and fear of envy, thus by the iron rules of sharing equally and receiving the same as you gave. You must give (receive) the same value as you received (gave). (An eye for an eye is the principle at work in matters of crime.) When it comes to exchange outside the band, these passions and rules become even stronger. Within the band the passions result in a great deal of conflict, including fighting, but the countervailing passions of love and caring combine with the adjudicative intercessions of elders to prevent almost all fights from escalating into deadly wars. These integrative passions do not extend beyond the family and friendship ties (with a few exceptions of generalized altruism).

Uncertainty (thus distrust) and anxiety (thus stigmatizing myths) about outsiders pervade the primitives' world. The insider-outsider, us-them, friend-foe dichotomy is even deeper and more absolute in most primitive societies than in our modern international relations. Warfare is, therefore, an ever-present danger. The stable wealth or *stasis* myth that pervades the primitive world leads to a zero-sum assumption that you can only get more by taking from someone else, thus increasing the incentive and probability of war. The myth of stasis sees the world as in a steady-state, so the amount of wealth is steady or constant. It includes the submyth of stable wealth, that is, the myth that wealth cannot be increased by human effort. One of the many modernist versions of this myth is based on the nonsequitur "Natural resources are inherently limited; therefore, wealth is inherently limited to what we have now." This bit of absurdity not only jumps from the implicit assertion that someday we will discover and use all resources to the implicit assertion that we've already done so—or very nearly so; but it also takes no consideration of the vast technological substitutability of natural resources—such as making gas from coal. Once you assume a stasis of wealth in the world, then anyone can only become wealthier by taking from someone else. That's a *zero-sum situation*. This danger is especially acute wherever there exists even one nearby society that adopts militaristic, predatory policies and intermittently attacks its more pacific neighbors to seize goods, women, slaves, or land. The response to this great danger is twofold: wage peace and prepare for war.

Almost universally, peace is waged primarily by avoiding the appearance of aggression (including punishing your own people for injuring others) and by developing intricate real and mythically ritualized webs of intertribal trade. Trade is by far the most important way to wage peace, for trade is normally even the initial step in building and reinforcing intertribal friendships ("people-to-people programs") and the very integrating kin ties of marriage.[22] Even people who are too distrustful and anxious about each other to maintain patterns of ritualized friendship and bride exchange can often build weaker webs of trade, at least through intermediary tribes (like the Manus and Phoenicians) who specialize in trade with many cultures and grow rich from it.

Some patterns of trade, such as the famous *kula* exchange of the Trobriands and their neighbors,[23] are predominantly ritualized exchanges of noneconomic "treasures" intended to wage peace, but even these almost always allow parallel exchanges of economic goods (the *gemwali* of the Trobrianders) to develop. There is a continuum, ranging from pure peace waging trade to pure economic trade. Clearly most trade is both peace-waging and economic. Though I know of no careful assessment in these terms, it seems very likely that, the lower the threat of war, the more trade will shift toward the purely economic pole of trade, and conversely.

Because the passions of envy, resentment, fear, and hatred are so dominant in these relations, in direct proportion to the distrust and anxiety over the threat of war that exists, trading is carried on very differently from the way it is in a peaceful free-market system. The first imperative, as long as the primary purpose is to avoid warfare, is to avoid arousing envy and, thus, the hatred and attack that could arouse. The Manus, and probably all rich traders, hide their real costs and their wealth from trading partners. The second imperative is not to be cheated and thus become envious yourself. These two goals have led people around the world, by vastly complex and probably largely preconscious processes, to approximate one specific solution. One trader "gives gifts" to his foreign partner ("friend"), who returns these with strict reciprocity at a later time. In fact, the greater the potential conflict, and thus the greater the risk of arousing envy and attack, the more they give each other a "war-risk premium": each gives a bit more than he was given the time before, thus challenging, demanding under threat of envy, his partner to return even more. The appearance of generosity communicates an appearance of friendliness, but it also establishes an obligation determined by the iron rule of equivalent reciprocity.

All of this is necessarily still at work in our modern corporate world. Contrary to all the myths of the predatory corporate executives purveyed by our "experts" on corporate behavior, like Jane Fonda and Paddy Chayevsky, our executives use reciprocal gift giving rather than murder to build their international webs of trade. Reciprocal gifts, wining and dining, and favors are a massive part of the gigantic kula and gemwali exchange systems ringing our world. Even takeovers of one corporation by another normally produce successful mergers only when these ancient principles of reciprocal altruism are followed scrupulously. George Gilder was right in arguing in *Wealth and Poverty*[24] that each business act, especially each entrepreneurial act, is commonly altruistic; but these acts are reciprocally altruistic, based on the expectation that on average over the long run one will give and receive equally, not in a one-to-one way, but in *all* the goods and services exchanged. Those self-proclaimed spokespeople for business who deny that they have greater responsibility because of their greater rewards do more than all the collectivist mythmakers to destroy the respectability of business.

Though the processes of primitive trade are shrouded in ritual secrecy and dissimulation, even Marshall Sahlins,[25] who often sneers at free-market economic theory, shows that the customary exchange prices (two axes for one bow, etc.) slowly adjust over time to relative supplies and demands and, thus, reach roughly the same price Adam Smith would have. *Homo economicus* never exists in reality, but he does serve as a beacon for our rational minds to home in on. And reason moves in many and wondrous ways to achieve our economic goals.

The Origins of State Power

Trade, of course, allows all sides to become richer by the law of comparative advantage; and, by overlaying the trade with actual and simulated familial and friendly reciprocity, it allows everyone to grow safer. Of course, as many observers have recognized, some grow richer than others. It is the traders who specialize in finding the greatest supplies and greatest demands, and who can isolate these from each other and all possible competitors, who profit the most. They minimize the envy by pretending reciprocity: e.g., they pretend they paid far more for it, ran greater risks, worked harder. The Manus are an excellent example of such traders. Each trade exchange, as long as carried out in accord with the principle of reciprocal altruism, makes each partner richer and happier, thus cementing the relation. Each in turn can trade some of the goods received with other people, who can do the same, and on and on. When not broken by warfare, these "spontaneous" chains of trade-order could build up over hundreds of miles, maybe at times over thousands of miles, without any of the people traveling more than a few miles in their safe territory. Trade was the medium by which technological progress was slowly diffused around the world. But, with little means of storing value and with the stern rules of total reciprocity dictated by extreme scarcity, emotions and values, trade produced *very* slow increases in wealth for hunters and gatherers. Its great potential was first unleashed by the coming of agriculture and herding between ten and fifteen thousand years ago. Regardless of why human beings started farming and herding, as soon as they did they were able to accumulate more wealth and in certain fertile areas with water were able to produce far more wealth. Once they recognized this, they broke the culture patterns of all earlier periods and soon ignited the autocatalytic process of economic development that led eventually to civilization. A little more reward led to more effort, thus more reward; and some people began to adapt their cultures to allow more and more. These changes then precipitated both more wealth and more culture change. The process still seems to be accelerating except when regulated by bureaucratic powers, while we limp along with the same genes, always yearning at the same time for a return to the steady state of liberty, equality, fraternity and the nirvana of universal stasis.

An increase in wealth seems enough in itself to relax somewhat the iron rule of redistributive sharing. Almost all the Bushmen, a hunting and gathering people, live in great scarcity and sternly enforce the iron rule of reciprocal sharing. But one group, the //Gana, have found a niche that allows them to save water and accumulate goats. They are able to store wealth and do, thus becoming richer than any other Bushmen. They are still egalitarian, but less so than those in the areas of greater scarcity with no means of storing value. Of course, a value on total sharing greatly decreases the incentive to develop technologies of storage. The genes and culture values that allowed survival under great scarcity almost guaranteed the continuance of that scarcity. Since our emotions and values, even those powerfully influenced by our genes, are partially affected by our environmental and practical situations, this increased wealth *allows* a decreased emphasis on sharing. And the //Gana have relaxed the rule, thus leading to more inequality in wealth and political power. Specifically, the Big Men are allowed to accumulate more without triggering more envy, but I would predict this has stringent limits and that in droughts the Big Men would be expected to share totally.

The accumulation of wealth combined with this partial relaxation of the rules of sharing and equality may have been one of the bases for the origins of the proto-state phenomena known as chiefdom. A Big Man is commonly a leader of a lineage of kin, so he is still within the realm of family. A chief transcends his own kin ties and is believed to symbolically represent at least two lineages. Some analysts, such as Elman Service, distinguish between a chief and a state, but the difference is more one of degree than kind. The crucial point is that people feel dependent on a chief for reasons that go beyond all the forms of dependency found in the hunting and gathering societies. This was a crucial juncture for all human life. This process would be especially important when combined with any system of private property rights which allowed transference of ownership. The more efficient group, normally consisting of cooperating kin, might become more powerful, either by taking over the land of others or by insisting on a form of tribute or "rent" from the tenants. Marxist archaeologists, prehistorians, and anthropologists generally see some such process of greater efficiency and property accumulation as the beginning of state powers. They believe that the coercive state powers of laws and enforcers were then created to protect the material inequalities and to produce more. Service argues that the opposite is true: there is a mass of evidence indicating that chiefs were more the causes of material inequalities than the effects of them.[26] Chiefs, he argues, built their other powers on their initial power to redistribute goods the people wanted. Having reviewed the evidence, I am convinced that the evidence concerning the original formations of state powers is extremely skimpy and its interpretation *highly* problematic. The evidence seems to me to indicate that, as with such major processes as economic development, there is no single path to state powers. Rather, as we saw in chapter 2, there seem to be a number of specific paths, but all of them make use of some basic elements (just as all the successful paths to economic development make multiple uses of the means of producing the universal factors of production that increase efficiency).

We know that highly valued, emotionally arousing personal qualities, so-called "charisma", such as beauty or lovability, have enslaved many individuals and can stimulate great social movements. We know they are very valuable in fostering dependency even in whole nations, but all of these exist in plenty in hunting and gathering societies and do not produce state powers. They are not necessary (as we see in the terrible Shaka who used terror to build the Zulu state), and certainly they would not be sufficient. The adoration of rulers is far more commonly the effect of the myths of power, and this love of the leader produces in turn the myths of love, so that even Adolph Hitler appeared beautiful and kindly to his devotees. Though his charisma was very powerful (as we saw in the case of Albert Speer), far more people loved him or saw him as beautiful *after* he was The Leader and the mythmakers had gone to work overtime. (Albert Speer notes with wonder how his growing disenchantment with Hitler led him suddenly to see Hitler as ugly.[27])

In the same way, an already existing inequality of goods is certainly not sufficient and is probably not necessary. There are lots of segmented lineage societies in which the Big Men leaders of some lineages become the possessors of far more wealth than all but a few other members of the society. Actually, however, they do not normally have property rights to the goods in the way we do. They are Big Men because many are dependent on their ability to redistribute goods and services to them which are owed to the Big Men. They are rich overwhelmingly in reciprocal obligations. The Manus are a good example of this. The unequal distribution of material goods is important because it allows some men to *give* more to others, thus making them dependent until they pay off their obligations. These "gifts" are the primitive form of "wages" and the man who receives them is sometimes far more of a "wage slave" than any nineteenth century industrial "drudge" in London ever was. The furnish system, by which the owners of capital "give" sustenance to laborers before they do the work, involves a greater sense of submission or subservience on the part of the laborer. It was used by feudal lords around the world to help tie the workers to the soil. Peasants wanted to become wage earners to become freemen. In modern industry the laborer does the work first, making the wage payer the obligee until he reciprocates with wages.

The threat of external force is another factor that has always helped to breed dependency relations but does not seem to be necessary for the establishment of state powers. The greater an external threat, the more people have been willing to depend on common military leaders, from the hunting societies and the Iroquois League up to NATO. But, as far as I know, these confederations always break down once the threat disappears or becomes overwhelming, unless the core state myths and operating factors are used effectively.

Each of the core factors that generates dependency has been seen by many theorists as *the* one necessary and sufficient source of state powers.[28] Just as totemists and monotheists worship only one God, so are most social theorists monocausalists. The primary reason for this intense partisanship seems to be the obvious fact that all state rulers about whom we have much reliable knowledge have used some combination of these, and most have used all of them in many different forms at different times. Though I won't take the time to do it, you can easily convince yourself of this by merely reviewing the history of any well-documented state. For example, it is easy to see how Chinese dynasties have used all of these in different forms and to vastly varying degrees over the past twenty-three hundred years. Since we can see the same thing happening throughout history almost every place in the world, it is extremely likely the same thing happened at the very beginning of state powers.

I have ranked the factors in what I think is a rough order of their importance in generating emotional dependency on state rulers in most situations. A reasonably high degree of mythopoetic dependency has always been a necessity for rulers and seems normally to be the opening wedge against our natural fears and protective armor against unreciprocated dependency. The Enlightenment myth of rationalism made the story (or myth?) of the social contract very appealing to social analysts, until the scripts of the ancient states were deciphered and until anthropology developed. Then the importance of the myths of divinity and other magic powers was so obvious that most theorists decided that the myth of the king's divinity was *the* crucial factor. Certainly myths are necessary: all successful rulers have used mythopoetic rituals and justifications to legitimize their rule. Most of the time they have not been priests or magicians, but the priests and magicians have sanctified their rule. And priests have normally been the primary creators, embellishers and transmitters of the myths of the legitimacy of the rulers' dominance: they and their closely allied intellectuals have been the myth-makers and transmitters.

No one, not even John F. Kennedy, has been more thoroughly mythified by intellectual media propagandists than Augustus was by the imperial poets Virgil, Horace, and Propertius—who were quietly paid with grants by the emperor's friends, the first foundation. (Note how much more plausible it was for them to say the king rules by divine right than for the king to make this claim.) In the ancient world the priests were also the astronomers and calendar keepers who made it possible for the kings to "predict" when the Nile would overflow, when spring would come, and so on, thereby tricking the people into believing they controlled these life-giving powers or had divine contacts who did. The later, far more autocratic Chinese emperors imposed severe punishments on any commoner found to possess a book of astronomy. The priests were also the ones who fabricated the holy texts purporting to tell how the world was created, how God decreed the ruler's power, how the king was necessary for everyone's welfare, and on and on. They were the ones who developed (though they may not have discovered) the "magic" of writing and who preserved the "magical" records. Their power was so great that they were often tempted to try to seize the king's secular power, as Amenhotep and many later kings learned the hard way. Some theorists, especially Max Weber, have argued that in our modern world the mythical legitimacy of states has waned with the waning of Christianity and been replaced by *rational-legal* legitimacy.[29] The legal legitimacy is still there (see below) and always was. But, contrary to this modernist myth, there has been no waning of statist myths. The explosion of nationalist myths and, once those failed, of the myth of the modernist welfare states has more than replaced any decrease of dependency due to the slow waning of Christianity. Besides, Christian priests have become more nationalistic at times and Christian socialist or welfare statist at others. Today the "liberationist-Marxist" priests of the Catholic Church are leading their flocks of ignorant peasants down the well-worn path to the modernist totalitarian welfare state.

But is mythical dependency strong enough to build a state? Some prehistorians have thought this was the primary basis of the first state powers in Sumeria and, thus, of what was probably the first statist civilization. Yet most of these analysts also insist that these priests of the "ziggurats" (pyramids) also were redistributors of goods and lawgivers. I suspect they will eventually recognize that these priests merely used myths as their most effective generators of dependency. There have been very successful leaders of social movements who used only mythical dependency. But these have normally been millennial leaders reacting to severe external threats, as we see in the leaders of Ghost Dances (see chapter 6), in Savonarola or Martin Luther, and in Joseph McCarthy. They do not seem to last long unless they combine mythical dependency with the other forms. The popes based their power firmly on their supposedly direct historical link with God, on their intercession with God through ritual and prayer, and on the myths of the Great Chain of Being. But their greatest power did not come until they synthesized this mythical dependency with Roman and canonical law and with the massive redistributive bureaucracy of the Church, as Dostoevski's Grand Inquisitor noted. They got tremendous support for waging peace at home—that is, for their "Peace (Truce) of God" program from the eleventh century onward against pervasive feudal violence. Their development of canonical law, combined with secular enforcement of their decrees, vastly expanded this dependency over the centuries. But then they built their vast system of redistributive dependency—the church charities, schools, and so on. Of course, even with all this, their power was normally shown to be less than that of the kings they opposed when the kings used all these same powers plus force. And of course, before the Church undermined its mythical divine power with polluting corruption, the kings generally could win only over the long run if they appeared to do so in a Christian way. Few kings seemed to have forgotten the lesson of the pope's mythopoetic power that Henry IV learned at Canossa. Far more popes, perhaps overawed by the presumed power of their own righteousness, have underestimated the statist mythopoetic power of the kings and forgotten that even Gregory eventually lost in his struggle with the iniquity of the secular statists.

Hobbes was obviously wrong about the degree of rationality involved in the origins of state powers, and about the degree of brutishness in stateless societies, but his intuition was right when it told him that human beings will accept considerable dependency to escape pervasive violence. Wherever life becomes very uncertain, human beings will accept a great deal of dependency to escape the dread that situation inspires. The most powerful forms of mythical dependency are based on that fact and so are the powers of "peacegivers" and modern doctors. Rulers always try to maintain law and order and redistribute justice. Normally they start out by trying to stop murderous conflicts and, once this is done, they use it to extend dependency step by step by dealing with progressively less potentially violent conflicts. They begin with maintaining peace because people want above all to escape from violence. For example, most historians have noted how "relieved" the Romans were to accept Augustus's "benevolent" emperorship after a century of terrifying civil wars. And, of course, would-be dictators can use gangs and terrorist forces to spread violence through agents provocateurs and guerrilla actions they alone can end—and will, if only you obey. To end violence they must have more force. Once this force is in place and legitimized, they increase dependency by taking legal jurisdiction over all crimes, then over all major civil conflicts, then over all contracts (including once-sacred contracts like marriage), then over any major conflicts over equity. Probably the most telling justification in establishing the American federal government (and the Iroquois League, the League of Nations, the United Nations, and the EEC) was the argument that it would prevent warfare between the states. This was also the rationale of statesmen in the nineteenth century for holding together the weakening Austro-Hungarian and Turkish empires. When they withered away, south-central Europe was Balkanized and violence grew rapidly. At that time no politician would have imagined arguing that the government leaders would think they could change property rights by legislation or legislate other matters of equity. Today a high percentage of our politicians insist moralistically that it is is their sacred duty.

Rulers have almost always used whatever forms of redistribution of goods and service they could to generate dependency on themselves or their close allies, such as priests or delegated rulers in empires. It is the universality of redistribution that led Elman Service to argue that redistribution is the origin of chiefdoms, of full-blown states, and of the empires that weld together states. It is obvious that the more any people can control vital services or the importation or production of essentials, luxuries, and status goods, the more they make the recipients of these gifts dependent on themselves, both immediately and for the future, since these recipients can only get the goods by continuing to support the ruler. There is at least one situation in which redistribution powers may be the best foothold for building state powers. This is the situation in which the would-be state builder gets control of a great deal of wealth, or of special knowledge of production, from abroad which he can redistribute to legitimize his regime. Big Men are constrained in their efforts to get power from redistribution by their normative dependency on their kin and by all of the internal competition. But a Big Man who becomes the conduit for foreign wealth can circumvent some of these controls: he has gotten this wealth without becoming reciprocally obliged to anyone inside his society, so he builds one-way dependencies on himself by redistributing his foreign wealth as gifts. If the recipients want the gifts to continue, they must become more dependent, more submissive. In the South Pacific the arrival of Europeans was often extremely threatening to Big Men, because many little men could earn a great deal of money (such as by pearl diving) and then buy great quantities of status goods to distribute at home, thus making an end run around the traditional authorities and making themselves Big-Big Men. Peisistratus, tyrant of Athens, opened the great silver mines and began minting the Athenian "owls." Peter the Great imported the secrets of Western technology, a practice continued to this day by massive industrial espionage and theft by the KGB. Today all would-be dictators clamor for more and more foreign aid, with no reciprocal obligations attached, which they can give their people to breed dependency. It makes the people less able to create wealth, because it breeds dependency, but it makes the dictators more powerful. In the same way, rulers have normally tried to control imports, especially of vital foods for commoners and of war-making materials and status goods, which are forbidden to commoners by sumptuary laws, but are necessary to leaders as part of their mythical symbolism. At the extreme, as under the Tokugawa regime of Japan and the Ming Dynasty of China, they have tried to ban all private trade so that they could completely control it. I believe this led Michael Polanyi and his followers to believe that foreign trade in the ancient empires was created by the rulers.[30] This impression was gotten from the official records, but it is not true.

Foreign trade was easier to control and tax for redistribution purposes than domestic trade and production, but these too were subject to redistribution. The imperial state bureaucracies were especially important in building public works and controlling them to breed dependency. Karl A. Wittfogel[31] argued that the ancient rulers created the massive irrigation works and this gave them despotic power. It now seems clear from all the evidence that this was another official-records illusion. Anthropologists have found that even very extensive irrigation systems are built and maintained by societies without state powers. And probably most archaeologists now believe that local groups (kin?) built the first irrigation systems in Egypt, Mesopotamia, and elsewhere.[32] Once the rulers got power, they took control and greatly expanded these public works, then proclaimed their benevolence—and the ever-greater dependency of the people. This is roughly the process that was followed in historic times in Tokugawa Japan, Ming China, Stalinist Russia, and Roosevelt U.S.A. (One of the unintended consequences of these great irrigation systems was the debilitation of the peasants by shistomiasis, a disease contacted from snails in the water. William MacNeill argues that this debilitation probably did more than anything else to prevent successful rebellions.[33] But, of course, there were rebellions, especially when the bureaucratic regimes eventually produced their other unintended consequences—stagnation, inflation, and generalized hatred of the regimes.)

Destroying the Balance of Power

The manipulation of the balance of power among nations has always been one of the most important strategies of statecraft. All rulers of states, except some of those suffering from our virulent myth of modernism, have taken it for granted that each individual will expand his own power until something (like sickness or the English Channel) or someone stops him.[34] The reason the statesmen grasped this strategy so easily was that it is also basic to all of our everyday lives. Dominance, the dependency of some people on others, is one of our primary goals in social interaction. The reason for this is almost self-evident: since almost all our most important goals in life are actually or potentially dependent on other human beings, the more they are dependent on us the more we are likely to satisfy our most important goals. We learn this as babies. If our mother loves us, she is emotionally dependent on us and we get fed. If she's bigger than us, we're dependent on her and better do what she says—unless she loves us so much she wouldn't dare hit us, in which case she can be walked all over (and will be, if we do not love her in turn). Dependency is the foundation of all human society, of all human relations. All that varies is the type of dependency and the degree of asymmetry or symmetry of the dependencies.

On the surface it might appear that this fact of life, coupled with the obvious dangers of dependency, might lead everyone to adopt a strategy of total independence—of "splendid isolation." But, of course, that would lead to the extinction of human genes. The only people who pursue this strategy are those who are excruciatingly insecure (such as narcissists). These in fact are the people who become anchorites or, more commonly, the "power-hungry fiends" of whom we shall see more. Most of us want to be emotionally independent and at the same time we want all those things that make us dependent on other human beings—love, help, protection, and so on. We are ambivalent. Nowhere is this more obvious than in powerful love partnerships. Anyone deeply in love easily swings from blind devotion (when you feel safe in the other's love for you) to bitter, angry rejection and flight (when you feel the other rejects you or is using you).

The optimum solution to this human dilemma is the balance of power, or, more specifically, the balance of identification and emotional dependency. Your identification and emotional dependency must be balanced by theirs. If you are mutually identified and dependent to the same degree, you are both equally safe—and equally at risk. People falling in love are continually alert and testing to see how much the others love them.[35] Only those who do not yet know how painful unrequited love can be are sometimes willing to jump first and wind up far more dependent than the other. (That's the same as unilateral disarmament in nuclear strategy.) Most people are not very conscious of this strategy, since much of it is already built into automatic genetic programs or goes on subconsciously. One automatic program is "Reject the Rejector Immediately." Even small children will almost instantly reject someone who rejects their offer of affection. The sexually aggressive adult may persist, but that's sexual aggression, not love. Sexual aggression does not make you dependent. At the opposite extreme of conscious planning is the strategy of playing several suitors at once to avoid too much dependency on any one; if one hurts you, you increase your alliance with the other, just as the U.S. builds its relation with China when things turn very bad with Russia. Of course, people make mistakes, including taking deceitful presentations of love for the real thing, and they suffer terribly for them. Hence the need to be ever vigilant in love—and in maintaining a balance of power within society, thereby preventing anyone from getting much power for long.

In hunting and gathering societies, the balance of power is maintained by continual minor adjustments at the margins, just as it is in most families today. Certainly there are attempts by some people—especially power-hungry bullies—to get more power over others, one little step at a time or, far less successfully, by power grabs. Regardless of the stern values on liberty, equality, and fraternity, and regardless of repeated failures, there are even some bullies who try to subordinate everyone—and there is even an occasional murder. But most people are vigilant and immediately coalesce to put down any such power plays. The balance of power preserved individual liberties, fraternity, and equality.

Even in the vastly larger segmented lineage societies made possible by the development of herding and agriculture, the balance continues to work. The Big Men who head the lineages do have more power because of their control of property for redistribution, which, of course, breeds the dependency of reciprocal obligation. But the kin are still able to make sure the actions by their lineage head are in their favor. In addition, the Big Men of the different lineages check the growth of too much dominance by others. In most of these societies, as one can see in Paul Bohannan's classic analysis of the Tiv of Nigeria,[36] conflicts between lineages lead to a series of spreading alliances which eventually produces, almost automatically, a balance of power that checks the further growth of power and of warfare.

The apparently automatic nature of these checks and balances on conflict in stateless societies is partly misleading. These systems have evolved over very long periods, and their historical roots are lost in the mists of the historic amnesia of societies without written records. It seems most likely that the checks and balances were built by innumerable small, purposeful steps intended to resolve conflicts and maintain local social order. They followed the social drift process into ever greater "spontaneous social orders" analyzed by Burke, Maitland, and Hayek.[37] By carefully planning local orders to deal with problems as they arise, then changing taken-for-granted rules marginally to encode those new bits of information, each Big Man moved over time toward an overall better—more peaceful—situation for the great majority of people and built rules that, when followed, would almost "automatically" solve the new problems that arose. Aidan Southall has analyzed stateless social order in these terms and noted how they resemble the "spontaneous," non-centrally planned ordering of trade relations known as laissez-faire economic orders:

> The remarkable spectacle of societies positively maintaining themselves at a high level of integration without any obvious specialized means of enforcement has undoubtedly led to new insight and attention to the fundamental responsibilities of all citizens, which for most people are obscured by the ubiquity of specialized political institutions. In stateless societies every man grows up with a practical and intuitive sense of his responsibility to maintain constantly throughout his life that part of the fabric of society in which at any time he is involved. Stateless societies are so constituted that the kaleidoscopic succession of concrete social situations provides the stimulus that motivates each individual to act for his own interest or for that of close kin and neighbors with whom he is so totally involved, in a manner which maintains the fabric of society. It is a little like the classical model of laissez-faire economics translated into the political field. But if every man is thus for himself he is so only within a very tight framework of reciprocal obligation that he cannot avoid absorbing. The lack of specialized roles and the resulting multiplex quality of social networks mean that neither economic nor political ends can be exclusively pursued by anyone to the detriment of society, because these ends are intertwined with each other and further channeled by ritual and controlled by the beliefs which ritual expresses.[38]

As I have noted, I doubt very much that we shall ever have enough facts to know how the first states were formed. The worldwide spread of Western culture now probably even precludes our observing any new state formations that are not affected by the example of our state powers or those of other civilizations. But my guess is that some especially aggressive, intelligent, and magically potent Big-Big Man, or, far more likely, a team of Big Men created a way to break these tribal balances of power. They probably did it by appealing to the power ambitions and greed for women, wealth, and possibly slaves: if others would support their new powers, they would lead them to victory against neighboring tribes and redistribute their goods to the victors. But this situation would have to be one in which victory would lead to a nearly permanent need to remain partially mobilized to suppress the opponents, or to defend oneself against constant threats. They probably already had great mythic powers and the booty of victory would greatly increase their redistributive powers. Once enthroned as chiefs, they could work furiously to get power over mythmaking and education to breed statist identification, law and order, property, and so on, seizing whatever stratagem seemed to work in each situation. And, of course, the great new powers would produce soaring power lust, conflicts, and wars among the little chiefs until one paramount chief was able to enforce sovereignty over others. Once one society was subordinated to a statist ruler dedicated to conquering other tribes, the military advantage of his statist operations and apparatuses would exert tremendous pressure on others to organize in the same way, so primary states would produce *reactive states.*

I guess this is roughly how early chiefdoms were formed because there are clear instances of this process at work in the conquest by herders of agriculturalists,[39] and, moreover, this is how the gigantic states and empires of today were built. All of the nations of Europe were built this way. Even the most seemingly homogeneous and pacified nations today were forged in the crucible of soaring myth, ferocious battle, law-and-order giving, redistribution, and so on. The very same process is going on all over the world today within nominal states and between them. There are a few instances, such as the Iroquois, Switzerland, and to some extent, the U.S., in which rational coalitions were formed, generally in common defense against very threatening enemies. But almost all merely rational coalitions fall apart when the threat wanes. (The Iroquois League in Iroquois legend was first inspired by the divine leader, Deganawidah, then promoted by his secular devotee, Hiawatha.) The American federation nearly fell apart immediately, then under the Constitution New England threatened to secede, then brutal force had to be used against the South—then an incandescent cloud of nationalistic mythification increasingly welded the mythical bonds of statist dependency. Switzerland remains to this day a mutual-defense league in which every able-bodied adult male is ready to man the mountain passes.

Almost all states and empires have been built first by mythification and force and then strengthened by the creative use of the mythification of the statist powers, waging law and order internally, redistributing goods and justice, and so on. The mythification we now call agitprop becomes immensely more successful in states and empires. The primary reason for this is the tremendous control the rulers have over information about their persons, their subordinates (eventually bureaucrats), and their operations. As long as human power was kept to the Big Man stage, the leader and his actions were known and directly observable by a reasonably high percentage of adults. With the coming of the giant state bureaucratic apparatuses, the ruler becomes increasingly distant, unknown, and purposefully very mysterious. He can now carefully control how people see him or whether they see him at all. He can present his public images and construct his magical official information to mythify his powers—creating uncertainty (mystery) and showing the people how absolutely necessary his growing powers are for their welfare, how benevolently paternalistic he is to all his "sons" and "daughters." By approximately 2800 B.C., the rulers had developed the rudimentary forms of the state bureaucracies that have ruled empires down to our own day in roughly the same ways. From then on the most powerful rulers have had these official bureaucrats to wage war abroad, wage law and order at home, redistribute the subjects' net national product, and, above all, to mythify their powers at home and around the world and to "educate" the masses in the statist myths.

The day of the experts in public relations and propaganda dawned in Egypt in 2800 B.C. when the state artists developed the mythical image of the pharaoh synthesizing the symbols of Upper and Lower Egypt to sanctify this wedding-by-conquest. These experts have continued to develop their strategies for victory through mythical official information up to this day. Over the centuries they have added key elements, such as massive state education, practiced at least from the Roman Empire onward, to their mythmaking powers. It is these myths more than anything else which lead people to see the imperial powers to wage war, wage law and order, and redistribute as legitimate. These powers in turn are used to build further legitimacy. As new empires have been built on the ruins of old ones, they have had to start the ancient processes over again, beginning with weak powers, nourishing their myths of power, expanding their bureaucracies, redistributing and giving law and order, waging war abroad and peace at home, and becoming more and more powerful. It is precisely this process that has been going on with fits and starts in our Western nations. The myths are partially new, especially in their outer forms, as they must always be for new imperial powers, and they are largely hidden by our *exclusionary myth of modernism* which assures us we are above all myths—we are too rational and scientific to be the victims of ancient statist myths. But they are really basically the same. Today the myth of the rationally planned, scientifically run welfare state is our most virulent imperial myth.

Anyone who accumulated large amounts of wealth while remaining independent of military-political command structures faced the problem of safeguarding what he had gained. Unless a merchant could count on the protection of some formidable man of power, there was nothing to restrain local potentates from seizing his property any time his goods came within reach. To gain effective protection was likely to be costly—so costly as to inhibit large-scale accumulation of private capital.

Moreover, in most civilized societies, the prestige and deference paid to men of power, i.e., to bureaucrats and landowners, was matched by a general distrust of and disdain for merchants and men of the marketplace. Anyone who succeeded in profiting from trade, therefore, was likely to see the advantage of acquiring land, or in some other way of gaining access to a place in some local command hierarchy.

Accordingly, trade and market-regulated behavior, though present from very early times, remained marginal and subordinate in civilized societies before A.D. 1000. Most persons lived out their lives without responding to market incentives in any way. Customary routine dominated everyone's behavior. Large-scale changes in human conduct, when they occurred, were more likely to be in response to commands coming from some social superior than to any change in supply and demand, buying and selling. . . .

We can gain a juster perspective on the remarkable European venture toward the sovereignty of the market in military as in other forms of management by recognizing it as an eccentric departure from the human norm of command behavior—the sort of behavior that dominated ancient times and has reasserted itself with remarkable power since the 1880s.

William H. McNeill

Notes

1. For the evidence on Cyril Burt, see L. S. Hearnshaw, *Cyril Burt, Psychologist* (London: Hodder and Stoughton, 1979); and Stephen Jay Gould, *The Mismeasure of Man* (New York: W. W. Norton, 1981). On Margaret Mead see Derek Freeman, *Margaret Mead and Samoa* (Cambridge, MA: Harvard University Press, 1983).
2. For an overview of the massive literature on political corruption, see Jack D. Douglas and John M. Johnson, eds., *Official Deviance* (Philadelphia: Lippincott, 1977).
3. *Los Angeles Times*, "U. S. Double Standard Seen on China's Rights," Nov. 23, 1987.
4. See "Songsten Gampo and the Tibet Question," *The Economist*, Oct. 10, 1987, p. 33.
5. John King Fairbank, *The Great Chinese Revolution, 1800–1985* (New York: Harper and Row, 1987), pp. 9–10. Western intellectuals had contact almost exclusively with Chinese "high culture," that of the mandarinate bureaucrats honing the statist myths necessary to their suzerainty. See Leon E. Stover, *The Cultural Ecology of Chinese Civilization* (New York: New American Library, 1974).
6. This is the general theory shared by almost all geneticists and biologists. See Richard Dawkins, *The Selfish Gene* (New York: Oxford University Press, 1976); and Edward Wilson, *Sociobiology* (Cambridge, MA: The Belknap Press of

Harvard University Press, 1975); also *On Human Nature* (Cambridge, MA: Harvard University Press, 1978).

7. Leadership and authority in these hunting and gathering societies are of the forms analyzed by James MacGregor Burns (in *Leadership* [New York: Harper Colophon edition, 1979]) with a strong strain of paternalism.

8. This theory of power is radically different from that of earlier social scientists. It is closest to the theory developed by James MacGregor Burns, Ibid. As will become apparent, it is an adaptation for human beings from the theory of dominance developed by behavioral biologists.

9. Ibid., pp. 15–16.

10. See Edward Crankshaw, *Bismarck* (New York: Viking, 1981).

11. The literature on heroes is extensive. All nonmoribund societies have heroes. (See Joseph Campbell, *The Hero With A Thousand Faces* [New York: Pantheon, 1949].) But only great anxiety, normally potentiated by hope, inspires the mythification of heroes into Savior-Leaders. It is easy to see this in individual hero-worshipers (such as in the German people's heroization of Hitler). Richard Schickel has argued that we see this in the phenomenoa of "fans." See Richard Schickel, *His Picture in the Papers* (New York: Charterhouse, 1973). Most of this argument was developed by Erich Fromm in his classic work on *Escape from Freedom* (New York: Holt, Rinehart and Winston, 1941).

12. Albert Speer, *Inside the Third Reich* (New York: Avon, 1972), pp. 46–47, 84–85, 105.

13. Ibid., pp. 44–45.

14. See, for example, Tim Ingold, *Hunters, Pastoralists and Ranchers* (Cambridge: Cambridge University Press, 1980); Elman R. Service, *The Hunters* (Englewood Cliffs, NJ: Prentice-Hall, 1966); and Carleton S. Coon, *The Hunting Peoples* (Boston: Little, Brown, 1971).

15. *International Encyclopedia of the Social Sciences* (Crowell Collier and Macmillan, 1968), vol. 7, pp. 24–25.

16. A. R. Radcliffe-Brown, *The Andaman Islanders* (Glencoe, IL: The Free Press, 1948), p. 45, quoted in Elman R. Service, *The Hunters*, p. 53.

17. June Helm MacNeish, "Leadership Among the Northern Athabascans," *Anthropologica*, no. 2 (1956), p. 151; quoted in Elman R. Service, *The Hunters*, p. 54.

18. See Helmut Schoeck, *Envy* (New York: Harcourt Brace and World, 1969). This theory agrees exactly with Tocqueville's observation that envious conflict is greatest precisely where equality is the greatest. Again, Marx had it exactly the opposite of the truth. It is normally the educated upper- or middle-status-and-income people who revolt against their slight superiors, not the poor. The poor revolt only under *extreme* suffering and threat combined with hope. As Lenin saw, the hard-core can offer (mythical millennial) hope, but the threat (such as by starvation) must be great to finally arouse the poor and uneducated.

19. See G. Lefebre, *The Great Fear of 1789* (New York: Pantheon, 1973).

20. Michael Grant, *The Twelve Caesars* (New York: Charles Scribner's Sons, 1975), pp. 66–67.

21. See P. A. Sorokin, *Social and Cultural Dynamics* (New York: Bedminster Press, 1937, rpt. 1962).

22. Marshal Sahlins, *Stone Age Economics* (Chicago: Aldine, 1972).

23. See Bronislaw Malinowski, *Argonauts of the Western Pacific* (New York: Dutton, 1961).
24. George Gilder, *Wealth and Poverty* (New York: Basic Books, 1981).
25. Sahlins, *Stone Age Economies*.
26. Elman Service, *Origins of the State and Civilization* (New York: Norton, 1975).
27. Speer, *Inside the Third Reich*, p. 429.
28. Ronald Cohen is the most important exception to this ungenerous generalization. See "State Origins," in H. J. M. Claessen and P. Skalnik, eds., *The Early States* (The Hague: Mouton, 1978).
29. See Hans Gerth and C. Wright Mills, eds. and trans., *From Max Weber* (New York: Oxford University Press, 1946); and "The Three Types of Legitimate Rule," in A. Etzioni, ed., *Complex Organizations* (New York: Holt, 1961), pp. 4–14.
30. K. Polanyi, *Trade and Markets in the Early Empires* (Glencoe, IL: Free Press, 1957).
31. Karl A. Wittfogel, *Oriental Despotism* (New Haven: Yale University Press, 1957).
32. See R. Cohen and E. Service, eds., *Origins of the State* (Philadelphia: Institute for the Study of Human Issues, 1978).
33. William McNeill, *Plagues and Peoples* (Garden City, NY: Doubleday Anchor, 1976).
34. They have recognized the Clausewitz principle.
35. My extensive use of love partnerships is based on commonsense experience and years of life studies I've done. See J. D. Douglas and Freda Cruse Atwell, *Love, Intimacy and Sex* (Beverly Hills, CA: Sage, 1988).
36. Paul Bohannan, *Justice and Judjment Among the Tiv (London: International African Institute / Oxford University Press, 1968)*.
37. See the general synthesis of these ideas in Friedrich Hayek, *Law, Legislation, and Liberty* (Chicago: University of Chicago Press, 1973), vol. 1.
38. A. Southall, "Stateless Society," in David L. Sills, ed., *The International Encyclopedia of the Social Sciences* (New York: Crowell Collier and Macmillan, 1968), p. 167.
39. Herders had great military advantages over agriculturalists, especially when they rode horses or camels. The Mongols used this advantage to conquer a vast empire of agriculturalists. See James Chambers, *The Devil's Horsemen* (New York: Atheneum, 1979), pp. 51–70; and T. N. Dupuy, *The Evolution of Weapons and Warfare* (London: Jane's, 1982), pp. 71–80.

4

The Drift into the Modernist Megastates

"...the great danger in this matter lies in the fact that 'plain men' do not appreciate the enormous cumulative effects of these many small infractions of sound principle. They do not seem to realise that all this legislation means the gradual and insidious advance of a dull and enervating pauperism....it is very necessary that men should abandon the policy of indifference, and that they should do something to enlarge the atmosphere of Liberty. This is to be accomplished not by reckless and revolutionary methods, but rather by a resolute resistance to new encroachments and by patient and statesmanlike endeavour to remove wherever practicable the restraints of regulation, and to give full play over a larger area to the creative forces of Liberty, for Liberty is the condition precedent to all solution of human difficulty."

Thomas MacKay, 1891

"In all well-attempered governments there is nothing which should be more jealously maintained than the spirit of obedience to law, more especially in small matters; for transgression creeps in unperceived and at last ruins the state, just as the constant recurrence of small expenses in time eats up a fortune. The expense does not take place all at once, and therefore is not observed; the mind is deceived, as in the fallacy which says that 'if each part is little, then the whole is little'. And this is true in one way, but not in another, for the whole and the all are not little, although they are made up of littles."

Aristotle

It is remarkable testimony to the natural tendency of human beings to conserve their pasts, and to repeat even the worst mistakes once the passage of time has dulled their memory, to see how some of the most ancient myths of statism can mesmerize masses of people in our modernist age. Mussolini basked in the ancient glories of Roman power, which had been kept alive by the glowing accounts of historians like Edward Gibbon, and promised a

141

return of those glories; Hitlerian Germany marched to the Wagnerian strains of Valhalla's heros; and Mao's Great Leap Forward was purposefully portrayed as a second coming of the First Great Emperor of ancient China. The most ancient and disastrous mythical convictions of statism still echo down through all of these centuries.

It is easy to see that the trappings—the external signs—of statism and other magico-religious ideologies can have these remarkable echo effects, even with new twists, as we see in the recreation of the ancient mandala in the Nazi swastika. But by far the most powerful effect of the statist myths is seen in the idea of the state itself as a separate and higher level of existence. The idea of the sacred essences can haunt folk memories and intellectuals over the millennia and return with a vengeance to mesmerize new generations. Just as children orphaned at an early age generally forget any conflicts with the beloved parents and come to see them as the ideal embodiments of all goodness, so whole nations beset by dreads or sufferings can look back longingly to the golden ages of advertised statist glories, and forget all about the very real agonies of statist repression and Caesarism.

The most powerful bureaucratic states soon stagnate their societies, even when they have been among the most creative in the history of the world. This iron rule of bureaucratic stagnation has been repeated over and over again in most civilizations, and in all very successful big business organizations today. (The reasons are dealt with in chapters 8 and 9.) Thus, even the most homogeneous states that start with great morale generally stagnate in a matter of decades, slowly ratchet-downward in adaptations to the always-changing situations they face, enter times of troubles, explode under the pressure of foreign attacks, or implode from revolutions, or, more commonly, do both, then disappear culturally or begin rebuilding under new creators and managers.

One of the myths beloved by historians, as we noted, is that state bureaucracies produce the growth and concentration of creative activities called civilization. Since all historians know that the great primary states were annihilated by comparatively small groups of barbarians armed with new weapons they created (or adopted from unknown places), the idea that the statists are far more creative is patently absurd, even in the realm of weapons which is crucial to their survival. In the Middle East the primary states were quickly swept into Marx's mythical "dustbin of history" (that is, statist bankruptcy and dissolution) by the comparatively small barbarian military organizations using the new chariots. The huge bureaucratic states the charioters created were in turn annihilated by small new military organizations using the newly discovered iron weapons. This great cycle of statism, from birth to decay and destruction, has been recognized for centuries by historians not chained by statist myths and continues to this day. (Ibn Khaldun presented a broad picture and analysis of this waxing and waning of states in his famous work, the *Muqaddimah*, in the fourteenth century.) Even the vastly creative private manufacturers and other groups still remaining in America could not save our immense statist military machine, with all of its colossal fire power, from defeat by the Vietnamese barbarians who created extremely simple but new weapons (such as handmade tunnel systems) and strategies of guerrilla and political warfare. The reason is the same it has always been: the bureaucrats soon become so inefficient at recognizing and using creative ideas and products that they repeat failures over and over again, even when they are surrounded by a vast explosion of creativity. Almost no serious analyst of business bureaucracies now doubts this to be true of them, even when they face continuous competition.[1] If this is so obvious to anyone studying such small bureaucracies, why is it not obvious to historians and others that it is far more true of the immense statist bureaucracies, especially in view of the awful misery and the colossal pyrotechnics that normally accompany their declines and falls?

There seems to be more at work than the obvious fact that the historians and others surveying these facts are commonly the aspirants and grantsmen of statist powers. One other important factor is the very real increase in creativity that normally accompanies the early drift into statist powers, the *proto-statist period*, the period of the spring flowers of states. Business organizations that eventually become very big do so precisely because their early growth period involves an acceleration of creativity or, at least, an explosion in the application of creations. Ford, General Motors, and International Business Machines became huge only because they were very creative in their early decades of growth. This may be creativity in marketing, technology, finance, or other factors. The combinations vary widely. What works depends on the situations they face. Some proto-statists show the same burst of creativity and production—of spring flowers—and they are on average the ones that build the hugest and most powerful states. Other factors, notably accidents and the power of competing groups, are also very important. The most creative statist can be felled by disease or by a neighboring statist. It takes brilliance and creativity to build colossal new bureaucratic cultures inspired by morale, new political coalitions, new military strategies, new strategies of political deceit, and so on. The brilliance and creativity of the world's Lenins, Stalins, and Hitlers in their early days, before the rigidity inspired by hubris, paranoid dread, and bureaucratic degradation sets in, is galling and frightening to those of us who are their enemies. Most people try to escape the dread it inspires by denying it but, as Cassirer warned us, it is vitally important to know our political enemy. Their chosen operators and bureaucrats commonly show the same flairs for statist entrepreneurship in these halcyon days of exploding state powers.

However, it is most likely that little of the creativity and production of this proto-statist period is due directly to the new government bureaucrats. Instead, they seem due mostly to the rapid increase in cultural homogenization, to the morale born of the early victories, to the explosion in the size of the market (leading to economies of scale and scope), to the destruction of trade barriers, to the new peacefulness of the realm (which means no one is burning crops and murdering able-bodied men), to the import of new wealth from conquered lands or tributary states (slaves, gold, and other booty), and to the explosion of state expenditures on monumental artifacts of civilization made possible by the new booty and the great expansions of the tax roles to newly conquered subjects. All of this produces some short-run bursts of creative efficiency and far more lasting *illusions of statist creativity and production*, simple fallacies of correlations of the growth of the statist apparatuses and myths with the growth of creativity and production. The most important contribution to this illusion among historians has been the vast new expenditures of the statists precisely on the huge—Caesarist—monuments that last the longest and were intended to make the greatest impression of creativity and production—pyramids, statues, castles, and televised space shots.

The most creative statists, in other words, purposefully create these artifacts so that they will last and produce precisely the illusion they do among historians and even more among their subjects. Their tax booty, brilliance, and creativity are poured into the artifacts of "civilization"—which means precisely those activities and objects that awe and inspire submission more than anything else—precisely for the purpose of building the statist myths on which further expansions of their power so heavily depend. Historians have merely fallen into the "trappings trap" set for all submissive victims by superior minds and lion hearts. The pharaohs inspire awe to this day through the giant and mysterious pyramids they had built and the Soviet rulers launch giant rockets into the heavens for all to marvel at, even as the plaster from their new buildings cracks and their nuclear generator spews radiation over their countryside. Purposefully constructed statist illusions mesmerize our mass media every day, over and over again, regardless of the mountains of less mesmerizing evidence of the perpetual failures and awful dangers of statism over the long run.

The Rise of the Renaissance Welfare States

The waning and near disappearance of the material trappings of the Roman imperial state, combined with the inaccessibility of the scarce written documents of the "Dark Ages" and the early medieval period, led to the easy assumption that statism died with the "fall" of the empire. This assumption is still found in popular treatments of Western history, but has been progressively replaced in serious historical analyses by the recognition that the basic Roman ideas of the state as a corporate body—a "sole corporation," separate from its members yet a body—was transmitted down the centuries and was made more absolute and far more explicitly holy. In Byzantium, the Eastern part of the empire, the ideas were transmitted and strengthened both by those who shared the more absolutist or despotic ideas of the Eastern states and by the Church rulers. They became the mythical foundations of Russian statism and eventually of Soviet communism. In the West the Church rulers became the primary transmitters of the Roman ideas and added greatly to their divinity. Because the Church trained everyone through its increasingly massive bureaucracy of centralized education—preaching and ministering, as well as the narrower activities we now call "education"—the Church became the primary fount of statist ideas. Throughout most of its history, however, it did not merely adopt the subordinate role of supporting secular statism with which we are so familiar in the absolute monarchies, and which became a central idea in the modernist revolt against the "ancient regime." The Church trained people in the myths of statism in pursuit of its own goal of sacred statism and only compromised these when it was not powerful enough to pursue them openly, reverting to the secret nurturance of theocratic absolutism during those periods.

The idea that the state is only a secular body that makes claim to exclusive or sovereign use of violence caused endless confusions over the whole history of statism in the West. These confusions were actually encouraged by the papal statists and others by their insistence that the state powers were *merely* secular rulers who used violence, not the grace of God, to achieve their petty ends of worldly power. This massively advertised "product differentiation" became a taken-for-granted truth in social science theories, which makes about as much sense as defining IBM as "reality" because its executives prefer that image in their advertising. The Church was far more statist in every other respect than any merely secular ruler and several times came close to permanently subordinating the secular states under its imperial sway. The Church not only made far more extreme use of the core enabling myths of the welfare state, but was in fact vastly more important than any secular states in the exercise of most of the core operations of statism, except those directly using violence, and has always had a vastly greater statist apparatus—bureaucracy—than any secular state before the Soviets and Chinese communists. In our own day journalists almost universally argue that the modernist welfare state has revolutionized the world because for the first time ever the state has assumed the powers and responsibilities of giving alms and security. What changed was merely that the secular rulers saw that they could profit in power by usurping these from the Catholic church and the

Protestant churches, and that they could get away with this because the Church was stagnating too badly to be able to prevent it. Toyota's winning market share from General Motors does not mean that Toyota invented the automobile, and Bismarck's social security system for German workers did not mean that he invented alms giving or the promise of state succor in times of need. The tithe, or one-tenth of income, has been the standard Christian church state welfare program for the poor and helpless (and for the bureaucrats) and was far greater proportionately than is now given by most secular states. The fact that the Mormons strongly oppose most federal welfare programs today does not mean that they are against statism. It means they have their own state in the Church of Latter Day Saints, which rules both directly and indirectly through elected officials in Utah, do not want secular rulers stealing their market or show, and do not relish paying both the church state and the secular state for the same services.

The dominant Pauline Christian theology and theory of politics saw Christians as united in the corporate body of the Church and as necessarily and absolutely subject to the decisions of the Church officials or rulers about the common welfare. By the fourth century A.D., when Augustine wrote the great synthesis of Church doctrine, the Church rulers saw baptism as the official rite by which the secular self of the individual (his *humanitas*) was shed or transformed into the Christian self (of the *fidelis*) who owed absolute faithfulness (*fidelitas*) to the Church hierarchy, which was thought of and referred to explicitly in absolutist monarchic terms. The corporation of the Church quite literally was thought to absorb the very selves of individuals and thenceforth the sacred Church monarchs rightfully ruled their wills by the grace of God. As Walter Ullmann put it in his classic study *The Individual and Society in the Middle Ages*:

> The individual became absorbed in and by the corporation itself, by the Church, which itself, however, was governed on the monarchic principle, according to which original power was located in one supreme authority, from which all power in the public sphere was derived—a system which, for want of a better name, I call the descending or theocratic theme of government and law. . . .Conceptually it was impossible to maintain that the fidelis could share in government. . .by virtue of his baptism and the consequential incorporation into the Church, [he] had no autonomous character. Because he had instead the required faith, he accepted—or perhaps I should say, was supposed to have accepted—the will of him who was set above him, the will of the superior.[2]

This, of course, was the statist theory of the Church rulers, not the whole definition of the common welfare shared by the simple body of the faithful. As usual throughout history, we have almost no records of what the faithful who were not members of the Church bureaucracy really thought. Even when they began to write things, for centuries they had to use secretive Aesopian language to communicate thoughts that deviated from the "party line" of the Church rulers. What is obvious is the extreme totalitarianism of the Church doctrine of its powers over the faithful. Canon law continued this same extreme view right into the modernist world, in spite of all the catastrophes of corruption and rebellion suffered by the Church over the centuries.[3]

The Church "Fathers" repeated over and over again through the centuries that obeying the "weight of authority," as Augustine called it, is the very hallmark of the true Christian. The only real problem over the centuries, until the rise of classical liberal thought and action, was that of demarcating the sacred statist powers from the secular statist powers. Since the Church generally had serious competition for power over its subjects from secular rulers, and since these rulers frequently used violence to enforce their definitions, the Church rulers frequently had to be circumspect, even using Aesopian language to communicate with true believers in their claims to total power. Though we obviously cannot indulge in a full-scale history of the Church here, it seems clear that Church rulers have been far more prone to hubris, in the name of God, of course, than secular rulers. Very roughly, whenever they saw a chance to gain greater powers, they moved irresistibly in that direction, until stopped by secular rulers or internal revolt (especially the Reformation). Most of the time the competition has been so great that they have had to accept a power-sharing compromise. In general, the Church hierarchy has seen itself as absolute in the roughly defined sacred realm and yet rendered unto Caesar in the nonsacred, to the extent they thought necessary, including rendering unto Adolph Hitler when that seemed necessary.

The overall significance of this huge Church state in the Western World has been immense. It has made the West a far more inherently pluralistic and conflictful civilization than most of the other great civilizations. The Church has helped mightily, contrary to its own worst intentions, to keep the West a "house divided against itself," and, thus, a far freer and more creative community of nations. In the other civilizations there has either not been a powerful church, as in the more secular or pantheistic Chinese civilization, or, more commonly, the powerful church has been effectively subordinated to or absorbed by the secular rulers, as in the ancient primary states and in Indian states. (Christian Byzantium and the Islamic kingdoms have been in between these extremes and more variable. Sumeria probably involved the same conflicts among church states and secular states in the early period.) Wherever the secular rulers have been unchecked by the dominance drives of sacred rulers, and even more wherever they have been able to absorb or fully dominate sacred nations, secular rulers and their governments have verged toward the totalitarian end of the spectrum of statism in claims and practices. The Russian Orthodox Church was dominated by the czars and is now almost completely absorbed by the Soviet Party. The other most totalitarian states in the West have normally arisen when the Church has been fragmented, weak for other reasons, or allied with the secular rulers, however uneasily. The alliance of the Church with the secular state in Spain made it the most totalitarian state in the West for centuries, thereby destroying the earlier vast creativity and productivity of the many nations living under this vast empire. To this day the rulers of the allied sacred state and the secular states immiserate Latin American nations with vast natural resources, most of all through their control of almost all education. And it is all done in the name of Christian caring. Mussolini made grandiose claims to totalitarian power, but the Church was far too powerful in Italy and both Church and localities too opposed for him to make good on his claims, while Hitler was less checked by the fragmented Protestant churches and local governments in his quest for total power.

Of course, the West has also had the great fragmentation of national groups and of secular states. These have played the eternal game of checks and balances known as "the balance of power" grand strategy, each national leader or statist ruler forming ever-shifting coalitions to try to gain power, while building federation-coalitions to check anyone else who gained much power. This inherent federationism and checks-and-balances strategy of the West has long been seen as crucial in preventing the rise of a great totalitarian state ("oriental despotism") and is certainly the dominant factor today. However, this same ever-shifting fragmentation and federationism existed in all the areas that became the territories of the most absolutist states. In all of them eventually one of the statists was able to tip the balance of power play his way enough to establish a totalitarian empire that was then built through mass agitprop and other state operations into a totalitarian state. China is the classic case of this process of total state building because it is so highly documented from the time of Ch'in on, but many other cases are well documented. The history of the Russian Empire is one of the most important today. The existence of the huge sacred Church state in the West seems to have been of crucial importance in both the creation of secular states, by training the masses to believe in statism in general, and in preventing any of the many would-be Caesars from succeeding thus far in building the universal secular state. The core welfare statist powers of the Church were an ever-present threat of a counterweight to any secular state that gained very much power. Of course, with the waning of the Church state powers in the Reformation, the counterweight was greatly weakened, and in a few short centuries Napoleon, Hitler, and Stalin have come very close to succeeding where all others had failed. With the near paralysis of Church powers by modernism, either Hitler or Stalin would almost certainly have succeeded had it not been for the massive counterweight of the United States.

The Church rulers of Augustine's day were already highly enmeshed in the struggle for secular statist power as the secular powers of the Roman officials waned. They had come a long way since Constantine submitted—nominally and for public presentations—to the mythical sacred state powers of the Church rulers. There were even instances of successful Christian rebellion against the secular rulers when they tried to extend their nominal sovereignty to Church members. The invasions of Rome by the infidels caused a great potential scandal and loss of legitimacy for the Church, since the Roman rulers were nominal Christians. Augustine's *City Of God* was written as the great defense of the Church and its theodicy, the justification of its sacred statist rule over the corrupt rule of the secularists. As the secular statism of the Romans waned, the sacred statism of the Church waxed. By the late sixth century the intermittent powers of the secular rulers presented tempting opportunities to the Church rulers to extend their powers into the secular realm.

Pope Gregory I (the "Great" of Church history) was a man of the people, a lifelong monk, and so nominally humble that he proclaimed himself officially to be "the servant of God's servants." But this most professedly humble man extended the Church's conceptions of secular statist or absolutist authority and of direct secular statist authority in all directions. He greatly increased and reformed the bureaucracy; expanded the bureaucratic giving of alms and relief in times of political crisis; taxed the richer and redistributed wealth to the poor; built the foundations of the papal secular states, territories, and powers; negotiated treaties with secular rulers; allied himself when under pressure with one of the most hated tyrants of the age, Phocas; and exhorted secular rulers to launch holy wars against the heathens. Above all, he built the firm bureaucratic foundations of absolutist papal authority and fought successfully against the Arian heresy of pluralism which denied the monolithic conception of the godhead and, thus, the monolithic conception of statism. And he vastly extended the mass education programs of the Church and the great monastic orders and institutions, including Augustine's peace corps in Britain. These vast bureaucracies of Church agitprop more than anything else became the builders of the firm mythical foundation of statism which has lasted throughout Western history. Both Church and secular statism have waxed and waned in vastly complex ways over the centuries, but the ancient myths of welfare statism have always been there, ready to be revived by those enflamed with power lust and used to build their core statist operations and bureaucracies.

The myths of statism are hard to detect during the "Dark Ages," better known as the Era of Few Surviving Records, but, as soon as Charlemagne managed to recentralize secular power in the eighth century, the myths reappeared in their full-blown, ancient form. Louis Halphen has shown that Charlemagne proclaimed that all of his subjects must serve him *pro nostra omnium communi salute*—"for the common welfare of us all."[4] Having temporarily managed to gain the upper hand on the Church rulers, he coerced them into coronating him as both sacred and secular ruler of the born-again Roman state, "Holy Roman Emperor." This grand claim to the unified—hybrid—command of secular and sacred powers was to echo down through the centuries of Western statist struggles, right into the hybrid statist rhetoric of Mussolini and Hitler.

The decline of the Merovingian kings after Charlemagne and the drift into feudalism to meet the great crisis of foreign invasions led to the disappearance (thus far) from historical records of most of these great myths of the state. Historians, too used to identifying statism with the symbolic forms of Roman statism, have almost all argued that private law and welfare completely displaced statist law and the common welfare. It seems more likely that the myths merely devolved upon the more local rulers as they undertook the real but much-reduced statist operations and apparatuses. In any event, as soon as the operations and apparatuses appeared once again in their comparatively huge and centralized forms in the twelfth century, the myths of the secular state as a separate and higher level of reality and of the common welfare represented only by the rulers reappeared. Gaines Post has argued that theorists, especially those inspired by classical liberal ideals, were too mesmerized by local and private rights to see how pervasive and important the ancient ideas were:

> In short, the authorities referred to, from Gierke to McIlwain and Lagarde and Lousse, are too absorbed in the importance of private rights, and in the cellular, corporate nature of the medieval society, to appreciate how not only Roman and Canon lawyers but kings and popes frequently appealed to the 'public welfare clause,' the 'state of the realm' (*status regni*), and the 'state of the Church' (*status Ecclesiae*), and thus demanded a sacrifice of private rights and of the law that protected them; how, indeed, they were, in an earlier period than generally supposed, developing the theory and practice of public law and the State.[5]

From the eleventh to the end of the thirteenth centuries, the Western world drifted rapidly into a great age of intellectual and economic expansion—a first Renaissance and the first industrial revolution—and then into an age of sacred and secular statism and Caesarist warfare. (From this time on Western history is so complex and pluralistic that there are always smaller trends running counter to the dominant trends, which makes it easy for "specialists" with little concern for broader concerns and much concern for protecting their professional territories, to dispute anything said. Let us keep in mind the existence of these many countertrends, the waxing and waning of broader trends, the wide cultural and individual variations on any such trends, and get on with the important task at hand.) This was the first great age of science, technology, and entrepreneurial business in the West since the Roman megastate had begun to seriously erode creativity and productivity in all realms of life, except the theology of the afterlife, a thousand years earlier. Historians have discovered ever more direct links, more through subcultural transmission than written records, between them and us. The written protoscience of Albertus Magnus and Roger Bacon has been known ever since and has been seen as the early roots of modern science, and the importance of international trade and banking for later developments has long been known, but only in recent decades has it been recognized that this was also an age of industrial revolution (as seen in dams and mills) and of great economic growth. With these explosions of worldly creativity and wealth came a first small explosion of the secular millennialism so obvious in our modernist world (see chapter 6) and a great explosion in the statism that normally aids such development in the spring flowers stage, then feeds upon it, and finally produces the rapid declines of the fall canker bloom stage.[6]

The explosion of statism was most obvious in the sacred statism of the Church. This was the period during which the popes and their massive phallanxes of priestly bureaucrats attempted to dominate the secular rulers with the greatest displays of papal absolutism in the history of the Church, carried out completely successful holy crusades against the Cathar and Albigensian heretics within Europe (including the burning of whole cities), and launched Caesarist crusades against the Moslem infidels abroad. All of this was done in the name of Christian peace, humility, and charity. It was carried out with the help of vast new phallanxes of the most dedicated Christians, such as the Franciscans, who intended only the opposite of what they blindly helped to produce. They clearly intended only to help the poor, and wound up helping to murder the "poor men" of the Cathars and Albigensians; to bring peace and love to the whole world, and wound up bringing the sword to the innocent and ignorant poor of the Arab lands. It was also in this burst of neostatism that the Church began to lay the foundations for the later centuries of Inquisition in which the well-meaning Dominican friars would condemn tens of thousands of little old ladies and others to the flames for their "evil conspiracies" with Satan. This was the first great age of Western statist hubris, and the Church, acting in the full conviction of its own absolute virtue, was the worst perpetrator and victim of the ancient myths of statism.

The secular rulers, however, soon outdistanced their sacred mentors in statism and in the uses of creative agitprop. They and their intellectual supporters adopted or created most of the fundamental ideas, bureaucratic apparatuses and practices of Western welfare statism which have been transmitted and further developed by statists up to our own day. While they inherited the core enabling myths full-blown from the ancient world, as transmitted by the Church, they had to recreate many of the ancient core operations and apparatuses and create some of their own. They also inherited from the Church the basic forms of bureaucracy, taxation, and redistribution (of both goods and justice), but the ideas of professionalism and rational central planning, though found in the bureaucratic administration and budgeting of the Church, were only slowly recreated. The newest ideas, such as those of official statistics (which existed only in rudimentary form in the ancient states), were created more slowly and intermittently, but even they were begun by the twelfth century. Little is known about the early growth in these, presumably because historians have not generally been interested in such things. But there is a large and well-known historical literature on the massive systems of mercantilist state planning and bureaucratic regulations that began in these centuries.[7]

Except for the great explosion in modernist millennialism, rationalism-scientism, and the vast expansions into megastatism in the last century, little that is totally new has been added since the development of these medieval paternalist-mercantilist welfare states. Their importance and basic similarities to our modern explosions in secular statism were long ago recognized by some historians. In 1914 Henri Pirenne argued that the dynamics of the great waxings and wanings of state powers in that age were very similar to those of later periods, including the new age of massive central governments he so presciently saw developing in his day. Some historians, notably Reinhold Dorwart in his work *The Prussian Welfare State Before 1740*, have emphasized the continuities since the explosion of medieval welfare states, see the Enlightenment political economists (at least the physiocrats and the Scottish moral-political philosophers) as the first great break with that tradition, and see the rise of the modernist welfare states as a counterrevolution against this Scottish Enlightenment (a major point in the works of Friedrich Hayek):

> The common denominator of all three stages is the police power legally inherent in the state and the exercise of that power to promote "welfare." The distinguishing marks of each stage involve differing attitudes toward the extent of state intervention, the areas of intervention, and the definition of "welfare," both individual and general, to be promoted by the state. The evolution of the welfare state is a dynamic process adjusting in theory and actuality to historical changes in political and social institutions and in human values. The underlying philosophy, the ultimate goals to be achieved, the degree of intervention in public and private life, the element of coercion or restriction of the rights of the individual, all are a composite mirror which reflects a particular definition of "welfare state."[8]

Clearly there are great continuities. Nevertheless, in most of the most successful medieval welfare states, in England and most of all in France, there was a great interregnum. The great expansions of bureaucratic statist powers led them into the quagmire of Caesarism, the Hundred Years War and its aftermath of prolonged decline in the economy and in government powers, which was greatly exacerbated by the outbreaks of the Black Plague in the second half of the fourteenth century. The decline of statist powers was so great, and alienation and rage against the officials so great, that serious revolutions erupted. However, the most famous of these peasant rebellions, that nominally led by Wat Tyler in England, also shows that the sacred state of the king was still enshrined, if a bit shredded. The revolution was so widespread that its leaders had a real chance of either building their own state or doing away with the centralized state. The representatives of the king then intervened personally and convinced Tyler to trust him enough to negotiate for a peaceful resolution to their differences. When he did he was struck down. The revolt fell apart when his followers quailed before the prospect of attacking the sacred person of the king. They were later hunted down and killed. They were among the many human beings who have lost their heads from too much trust of the sacred state and its sacred rulers. By this time the often-uneasy alliance of Church and secular state was apparently succeeding in convincing most of the people that their rulers ruled by divine right, a mythical conviction that was to reach its apogee only three centuries later. The great enabling myth of The Great Chain of Being was increasingly becoming a background, taken-for-granted truth, so that more and more people assumed that God had decreed the statist hierarchy as absolute. The Great Chain of Being permeated this age as much as the great myth of The Failure of Economic Freedom in The Great Depression and salvation through statist planning permeates our age.

In the fifteenth and sixteenth centuries, both secular and sacred statism grew to new heights. This is the great age of the immensely corrupt and tyrannical Renaissance popes and of what Hugh Trevor-Roper has called the Renaissance Welfare States.[9] Bureaucracies, legal codes, mercantilist economic planning and regulation, monopolies, payoff systems, rampant inflation, government bankruptcies, stagnations, depressions, exoduses and expulsions, show trials, secret police, Inquisitions, absolutism veiled by propaganda, Caesarism, and even open claims to totalitarian powers by new tyrants grew massively across the continent. It was almost a dress rehearsal for the explosion over the last century of our modernist megastates.[10] Perhaps the only things that prevented Renaissance secular statism from reaching our megaproportions was the continuing countervailing absolutism of the Church, the countervailing local corporatism of the guilds in many areas, and their relative lack of rationalism-scientism, modernist secular millennialism, and the full panoply of the modern technologies of agitprop. The monstrous deceits and murderous actions of the absolutist kings and popes, and the absurd statist theories created by their intellectual grantsmen to rationalize their soaring statism may seem pale beside our modernist creations, but they went far in the same direction and were remarkably similar in their basic forms.

Today's vast secular statist bureaucracies of France, Spain, Russia, and elsewhere have been "reformed" many times over the centuries in the never-ending struggle of statists against the fatal stagnation eventually produced by bureaucracies, but they remain remarkably similar to their predecessors of this long-ago era of monarchic absolutism. The Hapsburg monarchs are gone, but the ossified Spanish bureaus they built on the dry and dusty plains in the new city of Madrid still strangle the pluralism and smother the native creativity of the Spanish people, impoverish them, and incentivize a sense of fatalistic resignation. (We can, however, still see the cultural entrepreneur-ship of the Catalonians and other peoples bubbling in the ever-present under-grounds.) Even Ivan the Terrible might be shocked at the immensity of the tyrannical powers of the KGB, the descendant of his own terroristic *oprichniki*, but he would recognize and applaud their statist rationales and operations. Colbert, the most famous head of French economic planning and regulation in the seventeenth century, would be filled with envy by the vastness of the modernist French bureaucracies and their labyrinthine regulations of life, but he would recognize them as legitimate descendants of "Colbertisme," so well described over a century ago by Henry Thomas Buckle:

> In every quarter, and at every moment, the hand of government was felt. Duties on importation, and duties on exportations; bounties to raise up a losing trade, and taxes to pull down a remunerative one; this branch of industry forbidden, and that branch of industry encouraged; one article of commerce must not be grown, because it was grown in the colonies, another article might be grown and bought, but not sold again, while a third article might be bought and sold, but not leave the country. Then, too, we find laws to regulate the interest of money; custom-house arrangements of the most vexatious kind, aided by a complicated scheme, which was well called the sliding scale—a scheme ot such perverse ingenuity that the duties constantly varied on the same article, and no man could calculate beforehand what he would have to pay. . .A large part of all this was by way of protection: that is to say, the money was avowedly raised, and the inconvenience suffered, not for the use of the government, but for the benefit of the people; in other words, the industrious classes were robbed, in order that industry might thrive.[11]

Trevor-Roper argues that the massive growth of statist, bureaucratic powers over the economies produced growing inflation and stagnation by the seventeenth century and these in turn led to revolutions throughout Europe. No doubt the relations between the economic and political realms were vastly complex, all the more so because of the great importance of religious factors that were partly independent yet interacted with both. But it is at least clear that there were great revolutions and that in good part they were reactions both directly against the state absolutists and the economic problems they produced or exacerbated. Each nation followed a somewhat different path, but they drifted in the same general direction in the West and the opposite direction in the East. (I shall not be directly concerned with the great expansion of state totalitarianism in Russia which, with waxings and wanings, continued up to the Stolypin reforms after the revolt in 1905. Jerome Blum has shown how Russia moved in the opposite direction from the growing freedom in the West.[12])

The Western European states had widely varying degrees and dimensions of powers, some multiplied by the Church statist powers revived by the Counter Reformation reforms, some freed from these by Protestant rebellions. Very roughly, the Church remained powerful in the south (and in Poland), in all of America from Mexico south, and in the Philippines. This waxing and waning alliance—multiplication—of Church statist and secular statist powers produced the growing stagnation of the economic, scientific, and technological realms of life which has continued in *all* of those societies in comparison to the northern Protestant societies freed from the grand alliance of statist powers. This remarkably consistent correlation had little to do with religion in itself, contrary to what Max Weber argued, and everything to do with statist repression of creative worldly activity. When the Church was weak, or merely not concerned with the worldly realms, or not effectively allied with the secular states in repressing them, the southern European societies were the most creative and productive in the world. They created the basic forms of economic freedom and the spirit of it that Weber called "the spirit of capitalism," and they lost it all in direct proportion to the degree of effective alliance between the Church and secular statist bureaucracies regulating worldly life.[13] At times the alliance was so complete that Church bureaucrats became the most effective secular statists in building the power of the secular absolutists, in support of their Church absolutism as well.

Cardinals Richelieu and Mazarin were the very epitome of this holy Church and secular state alliance, though their policies aided the soaring growth of French absolutism at the expense of the overall Church absolutism, even by forming alliances with Protestant states to defeat Catholic Hapsburg Spain. They built the massive system of French bureaucratic regulations to be known later as "Colbertisme" in honor of their more secular heir.[14] In the short run their policies were immensely effective in building the powers of the French secular state both at home and abroad. At home they vanquished both the rapidly growing powers of the creative and productive Protestants and those of the nobles and judges opposed to monarchic absolutism. Their short-run legacy to France was the soaring military power and hubris of the "Sun King," whose boast "The state is me" remains to this day the cliché for absolutist pretensions. Their long-run legacy was the fall canker blooms of statist absolutism that follows the spring flowers. France, which had far greater natural resources than any other Western European state, and a culturally vastly creative people who made France the center of the "civilized" arts so closely associated with statist powers, spiraled downward into economic stagnation and one crisis after another throughout the eighteenth century. While their tiny rivals across the English channel, cursed with the blessing of few natural resources and the social chaos of weak state bureaucracies, were soaring onward and upward in creating science, technology, industry, and a world empire (which was soon to become a bureaucratic albatross on all her creative forces) at the expense of vastly endowed France. France limped from one failing bureaucratic and economic reform to another. The liberal physiocrats and intelligent businesspeople in general knew very well what was needed to stop the spiral downward into regulatory stagnation, deficit spending, inflation, and bankruptcy. A.R.J. Turgot spelled out the program needed, including the trio of "No bankruptcy, no new taxes, no loans," but was thrown out after the interest groups coalesced against him during a crop recession and inflation he did not cause. He was replaced by Jacques Necker, an avid advocate of Colbertisme, but also a banker well aware of the need to stop financing the state into bankruptcy. Even his neo-Colbertisme, which included the very modern political tactic of disguising a soaring deficit as a slight surplus, proved too much for the interest groups and the king to bear. The dismissal of this very moderate tax reformer on July 11, 1789, led to immediate outcries in the streets from a people sick and tired— "alienated"—of the endless illusions of nominal "Reforms, Reforms," and the very real ratchets-downward of economic life. On July 14 the people stormed the Bastille and the absolutist statists limped toward their destiny with the purifying absolutism of the guillotine.[15]

Classical (Conservative) Liberalism
versus Modernist Liberalism

The bias of intellectuals in favor of the power of abstract (theoretical) thought has been more extreme in Western civilization for eons than in any other civilization. This bias is found in almost all analyses of the rise of the modern democracies and of the modernist megastates. The prime movers in these analyses are almost always the carefully written, published, and preserved abstract theories of philosophers and other intellectuals. This is an obsession of great convenience and comfort to us intellectuals, but, unfortunately, any careful study of the world reveals that it is a vast oversimplification. The ideas of nonintellectuals are normally inspired by the practical realities of concrete situations to some major degree, except in people who act so "out of situation" that they are seen as insane. Ideas in turn inspire actions that change practical realities, which in turn inspire ideas, and so on. Keynesian ideas, as noted earlier, were long thought to have caused governments to launch deficit-financed programs, then were shown to have their roots in very old ideas about public works and pump priming through "easy money" (inflation) and were seen as old hat, and finally were shown to have been inspired by earlier ideas, shaped by the practical problems Britain faced in the 1920s and analyzed by Keynes in stages, formulated and reshaped by experiences and politics in the early days of the Depression, to have had little effect until the 1960s, but then to have had a great impact by providing the mantle of science for inflationary policies politicians wanted to follow to meet practical political problems they faced.

The same complexities are seen in the interactions between practical, situated realities and the theoretical ideas of classical liberalism. It is easy to show direct links between the political ideas of ancient theorists, especially Aristotle and the Stoics, those of medieval thinkers, especially Saint Thomas, and those of the early liberal philosophers, especially Locke, Montesquieu, and the American constitutionalists. So-called "histories of ideas" have done so in vast detail and assume that these inherited ideas then caused or inspired the Americans to create the roots of classical liberal democracy. These historicist eschatologists commit the same rationalistic fallacy we see in the popular eschatologists of the modernist welfare state. They assume that the liberals were responding to real oppressions, just as they said, in terms of the inherited theories of liberal philosophers. This nice and simple explanation is absurd. The Americans suffered from the least statist oppression of any of the Western peoples at the time they proclaimed eternal warfare against statist tyranny, and the statists had their own vast literature justifying absolutist welfare statism and all other degrees to throw at them as agitprop opposing all rebellion—and did so. Plato was the fount of absolutist conservatism and central planning by rationalist kings known in detail to all educated people. Thinkers like Locke were self-contradictory and obscure in the extreme compared to the brilliant statist rationalisms of Hobbes and many others. (As some historians have noted, it is remarkable that the colonists, or anyone for that matter, could make much of Locke's writings even with painful effort.[16]) The age of the American constitutionalists was also the age of Tory cries from the heart over the fall of Imperial Roman absolutism. Montesquieu now glows brightly in history, but at the time he hardly glimmered in France compared to Descartes, Bodin, Bossuet, Malebranche, and many others. As we shall see, the American constitutionalists, even at times the Jeffersonians, retained some important shreds of Platonic Toryism, especially shreds of statist ideas of the common welfare. There was no simple or homogeneous application of ideas of freedom to revolt against the mercantilist welfare states.

As Carl Becker has shown, the American constitutionalists' choices of their intellectual sources and their interpretations of these were deeply grounded in their own practical experience of English constitutionalism, of representative government in the "backwoods" where the long arm of the British bureaucracies weighed lightly, and in the political-drift processes they helped to create:

> Locke did not need to convince the colonists because they were already convinced; and they were already convinced because they had long been living under governments which did, in a rough and ready way, conform to the kind of government for which Locke furnished a reasoned foundation. The colonists had never in fact lived under a government where "one man. . .may do to all his subjects whatever he pleases." They were accustomed to living under governments which proceeded, year by year, on a tacitly assumed compact between rulers and ruled, and which were in fact very largely dependent upon the "consent of the governed." How should the colonists not accept a philosophy, however clumsily argued, which assured them that their own governments, with which they were well content, were just the kind that God had designed men by nature to have![17]

The continental intellectuals shared the same general tradition of thought as the Americans and British and were probably on average better versed in it. They commonly had suffered far greater oppression from the mercantilist welfare states, both sacred and secular; and many of them, notably the French philosophes, were far more enraged by it than the Americans were at the relatively weak British monarch, ministers, and bureaucrats. The great majority of continental intellectuals later revolted against the oppression, stagnation, and inflation of their statists, ushering in the vastly complex drifts and protracted conflicts of *The Age of the Democratic Revolution*, as R.R. Palmer has so aptly described it. But even those living in nearby nations went off in different specific directions. Some, notably the Dutch, nearby neighbors of the French and long oppressed by the Hapsburg sacred-and-secular welfare state, drifted in the same general direction as the Americans and British. Many of the continentals wound up far more modernist, rationalist, millennial, and violent.

The obvious common intellectual sources and revolt against the bureaucratic oppressions of the ancient regime had led historians of ideas to emphasize the commonalities in *The Liberal Tradition In European Thought*, with due allowances for the many individual variations.[18] Jacob Talmon, however, has shown that the many shared sources and abstract ideas obscure the far more important differences of political ideas and practices between the American and British classical liberals on the one side and what he calls the tradition of "totalitarian democracy" that came to dominate the philosophes and the French revolution.[19] The French were also drawing upon Augustinian Catholic and French sources, little known to the Americans, which emphasized far more sacred statism, absolute and rationalistic truth revealed by emanationist means, and thence modernist millennialism. (See appendix IV.) Such ideas definitely existed in the colonies and the new federation and even show up on the American dollar today. But Americans overwhelmingly rejected the absolutist implications that the French drew from them. The most important factor leading to the differences in selections from generally common sources and their applications to specific political ideas and practices seems to have been the far vaster sacred-and-secular statism suffered by the French and most other continentals. It was this which inspired the far greater rationalism and millennialism of the French, which Talmon called "political messianism,"[20] a far greater rationalism and secular millennialism that led to the explosion of modernist millennialism in the French revolution (for reasons explained in chapter 6).

American Welfare Federationism versus Welfare Statism

The conserving passion of human nature is the foundation for traditional legitimacy found in all human societies, even in our more futuristic modernist age. And it is this traditional legitimacy that makes historicistic eschatology, or the explanation of sacred final causes in terms of origins, such a vitally important part of the real and mythological histories of all families, nations, and states. The Western Judeo-Christian ideas of the compact between God and man and of the millennially directed nature of history greatly accentuate this natural tendency. The secular-yet-sacred compact that is the foundation of all American legal and political life, the Constitution, has made the history of the origins of our present political values, ideas, and laws of vital importance to us all. American history has always been a battleground for our legal and political differences. Our modernists, regardless of their preference for historical amnesia and for living in not-yet-existing futures—the utopias of science fiction and of scientistic central planning—have invaded this battleground with crusading fervor. Hardly an iota of historical facts has been left unreconstructed by our avowed "revisionists" or their unavowed allies. At the extreme, they have tried to show that there is a direct—and necessary—historicistic line from the supposed welfare statism of the constitutionalists up to our modernist megastatism.

Reconstructionism, deconstructionism, and revisionism of numerous stripes and shades can always find some strands of empirical support in the American record. Colonial America was a vastly pluralistic set of societies open to all the world and steadily became more so over the next two centuries. Many of the Tories most publicly committed to statism fled after the revolution, but many statists of all degrees remained. While it is hard to find any Rousseaus or Condorcets among native-bred Americans in the early decades, it is easy to find many Thomas Paines dedicated to somewhat-less-extreme modernist ideas of welfare statism and central planning. And one thing that is clear about the real American history is that the great political conflicts between the federalists and the Jeffersonians revolved around ideas and practices that were quite similar, though by no means the same, as those around which our present political wars rage. Fortunately, we need not get embroiled in most of these conflicts. What matters for our analysis is only the broad trends of developments, which are much clearer, if not uncontroversial.[21]

The distrust of any strong central government is obvious in the fact that the Americans refused at first to form anything but a loosely confederated set of ideas and practices for negotiating their common interests and differences. This was in spite of the obvious benefit of providing for the common defense against a still feared and powerful Britain by forming a strong central government. Many Americans, especially those on the frontier, were obviously gut-level anarchists who took such slogans as "Give me liberty or give me death" so seriously that they were willing to run any danger rather than run the danger of having a central government that might drift into the awful imperial powers of earlier states. They strongly opposed the mercantilist central planning they knew so well from the British navigation acts. As Patrick Henry said, "Fetter not commerce! Let her be as free as air. She will range the whole creation, and return on the four winds of heaven to bless the land of plenty with plenty." Thomas Jefferson summed it up: "The system into which the United States wished to go was that of freeing commerce from every shackle." Even moderates such as Benjamin Franklin warned, "Those who would give up essential liberty to purchase a little temporary safety deserve neither liberty nor safety."

Though they did not have access to the vast historical evidence we do, the American leaders, and the Scottish "moral philosophers" who inspired them, were well aware of the specific forms of welfare states in the ancient world, both in Periclean Athens and in the totalitarian empires, and in European totalitarian (monarchic) mercantilist welfare states, especially the "benevolent absolutism" of their own day. It was not only King George III who moralistically and militarily insisted that his imperial policies in America were necessary for the common welfare. Indeed, Frederick was far more famous for his insistence on the "necessity" of "benevolent absolutism," including his planning and funding of massive state industries, for attaining the common welfare of his Prussian welfare state.

They knew the arguments in favor of absolutist (totalitarian) welfare states so well they took it for granted their fellow citizens and readers everywhere would too and would see that it was precisely this form of welfare state against which they were rebelling. They knew very well what a fatal temptation it was to the insecure, the envious, the greedy, and, above all, to those ignorant of history and practical experience to believe in the sincerity and practicality of these honeyed snares. Even Thomas Jefferson, one of those most tempted to believe over much in the efficacy of rationalism, pleaded with the people to heed the lessons of history and thus to reject all activist governments, above all those wrapped in the mantle of "caring" controls of the citizens' lives. As he was to sum up this view: "Beware of energetic governments. They are always oppressive. . . .If we can prevent government from wresting the labors of the people under the pretense of caring for them, we shall be happy."

It is commonly assumed in our age of greater statism that the great problems experienced under the confederation of American ex-colonies proved the necessity of having a strong centralized state to "order" social life through central plans, at least of the minimal form known as legislation, if not of the more extreme form of regulatory fiat we now have. This is quite unfounded. The problems they experienced were the result of having thirteen central governments, with widely varying degrees of federationism and statism found in them, most pursuing the usual welfare statist programs of regulating trade, trying to begger their neighbors and aggrandize their own powers. What they experienced were all the problems of statist conflicts so obvious throughout the first five thousand years of the history of states, and toward the extreme known as the "Balkanized" situation in which many states of roughly equal power compete against each other. They were clearly not very statist compared to the average imperial state, but their problems were merely less as a result, not different in kind. Had they drifted jointly toward even fewer statist powers at their local levels, their problems of statism would have drifted away. Since they did not, their inter-statist (not international) problems were as painful as they have always been.

Since the understanding of this was not widespread enough, and since they would still have faced the ever-present threat of the great state powers of Britain had they moved toward fewer state powers in general, they drifted toward a centralized federation. This was clearly a drift process at work, not a matter of conscious choice by many. The convention called to discuss solving the problems was not entrusted in any way with forming a strong central government. The convention, possibly caught up in the mob passions of statism, became a "run away" or "rogue" convention and wound up proposing a federal union. As elementary school children still learn, even the writers of the proposed constitution knew that most people would likely reject it out of their ingrained dread of the benevolent absolutist statism of their day. The Bill of Rights was added as a verbal and, hopefully, legal guarantee against the central government ever becoming very powerful, and a team of the most brilliant journalists in history set about selling the plan to the people in the essays later published as *The Federalist*, in spite of the antifederalist and profederationist ideas they generally presented.

The entire political theory of *The Federalist*, and the works of political philosophers like Jefferson, show that they believed *all powers must be checked by other powers because any unchecked power will expand inexorably to serve its own interests, not someone else's, nor everyone's in common.* The elected representatives were to check the power of minorities who seek to oppress everyone else (criminals and rebels) and of foreign powers. The customs, self-control in the service of rationally calculated interests, the Constitution (especially the Bill of Rights), the courts, and the elected officials were in turn to be the checks on the tyranny of majorities, the mobocracy dreaded since the ancient world. But the ultimate election of officials by the people (or the roughly 5 percent of them who could vote at that time) was the ultimate check on all official powers. King George III and other "tyrants" had taught them to be quite suspicious of rulers' interpretations of the common interest of the body politic. Even Hamilton, far more conservative than any of the others, wrote stingingly of those who "assuming the pretext of some public motive, have not scrupled to sacrifice the national tranquility to personal advantage."[22] He was also so aware of the great multitude of conflicting passions and interests in society, including class passions and conflicts, that, rather than calling for a ruler who would serve the common interest of them all, he called for an "umpire or common judge to interpose between the contending parties;"[23] but, of course, the players would ultimately check the umpire's powers, or else. In spite of Hamilton's extreme conservatism, when he wanted to convince Americans to enact even this weak central government he presented it as an "umpire."

Of course they believed a central government in America should promote the general welfare. It would have been absurd to propose a government for any other purpose. (Who would conceivably support a government intentionally useless—or dedicated to the general misery!?) But their classical liberal welfare federation was to be the exact opposite of the absolutist welfare state. In the classical liberal welfare federation, liberty was the very heart, the soul, the foundation of the general welfare: without liberty *from* almost all government constraints, there could be no general welfare for Americans. But, in addition, it was liberty that would do more than anything else possibly could to promote the general welfare, for liberty *from* government power would at the same time be individual freedom *to* pursue their own welfare—their own happiness—more efficiently than anyone else possibly could, and certainly vastly more reliably than anyone else ever would. J.B. Say, whose works simplifying and interpreting *The Wealth of Nations* were extremely popular in the United States in the early nineteenth century, made this very clear.

All of this would have been enough to justify the conclusion that the American experiment in the System of Natural Liberty was a most thoroughgoing revolution against the absolutist welfare state. But their revolt went even further. All pursuit of the general welfare was to be sternly constrained by the rule of laws that were themselves ultimately to be derived from the laws of nature, including human nature, ultimately decreed by God. The American government was specifically forbidden by the Bill of Rights from constraining a whole series of forms of behavior believed to be vital to the preservation of liberty; and all government powers allowed by the Constitution were to be severely constrained by the ancient precedents and forms of the common law.

The Counterrevolution against the
Classical Liberal Welfare Federation

The original goals of Americans in establishing our federal government were stated with stark simplicity in the preamble to the Constitution: "We, the people of the United States, in order to form a more perfect Union, establish justice, insure domestic tranquility, provide for the common defense, promote the general welfare, and secure the blessings of liberty to ourselves and our posterity, do ordain and establish the Constitution for the United States of America." We see from this that one of the basic goals of our central government from its beginning was to "promote the general welfare." Indeed, its only other general goals of equal importance were those of providing for the common defense and securing the blessings of liberty, since it was intended that justice and tranquility (law and order) be provided overwhelmingly by the states and local governments. Our central government, then, was always intended to be a welfare government *and* a securer of liberty.

How, then, was the federal government to promote this general welfare and secure the blessings of liberty? That, of course, was the one crucial question that concerned all of the founders of the republic in their earnest anguish over whether there should be any central government at all. It was more or less clear how to provide for the common defense (though there were to be bitter arguments over the militia and the standing army), so these other two coequal goals were the focus of their concerns. And their concerns were grave indeed, for they knew from their scholarship and from personal experience how central governments throughout the history of the world have striven mightily under every conceivable guise to usurp local powers and to oppress the liberties of the people. Above all, they knew how the British monarchy had grown, largely under its self-proclaimed "necessities of warfare," which had actually been created by statist struggles for power, in the previous century from the meager powers given to William of Orange (and constrained by the Declaration of Rights in 1689) to the oppressive "tyrannies" of George III. How was it at all possible to have a central government that would provide for the common defense but at the same time promote the general welfare and secure the blessings of liberty to all the people?

The classical liberal answer to this question was the true genius of Thomas Jefferson and the mass of common Americans who launched the Revolution of 1800 and thence the Great Experiment in the System of Natural Liberty of the American Republic. Their answer, in total opposition to the ancient mercantilist ideas of the European governments which assumed the necessity of the ancient forms of Big Government, was startlingly simple: "That government governs best which governs least." In other words, that government which most secured liberty to the people would also do the most to promote the general welfare. They believed the entire success of this great but perilous social experiment in liberty rested on that one basic principle, that bedrock principle of the System of Natural Liberty which they believed to be as basic to a free human society—and as revolutionary—as Newton's principle of gravity is to the physical universe. If the central government could be kept as small and weak as possible, while still allowing for the common defense and some minimal powers to maintain law and order among the states, both essential to the preservation of individual liberty, then individual liberty and all other dimensions of general welfare would be optimized. All the people would be as free as is possible in man's necessarily social condition, as Locke, Montesquieu, and many others had argued; and as prosperous as possible, as the physiocrats and the Scottish moral philosophers (Adam Ferguson, Adam Smith, David Hume, and many others) had shown. Yet social order would be optimized by the operation of the "invisible hand" of the spontaneous natural order that grows out of the free, rational but common law-and-custom-bound calculations of interests and reciprocal altruism, as Mandeville and his successors had argued.[24] Rather than pursuing the interminable warfare dictated by the logic of mercantilist collectivism, individual liberty and decentralized government would lead to peace and order, just as Spinoza had argued a century earlier that the freedom of religion protected by tolerance and law produced peace and piety: ". . .not only is perfect liberty to philosophize compatible with devout piety and with the peace of the State, but. . .to take away such liberty is to destroy the public peace and even piety itself."

Independence, individual freedom (including the all-important spiritual freedom), prosperity, peace, mutual caring, and withal equal justice before the law and social order—unity in diversity. What could be more conducive to human happiness? That was the general welfare ideal of the System of Natural Liberty. The goal of keeping the government inherently weak and small then became the central operational goal of the Constitution. The

Constitutionalists tried to do this by ingeniously elaborating upon Locke and Montesquieu's theory, which was based largely on the model of the Roman Republic and on the Whig (Burkean) model of the British Constitution as they practiced it in their own colonial legislatures. They divided the government into three more-or-less equal parts and put them into conflict with each other. They soon weakened the government even more by explicitly setting stern restrictions to its powers in the Bill of Rights.

It seems most likely that some of the federalists supporting the new constitution, notably the Hamiltonians, were somewhat deceitful in their purposes. Though they did not know it by our name, most of these political philosophers were well aware of the basic idea of the *iron law of oligarchy* by which states and their bureaucratic regulators drift toward ever-greater powers, until they pass into the critical range beyond which they erode their powers more rapidly than they can build them. They had excellent historical reasons to expect that once the people had entered into the realm of central controls, under whatever pretexts or truths, they would be subjected to the ever-increasing powers of the rulers and bureaucrats. Since most of the people were obviously afraid of just that, they had to be given every rhetorical guarantee. The one that counted most was the *structuralist fallacy* that was to become central to the social scientism of the next two centuries, but which was really a new version of the basic idea of the state as a separate and higher level of reality. The constitutionalists and federalists argued that the checks and balances provided for by the Constitution would prevent any one branch or any group of individuals from getting enough power to cause a tipping or tilting in its direction that would lead by drift into the massive statism they dreaded. The best theorists recognized that there could be nothing extrapersonal, automatic, or structural to any such human social processes. They recognized that only eternal vigilance and action by the people to prevent that drift would check it. Those who did and who at the same time recognized that the people would be lulled into nonvigilance and the iron law of oligarchy would come into full sway, recognized how perilous the experiment was, and opposed it. Others, such as Jefferson, knew it was a perilous experiment indeed, but hoped the people would remain vigilant enough. They did for many decades, but then the understanding of all of this waned under the ever-growing pressures of the modernist myths and rhetorics, and the drift into megastatism began to accelerate.

As soon as they came to power, the federalists began drifting toward ever-greater powers. While Congress rejected some of Hamilton's more extreme mercantilist proposals for the central statist planning of the economy, the "industrial policy" of the early days, other ratchets-up in statism were widely accepted, notably the Bank of the United States, and some were enacted but rejected in practice, notably the Alien and Sedition law. The statism of the federalists looks puny by our megastatist standards, but it frightened the American people enough to produce a massive ratchet-up in vigilance and the Jeffersonian revolution, the first great American ratchet-down in statist powers under the Constitution. Bernard Bailyn and his coauthors have described this second American Revolution of 1800 in striking terms:

> Believing that most of the evils afflicting mankind in the past had flowed from the abuses of political establishments, the Republicans in 1800 rejected outright the traditional eighteenth-century conviction cherished by the Federalist that government was the most effective mechanism of social integration. They set about deliberately to carry out what they rightly believed was the original libertarian aim of the Revolution of 1776—to reduce the overawing and dangerous power of government. They wanted to form a national republic based on their inherited country-Whig opposition ideology and cast in the image of the Revolutionary state governments of 1776 with their diluted executive powers. They envisioned a central state whose authority would resemble that of the old Articles of Confederation more than that of the European type of state the Federalists of the 1790s had thought essential in the modern world. They sought in fact to create a general government that would rule without the traditional attributes of power. . . .The Republicans in fact meant to have an insignificant national government. . . .Thus the roll of federal officials was severely cut back. All tax inspectors and collectors were eliminated. The diplomatic establishment was reduced to three missions—in Britain, France, and Spain. The Federalist dream of creating a modern army and navy in emulation of Europe disappeared; the military budget was cut in half.[25]

Yes, Jefferson said, the American nation too was to be an empire, but it would be an "empire of liberty," not a bureaucratic state oppressing the freedom of the people.

The Jeffersonian revolution produced a great ratchet-down in federal government powers for at least three decades and continued to affect American political decisions up to the present, obviously with decreasing effects. But this was not an era of total laissez-faire policies, nor one devoid of powerful statist ideas and policies. It is obvious that there has never been an era in American history in which "every heart beat to that iron string" of self-reliance, as once popular myths would have us believe about the era of supposed "laissez-faire." Local governments, especially at the appropriately named state level, were the primary loci of statist ideas and powers. They were extremely mixed, but some of them were statist enough to please most Tories in disguise as federalists. At the national level the federalists built a power base in the Supreme Court under John Marshall, in spite of the Jeffersonians' bitter struggles to curtail the powers of the federal courts. The Jeffersonians themselves continued their uneasy alliance with some statist ideas in allowing slavery, tariffs, and a much-weakened U.S. Bank. Even Jefferson consciously and anxiously compromised his own principles of federationism in some of his dealings with massive foreign states, notably in his purchase of the Louisiana Territory and the war-power trade measures against Britain.

State powers always have a great advantage in concentrating military powers (as long as morale is high and the bureaucracy not too gigantic or entrenched) and the nonstatist or very weak statist group attacked by them normally resorts to greatly increased statist powers to cope with them, or becomes their subjects. The serious questions in American history, all faced by the Jeffersonians, have been how to keep these to a minimum consistent with the survival of our liberties and, most difficult of all, how to ratchet-down state powers once the crisis is over.

The Slow and Erratic Drift into the Modernist Welfare State

The theodicies of our megastates normally present Count Bismarck as the first of the "welfare statists." They argue that his social security programs for industrial workers were intended to gain political support for the rising Prussian and all-German state from their new parliamentary representatives, thereby undermining their support for more sweeping socialist and internationalist programs. They seem to be right about some of his motives, but fail to see the vastly more important fact that this was merely an extension and modification of the vast welfare statism of the Hohenzollern dynasty that stretched back centuries, as Dorwort has shown. They also fail to note that this same drift process was at work in all of the other huge bureaucratic states and was merely an adoption of new bureaucratic and political tactics to meet the new situations emerging with industrialism, the relative decline of Church welfare statism, the growth of parliamentary powers, the widening of the electorates, and most of all the growth of modernist millennialism. In none of these nations was there ever much knowledge among the general population or the educated people of the basic ideas of classical liberal political economy and Whig conservatism. There is an obvious gradient of knowledge about these ideas running from the high plateau in America and Britain steadily downward as one moved east (with some exceptions of important outposts, such as some economists in Vienna). The practices of economic freedom and political freedom—democracy—were everywhere very highly correlated and the knowledge of the liberal and conservative ideas of economic and political freedom were everywhere highly correlated with both, though more roughly. The interdependencies were vastly complex, but they are quite obvious with telescopic hindsight.[26]

In France there were well-known writers such as Say and Bastian who continued the traditions of the physiocrats and the Scottish moral philosophers and interpreted them for the mass of general readers. In Germany there were very few of these liberal or Whig thinkers, and economic thought was dominated by the so-called institutional or "cathedral" economists, whose ideas are now well represented in America by the phallanxes of Galbraithians and industrial policy central planners. In Russia there were some important liberal thinkers by the early twentieth century, when Russia was rapidly reforming after the terrible loss of a war to Japan, under the decentralizing policies of Stolypin and with the growing powers of the Diet. But the ideas and practices of freedom, especially in the economic realm on which all of life ultimately depends, were weak even in France, were easily swept away by the socialists of the Weimar Republic and the National Workers Socialist Party, and left Russia in the boxcars with the officials of the deported Kerensky government.

Today the general knowledge of those ideas of economic freedom and political freedom, of the great System of Natural Liberty that inspired the American founders and their British counterparts in Britain, is so vague that it is hard even for historians to understand how important they were at the time. Today American and British college students are far more likely to study Marxism and neo-Marxism in detail, to delight in witty slashes at the ideas of economic freedom by Galbraith, and to dream with popular economists of industrial policy miracles than to read the classical works on the System of Natural Liberty by Locke, Montesquieu, Smith, Burke, Jefferson, the writers of *The Federalist,* or any of their legions of heirs. Hardly any of our social scientists have read them, unless they were forced to do so in survey courses by some "conservative" professor. Instead, they insist that all of those ideas were merely myths foisted upon the workers by "the capitalist class," "special interests," "monopolists," "robber barons," or others on the rolls of their litany of stigmata. This has encouraged them to assume that the American and British workers ("proletariat") suffered from "false consciousness" and that, had they had any serious and truthful thoughts about economics, they would have voted in our current welfare state programs at the time. Their argument that the "have-nots will use democratic votes to take from the haves" has become the conventional wisdom of Marxists and almost all economists, other social scientists, and journalists. It is basicly the same "selfish interest group theory" handed down from the ancient social thinkers, who had seen the demogogues get the support of the people by using the state treasuries to pay them off. It was probably experience with the Periclean political machine paying off the Athenian "mob" that led Plato to declare what became the Tory political critique of democracy over two thousand years: "When a tyrant comes into being, the root he springs from is the people's champion and no other." Down through the centuries the evidence seemed to confirm this interest-group theory over and over again, and it is obvious today that most of our politicians are involved in paying the voters for their votes with promises of material gains on a colossal scale and with more skimpy real goods. (See appendix III for other details on the argument presented below.)

Tories everywhere and many non-Tories finally believed that the new democracies would quickly succumb to the most obvious fatal flaw of the ancient democracies and republics, the tyranny of "mobocrats" and other demogogues who would use the powers of government to legalize robbery of the capital—the savings—of the haves by the have-nots. Jefferson himself had admitted, in view of all the evidence, that America was undertaking a perilous "experiment." The spread of suffrage to the less propertied and finally to the respectable poor enflamed these ancient dreads. The Jacksonian Revolution of the "common man" caused panic among many.

No one put it more forcefully or blatantly than Chancellor Kent did in 1837, at the height of Jacksonian policies: "My opinion is that the admission of universal suffrage and a licentious press are incompatible with government and security to property, and the government and character of this country are going to ruin. . . .We are going to destruction—all checks and balances and institutions in this country are threatened with destruction from the ascendancy of the democracy of numbers and radicalism and the horrible doctrine and influence of Jacksonism."[27] William Sullivan concluded, "I think that our experiment of self government approaches to a total failure."[28] Even Noah Webster, the famous Whig aspirant for the presidency, despaired and proposed one house of Congress be restricted to those of a proper age and wealth, "thus the supremacy of property may be assured, and America yet saved from democracy."[29]

This ancient Tory theory sounds so reasonable to many people that it has become the hidden foundation for most of the rationalistic explanations of the rise of the modernist welfare states (see appendix III). The best refinement of it is found in the idea of many economists that any potential recipient of government favor has a greater incentive to seek it than the average citizen has to resist it. The cost to the potential recipient is small compared to the hoped-for gain; whereas the potential opponent would bear a roughly equal cost to stop him, with no gain in sight (unless he hopes to get it instead, in which case his costs are minimized and expected gains maximized by cooperating with the other supplicant, that is, forming or joining an interest group). Gordon Tullock, who has given one of the finest expositions of the rational interest-group theory, quotes approvingly the classical statement of it almost a century ago by Vilfredo Pareto:

[Imagine] that in a country of 30 million inhabitants it is proposed, under some pretext or other, to get each citizen to pay out one franc a year, and to distribute the total amount amongst 30 persons. Every one of the donors will give up one franc a year; every one of the beneficiaries will receive one million francs a year. The two groups will differ very greatly in their response to this situation. Those who hope to gain a million a year will know no rest by day or night. They will win newspapers over to their interest by financial inducements and drum up support from all quarters. . .In contrast, the individual who is threatened with losing one franc a year—even if he is fully aware of what is afoot—will not for so small a thing forgo a picnic. . .In these circumstances, the outcome is not in doubt; the spoliators will win hands down.[30]

Many variants of this basic idea have been proposed, but they all suffer from a few embarrassments. The most telling argument against the ancient theory and Pareto's special application of it is that America's common voters did not vote that way. There were always multifarious schemes by political and business con artists to milk the federal treasury of the United States, as their legions of brethren have always sought to milk any source of wealth by equally deceitful means. *But in the overwhelming majority of cases the political schemes failed completely,* even when the conspirators had immensely more loot to gain than a paltry million francs a year.

Even after the Republicans had launched the first programs of the business welfare state (see below), Jay Gould and James Fisk suffered a disaster in 1869 when they tried to lure and bribe government support for their gold-cornering scheme, in spite of the immense loot that might have been taken and the immense sums at their disposal to lobby the politicians and bureaucrats. Almost all lesser schemes were routinely stigmatized as the schemes of "hogs" (or similar contemptible creatures) trying to stuff themselves at the federal "trough" and were soundly defeated. The Bank of the U.S., a rare success, was sold by the politicians initially as something good for everyone because it would end the inflation so endemic to many of the local banks, but the people became aroused over its monopolistic privileges and cancelled it, in spite of the success the first bank had in stabilizing the currency, in spite of the immense vested interests its owners and other beneficiaries had in continuing it, and in spite of the immense effort they put into trying day and night to save it. Only on those extremely rare instances, specifically those of government subsidies for land purchases, roads, mails, and the tariffs, could the people be convinced to grant interest-group privileges, and in those major ones they were convinced because they could see the real gains to most of them of mails, roads, and land subsidies and, apparently, failed to see the real (but hidden) losses to most of them incurred by the tariff violation of consumer freedom or sovereignty. Moreover, even these rare instances were administered to avoid establishing huge government bureaucracies (the mails probably being the biggest exception) so the direct, visible costs were roughly minimized and the ancient specter of bureaucratic tyranny was exorcised.

It is obvious that in almost every case of special-interest pleading the supplicants, whether con artists or sincere would-be saviors of the common good, were vehemently denounced as "selfish interests" and "criminal monopolies" by everyone from Adam Smith to Andrew Jackson and Jimmy Carter. It has always been vitally important to the success of selfish interest groups that they present themselves as a public-interest group dedicated to the common welfare. Most people have known this, and, as a result, were normally extremely suspicious of any such proclamations of public spiritedness by any supplicants for public favor. As long as there was little conception of a common interest as distinct from the aggregated general interest of all individuals, and as long as the direct and external costs of bureaucracy were not hidden by the myth of rationalistic planning by bureaucrats, it was extremely difficult to convince the people that any special-interest group privileges served the public interest. Moreover, thoughtful Americans (perhaps anticipating the modern "rational expectations" theory) generally argued that it was to the benefit of everyone to be extremely vigilant in opposing all such creeping accretions (drifts) of federal government favor because they would lead in time to monopolistic powers and to an explosion of special-interest privileges detrimental to the real general interest. Interest-group theory fails to see that there is even a cliché of common sense that points to the inherent weakness of interest-group politics. A student who speaks out without permission is routinely reprimanded by the teacher for endangering class order. The student commonly insists, "But my speaking out did not in fact create disorder." The teacher then informs this young egoist, "Yes, but, if I let you speak out, everyone will soon do so and social order will be destroyed." In fact, new teachers who do not recognize this commonsense truth often let little bits of deviance go unpunished and soon there is a drift into an explosion of deviance that, once unleashed, is exceedingly difficult to reverse. To fail to see this truth is to fail to see *the principle of social order decomposition*: that is, to fail to see that a given social order can only be maintained by trying systematically, universally to enforce its fundamental rules (including, of course, enforcing the rules by which the rules are changed). Deviance unchecked will spread, so that what one individual gets away with will tend to become more general. Exceptions to the rules tend to become the rules and, thereby, to destroy the foundation of the original order. This is precisely what conservatives insisted was true about special-interest pleas, and the classical liberals were truly conservative in this way.

The classical liberal abhorrence of monopoly, and of business groups demanding favors—regulations of the market—that led to them was very explicit in Adam Smith. In 1834 William Leggett put it succinctly, "If we analyze the nature and essence of free government, we shall find that they are more or less free in proportion to the absence of monopolies."[31] It was probably during the Jacksonian "era of the common man" that this opposition to special interests and favors, even for the poor, was most intense, because it was believed that in the long run they would really work against the interests of most citizens, including those (such as the poor) they were intended to help. The average educated American of that day knew that for hundreds of years the mercantilist welfare states had proclaimed they were serving the common interest by mandating and subsidizing monopolies. They knew the fact was that government programs for the common interest wound up drifting to the interest only of the most powerful, the rich special interests—the monopolies—and the politicians who milked them.

It wouldn't surprise the most knowledgeable of them to learn that our "regulatory" agencies, supposedly intended to serve the public interest, drifted into regulating, or better, rigging the market monopolistically for the benefit of the biggest railroads, trucking firms, airlines, and so on; or that our War on Poverty in fact wound up being a secret war on the poor in which the poor were largely statistical phantoms serving as the pawns of a vast "poverty industry" who milked off much of the money for the poor, used the poor as a moralistic shibboleth to attack the moral susceptibilities of caring Americans, put the poor in a state of dependency on themselves through a mass of regulations ranging from minimum-wage laws to certification laws, and used part of their "poverty profits" to reelect the politicians who made all of this possible. As Jefferson and Jackson knew so well, and proclaimed so stingingly, when governments become caring they wind up supporting monopolies and oppressing the common people. In their own day the Federalists' Bank of the United States had repeated this ancient scenario (though only in miniature), giving the people a striking reminder of all the evils of government caring. What they and the voters demanded was an end to *all* privilege or, simply, equal opportunity. Jackson abolished this "development" bank with overwhelmingly popular support and against immense political pressures from the special interests.

Modernist critics of America of all varieties and degrees, from the Marxist-Lenninists to our current "liberals," have insisted in their revisionist histories that "social class"—"inequality"—was the great secret cause of the historical process emerging in America at this time. This more radical interpretation of the ancient theory of the "rich versus the poor" comes in various forms, but they generally agree that Americans were deceived by the "bourgeoisie" into believing their ideal of "equality" had been achieved, thus did not at first see how they were being oppressed by their class enemies; that they gradually became aware of this, and that the Jacksonian era of the "common man" was a first "New Deal" in which the "workers" began to "throw off their chains" by turning government into a force for their equality. This theory is wrong on almost all fronts.

Americans at that time were extremely sensitive about "class" differences and tyrannical oppressions precisely because they had lived under a statist system in which class differences were still explicit and very important, though decreasingly so, in Britain. In *The Federalist* (no. 10) James Madison proposed a theory of interests, class conflicts, and *false consciousness*—the effects of the passions on reason—which was far more explicit, systematic, and true than anything Karl Marx ever did.[32] Above all, unlike the modernist and millennial-utopian Marx, the founding fathers realized from history and their own experience that conflicts and competition, including those based on economic interests, are an inherent part of human nature in the human condition of civilization, that promises of complete equality were an ancient guise of demogogues used to tempt the ignorant masses into tyrannical oppression, and that "relief is only to be sought in the means [representative and constitutional democracy] of controlling its *effects*."[33] Had Marx and his honest followers understood class conflicts as well as the founding fathers did, they might not have lured the illiterate masses of Russia, China, and many other nations into the most class-based, totalitarian form of slavery ever endured by human beings. The constitutional means adopted by the founding fathers did increasingly allow the most political, economic, and cultural equality ever found in any civilization, as attested to fearfully by the aristocratic Tocqueville.

No major American political leader, from the Founding Fathers to Jackson and Lincoln, ever thought we were "innocent" of all materialism, or of status differences, or that we ever could live perfectly in accord with our spiritual ideals. As Seymour Martin Lipset argues in *The First New Nation*, Americans from Revolutionary days onward have been torn ambivalently by the conflict between our primary commitment to liberty and our secondary commitment to equality (and, I would add, to caring).[34] Americans were able to use some political means to decrease some of the worst conflicts by progressively instituting equal treatment by law in public settings for all adults, including spreading the franchise to broader segments of the population. In practice, though some forms of increased freedom also constitute increased equality, there is ultimately a degree of inherent conflict among liberty, equality, and caring such that one can achieve more equality or caring only by infringing general liberty. "Equal opportunity," "equal treatment before the law," and private philanthropy became the catchwords for the optimal solution of this conflict, allowing Americans to achieve a maximum of liberty commensurate with equality and caring. Andrew Jackson seems to have clearly understood this and strongly supported government action to enforce equal opportunity and treatment, while opposing attempts to produce equality beyond that, because he saw that these efforts would actually wind up producing inequality, just as the Founding Fathers believed. As he said:

> It is to be regretted, that the rich and powerful too often bend the acts of government to their selfish purposes. Distinctions in society will always exist under every just government. Equality of talents, of education, or of wealth cannot be produced by human institutions. In the full enjoyment of the Gifts of Heaven and the fruits of superior industry, economy, and virtue, every man is equally entitled to protection

by law; but when the laws undertake to add to these natural and just advantages artificial distinctions. . .to make the rich richer and the potent more powerful, the humble members of society—the farmers, mechanics, and laborers—who have neither the time nor the means of securing like favors to themselves, have a right to complain of the injustice of their government.[35]

There is every reason to believe this erstwhile "common man" proclaimed here the belief of the great majority of Americans. Jackson's common man supporters also demanded and got a gold currency because they believed the paper money of the Hamiltonians did not produce real "increases in capital" (real wealth) as Hamilton claimed, but did produce roaring inflation. And it was Jackson who stopped the paper inflation fed by state banks, by refusing to accept the paper in payment for government land. One popular cliché against paper money was "As the currency expands, the loaf contracts."[36] Economists today put it more precisely and elegantly, but those average Americans had the right ideas. They had learned the hard way the quantity theory of money which modernists later denied, thereby igniting our fire storms of inflation. The core idea of the quantity theory of money is many centuries old and was clearly stated by the sixteenth and seventeenth centuries. It states that an increase in the amount of money relative to the goods exchanged will produce a decrease in the value of money: i.e., increased money supplies relative to goods supplies produce rising prices—inflation. Modern theorists have refined it by noting that the rate of exchange, or velocity, also affects the value of money; and that the ultimate reason the relations hold is that more money is simply more supply relative to any given demand for money, and thus reduces the price in the same way the increased supply of corn at harvest reduces the price, when there are no government supports to keep corn off the market.

These "common man" ideas of Americans were extremely consistent with the basic ideas of classical liberal and (Burkean) conservative economic and political theory. This is not so remarkable when we remember that both grew from the same general experience, were selected in the light of that experience from the same traditions of Western thought, and then reinforced each other through the nineteenth century. Perhaps the one remarkable fact is how widespread the knowledge of the classical works were, at least in the somewhat popularized forms in which they were printed massively. We see the ideas repeated over and over again by American presidents, and far more so by the representatives of the common man than by others. Abraham Lincoln even made explicit reference to the crucial difference between the short-run benefits of government action and the long-run costs:

You cannot bring about prosperity by discouraging thrift. You cannot strengthen the weak by weakening the strong. You cannot help the wage earner by pulling down the wage payer. You cannot further the brotherhood of man by encouraging class hatred. You cannot help the poor by destroying the rich. You cannot keep out of trouble by spending more than you earn. You cannot build character and courage by taking away man's initiative and independence. You cannot help men permanently by doing for them what they could and should do for themselves.[37]

Of course, the presidents were not really "common" men. Most voters did not have such clear and systematic ideas, nor did they understand the classical liberal and Burkean synthesis. They relied far more on gut-level feelings growing out of the experience in which those ideas were embedded, and sometimes expressed, and on the faith of myths built on these. The revisionist, modernist historians have documented the faith in these myths, especially the myth of the vastly popular Horatio Alger "rags-to-riches" story. The modernists have been avid to show the obvious—that such myths distorted reality, at least if readers really believed a high proportion of people could soar from rags to riches. It is a vital part of their program to show Americans suffered from false consciousness about economic realities. What they have not generally noted is that these mythical convictions reinforced the widespread belief in the classical liberal and conservative synthesis, that this formed a strong bulwark against the "caring" deceits and myths of statists, and that the American people thereby soared onward and upward at a faster pace and further than any other people before or since. There is a vital difference between the waking dreams of *beneficent myths* that have some (but rarely all) of their intended consequences and the *disastrous myths* that have the unintended and dreaded consequences of statist oppression, as the myths of modernist statism have had.

The Beginning of the Drift into Modernist Statism

The widespread commitments to the ideas of the liberal and Burkean conservative synthesis, the System of Natural Liberty, and the far more widespread beliefs in the myths consistent with this synthesis formed a *cognitive bulwark* against the growth of statist ideas, myths, and operational powers. Statist ideas were always there, they were quite important in some areas of life (see below), and they were inflamed by various situational shocks, especially by war and threats of war which (in a nation not yet demoralized) produce a "rallying around the flag," the symbol of common identity that is the cornerstone of the statist myths. When these shocks were very great, as the Civil War was in both the northern nation and the southern nation, the statist myths and powers soared. This did apparently produce a longer-run weakening of the synthesis and its attendant myths, yet the bulwark, while breached, remained intact and was rebuilt after the situational threats were overcome.

The result of this interaction between the cognitive-emotional factors and the situational shocks was the irregular step-function now so well known from economic studies of the growth of our federal budgets in this century: situational threats to the nation, especially wars, produce soaring federal budgets, monetary growth, regulatory powers, and so on; the end of the threat leads to a decay toward the longer-run, prethreat trend, but this decay levels off at a higher plateau than before the threat; then another threat comes along and the ratchet-up cycle begins again. Higgs has analyzed the information and complexities of this protracted drift process in this century.[38] The same process was at work in the last century, but the decay to trend (that is, to the starting plateau) was far more complete then. It seems clear that the tendency to go back downward in statist powers weakened. Even the most powerful shock Americans have ever faced, the Civil War, was very largely overcome and the federal government reduced to far more prewar size rather quickly. (Even the great ratchet-up in monetary powers, which included federal licensing of banks, was largely undone in a few decades.)

As Higgs, Friedman, and other economists have recognized, the ultimate factor lying behind this great drift process has been the "ideological" one— ideas and myths. The specific irregular step shape of the drift in response to the great situational shocks seems best explained by a general weakening of the ideas and myths of the great synthesis against statist powers resulting from the shocks, especially the seemingly successful statist operations to overcome the threats. The catastrophically unsuccessful core operations of the southern Confederacy produced a catastrophic ratchet-downward in the welfare statist beliefs and myths in it. Waving a Confederate flag and vowing "The South Will Rise Again" has lingered as a wistful daydream, not a myth that inspires conviction. It has been noted by many, for example, that the beliefs in the efficacy of government central planning, price controls, and so on, spread and were much stronger after their apparent successes in both World Wars. I believe the evidence shows that these supposed "successes" were overwhelmingly the result of the statists' successes in managing the official information and media images. We know that blackmarket free pricing was massive at all levels of the economy, in spite of the grand proclamations of price czar John Kenneth Galbraith. But it is clear that most people believed they worked. The same can be seen in the present myths of the New Deal successes in dealing with the problems of the Depression. The actual failures were too complete for people to believe the New Deal ended the Depression, but there is great belief in the myth that the federal government did much to alleviate the problems, and very few people know any of the evidence that the government actions did the most to precipitate it and to prolong it.

It seems clear, however, that this is only one vital part of the explanation, necessary but not sufficient. The Jeffersonian Revolution of 1800 against the big government of the Federalists came after a solid decade of such big government and after it was seen as successful in overcoming many of the perceived problems of the confederation which led to the adoption of the constitution in the first place. To the Jeffersonians, and to anyone committed to the basic ideas of the great liberal-conservative synthesis, it is the very success of statist operations that is the most frightening prospect of all. It is precisely when government seems to be the most successful, either in the light of reality or by the bright glow of false official information and media images, that we have the most to fear from ever-growing statist powers, since people are hardly likely to support the growth of known failures, or dyswelfare states. As Jeffersonians would say today, successful statist powers beyond the minimum necessary for maintaining freedom from foreign tyranny or domestic tyranny are the greatest problem, not the greatest solution. The Jacksonian common men felt the same way about the U.S. Bank. The bank was not a failure in expanding credit and the money supply or in providing indirect government leverage throughout the economy. It was a danger because of these "successes," and that was the best reason for doing away with it. In the same way, the federal government's attempts today to end poverty for all time arouse resentments from some taxpayers, but hardly arouse fears over competition from the poor or for any other reasons because they are an obvious failure, whereas taxes arouse both resentments and fears because the taxation powers are real and successful.

Even more importantly, any explanation of the ratchet-up process that relies only on the shocks that preceded the ratchets-up would be largely begging the question. Consider, for example, the argument above about the importance of the appearances of the successes of the massive government central planning of the economy in World Wars I and II and in the Depression. They did indeed become important pseudo-proofs of successful government economic planning operations, but why were they tried in the first place, and why was it so easy to convince people of these pseudo-successes when there was such massive evidence to the contrary? It was not assumed to be natural for the American central government to seize control of the economy during wartime and economic shocks until this century. The Civil War was by far the greatest shock in our history. The Confederate state was seen to be attacking the most basic ideas of the Christian self and of political freedom. The federal armies lost most of their early battles, and the federal government was almost captured. Lincoln greatly ratcheted-up federal powers over legal rights, even doing away with some individuals' sacred rights of habeas corpus and speedy trials, and over some monetary powers, but he did not try to plan the economy through production czars and price czars. Central planning, even in such a small and simple government and economy as that was, is very counterproductive, as explained by the System of Natural Liberty. The same was true of economic shocks, so that economic depressions in the nineteenth century were seen by most Americans, especially the better-educated ones, to demand *less* government intervention, not more. That, of course, is what the great majority of economists and businesspeople said during the Depression. In the nineteenth century all of the basic ideas of economic planning, including the Keynesian ideas, were proposed over and over again by institutional economists and others. They were firmly rejected. And the government that lived most by the great liberal-conservative synthesis, the American government, floated upon the most creative and productive economy and society in the history of mankind—not the least. As economists like Friedman and Higgs are well aware, it was not the ratchet-up process itself that produced the vitally important shift in the tidal drift of ideas and myths.

A great many single factors have been torn from the great drift process in attempts to explain it. These range from Marxist theories of the inherent contradictions of capitalism, to Keynes's theory of the inherent tendency toward oversaving in mature capitalism, to Joseph Schumpeter's theory of the inherently superior efficiency of bureaucratic planning and production (and the current industrial policy variants of this), to the theory of the decreasing marginal utility of disposable income, to the theory of deceitful and corrupt politicians and interest groups. Most of those proposed by serious social thinkers have been plausible at certain times in explaining certain specific aspects of the drift, and I shall draw upon them at times for those purposes. (Payoffs, for example, while generally highly irrational over the long run, are very important in all megastates today. They were not important in the early stages of the drift process.) In general, however, they suffer from the fatal flaws of having been wrong in their extrapolations—as Marxists seem to delight in doing every time they predict the next final end to capitalism—and of trying to explain the systemic drift of a vast and pluralistic civilization by factors that only apply to some small parts of the civilization at certain times—as Keynes did when he used the British inter-war experience to explain the whole vastly complex drift of the world economy into the Depression. (I provide a summary and critique of the most important of these many theories, and of the more recent and useful theories of rational interest group politics in appendix III.)

Most of these specific factors seized upon have been *epiphenomena* (symptoms) or proximate contributors (amplifiers) to the *core drift process* at work, not ultimate causes. Just as the theorists of disease were misled for millennia by the symptoms of disease, mistaking such phenomenon as fever for the cause of the disease when it was the result of it, so have the theorists of our megastatism mistaken the symptoms of megastatism, such as the Great Depression and our growing stagflation, for its core (ultimate) causal factors. In the same way that fever can become a complication of the disease that led to it, so can the problems caused by growing statism become problems that lead to ratchets-up in the megastatism that caused them in the first place, but they must not be mistaken for ultimate factors—the core factors in the core drift process. Once a drift process is well under way, many other parts of the culture are reoriented to fit it, as more and more people hop on the bandwagon. Some of these become ancillary amplifiers of the drift, but they are not necessary to its continuance, and most *bandwagon factors* are merely correlated with it, not amplifiers.

There appear to be four core factors at work in complex ways in our core drift process into megastatism. First, there are the ancient myths of statism. These were strongly opposed by the classical liberals, and less strongly opposed by the Whig conservatives, but they never fully understood them and wound up unknowingly retaining within their own theories the most important myth of statism, that of the common welfare, in their ideas of public goods and factors assumed to be externalities to the market—that is, not considered by the individuals making up markets. (The idea of "externalities" assumes there are omniscient people outside of the decision-making situation who could see costs that those inside cannot. This would obviously be true with perfect hindsight, but a fatal mistake about the future. Economists who pretend to have this omniscience about externalities are almost never rich investors. They are scientistic poseurs, not Merlins.) The liberals themselves actually transmitted some of the seeds of their own destruction (which will delight Marxists committed to the idea of "fatal flaws"). This was very important, but it is obvious that this factor had to be ignited by something else. It was always there, like a charge of dynamite, but it did not reignite itself. Unfortunately for Marxists, spontaneous combustion is not really spontaneous. Something has to hold in the heat to cause it to build up.

The second core factor was this ignition factor, the spark of our modernist statism. This is the general factor of *modernist hubris*, as the Greeks called overweening pride or arrogance. It is produced in the modern Western world, and in many other societies so greatly affected by the West, by the *myth of secular millennialism* which was produced by the great and sudden successes of freedom itself, amplified by Christian millennialism in the West.[39] Great and sudden success tends to produce hubris. (We shall see in chapter 6 that great uncertainties and anxieties—dreads—that coexist in ambivalent conflict with or alternate with the great hopes inspired by great and sudden success produce the greatest hubris.) The powerful passion of hubris then distorts our perceptions, thinking, and moral feelings. This distortion—mythical thinking—then leads to highly irrational actions, that is, actions that would not be taken when calculated with reason alone, which then have unintended and hated consequences. As the Bible states so well, "Pride goeth before a fall." The disastrous consequences of the mythical distortions of thought wrought by pride are most glaring in the monumental mistakes eventually made by the greatest conquerors in history, from Alexander and Caesar to Napoleon and Hitler. But we see it writ large in the greedy irrationalism that seizes the vast majority of investors at the top of every boom in every business cycle in real estate, stocks, chickens, oil, cattle, and so on. Today every good investment counselor is aware of this greed factor—the "soaring onward and upward forever" myth that seizes even most investors who were extremely cautious before the sudden riches swept away their reason. These ever-so-rational counselors use such hot flashes of greedy optimism as an indicator that distortions of thought and action are getting so great that a fall or crash will soon follow.[40] Of course, when they are swept up in the get rich quick boom, they too temporarily lose their minds and crash with the rest. The opposite is extreme dread, the doom and gloom mythical thinking that comes at the bottom of every series of sudden and prolonged losses, which merely shows that dread cometh after a great fall. As people say, they feel "jinxed" and think nothing will ever go right for them again.

The great personal freedoms in thought, science, technology, investing, producing, and consuming which became so great in some Western nations with the decline of the Renaissance secular state and sacred state led to rapid increases in wealth. (As we saw above, the same apparently happened with earlier booms, especially the first industrial revolution of Medieval Europe.) This led to the erratic cycles of economic booms and busts, the tops and bottoms of the business cycles, and especially to the explosions of wild enthusiasms or bubbles at the top of cycles and of wild depressions or busts at the bottom which have been so obvious in the West since the seventeenth century and which are now devastating societies that have not yet learned to spot the symptoms and at least partially discount the passion-inspired myths.

These cycles and their booms and busts are affected by other factors (such as cycles of inventory buildup and divestment; because of this, they are not clearly and simply periodic, as analysts such as Nikolai Kondratieff have claimed.) But the triggering of hubris at the top of the sudden and protracted successes and of dread at the bottom of the sudden and protracted losses are the most important factors. The sudden buildup of inventories, for example, is probably due both directly to the greedy overoptimism in the merchant and indirectly to the greedy overoptimism of consumers which leads them to escalate their own expectations, rather than to any simple miscalculations. However, there probably are *error functions* at work as well. Our societies are now subject to the great cycles of boom and bust, of overenthusiasm followed by underenthusiasm. Most of them are merely seen as cycles of styles, fashions (which are even shorter-run than styles), and fads (which are even shorter-run than fashions). There are styles, fashions, and fads in ideas, dramas, gestures, political personalities, hair styles, sexual mores and practices, and so on. Arthur Schlesinger, Jr., has documented the roughly thirty years, or generational, cycles in political rhetoric fashions,[41] but he failed to note that these are partly rhetorical epicycles built over the great drift cycles that ratchet-up or down. Pitirim Sorokin long ago provided the definitive analysis of linear drift processes, cyclical drift processes, epicycles, and so on.[42]

The most fateful form of hubris for everyone is *political hubris* and this proved to be the Achilles heal of Western freedoms. Political hubris may be produced by direct military victories that are protracted and sudden, as we see in "great" military rulers and their Alexander-cycles throughout history. This was not the most important factor in most of our Western nations, especially in the most free, the United States. Political hubris was triggered in our free societies primarily by the great, prolonged, and relatively sudden superiority in knowledge and wealth made possible by the relatively weak governments that allowed freedom to produce its explosions of efficiency (due to the law of situated efficiency—see Chapters 7, 8, and 9). The nineteenth century was the peak of freedom in our societies. This was also the peak of growth rates in knowledge, wealth, and almost everything else. By the middle of the century, the belief in Secular Progress had become such a sacred idea that it was literally made into a universal theory of nature, and the Western nations, especially the Anglo-Saxons, were arrogantly asserted to be the very peak of perfection in everything—literally everything.[43] The millennialists like Auguste Comte developed Grand Theories about all of reality which "proved" absolutely—"positively," as the positivists put it—that all of reality was moving in the direction the Western peoples were moving.

Political hubris—the most important part of this millennialism—was most obvious in the national-statism and imperialism that erupted everywhere in the West, though to widely varying degrees at different times.[44] National-statism and imperialism were completely interwoven with each other and with all the emerging strains of modernist megastatism. In the early days they were by far the strongest strains and were used rhetorically to justify almost all of the others. National-statism and imperialism were the most important because they inspired the powerful passions of power-lust and greed and inspired everyone in the nation and empire to identify with the common essence of the state, thereby inspiring soaring feelings of dominance and hope for wealth. The explosive bursts of statist morale which can be temporarily produced by this passionate identification of the mass through holy communion in the mythical essence of the state was first revealed in the

Napoleonic Crusade for French Empire, even before the hubris of soaring economic success began to amplify it. They became the key by which Tory conservatives joined forces with the most insecure and ignorant to overthrow the individual freedoms and general welfare federations of the classical liberals and the Whig conservatives.

National-statism and imperialism were a complete inversion, the political antipode, of all the basic ideas of the liberal-conservative System of Natural Liberty. The imperialists, like statists of all time, sternly pronounced their international statism to be the one and only possibly true welfare state— absolutely necessary for the well-being, both sacred and secular, of every poor native. It was the white Christian's "burden" to bring all the blessings (welfare) to people of all nations, and most certainly of their own. The nationalistic and imperialistic Tory conservatives became the foremost proponents of the early forms of all that is now called *the welfare state*. They had always hated and sternly resisted the economic freedoms and industrialization of the bourgeoisie, the shopkeepers, engineers, small bankers, and skilled craftspeople. Now they found the key to defeat their enemy and to undo the System of Natural Liberty that had undermined their own monarchic, aristocratic, and church statism.

The arch-national-statist and imperialist of the age was Count Otto von Bismarck. As noted already, the traditional hagiographers of the modernist megastates present him as the founder of their welfare stastism. In fact, he merely adopted new forms of centuries-old conservative payoffs and regulations to co-opt the new socialist voters in the urban factories, who had quite different needs, desires, and political powers from the earlier rural workers. It is also a great mistake to think that he was first or alone at the time in creating the new forms of "social insurance." Much of the mistake is due to his genius in advertising. He either coined or first used the basic terms in mass publicity which were later adopted by the British conservatives. As Otto Hintze concluded in 1915, in a book celebrating five hundred years of the Hohenzollern monarchy, while social insurance did not stem the tide of socialism, "it provides the government with a good conscience, and enables it to take a strong and decisive position vis-à-vis the lower classes and their demands, as is befitting the traditions of the Hohenzollern state."[45] Social insurance, then, was merely an extension of the "noblesse oblige" European monarchs and aristocrats, especially the most absolutist of them, always used to try to legitimize their power. The intellectual supporters of the Hohenzollerns even developed the more general idea of the "social monarchy," a general program of monarchic paternalism more sweeping in its "protections" than earlier programs.

Some of the most vital measures extending the suffrage to the less educated, co-opting socialist unions, and providing subsidy payoffs of many forms were first promoted massively in Britain by the Tory conservatives and were well in place and entrenched by the time Benjamin Disraeli launched the full-scale and open program of British imperialism. From the 1840s onward, Disraeli was a stern enemy of the Whig conservatives and classical liberals (and their allies the radical utilitarians). He denounced them for failing to provide for the welfare of the workers and pushed to extend the suffrage, union powers, and so on. And always he preached the divine mission of British imperialism. The two programs of modernist welfare statism and imperialism were part of a single program of building statist powers.

American Tory conservatives, joining forces in the new Republican Party, followed in the same general path, but generally a few decades behind their British counterparts, a rough pattern that persists to this day. The Mexican-American War was one of the first outbursts of the growing American nationalism and imperialism, euphemistically called *manifest destiny*. Though Abraham Lincoln had opposed that war on classical liberal and Whig grounds, he drifted into becoming the foremost architect of American statism and with the thirty-seventh Congress in 1862 launched the *business welfare state* that dominated late-nineteenth-century American government actions.[46] Theodore Roosevelt became far more outspoken in favor of American statism, which he called The New Federalism, and of imperialism than any other American president.[47]

The third major factor igniting modernist megastatism was the tremendous growth of rationalism, technicism, scientism, expertism, and all the other forms of mythical thought associated with the very real successes of rationality, science, and technology in the modern world. The myth of rationalism-scientism, as I shall refer to this whole complex of ideas and practices, inspired our megastatism both by inspiring the passions and by providing the cognitive forms of the whole myth of modernism. The real powers and successes of rationality, science, and technology first inspired the passions that fed into secular millennialism. We can already see these passions stirring in the sixteenth-century works of mystics like Giordano Bruno, in the fanciful political legend of Sir Thomas More's *Utopia*, and, far less, in the quasi-scientific work of Francis Bacon. But these passions were rarely felt or inspired directly by the scientists and technologists themselves. Astronomy as a science does not inspire passionate hopes of conquering your enemies by predicting their moves, becoming wealthy by predicting the movements of the stock markets, gaining love, or otherwise promising to fulfill all the passions of human nature. It is astrology, the scientistic myths built on the symbolic forms of astronomy, but violating its real ideas, which promises and inspires all of these. The Tycho Brahes and Copernicuses of this world do not get rich and famous in their own days, because they do not promise great power and wealth to rulers and other patrons. Astrologers have for millennia gotten rich and sometimes famous for their soothsaying, in spite of the immense disasters they have inspired. Rulers driven by the madness of political hubris commonly turn to astrologers to make their most insane grabs for power, even when they have never shown an interest in it earlier. Knowing that others see it as insane, the rulers commonly hide their astrological proclivities and astrologers never advertise the facts after the disasters. The same has remained true to this day. All serious, scientific economists know that the vastly complex international economy is largely unpredictable in detail and make this the most important assumption of their rational and empirical theories and guesstimates. It is precisely their knowledge that it is scientifically unpredictable in detail which leads them to advise caution, and nonintervention except when something is very wrong and then at the margins: "First do no harm;" "Don't fix it unless it's broken—and then do so most sparingly." But the world is awash with grandiose economicistic predictions and plans for getting rich quick, overcoming the limitations of economic realities, and transcending history itself.

The modernist social sciences were created in the last century almost entirely by prophets who sought the holy grail of absolutist knowledge which would allow them to explain everything by their Grand Theories, predict everything, and thence control everything. As Friedrich Hayek has shown, they were overwhelmingly ignorant of human history and of practical successes in working with people.[48] They were ablaze with political ideologies before they ever sought to create "science" to give them omniscience and omnipotence. They hated the highly empirical and extremely cautious social scientists who came before them, especially the Scottish moral philosophers who built the foundations for all of what is really a scientific understanding of human beings, and those who continued these activities. By the late nineteenth century these scientistic prophets had built the foundations of modernism which remain largely intact, but increasingly modified by "postmodernism." The theorists now presented to millions of students every year as the founders of the social sciences were these prophets and their heirs, especially the macrostructuralists and mathematizing model builders and simulators. With few significant exceptions, these founding fathers of modernist social scientism were inspired by dreams of megastatism and became inspirers of that dream in millions of people drilled to believe their theories are truth.

The fourth and final factor in the early growth of the modernist megastates was that of *autocatalysis* or *positive feedback*. This factor accelerated rapidly as the state powers and bureaucracies grew, but it became important early in the whole drift process. The autocatalysis in the later stages of the ratchets-up are due more to the informational pathologies and consequent inefficiencies inherent in bureaucracy (see chapter 9). The early autocatalysis is found primarily in the *breeching of the dam* phenomenon and then in the *pay me for it* and *leave it to Sam* phenomena. As noted above, the liberal-conservative synthesis was like a bulwark or dam against statism. A crucial part of this bulwark was the *unwritten rule of equal nonfavoritism*, a vital correlary of equal opportunity and equality before the law, which prevents both envy and hope of favoritism in payoffs. As long as no one could expect special treatment or payoffs from the government, there was no cause for envious rancor over government assets and no rational hope of getting rich or powerful quickly by government intervention. At least roughly, the government's interest was the equal interest of everyone, and everyone's interest was best served by equal interest in the minimum of government consistent with its serving as a bulwark against tyranny, both domestic and foreign. Anyone who sought to breech this bulwark was stigmatized as a "pig" eating at the public "trough." As soon as people saw some people getting special treatment, eating like pigs at the public trough, then they were likely to be inspired by both greed and rational expectations to demand special treatment at the trough. (As any parent is likely to suspect, "If Johnny can do it, why can't I?" seems to be part of human nature.) A highly pluralistic and conflictful society like the United States is far more apt to generate envies than a culturally homogeneous society like Japan. This society, then, had the greatest reason to enforce the rule against breeching the dam and did so more firmly and longer than any other nation. Once the dam was breeched with the business welfare state, especially the great "giveaways" to the railroads, the dam quickly broke and demands for the government payoffs soared. Once people get paid for something that they previously did for free, they no longer want to do it for free and feel resentment if they must. Once the government no longer is seen as the representative of the general welfare and is not yet seen by most people as the embodiment of the common welfare, all people want to let the others bear the costs and themselves to reap the benefits. "Let Sam do it" is a rational choice once the community spirit working for the general welfare is destroyed by special-interest-group calculations. By the late nineteenth century the United States was already in a frenzy of welfare-statist conflicts, led by the Teddy Roosevelt who proudly proclaimed his New Federalism and imperialism.

The Ratcheting-Up of the British State

As noted in the last section, all of our modernist states go through vastly complex cycles of many forms, with some acting as epicycles on greater cycles, and all of them affected by more situational factors. These vast complexities greatly obscure the general drift processes, so much so that even most people unblinded by myths do not recognize the most powerful drifts until they are reaching an apogee or trough. Often it is only the *turning point*, with the consequent contrast between the very new and what was going on for so long, that "shocks" them into recognizing what was happening. Most journalists today are still drifting along contented with their unidimensional models of "leftists versus rightists," "capitalists versus collectivists," and other cozy simplicities. But journalists also perpetrate many of the opposite illusions about our politics, those of the media fads which have little to do with real changes in the ideas and actions of people and much to do with the need the media people have for "newness." ("Todayness" was the literal meaning of the French term, "journalism"). Every new Soviet general secretary of the party, for example, has produced breathless expectations of utopian changes in the news media and opinion surveys that probe no deeper than "popularity ratings," which soon give way to the "doom and gloom" trough of the media fad cycle.

One of the crucial complexities which produces the cycles and at the same time obscures them is the great political pluralism of our huge societies, especially our Anglo-Saxon societies. The arguments of historians, such as Pirenne and Dorwart, that there are great ages or eras of state powers and others of individual freedoms easily obscure this pluralism.[49] In our societies there are always many large collectivities and organized groups committed to the slowly changing systems of political perspectives and ideas (now often called "ideologies," though this term should be reserved for perspectives that are mythified by passionate commitments). There are the great and shifting coalitions of Tories, classical liberals, anarchists, Burkeans, socialists, populists, and many others operating both within and outside our major parties, generally overtly, sometimes covertly. Just as in military matters—politics using physical force—it is the *shifting balances of military powers* that matter, so in all politics it is the *shifting balances of political powers* that matter. Though megastatism is rapidly politicizing everything, most people in our Anglo-Saxon societies are still not highly polarized, that is, highly committed ideologically, to their political perspectives and ideas. This is a crucial reason why they still join the umbrella political coalitions that give our politics the external appearance of being exercises in Guelf and Ghibelline factionalism. Our parties are still barely dominated by practicality, not ideology. Except in the most catastrophic situations, such as that of the United States immediately after the attack on Pearl Harbor, most people change most of their political ideas and perspectives relatively easily as situations, especially problems and political fashions, change. It is normal to find rapidly shifting fads and styles in specific ideas such as rent control, arms agreements, and defense expenditures. Those general political perspectives affected by the great myths are not so easily subject to changes and account most for the long periods of systemic drift, but there are always major voting blocks committed to the major perspectives and always many individuals drifting from one perspective to another. We get long-run, or drift, changes in these balances and very short-run changes—the "trots" of fashions and the "gallops" of fads. When these complexities in real (private) commitments are combined with those resulting from the changes in rhetorical, public presentations, life becomes awfully complex for the analyst.

In understanding our great drift processes, it is crucial to realize that there was never an *age of laissez-faire ideology* in any of our societies in which classical liberal theory strongly dominated all of political life. There was a brief period during which classical liberal coalitions committed to various degrees of the dimensions of liberal ideas, and, far less, the general perspective of classical liberalism, held a reasonably strong balance of powers against their opposing coalitions in the economic realm. In general, this balance of liberal political power was stronger in the United States than in Britain, where political perspectives and ideas have been much more polarized and mythified by social class and other factors. However, in some parts of economic life, notably in the very important trade tariffs and protectionism, America was quite statist[50] in the style of mercantilist central planning. Until the General Agreements on Tariffs and Trade beginning in the 1950s, U.S. tariffs averaged about 50 percent and shut out almost all imports competing with American goods. As some modernist revisionists have delighted in arguing, the Founding Fathers and their immediate successors, especially the Jeffersonians after the Louisiana Purchase, were extreme interventionists and socialist equalizers in their land policies and often in their public school policies. They much overdo their case by failing to note that the government's goal was to sell the land to private owners. Nevertheless, land ownership was systematically subsidized and today the federal government still owns about 40 percent of the land in the West. That seven hundred million acres is quite a socialist kingdom unto itself.

Most importantly, the most famous of American classical liberals were often quite statist at the level of their home states. Thomas Jefferson himself was the leader in establishing primary, secondary, and higher education under the dominion of the state of Virginia, an instance of what most antistatists today would see as extreme statism because of its extreme effects in inculcating the myths of statism in the minds of the young. The most famous of the radical liberals in Britain, John Stuart Mill, was a firm crusader for various forms of government intervention to promote public goods that represented the common welfare, as bootlegged in the theory of the classical liberals. In realms of life such as the family, the classical liberals supported some freedoms (such as their opposition to the legal "entails" that restricted rights to the sale and use of property), but few of them took radical positions. The idea that there was ever an era of rugged individualism or "robber barons" when individualism dominated all realms of life was an absurd legend and myth created and purveyed by statist critics to make the classical liberals look evil and ridiculous to the mass of people. These revisionist ideas were created and sold well only after the balance had shifted far toward megastatism and people had forgotten what really happened. The most famous of these, Matthew Josephson's *The Robber Barons*, was published in 1934 when our nation was awash in mythical revisions of history and dreams of the utopias to be produced by statist planning.

The ever-shifting balance of political powers existed not only within each nation and each group within the nations, but also within each individual. The simple-minded and rationalistic view of politics as total war between ideological opposites has almost never been valid even when applied to single individuals. The people of our Anglo-Saxon societies have been especially subject to great conflicts within themselves over their uncertainties concerning the realities of concrete situations, over their values and interests, and over their passions and values. Even the few "rugged individualists" who may have believed rationally that "life is totally a matter of tooth-and claw-survival of the fittest" were almost always torn by natural pities and sympathies and by Christian values and training in exactly the opposite directions. Their "hard-headedness" told them that charity breeds dependency and must, therefore, be resisted for the sake of the poor and helpless, but their "soft-heartedness" and their militant protestantism told them the opposite. Anyone with common sense recognized that these omnipresent conflicts have to be dealt with situationally—carefully distinguishing between the permanently helpless and the slackers, between helping in a crisis that makes the long run possible and "helping" permanently that breeds weakness and dependency, and on and on endlessly—in all situations for all times. All of the great political battles of the nineteenth century, precisely like those of today, involved these anguished conflicts over the ideas of statism and federationism, common welfare and general welfare, individual rights and responsibilities, local government action and central government action. Slavery was probably the greatest and most anguishing of all conflicts for classical liberals and almost everyone else. The heroic appeal of Abraham Lincoln to Americans and others lies not in his being an ideologist who brought some absolutist program to bear on the tangled issues he faced, but precisely in his anguished struggle to do the best he could in a situation where there were no absolute rights and wrongs with ready-made decisions for concrete situations. Precisely the same anguished struggles were repeated internally and externally over all the great issues that emerged. As I have noted above, it was precisely this recognition of the inherently problematic nature of life, and the great positive value placed on that open-mindedness and pluralism, which separated classical liberalism from the absolutist or totalitarian pseudo-liberalism of the continent.

The result is that when we look at any brief period it is very hard to tell which way the overall society was drifting, and it was certainly impossible for anyone at the time to tell with any high probability. The same is obviously true today, which is why there is such vast, sincere disagreement over the matter. It is only with the long-run perspective of hindsight that we can see the directions of the drift process, and this is almost always made to appear far more one-sided than it was in fact by the *selective perception* of facts that are now known to be the most fateful. Our memories and our historical analyses reconstruct the past in good part to fit the outcomes, precisely as someone who falls in love reconstructs memories of the loved one to fit or be consonant with the new passion of love. Passions and outcomes determine the relevance of memories.

This is why we see even the greatest champions of classical liberalism, such as Thomas Jefferson or John Stuart Mill, championing some programs that had the exact opposite and unintended consequences and far more often going along with or compromising on programs known full well to have such consequences. Classical liberalism, like life itself, was seen by them to be an exciting experiment, full of hopes and fears, opportunities and threats, costs and benefits. Constitutional government was obviously one of the most perilous experiments yet tried by man on a large scale, because all previous ones had soon been defeated by totalitarian enemies, with the help of well-meaning but deceived democrats. This spirit of anxious hope was symbolized by Dr. James McHenry, one of the signers of the draft of the Constitution in 1887, in his report of one incident: "As the delegates of the Constitutional Convention trudged out of Independence Hall on September 17, 1787, an anxious woman in the crowd waiting at the entrance inquired of Benjamin Franklin, 'Well, Doctor, what have we got, a republic or a monarchy?' 'A republic,' Franklin said, 'if you can keep it.'"[51] The great struggles between the many opposing forces, both within and without, have never ceased. Only the relative balances have shifted, ceaselessly.

In Britain the balance was always far more equal, and thus the shifts far less wide, than in the United States. The Tories generally strongly opposed industrialization and the "new" bourgeoisie, so they commonly wound up supporting antiliberal forces and policies. Most fatefully, they commonly wound up supporting the emerging powers of labor unions that were to become so powerful in Britain's drift into statism, though at times they also strongly supported policies that hurt labor greatly. (Though noblesse oblige had real moral and emotional appeal to the aristocrat and the gentleman who succeeded him, this was also more a self-ennobling stance and a matter of self-interest, as such public stances normally are.) The period from the 1820s up to Disraeli's synthesis of labor interests with those of Tory imperialism shows this very clearly.

The Napoleonic Wars had caused all of the great disruptions of trade, credit, and currency that were to be repeated after World War I (and were cut short after World War II largely by American free-market policies and Marshall aid). The Bank of England returned to the gold standard in 1818 and pegged the pound to prewar price levels (parity), which resulted in a great deflation, very much in the same way the return to prewar parity for the pound in 1926 was to do after World War I. The wartime disruptions and the deflation, possibly interacting with more cyclical factors, led to a prolonged depression involving high unemployment and declining nominal incomes in Britain. It was the first shocks of this that led Thomas Malthus to publish his work on *The General Principles* in 1820, which anticipated Keynes's basic ideas that were to grow out of the similar experience of Britain in the 1920s. High unemployment and declining wages may have been exacerbated by the rapid influx of the rural poor to burgeoning industrial cities. Regardless, there was certainly a sense of anguish over what the British, especially the Tories, felt to be a traumatic transformation—the loss of the Arcadian bliss of country life and its replacement by slum living for the new arrivals. Whether they actually felt worse off may be impossible to determine. Almost all of the studies done to this day, and certainly the famous ones by British "social scientists" in the last century and early in this one, were highly politicized from the start and were intended to show the evil of the "capitalists." The urban immigrants probably felt great excitement, hope, anxiety, delight, and misery, much like poor immigrants today and for all time. The studies done almost universally fail to compare what they were leaving for what they found, and almost all of them focused on the "problems" and gave little or no attention to the "benefits." They were also almost totally static studies, looking only at people who at one time were poor and not following them to see the paths they followed. As new poor came in from rural shacks, the studies focused on them and paid no heed to the earlier poor who were rapidly ascending the bourgeois scales. We know that by the end of the century the British were predominantly middle-class and skilled workers and that they enjoyed the highest standard of living in history, so there was obviously an immense amount of unstudied soaring onward and upward going on. The glass was being rapidly filled with water, but the political eyes were focusing on the shrinking emptiness, just as is done today by our journalists and by most of our intellectuals and bureaucrats calling for megastatist "solutions." In any event, the prolonged problems led to the Parliamentary studies that resulted in the Blue Books, which provided Marx and other phallanxes of anticapitalists with their political weapons. All of this greatly reinforced the shifting political balance in favor of workers' suffrage and union powers, which were to have profound influence on the British drift into modernist megastatism.

In their famous work on *Industrial Democracy* Sidney and Beatrice Webb,[52] two of the most influential of the Fabian Socialists, hailed Britain as the motherland of collective bargaining and showed that this had begun as early as the late eighteenth century. These practices were legalized by Parliament between 1824 and 1825. Union powers took giant leaps with the passage of the Trade Union Act in 1871 and 1876 under Disraeli. By the turn of the century, unions had been granted some extreme monopolistic powers, especially legal immunities, which have never yet been granted in the United States. All of this was enacted by liberals (of the sort who were soon called New Liberals) and conservatives (before the Labour Party even existed) in the name of social "equity" and with the publicized goal of moderating class conflict. It did the exact opposite over the long run by encouraging the ancient British class conflicts and has given British politics and industry a Peronist tinge not yet found in any other industrialized, democratic nation, though a few, such as Australia, can challenge this.

Public opinion in Britain was drifting so rapidly away from the ideas of classical liberalism that in 1894 Sir William Harcourt, Chancellor of the Exchequer, remarked, "We are all socialists now." Between 1905 and 1914 the Liberal party, increasingly dominated by New Liberals, anxious not to be outflanked by Tories and Labourites, and working with the new Labour party, enacted numerous "social reform" measures, including noncontributory old age pensions, health insurance, and unemployment insurance. Government expenditures for these increased rapidly. They were paid for by direct taxation aimed primarily at the well-off (and were thus rejected by the House of Lords, but to no effect). Bruce Murray has noted that British experts were already publishing works showing that the increased government expenditures were slowing the rate of growth of the economy. As economic historians have shown, the "British Disease" started in the 1890s. Sir Robert Giffen, a noted statistician of the day and an obvious "supply-sider," even argued that the high taxes on the better-off were the main culprit because they were decreasing the incentives to invest at home. Most ominously of all, Murray notes that the ideas to be enshrined in Keynesian economics thirty-five years later were already being proposed even by Liberal politicians:

> Liberal theorists, by contrast, were beginning by the turn of the century to explore the notion that progressive direct taxation and government expenditure on social welfare measures might in fact prove capable of helping to offset cyclical depressions and to regenerate economic activity by promoting income redistribution and with it consumption. At the same time, Liberal politicians were also exploring the

potential capacity of direct taxation to meet higher new levels of government expenditure, and were investigating the possibilities for reforming the system of direct taxation so as to render it more productive of revenue, particularly the income tax.[53]

Lloyd George's Liberal "People's Budget" of 1909–1910 was intended to retain working-class support. It did this temporarily, but it drove many middle-class voters to the right and out of the Liberal party. Soon the workers defected to Labour, the Liberals declined, and the nation accelerated its drift into collectivism.

The 1920s and 1930s were a period of only slow growth in the modernist welfare state in Britain and, except for the deflating effects of the 1926 return to the gold standard at prewar parity, of only slow relative economic decline. The Depression was not as bad in Britain as in the United States, in good part because their deflated situation restrained speculation and they left the gold standard when the Depression hit. As I noted earlier, the great ratchet-up began with the solid election of Labour just after the Second World War. Nowhere has this forty-year trend been better summarized than in *The Economist* review of Sidney Pollard's book on *The Wasting of the British Economy:*

> Britain has performed an economic miracle of a kind since 1945. Despite enjoying political stability, ample energy resources, excellent sea communications, world-class financial institutions, access to advanced technology, a law-abiding population, an educated workforce, and an enormous headstart over almost all its industrial competitors, Britain has contrived in the ensuing decades to fall well behind its rivals in just about every important economic indicator: gross national product per head, share of world manufacturing exports, steel production and motor vehicle production. In only three fields has Britain stood out: currency depreciation, inflation and, in recent years, unemployment.[54]

But, as almost all British economic historians realize, all of this was merely an acceleration of the earlier trend that was obvious to many investors and some economists by the 1890s.

Americans followed roughly in the British political wake, generally several decades behind, always with a higher proportion of people intensely dedicated to the System of Natural Liberty and a lower proportion dedicated to Tory or socialistic extremes of statism. Our foreign policies, including the vital area of trade and tariffs, have generally been quite different because of our radically different situations. It is a remarkable fact, however, that the U.S. took on the "British burden" of worldwide interventionism and everything else after World War II. The policy of being the "world's policeman" is the exact opposite of almost all nineteenth-century American foreign policy and, since the millennial idealism of Woodrow Wilson and Franklin Delano Roosevelt, has been an extreme form of modernist statism, not any traditional form of imperialism. Federal legislation regulating labor practices began in the late 1840s under Martin Van Buren, at a much lower level than those in Britain, but drifting in the same general direction of monopolistic labor powers eventually mandated by federal laws in the 1930s and later (primarily by excluding unions from antitrust laws). This was also the era in which the ancient mystical ideas of rationalistic and millennial emanationism exploded in transcendentalism (see appendix IV) and the mystical and millennial ideas of manifest destiny contributed to the ambivalent proto-imperialism of the Mexican-American war.[55] It was a time of soaring Christian absolutist idealism, which enflamed the slavery issue that had plagued Americans from the beginning of the federal government. The fight against slavery rapidly took on all the aspects of a millennial crusade, and the crusade to make the world safe for free labor and liberty in general became the most powerful political force catapulting the northern nation into its first great bout of statism.

The rush to civil war and the government policies during the war were pervaded for more by traditional Christian millennialism and sacred statism than by modernist millennialism and statism, which were, however, strong and growing undertones in the North. It left a powerful legacy of statism which has waxed and waned, but has drifted ever upward. Before the war Americans referred to the United States government in the plural, the same way the British still refer to their government. After the war they referred to it as a singular monolith, as we still do.[56] Popular works began to extend the godly unity of the American nation, and Elisha Mulford even called the nation a "mystic body" in the terms of Hegel's sacred statism.[57] So powerful was this drift into statism that it stimulated a strong counteraction by more traditional constitutionalists. They slowed the drift, but the tide had drifted against them.

A large minority of Americans today probably assumes their "union" to be more of an essence, more homogeneous, mystical, and sacred than do most citizens even of the ancient European states. Abraham Lincoln, one of the most earthy and political of American presidents, remains canonized by popular will more than any European ruler outside of the communist world, and only Lenin has the same status within the Soviet megastate. The Lincoln Memorial and the Arlington Cemetery across the river are the American altars of nationalism. The Jefferson Memorial is not only unimposing by comparison but is shunted aside on a backwater, out of sight in the great media presentations and largely out of the public mind. In the nineteenth century George Washington was seen as the father of the nation, predominantly because of his wise counsel and strong leadership against all of the ancient follies of statism, including the awful dangers of entangling alliances. Today Father Abraham has usurped the role of patriarch. The man who united the nation in freedom is rapidly being forgotten, while the man whose election led immediately to the beginning of the war that tore the nation apart and produced more casualties than all of our other wars combined remains the hero in popular novels who "saved" the nation. In fact, he almost lost the nation, but forged the foundation of what was to become our megastate.

Relatively few Americans are able or willing, at least in public, to transcend the American statist myths sufficiently to analyze the irrationalism of the Civil War. The historians who led the way in doing so[58] did not exactly arouse widespread admiration, though the post-Vietnam waning of statism has now allowed a much wider hearing for these ideas presented by James McPherson.[59] The implicit assumption seems to be that the "union" was a necessary and transcendant reality, indivisible and sacred. Why it would be unthinkable or dreadful to have an agricultural nation of English speakers to our south, smaller and less industrialized than the English-speaking state of Canada to our North, and much smaller in population than the Spanish-speaking state we in fact have to our south, is hard to comprehend rationally—that is, from outside of the statist myths that were growing so rapidly in the union at the time and are now much stronger, if somewhat abated in the post-Vietnam era.

The moral argument that the war was justified by the necessity of stamping out slavery is absurd, since that was not the primary goal of unionists, and was used reluctantly by Lincoln later in the war as a political strategy to gain support for the war from freedom-loving Americans. It would also have been most impractical to sacrifice hundreds of thousands of lives to destroy a legal institution that was rapidly being eliminated around the world. Moreover, the military draft that Lincoln used to wage the war literally constituted a form of legalized, if temporary, enslavement of all able-bodied young men, tempered by their ability to escape abroad, by the provision that they could pay substitutes if they had the means, and by retaining some legal rights in military tribunals. Americans fought the War of 1812 in good part to end *impressment*, as they called the temporary British draft of American seamen to defend the freedom of the seas. How could it make any sense to legalize the temporary impressment of all young men to end the impressment of a minority which was rapidly dying out around the world? Taking possession of all able-bodied young men was an extreme act of statist powers by American standards, and it produced revolts in the streets. But it was endured and, as the people drifted deeper into the myths of statism, the draft became more untempered and was finally assumed to be the sacred right of congressional rulers, until the Caesarist crisis produced by the drift into the Vietnamese quagmire led them to make the draft a "standby" power. The Civil War made sense only to those in the North impassioned by the growing hatreds of the South and enflamed by the growing myths of American imperial statism. It is now assumed by Americans that the South started the war, but this is part of the myth of American statism. The southerners saw themselves as constitutionally withdrawing from the union and did not believe there would be a war. They saw union military bases, such as Fort Sumter, as foreign occupation. Secession violated the saga of manifest destiny preordained by Divine Providence. Just as the ancient Romans had drifted into their imperial statist powers, so Americans were rapidly drifting into imperial statist powers that would soon encompass the entire world, lead to Machiavellian deceits by their presidents about "threats" from abroad that did not exist, and finally to the international welfare state we are now planning and operating both directly and indirectly through our domination of world monetary institutions.

The Lincoln administration and its immediate successors created the American business welfare state, a moderate form of state capitalism by modernist standards which seems to have had more in common with medieval mercantilism than modernist rationalist-scientism and millennialism. Though Lincoln said many things that sound like modernist European socialism, the reason is probably more that we so easily transpose his statements into that historical context and that democratic socialism was so hybridized with Christianity, especially in the most Christian nation. Rather than trying to use business to build statism, as modernist state capitalists do, the original goal of the American business welfare statists was probably to use the growing state powers to aid business and its employees, which were assumed to be largely identical precisely because there was little class conflict in America at the time and the natural envies of human beings were not enflamed by political power. Regardless, the actual state operations constituted a massive ratchet-up in state powers and an even-more-massive reinforcement of the myths of statist powers to advance the common welfare.

The subsidies to the railroads were quite massive by American standards of the day. Federal and state governments subsidized the railroads with twice as much land as they "granted" and sold to individuals under the Homestead Act of 1862. The federal government also launched itself into the direct subsidizing of state education by making land grants for state colleges through the Morrill Acts of 1862 and 1890. The federal government launched itself on its programs of "aiding" farmers by establishing the Agriculture Department in 1862. The Interstate Commerce Commission, the first of the federal regulatory agencies, was established in 1887. It was presented as a protection of the common interest with its low and nondiscriminatory transportation prices, but became a scheme for monopolistic pricerigging and excluding new competitors. From the very beginning the regulatory agencies were presented as vital to the common interest, public interest, common welfare, and so on, but they have always eventually become fronts for central planning of the "fascist" variety that was to become so popular in Italy and

Germany and for the political milking of businesspeople, who found it expedient to make political contributions in many guises to those who ultimately controlled the regulation of their livelihoods.[60]

At the same time politicians were building the foundations of the business welfare state on which the more massive megastate of today was built, intellectuals were rediscovering and repackaging all of the essential roots of welfare statism. Political scientists took the lead in the creative repackaging of these ancient metaphysical essences in the guises of modernist rationalism and scientism.[61] The soaring rhetorical power of science, the rapid growth of social science pulpits in the new graduate departments in universities, and the rapid spread of state-mandated reading skills, unchecked by more critical classical education, led to an explosion of the new scientistic rhetorics of the state and scientific planning for the common interest. Theodore Roosevelt's New Federalism was synthesized with the rapidly growing progressive movement to become the most openly statist program in the history of the American presidency and was an integral part of his blatant imperialism and jingoistic Caesarism.

The social scientists provided the powerful scientistic rhetoric of "society as a separate level of existence" to synthesize the popular image of science with the ancient essences of the state, especially that of the common interest.[62] The new conquistadores of the mass media wedded this scientistic rhetoric to the moralism of populistic muckraking and progressivism to forge the powerful coalition of the ignorant poor and the college half-educated that has remained the dominant political coalition up to today, in spite of its many twists and turns. Walter Lippmann, the most influential journalist in American history, became the preeminent media spokesman for this coalition. The heart of this "progressive" and "scientific" message was that the common interest is a separate level of analysis that can only be made adequately by those who speak for the public, ergo "public officials" and self-anointed scientistic "experts." He argued over and over that the "real" public, the real society, is not the aggregate of voters who elect representatives at any one, concrete time, but the "invisible" yet "corporate" political body that transcends the generations, outliving the merely human forms of the members. He warned in direst terms that the Western democracies were rapidly declining relative to the collectivist states precisely because they had forgotten this ancient truth. As he summed up his lifelong philosophy in 1955, "This invisible, inaudible, and so largely nonexistent community gives rational meaning to the necessary objectives of government."[63] The "sole corporation" of the *res publica* and Rousseau's "conscience collectif" were given wing for the mass-mediated audiences of America and warned that decline and fall was their inevitable fate unless they bowed to the iron dictates of the "public interest" as decreed by the "public officials" and "experts" who alone could represent this invisible entity floating among us. Of course, he failed to note that the problems—the growing "crisis"—that so obsessed him were overwhelmingly correlated with the growth of the imperial presidents and imperial legislators with whom he sometimes secretly worked. Only great ratchets-up in statist powers could possibly solve the problems caused by earlier ratchets-up in those very powers. Though a brilliant and generally honest man, Lippmann lived so completely inside the hall of mirrors of the labyrinthine megastate that he could not see that the "public" problems that obsessed him, and the official information he was using to analyze them, were products of the megastate apparatus he expected to solve. It is little wonder that the modernist mythopoetic translations he provided of the ancient statist rhetoric completely entraps and baffles so many Americans officially "trained" in them throughout childhood.

Progressivism was a massive political movement that included many currents, including some of the leveling plans of American populism and European socialism.[64] But its dominant current among American intellectuals and politicians was that of scientistic, or technocratic, central planning for the common welfare. The populistic, moralistic muckraking of the new mass media rallied the mass vote for the new central planners, but the planners seem to have been more inspired by the soaring millennial aspirations unleashed by the seeming powers of rationalism and science. The creation of the Federal Reserve, the greatest ratchet-up thus far in the federal government's planning of life in the United States, was not preceded nor accompanied by any sense of crisis such as the Great Depression. There had been a serious threat of a great financial crisis in 1907–1908, but the private bankers had acted swiftly, courageously, and rationally to stop it as soon as the risk became apparent. As Milton Friedman and Anna Schwartz have shown, they were successful at stopping the same kind of run on the banks that the Fed completely failed to stop in 1932.[65] Their success, however, did not quell the outpouring of scorn and hatred, any more than the catastrophic failure of the Federal Reserve later led to any mass outcry of scorn and hatred of them. In the mind-set of the new statist technocrats, nothing failed worse than economic freedom, no matter how successful it was in furthering the general interest in sound money and prosperity.

Herbert Hoover is now enshrined in our mass statist education as the epitome and prime malefactor of the "chaos" of economic freedom under Capitalism. Actually, he was the exact opposite, one of the foremost devotees of the new science of central planning. As a young engineer-politician, he advocated a pretty thorough-going form of central statist planning. As he gained more experience in American politics, he moved to a form of what would now be called *indicative planning* roughly similar to that of the French bureaucratic state. He advocated a massive network of trade associations to voluntarily plan prices and much else. Though he quietly opposed the Federal Reserve's massive inflation of the credit system, which fed the great inflation in stock prices in the middle of the 1920s, he said nothing about this publicly after his election as president. The Smoot-Hawley tariff bill passed during his administration was a declaration of trade war against the world which led to defensive counterattacks that disrupted world trade and greatly amplified the financial contraction that slowly gained speed after the stock market bubble began to lose air. (It burst, but then regained much of its air, only to slowly leak it again.) By 1932 the Hoover administration had proposed most of what the New Deal was to put in place, had adopted much of it, and was prevented from adopting much of the rest only by Roosevelt's refusal to cooperate between his election and inauguration. In the election campaign of 1932, Roosevelt strongly attacked Hoover for the explosion of deficit spending during his administration. By being a verbal champion of *free-market capitalism* and the whole traditional American System of Natural Liberty, while pursuing contrary policies that undermined the whole system, Hoover may have done more than anyone else to stigmatize the free market as unworkable. He was, of course, even more entrapped in the labyrinth of statist rhetoric than men like Lippmann, since he was a well-meaning engineer with little understanding of politics.[66]

It is no accident that Franklin Delano Roosevelt and his vast coalition of intellectual social planners launched a crusade to save the free market from itself by vastly curtailing economic freedom at the same time Adolph Hitler launched a crusade to save the German people from the oppressions of freedom under the Weimar Republic. Other leaders were launching similar crusades in all the Western nations, with wide cultural variations in rhetorics and degrees. This was not happening because the Great Depression was a crisis of the old order, as the statist eschatologists never cease to chant. The Great Depression was a direct product of the progressive destruction of the ancient regime, the System of Natural Liberty, by the polychromatic forces of modernist rationalism-scientism and millennialism, often allied politically, as was partially true of the Nazi case, with Tory conservatives who deeply feared and resented the freedoms of the bourgeois order. The great and abiding faith of the age was, in simplest and starkest terms, "Freedom fails!" Freedom failed first of all because it did not and never could deliver utopian happiness. The System of Natural Liberty failed by comparison with the soaring and infinite aspirations of secular millennialism that had been partly inspired by the explosions of creative knowledge and prosperity under the partial System of Natural Liberty. But the greatest failures came from the progressive erosions of liberty intended to attain more perfect liberty. Stalin, Hitler, Hoover, Roosevelt, and myriads of other real opponents of economic freedom always promised the people greater new freedoms from ancient oppressions. Some of these oppressions were real, since the successes in the economic competition of the free market had some real power over the economic livelihoods, hence over the lives, of the less successful or less ambitious, and since those business rulers were every bit as human as anyone else. The business welfare state greatly ratcheted-up the oppressions of small-business people and consumers by the big-business people allied with the reborn statists. Many of the oppressions, however, were imagined, the products of the progressive entrapment in the official information hall of mirrors of megastatism. Some of the politicians realized this and manipulated the symbols to deceive the people into submitting to the far-vaster powers of the state apparatuses, in the name of far-greater new freedoms, including an end to all state powers in the most utopian case of all, that of the Marxist-Leninist-Stalinists. Far more seem to have been entrapped themselves.

There have been an immense number of twists and turns, new symbolic shibboleths and new political tactics, since the Square Deal of Theodore Roosevelt. The New Deal was a major ratchet-up in these shibboleths and twists and turns. The many newer political "Deals" that have come since then have never de-ratcheted the general powers, and there has really been little new under the political sun. In the 1932 election campaign, Franklin Delano Roosevelt sternly denounced Herbert Hoover for his welfare state policies, then after his election immediately "reformed" them, largely by cosmetic measures such as renaming them, and expanded statist powers. All of our presidents since have done roughly the same. There have been wide variations in rhetorics and styles, many variations in the forms of statist powers expanded, and some significant variations in the rates at which the powers were expanded. It is likely that a few presidents, notably Dwight D. Eisenhower and Ronald Reagan, would have liked sincerely to de-ratchet the civilian realm of statism, but in fact they expanded the military spheres—Caesarism—while merely plateauing the civilian spheres. They did trim and "reform" some of the civilian programs, but they seem clearly to have backed down from these policies in the face of political opposition and to have agreed to compromise in these areas in return for support in expanding the military sphere. They could have greatly expanded our defense capabilities by decentralizing the immense bureaucratic programs, especially by greatly expanding the national guard and reserve forces of the states. This partial debureaucratization has been proposed by many serious military thinkers, but no recent president has taken it seriously. Eisenhower drifted into the *massive retaliation* nuclear strategy, the most total of all total military threats in human history. Reagan oversaw the most massive military buildup in our peacetime history and almost all of it went into the standard operating procedures of the Pentagon's octopal bureaucracy, whose immense inefficiencies and demoralizing effects on our fighting forces have been detailed by Edward Luttwak and many others.[67] Our three most-recent presidents have all sternly denounced Big Government in their speeches, trimmed and reformed some small apparatuses and their operations, and expanded it ratchet by ratchet.

The Mythically Induced Blindness to Costs

Gordon Tullock has noted that economists from A.C. Pigou to Paul Samuelson (in his vastly popular economics text) have consistently *assumed implicitly* "that government reaches a perfect solution" to problems of the marketplace, that is, produces a complete solution at no cost.[68] Tullock and other *public choice economists* have been appalled at this blindness because it contradicts the most basic idea, the very purpose of economics, that of studying and analyzing the allocation of scarce goods to alternative (or partially conflicting) goals, which means that all choices have costs and, therefore, the only relevant question is the relative costs and benefits. But they have not tried to explain this appalling contradiction of the economists' own basic ideas.

As we shall see in the next chapter, the appearance of resolving otherwise irresolvable conflicts is the work of mythical thought. When we see otherwise highly rational thinkers contradicting their own basic ideas, we should look for the mythical preconceptions lurking in the background. When a whole generation of thinkers make the same contradiction, they are most likely in the grip of some great myth, such as the core enabling myth of the modernist welfare state. It is this which has led so many of our most sincere conservative politicians to drift ever more deeply into the thicket of government power and citizen dependency in their attempts to solve social problems. Dwight D. Eisenhower was especially susceptible because, as he told Arthur Burns, he knew almost no economic theory—and certainly did not know the liberal-conservative synthesis of the System of Natural Liberty. Eric Goldman has revealed one instance of the way Eisenhower's caring for people led him not to reverse New Deal powers:

> Any policy in any field had to stand the test of the President's persistent tendency to react less along the lines of doctrine than according to the human aspects of the problem. The journalist Steward Alsop has recalled an incident of the 1952 campaign. At first Eisenhower was strongly inclined to make a major issue of what seemed to him the excessively pro-labor attitude of Truman in dealing with a serious steel strike. Before committing himself, he asked to be briefed on the facts and some of his labor advisers explained the demands of the union in terms of what the benefits meant to the men's families in a period of rising prices. Eisenhower's reaction was, 'Why maybe they ought to have had more than that,' and the steel strike never became an important campaign issue.[69]

Why did Eisenhower not consider the effects of rising steel wages on the rising prices of steel and, thus, on the higher costs borne by the tens of millions of consumers of steel, most of them far poorer than the steelworkers? If he were to have assumed the increased wages would come from profit, why did he not consider the costs of decreased capital for investment in new technology, thus the decreased competitiveness of American steel against foreign steel, thus the likely loss of invested money and of jobs, thus the outcry for government protection, thus increased costs to consumers and the further growth of government power—increased costs in individual freedoms? In the same way, the conservative Eisenhower expanded welfare programs, with no apparent considerations of long-run costs in increased government power and citizen dependency. The drift continued.

In recent years we have been paying some of the costs. The largest American steel companies have had declining profits, they have not modernized, they have been firing massive numbers of workers (over one-fourth of U.S. Steel's workers alone in the last decade), they are in danger of bankruptcy, they have gotten trigger-price government *de facto* tariff protections, and so on. Millions of other Americans found it profitable to go on welfare permanently, so now any attempt to cut their benefits to increase their long-run independence and income causes them the tremendous distress of drastically rearranging their lives and is seen as an evil, pitiless attack on the poor. Why did Eisenhower not foresee any of this? Because he was blind to the costs. It is not much of a leap from Eisenhower's blindness to costs to New York Mayor Abraham Beame's moral rejection of economic realities in 1975. Bowing to political forces, he presented a plan to cut the city's budget by $200 million, but asserted, "We can take no pride in the plan, because it places a higher priority at this time on the grim economic realities confronting the city rather than upon the needs of our citizens." To allow the grim costs of reality to take precedence over desires was by then so immoral as to be almost unthinkable.[70] Why? Because they did not really believe there are any economic realities, or real costs. In the modernist balance sheet of secular millennialism, *only* desires have any real value.

Once the massive system of statist myths was widely shared, even most people who understood the System of Natural Liberty in general commonly found themselves blindly building massive statist powers in particular. William Simon saw clearly how liberal democrats were led by their blindness to costs to drift into ever-bigger government: "They appear to be compelled by their own distorted thought processes to keep rushing down the route to the destruction of our production system, emitting shrill cries of moral outrage all the way and staring with astonishment at the economic disasters that spring up, unaccountably, about them."[71] But then he found his fellow Republicans, and even himself in office, following the same route and trying to cover their feelings of guilt with rationalizations. Simon's *mea culpa,* in *A Time For Truth,* is a poignant confession of a man who, like the scientistic and modernist Dr. Frankenstein, set out to create the perfect human being and discovers he has created a monster.

The Great Christmas Tree of Modernist Myths

The big historical picture in both America and Britain is, then, strikingly clear. Though commitment to the basic ideas of the classical liberal system was widespread, especially in the United States, it always had some strong opposition and was never fully enacted. Though many classical liberals and situational allies always resisted, each widely shared problem that was proclaimed aroused widespread treatment as a "special case" that could be dealt with by increased state powers without bankrupting the System of National Liberty. Each statist solution of these problems was a tiny step in the growth of statism and state powers. At no time, not even during the New Deal, was there a decision by the people to go from a classical liberal society to our vast bureaucratic megastatism. The growths of the modernist welfare states in Britain and American were step-by-step, systemic drifts in which the end result of the drift processes—megastatism—was both unintended and hated when it was finally seen as Big Government. It is also strikingly clear that both of these modernist welfare states started very slowly against great opposition, accelerated (about ninety and fifty years ago, respectively) against rapidly decreasing opposition, then started stagnating and encountering rapidly rising opposition. The growth process has the obvious characteristic of becoming autocatalytic after the early phase and then self-dampening but by no means yet self-reversing. Each ratchet-up in the state powers produced unintended consequences in rough proportion to the size of the ratchet-up, but with the time lags usual in complex economic (and other) systems, so the new problems were not seen by most people as caused by state action. Each state-caused problem then led to calls for more state action, which led to more problems, onward and upward in state powers and problems. This was the autocatalytic drift process of the growth of the modernist welfare state. Once it came into full play, the state grew rapidly.

The monocausal explanations of the rise of our modernist welfare states all seize one part of the vastly complex processes at work and mistake it for the whole (see appendix III). These parts are important (and I shall deal with them in numerous instances), but they must always be seen in the context of the whole, the great tidal drift of an immensely complex, worldwide civilization. The citizens of great civilizations do not rise, fall, or transform themselves by any one factor or any one leader. Rome did not fall because of the rise of Christianity, or because of slavery, or lead poisoning, or merely because of the antibusiness, bureaucratic ethos of the ruling elites. As Michael Rostovtzeff and other great historians have shown, many factors such as these played a part, some certainly more important than others, but all in complex interdependent interaction with each other to produce the great systemic drift. The drift into welfare-statist myths and bureaucratic operations was made up of many factors and all of these interacted with contingent situational factors, especially the intense military pressures. The same is true of the rise and fall of our modernist welfare states. We have seen some and shall see many other important factors at work. But the focus of this work must be on the most important—the fundamental—factors at work. The most important, by far, are those of mythical thought and the statist bureaucratization of society, especially the myths and operations affected by our great myths of modernism, rationalism-scientism, and secular millennialism.

The most basic ideas shared by the individuals of any society are so taken for granted that they are rarely spoken clearly in everyday life. In everyday practical situations they would sound so trite that talking about them would make their proclaimer seem a terrible bore or worse (possibly mad). Medieval Christians did not have to profess Christianity in everyday affairs because almost everyone was a Christian (at least publicly) and everyone knew it. Thomas Jefferson and the other constitutionalists did not try to prove their "natural rights" because they were self-evident to most educated people in the English-speaking nations and to many French speakers. (They probably proclaimed them *only* because they obviously were not self-evident to the British monarch.) Americans today do not often say "I believe in individual freedom" because almost all Americans believe in individual freedom, at least publicly, and we all know it. Only on sacred occasions, like Fourth of July rituals, are the trite statements transformed into meaningful avowals of identity and commitment.

But these taken-for-granted ideas are the hidden foundations for much of what is said and done in everyday life, and anyone who wants to understand everyday life must know them in all their details. The vastly complex patterns of everyday life are woven out of and against the background of these basic ideas in specific combinations to deal with the concrete situations people face to achieve individual goals. Anyone who does not know the taken-for-granted meanings will see only the vast complexity of the everyday phenomena; and they will look like the multifarious ornaments on a Christmas tree, each one possibly dazzling and interesting in itself, but all of them seemingly standing miraculously on their own and disconnected—if one does not see the Christmas tree that holds them all together.

The mythical ideas and programs of our modernist welfare states are very much like Christmas ornaments in this respect. There is an almost unbelievably vast profusion of both the myths and the programs. People suddenly immersed in the details of just one realm of myths (say the myth of capitalist immiserization and of salvation by union power) or one set of programs (say American welfare programs) are apt to be dazzled and even overwhelmed by their vast, multifarious complexity and find them incomprehensible—if they do not see the great myths and lesser myths synthesizing and inspiring the multitude of minimyths and undergirding the proliferation of programs with a gossamer of pseudo-rationality. This, of course, is exactly what has happened to most of our experts on unions, welfare, air pollution, farm subsidies, child abuse, social security, and on and on. They have seen the ornaments only and not the tree of great myths and lesser myths lying behind, undergirding, and connecting them. Thus, they have seen their short-run failures, but they have not understood why and how they arise, and, by encouraging everyone to focus entirely on the minute details of each ornament, they have only encouraged incomprehension, the futile search for "Reforms, Reforms, Reforms" that will supposedly make them work, and obscured the contribution each makes to the tidal drift toward systemic catastrophe.

American welfare programs are an excellent example. Under President Eisenhower we already had around forty welfare programs. When Richard Nixon became president in 1968, a mere eight years later, there were somewhere around 100 to 400 depending on what was classified as "welfare." When Jimmy Carter took office he was determined to reform this immensely complex web of programs and bureaucracies. But his rage for reform was quickly dissipated and he declared, "The complexity of the system is almost incomprehensible." In California Governor Jerry Brown, less concerned with comprehension and far more adept at media dramatizations, displayed the row upon row of books of official regulations on welfare to illustrate the baffling immensity of it all—just for one state. In 1987 William O'Hare surveyed the great morass and concluded:

> No topic is more complex, confusing and misunderstood than our welfare programs and the people who use them. The reason is simple. The U.S. welfare system is a chaotic collection of more than 100 programs that has evolved in a haphazard, piecemeal fashion and left us with a set of complicated and often counterproductive eligibility standards, benefit levels and responsibilities.

> Because hard facts about the programs and the people who use them are rare, perceptions are often shaped more by anecdote and misinformation than by research.[72]

But what if one individual, or a whole team, could agree on what these programs are, could assimilate all of the official information on the legislative origins of the programs, on the regulations, on the operation of the programs, on the welfare workers, and on the recipients? Would they then understand how these convoluted welfare programs operate, what effects they have on the recipients and on our entire society over the long run? Certainly not. The official information spewed forth by these colossal bureaucracies is largely misinformation—bureaucratic propaganda[73] carefully constructed in good part to hide, protect, and advance the information creators (see chapter 9). The answers provided by recipients and journalists is equally distorted. And there are so many convoluted overlaps and interdependencies that no one could get a clear picture. It might seem simple enough—and certainly vitally important—to determine how much the recipients benefit from these polymorphously perverse programs. But Martin Anderson and many other researchers have found that even the number of people left under the official poverty line has been overestimated consistently by about 300 percent.[74] "Information" that misinforms by 300 percent on one of the simplest and most vital details is what computer analysts call *informational garbage* and is far worse than no information at all, because without the illusion of information you would see the need to get good information. But suppose there were no such information pathologies. Indeed, assume perfect official information. Would we then be able to understand *why* the programs were enacted and what their effects are and will be over the long run on our society? Not at all. Even perfect information about the reasons legislators give for enacting such programs would not directly reveal the vital forms of mythical self-deceptions and the deceptions of others involved in such deliberations. And even perfect information on all the effects on our society in these early years of their operation would not yet reveal their long-run (trend-lag) effects on dependency, bureaucratic pathologies, and the ratchet-up growth of government power toward collectivist tyranny.

As we shall see, the trunk and the strongest limbs of our welfare-state Christmas trees are woven of the mystical gossamer of myth, above all of the core enabling myth of all welfare statism, the myth that the state and its rulers are a higher level of existence—a sacred reality—necessary to the common welfare. These sacred myths are not revealed directly by official information and their most revolutionary effects are normally only apparent after many years, exactly as the greatest effects of drug addiction are normally apparent only after many years. By then, because of the many ratchet-up resistances to change, it is almost always too late to reverse the process by democratic means, except, perhaps, in nations with the most passionate commitments to liberty.

[Suetonius] records with interest the uncanny atmosphere in Augustus' nursery at Velitrae (Velletri), where the local inhabitants believed that the emperor had been born. People were afraid to enter this room, reports Suetonius, because strange things had happened to those who had made the attempt before.

Michael Grant

The new awe for the presidential role rubbed off on the President's very working space. Sorensen wrote:

The whole White House crackled with excitement under John Kennedy, but the soundproof oval office, the very center and stimulant of all the action, symbolized his own peace of mind. . .

Breathless description of that office became a set piece in post-Kennedy hymns to the presidency. Hugh Sidney called the last chapter of *John F. Kennedy, President* "The Oval Office":

There was an awesome presence in that Oval Chamber which was then quiet, cool, sunlit—the very heart of his nation's meaning, the very core of freedom, thirty-five feet long by twenty-eight feet, four inches wide. To an outsider the feeling of awe is always there—any man who walks into that office senses it. I wondered if the President ever got used to it, and then I decided that he never does either.

The office itself was now a superhuman dwelling place, as Theodore White made embarrassingly clear in his genuflections at the shrine in *The Making of the President 1960*:

For the laws of Congress cannot define, nor can custom anticipate, the unknown—and this is where the great Presidents must live, *observant of the law yet beyond the law, Chief Executive and High Priest of American life at once.* (Italics added)

Notes   George Will

1. Probably the best analysis of the bureaucratic stagnation of the American military in Vietnam is by Edward Luttwak, *The Pentagon and the Art of War* (New York: Simon and Schuster, 1984). The stagnation of business creativity by bureaucratization is now so obvious that it has been mass-mediated into a stereotype that overlooks the real values of small bureaucracies. The best treatment of the dangers of bureaucracy is probably the popular work by Thomas Peters and Robert Waterman, *In Search of Excellence* (New York: Harper and Row, 1982).
2. Walter Ullmann, *The Individual and Society in the Middle Ages* (Baltimore: The Johns Hopkins Press, 1966), pp. 12–15.
3. Ibid., p. 12, f.n. 18.
4. Reinhold August Dorwart, *The Prussian Welfare State before 1740* (Cambridge, MA: Harvard University Press, 1971), p. 7.
5. Gaines Post, *Studies in Medieval Legal Thought* (Princeton: Princeton University Press, 1964), p. 12.
6. Jean Gimpels, *The Medieval Machine* (New York: Penguin Books, 1977) is the classical analysis of this period. His analysis, however, is based on the culturalogical and psychological theories of civilization developed by Spengler, Sorokin, and so many others. Their theories see civilizations as necessarily following a great cycle from birth to exuberant growth to mature plateauing and finally the decline of old age. They generally agree with the great importance of economic freedom (entrepreneurship) in producing the growth of statist bureaucratic centralization and Caesarism in producing the stagnation and decline. Gimpel, for example, sees all of this in the medieval era. But they do not see the drive for power, statist bureaucracy, and so on, as crucial in this drift

process. Moreover, since they believe it a necessary cycle, they easily fall into simple extrapolations, including disaster scenarios of Spenglerian proportions. Gimpel, for example, predicted that the West would have no technological breakthroughs after 1975 (ibid., pp. 237–52), just before the explosions of biotechnology, personal computers, superconductivity, and so on.

7. See, especially, Eli Heckscher, *Mercantilism* (New York: Macmillan, 1955); Charles Cole, *French Mercantilism* (New York: Octagon, 1965); Philip W. Buck, *The Politics of Mercantilism* (New York: Octagon, 1964); Joseph Schumpeter, *History of Economic Analysis* (New York: Oxford University Press, 1960); Jacob Viner, *The Long View and the Short* (Glencoe, IL: The Free Press, 1958). On the vital matter of mercantilist bureaucracy, see G. E. Aylmer, "Bureaucracy," in Peter Burke, ed., *The New Cambridge Modern History* (New York: Cambridge University Press, 1979), vol. XIII, pp. 164–200.

8. Dorwart, *The Prussian Welfare State before 1740*, p. 3.

9. Hugh Trevor-Roper, *The European Witch Craze* (New York: Harper and Row, 1969). For a more specialized view of the economy in this period, see Jan de Vries, *The Economy of Europe in an Age of Crisis* (New York: Cambridge University Press, 1976).

10. The literature on the statist absolutism of this era is huge. See especially Ragnhild Hatton, ed., *Louis XIV and Absolutism* (Columbus: Ohio State University Press, 1976).

11. Henry Thomas Buckle, *History of Civilization In England*, 2d ed. (New York: Appleton and Co., 1874), vol. I, pp. 201–2.

12. Jerome Blum, *Lord and Peasant in Russia* (Princeton: Princeton University Press, 1961).

13. There is now a huge literature discrediting Weber's theory. The most important earlier sources for my argument about the relations between Church, state, and economics are David Landes, *The Unbound Prometheus* (New York: Cambridge University Press, 1969); and Jean Baechler, *The Origins of Capitalism* (Oxford: Blackwell, 1975).

14. See Charles Cole, *French Mercantilism*.

15. The explanation of this crucial revolution is derived from the argument of this whole book, though I shall not be specifically concerned with the dynamics of revolutionary movements. The most important sources for my general argument have been Jacob Talmon, *The Origins of Totalitarian Democracy* (London: Secker and Warburg, 1955), and James Billington, *Fire in the Minds of Men* (New York: Basic Books, 1980). See appendix IV and chapter 6.

16. See Carl Becker, *The Declaration of Independence* (New York: Knopf, 1966).

17. Ibid., pp. 72–73.

18. David Sidorsky, ed., *The Liberal Tradition in European Thought* (New York: G. P. Putnam's, 1970).

19. Talmon, *The Origins of Totalitarian Democracy*.

20. Ibid., pp. 1–2. Talmon seems to assume too readily that the American thinkers of the Enlightenment all fell into the liberal camp. Henry F. May has shown how active some of the more millennial, rationalistic radicals were among Americans (see *The Enlightenment in America* [New York: Oxford University Press, 1976]). May's argument that the dominant American social philosophy that evolved in the eighteenth and nineteenth centuries was a compromise between Protestant conservatism and Enlightenment ideas underlies my interpretation.

21. The historical interpretations of the American Revolution, Constitution, and all related subjects are now a vast intellectual battleground. I am concerned only with the most general and clear patterns. Where I cannot avoid entirely the controversial issues, I have reference to specific works or follow the general interpretations of historians such as Forrest McDonald, *Novus Ordo Seclorum: The Intellectual Origins of the Constitution* (Lawrence, KS: University Press of Kansas, 1985).

22. Alexander Hamilton, from *The Federalist* (New York: The Modern Library, no date), p. 28.

23. Ibid., p. 35.

24. See Albert O. Hirschman, *The Passions and the Interests* (Princeton: Princeton University Press, 1977).

25. Bernard Bailyn, et al., *The Great Republic* (Boston: Little, Brown, 1977), pp. 362–64.

26. As far as I know, no one has attempted a careful historical comparison to demonstrate or disprove this crucial point. The idea underlies many important works, notably Jean Baechler, the *Origins of Capitalism*.

27. As quoted in Arthur M. Schlesinger, Jr., *The Age of Jackson* (Boston: Little, Brown, 1945), p. 267.

28. Ibid., p. 267.

29. Ibid., p. 268.

30. Quoted in Morgan O. Reynolds, "The Middle-Class Welfare State," in *Fortune*, March 21, 1983, p. 176.

31. Quoted in Schlesinger, *The Age of Jackson*, p. 315.

32. *The Federalist*, no. 10, (New York: The Modern Library, no date), especially pp. 54–57. As Reinhard Bendix and Seymour Martin Lipset have said of Marx: "Karl Marx's theory of social classes was of great importance in his work and it has had a profound influence on modern social thought. Yet the writings of Marx, voluminous as they are, do not contain a coherent exposition of that theory. They contain, instead, many scattered fragments on this topic." See "Karl Marx's Theory of Social Classes," in Bendix and Lipset, eds., *Class, Status and Power* (Glencoe, IL: The Free Press, 1953), p. 26.

33. *The Federalist*, Ibid.

34. Seymour Martin Lipset, *The First New Nation* (Garden City, NY: Doubleday, 1967).

35. Andrew Jackson, message of July 10, 1832, as quoted in Schlesinger, *The Age of Jackson*, p. 90.

36. Ibid., p. 315.

37. Quoted by Ralph Mango in *The Wall Street Journal*, December 12, 1987.

38. Robert Higgs, *Crisis and Leviathan* (New York: Oxford University Press, 1987).

39. Gordon Prange has recently shown in meticulous detail, both documentary and interview, how hubris was the crucial factor producing the naval disasters at both Pearl Harbor and Midway. See *At Dawn We Slept* (New York: Penguin Books, 1982) and *Miracle at Midway* (New York: Penguin Books, 1982).

40. See John Train, *Preserving Capital and Making It Grow* (New York: Penguin Books, 1983).

41. Arthur Schlesinger, Jr., "America's Political Cycle Turns Again," *The Wall Street Journal*, December 10, 1987.

42. Pitirim Sorokin, *Social and Cultural Dynamics* (New York: Bedminster Press, 1937; rpt. 1962).

43. See Robert Nisbet, *History of the Idea of Progress* (New York: Basic Books, 1980).

44. See Hans Kohn, *The Idea of Nationalism* (New York: MacMillan, 1944); Hans Kohn, *The Age of Nationalism* (New York: Harper, 1962); Louis Snyder, ed., *The Dynamics of Nationalism* (Princeton, NJ: Van Nostrand, 1964); Hans Morgenthau, *Politics among Nations*, 3d ed. (New York: Knopf, 1960); A. P. Thornton, *The Imperial Idea and Its Enemies* (New York: St. Martin's, 1959), and *Doctrines of Imperialism* (New York: Wiley, 1965); and Raymond Aron, *The Century of Total War* (Garden City, NY: Doubleday, 1954).

45. See Peter Flora and A. J. Heidenheimer, "The Development of Welfare States in Europe and America" (New Brunswick, NJ: Transaction, 1981), pp. 17–18.

46. See William Appleman Williams, *America Confronts a Revolutionary World, 1776–1976* (New York: William Morrow, 1976), especially chapters 6 and 7.

47. "Outspokenness" must not, of course, be the complete index of real intentions. Living in an openly imperialist age, Roosevelt could boast of what current presidents would hide behind nested fronts of incandescent, nominal humility.

48. Frederich Hayek, *The Counter-Revolution of Science* (Glencoe, IL: The Free Press, 1955).

49. See Henri Pirenne, "Stages in the Social History of Capitalism," *American Historical Review*, (1914), pp. 494–515.

50. See, for example, the overdone argument of Daniel Elazar, *The American Partnership* (Chicago: University of Chicago Press, 1962).

51. Quoted in the Frontispiece of Earl Warren, *A Republic, If You Can Keep It* (New York: Quadrangle Books, 1972).

52. Sidney Webb and Beatrice Webb, *Industrial Democracy* (New York: Longman, 1920).

53. Bruce Murray, *The People's Budget, 1909-10: Lloyd George and Liberal Politics* (New York: Oxford University Press, 1980), p. 23.

54. *The Economist*, May 8, 1982, p. 105.

55. Historians have differed greatly in their analyses of American "imperialism," especially in these early decades. I believe this is because a high percentage of Americans, normally a majority, have always been highly ambivalent about all "foreign entanglements." Victories and possessions inspire soaring pride, as well as embarrassment; and defeats and threats inspire desires to reject all entanglements, as well as lusts for revenge. The situations and the rhetorics of politicians have great impacts on which ways the ambivalent forces swing, as the Japanese demonstrated in a marvelous twenty-four-hour experiment. Americans are generally quite ignorant of foreign affairs, are generally aware of this, and have few stereotypes to replace this ignorance (except in great conflicts or the few protracted conflicts such as with Mexico). Their high uncertainty allows situational passions to inspire very mystical foreign policies, as Robert Dallek has argued in *The American Style of Foreign Policy* (New York: Knopf, 1983).

56. See Hans Kohn, *American Nationalism* (New York: Macmillan, 1957) and George Fredrickson, *The Inner Civil War*, Harper and Row, 1965.

57. Bernard Bailyn, *The Great Republic*, p. 770.

58. See, especially, Williams, *America Confronts a Revolutionary World, 1776–1976.*

59. James M. McPherson, *Battle Cry of Freedom* (New York: Oxford University Press, 1987).
60. There is a vast literature on the rhetorics and realities of regulation. For both the evidence on one crucial agency and the general implications, see Michael Parish, *Securities Regulation and the New Deal* (New Haven: Yale University Press, 1970). For the general argument see Robert Poole, ed., *Instead of Regulation* (Lexington: Lexington Books, 1982).
61. See Daniel T. Rodgers, *Contested Truths* (New York: Basic Books, 1987).
62. Most of my earlier works have dealt with some of the many aspects of social scientism, absolutism, and so on.
63. Walter Lippmann, *The Public Philosophy* (Boston: Little, Brown, 1955), p. 36. And see Ronald Steel, *Walter Lippmann and the American Century* (Boston: Little, Brown, 1980).
64. Progressivism and all related terms, such as populism and socialism, are, of course, political shibboleths. This is all-too-rarely considered in standard histories. See, however, Daniel Fox, *The Discovery of Abundance* (Ithaca: Cornell University Press, 1967); and James Gilbert, *Designing the Industrial State* (Chicago: Quadrangle Books, 1972).
65. Milton Friedman and Anna Schwartz, *A Monetary History of the United States* (Princeton: Princeton University Press, 1963).
66. See Martin Fausold, ed., *The Hoover Presidency* (Albany: State University of New York Press, 1974); and David Burner, *Herbert Hoover* (New York: Knopf, 1978).
67. See Luttwak, *The Pentagon and the Art of War*.
68. Gordon Tullock, *The Vote Motive* (London: The Institute of Economic Affairs, 1976), p. 10, including note.
69. Dean Albertson, *Eisenhower as President* (New York: Hill and Wang, 1963), p. 41.
70. See my essay on "New York's Fiscal Crisis and the New Political Machine," in J. D. Douglas and John M. Johnson, eds., *Official Deviance* (Philadelphia: Lippincott, 1977), pp. 90–106.
71. William Simon, *A Time For Truth* (New York: Berkeley Books, 1979), p. 80.
72. William O'Hare, "Separating Welfare Fact from Fiction," *The Wall Street Journal*, December 14, 1987.
73. See David L. Altheide and John M. Johnson, *Bureaucratic Propaganda* (Boston: Allyn and Bacon, 1980).
74. Martin Anderson, *Welfare* (Stanford, CA: The Hoover Institute Press, 1978).

5

The Power of Political Myths

The golden age of humanity is not behind us; it is to come, and will be found in the perfection of the social order. Our fathers have not seen it; our children will one day behold it. It is our duty to prepare the way for them.

Comte Henri de Saint-Simon

...we have been drifting unconsciously, rather than plunging into state socialism deliberately. And the reason that we drift is that as a people we do not understand. We still believe in fairies...

Would there be a rush in this direction if the citizens generally regarded each of these bills as merely a way of shifting funds from one group within the country to another, with the intervention of a growing governmental bureaucracy? Would we appropriate so freely to aid this or that group if the taxpayers generally really recognized that they would pay the bill, either directly or by indirect taxes they hardly see? Not at all. There is still, in this country, some sort of belief in a magic wand.

Vannevar Bush

There are eras in human history when whole societies, even great civilizations, are swept along blindly to their fates. In his monumental study *The Social and Economic History of the Hellenistic World*, Michael Rostovtzeff noted the blindness of the ancient Ptolemies in the third century B.C. and their citizens to the sinister erosion of their economy by massive bureaucratic planning: "The sinister phenomena of which I have been speaking were, however, hardly perceptible to contemporaries, even if good observers. The dominant note was splendour and rapid progress."[1] Like almost all previous and succeeding emperors, kings, and presidents of imperial state bureaucracies, the Ptolemies did not see that the very programs of bureaucratic controls and vast increases in taxation which allowed them to greatly expand their realms and public consumption, thus producing a temporary explosion of public wealth and power, would soon erode their real economy terribly and, thus, the bureaucratic state itself.

Rostovtzeff also concluded that the Roman Empire grew without any plan and without any significant recognition that the Empire would be the outcome of the multitudinous, step-by-step choices they were making:

> Thus in the course of little more than half a century the Roman state ceased to be a federation of Italian cities and clans, and became a great empire without a single rival either in the West or in the East. The Romans did not work for this position, or prepare for it, or desire it; it was the natural result of a series of incidents, whose consequences no one at Rome foresaw or could foresee. Yet this growth of Rome into a worldwide empire is one of the main events in the history of the world and has changed the course of that history. It also imported many new elements into the life of Rome, political, social, and economic—elements which worked a radical change in the whole aspect of the Roman state.[2]

More recent historians have argued that some Roman general strategists were more conscious of this drift to empire and hid their plans to help its success. While I believe this likely, the vast majority of Romans apparently drifted blindly.

In the second century B.C. Polybius, a Greek historian sent as hostage to a victorious Rome, surveyed the splendours of the new Roman Empire and in a stunning display of human foresight predicted that Rome had already sown the seeds of its internal disintegration and would soon reap the bitter harvest of the ferocious internal struggle for power. But the Romans, filled with pride and greed by their new power and the tribute pouring in, could not see it.[3] The beginning of the end for Roman freedom soon struck. In 133 B.C. two young noble brothers, the Gracchi, launched their bids for total political dominance by proposing an idealistic program of social "justice," land redistribution, and food for the urban poor. Certainly their call for justice was not intended to ignite the roaring flames of political combat and civil war that engulfed Rome for a century, and obviously the Gracchi could not imagine that their "welfare" programs would be finally realized only by Augustus after he had waded through rivers of Roman blood, nor that they would be a pillar of his imperial welfare state.

Fernand Braudel argued that the long-run trends of societies are normally unseen, and, thus, unintended, by the vast majorities of their members.[4] The people are swept along by their "unconscious history," what economists today call *systemic drift* and linguists call *cultural drift*. These unconscious drift processes are most obvious and demonstrable in language and biological evolution, but they are far more important to us in the ways they eventually transform our economic and political lives. The feudal lords of Britain had no idea whatsoever that their checking the powers of the king in the Magna Carta was one step in the direction of classical liberal democracy, any more than millions of other checkers of the divine statist myths of kings and popes realized they were taking tiny steps in the same great historical drift process. In the same way, there is no evidence that politicians like Abraham Lincoln and Franklin Delano Roosevelt realized they were taking a multitude of small steps in the rebirth of the ancient myths of statism and bureaucratic planning in the very names of freedom, justice, and equality.

Sometimes the trends of history, even if unseen by the mass of people, are recognized and used by politicians to gain more power and by economic entrepreneurs to gain profit. Sometimes the drift mystifies and victimizes the political leaders even more than the common people. Rulers who create powerful empires by crushing their rivals often unleash an era of both economic boom and public splendor. The economic boom comes from the simple elimination of the earlier trade barriers, the decreased cost of warfare, and the increased political certainty that encourages investment. The sudden elimination of the earlier tariffs and proscriptions on trade produces an explosion of efficiency through the simple but normally unrecognized workings of the law of comparative advantages; and the vast increase in the size of the market allows some producers to become more efficient through the economies of larger scale. At the same time, both the pooling of taxes and the boom produce a gusher of revenue that can be used in public investments (roads, dams, irrigation) to aid the boom and in lavish displays of the ruler's power which overawe would-be rebels and exhilarate him and his loyal supporters with soaring pride.

These are the heady days of the spring flowers of the imperial state, but neither the rulers nor their subjects recognize that the flowers are bought at the cost of vast new bureaucratic powers necessary for administering the vast empire and the loss of the countervailing powers that once constrained the explosion of imperial bureaucratic powers. The spring flowers also tempt the rulers into believing they and their bureaucrats can create wealth, and the era of "rationalized monopolies" and "rational planning" is decreed which will eventually combine with the bureaucratic regulations and taxes to stagnate the economy, then erode the tax base as the declining wealth of the realm causes the real rates of taxation to soar to pay for the costs of bureaucracy and the rising costs of warfare, resulting from the fact that the decline in wealth produces a decline in power, which increases the incentives of attack for aggressive powers. The soaring hubris of the most successful empire builders even tempts them to lay claim to divine status, as we see in the absolute monarchs of the Renaissance welfare states. The fall canker blooms of imperial bureaucratic regimes are the inherent costs of their spring flowers, but they are almost never seen because they lag so far behind and because empire builders are never good economists. Ibn Khaldun saw this dynastic cycle occur so universally in the Islamic world that he decreed it a law of nature,[5] but he remained unaware of the bureaucratic dynamics at work producing the inevitable stagnation and waning of the dynasties.

In the fourteenth and fifteenth century, the Iberian peninsula was a site of vast creativity and productivity rivaling the achievements of the many free cities of Renaissance Italy and Germany. This was one of those eras of great competitive struggle which inspire us human beings to aspire and strive for greatness. But out of the struggle came one victor, a centralized Spanish empire under the dominion of the ruler of Castile. J.H. Elliott has described this "glorious springtime" of the new empire, an age he calls "the open society," and the sowing of the canker blooms that would eventually grow so lushly, but which in the glorious spring were completely unseen:

> The reign of Ferdinand and Isabella was called by Prescott "the most glorious epoch in the annals" of Spain. Generations of Spaniards, contrasting their own times with those of the Catholic Kings, would look back upon them as the golden age of Castile. The conquest of Granada, the discovery of America, and the triumphant emergence of Spain on to the European political stage lent unparalleled lustre to the new State created by the Union of the Crowns, and set the seal of success on the political, religious, and economic reforms of the royal couple.

> Against the conventional picture of a glorious spring-time under Ferdinand and Isabella, too soon to be turned to winter by the folly of their successors, there must, however, be set some of the less happy features of their reign. They had united two Crowns, but had not even tentatively embarked on the much more arduous task of uniting two peoples. They had destroyed the political power of the great nobility, but left its economic and social influence untouched. They had reorganized the Castilian economy, but at the price of reinforcing the system of *latifundios* and the predominance of grazing over tillage. They had introduced into Castile certain Aragonese economic institutions, monopolistic in spirit, while failing to bring the Castilian and Aragonese economies any closer together. They had restored order in Castile, but in the process had overthrown the fragile barriers that stood in the way of absolutism. They had reformed the Church, but set up the Inquisition. And they had expelled one of the most dynamic and resourceful sections of the community—the Jews. All this must darken a picture that is often painted excessively bright.[6]

The springtime of imperial Spain was prolonged by the vast treasure of gold and silver that poured in from the American conquests. The mighty empire came close to conquering and uniting all of Europe. But with the vast treasure came a mysterious epidemic that afflicted everyone—inflation. E. J. Hamilton[7] has shown that, while all Spanish citizens and leaders almost universally saw the spiraling price inflation that swept their empire throughout the sixteenth and seventeenth centuries, they almost universally failed to realize it was caused by the increased money supply minted with the new American silver and gold. Instead, they turned in moral outrage against the businesspeople, especially foreigners like the Genoese, accusing them of monopolistic "profiteering," just as in our own day inflation is blamed on monopolistic "price setting" rather than on government expansion of the paper money supply. Not seeing its long-run effects, the rulers of Spain used the vast increase in money supply to build a vast patronage system and to build even-more-vast bureaucracies to regulate the economy and rule the newly formed nation state.

The king commanded and the bureaucrats built him a vast capitol—Madrid—on a barren plain in Castile. The people were awed by the royal splendor and by the apparent might of the new empire. But, while the politicians and people railed against the businesspeople, the inflation soared. Soon the government was borrowing massively, taxes were soaring, and the economy was declining rapidly. Businesspeople and peasants were ruined on a massive scale. Many fled and whole regions were depopulated. By the late sixteenth century the government was bankrupt. But the vast bureaucracies and their massive regulations remained. Spain, which had been the fastest growing, richest, and most powerful area of Europe before the Hapsburgs created their "Renaissance welfare state," declined into the "sick man" of Europe.

Roughly this same scenario was enacted on a smaller scale throughout Europe. The Spanish inflation spread as the bullion was disseminated and the Renaissance courts built their mercantilistic regulatory bureaucracies—all intended, of course, to vastly increase their wealth by planning new industries and their power by increasing taxation. Hugh Trevor-Roper has shown how the inflation and these regulations and taxes led to the general twenty-year depression starting around 1618.[8] Most of the rulers were overthrown by revolutionary violence. France went bankrupt repeatedly, but Colbert's mercantilism, tempered by a massive black market and evasions of regulations, limped on to its own destiny with the guillotine more than a century and a half later. The few Cassandras who saw what was happening and tried to rid the land of the pestilential bureaucracies, regulations, and taxes, as Turgot later did shortly before the French Revolution, were repaid with shocked outrage and ostracism by the vast coalition of interest groups. Their politicians' and bureaucrats' most "rationally" planned actions led to their own destruction because they would not see what to us seem the too obvious consequences of their actions. They were blinded by the rationalistic myths of mercantilism and drifted into the political and economic catastrophies produced by the bureaucratic gigantism of all megastates.

Americans commonly see the Founding Fathers as the perfect example of how rational men of good will can construct a society that works the way they intended it to work. After the octopal political plots and usurpations of Watergate had been disclosed and extirpated, these optimists proclaimed

"The system still works!" But this belief is actually an example of the historical blindness that can hide the sweeping systemic drift of a society from common view and, thereby, prevent any effective resistance to it. The American System today, that of highly centralized and massive government, is certainly the exact opposite of what our culture creators intended.

Explaining Blind Systemic Drift

Blindness to the great tidal drifts of history has at least two sources. There are, first, the ever-present complexities and irreducible uncertainties in the outcomes of human action. Given these complexities and uncertainties, it is not hard today to understand how rulers from the earliest civilizations have been enticed in periods of costly bureaucratic government to debase the coinage, then fight the inevitable inflation with price controls, then watch unbelievably and with outbursts of moral outrage against the "criminal" businessperson as investment and exchange died away, the nation was further impoverished, and inflation was eventually made worse. Yet, in spite of all this recorded and well-known history of the catastrophes wrought by inflation and price controls, this same process of politically induced immiserization has been repeated blindly in our own century by the bureaucratic governments of our welfare states. There are many once-great nations today that are enacting our modernist variation on that ancient theme, as if they were puppets dancing on the strings of centralized planning pulled by some ancient Ptolemy. Yet the people and most of their leaders, even brilliant men like François Mitterrand, are long mystified by the outcome of their actions.

The second major source of such historical blindness that allows society to drift into catastrophe, long after all the dire signs of the new "times of trouble" are omnipresent, is our symbolic and moral *inertia*, that is, the tendency of our symbols and morals, our beliefs and values, to continue along old lines while our feelings and mythical symbols and concrete actions are leading us to drift in wholly new directions. Most human beings all too easily deceive themselves about the symbolic meanings and consequences of what they are doing when those actions contradict what they wish to think morally about themselves (their "ego-ideals") or when they are influenced by the powerful passions of power lust, money lust, and sexual lust. Studies of deviance have shown us that most people who drift into wholly new deviant patterns of life, such as prostitution, resist talking about themselves in those terms for years and insist sincerely on using terms like "sex therapist," "playgirl," or no words at all. By not using these emotionally loaded moral categories, the stigmatizing labels, they partially avoid feeling guilty or ashamed and, thereby, deceive themselves into drifting blindly into a life they once abhorred. In a very real sense, their emotions conspire successfully against their minds and traditional morals.

In societies with intense pride in earlier forms of social life, such as democracy or individual enterprise, the whole society can subconsciously deceive themselves in conspiracies of blind drift into all those things they once abhorred and only later, if ever, admit what they have become. This is, in fact, the normal process of social deceit by which proud and enterprising democracies or republics became meek and submissive tyrannies. Most of the Greek city-states, for example, went through this process at some time from the sixth to the third centuries B.C., many more than once. Peisistratus, the first famous tyrant of ancient Greece, was a theatrical master at building fronts of legitimacy for his tyranny (see appendix I). Augustus, whose reign, beginning in 30 B.C., transformed the Roman Republic into an imperial tyranny, always carefully concealed his tyrannical powers behind the once-proud forms of republican freedoms, and behind his masterful mien of egalitarian humility. Not until Diocletian and Constantine in the third and fourth centuries A.D. did the Roman tyrants openly proclaim their absolutist powers with success. In fifteenth century Renaissance Italy, the Medicis exercised tyrannical powers in Florence but always hid behind democratic masks—and rarely assumed any public office. This is the key to success for the tyrannical prince, as Guicciardini and Machiavelli realized from their own experience—and as recent experience has warned us over and over.

It is a lesson that has not been lost on our modern tyrants. Not a single totalitarian tyranny today dares proclaim itself either totalitarian or tyrannical. The most terrible totalitarian regimes in human history now oppress hundreds of millions of human beings, but nowhere do they dare to name themselves for what they so obviously are—totalitarian slave states. Of course, this is most obvious to those of us outside. Many of those inside prefer not to see the obvious and pretend to be "good Germans" or "good Russians" until their sufferings become so great they prefer to confront the realities. Everywhere these murderous dictators proclaim their totalitarian regimes to be "people's republics" or hide behind some other shining symbols of freedom and democracy. The dictators of the Communist Party of Russia rule over an imperial bureaucracy whose death camps and gulags have murdered many more millions than any previous government in human history, whose secret police have terrorized their entire population as thoroughly as any previous government, whose armies tyrannize the largest contiguous empire in human history. But these new Russian emperors hide behind the names of democratic freedoms and republican constraints and publicly denounce all forms of imperialism. The very name of their empire, Union of Soviet Socialist Republics, is a lie. It is "united" only by brutal force; the party destroyed the basic idea of the Soviets; and they are the opposite of republics. Even "socialism" steals the name of a utopian myth of total equality to label a total-itarian dictatorship in which the party members, who make up less than 7 percent of the population, have special stores and resorts and vast political powers. The murderous brutalities of their death camps are hidden behind the scientific labels of psychiatry; their economic tyranny and exploitation of the masses is hidden behind a symbolic facade of economic democracy.

The Power of Social Myths

Social myths are a vital ingredient in most periods of sweeping systemic drift in a society and in all successful forms of political deceit that move a people away from their sacred values. Most of the time we human beings are rational animals who consciously choose our paths of action to try to "optim-ize" or "satisfice" our movement toward our many basic goals, set by human nature, cultural, and individual experience. Certainly we are often misled by mistaken ideas and, thereby, frustrated in seeking our goals. But normally the pain of our frustrations quickly leads us to give up our mistaken ideas and either to find an idea that works or another mistaken one that will in turn soon be surrendered to our new pain of failure. In this way human life is normally a complex process of trial and error that inches forward by discovering, largely through our many failures, what does not work and what does work in our world of painful but necessary uncertainty. When we discover patterns of action that work to satisfy some of our basic desires, we develop norms (values, morals) that prescribe these patterns of action as the "right" ones in the future, thus making it more likely we'll perform them—and thus succeed—the next time. When we find what doesn't work, we proscribe them normatively and, thereby, hope to avoid future pains. Norms may be presented as absolute by those who want others to continue acting in accord with them, but in fact they normally change in a slow step-wise drift when they lead to systematic frustrations of our basic desires.

The most tradition-bound norms, those hoary with the encrustations of the "cake of custom," normally soon fall before the pains of repeated frustration. Many anthropologists and experts of economic development long assured us that if they were to avoid mass starvation, cultural revolutions would be necessary to destroy the customary, normatively prescribed patterns of tradi-tional agriculture in many poor societies. But the dwindling per capita pro-duction on their small farms opened the eyes of almost all poor farmers throughout Asia to the advantages of new strains of rice, thus producing the Green Revolution without any cultural revolution, and thus producing sur-pluses for export where so many experts had predicted starvation. Before the Meiji restoration in 1868, Japan was one of the most tradition-bound (feudal) and economically primitive nations in the world. The Tokugawa Regime greatly restricted contact with all foreign ideas for centuries. Yet, by opening their nation to all forms of Western technology and allowing far more free enterprise in using that knowledge, the new political leaders allowed their people to take a rational leap into prosperity and power in one generation. This same leap is now being taken by the newly industrializing societies of Asia—Hong Kong, Taiwan, Singapore, Thailand, and South Korea. Individual human beings are marvelously adaptive when their rationality is allowed relatively free reign in fitting their practical means to their own ends and reap the consequences (both gains *and* losses) of those actions.

But, of course, individuals have rarely been very free to organize their lives by reason alone. There have normally been external restraints, ranging from the benevolent pressures of relatives and friends to the commands of government regulators. These external restraints will concern us a great deal throughout this work, but it is the internal constraints on the exercise of reason that must first concern us. For it is these internal constraints that underlie almost all submissions to external restraints over long periods of time. Individuals will not long submit to external restraints on their rationality unless there are internal restraints that support submission to the external restraints.

The internal restraints on rational action come in two forms. The first form is *mistaken beliefs,* which may be more situational or more culturally transmitted in the form of normatively prescribed beliefs. The value of norms is that they serve as a social memory that encodes heuristic or flexible plans for success and failure. But when the situation changes, our norms may be pushing us in the wrong directions. The second form is *mythical beliefs,* or, more simply, myths. *Myths are mistaken beliefs shaped by and supported by powerful emotions.* It is these powerful emotions that make mythical beliefs so extremely resistant to change. When the emotions are most aroused, myths may be retained and acted upon regardless of any amount of evidence showing them to be wrong. This, however, is true only of a small percentage of people—the "diehards."

Myths, as the greatest mythologists have all realized, are very much like dreams. (The Australian Aborigines explicitly refer to their myths as accounts of events that happened in a distant "Dream Time.") We might even call them our *waking dreams.* While they are more subject to the demands of rationality than dreams, they still share more of the special structure of dreams than the logic of reason. As G.S. Kirk[9] has said, myths, like dreams, look inward more than they look outward. They appear to be responses of our largely preverbal, prelogical mind to our strongest emotions. They express and objectify these passions in the forms that can be shared in common identifications and rituals with our Soul-mates.[10] Myths are, in fact, communicated best—most emotionally—by the nonverbal imagery of ritual and body language. Sound, color film is the "miraculous" way to communicate the miracles of myth. "The Wizard of Oz" and "Gone With the Wind" are known to be fictitious stories, but they appeal to American emotions so powerfully that when we are experiencing them we automatically tend to suspend our disbelief—to be transfixed—and they become great American myths—until the lights banish them once again to the realm of stories.

Claude Levi-Strauss,[11] Edmund Leach[12] and many other mythologists have even argued that when we do communicate myths verbally our words commonly are given a structure (almost a cadence) that tends to mislead or even paralyze our rational mind so that logical contradictions appear to be resolved. For example, this structure of myth encourages our minds to believe that what we would rationally see as violations of our basic values are not violations at all but are actually totally in accord with those values.

Myths, then, are predominantly the voice of our emotions, the images of our passionate hopes and fears, of our passionate longings and hatreds. It is, in fact, easy to see myths being created by people in the full heat of love or hatred. Everyone who falls in love has a tremendous tendency to idealize the loved one; to see him or her through "pink lenses." The most remarkable thing of all is that, not only do our thoughts about the loved one become idealized, but our very perceptions of their physical features are transfigured and someone who before was of average attractiveness suddenly becomes "the most beautiful person in the world." But once the love dies, this paragon of perfection once again turns into a pumpkin and we wonder, "How could I ever. . .?!"

Albert Speer has presented a stunning picture of how Hitler wove a magical spell of myths that expressed his and most other Germans' passions of the day, thereby tempting them to fall in political love at first speech and from then on hear him and his unknown program through the pink lenses of love possession:

> Hitler's initial shyness soon disappeared; at times now his pitch rose. He spoke urgently and with hypnotic persuasiveness. The mood he cast was much deeper than the speech itself, most of which I did not remember for long. . . .Both Goebbels and Hitler had understood how to unleash mass instincts at their meetings, how to play on the passions that underlay the veneer of ordinary respectable life. Practiced demagogues, they succeeded in fusing the assembled workers, petits bourgeois, and students into a homogeneous mob whose opinions they could mold as they pleased. . . .But as I see it today, these politicians in particular were in fact molded by the mob itself, guided by its yearnings and its daydreams. Of course Goebbels and Hitler knew how to penetrate through to the instincts of their audiences; but in the deeper sense they derived their whole existence from these audiences. Certainly the masses roared to the beat set by Hitler's and Goebbels's baton; yet they were not the true conductors. The mob determined the theme. To compensate for misery, insecurity, unemployment, and hopelessness, this anonymous assemblage wallowed for hours at a time in obsessions, savagery, license. This was no ardent nationalism. Rather, for a few short hours the personal unhappiness caused by the breakdown of the economy was replaced by a frenzy

that demanded victims. And Hitler and Goebbels threw them the victims. By lashing out at their opponents and villifying the Jews they gave expression and direction to fierce, primal passions.[13]

After a decade of slavish devotion to Hitler, as the myth of the Third Reich was crashing all about him, and Hitler was venting his fury on all around him, Speer fell out of political love, his mythical blindness lifted, and he saw a new Hitler, one reconstructed by hatred into an ugly ogre.[14]

Goethe, having experienced this love idealization numerous times, portrayed Faust under the magical spell of love. He looks at what he thinks is Margarita and declares her the most sublime beauty, but he is actually only looking into a magic mirror (provided by Satan) that mirrors his own desires. It is his passion that magically transforms his perception of an ordinary young woman into an image of Helen, the most beautiful woman of all time in Greek myth. Stendhal, having been through this same universal process of creating love myths, argued that while our eyes still see the bad characteristics, the more our passionate love is aroused the more we focus our attention on the good characteristics, so our rational mind winds up processing only information about the good. My own experience with such "fits of madness" and my unimpassioned life studies of people in love lead me to believe the Goethe-Stendhal theory of love idealization is completely right.[15]

In precisely the same way, as we see in Speer's remarkable account, when we come to hate someone we deidealize them, that is, we automatically focus our perceptions and thoughts on their evil characteristics and thus see and think of them as evil. This is most obvious in *stigmatization processes* by which individuals come to brand others as monsters. Someone who hates Blacks, Jews, WASPS, Yanquis, gringos, wetbacks, capitalists, ad nauseum, focuses all his attention on any bad characteristic he can find, closes his mind to any good, and winds up seeing them all as the same monster. Of course, the less concrete experience they have with members of this mythical monster group, the easier it is to believe the stigmas. When one or a few are encountered who cannot be shoved into the category, they are actually partially idealized because they are so strongly *contrasted* with the monster myth. Thus we get the antisemites' "good Jews." A vast amount of research on the interactions among emotions, perceptions, and beliefs have shown these idealization and stigmatization processes to follow these general paths.

Creation Myths

Myths come in many different forms. In fact, there are so many different forms that anthropologists, historians, and other mythologists have often been mystified by them and wind up bewildering their successors by spinning out elaborate taxonomies to distinguish what they believe to be the "fundamental distinctions" (*fundamentum divisionis*) among types of myths. When we look beyond the taxonomies at the myths themselves, we find that the common element of myths is powerful emotion. It is powerful emotion more than anything else which makes it extremely difficult for human beings to give up mistaken ideas when they don't work in concrete trials. Many analysts of myths even include narratives and expressions that their tellers see as stories, rather than things they believe in. But these are rightly called stories or intentional fantasies. Myths are strong beliefs—convictions—that we can show to be mistakes in some of their fundamental aspects. As conviction wanes, the once "living myths" increasingly become "mere stories" that their tellers feel free to play with—to adorn, exaggerate, even invent from scratch.

There is, however, one distinction among types of myths which throws further light on why some are more resistant to change or rejection than others. This is the distinction between *magical myths* and *creation myths* (or general causality myths). Most forms of magical thought are reasonably simple cause-and-effect ideas. For example, it is a common belief around the world, and one generally supported by cultural norms and tremendous fear, that a man who has intercourse with (or touches, or merely sees) a menstruating woman will die, become impotent, or suffer some other calamity, unless he performs a prescribed purification ritual. Both the rule against his having intercourse, which is called a taboo, and the purification ritual are generally based on reasonably simple cause-and-effect ideas: you do it, you die; you do the purifying ritual, you're saved. These are the kinds of myths that nonbelievers find so delightfully funny and mystifying, because they would seem so easy to disprove. All you have to do is try it and see. But, of course, the natives' fear is so great that they almost never do try, so they almost never see the disproof; and, even worse for the true believers, when they do accidentally violate the taboo, they can literally go into a terror-induced state of shock, heart attack, and so on that actually does kill them. Nevertheless, these simple magical beliefs can be rather easily destroyed by an outsider. Tarzan often did this in the movies by violating the taboo (though not the ones about menstruating women) and living to tell about it. The natives watched in horror, then applauded when Tarzan lived, lynched the old medicine man who supported the taboo, and welcomed their great liberator.

But creation myths are different. They have both the universal property of myths, that is, being supported by great emotion (as Charles Darwin discovered) and two additional properties that make it extremely difficult to refute them through the use of common sense and everyday experience alone. Creation myths are, first, complex systems of beliefs and, second, they are removed (or hidden) by the system itself from everyday, rational experience and analyses. Creation myths are made up of many parts, some of which explicitly define everyday experience and the common sense built on this as irrelevant to establishing the truth of the system. The gods who caused it all always did it long before you or anyone you know was around to observe them; besides that, they insist on being invisible (not only to visual sighting but to detection by any means imaginable); moreover, they reveal themselves only in symbols or signs (like storms) that can be interpreted only by the most devoted true believers; and, if that's not enough, they insist that all this mystery is itself "proof" of why we should believe in them. And, since all of that is not usually enough to protect myths from the powers of rational criticism, creation myths are invested with "holiness" and, thus, protected by the rules against insanity and heresy, often including a death penalty for heretics. In exactly the same way, a creation myth might insist that an entire international economy is the result of a grand conspiracy that cannot be directly observed but can be indirectly inferred, but only by true believers; and, most ominous for would-be critics, that people who don't believe this inference are brainwashed by the conspirators' advertising, or, far worse, are part of the conspiracy, thus deserving liquidation. Heresy trials and censorship are always signs of creation myths being defended. If an American Marxist claims in *The New York Times* that our elections are rigged by a secret conspiracy, we shrug and say, "So what's new in the Marxist Cloudopolis?" If Russians were to say that in Stalin's *Pravda* (which, of course, censorship prevented), they'd be liquidated (or, still possible today, psychiatrized).

The great myth of modernism is protected by one of the most astounding exclusionary rules ever observed. Its assumption of the uniqueness and superiority of modern humans is easily shown to be absurd by all the vast historical and scientific evidence from many disciplines showing that there is a genetically determined human nature that makes us overwhelmingly similar to all human beings throughout the five thousand years of recorded evidence. But the modernists counter this massive evidence by denying there is any human nature and assuming absolute cultural relativism. Their only evidence to support their assertions is that we can generally find some cultures or individuals who do not share the properties of 95 percent of cultures or individuals. This "counter" evidence from Bongo-Bongo is actually one of the strongest supports for the genetic theory of human nature, as we shall see, but the modernists refuse to look at that fact, exactly like the theologians who refused to look through Galileo's telescope out of fear of seeing that geocentrism was wrong. By denying the relevance of historical evidence and then making ignorance of history a virtue—a symbol of "real science," the modernists exclude from consideration the evidence showing how absurd their modernism is. Did almost all previous governments use paper money to produce inflation? Exclude those irrelevant facts and full steam ahead with the printing presses! Did Martin Van Buren warn in 1843 that government paper money would lead to soaring debts, extravagant expenditures, and eventual financial collapse? Exclude such reactionary facts—we are too, too modern to commit such errors—indeed, when we did in fact do those things they were virtues, not errors! We have transcended history and human nature itself.

The Big Lie Made Truth

Though myths are mistaken thoughts, certainly not all of their elements are mistaken. Quite to the contrary, the most appealing myths are woven out of as many facts as can be fit into the whole cloth and they are woven by methods of analysis as rational as is commensurate with the properties of the whole cloth. The Greek gods and their beautiful playmates were extremely human (à la Grecque, as Herodotus noted) down to the most minute details of their lustful feelings, pronouncements, and actions. Moreover, the massive cloth of stories about them were related to the observable facts of everyday life (like storms) and were woven together very rationally so that they fit the observable facts and fit together to seem very plausible to the Greeks, who were obviously some of the most rational human beings of all time. Greek mythology was as realistic a production as any of our modern Cecil B. deMille movie productions.

But, of course, the realism of its "facts" only served to hide the vital fact that the whole cloth was a total mistake rationally. To paraphrase one of Adolph Hitler's crucial ideas in his masterful analysis of propaganda, the big lie works only when it is built firmly on a foundation of fact known to those to be deceived. Most of the detailed things (purported facts) Hitler said about the Jews were true. For example, some of the most important founders of Marxism, such as Karl Marx, were Jews. But Hitler, availing himself of the skills of Alfred Rosenberg, then spun off from this a monstrous whole cloth of creation myth that blamed Jews for every evil washing across the tortured nation of Germany. Contrary to the assumption of many historians, I suspect Hitler knew this creation was a big lie. One of his closest and most loyal collaborators, Albert Speer, eventually concluded that Hitler lied about almost everything even to him. Speer also presents overwhelming evidence of Hitler's "practicality" in political action. Hitler was more a user of ideological convictions than their victim, a nearly perfect picture in political deceit. But for the true believers among the Nazi masses, it became a great creation myth explaining many of their social evils and, thus, showing them they could exterminate the evils by exterminating the Jews. In general, then, there is an unspoken rule that the successful myth must be as factual and rational as is commensurate with its general claims.

There are, however, a few important exceptions to this general rule. We've already seen one of these. This is the *exclusionary rule* of myths: that is, myths are protected from rational analysis by the normative removal (thus concealment) of their most important aspects (the gods, the conspiracy, etc.) from direct observation and rational criticism. Closely allied with this rule in protecting myths is the *presentational-aura rule* of myths: that is, myths are protected from rational analysis by being presented in a general aura that invites—almost demands—the suspension of rational analysis and, thus, the suspension of disbelief. Most myths are presented in symbolic forms that appeal directly to powerful emotions and thus initially circumvent rational thought and then have the aroused emotions to suppress or counterattack rational thought. The older man who dangles a huge diamond and a lifetime annuity before a girl's eyes before he proposes to her can easily arouse emotions that cloud her balancing of opportunity costs against his promised assets. In the same way, mythologizers present their mythical ideas in a situation that envelops the initiates in a veritable cloud of signs and symbols that unobtrusively arouse powerful emotions supporting the myths. Mythologizers especially love to control awe-inspiring rituals, signs and symbols of power which make the initiates feel properly submissive toward them but powerful by identifying with them. Any sign or symbol of power (vast size, terrifying noise, etc.) can be used. Vast pyramids were used around the world when this was the form of construction that could produce the vastest structure and could reach nearest to the Gods. Later, vast cathedrals, then immense towering skyscrapers took their place. Albert Speer's use of one hundred and thirty searchlights to produce an immense, shimmering, luminescent "cathedral of ice" for a Nazi rally had such a dramatic effect that it seemed to inspire awe even in the British ambassador.[16] Oswald Spengler[17] rightly saw these vast and soaring structures as Faustian symbols of Western humanity's infinite, soaring aspirations for power. Today's most effective symbols of power are our giant, gleaming metal birds that soar to the heavens—747s for every dictatorial mythologizer around the world and far-more-gigantic space rockets for the super-mythologizers of the "super powers."

The most effective mythologizers orchestrate a mass of such symbols to envelop their mythical presentations in waves of emotion that sweep away all rational thought. Hitler's presentations in the sports arenas of Germany will probably never be outdone. The massive crowds, the columns of soldiers marching in unison, the soaring music, the thunderous waves of adoration and exaltation, the bright clouds of streaming banners and flags, the fierce eagles and archetypical swastikas—all built the mass of believers to a crescendo of excitement, communal identification, and love as the leader marched in to proclaim the truth from on high. Almost any human being's rational thought would be swept away by such an orchestrated assault of mythological symbolizing. Those who were trained since childhood to respond emotionally to such symbols were easily swept away and in their awed thrall could feel the absolute truth of the leader's mythical pronounce- ments and promises of Valhalla—of a National Socialist Heaven on Earth for all Germans to enjoy in total equality, of course.

None of our nation-state mythologizers today approach Hitler's success in using symbols to sweep away the rationality of the masses, not even the Kremlin dictators surrounded by their godly icons of Marx and Lenin, imperially staring down upon the strutting columns of troops and the huge nuclear-tipped rockets. But all of them envelop themselves in their nationalis- tic symbols to arouse the emotions that encourage their subjects to mythi- cally, symbolically identify themselves with the rulers, and the rulers with the nation-state. It is this irrational identification of the self with the leader and the mystical symbols of the nation-state which encourage the fatal willing- ness to subject oneself to the will of the leader and, supposedly, the fate of the nation and thus the common interest that the leader represents symboli- cally. Once this symbolic identification is made, individuals can easily make the fatal leap into the abyss by sacrificing themselves for the nation to gain immortal glory.

In his classical analysis *The Myth of the State*, Ernst Cassirer showed that the extreme myth of the state in Germany was first forged by the Romantic poets and philosophers of the eighteenth and nineteenth centuries. They saw reason as their enemy and myth and passion as the ultimate truths. They saw the symbols of poetry and music as the vehicles of emotion and myth, so poe- try and music became their primordial language. (This is why Wagner's soaring musical-poetic myths of Germany's gods were such an inspiration of belief and dedication in Hitler's supermen.) They were, of course, right that poetic symbolism and music are the most effective language for arousing the emotions that encourage belief in myths, a truth Plato first stated very clearly in *The Laws* twenty-three hundred years ago. Mythopoetic symbolism has been a bulwark of nationalistic state myths in all times, from the Menes of ancient Egypt to our modern creators of the Kennedy myth of Camelot.

Some of these statist myths may have sprung from the inspired visions of poets who were passionate believers in the great leaders they eulogized. This was probably true of those who invented the myths about George Washing- ton (such as the ridiculous cherry tree myth) and was almost certainly true of the creators of *The Lincoln Legend* that Roy Basler has documented so meti- culously.[18] Similar inspiration has probably been the motive of most of the mass of American literature that has sung the hosannas of those who pro- duced *The Miracle in Philadelphia* that created the American government. But successful politicians and their supporters have almost always under- stood and carefully manipulated the power of mytho-poems to give legitima- cy to their rule. Consequently, they have supported the media experts who sing their praises and the glory of their state powers in the mythic symbols of drama, literature, painting, statues, architecture, music, and all other arts and rituals.

Peisistratus used his vast wealth as an informal national endowment for the humanities and arts to support the mytho-poets who sang his praises. Some of the closest supporters of Augustus, the first emperor of Rome, subsidized Virgil to write *The Aeneid,* a panegyric to Roman imperial power which proved—in the emotional cauldron of mythopoetic symbolism—that the gods had decreed empire as the fate of Rome. Hitler, Stalin, and succeeding Soviet dictators used both terror and corruption to convince huge cadres of artists and intellectuals to create the myths proving the inevitability and supreme benevolence of their dictatorial state powers. And the nationalists of the United States, unwilling to leave their state powers to the vagaries of artistic inspiration, early in the century commissioned the most massive symbols of state grandeur ever attempted by mere mortals. The Washington and Lincoln monuments radiating along the mall from the Capitol, and pointing across the Potomac to Arlington National Cemetery, are the state shrines of the American secular religion that in this century has come more and more to inspire in our citizens awe and dependent submission toward the federal government. The Kennedy legend, our latest myth of the great leader, was consciously planned and forged largely by the loyal would-be-once-again knights of the Washington Round Table. (King Arthur, who, according to the myth, originally started the Round Table in the first Camelot, was actually a petty border raider who preyed upon his neighbors, more of a bandit than a noble of grandeur. But few myths of power are born in nobility or die with rational disproof.)

The Origins of Myths

A century ago it was commonly believed that "savages" (later euphemized as "primitives") thought in fundamentally different ways from civilized people. The "savage mind" supposedly thought in mythical forms, while civilized beings thought rationally. Claude Levi-Strauss and many other students of myth have tried to show that this is not true. The "savage mind" explanation of myths was largely a result of our modernist myth of our own rationalism and our human passions of pride and vanity. Mythical thoughts vary greatly both in their forms and their power from one society to another, from individual to individual, and from situation to situation for any one individual. But they are a universal potentiality of us all. It is a potentiality we must be continually aware of and continually correct for in our analyses or we easily fall into it in certain situations.

But what are these situations? Bronislaw Malinowski[19] provided the most important clue from his meticulous analysis of magical thought and rituals used by the Trobiand Islanders, especially in growing yams. As any back-yard gardener soon learns, growing food successfully is only possible when the gardener has and uses a great deal of practical knowledge, that is, con-crete facts about what is edible, how it propagates, when, in what kind of soil, with how much water, and so on. Trobrianders, like all agriculturalists, are extremely practical and use extensive facts about yam growing in the same way I do in growing sweet potatoes and "Irish potatoes" (really either a mistaken or mythical derivation, since they were first discovered in Peru).

Trobriand yam growing, unlike my potato growing, is extremely important to their entire lives. Since yams are their main food, growing them is almost a life-and-death matter. But yams are also vital in the Trobriand version of the human struggle for dominance over other human beings: those who grow the biggest, best, and most yams have the best chance to feel proud and to gain social status, and thus to gain women, children, and many other things. Yams and yam growing raises many strong emotions in the Trobrianders, especially in their growers.

As any gardener would suspect, growing yams is fraught with uncertainty. There are the uncertainties that result simply from the complexity of the prac-tical knowledge and its application. These uncertainties can be minimized by experience. But even with vast experience, there remain the large and neces-sary uncertainties resulting from the unpredictability of weather. These uncertainties combine with the importance of the yams to the growers to pro-duce the sense of the risk of yam growing. The uncertainty and the value of the payoff of an investment seem to multiply each other to produce the sense of risk, since the sense of risks increases rapidly with any increase in uncer-tainty or value of the outcome. Low levels of risk may produce no feeling and merely be handled in routine, even boring ways. Moderate levels of risk arouse excitement. High levels of risk produce anxiety (such as when you bet *all* of your money on a 50–to–1 long shot).

Growing yams is anxious business for the Trobrianders. Anxiety is a very loud hormonal call for human action to reduce the risk and, thus, the terrible pain of anxiety. But, having exhausted all of the practical means at their disposal, the Trobrianders would still be anxious. What will they do? Every human being knows immediately what they will do: pray or something equivalent. The Trobrianders do something roughly equivalent: they perform punctilious magical rituals intended to ward off the many possible evils. They resort to mythical thought and magical rituals (based on or implicitly justified by those thoughts) to ward off the anxiety and decrease the sense of risk.

Malinowski was thus led to argue in general that anxiety leads to magical rituals believed to control the outcomes of risky ventures. Once the magical rituals become habits, they are used in any risky situations to avoid the antici-pated anxiety, much as heroin addicts are desperate to get their fix in order to avoid the withdrawal pains they anticipate will come if they don't. Mythologists have often argued that we can never observe myths being created. But this is not true in the case of magical (mythical) rituals (or in the case of individual myths, seen, for example, in love-and-hate myths). Anyone subject to great anxiety will very likely become an instant magician and "There are no atheists in foxholes."

More recent mythologists have shown that Malinowski's analysis is right in its core idea but too simple. It is too simple first because he failed to see that *all of the powerful emotions can arouse or shape mythical thoughts.* The negative or painful emotions arouse or shape mythical thoughts that decrease, or promise to decrease, themselves. The positive anticipation can have analogous effects. Children waiting for Santa with vast expectations may devise rituals to "make him" bring that bike. Some South Pacific natives who were mystified by the vast wealth and power of American troops in World War II and wanted to get these for themselves, but did not know how or could not believe it could be done by natural means, created Cargo Cult myths, which involved the conviction that they would someday receive vast cargoes of American machines and goods from the gods.[20] Most people today who "pray upon a star" ("star light, star bright. . ."), pick the petals from a daisy ("He loves me, he loves me not. . ."), or perform any of the thousands of the cultural or individual magical rituals in our society are inspired more by hope (or greed or pride) than by anxiety.

We have already seen that uncertainty is vital in actually or potentially arousing anxiety and thus the myths to ward off evils. Uncertainty is also vital in titillating the positive emotions and, thus, myths and rituals to achieve our heart's desire. Consider, for example, the importance of uncertainty in titillating sex and love. It has been known by erotic performers since the ancient world that uncertainty is necessary to enflame desire to its peak. A normal man whose sexual desire has not been inhibited will initially be aroused by the sight of a beautiful nude woman, but, the more he sees her nude body, the more certain (habituated) he becomes and the less the mere sight of her body arouses him. (This is why nudists and the husbands of the most beautiful women are not driven to complete exhaustion). Recognizing this, the most successful practitioners of the erotic have always promised more than they actually show or deliver. The promise enflames desire, but the withholding, and the mere fact it has not yet happened, makes it uncertain it will be seen or received. It is this uncertainty that teases, or titillates, the desire to its peak. The striptease is a perfect example: the dancer reveals enough to arouse hope, but at the same time hides or withholds enough to peak uncertainty. Peak uncertainty multiplies peak value (the *most* beautiful body) to produce peak desire. Once all is revealed or possessed, habituation begins. If all is never revealed, the viewer eventually becomes certain it never will be and loses interest. The uncertainty of expectations is probably maximized for the longest possible time by pursuing an uncertain schedule of uncertainty, that is, mixing up, or randomizing, the amounts of exposure from one time to another. In the same way, romantic love is aroused by uncertainty and habituated by certainty. A Lady of Mystery (or a Mystery Man) excites more excitement than Always Reliable Nellie (or Solid John), and experts in the wiles of lovemaking have long known that "keeping them guessing," doing new things, personal growth, and looking different are vital to keeping the flame burning. Uncertainty and mystery captivate our attention and arouse our emotions. In fact, even our senses are programmed to respond primarily to variation or change. For example, when something moves we can see it far more easily and our attention is automatically drawn to it. So change, or uncertainty, is captivating.

Silence can induce a sense of vast uncertainty, and thus inspire mythifications because it does *not* focus our attention in a specific way: our attention is focused, riveted, *in general* and we search all possibilities of meaning. Since there is no specific information about what specifically the silence means, our dominant emotion, whether hope or anxiety, can then fill the information-void with its own sirens—myths. And these sirens then titillate the dominant emotion, which in turn increases the call of the sirens to the emotion. The Sphinx is the essence of profound wisdom, though it actually mirrors the dominant feelings and thoughts of the observer. In the classical western myths of American movies, the archetypical hero is almost always the tall and silent stranger.

The tallness of the hero, which is a sign of his strength, gives us a further clue to the mythification process. When emotions are extremely aroused, they can virtually make us see the things relevant to the emotions. Enflamed by satanic passion, Faust sees Helen in his mirror, just as a sex-starved saint saw a vision of a nude woman that was real enough to throw an inkwell at. (Ethologists have called this *vacuum activity* in animals.) But most of the time the mythification process is first triggered by some real events that are potentially very important to us and thus focus our attention and arouse our emotions; then the sense of uncertainty, such as that resulting from silence, triggers more emotion, which then weights our perceptions and interpretations of the events, thus allowing mythification. Great strength or power, such as that implied by tallness, is potentially very important. When we do not know for sure the strength is benign, our emotions normally are weighted toward the worst possibility—uncertain power (that of a stranger) is always potentially dangerous. If the tall stranger says nothing and gives no other clues, we begin feeling anxious and start thinking of all the terrible things he *might* do. The hero in the movies always disarms the suspicious minds of the good guys by smiling gently and speaking softly, thus inspiring myths of grateful love in the heroine, and the love-mythification is ignited at first sight and word. But he looks menacingly and speaks harshly to the bad guys, thus igniting myths of terrible retribution.

Psychologists have even been able to start mythification processes in experimental situations. In a typical anxiety experiment, children are read a blood-chilling story, preferably at night, to produce maximum visual uncertainty outside. Then noises are made outside and, as all readers of murder stories know, the children start imagining all kinds of horrible possibilities. Edward Crankshaw has shown that a very similar, but vastly more complex mythification process was ignited by Bismarck in Europe at the end of the nineteenth century. Having led Prussia to three stunning military victories in eight years, Bismarck had established the fact of Prussian power and his own. His main weapons had been secrecy, intrigue and the manipulation of uncertainty. While almost all men of power, especially in our mass societies today, are so removed from the people that they are largely uncertain quantities, Bismarck was far more so and was so by design. This, of course, might arouse only anxiety and, thus, invite stigmatization. Richard Nixon, who is strikingly similar to Bismarck in so many ways, suffered this fate in the news media. Something similar, though more mixed, befell Bismarck in the foreign media. But Bismarck, unlike Nixon, owned or corrupted most of the major news media in Germany, so they fed the victory-intoxicated people stories which mythologized this tall and silent stranger into the German hero—Siegfried returned from Valhalla, the first of the new supermen. After his stunning and exhilarating victory over the French in 1870, he made the mistake of stepping too much into the limelight while orchestrating his machination. His "image" (as Nixon liked to call such political myths) was gravely tarnished. After 1875 he withdrew into the shadows again and the mythologizing resumed: "Deep meanings were read into every action, into every abstention from action, so that the paradox arose that in a few years he recovered by passivity the reputation for statesmanship which he had jeopardized so sorely."[21]

We find, in general, then, that the value at stake multiplies uncertainty in arousing our emotions; and our emotions create a potential for, or susceptibility to, mythical imagery and thoughts. And, as we noted in the case of Nazi mythical symbolism, once the myth is created and believed in, then it too can arouse emotions, thus facilitating belief in itself. Consider, for example, a common pattern in love and sex. An individual who is sexually aroused by an archetype of beauty encounters a woman who fits the archetype; he is very sexually excited; this excitement starts the idealization process, so he begins to mythify her ("How kind *and* brilliant she is!"); this female myth is now more the type of person he can adore, so now he also begins to love her; and the love tends to lead him to mythify her beauty, thus arousing even more sexual excitement. Even more common, by interacting with someone, you begin to love them; this love leads you to mythify their beauty; this beauty then arouses you more sexually than you were before; and so on. Of course, there are conflicting, limiting processes at work that prevent myths from totally controlling our lives. We shall return to these, but first we must see the situational factors in our world today that give them more power to influence our actions.

Our Age of Modernist Myths

I've already noted that social scientists used to share the common belief that ours is an age of rationality and science which has banned mythical thought to the backward and dark interstices of our society where the light has not yet penetrated. And I noted that myth is a universal and ever-present human capacity, rooted quite obviously in human nature. All that is needed is the right kind of situation to call mythical thinking up from the vasty depths of our emotions and subconscious mind. We now see that in general this is a situation in which uncertainty is high, the stakes are high, and the basic emotions are high. The general stakes of human life and our basic emotions do not vary greatly from culture to culture or individual to individual. The most important variation in long historical eras is in the general factors, or trends, that produce uncertainties. But there are also situational and long-run variations that trigger powerful emotions. For example, sudden plagues or sudden increases in wealth trigger dread or greed.

Historians and philosophers have long noted that in comparison with earlier periods of Western society and with other cultures, our modern Western World is an age of uncertainty and anxiety. Some of them have meant that this uncertainty and anxiety are specifically the result of the waning of our religious faith. There has certainly been a waning of religious certainties, and it has triggered great anxieties, which have inspired many of our myths of security and savior myths. But I believe ours is an age of uncertainty and anxiety in other ways as well, and that this, as we would expect from what we know about myth, has made ours an age of modernist myths.

Let's look at one of our distinctively modern realms of activity and try to see what factors are at work producing mythification. Consider, for example, nuclear power. Let me first point out that I am not advocating nuclear energy. I believe nuclear energy in the U.S. would not be at all economically feasible if the government had not subsidized it vastly. The problems of nuclear waste and proliferation have been caused by government subsidies and, of course, they can only be solved by vast ratchets-up in government power. This is obviously a very modern realm with very high stakes—power, wealth, possibly life and death for millions. And, of course, it is a realm of vast uncertainty for most of us, thus arousing widespread anxiety. It is not a realm in which I can provide the analysis myself, but the scientists, engineers, technicians, and managers involved almost universally agree that the beliefs of their opponents about safety questions are totally false. (Note that on engineering questions there are always some uncertainties—the uncertainties inherent in artistic construction—and almost always some disagreements among the most knowledgeable people. The questions about storing the wastes are more uncertain scientifically, so I'm not dealing with them as myths.) Everything I've heard leads me to believe this; the experts seem very sincere *and* they are perfectly willing every day of their lives to bet their lives and the lives of their families on their rational assessments of safety. It also happens that, in stark contrast with conventional power plants, only one nuclear plant has become a real danger during their entire history and that was a Soviet reactor without a containment shield. Yet there are many people who have deeply emotional convictions that one or more of these plants will blow up and kill millions, that there is a massive conspiracy to hide the truth, and so on. These are predominantly mythical forms of thinking. In spite of this rational assessment, we sometimes feel the anxiety ourself because of our own uncertainties and the vast stakes involved; then we feel the myths surging up in us and we're about ready to flee.

The key question here is, what makes us so uncertain about nuclear generators? First, we know we're ignorant of much of the knowledge we would need to be sure rationally. Second, it's very complex and would take us years to understand it all rationally, so we don't do it. Third, the rate of change in knowledge and practice in this and most realms of science, technology, and industrial processes is geometric—so that we would have to be continually following developments to prevent an increase in our ignorance quotients. Since we can't without becoming more ignorant in our chosen realms, we become ever more uncertain. Fourth, we have no direct experience with the concrete operations of the generators or with handling any emergencies in them. Fifth, like most educated people today, we are more distrustful of scientists and experts than we used to be. We do not share the Frankenstein myth purveyed by our movies, but nuclear weapons have made us all more doubtful. Distrust makes us uncertain about what they say.

Known ignorance, complexity, change, lack of direct experience, and distrust are the five crucial factors producing our uncertainties. They are interdependent, since the more complex and changing something is, and the less direct experience with it we have, the more ignorant of it we are apt to know we are. These, then, are the situational factors that combine with the value of the relevant stakes to arouse our emotions and stimulate mythical thinking. Unfortunately, all these factors have been greatly increased by the vast development of science and technology.

As our collective knowledge has exploded, we have become aware that our average individual ignorance quotient (AIIQ) has exploded and thus made us more uncertain. As our world has become vastly more complexly interdependent, we also become more uncertain. Consider, for example, the uncertainty of the American farmer compared to the Trobriand yam grower. Weather is inherently uncertain for both of them, since the long-run predictions of the Farmer's Almanac and the U.S. Weather Bureau are both myths—and most farmers know it. Beyond that, the knowledgeable, experienced Trobriander has few uncertainties. He knows what he wants to grow, how much, and when. He does it in stable, patterned ways. The American farmer faces international competition, local competition, commodity cycles, general recessions, changing interest rates, and the ever-present possibilities of technological breakthroughs that may destroy (or save) his competitive position. He has some practical ways of reducing his uncertainties, such as hedging in commodity futures, if he's very big. But he still has lots of uncertainty about his livelihood, thus lots of anxiety and everlasting temptations to indulge in mythical forms of thinking—such as believing that farm subsidies, government loan guarantees, tariffs, and a full panoply of farm welfare state programs are good for him and for everyone economically, in fact, absolutely necessary to give him a secure floor to stand on. They *might* be good for him in the short run, but they're bad for him in the long run and bad for the rest of us all the time.

As our involvements with the whole world have grown and become ever more important, our average direct experience with things that we know matter greatly to us has declined. Only in the past thirty years or so has it really mattered much to us what happened in Russia, China, Vietnam, Mexico, or even New York (if we live elsewhere). But now it can be very important indeed to us what goes on in the Kremlin and around the world. On average, our direct experience has expanded, but this has been miniscule compared to the vast expansion of things that matter greatly to us. We could go to Moscow to sit in on some secret sessions at the Kremlin, or go to Washington to sit in on some secret sessions at the White House, the Federal Reserve, or any of the ninety-two separate regulatory agencies that now partly control our lives; but I doubt they'd let us. Our uncertainties have grown greatly because of this and they have combined with our scientistic myth-making processes to produce an explosion of mythical thinking in our modernist age that poses a grave threat to all of mankind. We shall see in the next few chapters how our growing uncertainties about economic life have combined with dread, produced by busts, and greed, produced by booms, to trigger and reinforce the three great millennial myths that help to produce the drift into statist powers.

Scientistic Mythmaking in the Modernist Age

It is obvious in one sense that ours is an age of explosive mythologizing. For one thing, we have been experiencing a reexplosion of the very same myths that exploded several times in the ancient world and eventually inundated science and destroyed the economic foundations of democratic and republican freedom. In the last twenty years astrology and many other forms of ancient occult practices have grown rapidly, especially among the young. As some of the close observers of these movements have argued, there is an important element of pop cult and even faddism involved. But there is also an equally strong element of belief in most participants, and conviction among many. It is these ancient myths, especially astrology, that swamped Greek science in the fourth and succeeding centuries B.C., then spread to Rome in the second and first centuries B.C..[22]

We have also seen the massive proliferation of "new religions" built on totalitarian salvation myths, and wholly new salvation myths, such as the extraterrestrial myths purveyed by books whose authors insist vehemently that they have ridden in these saucers and other space ships. We have had a massive revival of the nineteenth-century Romantic myths, ranging from the salvation-through-purity-and-innocence myths of *The Greening of America*[23] to the Arcadian myths of absolute "naturalness." And, of course, we are witnessing in the United States a gigantic revival of evangelical sects comparable to but more political than the revival movement in the early and late nineteenth century. Out of these evangelical sects has come the angry creationist movement, which is absolutely convinced that the myths of Genesis are the literal truth, something even few educated churchpeople in the late nineteenth century accepted.

These ancient and neoancient myths have spread so rapidly to tens of millions of our citizens that many scientists, aware of what happened to Greece and Rome, have banded together to oppose them. Certainly they are a grave sign of the deep and growing uncertainties, anxieties, and other powerful emotions in our societies. And it is possible that they could once again destroy the progress of human reason and precipitate a second Dark Age. But I doubt it very much. Myths such as astrology may delight even very rational people, but the historical and scientific evidence against such myths as astrology is so overwhelming that few intelligent people would support them with serious arguments once they were exposed to the evidence. Their revival is as much a symptom of the massive loss of historical knowledge among nominally educated Americans as it is of our myth-stimulating uncertainties and emotions. A few whiffs of historical knowledge would reveal all the hilarious absurdities of such myths and send their purveyors scurrying for the cover of something more respectable. It is the more respectable, the seemingly more rational myths we must fear. These are the rationalistic, scientistic myths of modernism, and it is these that have combined with some of the most ancient myths to form the economic and political myths I call the great myths of the modernist welfare state.

The Scientistic-Savior Monomyth

We shall be concerned throughout this book with the details of these scientistic myths and their effects in our modernist welfare states. But there is an immensely popular form of myth sweeping our Western societies today which reveals how prone to myths we are, *how rarely we see them as myths,* and how our most successful myths synthesize our ancient religious myths and our myths of scientific form (scientism). This is our scientistic-savior monomyth.

One of the most extreme forms of the scientistic-savior myth, one that Carl Jung saw as an obvious savior myth, but in scientistic garb, is the myth of the scientifically superior beings from outer space (superior and pure extraterrestrials) who come to earth in the many forms of UFOs to save humanity from the evils of its ways, generally by imposing external controls, as Klaatu threatened to do in "The Day the Earth Stood Still." Sometimes the superior being is a human being projected into the future who rules as a police officer of superior knowledge and purity (as in the case of the heroes of *Star Trek*), sometimes with the aid of a godlike, magical force (as in *Star Wars*). This theme has been presented in science fiction many times, but for many people the stories are a "reality"—powerful myths in which they subconsciously will a suspension of disbelief. When they enter the molten springs of the subconscious in childhood before the conscious guardians of rationality are fully developed, as we see in the case of E.T., these myths will haunt the emotions and distort the reasoning of millions.

In their book *The American Monomyth*, Robert Jewett and John Lawrence[24] have argued that in recent decades (roughly, I would say, the period of the most rapid growth of the modernist welfare state), one myth has come to dominate American popular culture so greatly that it can be called a monomyth like the myth of Hercules of the ancient world which came in time to pervade almost all other myths. The hero of this monomyth is strikingly different from the hero of classical Western myths but they evoke the same zealous belief, turning a fictitious story into a powerful mythical reality that hybridizes Christian millennialism with modernist scientism:

Whereas the classical monomyth was based on rites of initiation, the American monomyth derives from tales of redemption. It secularizes the Judeo-Christian redemption dramas that have arisen on American soil, combining elements from the selfless servant who impassively gives his life for others and the zealous crusader who destroys evil. The supersaviors in pop culture function as replacements for the Christ figure, whose credibility was eroded by scientific rationalism. But their superhuman abilities reflect a hope of divine, redemptive powers that science has never eradicated from the popular mind. The presentation of such figures in popular culture has the power to evoke fan loyalties that should be compared with more traditional forms of religious zeal; among those who resist overt fandom, the superheroes seem to offer a *mythic massage* that soothes and satisfies. It imparts the relaxing feeling that society can actually be redeemed by antidemocratic means.[25]

Jewett and Lawrence are able to show that this *monomythic modernist, millennial savior* has some roots in the cowboy hero from the 1930s onwards but increasingly has been invested with the supernatural powers of scientism. They are seen in their purest form in "sci-fi" films like *Star Wars* and *The Empire Strikes Back*, in which the pure warriors use both The Force and science-technology to fight the awesome and evil forces of the Empire. But they are also the heroes of the mass of catastrophe films, like *Earthquake* and *Jaws*, in which puritanical and, generally, scientifically superior heroes take the law into their own hands and with purification rituals and violence redeem the community and restore pristine innocence, happiness, freedom, and social order.

This monomythic hero of modernist America had no place in the Horatio Alger mythical heroes of nineteenth-century individualistic America. Alger was like the beneficiaries of the welfare-statist heroes, but, unlike them, he did not need a pure hero to deliver him. Alger did have to be Christian in his action, but above all he needed to work very hard, then have a bit of luck in the form of a reciprocally altruistic capitalist looking for a devoted worker and willing to pay well in exchange.

Jewett and Lawrence argue that this modernist savior monomyth has sprung from a sense of anxiety and dread that has beset Americans in recent decades because of a feeling of individual helplessness growing out of numerous crises. They do not note the relation of these crises and the monomyths growing out of them to much earlier millennial myths in which the saviors are otherworldly heroes, not modernist heroes, but the relation is obvious. They seem to think that the response to the dread so far has been a turning inward to story-myths, but they definitely fear that this savior myth is preparing the way for the political hero on a white horse (or rocket). I think it is obvious that the heroes of the modernist welfare state, ranging from Roosevelt, Kennedy, and Johnson to Ralph Nader, have fit the basic modernist, millennial pattern. The one major exception is that, while the more-recent ones, especially Kennedy and Johnson, did continually summon up crises from the rice paddies of Vietnam to the slums of Harlem, their rhetoric spoke even more of the lofty Great Society or whatever that is just within our reach if only we will give them more power to achieve it. We will reach for the heavens, clasp the moon in the ninth heaven, or bring heaven to earth. War on poverty! War on drugs! War on crime! War on cancer! War on inflation! War on a mere 2 percent or 3 percent annual rate of economic growth! Again and again our modernist welfare-state saviors have proclaimed the limits of reality themselves to be crises to be railed against and transformed into victories by the miracles of scientism. Above all, they have used millennial anxieties and soaring aspirations to sweep away political economics and replace it with economic quixotism in the names of Christian goodness, millennial utopias, and science.

Social Scientism Triumphant

The raw stuff of myths, their images and inchoate ideas, spring from the emotions and our subconscious mind. But they can only be fully born by sneaking past reason, that is, by being plausible to those who receive them. The ancient Indian myth that the earth is held on the backs of giant elephants finds few takers today in the United States, partly because of our space exploration and partly, I suppose, because we do not worship elephants as they did. (Even the denizens of our Flat Earth Society, who reassert their faith every time a space shuttle returns from orbit, do not defend this one.) Few of the millions of myths that have blinkered earlier human beings are plausible to us today. Myths must be believed to fit one's general conceptions of truth and reality before they can be seen as plausible. Only by being presented in the guise of what one sees as rationality can myths escape the stern criticisms of rationality which will inevitably come. In a Christian society the Antichrist must come in the guise of Christ. In a scientific society the antiscience must be presented in the guise of science. In a Christian and scientific society, the Antichrist and antiscience must come in the guise of both Christ and science—the caring savior who saves through the miracles of science.

Our Western societies today are obviously vastly more scientific and technological than ancient Greece. The triumphs of our science and technology have inspired such awe in people who do not understand the scientific perspective that they are almost worshipped as "the miracles of science." "Miracles" have always been the most potent "proof" of the truth of myths, a fact understood and used by all of the most successful magicians and mythifiers of all times. All of the most successful myths in our world today have been presented in the guise of science. And the most powerful new religions have commonly been presented as the absolute gospel of science. If the Antichrist ever comes to rule our modernist America, he will come in the mask of Christ and wrapped in the mantle of absolute scientific truth.

The natural sciences have been used as the mantle for innumerable myths. The ancient alchemists now don white coats and sometimes professional degrees to sell their perpetual-motion machines, their cancer panaceas, and their cryogenic ways to immortality. But natural-science myths will almost always be doomed to short lives by the high degree of certainty of the basic knowledge found in the natural sciences and by the certainty of the failure of the myths. These myths are almost always immediately analyzed to death by 99.9 percent of natural scientists and, if the project still sees the light of day, almost all the rest are quickly laid to rest by the bright light of failure. This is not to deny that there are some very rare instances in which this massive consensus against some totally new idea turns out to be proved wrong when the project is launched. Physicists rejected Edison's claim that he had produced light from electricity—but the light bulb worked anyway. But here we see a crucial difference between myth and scientific mistake. Because of the emotional commitment to the absolute truth of the myth, when the mythical prophesy fails the results are repeatedly explained away and the myth retained by true believers. Only protracted, repeated catastrophe will convince the diehard the myth is a myth. "Socialism has failed! Long live socialism!" could well be the subtitle of Mikhail Gorbachev's book *Perestroika*. When the scientific prediction failed, the physicists quickly accepted the fact and quickly and, for the most part, happily, revised their theories to incorporate this exciting discovery.

The most powerful myths sweeping our modernist world have all been wrapped in the mantle of the social sciences. Pseudo-scientists have expropriated the most complex, mysterious, and awe-inspiring forms of the natural sciences—mathematics, experimental procedures, hypothetical statistical verification procedures, laboratories, computers, etc.—but they have used these to get mass support for totally different kinds of theories.[26] The first social-science theories wrapped in the mantle of these awe-inspiring forms of the natural sciences were known as mechanistic theories. They were predominantly subject to the same kind of certain testing by observation as most theories are in the natural sciences. They were thus easy to prove wrong by direct observation and they were by the thousands over several centuries. But in the nineteenth century, some giants of social-science mythification found the key to avoid disproof by observation. They introduced absolute moral assumptions disguised as scientific concepts; they made their theories so general and universal that any attempt to disprove them by observation necessarily became entangled in massive complexities; and they wrapped their myths in the usual mythical defenses—exclusionary rules—to prevent any disproof. The three most powerful political movements sweeping our world today, Marxism, democratic socialism, and democratic welfare statism, were wrapped in the forms of the natural sciences and constructed in this way.

A totalitarian system which succeeded in perpetuating itself would probably set up a schizophrenic system of thought, in which the laws of common sense held good in everyday life and in certain exact sciences, but could be disregarded by the politician, the historian and the sociologist.

George Orwell

The influence that Marxism has achieved, far from being the result or proof of its scientific character, is almost entirely due to its prophetic, fantastic, and irrational elements.

Leszek Kolakowski

Notes

1. M. Rostovtzeff, *The Social and Economic History of the Hellenistic World* (London: Oxford University Press, 1941), vol. 1, p. 415.
2. M. Rostovtzeff, *Rome* (New York: Oxford University Press, 1960), p. 77.
3. Arnold J. Toynbee, *Greek Historical Thought* (New York: Mentor Books, 1955), pp. 109–10.
4. Fernand Braudel, *The Structures of Everyday Life* (New York: Harper and Row, 1979). On the crucial importance of uncertainty in free-market economic theory, see Frank H. Knight, *Risk, Uncertainty and Profit* (New York: Augustus M. Kelley, 1964).
5. See Ibn Khaldun, *The Muqaddimah: An Introduction to History*, 3 vols. (New York, Pantheon, 1958).
6. J. H. Elliott, *Imperial Spain* (London: Edward Arnold, Ltd., 1963), p. 115.
7. Earl J. Hamilton, *American Treasure and the Price Revolution in Spain, 1501–1650* (New York: Octagon Books, 1965).
8. Hugh Trevor-Roper, "The Crisis of the Seventeenth Century," in *The European Witch Craze* (New York: Harper and Row, 1969).
9. G. S. Kirk, *Myth* (Berkeley: University of California Press, 1970).
10. Ernst Cassirer, *The Myth of the State* (Garden City, NY: Doubleday, 1955).
11. Claude Levi-Strauss, *Structural Anthropology* (New York: Anchor Books, 1967).
12. Edmund Leach, ed., *The Structural Study of Myth and Totemism* (London: Tavistock Publications, 1967).
13. Albert Speer, *Inside the Third Reich* (New York: Avon, 1972), p. 44.
14. Ibid., p. 429.
15. See Jack D. Douglas and Freda Atwell, *Love, Intimacy and Sex* (Beverly Hills, CA: Sage Publications, 1988).
16. Speer, *Inside the Third Reich*, p. 97.
17. Oswald Spengler, *The Decline of the West*, 2 vols. (New York: Knopf, 1926–1928).

18. Roy Basler, *The Lincoln Legend* (Boston: Houghton Mifflin, 1935).

19. See Bronislaw Malinowski, *Magic, Science and Religion and Other Essays* (Glencoe, IL: The Free press, 1948); *Myth In Primitive Psychology* (London: Routledge, 1926); "The Role of Myth in Life," *Psyche*, vol. 6, no. 4, pp. 29–39; *Coral Gardens and Their Magic*, 2 vols. (Bloomington: Indiana University Press, 1965).

20. See, especially, Ralph Linton, "Nativistic Movements," in William Lessa and Evon Vogt, eds., *Reader in Comparative Religion* (New York: Harper, 1965), pp. 499–506; Anthony F. Wallace, "Revitalization Movements," *American Anthropologist*, vol. 58 (1956), pp. 264–81; Peter Worsley, *The Trumpet Shall Sound* (London, MacGibbon & Kee, 1957).

21. Edward Crankshaw, *Bismarck* (New York: Viking, 1981).

22. See E. R. Dodds, *The Greeks and the Irrational* (Boston: Beacon Press, 1957).

23. Charles Reich, *The Greening of America* (New York: Random House, 1970).

24. Robert Jewett and John Lawrence, *The American Monomyth* (New York: Anchor Press/Doubleday, 1977).

25. Ibid., p. xx.

26. Most of my earlier works have dealt with the details of social scientism in many realms.

6

The Explosion of Modernist Millennialism

> We can clasp the moon in the ninth heaven
> And seize turtles deep down in the five seas.
> We'll return amid triumphant song and laughter.
> Nothing is hard in this world
> If you dare to scale the heights.
>
> Chairman Mao

Our modern politicians know very well that great masses are much more easily moved by the force of imagination than by sheer physical force. And they have made ample use of this knowledge. The politician becomes a sort of public fortuneteller. Prophecy is an essential element in the new technique of rulership. The most improbable or even impossible promises are made; the millennium is predicted over and over again.

> Ernst Cassirer

Modern societies have substituted utopia for religion—utopia not as a transcendental ideal, but one to be realized through history (progress, rationality, science) with the nutrients of technology and the midwifery of revolution. . .

The socialist movement has (or had) the character of a secular religion, and only from this view can one explain its development and internal vicissitudes. . .

This is the permanent utopian—and even religious—component of socialism, a quest, as ancient as man's fall from grace, to unify himself with an ultimate and to find a world of freedom. It remains a world beyond.

> Daniel Bell

The three great modernist political movements—Marxism, democratic socialism, and democratic welfare statism—have some similar and some different ideals and means. Even more importantly, they appeal to somewhat different emotions to inspire mythical conviction. But all of them, though in varying combinations and to different degrees, synthesize the utopian myth of secular millennialism with the myths of modernism and rationalism-scientism, especially of social scientism. In addition, each of the political movements hybridizes and grafts many lesser myths onto these great myths. Each chooses somewhat different dimensions and degrees of these myths and their distinctive combinations are changed to meet new situations.

Marxism, for example, has synthesized an extremely large number of other myths with the three great myths and varies these in different cultures and eras. While purporting to be internationalist and antistatist, Marxists have grafted their great myth onto the powerful nationalist movements and statist parties around the world. It has, thereby, appealed to the widest spectrum of powerful emotions around the world. With the important exception of religious myths, the hybridized and grafted Marxist myths are like whole-dessert wagons with almost everybody's favorite sweets—all of them with no calories (costs) and chock-full of nutrients (benefits) guaranteeing everything good for almost everyone, except the few rich; yet all of them also are enflamed by fears and hatreds of the mythical Satans conspiring to steal the dessert wagon and immiserate all the rest of us. As Frank and Fritzie Manuel have noted,

> Marx combined the underthought of German philosophy in its Hegelian version with the rhetoric of the French utopians, which, unlike German philosophy, was easily adaptable to the styles of popular expression in any country, and with the rational argumentation of English economists amended and presented as science to give solidity to the whole structure. Marxists of later generations could stress one or another of these elements, transforming the whole in accordance with the passing needs of time and place. The amalgam became as flexible and plastic as the original Christian utopia of the ancient world, and it has enjoyed a signal success for much the same reason that Christianity and barbarism once triumphed over the Romans.[1]

It will be quite impossible in this short space to go into much detail about any of these myths. (Their historical grounding in ancient ideas of emanationism and Western Christian millennialism are dealt with in appendix IV.) The most important ones—the myths of modernism, rationalism-scientism, and secular millennialism—are dealt with throughout this book and in many sources to which I refer. This chapter will explain the great myth of secular millennialism and its importance in modernist welfare statism. Fortunately, most of the important aspects of my argument have already been dealt with in many excellent specialized works on which I have built.

Western Millennial Myths

Jewish, Christian, and Islamic millennial myths all involved the idea of an *inevitable* messianic (heroic) coming (a recoming or revolution—a revolving) that would follow a period of growing ungodliness and secular crisis and would usher in a period of heaven on earth to be followed by the beginning of the otherworldly heaven. There are similar recoming myths in most, and possibly all, societies, at least in the most myth-triggering situations, because of the probably universal importance of the myth of the eternal return,[2] which is built on the more basic great myth of eternal stasis. The myth of eternal stasis is probably one of the universal myths of human beings. It portrays the ultimate ground ("the ultimate reality," "the really real," etc.) of all reality as unchanging, as eternally the same. The changes that we perceive in everyday life are portrayed as epiphenomenal or as mere appearances, even, at times, as deceptions of human beings by the Evil One(s). These changes are always undone by the "eternal return," the revolution or re-turning to the eternal stasis. (Plato's "realism," as presented in the allegory of the cave, is a classic expression of this myth.) One of the submyths derived by mythical transmutation from the myth of eternal stasis is the myth of the eternal stasis of wealth or the myth of the conservation of wealth, which portrays all wealth and resources as necessarily always (ultimately) the same. This variant is seen in the socialistic idea of wealth as necessarily a zero-sum game: that is, since the amount of wealth is always the same, some can increase their wealth only by taking it away from ("robbing") others; they could not have created wealth because that is impossible. (A fabulous mutation of this Myth is the basis for Fred Hirsch's paradoxical critique of welfare statism in *Social Limits to Growth*.[3]) This myth is found also in most images of "spaceship earth," "littleness as beauty," and so on. However, the myth of eternal stasis is not the dominant myth in socialism. Rather, it is a subordinate myth in ambivalent conflict, and, thus, in tension, with the dominant myth of secular millennialism. The importance of this ambivalence will become clear in my discussions below.

Western Christian millennialism differs from most forms in that it is strongly *historicistic*, that is, it posits an inevitable, necessary process of historical unfolding, however great the cycles of waxing and waning good and evil may be, leading to the messianic recoming and a posthistoricistic period that is, one that will transcend history. Christian millennialism has provided a general sense of expectancy, of fatedness, of doom-and-gloom and hope which has partially inspired secular millennialism. The two have interacted with each other very closely since the great stirrings of naturalism and secular millennialism during the medieval economic boom. In the same way that soaring naturalism and scientific and scientistic observation and theory inspired centuries of natural religion, so soaring Christian faith, with its many Augustinian ideas of dualism and emanatianism, inspired these predominantly secular activities. The most devout Christian theologian might easily shift into natural (secular) religion, as we see in John Calvin, and the most practical navigator bent on finding worldly riches might be seized by visions of the Garden of Eden, as we see in Christopher Columbus's conviction on his final voyage that he had discovered the outer reaches of the sacred garden, a conviction that implied that heaven on earth was just around the next bend in the Orinoco.[4] There has obviously been a general drift toward ever more secularity in Western millennialism since about the twelfth century (see appendix II), but there have been many waxings and wanings of both. There has, for example, been a great upsurge in Christian millennialism in the United States in the last few decades.

This complex interdependency between Christian and secular millennialism, and the situational swings from one to the other, seem to be grounded in the great ambivalent tension between inner and outer, spirit and material, being and nothingness, reason and experience, rationalism and empiricism, good and evil, God and Satan, light and darkness in Western culture. All cultures show some of this ambivalence, but it has been extreme in the West. The inner world of God, rationality, light, and so on has always been the dominant Western strain—the overtone of Western culture. Even in our materialistic age, the pure rationality of scientific theory is accorded greater status than the dark forces of empiricism, and the *materialistic determinists* are messianic rationalists in disguise. In science today it is taken for granted that the scientific revolutions that are crucial in the progress of knowledge are the transformations of rationalistic systems—"pure theory"—rather than maps showing the relations between discoveries made by chance, accident, guess, and intuition. Almost all of the most fate-laden discoveries in the sciences have begun with shocking experiences—empirical discoveries—that totally confounded theorists, thereby precipitating *crises* that can only be resolved by *catastrophic* changes or revolutions in theory. The Michelson-Morley experiment *not* discovering the effects predicted by the theory of the ether, the Curies' astonishment at the decay of theoretically irreducible matter, and the potentially world-shattering discovery of superconductivity at high temperatures have all been bolts from the blue, but the great discoverers in science are almost all forgotten, while the theorists who come after them are seen as geniuses who have an inner light that penetrates the dark secrets of nature, casts this light of knowledge on a startled and resisting world, and after many trials revolutionizes the world for the better. Pure scientists are the demigods of spirit from whom emanates the absolute knowledge of the pure mathematical forms of rationality. In actual practice the vast majority of natural scientists are very empirical and look at theory as the helpmate of practice. Practice and theory are the yin and yang, the foreground and background of a seamless scientific understanding. It is precisely the inherent interdependency, the existential tension between practice and theory, which is the crucial superiority of science over the myriad forms of rationalism and radical empericism. The "pure-theory geniuses" almost universally report that their workable theoretical ideas come from immersion in empirical fact and other everyday experience and that their creative insights come from intuition, most commonly inspired by critical experiences, which must then be rigorously checked out by reason and experience. But the popular image is still of the ultimate and absolute truth of pure reason emanating from the head of the godly spirit—the "geniuses."

The ecstatic, mystical vision of the revealed godhead, the ultimate unity of all being, has been central to Western conversion experiences. The extreme denial of the world has in turn been central to the rationalistic or spiritualistic dogmas that have always tempted the intellectuals and devotees, and that have always before been ultimately rejected. Ascetics have tried to destroy the corruption of the flesh, to purify themselves, so they can reunite with God. Mystical monks have used their regimen of devotion, labor, asceticism, study, penance, and good deeds to the same end. Rationalist intellectuals have focused their regimen on abstract reason. All have sought a personal ascension and reunion of their souls with the inner light of God which denies the reality of the world. The goal of the accepted Christian personal quest, and of the aggregated quests of the community of Christians, has been salvation through purification and reunion with God in the afterlife, not denial of this worldly life. Conversion, receiving grace, and eventually the millennial Second Coming have been based on the basic idea of purifying and ascending in order to *return*—re-volve—to the original state of blissful union with God after living the best life possible in the world.

The goal of Christian *revolution* has been to *return* to the original state of purity, light, and all goodness experienced in Eden before the fall into sin. This was necessarily an individual quest and an aggregated quest of the Christian community. It was also necessarily imperfect, because after the fall people have only imperfect freedom ("libertad") to try to control their animal passions. Historians analyzing Western revolutions, even those concerned with their millennial roots, have generally seen modern revolutions as fundamentally different from earlier ones because they have the goal of building a "new humanity"—a utopia, not in returning to an original heaven after death or an imperfect melioration in this life. This is clearly true of the explicit statements of the Marxists-Leninists and their many heirs, because they deny the existence of any otherworldliness. But this public truth hides a far greater truth. Marxism-Leninism is the most absolutist and most millennial of the modernist political faiths and movements. Any idea that is absolute (and only ideas can be absolute) is true for *all* times, *all* persons, and *all* places. It is part of the ground of being. Thus, the "new people" of the Soviet "posthistorical" world that lies on the other side of the explosion of truth in the Great Revolution are necessarily what always was—and will be—perfect. The revolution that will transcend history will necessarily return to the eternal stasis, to the ground of being. Even if the most rationalistic party theologian asserts these "new Soviet people" must be constructed by historical materialism, and thus can only exist in the future, in fact they have always been the perfect Christians who have transcended greed, power lust, and any other worldly passions, but happen to mistake the party and the faith of the party for God and the holy writ. Russian prophets since Dostoevski expected that the Antichrist would have to triumph in the guise of Christ because of the devout and literal Christian millennialism of the vast majority of the Russian people. The Soviets made the political mistake of announcing they were the Antichrist, but largely recouped their losses in legitimacy by grafting the Party's revolutionary millennialism onto Russian "messianism," as Nicholas Berdyaev called it. This is a more otherworldly form of Eastern Christian millennialism.

The democratic modernists are logically less absolutist and purist. They are meliorists who believe in reaching perfection a step at a time, rather than leaping into "the ninth heaven." But all modernism is aimed at transcending the historical and traditional evil of the ancient regime and entering into a new world of light and goodness—the "good life"—which bears remarkable similarities to Eden. The ideals of equality, love, cooperation, peace, charity, abundance, joy, purity, immortality, and so on are obvious. The other ideal of modernists which might seem distant from the biblical account of Eden is casual sex or free love, but this is merely sex without sin or guilt—sex before the fall, sex as a natural act, in which nature has been transformed into Eden, heaven on earth. The good life is secular life made angelic or pure. Indeed, "beasts" themselves are not "beastly." They are not predators and prey. They too were corrupted by the dark evils of the ancient regime and will be revered little brothers (and sisters) in the pure realm of the good life. The lions shall lie down with the lambs. What, therefore, should be surprising about democrats lying down with the communists in Russia, Cuba, Nicaragua, and everywhere? Anyone who shares the modernist faith—the "good people" marching toward the "good life"—knows that enemies and warfare are merely caused by the dark ignorance and evil of the ancient regime. There is no human nature and no sin to inspire power lust in those who see the light of the inner truth, the ideals emanating from and revealed by rationality and science.

Like Christianity, the secular millennialism of modernism waxes and wanes, going through many bursts of enthusiasm and many lulls. Sometimes secular millennialism suddenly sweeps the Western world, as happened during the adolescent crusade of the 1960s and early 1970s, then recedes to the nooks and crannies of politics, entertainment, and everyday routine. Sometimes it flares intensely in one nation, while in others it goes in the opposite direction. The Labour victory in Britain after World War II ushered in a great explosion of hope for the first coming. The many grim years of socialist immiserization which led to the steady decline of Britain tempered even the adolescents, so there were few British millennial "demos" compared to those even in France and Germany during the love feasts of the flower children. But for two hundred years these lulls have eventually been followed by new outbursts.[5] Secular millennialism is grafted onto modernism and modernism is as much the deviant offspring of Western Christianity interacting with economic and scientific freedom as mystical millennialism has been the deviant offspring of emanationism and Christian millennialism (see appendix IV). The eternal recurrences of millennialism in the West tempt us to believe in the myth of the eternal return and the myth of cultural determinism.

Human Nature and Modernist Millennialism

Millennialism is both reactive and proactive, but the degree of each can vary greatly. There is almost always a major element of reaction to some situation felt to be a great threat—a crisis that cannot be explained or met by traditional means. There appear to be some individuals today, such as gambling addicts, who are only *proacting* (reaching out to the imagined future). These are especially the idle young of the upper-middle and upper classes who have been so unchallenged and so sated by consumption that, perhaps, boredom becomes a terribly painful crisis in itself. Since some of them are also unconstrained by any sense of moral duty, they easily become the champions of any utopian entertainment offered up for their jaded senses. Such are the welfare-state supported students of the "revolutionary festival," as Frank Manuel and Fritzie Manuel call it in their monumental study of *Utopian Thought in the Western World*. Theirs is the spirit of the graffiti message aerosoled across the walls of Paris in "the revolution" of 1968:

> Utopia now. It's the dream that's real. You'll all end up croaking of comfort. Make love, not war. God, I suspect you of being a leftist intellectual: Long live Babeuf! Anarchy, that's I. We want music that is wild and ephemeral. A revolution that demands self-sacrifice for its sake is a revolution *à la papa*. The passion for destruction is a creative joy. Invent new sexual perversions. The prospect of pleasure tomorrow will never console me for the boredom of today.[6]

Schopenhauer had foreseen the threat of boredom in the modern world when he predicted that, even if governments could solve all social problems, which he doubted, "boredom would at once occupy the place vacated by the other evils." But I suspect this "pall of boredom" cast over some of our young Western elites today by wealth, leisure, and extreme tolerance (such as of sexual "variations") inspires millennial thinking and action primarily when it becomes so extreme as to generate a threat of extreme boredom and, thus, extreme depression.

Millennial social movements are triggered only by a major sense of threat combined with some greater, counteractive degree of hope for the future. Culture is the great conserving force. Cultural rules tell us to act in roughly the same way as in the past in roughly the same situations. It takes a great and widely shared threat that cannot clearly be solved by traditional means—that is, a crisis—before many individuals will give up customary adaptations and try very new ones, especially the radical ones envisioned by millennialism. Even then, the new normally involves merely a recombination of the old with the new. It is this *reaction against* a dreaded crisis that starkly distinguishes millennialism from beliefs and actions based on the Western conviction that human progress is possible or even inevitable. It is one thing to believe firmly, even devoutly, that human beings can improve things by working long and hard at it, but quite another to believe devoutly that we can have vast improvements almost instantly with little or no work or other sacrifice—merely by redistributing wealth, or by central planning, or by some other miracle policy, by a great leap beyond all previous constraints of human nature in the human condition. The sacred Western idea of progress is inspired by vast historical knowledge and individual experience that give rise to hope tempered by our equal knowledge of the many severe setbacks along the path to progress. Millennial hopes are predominantly reactions against dread triggered by crises. Millennial hopes have normally been vast overhopings recoiling from the specter of despair. By trying to vault quixotically into the ninth heaven with one great leap forward, they prevent our taking the many little, arduous steps that alone can really move us in that direction.

Reactions to *politically defined crises*, then, have been the dominant themes in millennial movements. But the most powerful millennial myths and movements are those that combine a maximum of reaction to crisis and a maximum of proacting for the imagined future of euphoria. Almost all earlier millennial movements were dominated by the reactions to crises. But *modernist millennial myths and movements combine a maximum of reaction to politically proclaimed crises and a maximum of proaction to sustain them when the crises recede.* This is the secret of their vast power and their sustained, if diminished, momentum even during periods of rapid and prolonged economic growth surpassing anything ever before achieved in the whole history of humanity. Dread and ecstatic hope do not merely alternate with the shifting historical situation. They are both always there, waxing and waning, with dread dominating during busts and ecstatic hope during booms. And, very importantly, they *potentiate* each other. Just as a depressant drug such as heroine combined with an excitatory drug such as methamphetamine can produce an ecstatic effect that is a multiple of the two effects taken separately, so the ever-shifting but copresent, dialectical tension between dread and ecstatic hope multiplies to produce a frenzied explosion of utopianism unmatched in scope and duration by earlier forms of otherworldly millennialism. It is this explosive frenzy of *synthesized and potentiating reaction and proaction* to dreaded crises and dreamed-of utopias which is sweeping our modernist world today.

The Ancient Religious Millennial Myths

The ghost-dance myths and movements that swept the great American Western basin and plains Indians from about 1870 to 1895 were typical of traditional millennial myths and movements. They were overwhelmingly reactions to social crises in which a hoped-for future heaven was far more a desperate escape from or counteraction against the present than something the Indians could feel to be possible in itself—that is, when the dreaded crisis did not exist. The crises were very real and dreadful. The Indians were rapidly dying off from diseases transmitted by the whites. Their lands were being taken, their buffalo slaughtered, their braves were killed in warfare, and their traditions were being destroyed. All the most powerful negative emotions were aroused—pain, dread, grief, fury, hatred, envy, and the lust for revenge. All traditional means of overcoming the crises seemed hopeless. Even with all of these general enabling crises, the ghost dances seemed to arise mainly in concrete crises that threatened more-immediate destruction, especially periods of drought.

Though the specific beliefs and ghost-dance policies varied, the basic ideas were the same:[7] a few prophets, normally men with high traditional status, used traditional ideas and patterns to forge a radically new redemption myth. They claimed to have visited heaven (or to have special knowledge in some other way) and to have been told that ancestors would return to destroy the whites, or that a tidal wave would sweep the whites away. They prescribed purification rituals and then war. They led the people in ecstatic dances invoking the powers of the gods and the coming of the ancestors. The most famous outcome of the ghost-dance myth was the battle of Wounded Knee in 1890 in which Sioux men, women, and children wore "ghost shirts" to ward off the bullets of the whites. The shirts did not work and hundreds were killed. This extremely realistic "disproof" of the myth led to their quick demise. Human beings normally unlearn powerful myths the hard way. The initial disproofs commonly lead to a temporary redoubling of conviction unless the disproof is overwhelming. But they do eventually learn.

Millennial movements have swept most of the major societies subjected to the many moral, religious, economic, and political threats from Western world domination, especially in situations of colonial domination. These movements have generally involved a profound ambivalence between yearning for a purification of the debased present and a return to the traditional culture, on the one hand, and, yearning for the power and wealth of the West on the other. The millennial myth is above all a bridge of hope to get true believers from present impotence (the shame of submission) and relative poverty to future dominance over the West and Western wealth—all the while synthesizing this future with a highly idealized image of the traditional culture (a golden age), perhaps to alleviate the anxiety and guilt that would come from abandoning the traditional past. The millennial myth provides them with an image of the future which resolves the contradictions in these emotions, desires, values, and beliefs and shows them how they can achieve this heaven on earth.

The Taiping Rebellion in China (1850–1864) was typical in most of its forms, though unusual in its immense scope, resulting in the death of about twenty million Chinese.[8] It broke out only after a long period of Ch'ing Dynastic decay, corruption, disorder, and poverty and a briefer period of Western colonial policy which revealed the immense Western superiority in military power and wealth. Hung Hsiu-ch'üan, the rebel leader, was greatly affected by contact with Western culture and by Christian teaching, a common synthesis found in "nativistic cults." The rebellion released immense emotions that inspired the terrible fighting. Like most such movements, the release from the controls of customary rules inspired a tremendous yearning for the ancient human goals of liberty, equality, and fraternity (normally leading to some goal of primitive communism), but this was combined with a rigid puritanism demanding extreme conformity to some idealized, purified idea of traditional rules in the Golden Age before the decline. The totalitarian puritanism that springs up in these millennial revolutions is a form of purification ritual[9] that normally involves self-sacrifice in ascetic practices (no sex, etc.) to propitiate the gods and to restore universal or social order. But the freeing from customary rules can also produce the opposite and generally does in some followers and subjects. This opposite is known as *antinomianism* and asserts that what was customarily sin is now goodness itself and a sign of God's grace. Revolution turns the world upside down and the myths of revolution show opposites springing from each other. Puritans, especially Calvinists, had a subcurrent of antinomianism, as seen in their justification of worldly accumulation as a sign of God's grace.

The hippies released by the second great takeoff period of American welfare statism, from about 1965 to 1975, were overwhelmingly antinomian, transforming all bourgeois sin into hippy goodness. But even they showed the ambivalence that dominates millennial mythical thought, for they also aspired to purge bourgeois life of its evil cankers to achieve its *real* goals. They wanted "real love" to rule the world, not "hypocritical bourgeois love." They wanted a Christian golden age transformed into a future heaven on earth, which, of course, would finally achieve total liberty, equality, and fraternity. In the end a high percentage of these antinomians became traditional puritans by joining the Jesus Freaks and many other forms of fundamentalist religion.

The Taiping movement was intended to achieve all of this plus give China its traditional dominance over barbarians through a transformation into a modernized, industrialized society. This movement, like almost all millennial movements, was soon largely paralyzed by the absolutist disagreements among factional leaders once the promised land did not arrive. This revolt was put down by Western arms, but succeeding revolts, such as the Boxer Rebellion of 1898–1900, included the same elements of millennialism. Maoism, being a Chinese form of Marxism, was profoundly millennial. Movements such as the Great Leap Forward are insanely suicidal from a rational, empirical standpoint, but when seen through the mythical haze of secular, modernist millennialism they look like the true way to leap into heaven on earth—the ninth heaven.

One of the greatest failures of Western social thinkers and policymakers in the last two centuries has been their failure to understand the nature of millennial myths and their consequent failure to see them at work in our own societies and in even more extreme forms in most of the world today. The result has been that they try to understand extremely powerful and destructive social movements in terms of rationality. From a rational standpoint the movements merely look insane or suicidal—or even simply mistaken when, for example, they seek to achieve wealth by banning investment by multinational corporations when it can be shown empirically that the people are benefiting economically from trade with the corporations. But all of this is a misunderstanding that fails to see the emotional-mythical inspirations for these movements, their great powers, and their great weaknesses. When fully aroused these millennial movements are almost entirely beyond everyday, practical rationality, so they are largely beyond rational persuasion.

Rousseau, one of the great modernist mythmakers, protected himself against all these "irrelevant" worldly considerations at the beginning of his *Discourse on Inequality* by invoking a sweepingly romantic exclusionary rule: "Let us begin, then, by laying facts aside, as they do not affect the question." Thus spoke the true mythmaker. (Of course, some fellow travelers of the movements are quite accessible to reason, so one should always reason with them.) Since they are in good part the result of a profound sense of insecurity, including intense feelings of shame and even self-hatred for being submissive where once they were proudly dominant, attempts to shame them by showing how immoral or insane they are only inflame the myth and thus the movement.

Extreme millennial "true believers"[10] are filled with self hatred and projected, paranoid hatred of the devils who supposedly oppress them. As long as they remain true believers, they are so distrustful, and so confident of eventual victory, that they cannot be trusted and are extremely dangerous to the devils. Any attempt by the devils even to help them will be seen only as a plot and will probably inspire more feelings of shame, thus hatred rather than gratitude. Any expectation that they will trust the devils enough to honor treaties with them is absurd.

But, at the same time, these movements are very subject to internal disillusionment, factionalism, terrible civil wars, and eventual return to rational thought and action when the heaven on earth fails repeatedly to materialize.[11] Unfortunately, the first realization of failure of the prophesy tends to produce a desperate explosion of mythical counteraction (like Mao's Great Leap Forward) and in some instances there are even numerous cycles of hope-failure-despair-counteractive-hope before the myth fades. Santayana noted that fanaticism leads to "redoubling our effort when we've forgotten our aim." It leads even more to redoubling our efforts when the first (or second) disproof by reality begins to seep in.

All of these misunderstandings and resulting counterproductive policies have been seen, for example, in the American responses to the Shi'ite millennial movement being led by the Ayatolla Khomeini in Iran. The Shi'ite sect of Islam has been a highly millennial sect almost from its beginning in the seventh century. They have a profound belief in the wisdom, foresight, and intercessionary powers of Mohammad's successors, the Imams; and a profound expectation that when injustice in the world reached its zenith the Mahdi would come to restore ancient Islamic order, justice, and power. The ordinary followers in Iran felt the usual immense ambivalence toward Western secularization, both a dread of its defiling effects and a deep yearning for its power and wealth. For whatever reason, the Shah's regime and policies tipped the scales of the ambivalence to the dread side, and the powerful counteraction of a millennial movement was triggered, unleashing powerful attacks against the West, especially the most powerful representative of the West, the United States, and against the westernized Iranians.

In his beautifully illuminating account of his travels through Iran shortly after the revolution, V.S. Naipaul[12] saw posters all over Tehran which proclaimed ecstaticly, "Twelfth Imam, we are waiting for you." In Shi'ite myth the Twelfth Imam went into hiding eleven hundred years ago, waiting to return in a blaze of glory to cleanse the world of Satan. "Devils" who attack them morally and physically, short of using enough force to disprove the myth, only strengthen their belief, as the Americans and the Iraqis both discovered. But the movement is insane and suicidal, so, if left to itself, it will produce immense internal factionalism (especially once the Imam's light is no longer there to show the way to heaven on earth) and will disprove itself.

Millennial myths of this ancient, otherworldly kind still pop up in our Western societies in the ancient forms of Christianity, as we see in Jehovah's Witnesses, Seventh Day Adventists, Mormonism (to a lesser extent), and the many millennial fundamentalist sects now springing up everywhere. One of the most famous studies done by social scientists, *When Prophecy Fails*,[13] shows how resistant to "unlearning" their true believers are. Failures to meet the deadlines for second comings are routinely rationalized away. But only a few schizophrenics are totally impervious to failures. Repeated failures lead almost everyone to give up the myth. Human beings are both mythmakers and rational decision makers who weigh the situational consequences of past actions in deciding what to do in the present.

General Properties of Millennial Myths

There are some important variations among millennial movements, yet there is a remarkable patterning of the basic factors throughout the world. Even the variations, such as antinomianism in contrast to the far more common puritanism, follow certain basic patterns. Considering how many basic factors are involved, and the great variation we find in most complex human phenomena, it is remarkable indeed to find such a clear pattern in these myths and their situations of despair and hope. They clearly spring from some of the strongest emotions and linked ("primed") behavioral tendencies of human beings. They are deeply grounded in human nature and, once we grasp that fact, it is not surprising to find them popping up in our secularized Western societies in secularized masks. The general properties of the traditional religious millennial myths have been summarized by Yonina Talmon:[14]

(1) Millennialism is "the quest for total, imminent, ultimate, this-worldly, collective salvation."

(2) "...The new dispensation will bring about not mere improvement but a complete transformation and perfection itself..." and "...the impending redemption is ultimate and irrevocable."

(3) Millennialism "assumes that history has its predetermined, underlying plan, which is being carried to its completion, and...this predestined denouement is due in the near future." Millennialism, then, has what Karl Popper has called a "historicist" vision of human events: history is *fated* to develop in only one sequence (evolution) and this fate has been foreseen by the millennial prophet (seer) and, thus, his followers and their leaders.

(4) Millennialism "is dominated by a sense of deepening crisis that can be resolved only by ultimate salvation." The crises are not temporary or merely part of life's normal crises: the crises are a "sign" of the coming redemptive transformation; the crises are part of the "fated" progress of history.

(5) "Salvation is to be enjoyed by the faithful as a group." *Collectivism and, thus, the common welfare are vital parts of millennialism.* All true believers must bear the crises collectively and be transformed into heaven on earth collectively.

(6) Millennial myths and movements are basically "dualist": "A fundamental division separates the followers from the nonfollowers. History is viewed as a struggle between saints and Satans..."

(7) Millennial myths have to an extreme degree the common tendency of myths to give an appearance of resolving totally conflicting opposites. The divine power (God, spirit, history, etc.) "is transcendent and imminent at the same time," both of this world and beyond it. Heaven (beyond earth) will become earthly, yet remain heaven, in the heaven-on-earth. Progress is historical, yet will transcend history. Out of destruction and death (crises) will come creation and life (heaven-on-earth): out of X comes not-X. This is most obvious in the antinomian movements in which "sin" becomes "virtue" (in the "holiness of sin") and "virtue becomes sin." (These are "transformation myths.")

(8) Most millennial movements are messianic: "Salvation is brought by a redeemer, who is a mediator between the human and the divine. Another important mediator between the divine and the movement is the leader. Leadership tends to be charismatic."

(9) Millennial "movements tend to be ecstatic...we encounter in many millenarian movements cases of hysterical and paranoid phenomena, mass possession, trances, fantasies; and in others ecstatic dance figures prominently. Closely related to these phenomena are the antinomian tendencies, which appear in many guises. In some movements the antinomian element is moderate and mild, in others explicit and radical. Many millenarian movements deliberately break accepted taboos and overthrow

hallowed norms. Sexual aberrations and excesses and unbridled expressions of aggression are very common. Sometimes aggression is turned inward; the members may destroy their own property and even commit mass suicide. . . .

Millenarism usually evokes extreme dedication and fervor. . . However, in a minority of cases we encounter the direct opposite: religious fervor manifests itself in excessive self-discipline, stringent observation of rules, and extreme asceticism. The Black Muslims, for instance, insist on strict order and decorum; they prohibit any excess and any expression of religious enthusiasm."

(10) "Movements range from the fairly passive and nonviolent, on the one hand, to the extremely activist and aggressive, on the other. . . .All millenarian movements share a fundamental vagueness about the actual way in which the new order will be brought about, expecting it to happen somehow by divine intervention.

It should be noted, however, that there is a strong militant ingredient in the millenarian ideology which more often than not outweighs the passive and pacifist elements in it. The assurance of operating in accordance with the predetermined divine plan and the passionate confidence in ultimate triumph may encourage heightened activity rather than passivity."

". . .An alternative and equally prevalent reaction is active revolt. Radical negation of the social order engenders, in many cases, open aggression and violence."

(11) Millennialism "flares up, in many cases, as a reaction to cumulative deterioration of life conditions and as a result of awareness of prospects for further decline in the future. We note also the precipitating effect of sudden and dramatic crises that aggravate endemic deprivation and at the same time symbolize and highlight it. . .First, it should be noted that the predisposing factor is, in quite a number of cases, not severe hardship but a markedly uneven relation between expectations and the means of their satisfaction. In many cases it is predominantly the inability to fulfill traditional expectations."

(12) Millennialism "occurs mainly in periods of transition. . . .In modern societies we find that those who have undergone the double transition of intercountry and intracountry migration and are both new immigrants and new urbanites are particularly prone to millenarism. Millenarian movements have proliferated during the transition between premodern and the modern way of life in rural Spain and Italy. Millenarian outbursts abounded toward the end of the Middle Ages and the beginning of modern times."

(13) Millennialism occurs especially among groups who are blocked from organizing politically to achieve their goals by this-worldly, practical activity.

(14) Millennialists "are not always the worst-off among the underprivileged. Those members of the deprived group who are somewhat better-off are often better able to take stock of their situation, to react, and reorganize."

(15) All of the predisposing factors interact with each other and, very importantly, individual actions and historical accidents are important in determining whether they occur or not, even when many of the predisposing factors are there.

(16) "It is mainly when the authorities are not only unresponsive and inflexible but also somewhat ineffective, or at least permit some relaxation of control, that the millenarian movement has a chance to emerge and spread."

(17) "The predominant element in millenarism is inner certainty and hope, not despair." ". . .Millenarism arouses truly great hopes and therefore can make equally great demands on its followers. By promising complete salvation, it is able to liberate formerly untapped energies and generate a supreme effort without which no major break with the existing order can be achieved."

(18) The greatest strength of millennialism, its inspiration of immense hope, is its greatest weakness when heaven does not arrive as predicted.

(19) "The most important feature of millenarism seems to be its composite, intermediate nature. It combines components that are seemingly mutually exclusive: it is historical as well as mythical, religious as well as political, and, most significant, it is future oriented as well as past oriented. It is precisely this combination of a radical revolutionary position with traditionalism that accounts for the widespread appeal of millenarism and turns it into such a potent agent of change."[15]

It is, of course, unlikely that any one millennial movement will show all of the general dimensions. The weightings of dimensions vary greatly and each has some unique cultural, individual and situational characteristics. In general, however, the more of the predisposing factors present, the more the common factors and patterns appear. Though the anthropologists and historians have tended to look only at the extremes of millennialism, we actually see all different degrees of millennial responses, with different combinations of actors, to different degrees and kinds of threats to individuals and groups.

In general, millennialism is born of intense ambivalence and is a mythically inspired joy-and-hope counteracting an extreme dread-and-despair triggered by great crises. If the dread-and-despair go away, millennialism dies down. So it is only when there is a profound ambivalent tension between joy-and-hope and dread-and-despair that we get millennialism, but joy-and-hope must dominate or else we get extreme dread-and-despair, as we commonly see both before and after the uprising of millennialism. Any social situation that increases either side of the ambivalent conflict and yet allows joy-and-hope to remain dominant will increase the millennialism. This is why millennialism occurs especially in situations where there is both real crisis and yet there remains real hope of escape; and in situations where a great hope is felt to be gravely threatened by something.

The millennial response that I shall call *optimistic millennialism* (or optimism-led millennialism) has not been studied by anthropologists because it is so uncommon in the societies they have studied. These societies have almost all been impoverished by Western imperial bureaucrats dispensing dependency-breeding welfare and annihilated by great plagues imported from the West and local warfare triggered by Western arms. But in our free-market societies there have been repeated periods since the eighteenth century in which economic growth has been so extremely rapid that human reason has literally been swept away into mythical hope. These boom periods have been known for three centuries to have their own peculiar boom psychology. This is seen most starkly in individuals who experience extreme *and* sudden success of any kind. This "star phenomena" produces soaring optimism, but it is always shadowed by a dread of failure (falling from the high and slippery media-pinnacle) and it is this ambivalent conflict that produces their well-recognized insecurity, their soaring optimism during success, and their tendency to swing so easily from soaring optimism to crashing despair with any slight block to success.

The same tinge of dread or despair is seen in periods of "frantic" optimism we call boom periods. I believe the reason is the human mythical assumption of the steady state, the myth of stasis: when we go way up, or way down, we expect, if only subconsciously where our myths reign supreme, an imminent correction. Note the two extreme expectations of imminent correction in our popular statements, "It's so wonderful I can't believe it's true" and "Things have gotten so bad they can only get better." This myth of stasis and its submyth of corrections is well known to any gambler. A "run of luck," good or bad, always "runs out" and you can only "stay ahead of the game" by "quitting while you're ahead." The so-called roaring twenties were only the most extreme boom period of many in the past three centuries, but because of this they show most starkly the millennial, frenzied joy-and-hope of heaven on earth (infinite and eternal wealth right away!) shadowed by dread-and-despair and a sudden shift from extreme high to extreme low once the crash made dread-and-despair dominant. The entire cycle, from frenzied hope for imminent paradise tinged with dread-and-despair to crack-up, can be seen writ large in the famous lives of F. Scott and Zelda Fitzgerald.

Once extreme threat comes to dominate, we get inverse-millennialism: now rather than imminent heaven on earth, we get imminent hell on earth. Now every positive sign is heavily discounted as false. From soaring optimism we go to plummeting despair—the sky is falling, the world is about to end, and so on. Everything is black and bleak.[16] If a handful of people are seen suffering greatly, it means *everyone* is starving. And so we wind up with the great myth of the Great Depression which has been handed down in the photographs that focus on a minority of suffering people to depict an entire age. (The highest official unemployment rate was about 20 percent and the great majority of these were temporary.) And so we get mythical economic ideas that blindly assume gloom-and-doom are inevitable and eternal, that propose mythical transformations to produce heaven on earth, and mystical conversions of most economists to the new Keynesian, Marxist, or whatnot modernist faith.

The Fatal Flaw of Greed and Overoptimism

Many different prophets have proclaimed many different inherent, necessary, ineluctable, and inevitable contradictions in the system of economic freedom. All of these have been simple mistakes or else myths born of the myths of statism, such as the fallacy of structuralism. All of them mistakenly assume this so-called system is an essence or structure that is somehow independent of the free situational choices and actions of the individuals involved. But that would be the opposite of free enterprise, a system of relations imposed by some degree of force. (Unfortunately, as noted earlier, Adam Smith's talk of an "invisible hand" encouraged readers to interpret the so-called "shifting equilibrium" structurally.)

A system of free enterprise is self-adjusting (or "self-equilibrating") precisely because it is nothing more than the creative interactions of all the individuals and all individuals are free to adjust their lives to all the changes in their situations in life. If, for example, a great deal more gold is put into circulation, as happened from about 1851 to 1871 because of big gold discoveries, individuals will find they have more gold relative to supplies of goods, so they are willing to pay more of it for the goods, so the prices drift up all over the system of economic exchanges. The reverse can happen also. Of course, any individual can refuse to adjust—and some always did—but most people in such a system of interacting decision makers chose to adjust to their situational changes, so most of the holdouts would eventually go along. If, however, government power was used to stop these individual interactions and adjustments, then, of course, the system did not adjust. As we shall see, for over a hundred years our governments have used more and more power, especially in the form of legal, bureaucratic regulations enforced by police powers, to try to stop these free individual interactions and adjustments. This might be called an *external* contradiction of economic freedom, but it is quite ridiculous to call it an *internal* contradiction of economic freedom.

And, yet, it is true that freedom in general, and especially economic freedom, has thus far tapped a fatal flaw in human nature, a flaw greatly exacerbated in the West by Judeo-Christian millennialism. This fatal flaw is millennialism and inverse-millennialism, which have reinforced each other. Regardless of their resources, the more free individuals are from social constraints on their economic activities, the more they adjust their situational production methods, largely by responding to the incentives—rewards and punishments—resulting from normatively patterned behavior and from creative trials and errors, to fit their individual abilities and resources to become more productive and wealthy. Some individuals and even whole nations are more successful at such creative adjustments than others, but in general a high degree of freedom in economic activity tends to produce great readjustments in lives which produce great increases in wealth. This is most obvious in the United States because in the last century we had more economic freedom than any other large nation in history. If they had wanted to, all Americans could still be living on small farms tilling the soil with a horse and plow—or even with a shovel. There were no laws or government powers forcing people off the land (as the enclosure acts did in Britain). In fact, there are still some dirt poor farmers and survivalists who prefer precisely that life. And many thousands of American communalists have returned to the soil in the last twenty years to live such a simple, natural, life. But the vast majority of Americans in the last one hundred years have *chosen freely* to uproot their lives and move to cities and suburbs in order to become more productive—produce more wealth for themselves. These readjustments had become so numerous and fundamental by the nineteenth century that they constituted part of what the socialist economic historian Michael Polanyi called *The Great Transformation.*[17] Of course, it was only the "greatest" of such great transformations because they happen wherever people are economically free for long and they go on happening as long as people are economically free; and the degree of transformation varies directly, if roughly, with the degree of economic freedom. Even today, with all of our government constraints on economic freedom, we are in the takeoff phase of the Electronic Age in which we will vastly transform production with computers and robots and produce great increases in wealth—unless government power stops us. These transformations easily become transition stages that breed millennialism.

The second Great Transformation in Europe began (or, at least, "took off") in the eighteenth century. (The first Great Transformation of Medieval Europe has, as noted earlier, been all but forgotten until recently.) The initial impetus, even in Britain, seems to have been an extremely high rate of population growth. The best guesstimates indicate that the European population grew from 118 million in 1700 to 187 million in 1801; that of England and Wales from 5.8 million to 9.15 million in the same period; and that of France from 18 million in 1715 to 26 million in 1789. In spite of increased agricultural productivity, this great surge in human fecundity created a rapid rise in rural poverty, which only recently has been studied in detail, and a migration of these poor to the cities.[18] Most people who move to cities find them exciting centers of new adventures, but some find them threatening by their very rapid pace of change and their complexity. The poor obviously feel most threatened. Those who feel most threatened, but who see the vast possibilities, most easily become millennialists.

Though the major cause of the rural population explosion was probably the decline in rural disease,[19] in the early nineteenth century the great growth of cities had an ancient consequence few expected or understood. Cities have always been breeding grounds of germs and viruses far more than rural areas, because of the vast increase in interaction in close proximity. The vast growth of cities in the nineteenth century led to an explosion of plagues, especially of the dreaded cholera. In 1830 to 1832 cholera swept through Europe from east to west. In 1832 some 80,000 people died of cholera in London alone. Of course, all cities had been swept intermittently by plagues since they began in Sumeria five thousand years ago. Rural life, while less subject to plagues, had always been more subject to death from famine and disease combined than was true of city life in nineteenth-century Europe. Moreover, poverty was more widespread in the rural areas. That, as I noted, is probably the major reason people moved to the cities in such great numbers. They were lured by the sudden increases in the real average standard of living and by unrealistic glittering prospects. But when they first arrived, they were still poor and they were concentrated and, thus, could be studied by reformers who, not looking at the poor peasants (the "controls") in rural areas, concluded that industrial capitalism "caused" the poverty.

In retrospect this kind of social analysis would be ludicrous, if it had not done so much to inflame the already-smoldering millennialism. Everyone, regardless of ideology, agrees with Keynes's picture of England, especially London, as predominantly middle-class and the richest nation in the world by 1900.[20] That could not possibly have happened if any large percentage of the people had stayed poor permanently. What happened is obvious because it has happened to wave after wave of American immigrants—Irish, German Catholics, Italians, Jews, Japanese, Chinese, Puerto Ricans, Southern whites, and Southern blacks.[21] The people arrived in the cities from the poor farms (or from being poor laborers on richer farms) with almost nothing. They worked hard and slowly, most of them became more prosperous, some of them spectacularly so. It took the Irish approximately three generations to go from being starving exiles from the potato famine in Ireland to being indentured American workers, to being middle-class workers in America, and some in England and elsewhere. Every immigrant group has done the same, over and over again. In little more than a hundred years, the Irish had worked their way up to one of the highest per capita incomes of any ethnic group and one of them was elected president. It's monotonously patterned and perfectly obvious. But with equal monotony every new wave of poor being enriched by industrial society has been proclaimed by millennial messiahs to be the "victims of capitalistic oppression." Always the hidden, unspoken assumption of all of these proclamations has been that these people—all the tens of millions of them—*should* have been made instantaneously wealthy if our Western societies were politically moral ones. And, thus, moralistic politics swept away political economics.

Always before, throughout the entire history of mankind, it had been assumed that "you have always the poor with you" because the poor were always the great majority. Now, suddenly, the exact opposite was assumed. Free technology and enterprise had produced such vast increases in wealth so seemingly instantaneously that the new poor seemed intolerable—absolutely immoral—so immoral that the free enterprise that was making almost everyone unbelievably well off by any previous standard in the history of the world should be abolished and replaced by—by what? By heaven on earth.

This mythical transformation in perspectives is so unprecedented and so sweeping in its implications that it dwarfs the second Great Transformation in the mode of production. How could so many millions of people possibly come to share these Marxist, socialist, and democratic welfare-statist millennial myths? The most important "secret" to it all lies in the effects on human beings of the sudden and vast increase in wealth, combined with the mass ignorance of history and the theory of the System of Natural Liberty and, most importantly, the many transitional dislocations produced by free enterprise. The industrial phase did produce some widespread but temporary threats in plagues and economic problems in the cyclical "busts." But most of these were less than the ordinary threats of rural life throughout history. The difference is that free enterprise triggered greed in almost everyone, though to greatly varying degrees, and greed made any temporary threat seem like a terrible fall. The joy-and-optimism side of millennialism was now permanently triggered by the wealth produced by free enterprise and by the miracles of science and technology. From now on no amount of satisfaction of needs was sufficient, for each new satisfaction only unleashed many new ones, exactly as anyone understanding the hierarchy of motives would expect (see chapter 7). As all observers of our modernist world with historical perspective realize, we are being swept by an explosive revolution of rising expectations.

When the first great wave of utopian socialists, communists, anarchists, phalangists, communalists, anarcho-socialists, and others first washed across Europe in the early days of the industrial revolution, their ideas about "needs" were terribly paltry by modernist standards. "When the communist artisan Wilhelm Weitling tried to offer an example of capitulation to a wild, egotistic desire by a worker of the future with extra chits to spend in his utopia, the most self-indulgent act he could imagine was the purchase of a watch with a second hand."[22] How terribly paltry by the actual standards of life enjoyed by all workers in the West today—or even by our tens of millions of nonworking welfare cases. Little more than a hundred years ago, even the most utopian worker could not even dream of the reality of wealth enjoyed by today's average worker—or even by the semileisure class on the dole.

Once triggered by the realities of the immense productive capacities of prolonged free enterprise, greed inflamed utopian myth making among many millions. Anthropologists have studied a form of millennialism around the world which they call *cargo cultism*. Primitive peoples around the world who suddenly experienced the vast wealth and power of the West through cargo, especially in World War II when the vast cargoes sometimes arrived overnight like manna from the heavens, created magical rituals to bring the cargoes to them. In the same general way, but generally to less degree and in modern Western garb, Western peoples have been swept by vast political cargo cults. Most important of all, those greed-inspired myths made any temporary threat to their fulfillment, such as by recessions, seem both dreadful and totally unnecessary, thus absolutely intolerable. At the same time, greed inspired vast overoptimism in successful businesspeople and workers, tempting them to overinvest and overproduce when business was good and to go into debt to overproduce and to consume now on credit. This tendency to greed was always there and would have led many individuals to be swept away, but these individual booms and crashes would have been limited to rare situations, such as the inflation-fed boom of the 1850s, following the great gold discoveries that swelled the money supply, thus sending signals throughout the economic system of boom, and the crash of the 1870s. When governments changed or manipulated the basic rules of credit or the money supply to greatly expand the credit supply or money, then the inflationary signals triggered both greedy overoptimism and severe miscalculations (dislocations) of investment and consumption.

Greed-inspired mythical thinking became a crucial source of the business cycles, especially of the vast splurges in speculation such as we saw before the depressions of 1837 and 1871 and in the roaring twenties that ended in the third great depression. Greed-inspired mythical thinking thus inspired vast demands, business cycles that periodically frustrated even some rudimentary demands, and made all such frustrations seem intolerable—absurd because "unnecessary" by mythical standards. Greed and the El Dorado myths inspired by the vast successes of free enterprise and science and technology are the only "inherent contradictions of capitalism." This greed would normally be constrained in a very free market because credit would quickly become far more expensive when more and more individuals, inspired by greedy optimism, started demanding more and more of the lagging supply of credit. They would normally crash before the entire system of exchange had drifted into a great crash. But when government pumped up the credit and money supply throughout the system, as the U.S. Bank and state banks did in the 1820s and early 1830s by allowing land purchased on credit from the government to be used as collateral for new loans and as the Federal Reserve did during the 1920s, it vastly inflated both greedy optimism and distortions in other economic decisions. The entire system then drifted toward a great crash.

Greed, Secular Millennialism, and Modernist Revolution

Alexis de Tocqueville, looking at the history of the French revolution, noted that, contrary to the popular assumption, revolutions occur when things are getting better economically, not when people are getting poorer or remaining at the same level. There are often uprisings during periods of vast suffering, due to sudden impoverishment, such as the Jacqueries of France. But in our modernist world the desire to overthrow the government, to establish a new structure of government, seems to grow tremendously after periods of rapid economic growth. However, Tocqueville's idea must be modified. Greed is certainly triggered by the new situation of rapid economic growth and, as this greed soars, it sweeps away rational analyses of risk and caution. Utopia—a world of unlimited wealth, total freedom, unconditional love, sexual ecstasy—everything now seems possible, just within reach. People in the grip of this utopian greed will immediately hate anyone or anything that seems to block their reaching this utopia, in the same way anyone hates the person who frustrates their achieving a passionately desired goal just when it seems at hand. They are the "oppressors." If we destroy them, heaven is ours. It is utopian greed, the passionate belief in the myth of the earthly heaven, which first lights the fire in the minds of revolutionaries. This fire was stoked to incandescent heat by the first waves of hope unleashed by the French Revolution. Socialism, absolute freedom, total equality, sexual freedom, pornography, feminism, magical power—all were unleashed then and in the ecstatic, halcyon early days of each succeeding revolution.[23] It is the hatred of those believed to be keeping us out of heaven which then fans the flame into a moralistic holocaust. In time some revolutionaries—terroristic nihilists—become so obsessed with the hatred that the vision of Heaven is lost and there remains only hatred and the violence that grows out of hatred—violence for its own sake becomes a purification ritual that is felt to restore the cleanliness and the order of the world. Out of the chaos of violence springs the hope of everything. (Thus the antinomian Robespierre springs from the flames, the cleansing savior with a murderous guillotine.)

There have always been rebels, people who tried to overthrow governments and sometimes succeeded. These people almost always saw themselves as "revolutionaries" in the original sense of the word, that is, a returning to an original state of purity and order (just as a planet returns to its original place in its orbital revolution around the Sun). They were true believers in the myth of eternal return. Their basic idea was always that the necessary and pure (divine) steady state (stasis) was temporarily disturbed, thus producing or threatening evil and chaos, so now it was necessary to return to it by overthrowing—cleansing away—the evildoers. There have been millennial Christian revolutionaries (Abighensians, Cathars, Anabaptists) for centuries fired by the hope for a totally pure Church in place of the Roman Babylon, by hatred of that corrupt reality, and by the belief this pure Church would redeem mankind. But the modernist revolutionary enters the Western stage only in the seventeenth and eighteenth centuries and at first only cautiously. The first may have been the Anabaptists of Munster in the reformation or, more likely, the levelers in the English Revolution of the seventeenth century. While Cromwell and most of his followers lusted after God's heaven, the levelers seem to have been fired as well by a vision of a heaven on earth, or at least an immensely better earth. By the eighteenth century the basic myth of revolution was popping up almost anywhere in Europe, but it was most inflaming in Germany and France. The American revolution was one primarily in the classical meaning of the word, a return to the rights of all English citizens. But it did help greatly to fan the hopes of French revolutionaries, especially those of Mirabeau and Saint-Simon. Thomas Paine was the only famous American modernist revolutionary and he was British. The French Revolution was the first conflagration embodying the modernist myth of revolution on a large scale. The Jacobins began with a blaze of idealistic hope for communal (national) redemption, love, and glory on earth—heaven on earth is just around the corner, if only the ancient regime will let us exercise rationality and science.[24] Condorcet stands as a symbol of this first great explosion of modernist millennialism. At the very time he was being hunted down by the millennial terrorists he had helped to unleash, he wrote his millennial work of social mathematics, *The History of Human Progress*, then killed himself in prison—or was murdered.

The "evil" ones would not cooperate. Hatred grew rampantly and nihilistic violence became the only hope for heaven on earth. This same pattern was to be repeated over and over in the lives of individual revolutionaries and their followers. Once the leaders had created the synthesis of the myth of heaven on earth with a myth of monster oppressors (devils) barring the way to this heaven, they united the powerful emotions of greed and hatred. By promising this earthly paradise equally to all who would follow them, they presented themselves in the ancient mythical guise of the hero-savior inspired only by paternalistic love—and the power of love was synthesized with that of greed and hatred. Now their movements could appeal equally to gentle idealists and submissive masochists who dreamed of a world ruled entirely by the power of altruistic love and to the narcissistic, borderline-psychotics who loved only power and sadistic violence. The more massive, professionalized, and bureaucratized their movements became, the more the sadistic lovers of power were drawn to them and the more they became the dictators of the altruists and masochists. The more they could separate and hide themselves from the mass followings by ruling from above and by censorship, the less concrete information the followers had about them, and the more they could manipulate the mythmaking processes that would make them the gods of this heaven on earth. Mythmaking agitprop became a science and art in the service of the Antichrist and the antiscientist.

The Myth of Modernism

Though I shall analyze rationalism-scientism-technicism in chapter 7, it is important to see its major dimensions here. The great myth of modernism is a synthesis of the myth of the uniqueness (thus ahistorisity and incomparability) of modern humanity and society and the myth of the moral and intellectual superiority of modern humanity over the ancient regime. The awe-inspiring miracles of science and technology were the most important inspirations of both these submyths. The myth of modernism then is largely inspired by the myth of rationalism-scientism, but it also springs from ethnocentrism and the hubris that springs from military power. The myth of modernism is in basic conflict with some of the other myths, especially subordinate ones, synthesized in the three great political myths. Such conflicts are almost universal in great myths, but the nonlogical form of thought of myths commonly allows the conflicts to lie dormant, sometimes for centuries, until some "heretic" seizes the conflicting strain of myth to challenge the authority of the mythifiers. Today we are somewhat less awe-inspired and more sceptical, even anxious, about both. But most people in the eighteenth, nineteenth, and earlier twentieth centuries were still exulting in their sudden new powers, hope, and pride. The positive millennial myths, which tempted the uneducated with vast hopes of instant wealth and happiness through equality (redistribution), were irrational (and would take power and wealth from many of the educated), but over the long run science and technology could produce miracles. And so the fatal temptation to rationalize everything, to see the West as unique and the special bearer of moral strength and duty that so inspired nationalistic imperialism (colonialism) and warfare—and the great myth of secular millennialism.

Since the myth of modernism is now so taken for granted as dogmatic truth in our Western societies, and especially in the United States, it is vital to see what a revolutionary conception of humanity it involves. Almost all previous societies assumed that some time in the distant past was a golden age of truth, wisdom, knowledge, wealth, leisure, peace, virtue, beauty, and everything else good.[25] There was actually some truth to this, since most civilized societies do tend over long periods to degenerate economically and, to a far less extent, technologically and scientifically. (I shall argue that this degeneration is generally produced by the massive growth of imperial state bureaucracies, but accidents and foreign conquest can achieve the same end state.) This is evident, for example, in the degeneration of Mycenaen and Minoan Greece into a centuries-long dark age, and the degeneration of the Graeco-Roman civilization into another centuries-long dark age. But even in these degenerate civilizations the ancient golden age was seen by polarized contrast as far more golden than in fact they were and the dark ages far more dark than they in fact were. And in most societies we have no reason to believe the ancient Eden really existed. In general, the tight constraints on individuals that made any visible individual improvement very improbable greatly encouraged despair in the present (thus inspiring the myth of eternal stasis), while the subordinated hope was projected backward in a nostalgic memory of heaven on earth and forward to a better life after death.

This was the conviction that dominated Western thought into the seventeenth century, after many centuries of slow and intermittent economic, technological, and scientific development. In spite of the relative despair of progress this conviction inspired, Westerners were slowly gaining hope and confidence from their real, piecemeal accomplishments, and by the seventeenth century they were openly challenging these abstract "idols of the mind" that chained them down. At first they saw themselves as "dwarfs on the shoulders of giants"—very small but still able, by building on the ancients, to get higher than they did.[26] By the eighteenth century this pall of despair and inferiority was rapidly giving way to soaring pride in modern science, then in technology, and finally in economic prosperity.

By the middle of the nineteenth century, Westerners were being swept away by the ancient sin of hubris. Theories (dogmas!) of racial superiority, cultural superiority, and unilinear evolution—progress!—were sprouting everywhere.[27] "Civilized mind and virtues" were compared to "primitive mind and nonvirtue" in categorical terms. Primitives were not only inferior morally, which one might have thought bad enough, but they had no choice since they were so intellectually inferior they could not see what was really their own good. (The "white man's burden" would soon save this primitive with colonialism.) Soon it was argued (by Benjamin Whorf[28] and his many followers) that other cultures actually made primitives see things like colors differently from Westerners.

Modernism came to pervade almost all aspects of Western thought and action, from hideous art forms and absurd poetry to imperialist warmongering. But it has had two really fundamental and sweeping effects. First, it has led to an implicit assumption of *cultural relativism* which denies (often violently) any form of human nature, in spite of all the obvious universals in human societies and in spite of our knowledge of genetics and comparative studies of emotion and behavior (see chapter 7). This cultural relativism and denial of human nature are vital foundations for all of the millennial political myths, for they all involve some explicit (in the case of Marxism and some socialisms) or implicit (in the case of democratic welfare statism) assumption that the human beings of today can be remade by government power (especially used to "rebuild the economic structure") into "better" human beings. Second, and a close complement to cultural relativism, the modernist myth leads Westerners today to take it for granted that history is irrelevant to our situation: we are unique, so special and superior that all earlier experience is irrelevant; we have nothing to learn from history. This strain of modernism is denied or muted by Marxists because it conflicts with Marxist historicism. But Marxists promise to transcend *all* history. It is obvious historically that the growth of vast government power eventually destroys individual freedoms and, thus, eventually reverses economic, technological, and scientific progress. So what? Our bureaucrats and politicians are modernist ones—we can simply assume they'll be different, superior—the opposite of all past experience. And so the millennia of human history are brushed aside, relegated to increasingly irrelevant experts on history, and so we plummet onward in our growing ignorance toward the promised land.

It is the myth of modernism which more than anything else has been the implicit rationale behind the belief of welfare statists that all of the ancient and Renaissance history of the ways imperial state bureaucracies erode economies is irrelevant to our modern world. All of the warnings by conservatives, who rejected modernism and retained historical perspective, that the New Deal was really the same old ancient deal of imperial state powers, were stigmatized as ignorant prejudices. They warned, as Aristotle had done more than two thousand years earlier, that all of the "new" programs were merely small steps that would add up over the years to become massive usurpations of the most basic constitutional rights. All of this was vehemently denied and when it happened their warnings had been totally forgotten. And thus we were tempted to repeat all of the ancient and mercantilist policies of massive regulation and inflation and reap the long-run economic and political whirlwinds. We shall see the details throughout this book of how modernism was involved in this great temptation. But we can see the essential features of modernism at work in microcosm by looking briefly at the American Vietnamese war.

All great and successful military strategists have known that the *moral factor* is by far the dominant one in military action.[29] In military terminology "moral" refers to all mental or meaningful factors—all effects on the emotions and thoughts. The "moral," then, is everything that is not "physical." Morality is one important part of the moral factor. Sun Tzu effectively summed up the fundamental principles of concentrating on the moral in his great work *The Art of War*—in 500 B.C. (Hannibal and Caesar were real latecomers, but quick learners.) In the modern world Napoleon put it succinctly and epigrammatically: "[In war] The moral is to the physical as three to one." Lenin applied the general dictum in detail: "The soundest strategy in war is to postpone operations until the moral disintegration of the enemy renders the delivery of the mortal blow both possible and easy." B.H. Liddell Hart enshrined these ancient principles as the foundation for his own masterful study of *Strategy*, which has rightly become the handbook of modern strategists.

The American disaster in Vietnam was overwhelmingly due to the implicit modernist assumptions made by our political and military leaders. They assumed that history was irrelevant to them; consequently, they did not have to give much consideration to all these ancient injunctions about the preponderance of the moral factor. Nor did they have to learn from the French experience in Vietnam or from their own earlier failures of using massive strategic bombing in World War II (which may have merely increased the moral resistance of the enemy and, at the least, was a terrible waste compared to what tactical bombing on that scale could have accomplished). They assumed that the might of rational-scientific-technological forces could easily and cheaply destroy a technologically backward military force. And they assumed that people of good will everywhere, and certainly among our allies in Europe, would see their cause as a just one and, thus, support it.

Those of us who were aware of the modernist myths of social scientists in general were first alarmed by the McNamara Pentagon's use of official statistics like "body counts" and massive computer simulations of the war. I myself had originally done some work using such official statistical data and work on mathematical models (of the sort used in computer simulations) using that kind of data. But I had rediscovered what isolated social scientists knew from the beginning: all such official information is subject, in widely varying degrees, to very important forms of falsehood, including outright lying by officials themselves to protect or advance themselves within their bureaucracies. In 1967 I published a book about the falsehoods involved in one form of official statistics and argued that they should never be used without very good evidence concerning their degree of truthfulness. Many other studies were showing the same thing with all kinds of official information, ranging from Morgenstern's classic work on government employment and unemployment statistics to a massive amount of work on the problems of crime statistics. We immediately suspected from this experience that data such as body counts being fed to the computers were "garbage," as computer analysts call false data; that the mathematical models being computer simulated were absurdly oversimplified and biased; and that the two combined would multiply specific mistakes into general absurdities of strategy and tactics. Our expectations about body counts and other official data were later confirmed by John M. Johnson, who served as an officer on a Navy destroyer shelling North Vietnam, later did a paper on how body counts were done, and then did a general work with David Altheide on official information, *Bureaucratic Propaganda*.[30] Suffice it to say that bodies were rarely counted. Instead, optimistic and self-serving guesstimates were made by processes known in the Navy as "gundecking." Other reports have shown how the same types of guesstimates were made for all the damage reports showing that the North Vietnamese were being bombed into the Stone Age and would, presumably, thus be forced to quit the war any day. As one Navy flier told me, "Every time we had to jettison our bombs, we counted up some more bridges."

The falsehood of the models and the computer runs was demonstrated by the growing strength of the enemy and the outcome of the war. But the most convincing demonstration of the importance of the modernist myth in producing this first-order disaster is found in the army's own study of how it happened. Colonel Harry G. Summers, Jr., was assigned the task and eventually published his report. His reports show vividly how the modernist assumption of the irrelevance of history and the vast superiority of the rational-scientific-technological had pervaded both his own thinking and the general planning for the war, leading above all to forgetting the importance of the moral, even to the point of forgetting to first get a clear idea of their own general goal and to work out a general strategy for achieving this. Summers found in general that, "we had been so blinded by nuclear weapons, so confused by the computer age, with its emphasis on quantified analysis, and so enamored of the new strategy of counterinsurgency that we forgot what war was all about."[31]

Social Scientism

The fledgling social sciences and the humanistic disciplines became the foremost promulgators of the modernist myth and some of its worst victims. The systematic, comparative, empirical and objective study of human beings had developed parallel to the natural sciences for several centuries. Machiavelli, Guicciardini, Montaigne, Montesquieu, Quesnay, Turgot, Hume, Ferguson, Smith, Burke, Say, Tocqueville, and a great many others had forged the foundations of these disciplines. They had started with careful, systematic observations of the social world and worked out methods suited specifically to discovering the truth about human beings, especially the basic dimensions of human nature. They studied human beings the same way Darwin studied all animals, but with the added advantage of being able to listen to their "specimens'" reports on the meanings of what they did and to observe them indirectly over the millennia of historical records.

These naturalists had made remarkable progress. In economics they had discovered the basic ideas of free markets, competitive prices, and economic growth that were used in the nineteenth century to free individuals and thus allow them to create an explosion of wealth, technology, and science. Their successors have continued this progress up to today. But most of the so-called social sciences and some parts of the humanistic disciplines were turned against them. Friedrich Hayek has called it *The Counterrevolution of Science*.[32] He was certainly right about its cataclysmic, reactionary implications. But it would be wrong to imply that the naturalists like Adam Smith thought their works were revolutionary. They saw themselves as philosophers building on all of the best early works, certainly rebelling against what was wrong, especially mercantilism, but not revolutionary in the modern sense. None of them suffered from the delusion that they had discovered something totally new about human beings, nor had they any hope that the adoption of their ideas would usher in an age of millennial and redemptive glory. They were scholars who drew on earlier wisdom and grounded their theories in massive evidence about human nature (which I shall develop further in later chapters). They knew all too well what human beings were like to expect a millennium. They were trying to reform and improve, not transform. Very importantly, while they generally took state powers for granted, they took it for granted, as Darwin was later to do, that human society is nothing more than the sum of its individuals and that any truthful understanding of society must be based on an analysis from the perspective of individual feeling, thinking, and action. Their theories are now called *micro-theories*, but it would be better to call them *individualistic theories of society*. They certainly analyzed things at the macro- (systems) level, even sometimes analyzing the movements of vast empires over centuries, but they did this by showing how the aggregated individuals made their decisions, the effects of these, and so on. Society *is* the individuals, and the goals and goods of society are simply the goals and goods of all the individuals. They believed there are some nearly universal goals, interests, and goods because there is a human nature and the shared customs of cultures. These universals were determined by observing oneself and others through history and in everyday life. From such universals they inferred "natural laws" (though some also saw these as guaranteed by God), and these natural laws were assumed to be the principles that must constrain all individuals, thus all social policies. Any individual could see them by introspection and by observing others, so they appealed to common sense, not to the mysteries of holy books or science (though they believed these, rightly done, reveal the same things). And so their theories led to the assumption that social welfare could be maximized by guaranteeing certain rights that embodied these universals: life, liberty, and the pursuit of happiness (property) were the universals that most concerned them—and the ones now included in our constitution.

The naturalists of the social world rarely saw themselves as doing exactly the same thing as natural scientists. The "counterrevolutionaries" of social thought were what today we would call scientists with a capital "S." They had commonly been engineers, physiologists, and so on, and were bursting with revolutionary hope for creating sciences of humankind and using these to transform human society into a heaven on earth, but by reason, not by redemptive violence. The most important early ones were French people who had been inflamed by the rationalism and the maniacal popularizations of science of the philosophes. Marx and many others who came after him synthesized their ideas with the economic ideas of the British political economists to produce various forms of utopian-economic-scientism. Almost all of them, especially Marx, believed individual actions were determined by some social, "structuralist" factors external to the individuals.

Saint-Simon, Fourier, and Comte were visionary prophets who created sociology to be a positive science of society which would provide the absolute knowledge about society, including morality, which could be used to usher in a brave new world. Though they varied in their interpretations, they synthesized their scientific methods and rhetoric with Rousseau's "common will," which was supposed to be some kind of spirit (or transcendental embodiment) of the goals, interests, and goods of a society. The fatal difference from the individualistic theories is that this common will, which was soon made to look more scientific by calling it "social structure" or "social system," was asserted to be a separate and higher level of reality.[33] Not only is social structure supposed to be inferred independently of the feelings, thoughts, and actions of individuals, but it also supposedly determines what individuals do, independently of their individual wills and decisions. Social structure is the reality, not the individuals. Social structure trundles on independently of the individuals, at times even crushing them like a juggernaut. (For the Marxists this external structure is "the mode of production.") But that was not all: individuals in the society were believed incapable of knowing this social structure by common sense. Who, then, could know this vital reality of social structure? Only social scientists, of course. Since only the one who knows the social structure can make effective social policy, only the technocrat can rule. And so the social scientists become the scientific oracles of modernist society. Recent generations of structural social scientists generally argue that society is not a separate reality, but a separate mode of analysis. But this is only rhetoric. They still believe society causes what individuals do—and how can a mere mode of analysis cause anything?)

Each of the social sciences has followed a somewhat different path. Each profession now includes some very important subcultures that study human beings from the individualistic perspective. (Micro-economics, especially of the Austrian economists like Mises, Hayek, and Rothbart, and the sociologies of everyday life are examples of this.) But the dominant perspective in each of them is structuralism, except in psychology where "the unconscious mind" known only by the psychologist often performs the same magical trick of disappearing the individual. In most of them (but not yet much in anthropology), structuralism has been wrapped in the scientific mantle of the mathematical forms of the natural sciences. This synthesis was created in the nineteenth century, especially by Emile Durkheim in sociology and Vilfredo Pareto in economics. In other chapters we shall see some of the massive evidence showing how invalid and distorting much of this mathematical information and theorizing is. But today the juggernaut still trundles on, crushing both truth and individuals.

Millions of students in our colleges, and now even in our high schools, have been drilled in this structuralist faith by our "new class" of would-be technocrats. In the United States, where "higher" education has expanded far more than in any other nation, nearly half of our young people are now processed through social scientistic courses. This now includes almost 100 percent of our journalists, our elected officials, and our bureaucratic elites in government, business, and labor. Little wonder that a widespread cliché of the educated in the most individualistic major nation has become "The system made them (me) do it." The very social scientists who fret over the conformism supposedly shown by the fad of designer jeans are inculcating "designer minds."

Derek Freeman's expose of Margaret Mead's book *Coming of Age in Samoa*[34] provides the most striking example of the extreme absurdities to which the media canonization of social scientistic modernism has gone. Throughout the entire era of the American modernist welfare state, Mead was by far the most famous of all anthropologists and probably of all social scientists except Freud. This fame began with *Coming of Age in Samoa*, based on "fieldwork" she did in Samoa at age 23. After its publication in 1928, this book and Mead's later ones in the same vein (especially *Sex and Temperament in Three Primitive Societies*[35]) were the handbooks of anthropological modernism for generations of students in introductory courses. (It was the first required reading in the introductory anthropology course I took as a freshman at Harvard in 1955. There was no hint given of the unbelievably shoddy methods used. Many American anthropologists rejected it before Freeman's expose, but they did so very quietly.)

Mead's message is simple and alluring: human nature, if there is such a thing, is "the rawest, most undifferentiated of raw material"; society, culture, determines what we are, whether we are competitive or altruistic, aggressive or kindly, happy or miserable; Samoan youth, unlike Western youth, are uncompetitive, kindly, nonviolent, unrepressed, nonjealous, happy-go-lucky—life is one long sigh of casual erotic bliss under the palms; therefore, we can be equally blissful by merely transforming our society. Freeman, who lived in Samoa for years and studied it intensively, shows that Mead lived there briefly with a white family, never learned much of the language, talked through an interpreter with a number of school girls (chosen from 125 adolescents in one school) who may have purposefully put her on, and discovered in far more extreme form what her culture-determinist mentors had primed her to expect. The earlier and later researchers, especially Freeman, have been finding for almost two centuries that Samoans were exactly the opposite from what Mead said, remarkably similar to Western people except for being more aggressive, jealous and violent—even extremely rapacious in the literal sense. None of those has become a best-seller, a standard reading in massive introductory courses, or a media sensation—not even after Freeman's book tore away the media fig leaf and exposed this myth of sexual modernism.

In a review of Freeman's book, Ernest Van Den Haag concluded,

The expectations that Boas placed on Mead, and the theories she absorbed from him, do not fully explain her misinterpretation of Samoa. On a deeper level she was also responding to the widely experienced immemorial longing for some equivalent of the prelapsarian paradise of Genesis. Even in prebiblical times, the Garden of Eden was thought of as in the past: paradise lost. But with the rise of Christianity, paradise was something hoped for in the future as well: paradise regained. Finally, as Christian nations were increasingly secularized, more and more people thought they could create, or find, paradise here and now. Margaret

Mead found it in Samoa. Many persons more experienced and sophisticated than Mead was at 23 have found the paradise they looked for in their political wanderings—in the Soviet Union, China, Vietnam, Cuba. In their cases, too, we sense an emotional longing for an elusive paradise lost. That longing has often led to illusions far more disastrous than Mead's. But *Coming of Age in Samoa* is a testimonial to the force and pervasiveness of the longing.[36]

Van Den Haag should have noted that this "immemorial longing" had reached a feverish level in the Western world rarely reached by any previous society, that the extreme secularization of this intense millennial fever had almost no precedent, and that the modernist social scientism of Mead and many others powerfully inflamed these longings by giving plausibility to the myth that heaven on earth could be achieved by a simple, revolutionary transformation of social structure. The powerful thrust of all such modernist social scientism was summed up by Allyn Moss in the title of his biography, *Margaret Mead: Shaping a New World.*[37]

Except in anthropology, structuralist ideas did not become important in the social sciences in the United States until the 1930s and were not dominant until the 1950s. Before then American social scientists were overwhelmingly individualistic in their theories. It was only in the deeply anxious years of the Great Depression—the enabling crisis of the American welfare state—that more and more American social scientists, like their colleagues in other Anglo-Saxon societies, were suddenly "converted" to the structural theories that rationalize core ideas of the welfare state. But these ideas were already quite dominant in France and overwhelmingly so in Germany, especially in Prussia, the most authoritarian nation in the West and one of those in which the modernist welfare state, beginning there in the 1870s, was a direct descendent of the absolutist monarchic welfare state in the eighteenth century. The mercantilist French welfare state was destroyed by the revolution, but the modernist one Napoleon began was based on it in important ways.

The Revolutionary Transformational Myth of Marxism

Karl Marx was only one of the many millions of mythologizing revolutionizers who have been inspired by our Judeo-Christian millennialism, by our soaring technology, science, and wealth, and by our periods of business-cycle crisis psychology, to proclaim the coming of heaven on earth—after the revolution, for Marx. Some of our most successful technologists, scientists, and businesspeople have succumbed to the same temptation precisely because their real success does produce vast material progress and promises to deliver far more. These "geniuses" ("supermen"), like Thomas Edison and other "electronic prophets," have fanned the flames of El Dorado greed, but most of the time they have been too aware of the immense amount of effort and time needed to create even a small improvement to believe in the miracles of a mythically redeeming revolution. Almost all of the modernist prophets, like Marx, have been inexperienced teenagers, intellectuals, academics, and low-level workers. They have written our "communist Manifesto," our *Walden Two*,[38] and our *Affluent Society*.[39] But few of them have had the incandescent appeal of Marxism.

Marx himself embodied all of the immense ambivalence shown by our modernist movements of political millennialism. It is well known how dismal he was about the "inevitable" failure of capitalism and how much he hated the bourgeoisie. It is all too often forgotten that there was a (largely repressed) underside to this dismal view. Marx saw the bourgeoisie as the historicistic destroyers of feudalism and the builders of the vast economic productivity, technology, and science he believed would be necessary to usher in the age of "true communism" (when the socialist state would wither away and complete freedom begin). At times he became almost rhapsodic in describing this modernist age, showing how its "miracles" had triggered his own hope for the millennium. Of course, since Marx insisted this wealth would be stolen by the bourgeoisie, while the masses of workers would be immiserated, his rhapsodies inspired both millennial myths and envious hatred, thus a lust for revolution. The power of Marxism comes overwhelmingly from Marx and Engel's immensely successful abilities as sincere poets and deceitful propagandists in synthesizing many divergent and often-conflicting myths that are inspired by and inspire so many powerful emotions—all in ways that hide the conflicts and telltale propagandistic stitching, such as by using transformational submyths, as we shall see.

Certainly Marxism has not been influential because of any realistic ability to predict the developments in our complex societies. All human societies are vastly complex. Our modern societies are immensely complex. This complexity alone would be enough to make almost impossible the creation of a general theory of society capable of predicting its specific changes—and certainly enough to guarantee that, if such a theory can be produced, it will take centuries to do so. In spite of this complexity, a few social thinkers in almost every major age have been remarkably prescient in predicting some of the basic trends in their societies. In the eighteenth and nineteenth centuries, many thinkers were able to predict with remarkable (but certainly not perfect) precision the general trends their societies or others would follow for many decades. Alexis de Tocqueville was probably the most successful in foreseeing the general directions in politics, somewhat less so in economics. Tocqueville also wrote objectively, clearly, and beautifully in the *lingua franca* of the age. His achievements have been hailed by many Western scholars for over a century. He has not gone unsung among conservative and classical liberal intellectuals, but neither has he ever been the subject of popular veneration and mythification. Nowhere do the masses hail

Tocqueville as a hero: nowhere do they enshrine his memory in towering monuments; nowhere do they march in unison beneath the (nonexistent) banners of Tocquevillism; nowhere do they dedicate their lives to the (nonexistent) party of Tocquevillism. Early in our own century, great social thinkers like Mises, Schumpeter, Hayek, and Robbins predicted with remarkable precision the general paths now followed by our collectivist societies of all kinds for fifty years. And how many college bookstores now contain one book by any of them?

Though the contenders for the most false prophet of recent centuries would be legion, surely one of the foremost would be Karl Marx. Marx was wrong about almost every major trend except those that almost anyone could see. He believed industry and its workers would become more important in the same way we can all see that computers and their workers will become more important—because it was already a centuries-long trend. Yet, even this one is now the opposite of the truth in all of the most developed nations. In these nations industrial workers have declined as a percentage of the work force and are now less than 20 percent in the U.S. I shall not take the space to catalog even his major misprophesies, since they are so well known. As Schumpeter said about both Marx and Keynes many years ago in *Ten Great Economists*, "As with Marx, it is possible to admire Keynes even though one may consider his social vision to be wrong and every one of his propositions to be misleading."[40] Even his one potentially important contribution—a reemphasis of the ancient truth that the have-nots generally envy, resent, and hate the haves, a truth upper-class mythologizers love to hide—was vitiated by channeling it into a theory of class conflict that is so universal and monomaniacal that it becomes a parody of serious social thought.

Yet this major contender for the title of the most false prophet of all has become the most powerful new hero of our modernist age. It is Marx who is venerated by some workers, by many ignorant peasants, and by the masses of intellectuals around the world. It is Marx, the absolute scientific determinist, who has become the god of the most violent secular religion the world has ever seen. It is Marx who has ignited the revolutionary fire in the minds of hundreds of millions of modernists around the world. It is Marx who has inspired the powerful myths of communism and statist socialism (not anarcho-socialism).

Why? Why has Marxism become such a powerful myth in our world today? It is certainly not that human beings have a perverse adoration for irrationalism and thus for false prophesy. Marx's massive misadventures into prophesy are a great embarrassment to those who share the myth but have not thereby been totally blinded. That's why they put such immense emotion and paper into their Marxist apologetics about "the young Marx," "what Marx *really* meant" (versus what he only meant jokingly?), and so on endlessly. It is also not that Marx was such an endearing person. Marx had none of the law-abiding qualities of Abraham or Mohammed, none of the gentleness of Buddha, and certainly none of the lovingness of Christ. On the contrary, Marx was above all a dedicated, self-righteous, stern, and violently angry prophet of hatred and class war. He was also vulgar and petty, as Schumpeter noted with pity and disdain: "As every true prophet styles himself the humble mouthpiece of his deity, so Marx pretended no more than to speak the logic of the dialectic process of history. There is dignity in all of this which compensates for many pettinesses and vulgarities with which, in his work and in his life, this dignity formed so strange an alliance."[41] Hatred is the dominant theme in the life of Marx. Hatred was obviously the consuming passion that drove him: hatred for his Prussian and Jewish background, hatred for the British nation that took him in, hatred for the hardworking bourgeoisie everywhere and in all times, hatred for anyone successful. His abstractly professed love for the proletariat was merely a pretext for this consuming hatred, a pretext we have seen in most of the totalitarians who have since worshipped at his state shrines. But it is a vitally important pretext.

The historical Marx, the real Marx, is not the basis for the appeal of the Marxist myth. This myth has appealed to so many people primarily because it subtly inflames a number of passions and expresses them in all the forms of a pseudo-science of society which strike the chord of absolute truth in so many people today. Those forms are vitally important and I shall return to them. But, as with all myths, the emotions are the crucial ingredients, the searing bonds of faith. It is only these white-hot emotions that can carry the true believers through the thicket of obvious absurdities, false prophecies, half-truths, and unctuous reinterpretations. There are, of course, people who consider themselves Marxists, some of whom even stumble along with a party line, who do not really share the emotional commitments to the myth. These often-genial fellow travelers commonly shrug off the absurdities of the myth, insisting, "Well, of course, he made mistakes—who doesn't? But the core ideas seem right enough." They generally don't know much about the core ideas, rarely know anything about the vast complexities and mass of evidence concerning these issues, and commonly give up their pseudo-Marxism once they are advised of the facts. None of these things is true of the true believers in the Marxist myth. Contrary to common belief, they are not totally closed to evidence against their faith. They are closed to counterarguments, but the hard facts of experience can get to them over a number of years. This normally happens very quickly when they have been subjected to one of the deadly purges by the theocrats in charge of the faith, though even those being liquidated sometimes hold firm to their convictions, merely contending that the Anti-Marx has temporarily gotten control of the apparatus.

Otherwise it normally takes some years of hard experience; then they see the light. The new god fails, as some eminent ex-believers explained in *The God That Failed*.[42] There are extremely few true believers in Eastern Europe today over the age of thirty, and probably only a minority of the apparatchiki in Russia remain true believers for long.

In explaining the power of the Marxist myth, we have to always remember that it is first and foremost a utopian myth. Utopian myths always appeal to some combination of six of the most powerful emotions—love, hate, lust for revenge, envy, and the resulting lust for dominance (pride), greed, and the dread of death. The more of these emotions the myth can trigger in ways compatible with each other (or made to appear so mythically), the more powerful the myth will be. Marxism so far does not offer anything much for the dread of death, except the not too satisfying "immortal fame" to those on the side of the "inevitable march of history." This is a crucial weakness of Marxism, and one that it would take an awful lot of mythical reinterpretation to undo because of the basic ideas of materialistic determinism. (Of course, it is now being attempted by some Christian true believers.) But the Marxist myth appeals very strongly to all of the other five emotions.

Envy of the successful is inflamed to a white heat, since the "oppressors" are blamed for every evil imaginable and they are presented as if they had no problems of their own. In Marxist literature the bad-guy bourgeoisie somehow always sound, by implication anyway, as if they lead idyllic lives. If their audience were totally rational, they would all want simply to become bourgeoisie. And, in fact, there is a lot of simple-minded cargo cultism in many Marxist advertisements. The lust for revenge is absolutely justified, and made inevitable, by the idea that this idyllic state is entirely the result of their totalitarian oppression of the workers, whose state is always presented as totally and inevitably immiserated, at least by comparison, and "relativities" are always the important things to them. Marxist hatred is far more searing than the Puritan hatred for sinners or an Islamic hatred for infidels or of Shi'ites for all other Moslems. For the evil bourgeoisie there is no redemption, no brotherly forgiveness, nothing but unrelenting hatred. Envy, lust for revenge, and hatred are the dominant emotions of Marxism. But they have a powerful supporting cast in the El Dorado myth of Marxism (state planning and redistribution will produce wealth for all true believers) and in the myth of the community of love (the international brotherhood in Eden which will become all of mankind once the state shrinks away in the sweet by-and-by). It is not simply by accident that Marxism's appeal to envy, hatred, greed, and communal love has been so successful in the last two centuries in our free-enterprise societies. Some of the basic changes in our societies which are partly produced by free enterprise itself have vastly increased greed, and

Marx's greed was inflamed by the vast hope of scientific technology and private enterprise.

All of the powerful great myths that appeal to mass populations over the centuries are syntheses of a number of subordinate myths, each of which trigger and express powerful emotions in various ways. These emotions and submyths may conflict with each other logically, and in fact, some of them almost always do, but the genius of the great myth is that it transcends or hides the conflicts, seducing our minds by their complex structures and self-defenses into believing that the conflict does not exist, that the illogical is logical, that the impossible is inevitable and ineluctable. Transformational myths are an example of this power of myths. This kind of myth uses the strong tendency of our rational, verbal minds to polarize reality into dual opposites that cancel each other—right versus left, night versus day, life versus death, might versus right, freedom versus slavery, beautiful versus ugly, deviance versus repectability, etc. Each of these opposites has verbal meaning in relation to its opposite, by polar contrast. For example, what would beauty be without ugliness?[43]

As a result, each polar opposite seems to our rational minds to *imply* the opposite ("the extremes touch," "the extremes join hands"). As Plato once put it, you can only know life by knowing death; therefore, from death must come life. (He put it somewhat more complexly, thus confusing most people and, thereby, encouraging the mythical leap, but this was the basic idea.) Now, this rational slight of hand is easy enough to spot when you know about it, just as you can see background figures in a psychological puzzle when you know they are there. Plato was right to say we know the meaning of life in relation to death, because commonsensically we distinguish the live from the not-live relativistically; but he is logically absurd when he jumps from this level of conceptual meaning to conclude that this means or *proves* the phenomena we call death must lead to its opposite, life. We can see it, but how tempting these so-called "ontological proofs" have been to rationalists of all ages (for rationalists assert the absolute primacy of reason over all the rest of reality—what reason rules *is*.) Probably because of some genetically determined aspect of cognition, dualism seems a universal tendency of human thought, most obvious in the moral thought about good and evil. The gnostic cults and Manicheans introduced full-blown dualism into Western thought and religion quite independently of Platonism, but Neoplatonists were already addicted to it. Giordano Bruno's work in the sixteenth century includes ecstatic paeons to dualistic transformationalism.[44]

Transformational myths use this strong dualistic tendency of our minds to transform one extreme into the other to make us believe that out of one extreme will come the other. By asserting the existence of one extreme, the myth tempts us to believe the opposite is inevitable. In this world some people are rich and powerful, but what happens when this world is transformed into its opposite, the other world? The rich become the poor and meek.

Hegel drew upon romantic thinkers (who drew directly upon Bruno's dualistic transformational writings) to create the most thoroughgoing great transformational myth of all time. In fact, he created an entire theory of universal history around these mythical transformations. The heart of it is his idea of thesis-antithesis-synthesis, that is, the idea that out of one idea and thing *inevitably* springs its opposite and the two are then transformed into a synthesis. For example, one kind of government inevitably leads to its own downfall and transformation into its opposite; then the two are synthesized; then this becomes the thesis to be canceled by its opposite. But what lies behind this inevitable process? What is the source of this fate? The Great Spirit (God in mythical pantheistic disguise in an age of rationalism).

Out of this great transformational myth sprang a crucial worldly transformational myth. Hegel identified (mythically, of course) the Spirit with the nation-state and the nation-state with the will of the leader. Now the leader/nation-state became the inevitable engine of social change. The powerful myth of the godly hero was thus synthesized with this transformational myth of universal fate. Where does this leave all the other members of the nation-state? In submission, of course. That is inevitable, but note that freedom lovers have nothing to fear because absolute freedom is only possible because the opposite—absolute submission—exists. He who would find himself must lose himself; he who would be free must be a slave. Simple transformational "logic." (Rousseau had already discovered this in his argument that freedom was only possible when everyone totally submitted to the common will. In fact, Abraham had struggled with the same mystery.)

The genius of the great Marxist myth was to synthesize the many disparate passions and submyths of revolution with the great transformational myth of Hegel and with the ideas of classical economics (as interpreted by Ricardo) and wrapped in the mythical forms of natural scientism (precise definitions, equations, predictions, ad nauseum). Hegel's ideas are built on the primordial ideas of fate, of spirits, and much else inconsistent with science. Historical inevitability is impossible in science (as Karl Popper has argued so effectively),[45] but the Marxist myth synthesized the scientistic idea of objective truth with the ancient idea of fate found in Hegel and we get the scientistic-historicist myth of historical inevitability. He accepted the glories of capitalism, which is necessary because the revolutionaries want infinite wealth, but capitalism inevitably sprang from its opposite and will inevitably produce its opposite, communism. Under capitalism the few rich enslave the many, Marx asserts, so the many will inevitably be transformed into the many rich (not-x becomes x) and they will, during the transition, dictate to the poor few.

The capitalists preach brotherly love, but practice oppressive violence. The proletariat must practice oppressive violence to produce—what? Its opposite, of course, brotherly love and freedom. Greed shall become altruism; totalitarianism shall become freedom. Earth will be transformed into heaven, but to do this we must first negate earth (redemptive, transforming destruction)—not-x will become x by totally negating (not-x); the verbal double negative produces the positive.

Down through all the years, Marxists of all varieties have shown a remarkable obsession with these simplistic, dualistic transformational myths. Herbert Marcuse, whose main claim to Marxist deification is his synthesis of the myth of Marxism with that other powerful modernist, revolutionary myth of pop-Freudianism, became obsessed with the idea that "freedom is slavery" or "tolerance is intolerance" as seen in *Repressive Tolerance*.[46] Needless to say, it all proves the truth of communist double-talk: only a truly totalitarian society can be a truly free one; only a dictatorship with total political inequality can be truly egalitarian; only a malevolent war machine can be truly loving and peaceful.

Marxism is a great myth triggering and synthesizing some of humanity's most powerful emotions and submyths. It was born in the crucible of the emotions unleashed by our many simultaneous, rapid social changes—the rapid development of technology, science, capitalism, industrialism, urbanism, and individual freedom and insecurity. It still has vast appeal to poor, ignorant peasants and workers who live in feudal or semifeudal conditions and are totally ignorant of realities in Russia, China, Poland, Cuba, ad nauseum. It also retains some of its appeal to the most envious and hate-filled people in our Western societies, especially intellectuals secretly convinced they should be the rich and powerful and deeply resenting that they are neither. But it has passed its zenith in the West. The Marxist myth has "inevitably" failed and those who have embraced it the most heartily are now suffering terribly for it. The terrible economic and political decay of the communist nations has combined with the growing perception of their totalitarianism to convince all but the most ignorant or passionately self-deceived that communism has succeeded only in producing the opposite of anything we want and of everything it promises. We shall long face the terror of their war machines, which grow more menacing as the pathologies of bureaucratic central planning and control enter their terminal stages. But our internal dangers will not come from any temptations of the Marxist myth, unless our bureaucratic megastates produce an almost unimaginable economic catastrophe. We are still in grave danger internally from the passions we have unleashed and from the myths that have sprung from these. But the great myth we have to fear is the myth of the modernist, democratic welfare state that has synthesized some of the revolutionary passions with the El Dorado myth of pop-Keynesianism and with our deep commitments to individual freedoms and Christianity.

Christianity, Socialism, Marxism and the
Birth of the Modernist Welfare State

The many early forms of democratic socialism sprang directly from the many utopian novels and analyses that poured from Europe in the late eighteenth and early nineteenth centuries. These works, like Sir Thomas More's original *Utopia*, were inspired primarily by the morality and communal spirit of Christianity, but were progressively wedded to the rationalism and scientism of the Enlightenment. This synthesis of the rationalist-scientist myth with the millennial, redemptive myth of Christianity grew steadily throughout the nineteenth century. In Britain the Fabian socialists secularized this utopian myth of Christian socialism by grafting it onto the burgeoning social-scientistic myths, thereby giving it an appearance of intellectual legitimacy for the educated.[47] In America this modernist veneer was used, but the dominant theme was at first more that of Christian redemption and millennialism. Even in Britain this was clearly the main appeal to the mass of members of the movement, as seen in the ardent zeal for reform of the Evangelicals. The democratic socialist movement, then, did not draw significant emotional appeal from the secularized millennial and redemptive myth of revolution. Democratic socialism, thus, did not inspire the myths of millennial and redemptive violence. For this reason and because of its acceptance of democratic institutions, democratic socialism was able to fit into the established forms of constitutional republicanism. During the Great Depression the democratic socialists became the "permanent" majority party in many nations of Europe, leading many center and conservative parties to adopt their program (without changing political labels, of course). Only when the modernist welfare states had severely eroded the economy did some of the socialists move toward the myth of redemptive revolution.

National socialism, communism, anarcho-syndicalism, anarchism, and similar movements sprang originally from the same millennial myth of utopia, but most of them synthesized this myth with the myth of universal revolution and with various degrees of revulsion rejected the Christian myths and the institutional forms of democracy. These movements thus moved progressively toward the polar extreme of the myth of redemptive, millennial violence we see in such true believers as Frantz Fanon: "Violence, alone, makes it possible for the masses to understand social truths. . .frees the native from his inferiority complex and from his despair and inaction."[48] Since the myth of redemptive revolution had already been "cleansed" of Christianity and grafted onto the Enlightenment's myth of rationalism and scientism, it was natural for Marx and other communists to progressively synthesize their ideas with the myth of modernism. When Marx also synthesized Hegelianism into this vast hybrid, he did so to gain the emotional power of historical inevitability, but he unknowingly set the stage for the next mythical hybridization of socialism—nationalistic socialism. The synthesis of the myth of nationalism with the millennial, modernist myth of socialism was first fully consummated in Germany.[49] (The Babeuvists attempted this during the French Revolution but were opposed even by Jacobins and were severely repressed.) After winning power, Hitler subordinated the earlier egalitarianism of socialism (represented by Roehm) to the collectivist totalitarianism of nationalism and gave birth to the millennial "ex-stasis" (ecstasy) we know as Nazism.[50]

Ecstasy, known in the ancient world as *ex-stasis*, always involves a loss of the sense of self, a sub-merging of the sense of self in a greater being, an adored, even awe-inspiring being. Ortega y Gasset has described this "state of grace":

> The desire to "get out of oneself" has been the cause of all forms of orgiastic expression: drunkenness, mysticism, love. I do not mean to say by this that they all have equal "merit"; I am only insinuating that they belong to a common branch and that their roots are steeped in orgy. They are attempts to find respite from the weight of living separately by transferring ourselves to another being who will sustain and guide us. For this reason the simultaneous use, in mysticism and love, of the image of rapture or rape is not fortuitous. To be enraptured means not walking on one's own feet but feeling oneself carried by someone or something.[51]

The supreme leaders, the modernist totalitarians, may inspire only hatred and revulsion in their enemies, but to the true believers they are the loving Gods who inspire transports of ecstasy which sweep away all the doubts and dreads of too-frail selves. Charisma is precisely this ability of leaders to trigger the universal mechanism of ex-stasis.

To this day the Russian communists try to export their myth under the banner of universalism (internationalism, thus antiimperialism), but at home they have always found it necessary to hybridize their communism with the myth of the nation-state, even to maintaining the most important imperial rituals and symbols of the Romanov czars. It is nationalist communism that has ignited the fires in the minds of so many twentieth-century revolutionaries around the world and turned so many of them against Russian nationalist imperialism. As communism progressively erodes the economies of the Russian and East-European "republics," the myth of nationalism is progressively igniting fires against Russian nationalistic imperialism.

The modernist myth of the welfare state in the United States did not spring directly from the socialist millennialism, and its true believers have always been strongly against all forms of the myth of revolution and most forms of socialism hybridized with it. Certainly some welfare statists marching under various banners, such as progressivism and liberalism, have been knowingly and unknowingly influenced by socialism, but this has not been a primary source of their faith. Our true welfare statists, as distinct from political posers, have been true believers in the myths of modernism and social scientism. Our modernist welfare statists are millennial in their promises of eternal prosperity, winning the War on Poverty for all time, producing a world of equality and love, and so on, but millennialism is generally a muted background note in their great symphonies of the myths. They often strongly oppose the millennial, redemptive myth of Christian socialism, thereby emphasizing their "down to earth" American pragmatism. Being first and foremost true believers in the mythical extensions of natural science and technology to society, the American modernist welfare statists see themselves as very hardheaded, objective, policy-oriented, practical, down-to-earth-realistic. (We see all of this writ large in American Keynesianism and related forms of social scientism.) Our modernist and scientistic policy experts are virulently opposed to myth, magic, and superstition. But this is merely a modernist form of protesting too much: the more their cargo-cult dances are revealed for what they are, as mythical rituals intended to usher in their muted and secularized heaven on earth, the more they must assert their scientism to repress recognition of the truth. When the pro-Keynesian econometric mathematical model for eternal increases in wealth through multiplier effects produces stagflation, the time has obviously arrived for a ratchet-up to monstrous econometric models that can simulate the world economy into eternal progress, unimpeded by the imperfections of worldly evidence.

We shall be concerned throughout this book with the economic millennialism hiding behind the fronts of social scientism. But we should keep it in mind that this millennialism hidden behind moralistic protestations of being "progressive," "really scientific and modern" (being "with it" as Americans say) is far more pervasive and extreme in most other realms of our lives because the evidence is far more skimpy and subjectively manipulable than economic evidence. The millennialism, modernism, and scientism of the average Keynesian economist are pale by comparison to those of the average politician, sociologist, psychologist, and most other "professional experts." Preposterous schemes to do away with all crime by engineering total social equality may receive few mass hosannas, but millennial schemes masquerading as science that trigger more powerful, more immediate passions than the fear of crime have gained multitudinous acclaim. Nowhere is this more obvious or more destructive than in the mass-mediated schemes for sexual bliss through the "liberation" of pop-Freudian scientism. As even Bruno Bettelheim has now insisted,[52] Freud was actually a profoundly conservative thinker. But his ideas have been mistranslated, selected, reinterpreted, and purveyed by our sexual modernists in such ways as to turn them into a platform for sexual millennialism in the holy name of Freud and science. No doubt some of these purveyors are frauds, but most are quite sincere. They are simply so committed to the great myths of our modernist age that they screen out Freud's ideas and evidence that contradict their myths. The very man who grounded his ideas about sex in the agonizing scenarios of Greek tragedy is transformed by the miracle of mass-mediation into the modernist satyr of Bacchanalian corroborees. It is almost enough to convince one that Bruno and Hegel were right about the universality of negative transformations.

Conclusion

The ancients were convinced that "pride goeth before a fall." And, of course, pride did go before most of the great falls of the ancient world, for their falls were generally political catastrophes produced by the megalomaniacal myths inspired by soaring hubris and by the sycophantic adulation of courtiers: each victory, each growth in power, inspired ever more optimism in political predators and ever more deceitful plaudits from their underlings, until finally they lost most sense of the realities of power and believed themselves omnipotent, or nearly so. Alexander and many other emperors literally came to see themselves as gods. In his masterful survey *The Twelve Caesars*, Michael Grant has shown how the seemingly absolute power of the Roman emperors after Augustus slowly, progressively led each emperor, especially those who started with extreme inferiority feelings (as Tiberius and Caligula did), to feel soaring pride and then progressively to lose touch with reality.[53] Absolute power may not always corrupt morals (though it generally does), but it does corrupt even the most realistic thinking, turning even realists into mythmakers. Hitler was one of our modern victims of the mythifying powers of absolute power. In 1940, on the eve of his plummet into the abyss, he gave a vivid illustration of how his many early victories tempted him step by step into the most total absurdities of mythical thought, the realm in which the dreamer knowingly *wills* the replacement of realism by imagination. He, too, began as the extremely insecure nobody who counteracted his insecurity by asserting a mythical superiority. But in those early years he had a sense of reality that he later lost because of victories. In the foremost work of modern strategic thought, B. H. Liddell Hart has argued that "the fumes of victory intoxicated him," and this intoxication did more than anything else to cause his downfall.[54] Albert Speer has shown how megalomaniacal Hitler became and how this combined with the flattery and fear of his underlings to repress all serious consideration of the fiery apocalypse that was encircling them.[55] James Reedy, press secretary to Lyndon

Johnson, has shown how this ancient interaction of proud arrogance, fearful and flattering deceit, and mythical thinking now afflicts our imperial presidents.[56]

In the same way, the vast victories of free enterprise in economic life, in science, and in technology combined with the political hosannas over these "miracles" to tempt more and more people into thinking mythically—dreaming—about the world, until finally they lost much of their sense of the difference between the reality of progress and the myth of millennium. The Great Depression of the 1930s was primarily a direct (proximate) result of the Federal Reserve's "easy money" policy, but lying behind this policy was the ultimate cause: a soaring conviction that everyone could get rich quick, a typical El Dorado millennial myth inflamed by the greed triggered by each rapid increase in wealth. But when the crash came, people refused to blame greed or the myths. Many millions of them denied the reality that free enterprise produces vast wealth over the long run in order to grasp the El Dorado myth more firmly. In 1941 Franklin Delano Roosevelt, completely unchastened by a decade of the fall precipitated by greed and prolonged by statist regulations, continued to fan the flames of myth. The time was now ripe to spread the virulent El Dorado myth beyond the West, to engulf the entire world in the searing flames of millennial hope. And, just as Hitler at that same time was dreaming away political reality in the underground bunkers of Germany, so was Roosevelt declaring absolutely that this dream of the millennium was no dream at all, but a reality:

> In the future days, which we seek to make secure, we look forward to a world founded upon four essential human freedoms:
>
> The first is freedom of speech and expression—everywhere in the world.
>
> The second is freedom of every person to worship God in his own way—everywhere in the world.
>
> The third is freedom from want—which, translated into world terms, means economic understandings which will secure to every nation a healthy peacetime life for its inhabitants—everywhere in the world.
>
> The fourth is freedom from fear—which, translated into world terms, means a worldwide reduction of armaments to such a point and in such a thorough fashion that no nation will be in a position to commit an act of physical aggression against any neighbor—anywhere in the world.
>
> That is no vision of a distant millennium. It is a definite basis for a kind of world attainable in our own time and generation. . . .[57]

At the very time Roosevelt was asserting the imminence of this New Deal Millennium for all humanity for all time, Europe and Asia were being bombed into miserable poverty by militaristic tyrannies. But after four more years of this conflagration, the millennial myth sprang forth from the flames more virulent than ever. Britain, long on the decline, and whose very existence had so recently hung tremulously in the balance, proclaimed its soaring faith by embracing Labour and its Beveridge Plan for everything right away. After a century and a half of socialist dreaming, the dawn of the millennium had come at last. As the socialists took power, Hartley Shawcross exclaimed for them all, "We are the masters now!"[58] Hugh Dalton has described their exultant feeling at this *High Tide and After:* "There was exhilaration among us, joy and hope, determination and confidence. . .We felt exalted, dedicated, walking on air, walking with destiny."[59] But what a grim walk with destiny it was to be. They were absolutely convinced that by progressively destroying free enterprise, the very System of Natural Liberty that had allowed them to rise to the pinnacle of most wealthy and most powerful nation in the world in less than one century, they could achieve a real millennium.

Americans, less convinced than Roosevelt that the hour of destiny was upon them, were content in 1946 to adopt the Full Employment Bill. This Public Law 304 was only a pale reflection of the Beveridge Plan and of what the liberal democrats wanted. Liberals like Stephen Bailey[60] denounced this legislative "subversion" of popular will, little noting or caring for the fact that the checks and balances were still working, though with less force, against a mass tyranny. It took another two decades before Americans were transfixed enough by all the inflammatory promises of the great myths to launch our own great myth of the welfare state—the Great Society. But already Americans were propagating the myth to the entire world through such media as the United Nations' declaration of universal rights which embodied Roosevelt's ideas of economic freedoms.[61] At the very same time realistic Americans were trying to convince people around the world that their political and economic progress depended primarily on their own efforts, especially on their private enterprise, our government was furiously fanning the flames of the millennial myths that turned people toward the terrible myth of Marxism. Since Americans have repeatedly asserted that they have an absolute right to all they want *now*, why should Americans be surprised if they assert that we and their governments should give them all of these things for nothing right now? We have made the world drunk on our own millennialism and we have given hundreds of billions of dollars in foreign "aid" and "loans" to their bureaucratic states. In doing so we have unknowingly supported rationalistic statist plans that guarantee poverty and despotism, in direct proportion to their degrees of statism, rationalism, and millennialism. The millennial (quixotic) states of Latin American and the new African governments have had the most of these, so they have been rapidly immiserated. Some of the Asiatic nations have been spared most of these, and have received the least aid per capita, so they have prospered mightily.

It is certainly true that we cannot live by bread alone. And certainly it is true that we peoples of the Western world, above all we Americans, are peoples of bounding ambition and hope. We have for centuries been creators driven on by our hopes for a better and better world, by what Robert Nisbet rightly speaks of as our Western dogma of material and spiritual progress.[62.] It is our hope, our faith that we can create a better world, that inspired us to break out of the zero-sum world of the myth of eternal stasis and to build these vastly creative and wealthy nations upon the firm foundation of far greater, individual enterprise. But it is one thing to wish and to strive mightily to achieve that ameliorative wish for a better and better world against all the terrible obstacles of reality; and it is a completely opposite thing to believe that we are somehow fated by right or by historical inevitability to achieve a millennium regardless of obstacles. An ameliorative wish inspires creative striving. A millennial myth inspires blind assertiveness, terrible failures, and furious rages against the Satans believed to be barring the gates to the promised land. The great tragedy of the modernist world is that the great myths have been displacing both wishes and realities with a mythical dogma of modernist secular millennialism.

We live today in one of the lulls of modernist millennialism. It may even be hard for those ignorant of history to believe how intensely the flame of secular millennialism has burned in the minds of Western people and easy to believe that we are witnessing "the end of idealogy." We who have lived through "the war on poverty" only to see "poverty" as officially defined increase after hundreds of billions had been spent on it, and sweeping ("liberal") reinterpretations of the Constitution perpetrated to advance the impassioned dream, may find it hard to believe that true believers will once again come to power. But history shows us that we have been through many of these plateaus and even some temporary reversions in the great ratchet-up drift process—always before the flames fanned by pseudo-science have returned to burn away reason and the humble aspirations of real science.

I have always thought it was a most valuable trait to recognize reality and not to pursue delusions. But when I now think over my life up to and including the years of imprisonment, there was no period in which I was free of delusory notions.

The departure from reality, which was visibly spreading like a contagion, was not a peculiarity of the National Socialist regime. But in normal circumstances people who turn their backs on reality are soon set straight by the mockery and criticism of those around them, which makes them aware they have lost credibility. In the Third Reich there were no such correctives, *especially for those who belonged to the upper stratum.* On the contrary, every self-deception was multiplied as in a hall of distroting (sic) mirrors, becoming a repeatedly confirmed picture of a fantastical dream world which no longer bore any relationship to the grim outside world. In those mirrors I could see nothing but my own face reproduced many times over.

No external factors disturbed the uniformity of hundreds of unchanging faces, all mine.

There were differences of degree in the flight from reality. Thus Goebbels was surely many times closer to recognizing actualities than, say, Goering or Ley. But these differences shrink to nothing when we consider how remote all of us, the illusionsts (sic) as well as the so-called realists, were from what was really going on.

Albert Speer

Notes

1. Frank E. Manuel and Fritzie Manuel, *Utopian Thought in the Western World* (Cambridge, MA: Harvard University Press, 1975), p. 713.
2. Mircea Eliade, *The Myth of the Eternal Return* (New York: Pantheon, 1965).
3. Fred Hirsch, *Social Limits To Growth* (Cambridge, MA: Harvard University Press, 1976).
4. There is now a large literature on millennialism (often called millenarianism). The basic sources are George Boas, *Essays on Primitivism* (Baltimore: Johns Hopkins Press, 1948); Norman Cohn, *The Pursuit of the Millennium* (Fairlawn, NJ: Fairlawn Books, 1957 and 1970 [rev. ed.]); and Robert Nisbet, *History of the Idea of Progress* (New York: Basic Books, 1980).
5. William Martin, "Waiting for the End," *The Atlantic Monthly*, June 1982, p. 31.
6. Manuel and Manuel, *Utopian Thought in the Western World*, p. 805.
7. See, especially, David Humphreys Miller, *Ghost Dance* (New York: Duell Sloan and Pearce, 1959); James Mooney, *The Ghost-Dance Religion* (Chicago: University of Chicago Press, 1965); and Robert M. Utley, *The Last Days of the Sioux Nation* (New Haven: Yale University Press 1963).
8. See Yu-Wen Jen, *The Taiping Revolutionary Movement* (New Haven: Yale University Press, 1973).
9. Purification rituals are used in all cultures in situations of grave danger to reestablish purity and, thereby, dispel the danger. Sacrifice is basic to most purification rites. See Mary Douglas, *Purity and Danger* (London: Routledge and Kegan Paul, 1978).
10. See Eric Hoffer, *The True Believer* (New York: Harper, 1951).
11. See Leon Festinger, Henry W. Riecken, and Stanley Schacter, *When Prophesy Fails* (Minneapolis: University of Minnesota Press, 1956).
12. V. S. Naipaul, *Among the Believers* (New York: Alfred A. Knopf, 1981).
13. Festinger, et al., *When Prophesy Fails.*
14. Yonina Talmon, "Millenarism," *Encyclopedia of the Social Sciences*, vol. 10, pp. 349–60.
15. Ibid.
16. This period of neurotic depression following the "high" of the boom is described by F. Scott Fitzgerald in *The Crack Up* (New York: New Directions [New Directions Paperbook, 1956]).
17. Michael Polanyi, *The Great Transformation* (Boston: Beacon Press, 1944).
18. See Oliver F. Hufton, *The Poor of Eighteenth Century France, 1750–1789* (Oxford: Oxford University Press, 1974); William NcNeill, *The Pursuit of Power* (Chicago: University of Chicago Press, 1982), pp. 144–47 and 185–87; and *Plagues and People* (Garden City, NY: Doubleday, 1976), pp. 240–56.

19. W. McNeill, *Plagues and People*, pp. 219–20.
20. J. M. Keynes, *The Economic Consequences of the Peace* (New York: Harcourt, 1920).
21. See Thomas Sowell, *Ethnic America* (New York: Basic Books, 1981).
22. Manuel and Manuel, *Utopian Thought in the Western World*, p. 715.
23. See James H. Billington, *Fire In the Minds of Men* (New York: Basic Books, 1980).
24. The classic study of the Jacobins is Crane Brinton, *The Jacobins* (New York: Russell and Russell, 1957).
25. This is the dogma of "primitivism." See Boas, *Essays on Primitivism*.
26. See Richard Foster Jones, *Ancients and Moderns*, 2d ed. (Berkeley: University of California Press, 1965).
27. See Nisbet, *History of the Idea of Progress*.
28. Benjamin Whorf, *Language, Thought and Reality: Selected Writings,* edited and with an introduction by John B. Carroll (Cambridge, MA: MIT Press, 1956).
29. I've dealt with this in my essay "A Grand Moral Strategy for Waging Peace and War," in Robert Poole, ed., *Defending a Free Society* (Lexington, MA: D. C. Heath, 1984), pp. 317–430.
30. David A. Altheide and John M. Johnson, *Bureaucratic Propaganda* (Boston: Allyn and Bacon, 1980).
31. Harry G. Summers, Jr., "U. S. Army Strategy in Vietnam: A Critique," *Wall Street Journal*, April 21, 1982.
32. F. A. Hayek, *The Counter-Revolution of Science* (Glencoe, IL: The Free Press, 1955).
33. See my analysis of structuralism in *The Social Meanings of Suicide* (Princeton: Princeton University Press, 1967); *Understanding Everyday Life* (Chicago: Aldine, 1970); *American Social Order* (New York: Free Press, 1971) and (edited with John M. Johnson), *Existential Sociology*, (Cambridge: Cambridge University Press, 1977).
34. Derek Freeman, *Margaret Mead and Samoa* (Cambridge, MA: Harvard University Press, 1983).
35. Margaret Mead, *Sex and Temperament in Three Primitive Societies* (New York: Morrow, 1935).
36. Ernest Van den Haag, *Fortune*, April 18, 1983, pp. 100 ff.
37. Allyn Moss, *Margaret Mead: Shaping a New World* (Chicago: Encyclopedia Britannica Press, 1963).
38. B. F. Skinner, *Walden Two* (New York: Macmillan, 1968).
39. John Kenneth Galbraith, *The Affluent Society* (New York: New American Library, 1958, 1969).
40. Quoted in *Forbes*, May 23, 1983, p. 132.
41. Ibid.
42. André Gide and others, *The God That Failed*, Richard Crossman, ed. (New York: Bantam Books, 1965).
43. Since Plato, philosophers of beauty have realized that beauty is inherently comparative or contrasting.
44. Dorothea W. Singer, *Giordano Bruno* (New York: Henry Schuman, 1950).
45. Karl Popper, *The Poverty of Historicism* (Boston: Beacon Press, 1957).
46. Herbert Marcuse, "Repressive Tolerance," in Robert Wolff, Barrington Moore and Herbert Marcuse, *A Critique of Pure Tolerance* (Boston: Beacon Press, 1965).

47. Sidney and Beatrice Webb were the most important "researchers" preparing the way for the Labourites. See, especially, *Industrial Democracy* (New York: Longman, 1920).
48. As quoted in Billington, *Fire in the Minds of Men*, pp. 508–09.
49. As I noted earlier, Ernst Cassirer's *The Myth of the State* (Garden City, NY: Doubleday, 1955) is predominantly concerned with this rise of German statism. He did not give enough emphasis to the importance of socialism, including the only officially sanctioned form of economics in German education. Friedrich Hayek emphasized this in *The Road to Serfdom* (Chicago: University of Chicago Press, 1944), but did not give enough emphasis to the factors emphasized by Cassirer and many others.
50. The Dionysian ex-stasis of the Nazi communings is most obvious in sound films.
51. Jose Ortega y Gasset, *On Love* (New York: Meridian, 1960), pp. 73–74.
52. Bruno Bettelheim, *Freud and Man's Soul* (New York: Knopf, 1983).
53. Michael Grant, *The Twelve Caesars* (New York: Charles Scribner's Sons, 1975).
54. Quoted in B. H. Liddell Hart, *Strategy* (New York: Praeger Paperbooks, Inc., 1954), pp. 253–54, 261–63, and 328.
55. See Albert Speer, *Inside the Third Reich* (New York: Avon, 1972).
56. Quoted in Peters and Fallows, *Inside the System*, pp. 3–16.
57. James MacGregor Burns, *Roosevelt: The Soldier of Freedom* (New York: Harcourt Brace Jovanovich, Inc., 1970), pp. 34–35.
58. Pauline Gregg, *The Welfare State* (London: George G. Hurrap and Co., Ltd., 1967), p. 36.
59. Ibid.
60. Stephen K. Bailey, *Congress Makes a Law* (New York: Columbia University Press, 1950).
61. As early as the 1950s, Roscoe Pound severely criticized all such "promises" of the "super service state." See "The Rise of the Service State and Its Consequences," in Sheldon Glueck, ed., *The Welfare State and the National Welfare* (Cambridge, MA: Addison Wesley, 1952), pp. 211–34.
62. See Nisbet, *History of the Idea of Progress*.

7

Rationalism and Scientism
versus Human Nature

By one road or another, by conviction, by its supposed inevitability, by its alleged success, or even quite unreflectively, almost all politics today have become Rationalist or near-Rationalist. . . . The general character and disposition of the Rationalist are, I think, not difficult to identify. . . . His mental attitude is at once skeptical and optimistic: skeptical, because there is no opinion, no habit, no belief, nothing so firmly rooted or so widely held that he hesitates to question it and to judge it by what he calls his "reason"; optimistic, because the Rationalist never doubts the power of his "reason" (when properly applied) to determine the worth of a thing, the truth of an opinion or the propriety of an action. Moreover, he is fortified by a belief of a "reason" common to all mankind. . . . He has no sense of the cumulation of experience, only a readiness of experience when it has been converted into a formula: the past is significant to him only as an encumbrance. . .he is apt to attribute to mankind a necessary inexperience in all the critical moments of life, and if he were more self-critical, he might begin to wonder how the race had ever succeeded in surviving. . . . He does not recognize change unless it is a self-consciously induced change. . . . The conduct of affairs, for the Rationalist, is a matter of solving problems. . .by the appropriate technique. . . . He waits upon circumstance to provide him with his problems, but rejects its aid in their solution. That anything should be allowed to stand between a society and the satisfaction of the felt needs of each moment in its history must appear to the Rationalist a piece of mysticism and nonsense.

Michael Oakeshott

It is so obvious that we live in an age of rationalistic scientism and technicism, that we are very apt to take it for granted and, thereby, fail to see the overwhelming implications and consequences of this fact. Every day our massive pulp industries (newspapers, magazines, and pop books) and our broadcast industries spew forth technicist rules showing us "how to": pick up girls, find a mate, make a friend, fall in love, get married, solve sexual problems, achieve sexual bliss, get pregnant, have a child without pain or medicine, stay in love for a lifetime, fight fair and square while we do so, achieve a "creative divorce" when we can't, fight for every penny in the divorce settlement, avoid depression over our creative act, and have the courage after all of this to try again; choose a college, get in, make good grades by playing the system, write a résumé, choose a career, land a job, win friends and influence enemies, succeed at the job while loving it, start over again when we don't love it, make a million dollars in real estate with no capital, retire, find a pleasant burial plot or a warm crematorium, face death grimly or embrace it, make peace with God or live without Him; get a government grant, avoid our taxes legally, evade them when we can't, and fight the IRS when we get caught; solve the ageless problems of poverty once and for all, solve the problems of crime, rid the world of cartels and monopolies, end unemployment, provide everyone with free health care, plan the American economy, plan the world's energy programs over the next fifty years or more, and create a new world in space to escape from all of our failed plans on earth.

Do these rationalistic-scientistic techniques work? Of course not. Or, to be more technicist, while we cannot yet specify to the umpteenth decimal point the margin of error within which our analysis can be presumed to be acceptable until rejected by more precise measurements, we can say that every conceivable bit of reliable information indicates that living by these rationalistic techniques of modernist scientists, counselors, and religionists probably works almost as often as any of the ancient forms of technicism that used to be named magic, wizardry, or sorcery. These modern forms of rationalistic-scientistic technicism obviously do not work any more often than we would expect by chance. This is obvious in the case of the technicisms of psychotherapy because careful follow-ups have shown that the actual "cures" (however that might be defined) are no more common than one would expect by *spontaneous remission* (that is, getting well on our own, by individual initiative—"naturally"). It is obvious as well in some instances because there is an internal contradiction in many of the claimed solutions. The man who proclaims that he has a surefire formula to make you rich, which he will sell you for just $8.95, is invariably not rich; and the politician who promises to decrease government intrusions into your life, if you will only give him a powerful new bureaucracy of energy or education to do so, is obviously proposing rationalistic-scientistic technicisms that are ludicrous.

But the failure of the rationalistic-scientistic technicisms is most obvious because every major problem has inspired dozens, hundreds, or even thousands of different sets of technicisms for solving the problem. An encyclopedia of psychotherapies, for example, lists hundreds of techniques for solving psychological problems. Each ballyhooed technical solution commonly has some good effects in the very short run because of the effects of faith (technically known as *placebo effects* or *Hawthorne effects*), though they also commonly produce some instantaneous catastrophes. The short-run remissions make true believers out of a minority who go on to become highly addicted to this solution and are often so dependent on it that they feel they cannot live without it. The great majority of novitiates soon recognize that this technical solution solves nothing, and, in fact, often becomes a bigger problem than the initial problem was, so they go on to try a new technique, and then another and another. They become technique hoppers searching desperately, and almost always in vain, for the one ultimate solution to their love problem, sex problem, marriage problem, money problem, national economic problem, international liquidity crisis, or what not.

Rationalist techniques almost always fail to solve human problems and unintentionally produce highly dysphoric, dystopian consequences because their implicit assumptions about human beings are wrong. Most commonly they assume, either explicitly or implicitly, that human beings are a clean slate, a tabula rasa, upon which the technicist may write whatever theme he has the power to try. Most importantly, they assume that there is no such thing as human nature and that each society, culture, or expert can socialize its newborn members into any form dictated by rationalist techniques. Often, paradoxically, they also assume implicitly that people are, *by nature*, rational animals who can always control their emotions and who can choose to make their life decisions independently of the "cake of custom" and of the concrete situations they face. A few, such as Freudianism and its many offshoots, assume a very simplistic model of human nature (such as a monotheistic model built on sex), but see this as determining action independently of the concrete situations the actors face after early childhood and of any individual differences.

None of these assumptions is true and any understanding of human beings or any proposed solution to a human problem based on them will prove either worthless (except by chance) or actually harmful. As Michael Oakeshott has argued, technicists fail to solve their social problems precisely because of the nature of the techniques they presume to be superior to all others in understanding and acting in society. The rationalistic-scientistic social thinkers first destroyed the basic forms of social thought which are the only ones that prove of practical value in solving problems, then they lament the lack of practical solutions and launch themselves upon an endless succession of technicist solutions:

the Rationalist has rejected in advance the only external inspiration capable of correcting his error; he does not merely neglect the kind of knowledge that would save him, he begins by destroying it. First he turns out the light and then complains that he cannot see. . . .All the Rationalist can do when left to himself is to replace one rationalist project in which he has failed with another in which he hopes to succeed.[1]

The rationalistic-scientistic technicist and any society subject to his policy mongering is doomed to a karma of Reforms, Reforms, Reforms, an unending succession of technicist epicycles upon epicycles that merely replace old problems with new ones or, far more commonly, amplify the old and add new problems to them.

Michael Oakeshott, Karl Popper, Friedrich Hayek, and other conservative, classical liberal and neoconservative social thinkers have followed Edmund Burke's argument against the rationalistic-scientistic technicism that has so dominated the social thought of intellectuals and officials since Voltaire, Rousseau, Condorcet, and the many other philosophers of the Enlightenment.[2] (I should note that most classical liberal theorists agree with this part of conservative theory.) They see the crucial mistake of the rationalist, the crux of the myth of rationalism and scientism, in their failure to see the fundamental distinction between problem solving that is torn from concrete situations, which is what is known as *technicism*, and *problem solving grounded in concrete situations*, which is known as *practical wisdom* (or, alternatively, as common sense, horse sense, art, etc.). The commonsense distinction between theory and practice (as in, "That may be fine in theory, but will it work in practice?") underlies this conservative argument. As Michael Polanyi and others have argued for the sciences, abstract theory in science, even the most truthful, must always be put to use in concrete situations by artful forms of decision making which interpret how to apply the theory to the concrete situation at hand. These artistic forms of decision making are inherently problematic. Because the properties of the concrete situations that emerge are necessarily uncertain, the interpretations of how to apply the theory to the concrete situation is necessarily uncertain. These artistic activities, then, are necessarily *creative activities* and, while we now know a lot about creativity, we could never give any scientific rules prescribing how to create the interpretations of any theory for an emergent, concrete situation.[3]

This necessary uncertainty in the concrete application of knowledge means that some mistakes or failures are inevitable. In general, the newer, or more creative, the activity, the more mistakes there will be—necessarily. *Risk in direct proportion to the creativity of an activity is a necessary part of life.* Any idea or theory that assumes mistakes and risks can be eliminated is rationalistic, or, when presented in the guise of science, scientistic—a myth inspired by fears potentiating hopes. Mistakes and risks can be shifted and certainly their consequences—costs or losses—can be shifted from one account (or person) to another; but they cannot be eliminated. This is why bankruptcy, business cycles, failures of planning, and so on are necessary and why the more creativity we want the more we must be ready to absorb—even encourage—mistakes and their costs.[4] Ultimately, as Popper says, all truly practical learning is by trial and error—trying something new to learn probabilistically what works in a situation, and then continuing it, and what does not work, and then avoiding doing that again in similar future situations.[5]

The most successful way of minimizing the risks and costs of failures is through the accumulation of practical experience. Ultimately, this practical experience is necessarily individual. But it is possible for individuals to communicate and thus share this accumulated practical wisdom through direct interaction in the concrete situation. This learning takes place with maximum speed, minimal mistakes and, thus, minimal costs when it is observed and done together in the concrete situation. The ultimate reason is that in a given time our brains can learn and validly process immensely more perceptual information about the patterns in the world from direct observation than it can from verbal communication. If you doubt the truth of this ancient Zen theory of knowledge, you can easily convince yourself by direct experience. Learn how to surf, fence, play football, box, build, paint, do experiments in physics, fix your motorcycle, or so on, entirely by reading all the best accounts of these that have been written over many centuries. Then compete against individuals who have learned these arts entirely from direct experience with the appropriate artists. Your opponents will learn much faster at much lower cost and they will win—easily.

The major forms of cultural activity (carpentry, medicine, birthing, child rearing, politics, sculpture, and so on) all have *accumulated* (sedimented and culturally transmitted) *practical wisdom* associated with them which is largely unverbalizable by their practitioners, and thus cannot be completely communicated theoretically (by specifying technical rules). They can only be learned by observing and doing, by practical experience in concrete situations. Learning by observing and doing with someone who already has great practical experience and wisdom is what is known as apprenticeship and is known to psychologists and ethologists as *observational learning*. It greatly speeds up the accumulation of practical wisdom, but it never eliminates the need for concrete experience—in fact, it presupposes learning by observing and doing and interpretations in concrete situations.

These conservative thinkers argue that all scientific knowledge must be interpreted with accumulated practical wisdom in concrete situations, if we are to use it effectively. This reliance on experience must be overwhelming in dealing effectively with personal or social problems because we have so little valid, reliable, and precise scientific knowledge about these, and because human beings are genetically different (see below) and have such a wide margin of necessary freedom, hence necessary unpredictability (even to themselves) in their concrete actions—we and they must wait to see what precisely they choose to do in a concrete situation before we and they can know what precisely they will do.

When scientific knowledge is found to be applicable effectively to a stable type of concrete situation by a stable interpretation, we call this interpretation *technology*. Science gives us laws of gravity and stress; structural engineering technology gives us stable interpretations of how these fit certain types of concrete situations in bridge building. Scientific technology is tremendously valuable, but it must always be further interpreted to fit whatever concrete situation actually emerges—this situation may have these forms, but exactly which ones? It also has some unique properties. When specific rules are presented as if they will fit all individual cases without creative interpretations, we have rationalistic technicism (or technique) or the myth of rationalism.

Rationalism is built first on the assumption that mind (or symbolism) is *the* ultimate reality and ultimately determines all that happens in the world. (Plato was the philosophical fount of Western rationalism.) It is, then, built on a fundamental confusion and mistake about reality in general (easily demonstrated by thinking yourself into flight off the Empire State Building). But even more importantly it is built on a fundamental mistake about human beings: rationalistic theories of human life assume that our lives are—or can be—ultimately determined only by reason, with no necessary direction provided by outside factors (situations) or by genetically determined passions, like drives, feelings, or motives. (A huge literature in psychology tries to distinguish among these three and other categories. For the most part, these are ad hoc distinctions that obscure more than they clarify. I shall use them commonsensically and, thus, interchangeably.) In addition, social rationalism has almost always been built on the implicit assumption that the human mind is a tabula rasa, that there is no such thing as human nature (except, possibly, that of being the rational being), and that, consequently, human beings are entirely determined by their social or cultural environment. (There is a minority of modern rationalists who believe that the supposed lack of biological determinism in human life means that we are free to choose what we will become, but there are almost no social scientists who take this view and almost no policies of social planning are based on them. They, therefore, need not concern us here.)

These assumptions of the denatured human being and of cultural determinism underlie (or else lie hidden beneath) most major techniques of social planning, ranging from Marxist-Leninist state planning to Skinnerian planning for *Walden Two* and American bureaucratic planning of the War on Poverty. These largely unexamined, often hidden assumptions are based on a misunderstanding of the whole psychological and biological theory of human nature, as well as a complete mistake of the facts, and have led these social rationalists unintentionally to institute sweeping social policies that destroy economic efficiency and individual freedoms. Their plans have been intended to increase wealth (thus "freedoms from" deprivation), equality, and "freedoms to." In most democratic nations, both human nature and our traditional cultural experience have quickly undermined such plans, leaving little more than confusing and partially disruptive, yet vastly costly, *rhetorics of central planning* and *distortions of individual planning*. Everywhere these rationalist plans for freedom, equality, and prosperity have been significantly enforced for long, they have been enforced by tyranny and have produced far more inequality and poverty.

The Rousseau Myth of Denatured Society versus the Laws of Classical Economics

There are two very general perspectives on the relations between individuals and society which have dominated Western social thought since ancient Greece. One perspective is that of *human nature guidance*. From this perspective, human individuals are believed to have certain basic feelings and ways of perceiving and reasoning about the world that are always basically the same. Proponents of this perspective have always recognized the obvious, that is, that human beings show both similarities and dissimilarities. Individuals within a given society, such as Athens, have both similar feelings and different feelings. And Athenians in general were quite different in certain feelings from Spartans. These theorists have always argued in some way that the differences hide underlying similarities, and that the similarities are generally more important than the dissimilarities in inspiring what people do in concrete situations, especially in those realms of life that are most important to people—like love and sex, material goods, and death. Athenians and Spartans had extremely different forms of the family, but they both had sexual and family feelings and, thus, families. (Actually, if we can believe the meager historical traces, the Spartans were as unusual in this respect as any human society ever found, but they did retain strong family ties.) These theorists explained the differences in terms of different environmental and social situations leading to different ways or forms of expressing the unchanging human nature. The theorists have had all kinds of disagreements among themselves, especially over the factors they see as part of human nature or the weights they give to different factors, such as how important they consider the physical (geographical) or social environments to be. But the basic ideas have been similar from Thucydides to David Hume, Adam Smith, Adam Ferguson, and right up to contemporary sociobiologists, ethologists, and psychobiologists. Thucydides stated the basic idea very clearly 2,400 years ago in explaining why he wrote *The Peloponnesian War* to "last for ever":

> And it may well be that my history will seem less easy to read because of the absence in it of a romantic element. It will be enough to me, however, if these words of mine are judged useful by those who want to understand clearly the events which happened in the past and which (human nature being what it is) will, at some time or other and in much the same ways, be repeated in the future. My work is not a piece of writing designed to meet the taste of an immediate public, but was done to last for ever.[6]

The second major perspective has been that of *social (cultural)* or *institutional determinism*. Theorists who share this perspective have believed that the dissimilarities among human societies are far greater and more important than similarities. Since Herodotus argued that there was something distinctive about the Greeks (primarily their independence, initiative, and creativity) that gave them a crucial advantage over the Persians in warfare, these theorists have sought explanations of the differences between nations, and the different outcomes of their actions, in their social lives, that is, their shared values, laws, institutions, and so on. More importantly, they have not believed similarities are very important between nations, but when they have noted them they see them as arising from similar social values, geographies, or what not. While the basic idea is quite ancient, and was already highly developed by implication in Plato's theory of society in *The Laws*, it will be readily recognized as the dominant theory of the social sciences today. It is the mainstay of economic policy making, especially of general social planning.

The social theory of the Catholic Church and their allies, the monarchists, was actually a combination of these two. According to this Augustinian theory of the ancient regime of Church and monarchy, people were originally free to will whatever they would. But his (at the temptation of her) choice of evil fruit in the Garden of Eden damned all humanity to the necessary constraints of passions within and toil (scarcity) without—impassioned (evil) human nature in the human economic condition of scarcity. This theory asserted that, if people were left free to choose what they will, then they will necessarily choose evil (war, rape, theft, murder, etc.) because of the evil passions within them since the Fall. But God, in His infinite grace, gave people the gifts of Church and State to impose godly constraints on them to prevent them, as much as possible in this world, from committing evil. The Church and Monarch were, of course, human beings themselves and, thus, admittedly subject to such frailties, but they possessed the revealed truth and were *directly* descended from Christ and thus administered the word of God as constraints on evil people. Only this "Great Chain of Being"[7] linking the police powers ultimately to the absolute constraint of God (Christ) allowed them to perform what otherwise seemed the impossible task of lifting themselves by their own bootstraps—that is, only by being the vehicles through which God acted could evil human beings impose constraints on other evil human beings.

When the social philosophers of the seventeenth and eighteenth centuries created the foundations of modern social sciences and of the classical liberal and Burkean political theories, they recognized very well that they were doing something with frightening implications. Because they opposed the constraints on individuals of the ancient regime, they were commonly accused by Tories of releasing the demonic passions of human beings. The specter of anarchy and all the feared consequences of Hobbes's "war of all against all" haunted them. (Doestoevski's frightening portrayal of the evils perpetrated by the romantic anarchist Raskolnikov in *Crime and Punishment* is a classic statement of the belief that overturning the Church's moral authority would unleash the most terrible passions.) Hobbes recognized and spelled out the danger very clearly in secular terms and argued that one simply had to insist on absolute monarchy to provide the external constraint. But Locke and his successors thought this was not so. Locke and the Scottish analysts thought the Church and the monarchs had obviously succumbed to their own evil passions and that human beings could be constrained by "the laws of nature," which were moral laws outside of or independent of them to which they had to submit, and by their personal interests, defined broadly by Adam Smith to include all gratification of the natural passions.[8] Essentially, they argued that one could do away with the vehicles of God's word, the institutions of Church and Monarchy, without doing away with God's constraints as mediated by nature, that is, revealed by human reason guided by the natural human passions. Individual human beings would see and do what was necessarily right, and avoid the evil, if only they were not forced toward evil by powerful institutions like the Church and Monarchy. Individuals would constrain themselves with the help of God as much as those evil institutions would, because they can see directly, without Church or Monarch, what is good and what is bad. Their passions would be constrained by their recognition of natural law and their rational interpretations of their situational "interests." In *The Theory of Moral Sentiments*, Adam Smith[9] even went so far as to argue that our passions are so harmoniously and benevolently ordered that reason itself is largely redundant:

> . . .self-preservation, and the propagation of the species, are the great end which Nature seems to have proposed in the formation of all animals. . . .But though we are. . .endowed with a very strong desire of those ends, it has not been entrusted to the slow and uncertain determinations of our reason to find out the proper means of bringing them about. Nature has directed us to the greater part of these by original and immediate instincts. Hunger, thirst, the passion which unites the two sexes, the love of pleasure, and the dread of pain, prompt us to apply those means for their

own sakes, and without any consideration of their tendency to those beneficent ends which the great Director of nature intended to produce by them.[10]

By the time he wrote *The Wealth of Nations*,[11] he had rediscovered the great importance of reason in recognizing our interests and, thus, constraining our passions; and he saw the need for government to prevent tyrants (both foreign governments and criminals within) from preying upon others. But individuals would most serve their own and others' interests when these constraints were kept to the minimum necessary.

Rousseau became the great social determinist of the romantic movement and eventually of structural (macro) sociology, anthropology, political science, and economics. His basic ideas, while clouded, are simple enough. There is an entire literature analyzing what Rousseau, other philosophes, and the classical economic theorists "really meant." Their social thought was inherently ambivalent even on the most basic issues, as many analysts have shown. What I am concerned with here, the direct effects of Rousseau and others on later social theory, is much simpler and clearer.

"All men are born free (by natural Lockean law), but everywhere they are in chains." Why? Society, or ancient regime institutions, did it. The solution is first to "erase the infamy" of the ancient regime (as Voltaire had put it). But this must then be followed not by allowing individuals to make their own decisions free of external constraints, but by giving *all* power over to the new state in a dictatorship of the liberated, which would then, supposedly, act in accord with natural law, as revealed in what Voltaire called the "common will," to socialize human beings in the values and practices of liberty and justice. It may sound paradoxical to demand total subjection to society, especially to the new state organization, in order to achieve total liberty. But it is not at all once we remember that for Rousseau ". . .if all that comes to man from society were peeled off, there would remain nothing but a creature reduced to sense experience and more or less undifferentiated from the animal." (This is Emile Durkheim's summation of Rousseau's theory, which Durkheim saw as the beginning of sociology. This is especially important because Durkheim was the most important founder of the dominant stream of modern social thought, value-determinist structural-functionalism.) In short, there is no human nature distinct from that of other animals and no human nature that produces the general form of the social institutions within which people live. We are free, then, to create whatever institutions we wish, and most especially those that will generate total equality for everyone, but we must do so through social institutions, especially through educational ones, imposed by centralized state power that is necessarily unlimited because the very essence of sovereign power is to be unlimited: it must be unlimited, or it does not exist.

Rousseau's theories had a great deal of influence on certain British and American social thinkers. But, as I argued earlier, the common practice of grouping romantic Rousseauian liberals with the British and American liberals, such as Adam Smith and Thomas Jefferson, is justified by nothing more than the fact that they all wanted liberty from the ancient regime. The most important difference is that almost all the British and American liberal thinkers retained a firm belief in the existence of human nature, including its inherent conflicts and uncertainties, and in its importance in *influencing* what people *choose* to do in concrete situations. (Locke's argument against inherited ideas was directed against the dogma of church-revealed truth and did not mean that there is no inherited natural reason and natural passions.) This is of vital importance and makes these British and American thinkers conservative liberals, midway, more or less, between the romantic liberals of the continent and the liberal (Whig) conservatives best represented by Edmund Burke. (Adam Smith, the foremost British liberal, was a friend of Edmund Burke, the foremost Whig conservative, both personally and theoretically.)

David Hume, who was a close colleague and friend of Smith, has given the fullest statement of their conservative liberal theory of human nature in society.[12] Like Aristotle (and anyone with common sense), they knew that people are social animals and that this is of vital importance in any social theory. But they knew that they are social animals with distinctive animal properties, not mere by-products of socialization practices. As Hume repeatedly stressed, humanity is dominated by "human passions" such as vanity or pride. (Hume did not know that most of these passions are shared by other primates as well, so he tended to see them as more distinctive of human beings than they are.) He argued that we are normally very careful to hide such passions, and, indeed, to overpresent ourselves as just the opposite, as humble, precisely because we know that others will be expecting us to be vain or proud. But once we get behind these fronts, we find the passions dominating what we really choose to do in social life. Hume was very aware from his extensive historical works that these passions are given specific forms of expression by our choices of how to act in the concrete situations we face at any time and that social institutions, customs, and values are significant parts of the situations we face. One of the common assertions of social scientists today, and even more of our pulp intelligentsia, is that the classical economists like Smith and Hume did not know how social institutions affect the expression of human passions like greed for material goods. This view has been most widespread in sociology, both because sociologists almost never know anything about economics and because Durkheim mistakenly identified the radical utilitarians like Bentham with the classical liberal economists, whose works he apparently did not know directly. In fact, however, Adam Smith wrote a whole book on the effects of "moral sentiments," by which he meant what we would call social values or morality, in which he tried to show the effects of values and institutions on the ways in which basic economic motives are partially shaped by society. If anything, Smith and the other Scottish social philosophers went much too far in emphasizing the conformity of individuals to the shared moral sentiments. No educated Britisher was likely to be ignorant of the effects of the bloated Stuart bureaucracies on economic life in the seventeenth century. And Adam Smith insisted that the resurgence of monarchical monopolistic regulations in the eighteenth century had a very bad effect on economic efficiency and, thence, on the increase of national wealth. He was not likely to forget that different social institutions have a significant effect on economic life and, especially, on efficiency and, thence, on the wealth of nations. In fact, the very idea is ludicrous. If he had thought social institutions or customs do not have an effect on the key variables of national economic life, those of efficiency and wealth, it would have been ridiculous to write a book explaining why different societies have different levels of wealth. Indeed the fact that most social scientists could come to believe such a ludicrous thing is one more indication of the vast importance of mythical thought in the social sciences today.

But Smith and Hume's belief in the importance of social institutions in economic life never prevented their seeing the equally obvious fact that human passions in economics and politics remain basically similar everywhere at all times. It was, in fact, precisely their belief that universal laws of human nature underlie their laws of economic exchange that put them in direct contradiction to the later European, especially German, *institutional*, or *historicist economists*, who had such a profound effect on history and sociology, and to Marxist and Keynesian economists.

Human Nature in Politics and Economics Today

In the nineteenth century, intellectuals discovered the vast powers of greed when it is unleashed. In the first half of the twentieth century, intellectuals discovered what almost everyone had known privately all along, the vast powers of sex when it is repressed. In the third quarter of the twentieth century, everyone discovered the vast powers of sex when it is unleashed. In the last quarter of the twentieth century, we are rediscovering the vast powers of political lust, of the ferocious lust for social dominance, which Big Government has unleashed in all major societies. Only the intellectuals' ignorance of everyday life and their academic conformity to ancient ideologies prevents their seeing what is obvious to ordinary people today. While the myopic intellectuals are still bewailing the "unjust dominance" of the robber barons, a whole generation of ferocious political predators have come to dominate all major aspects of our public life except nonpolitical entertainment.

Almost all of our higher-level politicians have gladly quit business or professional life to endure the agonizing campaigns in the ferocious quests for political power, fame, and glory. Few higher-level politicians today willingly quit politics to become businesspeople or professionals. It is rare to encounter the old-fashioned, aggressive, business type on our elite campuses today, but they are overrun with ferocious young politicians of every type. Almost everyone knows the immense glory, power, and wealth of our politicians because it is all there on the TV screen every time the masses wildly cry their adulation of the great leader, every time the cameras mob the politicians as they step from the huge jet, every time the lowliest members of Congress berate the heretical oilmoguls or nominees to the Supreme Court on witch trial before the TV cameras. No amount of intellectual obfuscation can belie the sense of awe, the quavering thrill that sweeps through the body of the average person swept up in the majesty of the immense political power and glory in our mass statist rituals.

What we have seen in the last century is a progressive intellectual revelation of three of the most powerful passions of human life—greed, lust, and now dominance. These passions and many more have been obscured by the scientistic myths that have dominated most of our social thought since Saint-Simon, Fourier, Comte, and others carried out the *counterrevolution of science*. Ordinary people, of course, have not for one minute forgotten the power of those and many more passions in their lives. They continually use their concrete understandings of them to decide what to do. (Any pretty schoolgirl who does not yet know the power of envy in human life will soon learn.) But even they have been progressively trained by social scientists to think about social policies without any consideration of how politicians are driven by the lust for power and, instead, to think of politics in terms of political values on equality, social planning for equality, public opinion, and all forms of modernist rhetoric. As intellectuals have slowly begun to rediscover the passions, mostly by swallowing Freud whole, they have begun to search into the souls of our politicians with "psychohistories" to discover sex pervading their lives. Since most human beings are greatly affected by their sexual passions, it is about as easy to discover sex in the lives of these politicians as it is to discover sand at the beach. But mucking away at their sexual passions and actions only obscures the immensely more powerful passion of politicians—lust for dominance. I believe, in fact, that the obvious pervasiveness of sex in our politics today is primarily because sex is one form of dominance-display for our politicians. Political sex is a form of "scoring" in the dominance struggle. In our democracies we have unleashed sex and repressed most conscious consideration of the lust for dominance. Now our most ferocious political predators, people who are willing to suffer terribly and even to die for the fame, glory, pride, and power of political victory, are "exposed" as largely clownish philanderers.

Before the last two centuries, almost all major social thinkers saw the passions of power lust, greed, and sex as extremely important in human life.[13] Augustine made these three the triad of evil—the most important of the Seven Deadly Sins—which Christians should strive to control. Over the centuries, especially after Machiavelli and Guicciardini turned social thought from otherworldly to this-worldly matters, social thinkers slowly accumulated a considerable amount of empirical information and ideas about the strongest passions, their interrelations, the relations of passions to reason and will, of all of them to the situations individuals faced and, thence, to action. Almost all of this is contained explicitly in the works of David Hume and Adam Ferguson, and either explicitly or implicitly in the economic and political work of their colleagues, Adam Smith and Edmund Burke. The same ideas about human nature in society are found in the theories of politics and economics used to justify the weak and divided government of the United States in the *Federalist Papers*. While they disagreed on many specific ideas, it is of crucial importance to see that there is a remarkable fit between their basic theory of human nature and the theory that is slowly evolving from the many disciplines that have recently resumed the study of human nature in society. These are especially the disciplines of ethology, primatology, physiological psychology, comparative psychology, developmental psychology, the many brain sciences, psychobiology, sociobiology, and the many related behavioral biologies.

The Basic Model of Human Nature

The present biological idea of "human nature" is very different from that assumed in most of the criticisms of it by cultural determinists.[14] These rationalist cultural-determinists implicitly assume that human nature means a set of (almost?) invariant drives, ideas, and actions dependent on those. This is seen, for example, in the idea that selfishness, private property, and aggressive acts of competition are inevitable because they are part of human nature; and in the opposite idea that altruism, communal property, and cooperative acts are inevitable (or the inevitable course of history) because they are part of human nature. The biological idea of human nature sees almost no behavior as totally invariant, or, as they would normally put it, as "hard-programmed" or totally *closed* to the environment (which includes the physical and cultural or social environment). The hard-programmed theory of human nature is what we can call *absolute biological determinism*. It dominated social Darwinist thought early in this century and is generally found today in what Donald Ball so felicitously called "pop-ethology" and Marshall Sahlins called "vulgar sociobiology."

The new biological theory of human nature, the foundations of which are probably best presented in Richard Dawkins's work *The Selfish Gene*, in John Bonner's work *The Evolution of Culture in Animals*, and in Wilson's later work *On Human Nature*,[15] argues that the genes inherited by each human being *predispose him or her to varying degrees in vastly complex ways* to choose certain alternative ways of interacting with the environment over other ways. These *genetic predispositions of behavior*, which might also be called *behavioral primers*, are almost never absolutely closed or totally programmed in human beings in the way standard behavioral responses are fixed in response to standard releasing mechanisms in very simple animals. Even the simplest reflex actions in human beings, such as the blinking of the eye in response to a suddenly approaching object, can be *overridden* by willpower and learning, except possibly when there is no warning—when we are taken by surprise and cannot consciously *set* or program ourselves to inhibit the reflexive reaction. Our vast array of genetic inputs predispose us, largely through our vastly complex array of interdependent and hierarchicalized drives (inborn motives), to respond in certain ways with greater frequency to certain situations. The genes *partially close our responses with a probabilistic weighting (strength of emotion)*. But the obverse of this partial closedness in response is our partial openness of response choice: human beings are almost always partially open, or free, to choose how they will act in concrete situations. But this partial freedom of human action is not a denial of genetic determinism. Our partial freedom to choose how we shall will and, thence, act is a direct result of genetic determinism. *Human beings are partially free because our genes force us to be partially free* and, I would argue, predispose us to choose an optimum of freedom in all situations. Sartre was wrong in believing that we are absolutely free, but he was right to believe that we are condemned to be free. Contrary to what almost all the opponents of human nature have believed, human freedom of choice is grounded firmly in the iron law of genetic determinism.

In *The Evolution of Culture in Animals*, John Bonner has shown how behavior becomes partially open to choice at a very low level on the phylogenetic scale and increases rapidly as the higher brain, the *telencephelon*, develops. Certainly almost all such choices are highly conditioned by our memory traces of past similar and associated experiences, but even at low levels of complexity in neural processing of information there is some openness to the situation at hand, some decision making about the choice to make in this situation, because the past experience is almost never complete enough or fitted enough to our emerging situations to close the response totally. Once animals developed teaching and observational learning as a highly economical way (in terms of neural storage and information processing capacity) of transmitting behavior and information (especially through socialization of the young), the genetically determined openness to environmental inputs increased very rapidly and the stage was set for the development of cultural transmission of learned experience.

Just as human freedom is genetically determined, so is culture genetically determined. Social scientists over the past century have insisted adamantly upon the Rousseauian assumption that the creation and social transmission of shared symbolic experience, which is what is meant by culture, is distinctly human and has freed human beings from any genetic constraints, that is, from any form of human nature. For example, in his book *Societies: Evolutionary and Comparative Perspectives*, Talcott Parsons maintained that "in the realm of action, the gene has been replaced by the (cultural) symbol as the basic structural element." In his book *Social Sciences as Sorcery*, Stanislav Andreski quoted and replied to Parsons's antigenetic assertion: "As if we could be here at all if our genes had been replaced by symbols, or as if our capacity to use symbols did not depend on the nature of our genes. After all, worms cannot speak and crocodiles cannot write."[16]

Andreski's defense of the gene is obviously convincing, but it is easy for any neuroscientist to show not only that our human genes dictate our use of language, but that they dictate remarkably precise linguistic functions for relatively specific areas of the neocortex, especially for the temporal lobe of the left hemisphere in 98 to 99.9 percent of individuals. Lesions, tumors, interference with blood supply, or deterioration of neurons or synapses for any other reason in specific parts of these regions of the brain can produce remarkably specific and stable problems of linguistic symbol processing known as the aphasias, alexias, and agraphias.

All human beings with healthy, normal brains and family experience are cultural animals, that is, symbol creators, users, and transmitters, precisely because our genes have constructed our brains with almost unimaginable intricacy to create and process symbols in accord with the universal deep rules of grammar, as Noam Chomsky has shown;[17] because our genes have primed our infants' learning of symbols so that they learn symbols remarkably easily; because our genes have endowed us with our love of symbols that leads our babies to thrill to their own babble and to story, poem, and song as exciting forms of fantasy and expression in all human cultures; and because our genes have dictated that we will be born into a nuclear family in which we will be immediately immersed in a vastly complex body language and verbal language that are partly universal and partly unique to each culture that will be our lifelines to other human beings through all our days.

The cultural determinists have generally believed, or implicitly assumed, that culture actually takes over the function of absolute genetic determinism.[18] Culture supposedly does this by developing absolutist rules that are then enforced effectively against any deviants from the rules. As the biological theorists have argued, culture certainly does mimic the genes by remembering (sedimenting) through its normative code what has worked in the past and enforcing these adaptive forms of behavior on the members of the culture. The biological reason culture evolves, of course, is that it is more adaptive than the greater genetic *closedness* of behavior. Cultural rules mimic the genes, but can change far more rapidly to meet changing situations than the genes can, so natural selection leads to a drift to the genes that increase cultural abilities.[19] But the cultural determinists have been quite wrong in two of their basic assumptions about cultural determinism. We have already seen that they were also wrong above all in assuming the genes are made obsolete by cultural symbols and rules. They were wrong first in assuming that absolute cultural rules produce almost absolute closedness of behavioral responses, hard programming, to culturally defined situations. They replaced the pop-ethology assumption of absolute genetic determinism with the pop-sociology assumption of absolute cultural determinism, that is, with the iron law of cultural conformity. A whole generation of the sociologists of deviance have amassed a huge amount of evidence showing that, even when the rules are presented as absolutes, they rarely are used absolutely and, even when they are used absolutely, they cannot prevent a major degree of individual freedom of choice from cultural rules.[20] We are necessarily partially free from cultural norms because no culture can ever symbolically anticipate precisely the properties of situations that emerge. As anyone can see in our own society, individuals do violate cultural norms. They most frequently violate those they do not agree with, a situation that is very common in civilizations because all civilizations are made up to some degree of pluralistic subcultures. But they also sometimes violate even those rules to which they are highly committed. They do so primarily through protracted drift processes when the cultural rules come into conflict with their passions and mythical thinking unleashed by changing situations.

The second basic mistake of the cultural determinists was the failure to see that, even though our genes determine that we shall be partially guided by cultural norms, they also continue to guide us in a crucial way that puts all individuals into conflict to some degree with their culture and which puts all individuals of our complexly pluralistic and more "repressive" statist civilizations into a high degree of conflict with members of other subcultures and especially with the statist bureaucrats. When the genes progressively freed animals from direct genetic determination of their actions, they created (by mutations and successive natural selection) a fail-safe system to partially guide animals in their situational choices of action. They were made free to choose, but only within limits set by this fail-safe set of guides. These guides are the natural passions, otherwise known as basic emotions, motives, or drives. Through the passions, the genes do not dictate that we *must* act in a certain way. Rather, they indicate by the way we feel a *general* direction we should take in our free choices in order to satisfy eventually the demands of our emotions. The culture determinists swept aside all consideration of the emotions, seeing them as either nonexistent or as completely subordinate to our symbolic, hence our rational, side. This assumption that symbols and reason (cognition) totally dominate our individual lives is a crucial mistake leading to the myth of rationalism and to the follies that flow from that, such as the folly of central planning (see chapter 8). Today even psychology is dominated by *cognitive psychology* which systematically denies the most obvious emotional realities of human life.[21]

As remarkable as it might seem to the rationalists and cultural determinists, people appear to be the animals with by far the most complex and powerful set of emotions. And, what must seem truly remarkable, even paradoxical, to cultural determinists, *people are the most emotional animals precisely because they are the most free and rational animals.*[22] Emotions are our benevolent overseers, our inner guides that thrust us into the world, reward our life-enhancing plans and actions with sweet pleasures, and punish our life-diminishing plans and actions with bitter pain. Our emotional guides do not tell us exactly what we must do, nor how we should go about doing it, though some of them speak more precisely and sternly than others, especially in certain situations in which they are so aroused as to override our will power and dictate rather specific paths of action. Rather, our emotions normally insist, to varying degrees, that our vast powers of reason find some ways to plan and to act in certain general directions to fulfill and enhance themselves; and then they reward the plans that succeed in that, thus increasing the probability those plans will be followed again when the emotion grows, and punish the failures, thus decreasing the probability of those plans being used again.

Without these benevolent guides insisting that reason and action move in general directions that enhance life, and shun directions that diminish life, reason and action might not only wander off aimlessly, but might even be turned against life and end it. Without, for example, our fear of death and our love of self, we might "rationally" kill ourselves. The ultimate "reason" why it is irrational to kill ourselves is that thinking of doing so produces immense dread and grief: our emotional overseers are the ultimate costs and benefits that reason will sum up to determine what is rational, what is success, and what is failure. We are obviously genetically free to commit acts that result in our own death. But since we are condemned by our genetic guides, our emotions, to suffer terribly when we do, very few human beings do.

The more animals are free from specific genetic programs of action, that is, the more they are free to create, choose, and will from alternative plans of action, the more powerful and numerous their emotional guides must be to guarantee genetically that they will act in general over the long run to enhance their lives (that is, adaptively). Thus it is that humans must have the most powerful and multifarious emotions to guide their rational planning, their free willing, and their acting. Our will is free, not determined, but it is emotionally guided and in that sense it is partially constrained in general directions. All animals die in dread and agony; humans alone are born in great pain and die with a strong hope, or peaceful faith, that death is merely the dreaded door through which they must pass to reach eternal life. We have probably inherited the full panoply of the emotions of the lower forms of vertebrae life, including the fishlike peacefulness of floating in water and the birdlike thrill of soaring through the air. Some of our most primitive experiences, especially that of smell, may be relatively less intense than in some animals, but this is true only because we have developed a whole panoply of visually aroused sensations to complement those of smell. Humans alone thrill to the beauty of art, are smitten with love by the sight of the beautiful human face and body, and are transfixed with awe before the visual immensity of the universe.

Like all of our close relatives, humans obviously have a large number of drives that constitute what earlier thinkers called the "natural passions." These are basically the ones concerned with immediate survival, like hunger, and desire for air and water, and include the very powerful fear of death that reinforces all of the others. In addition, there are the generalized drives for pleasure and avoidance of pain. After these many drives, there is the whole second level of powerful drives we have been discussing—those of sex, dominance, greed, envy, jealousy, shame, pride, anger, fear and anxiety, hate, love, and friendly reciprocal-altruism. In addition, there are a number of drives that clearly are genetically inherited and specific, but that seem to be significantly weaker than these—such as those of curiosity, playfulness, desire for excitement and new experience, and aesthetic experience (a pleasurable response to art). Certain common feelings, like the feeling of awe or joy in triumph, may be independent enough to be considered basic feelings or drives, or they may be derivatives of these. Most of our common everyday feelings are complex derivatives, emotional Gestalts, of these, which, of course, makes it very difficult to be sure about which are basic (inherited) and which are derivative. But, whether basic or derivative, we know that all of these are of pervasive and fundamental importance in all human life.[23] The most obvious evidence for the universality of, and thus the genetic basis for, basic emotions are the universal facial expressions for them and their expression in basically similar situations.[24] Most of our basic emotions are also pervasive and fundamental in all primate life, for most of the major differences in drives among primates are matters of degree. Chimpanzees even show very clear signs of curiosity when they gather around a new object to poke it and observe all its properties. But, of course, drives most closely associated with symbolic life do seem to be much more developed in human beings.

It is obvious that certain of the drives are in conflict with others. Greed and dominance are obviously in conflict with altruism; love and altruism with hate, envy, and aggression; fear (and flight) with curiosity; and so on. Just as the early social thinkers came to realize from observing the history of human society that some of the passions are in conflict with each other, so have the modern scientists found that drives are in conflict within the same individual and, obviously, between individuals. Conflict within and between ourselves, and thus within any culture, is part of our genetic endowment.

But this does not mean that the simplistic early versions of social Darwinism, which often sang bloodcurdling paeons to the war of all against all, were true. Life is much more complex. Not only are so-called "selfish" genes partially counterbalanced by reciprocally altruistic ones (at least within the nuclear family and all friendly, intimate, and loving relations), but, more importantly, the drives are elicited in varying combinations by the situations we face, so that many possible conflicts do not in fact arise, while others hold us in a state of dynamic tension between opposing drives. *The situatedness of drives is of overwhelming importance in life,* even in extremely simple forms. Our perceptions of situations operate on an *inherited hierarchy of motives* modified by our experience and our interpretation of the situation to produce a *situated hierarchical ordering of drives.*[25] The meaning of this fundamental fact of life is simple enough, though the exact details of how it operates in our lives will probably take centuries to work out.

The reason I distinguished the drives for life, air, water, food, etc., as a separate and primary set of drives is that in situations in which they are threatened they take precedence over all others. Anyone whose air supply is threatened immediately becomes concerned only with getting air. Since few things in the early history of humanity threatened life more immediately than losing air, this drive came to dominate almost all others when threatened in a given situation. But note the very important fact that as long as our air supply is unthreatened we pay almost no attention to this vital drive. Our bodies are programmed to provide us with air subconsciously, automatically, as long as there is no threat. In fact, we all know from our experience that consciously thinking about breathing makes breathing much more difficult than doing it subconsciously. Worrying about breathing, or being highly conscious of each breath, can produce a real crisis of breathing. The same automatic programming can develop for any highly integrated task, such as walking or typing. Consciousness is a highly specialized part of life, one that is concerned with probing the unknown, working out problems, and abstractly thinking up something better. But this planning activity of the brain works well only when almost all other activities are working automatically, with no need to plan. Anyone who was confronted with the need to plan his breathing, walking, heartbeat, and a few other things all at the same time would not be long for this world. The planning circuits would be quickly overloaded and would lead to panic, which would probably save us from ourselves by allowing us to faint, thus returning us to automatic, non-planned life.

What we see at work here is the *brain economy* operating on a basic *principle of marginal efficiency*. That is, our bodies need air, water, food desperately, but only so much of them. As long as they are adequately provided, the brain and its subsystems that respond to threats (mainly the sympathetic and parasympathetic neural nets interacting with the neuroendocrinological subsystems) allow us to be totally concerned with other things. This maximizes our overall development. But as soon as there is some significant degree of problem, the greater the threat, the greater our total system effort to meet it, until we are quickly mobilizing all systems to deal with the threat to all systems.

The operation of these primary drives (what early social thinkers called the natural passions) are reasonably simple and obvious, so much so that they operate as complex reflex activities. The second set of drives is not so simple, nor are they totally independent of the primary drives. The dominance drive, and the closely related ones of envy and hate, are related to such things as food, at least in situations of relative scarcity such as has existed in almost all of human life. The reason for this is obvious: the dominant animals might get more of those things. At the same time, some of the other drives I've spoken of as secondary, such as sex, are also largely dependent on these in the same way—the dominant animals might get more sex. The result is that the dominance drive and the closely related ones seem to be more immediately related to or interdependent with some of the primary drives. Consequently, they may constitute a set of drives in between the primary and what we are calling the secondary ones. But for our purposes here we need not be so precise and will take the safer route of treating them all as secondary. It is the safer route because it means the rest of the argument does not hinge on such controversial assumptions.

These secondary drives are also far more problematic to study and understand because they are so much more complex and changeable. The needs for air and water are simple. Dominance and sex drives are just as genetically inherited, but they seem to vary individually far more in intensity and take far more complex forms. The genetic reason is obvious. The organism's continued existence and, thus, its chances of spreading its genes to the next generation, is clearly dependent on such secondary drives, but less immediately and completely so than on the primary drives. A man obviously must copulate (or become a sperm donor) to spread his genes, but he does not have to do it right now with this particular mate. In fact, a male's overall genetic success will commonly be enhanced by being careful not to copulate in most situations, since in most situations this act will lead to attack by more dominant (more deadly!) competitors. Similar arguments are even more telling for the females, so they are generally "coy," driven forward by love and sex and backward by the fears and uncertainties over whether this is the best mate and mating situation for genetic success.[26] Moreover, these secondary drives are not so clearly hierarchicalized. Instead, they are often in partial or total conflict, as we all know from our everyday experience. Sex is often in conflict with hate, love, dominance, altruism, etc. That is obvious to anyone who has reached adolescence. The same is more or less true of the others. The result is that this second level of drives is necessarily problematic for all human beings. Everyone faces conflicts over them, must worry about them, strive to clarify them, put them in perspective, and so on endlessly throughout life.

How do we make sense out of our complex, conflicting secondary drives? No one knows very much about this in general. What we do know very reliably now is that *we rely on concrete situations we face at any given time to provide the crucial information we use to resolve the problematic conflicts among them.* This *principle of situated action* is one of those simple but absolutely fundamental facts of life, the understanding of which revolutionizes our understanding of human beings and other animals as much as the realization that the earth circles the sun revolutionized our understanding of our whole world. Almost all social science theories, other than those of classical economics and the sociological and psychological theories known as everyday-life, or existential, theories, still assume human actions are determined by variables that are basically unaffected by the concrete situations the actors face. Sociologists, anthropologists and political scientists assume that values transmitted from one generation to another, and, thus, completely, or, at least, highly independent of the concrete situations faced by the actors, are the ultimate determinants of social action. This is another example of the rationalistic theory of cultural determinism. As we shall see, it is this assumption of nonsituatedness combined with a failure to see feelings or drives as the ultimate determinants of action that leads them to mistakenly believe that human life can be rationally planned by experts who have no direct information about those concrete situations faced by each individual.

The reason for this situatedness of feelings or drives and, thus, of action, is reasonably simple. It can be understood best by looking first at very simple animals. Consider, for example, the twelve-foot-high, air-conditioned, insulated mounds (really incubator hotels) built by thousands of termites. The complexity of these insect hotels was astounding to entymologists who first discovered their structure and functioning. The insulation and air conditioning was so ingeniously constructed that the entire inside was maintained at a temperature that varied no more than one degree centigrade, in spite of wide swings of temperature outside. It seemed almost unbelievable that these thousands of tiny insects, with extremely primitive brains, could build such a thing. Some students were inspired to think there might be some new force at work here, perhaps a mystical combination of thousands of simple brains into a vastly complex one by the linking of antennae. Had that idea become generally accepted, it might have produced a holy crusade against the termite threat more ferocious than the Moslem crusades against the Christians or the Christian crusades against the Moslems. Fortunately, a less awe-inspiring, but almost equally important explanation was provided, and subsequent experimentation showed this was the right one. The mounds are not built by central planning, which would demand a brain capable of assimilating, analyzing, and processing vastly more information input than any termite brain can. Instead, they are built very situationally entirely on the basis of individual actions. All termites' brains are programmed to respond to the immediate, concrete situation they face in such a way that all efforts go together to produce an immensely complex operating structure that none of them could possibly plan. In simplest terms, it was found that each termite is neurally programmed to respond to very specific, small amounts of information in the immediate situation, especially to the angle of incline of small pieces of material. Each effort interacts with those of other termites to produce a new, second-stage situation to which the termite is then programmed to respond in a new way. This is called *dynamic* or *sequential programming*. By responding to the concrete situation, the animal is able to achieve maximum results with minimum complexity of information processing, so even a very simple brain can achieve extremely complex things without ever being able to process all the mass of information that would be needed to plan it from the beginning. This situatedness of drives and actions maximizes the efficiency of the termite's use of survival information from the environment, thereby allowing greater adaptive success. This is the simplest part of what I call the *principle of situated efficiency of information utilization and of drive satisfaction*.

The termite is, then, extremely situation-bound. The human being is at the other extreme: we are the most "transcendent" of animals, or what we would call the most *trans-situational*. Our highly developed memories, consciousness and symbolic abilities, including reason and creativity, have as their specific function that of abstracting us from the immediate situation, allowing us to think about things of importance to our drives that are beyond or outside of our concrete situation. All of these vast abilities have developed because they give us far greater adaptability, or greater ability to adapt to the constraints of our world, especially by creating new modes of adaptation. These symbolic abilities tend in that way to progressively free us from situated programming. They do this initially by combining with our centralized powers of self-control or willpower, which act to inhibit the ancient animal tendencies of our drives to respond to the immediate, concrete situation we find ourselves in. Let's take a simple example, that of sex. When we encounter a "sex object" in our immediate situation, our sensory organs send perceptual messages to the feeling centers of the ancient lower and midbrain. (Perceptions normally come up through the ascending reticular system and first reach the lower, feeling brain, which is called the hypothalamic-limbic systems. But such complexities need not concern us here.) Our immediate drive response is sexual in that situation. But, while we all know that it is impossible even for saints who have lacerated the flesh for years to totally repress those feelings of lust, it is also the case that we act sexually in only an extremely small percentage of instances in which we feel lust. The same messages about the sex object and the feelings of lust are relayed to the higher centers of the brain, which then relate them to past learned experience and assess the relation of this situation to past situations, to the overall present situation and to probable future situations. In almost all cases in all human societies, our higher brains then inhibit our primal urges to act sexually, because sex involves such a huge investment and risk for all our other situations, especially for women who are likely to become mothers as a result of the sex act, that all kinds of experience and anticipations stimulate other feelings that conflict with and restrain the initial ones. The result normally is that our fears of attack from others, of rejection, of future responsibilities, and so on, lead us to hide our lust, or to reveal it only sequentially in such a way that we only partly reveal our desires, thereby risking the least possible, and can flee if we suddenly discover the dangers are too great. Thus, in almost all situations we act very polite, look away, and control our voices to prevent any lust-revealing quaver.

In the same way, and far more importantly for our purposes here, individual human beings are able to partially transcend their immediate drives to be greedy. Greed (or immediate selfishness) versus altruism has been the dilemma of most modern social thought. As I noted earlier, most social thinkers have lined up on one side or the other in an either/or fashion. Modern biology and ethology show animals in general, and humans especially, to be much more complex in this and all other ways than the traditional social thinkers imagined. Humans are genetically programmed to be both greedy and altruistic in different situations, especially in response to different individuals with whom they have different kinds of relations. Newborn children are, of course, overwhelmingly selfish. But as soon as they begin to develop the social bonds of intimacy and love with the members of their family, and later with friends and lovers, they become altruistic. In fact, children show all the basic patterns of pity and even sympathy by about the second year. Later, as parents they will become unilaterally (or asymmetrically) altruistic toward their own newborn children, sometimes even to the extreme of dying for them. At the same time, individuals remain predominantly emotionally selfish toward almost all other human beings with whom they do not develop a bond of intimacy or love. There is an important exception that has caused confusion and distortions ever since Mencius first pointed it out in ancient China. That is, human beings will act altruistically toward others, predominantly children, in short-run situations that do not demand much of them, without any expectation of reciprocity. This is similar to what is found in other primates, who generally show solicitude and care for children other than their own—but to much less degree most of the time. But this emotional commitment to selfishness does not mean that individuals always acts selfishly in a direct and simple manner. A glance at any society, and certainly our own, shows that is not true. Rather, mature individuals give up much immediate self-gratification for longer-run self-gratification. Specifically, maturing individuals develop *reciprocal altruism*, that is, a pervasive tendency to act according to the ancient maxim of common sense, "You scratch my back and I'll scratch yours." In primates this is literally what goes on all the time in the form of grooming behavior. Reciprocal altruism involves giving up some immediate self-gratification in the clear anticipation of getting some later gratification in return because individuals reason that they will be better off for that. When individuals decide they will be better off in this way by doing a specific thing for other people, they perform an exchange of precisely the sort the individualistic (Austrian) economists have made the basis for their general economic theories. The rudiments of what Adam Smith called "trucking and bartering" can even be seen in the hand motions, open palm for beseeching and giving, the looks of friendly beseeching and benevolent giving, and so on, in other primates. These reciprocally altruistic exchange relations are the basis for all free-market systems of exchange and, of course, they are found in all societies, even in rudimentary form where more powerful individuals try to repress them for dominance reasons. They are often bound up with other meanings as well in any specific situation (as seen, for example, in the kula exchange of the Trobriand Islands), but this is true of most human relations and must not be allowed to obscure the basic drives at work. As Jean Baechler has argued, if these free-market exchanges are not successfully oppressed by dominance seekers, then the market evolves into ever-more complex, rationalized forms of exchange. Free markets can be seen in the early stages of the development of all civilizations. If they are allowed to develop, they eventually develop very distant exchanges, complex banking systems, and so on. These *spontaneous (unplanned) systems of reciprocally altruistic exchange relations* evolve in the same step-by-step (iterative) fashion into vastly complex *spontaneous natural orders* that termite nests do, but by the use of situated reason in the service of self-interest, rather than by deterministic genetic programming.[27] Though there are always imperfections, such as some individuals cheating others, and, very importantly, using force and state powers to rig such exchanges for selfish purposes, these market systems have been built up again and again in all the civilizations into vast systems that retain a high degree of legitimacy because they are built ultimately on the individuals' calculations of their own selfish interests.

Discounting the Future

But all of that ability to be transsituational, to inhibit our drives in a concrete situation because of the relation of other situations to them, while very important, must not mislead us into thinking we can somehow totally transcend sex drives or selfishness. The Catholic Church fought the war against sex for many centuries and lost. Economic utopias have fought selfishness innumerable times—and eventually lost every war. There are two vital points about such experience. First, we all know from experience that whether we respond sexually or selfishly depends very heavily on the situation. While human beings are the most transituational of animals, *the more basic a drive and the more it is aroused, the more the concrete situation dominates thinking and action.* If our air supply is suddenly cut off, we can hardly think at all and everything else is swept away in our panic to get more air. Sex is not that hierarchically dominant, but it is strong. The more excited we are by a sex object, the more we are apt to forget ourselves and be swept away by the situationally triggered emotion. The level of excitement or arousal is known by everyone to be the first vital ingredient of temptation. But there is a second ingredient, as we also know. This is the ingredient of countervailing aspects in the concrete situation.

The less the concrete situation itself arouses conflicting drives, the more probable a sexual response, regardless of the information inputs about past and future. As we all know, the more likely it is that people can get away with it in the immediate situation, the more tempted they are to do it and the consequences be damned. This is true because *human beings are programmed to discount transsituational information input progressively.* The more out of sight, or the further in the future something is, the more out of mind it is; or, more importantly, the further removed it is from the concrete situation, the less effect even thinking about it has in eliciting our drives. This principle, which we might call the principle of *transsituational discounting*, is vital in understanding everything from sex to interest rates.

Just as sexual temptation and being swept away by the situation to do sexual things is a universal part of human experience, so are interest payments for foregone consumption a universal thing in human society. Because all human beings discount the future, that is, are less driven by what might happen in the future than by the same thing when it is happening in the present, very few people will forego present consumption unless they expect to get something more for doing so in the future, or something worse by consuming now. The result of this simple discounting property of human nature is that interest rates and profits in some form are universal properties of human societies that have enough to save anything, and that have devised means of investing savings to increase production.[28] For centuries the Catholic Church fought interest rates, which they stigmatized as "usury," and which they believed to be an invention of the forces of Satan. But, at the very time they were denouncing them, they were commonly paying very high interest rates to bankers for the use of their funds to pay for the steadily increasing burden of their public employee union, the clergy, and of their welfare state. As we saw earlier, the Church was above all else a sacred imperial state bureaucracy with all the usual problems of public employee unions. Religion, justice, and equality before God were justifications in the same way justice and equality are the justifications of the welfare states, but they had no significant effects on the Church's actual operations except that of making it necessary to carry on expensive public relations campaigns in the form of the mendicant orders. The Soviet secular church has carried on the same glorious struggle against the genetic wisdom of our bodies in discounting the future and have thereby bred a massive system of underground corruption, as Hedrick Smith[29] and other careful observers have revealed. (We should note that the hierarchy of motives is commonly considered by individualistic economists. Some of them, however, assume a total ranking of motives and a largely unsituated one. This leads to a far more rationalistic view of human action than they generally seem to hold.)

Once we understand the way in which the hierarchy of drives works, we are able to understand one of the vital things about human life which has seemed so paradoxical to social thinkers. We have seen that a stable satisfaction of the primary set of drives (life security, air, water, food, etc.) frees the individual to try to satisfy the less dominant ones, the secondary drives of dominance, sex, and so on. Secure affluence gives one secure satisfaction of the primary drives, thereby unleashing the secondary ones to a far greater degree. The result is quite obvious to anyone in our affluent Western societies. Instead of becoming satiated, happy, quiescent, and dull with affluence, the affluent become more unsatisfied with their sex and love lives, their position in dominance hierarchies and with their level of satisfaction of other secondary drives. Or, as Rimbaud put it in nineteenth century France, the securely affluent become like "drunken boats." No longer anchored by the immediate situational demands of survival, these individuals now want more and more sex, dominance, excitement, and so on. Since there are far more of these drives, and since they are not so clearly defined and hierarchicalized, the individuals are pushed and pulled in many different directions, not knowing clearly what they want but wanting more and more of any of these secondary things and wanting them far more than ever before. Moreover, there appears to be no physiological limit to certain of these drives.

Even more ominously, there may be certain of the drives that are increased by gratification so that achievement leads only to a more intense drive, at least over very large ranges. Sexual activity does appear to have certain limitations. In the short run, there is obviously satiation at some level for anyone. While it is true that the early stages of involvement in "casual sex" produce an explosion of sexual motivation and action, almost everyone eventually gets "burned out" and "settles down" after "sowing wild oats." The same thing is true of any of the simple forms of pleasure seeking. This is true even of the extremely pleasurable psycho-active drugs like heroin. As with pleasures generally, heroin users quickly develop an adaptation, or tolerance, level to the drug, which means that if they keep taking the same amount of the drug they experience no pleasure. They have to increase their intake to get pleasure, so they continually increase their drug intake in step-wise fashion, but eventually they burn out or get no more pleasure from the drug. They then must find pleasure in new dimensions of experience.

One of the only drives that may be unlimited, that may never get burned out, but which, instead, seems to feed upon its own gratification is that for dominance. Maslow and some of the humanistic psychologists of ethics have argued that once our need for a feeling of self-worth or dignity is fulfilled, we can go on to the higher (or hierarchically less dominant) motives of curiosity, altruism, and so on. These theorists commonly see the ferocious seekers after unlimited power, prestige, and pride as pathological. While there is certainly an important distinction between the egocentric "madness" of an Alexander, Napoleon, or Hitler which drives them on to destruction, as contrasted to the more "reasonable" acceptance by Augustus of certain situational limitations on his power hunger, the difference may consist entirely in different perceptions of the situations they face. We have no reason to believe that Augustus, Narmer (the founder of the first united Egyptian empire), Shih Huang-Ti (the First Great Emperor of China), Lenin, Stalin, or Mao Tse

Tung were limited in their dominance drives simply because they turned their attentions to solidifying their internal dominance rather than rushing head-long into further conquests. A drive may be constrained by situational dangers and by reasonable expectations of those without itself decreasing. Having built his power base at home, Stalin lost no chance to expand it immensely after World War II and his military probes continued until his death.

The opposite theory, that of a power drive that can only be limited by greater countervailing forces, has been developed by Clausewitz, Aron, and Baechler[30] to explain the massive historical evidence concerning warlords and politicians. While it may not be true that nature abhors a power vacuum, we know well that human nature is inflamed by a power vacuum, that politi-cians and warlords love such weaknesses, that they probe continually for them, and that when they find one they rush in to dominate. Dominance is such a powerful and pervasive drive in human life that it touches almost everything in some way. All of us are aware of the ways in which domi-nance striving pervades sex. (No one has ever said it better than the word used by adolescent American males to describe sexual triumph—"scoring.") Few who know many businesspeople will doubt that the rich are driven more by desire to dominate, to triumph, than by greed. Malcolm S. Forbes, Sr., surely one of the most experienced of people in the inner circles of business, puts it sweepingly: "It's clear to me, having seen so many chief executive officers over the years, that the ablest thrive on power, on the ability to decide what should be done and then to get it done. The prestige and the psychic income that accrue from positions of corporate power far outweigh the lure of any amount of dollar income. The dollars are important principally as an expression of the power."[31] Greed seems to get burned out at rather low levels for most people, but the quest for dominance—for winning the com-petitive struggle—can go on forever.

Perhaps the most remarkable thing is the way in which the apparent debasement of the self and even the destruction of the self can be used by human beings in the unrelenting war for dominance. Anyone who has read much about saints and puritans, whether it be Saint Bernard, Cromwell, or a college "poor man" in the 1960s knows how ferociously they asserted their dominance (pride) by being aggressively more "humble" than anyone else. When Saint Bernard was called into a French town to help subdue (dominate) the heretics challenging the Church's dominance, one of the onlookers chal-lenged his supposed virtue by pointing out how emaciated the heretical poor men were. Almost all the heretics, especially the massive movement of Albi-gensians and Fratecelli, presented themselves as "poor men," which to Chris-tians was a badge of superiority and, thus, supposedly made them better— more Godly— than the rich Church. Saint Bernard then angrily pulled back the cowl of his robe to display with unrecorded pride and belligerence that his neck was even more emaciated. Probably the most creative—and insane—form of human dominance display is killing yourself to show how superior you are or to get revenge on someone who has dominated you, yet both are common motives of suicide.

The way in which dominance "feeds on itself," or in which successful dominance striving increases the drive instead of decreasing it, has been commonly noted in the form of "power (pride) going to one's head." It probably does so with decreasing rates of increase, since a decrease in the rate of increase of satisfaction at higher levels is the common thing with human drives. (Economists deal with this in terms of the "decreasing marginal utility" or decreasing satisfaction of each additional bit of satisfaction.) But the crucial thing is that successful dominance increases the drive, or releases it further. Successful politicians become more and more ambitious, not less and less. At the highest levels of politics, the drive for dominance is ferocious and drives individuals relentlessly. This very important fact has often been obscured by social scientists who point to some small tribe of primitive people as evidence that human beings are not necessarily competitive and dominant. (The Pueblo Indians, the Zunis, and the Tongans have long been used by anthropologists and utopian socialists for this ploy.) While, as we saw in chapter 3, it is certainly true that in most simple societies no one has succeeded in achieving much dominance over others, this use of peculiarities of the human condition to prove its general properties, which Mary Douglas aptly calls the Bongo-Bongo Syndrome, is hardly acceptable.[32] No civilization has ever remotely approached that condition except in periods of decay and panic before tyranny is established.

All civilizations have involved high degrees of dominance compared to most small, primitive societies. Nevertheless, even in primitive societies the Big Man system or chiefdom of warrior bands long ago became vastly more common than the "uncompetitive, placid, happy savage" type of hunting and gathering. Certain civilizations, especially certain periods of Western civilization, have had a minimum of warrior-police and politician-priest (bureaucratic) dominance. These have been rare periods of vast individual freedom and creativity in economic activity, science, and art, as we see in pre-Periclean Athens and pre-Alexandrian Greece more generally, late-medieval and early-Renaissance Europe, and some parts of eighteenth- and nineteenth-century Western society, especially Britain and America. Those are, indeed, the periods of civilized life which I think we should cherish and try to create, but we must not allow Bongo-Bongoism and other forms of mythical utopian thought to hide from us the fact that they are rare situations. Rather than proving that human nature does not include a powerful drive to dominance, the rarity of such eras indicates the opposite. They arise when the environmental and social situations (including freely chosen collective opposition to the centralization of power) elicit minimal dominance drives and prevent the ferocious seekers of dominance from achieving their goals. When the political means to dominance are blocked, human beings strive for dominance in other ways, through contact with God (so religion flourishes), through control of the forces of nature (so magic and science flourish), through economic production and material dominance displays (so wealth accumulates and conspicuous consumption flourishes), through sexual dominance (so sexual activities and displays, especially the use of fashion in clothing to excite sexual interest and communicate dominance, flourish), and through almost every other conceivable means.

Political and military dominance, or direct power over the persons (including sex and reproduction) and properties of other individuals, is the primary goal of dominance drives in human beings. Though it is not necessary to explore the intricacies of dominance here, we should note that fame is a secondary goal of the dominance drive that normally supports the achievement of power. Fame becomes almost an end in itself in our mass-mediated societies. The ultimate explanation of these dominance drives, of course, is genetic. It is through control of others' bodies that the genes are spread and through control of their bodies and properties that the offspring are reared to further spread the genes. The result is that the dominance-drive genes were highly selected for through natural selection. About five thousand years ago, some of the more intelligent members of the species found that they could use some of the cultural forms of civilization to vastly expand their political-warrior dominance. They used magical and mythical thought to convince less intelligent members of their societies that they could achieve wealth or power, or eternal life by supporting them, and when they were victorious they actually increased the dominance and, thus, the genetic success of even the lower warriors—at least, those who did not die in the assaults. In the most ferocious early stages of this civilized warfare the politicians, priests, and warriors commonly directly expropriated the bodies and properties of the defeated. Indeed, they also often slaughtered the men and their children, or turned them into nonbreeding slaves, in much the same way the hanuman langurs of Asia kill the offspring of formerly dominant males to spread their own genes more quickly. As in so many other things, the Nazis partially revived these ancient ways of the "blood." But doing that threatens everyone else to an extreme degree, so it unites one's enemies, making its "genetic rationality" highly doubtful.

Once they had achieved thorough political-military dominance, these politicians, priests, and warriors then used massive training of all the young, mainly carried out by the priests, to make the mythical thought that supported their dominance more powerful. As we have seen, these myths of the church and state have been of vital importance in maintaining their dominance. They have been used in roughly the same way since the very dawn of civilization under Narmer in Egypt in about 2800 B.C. The myths of the state and the church that are always used are some variant of the enabling myths of the welfare state. There are periods when the competing warrior-priests checkmate each other. These tend to be periods of great struggles when the warriors and priests of smaller bands struggle ferociously to achieve dominance, as in Renaissance Italy. These are periods in which the once-dominant welfare state myth is no longer believed, in which once-subordinate novelists parody the quixotic feudal lords, and commoner philosophers write paeons to individualism. But, then, of course, a new coalition of warriors, politicians, and priests begin to mold the warrior-police powers and the mythical foundations of their imperial state bureaucracy, new forms of the core myths of the welfare state are created which scoff at, or bitterly denounce, all the earlier ones as superstition, but present the new ones as the only truths. Once the name "welfare state" is discredited by the terrible effects of massive bureaucratic controls, then the new welfare-statists attack the welfare state to gain greater power. The Nazis attacked the welfare state of the Weimar Republic to help them get vastly more power to pursue the "true" welfare of Germany.

As Otto von Gierke showed in such detail, as the imperial Church waned, individualistic philosophy increased, so that from approximately 1500 to the nineteenth century, almost every major social thinker had an individualistic view of humanity and, of course, were very concerned with individual human nature as opposed to the cultural training of the mind by the church and state. But in the nineteenth century the intellectuals, led by men like Auguste Comte, began to create the new collectivist myths that would later form the magical foundations of the now myths of the modernist welfare states. It is not surprising that the myth of the modernist welfare state grew at the same time as what Ernst Cassirer so rightly called *The Myth of the State*. It is also not surprising to find that the two myths were synthesized and applied in Prussia by Bismarck, nor to find that this synthesis was carried to the extreme by Hitler in Germany in the name of equality. The myth of equality had by then become a central component of the myth of the welfare state: everyone was trained by extreme measures of thought control to believe that everyone in the Nazi state was equal,[33] while in fact everyone was equal in their total subordination of person, mind, and property to the Divine Fuehrer, and his warlords and his imperial state bureaucracies. Meanwhile, the same process was being followed to different degrees in almost every other Western nation under different symbolic forms, but all in the name of national security, the welfare state, science, freedom from economic inequality, total equality, and a full panoply of lesser myths and goals.

The new priest-magicians, the social scientists, replaced the ancient priests as a vital part of the warrior-politician-priest coalition. Everywhere the new myths of the modernist welfare state flourished. The new myths are as disastrous as the ancient ones, but each failure was used to prove the need for more of what produced the failure, just as military disasters in ancient Sumeria proved the need for more militarism and kingly power. These magical transmutations of failure into success were a key function of the social priest-scientists, in much the same way earlier priests had shown death to be proof of the Church's power because it was the only door to eternal life.

Almost all successful dominance-predators strive for dominance in ways that hide this crucial fact from everyone else, generally behind the public fronts of humility ("I am only submitting to the will of God to do what is necessary for your eternal salvation when I cut your head off or burn you at the stake, so how dare you complain about my sovereign powers?"). This is especially true in an era in which no one has yet achieved great dominance. Indeed, in such an era all really successful dominance-predators fight ferociously for dominance in the very name of equality. Once again, the ancients had seen human nature at work long enough to see the same facts. As Aristotle said, "Inferiors revolt in order that they may be equal, and equals that they may be superior. Such is the state of mind which creates revolutions." All dominance-predators try to tear down their rivals by insisting on more dominance for themselves ("Erase the infamy!" or "End capitalistic tyranny by creating the dictatorship of the proletariat—*under* my benevolent guidance, of course."). One of the greatest predators in the history of the bloody human struggles for dominance said it all when he blandly noted that, "Vanity made the revolution, liberty was only a pretext." But, of course, Napoleon only said this after it was all over and liberty was totally subordinated to vanity, to arrogant pride in dominance.

When a dominance-predator proclaims "All power to the Soviets," he may or may not be feeling a blaze of idealism, but it never matters because his mind almost always responds to his human nature to identify the Soviets with himself and his dominance whenever he gets the chance. Marxists have always bitterly attacked the hypocrisy of big businesspeople who call for economic freedom (equality of opportunity) so that they can become more dominant. They are obviously right that this is precisely what most big businesspeople do. They are also precisely right to argue that most businesspeople always used government power or any other power they could get hold of to increase their own dominance over other human beings. Adam Smith had seen this very clearly almost a century earlier. Their success in this led to the business welfare state of the late nineteenth century and to various forms of corporate statism, such as fascism, when their dominance was threatened by mass politics. Unfortunately, the Marxists failed to note that this was due to human nature, not to some immoralism bred by the ancient regime of capitalism, and so they fought in the name of equality and produced the terrible tyrannies of Russia, China, North Korea, Cambodia, and most of the other tortured lands now dominated by ferocious human predators.

Any human being who believes the grand Rousseauian myth that there is no human nature and that we can trust the good human being committed to equality to make us all equal easily winds up the slave of Lenin, Stalin, Mao, Hitler, or some other brand of rationalistic "idealist." The vanity is the same, only the symbolic forms vary. The miseries of statist subordination, of some degree and form of slavery, are also the same. But as long as these opportunities exist because people believe the myth, they will create the tyrants—that is, excite their dominance drives and tempt the people to see their dominance as necessary—or even desirable in itself.

The people who believed them, and very possibly they themselves, were ignorant, they made a basic mistake about human nature, and paid in misery for it. As the American constitutionalists said, the only government that truly serves the general welfare of the people is a weak government, a government that is strong enough only to stop anyone from severely dominating all the others; and, ultimately, the only way a government can be kept that weak is by the citizens' being ever vigilant to refuse to allow it to be any more powerful. Therefore, the dominance-predators, the warrior-politicians and their priests, must convince the people that their welfare is really served *only* by a very powerful government, that only big government is a true welfare state. And thus they create or appropriate for political purposes myths such as the myths of the modernist welfare state, which includes at its core the myth of rationalistic state planning.

Modernistic Hubris versus Human Nature and Its Iron Laws of History

We all know, both from history and from our own lives, that Santayana was right when he said that those who do not know history are doomed to repeat its failures. We also know that even many of those who do know history keep repeating its failures. For example, all European statespeople and military strategists have known for centuries that in a multipolar pluralistic society like Europe it is almost impossible for any one group or minority coalition to defeat all the others. Indeed, because they have known this, they developed the balance of power theory centuries ago to show how any "insane" aggressor could be defeated by such coalitions; and they acted in accord with the theory to make it come true. It worked over and over down through the centuries. But those centuries were centuries of warfare as aggressors continually cast their fate against all the odds beautifully sketched by the theory. Napoleon and Hitler, the two best-known casualties of the neglect of this historical truth, even went the others one better by running amok in the face of a corollary of the theory. This corollary warns that the greatest danger to the aggressor, and the greatest good to the users of the balance of power, comes from fighting a two-front war against independent partners in the coalition, who are equal in relative strength to the aggressor. Why do people insist, in full knowledge of all the past failures and, thus, the general validity of the theory, on doing step-by-step what has produced the past failures?

There is, of course, the argument that this is all due to "madness." If one is speaking of madness in the usual sense, this argument is so much moralistic twaddle. People like Napoleon and Hitler were brilliant strategists who came closer than anyone else to winning, even against greater odds. The madness argument is true only in the sense that these men, and probably most of the others, were increasingly dominated by a lust for power in their thinking. That is, as they won earlier battles—became more powerful—so they came to want more and more. Moreover, and very importantly, those earlier successes, which are exactly the factors that galvanize their opponents to fully enact the strategies and tactics to counterbalance their growing power, led them to believe they were close to the ultimate prize—total victory; and those earlier successes, combined with their growing isolation and sycophantish and fearful lies fed by subordinates to such "great men," encouraged an irrational overestimation of their abilities to assess the situation correctly. The soaring lust for power makes them willing to take bigger chances, but it is still unlikely they would take such huge chances if they did not miscategorize and, thus, misunderstand the situation. It is of crucial importance that, knowing full well the experience of others before them and, thus, the general validity of the theory, they believe they will not meet the same fate because the situation is different; and their power lust inspires a reconceptualization of the situation that convinces them this is so.

The crucial reason why some people continually fail to learn even the most obvious lessons of history is that they reconceptualize their situations so that they think these "new" situations do not fit the earlier situation. The reconceptualization is certainly encouraged by the obvious fact that every situation and person is in fact partially different, so there is no precise predictability from the not-so iron laws of history. Only a social rationalist, such as a Marxist, believes learning from history is not inherently problematic.[34] In accord with the conservative (or ancient Zen) theory of knowledge, William James was clearly right when he concluded that "it is folly, then, to speak of 'the laws of history' as of something inevitable, which science has only to discover and whose consequences anyone can then foretell. . . .Why, the very laws of physics are conditional and deal with *ifs*. . .the evolutionary view of history, when it denies the vital importance of individual initiative, is, then, an utterly vague and unscientific conception." But, of course, we also know that all situations and people are more like past situations and other people than they are different. So that rationale is a clue that the reconceptualization is a rationalization, not a truth. The only truly rational thing is to search history for the previous situations most like this "new" one, not to assert that this one will come out differently because previous ones don't apply. The reconceptualization really comes about because people are inspired by great emotions like power-lust to create new conceptions—myths—that inspire hope in opposition to past experience.

Very importantly, people are aided in this reconceptualization by any egocentrism—arrogant pride or hubris—that makes them think they are far better, superior, more rational than those who previously failed. In the modern world they are strongly encouraged to believe this by the modernist hubris, the belief that we in the modern world are making such vast progress in scientifically understanding our complex world that we can do things that are fundamentally different from what was done in those old situations, so there are no lessons of history or economics or life relevant to us. Our myth of rationalism-scientism inspires the hubris of modernism and leads to all the calamities hubris always brings—because it supports mythical reconceptualizations of the otherwise most nearly iron laws of history which tempt us to take terrible chances we would otherwise recognize and reject.

Most of us know this modernist hubris primarily in the form of adolescent hubris. The whole idea is a stereotype now because it is repeated in almost each life. The adolescent decides that, in spite of all the messes people have made of their lives in the past by getting married very early, going deeply into debt at high interest rates, and on and on, she will not suffer the same fate because she is smarter than they were—and just a bit too special. After all, this adolescent has gone to college, whereas the parents didn't even finish high school; she knows calculus and some chemistry, and they hardly know what those are. Her basic mistake, of course, is in not noting that none of those things have anything to do with practical activities like love, sex, marriage, or the nearly "iron laws" of the market place. Those things are even more complex, just as dominated by emotionalism and, thus, irrationalist thinking, as ever. As most of us recognize, especially in looking back on our own lives, many of the young are tempted by their hormones to reconceptualize the early "iron laws" that the older generation learned the hard way, so they learn the hard way in their turn.

In government policymaking we see modernist hubris at work in similar ways: we know so much more about economics, government, etc., that we can do things they could not—we can even violate the most nearly iron lessons of history. This argument often springs directly from a great deal of ignorance about history, which has been growing very rapidly in nations like the United States which have steadily decreased humanistic education at the same time scientific and social scientistic education has increased vastly. Most people who reject the iron laws do not know what they are because they have simply not read Thucydides, Aristotle, Hume, Burke, Jefferson, Hamilton, Acton, and others. If they have, they are still encouraged by modernist hubris—not subject to even the most iron laws.

There is, of course, an obvious validity to the argument that we know more absolutely about those things than earlier thinkers and actors did. Hume and Hamilton may have clearly formulated the quantity theory of money and drawn the implications that governments should not inflate the money supply because this will only produce price inflation; but we do know more about those processes today, or, at least, some experts do. So why should we be concerned about the quantity of money the way they were? We know more, so we can do more. Hence, government activism in monetary policy is justified and we can escape the old iron laws of monetary history.

What these modernist reconceptualizers fail to note is a simple and obvious fact: we live in a vastly more complex world than they did. As our knowledge has increased, our level of complexity has increased. I myself believe that in social matters our level of complexity has increased far more rapidly than our knowledge of that complexity, for the simple reason that we do not yet have the firm foundations of a general science of human society. Anyone who thinks we do have those firm foundations simply does not know the chaos of bitter argument that grips every social science and should go back and look at the news accounts of the Economic Summit Meeting President Ford held to solve the problem of inflation (the one at which they sported WIN buttons—Win Against Inflation). It should have been entitled The Tower of Economic Babel. Not only do we now have vastly more kinds of economic activity and financial dealings on an international scale, but it seems clear that the vastly complex, highly reactive international market system has introduced more inherent uncertainty, or indeterminacy into our situation—so that even if our *relative knowledge quotient* (the ratio of reliable knowledge to complexity of reality) were as great, one of the crucial things it would tell us is that we can't know as much as we would need to know to predict precise outcomes of our actions. The belief that we have a higher relative knowledge quotient is based on the rationalist and modernist myths—on modernist hubris, not fact.

It is modernist hubris that leads sincerely democratic leaders to believe, contrary to all we know from the historical evidence, that they will not be subject to the nearly iron law of the corrupting influence of power. Louis the Fourteenth, Napoleon, Hitler, and all such men suffered from the corroding influence of power, the delusions of grandeur that come from isolation and from the lies told them by the sycophants who surround all people of power and from the soaring lust for power that is triggered by growing power. But all leaders today, even more than those people in their days, tend to think of themselves as superior and, thus, able to transcend that iron law, that fatal flaw of the situation-and-character of those earlier failures. In the same way, quite contrary to what they expect, all of our imperial presidents have failed to see the way the imperial powers of the American presidency today corrodes their ability to truthfully interpret their situation, so all fail to see how they are marching along the path to further corrosion of their vision and to ever greater lust for power. Most of them even come to believe they *should* do what was technically illegal *because they meant well* and had the highest moral goals in mind; all have thought their moral strength would allow them to limit the evil effects of those activities so obvious throughout history. The heads of the CIA, FBI, and, indeed, probably every other arm of the imperial presidency, imperial congress, and imperial local governments have followed the same path of self-delusion by believing in their superiority.

Worst of all, our assumption of greater knowledge and moral superiority over our predecessors, combined with our growing greed for more and more monies and services from government, have led us to reconceptualize our situation so that we can no longer see the relevance for us of the one great iron law of history on which American government was built. That iron law is that power corrupts leaders, so that they can no longer rationally assess their situation, and that, consequently, that government governs best which governs least and that big government inevitably produces tyranny. What educated American does not know that this was the basic idea on which our government was built? Indeed, who does not believe it abstractly? Yet, when making concrete decisions about government, how many believe it applies to our leaders and us?

Lord Acton. . .wrote: "Power tends to corrupt, and absolute power corrupts absolutely. Great men are always bad men."

In the second part of that statement there is a great deal of truth. To gain or keep an important position without performing unpleasant or at least self-seeking action is almost impossible. . .

It was not so much that it corrupted them after they had obtained it, but already, before that, it was what had tempted most of them to try to obtain the imperial office. In view of the alarming perils involved, it may seem difficult to understand why anyone could be eager to become ruler of the Roman empire. Yet signs of reluctance were not greatly evident. Even in the third century A.D. when a would-be usurper scarcely needed to be a statistical expert to note that the average reign ended rapidly and violently, candidates for the throne still proliferated on every side. . .

In a number of. . .cases. . .this. . .sense of duty played a part in driving emperors on. But a far more frequent inducement was the plain love of immense power and its breathtaking possibilities.

Michael Grant

Essential though it may be to understand Lyndon Johnson. . .this understanding is hard to acquire. He made it hard. Enlisting all his energy and all his cunning in a lifelong attempt to obscure not only the true facts of his rise to power and his use of power but even of his youth, he succeeded well. He told stories readily and repeatedly. . .And not merely many but most of these stories were false. . .

The more one. . .follows [Lyndon Johnson's] life, the more apparent it becomes that alongside the thread of achievement running through it runs another thread, as dark as the other is bright, and as fraught with consequences for history: a hunger for power in its most naked form, for power not to improve the lives of others, but to manipulate and dominate them, to bend them to his will. For the more one learns—from his family, his childhood playmates, his college classmates, his first assistants, his congressional colleagues—about Lyndon Johnson, the more it becomes apparent not only that this hunger was a constant throughout his life but that it was a hunger so fierce and consuming that no consideration of morality or ethics, no cost to himself—or to anyone else—could stand before it.

Robert Caro

Notes

1. Michael Oakeshott, *Rationalism in Politics* (New York: Basic Books, 1962), pp. 31–32.
2. See Russell Kirk, *The Conservative Mind* (New York: Avon Books, 1968).
3. The inherent uncertainty of situations that will emerge, and, consequently, the inherent situatedness of *effective* actions is *the* basic principle of all valid sciences of everyday action. All macro-structural theories failed to realize this, and, therefore, proved incapable of understanding action. See my earlier works, especially *American Social Order* (New York: Free Press, 1971), and, edited with John M. Johnson, *Existential Sociology* (Cambridge, MA: Cambridge University Press, 1977).
4. The intentional pursuit of risk and uncertainty is an inherent and well-recognized aspect of the pursuit of excellence (success) in science and business. Dealing with uncertainty is the essential purpose of creative business activity—entrepreneurship. See, for example, Thomas J. Peters and Robert H. Waterman, *In Search of Excellence* (Philadelphia: Harper and Row, 1982).
5. Karl Popper, *The Poverty of Historicism* (Boston: Beacon Press, 1957).
6. Thucydides, *The Peloponnesian War* (Baltimore: Penguin Books, 1954), pp. 24–25.
7. Arthur Lovejoy, *The Great Chain of Being* (New York: Harper Torchbooks, 1960).
8. On the way in which the interests recognized by reason were believed to check the passions, see Albert O. Hirschman, *The Passions and the Interests* (Princeton: Princeton University Press, 1977).

9. Adam Smith, *The Theory of Moral Sentiments* (New York: A. M. Kelley, 1966; rpt. of new edition published in 1853).
10. Quoted in Jacob Viner, *The Long View and the Short* (Glencoe, IL: The Free Press, 1958), p. 218.
11. Adam Smith, *The Wealth of Nations* (New York: Modern Library, 1937).
12. David Hume, *An Inquiry Concerning Human Understanding* (Indianapolis: Bobbs-Merrill, 1955).
13. See Stanford Lyman, *The Seven Deadly Sins* (New York: St. Martin's, 1978).
14. See, for example, Marshall Sahlins, *The Uses and Abuses of Biology* (Ann Arbor: University of Michigan Press, 1976).
15. See Richard Dawkins, *The Selfish Gene* (New York: Oxford University Press, 1976); Edward O. Wilson, *Sociobiology* (Cambridge, MA: The Belknap Press of Harvard University Press, 1975), and *On Human Nature* (Cambridge, MA: Harvard University Press, 1978); and John Bonner, *The Evolution of Culture in Animals* (Princeton: Princeton University Press, 1980).
16. Stanislav Andreski, *Social Sciences as Sorcery* (New York: St. Martin's, 1973).
17. See Noam Chomsky, *Aspects of the Theory of Syntax* (Cambridge, MA: The M.I.T. Press, 1965), and *Reflections on Language* (New York: Pantheon Books, 1975).
18. Derek Freeman (*Margaret Mead and Samoa* [Cambridge, MA: Harvard University Press, 1983]) has presented the history of cultural anthropologists' war against the social Darwinists and their subsequent denial of genetics and the behavioral biologies. As far as I know, no one has written the parallel histories for the other social sciences.
19. See Bonner, *The Evolution of Culture in Animals.*
20. See Douglas, *American Social Order*, and Douglas and F. K. Waksler, *The Sociology of Deviance* (Boston: Little, Brown, 1982); and Douglas, *Creative Deviance and Social Change*, forthcoming.
21. For one extreme example, see Robert J. Trotter, "Baby Face," *Psychology Today*, vol. 17 (Aug. 1983), pp. 14–21.
22. See the argument on this in M. Midgley, *Beast and Man* (New York: New American Library, 1980).
23. The best general source on the psychology of emotions is Robert Plutchik and Henry Kellerman, eds., *Theories of Emotion* (New York: Academic Press, 1980).
24. See Carroll Izard, *The Face of Emotion* (New York: Appleton-Century-Crofts, 1971); Paul Ekman and Wallace Friesen, *Unmasking The Face* (Englewood Cliffs, NJ: Prentice-Hall, 1975); and Irenaus Eibl-Eibesfeldt, "Strategies of Social Interaction," in Plutchik and Kellerman, *Theories of Emotion, pp. 57–80.*
25. This idea is now basic to works on emotions and behavior.
26. See Wilson, *On Human Nature*, and Dawkins, *The Selfish Gene.* For some striking pictorial evidence of the universality of the very complex bodily expressions of coyness, see Eibl-Eibesfeldt, "Strategies of Social Interaction."
27. Friedrich Hayek has most fully developed the theory of spontaneous natural orders. See *Law, Legislation and Liberty*, 3 vols. (Chicago: University of Chicago Press, 1973).
28. Some of the evidence to support this admittedly "sweeping" hypothesis is presented in the classic work on interest rates by Sidney Homer: *A History of Interest Rates* (New Brunswick, NJ: Rutgers University Press, 1977).

29. See, for example, Hedrick Smith, *The Russians* (New York: Ballantine, 1976).
30. See Jean Baechler, *Revolution* (New York: Harper and Row, 1975).
31. Malcolm S. Forbes, Sr., *Forbes Magazine*, February 14, 1983, p. 27.
32. Mary Douglas, *Purity and Danger (London: Routledge and Kegan Paul, 1978).*
33. See Milton Mayer, *They Thought They Were Free* (Chicago: University of Chicago Press, 1955).
34. Robert Solomon (*History and Human Nature* [New York: Harcourt Brace Jovanovich, Inc., 1979]) has argued that the eighteenth- and nineteenth-century Western theories of human nature were based on the assumption that the induction of knowledge about human nature from history is not problematic. He is probably right about the continental rationalists, in so far as they believed there was such a thing as human nature. The rationalistic philosophes approached history as a source of illustrations for their preconceived ideas, as Jacob Talmon (*The Origins of Totalitarian Democracy* [London: Secker and Warburg, 1955]) was aware. The works of the empirical British and American theorists of human nature were profoundly different. While they tended to assume human nature to be far more invariant (in relation to situations) than is the case, they largely took it for granted that it is quite problematic to infer from history just what human nature is. That is why they went to such pains to try to show by the analysis of history just what human nature is and how it operates in such important realms as the quest for political power. People do not normally write books about "self-evident" truths. (Solomon seems convinced that the French and German philosophers' idea of human nature was really a figment of their "bourgeois" status in life. But his entire argument seems based on the normal academic presupposition that there is no human nature—or none worth writing about. For all that I think he has a point about the rationalists, it is more likely that Solomon's ideas about them are based on his academic status in life than that theirs were based on their status. But by now this should be self-evident—almost.)

8

Central Planning versus Individual Planning

The main point to be made is that planning has succeeded in avoiding the main inconsistency in unplanned economies of the pre-1914 type, namely, the underutilizing of productive capacity as a consequence of business cycles and of structural disequilibria. It is highly probable that the disappearance of the business cycle after World War II has been obtained with the aid of macroeconomic planning. . .

Jan Tinbergen, 1968

Over time, Fed officials almost always have said exactly the right thing and then proceeded to do the wrong thing. . .the Fed's record in fine-tuning is consistent—consistently bad.

Lindley H. Clark, Jr.

The fundamental problem facing the economy today is that the Federal Reserve has no reliable compass to determine whether it is printing too much money, too little money, or just the right amount. It is comparable to businessmen running their companies without income statements, without balance sheets.

This astonishing fact—that the Fed is flying. . .blind—has received virtually no attention from policy-makers or the press.

M. S. Forbes, Jr.

While there is nothing in modern technological developments which forces us towards comprehensive economic planing, there is a great deal in them which makes infinitely more dangerous the power a planning-authority would possess.

Friedrich Hayek

"The more complicated the forms of civilization, the more restricted the freedom of the individual must become." This is an idea that seems to have rapidly, but very quietly, become a basic assumption in the thinking of many Western people, especially of the highly "educated." I suspect 90 percent of my academic colleagues would accept it without question. While it might arouse a bit more scepticism, and even some overt opposition, in the U.S. Congress, it would surely seem almost a law of nature to most of our liberal legislators. It could equally well serve as a slogan for the vast hordes in our land who agree with John Kenneth Galbraith that price controls enforced by government power are essential in our complex society; or those who insist that only centrally planned redistributions of students by judges can produce justice in our irrational society; or those who push for affirmative action programs and racial nonquotas to overcome the "irrationalities" of the market place; or those who support new laws in states like California to impose a central land use plan on the entire state to "rationalize" land use by forcing individuals to use it only in accord with The Plan.

Perhaps the only reason this quotation has not been used as a slogan for these diverse and vast programs sweeping our land is that its source is historically tainted. It is, after all, a famous pronouncement by Benito Mussolini and was used to justify his totalitarian central planning of the lives of Italians. I am not using this historical point in the usual manner of a political ploy, that of tarring one's opponents with the now universally despised label of "fascism." The point is far more serious. The Italian society Mussolini considered so complicated that it demanded extreme central planning was at that time exquisitely uncomplicated in comparison with American society today or with any of the other industrial societies. In fact, Italy was in many ways closer to medieval communalism than to the complex forms of the technological society in which we live. Mussolini's felt need for planned controls had nothing to do with the real nature of Italian society. It had everything to do with his too obvious lust for power.[1]

All bureaucratic systems drift—or gallop—toward some specific form of the generalized practice of rationalistic planning and control. The reasons are almost obvious. The bureaucracy is intended to control society, to extend the power of the rulers of the bureaucracy. As we saw in the last chapter, all planning at all levels is one basic method by which human beings try to control their world. Hence, when a bureaucracy is set up it is intended to plan the lives of the people—to control them. In addition, all bureaucratic organizations drift toward a legalistic, rationalistic plan of internal controls (for reasons explained in the next chapter). Consequently, the everyday practice of bureaucratic management instills a model of legalistically and rationalistically planned social organization, which is then implicitly projected onto the rest of the world as the only (absolutist) effective model of action. This, of course, is the reason why most bureaucrats drift toward literally loathing creative, entrepreneurial action and, thus, all free markets. The "entrepreneurial bureaucrats" are quite rare.

As M. Rostovtzeff[2] and Pierre Leveque[3] have shown, all of the basic ideas of rationalistic state planning of the mixed economy were already clearly formulated and used by the bureaucrats of the ancient Ptolemaic dynasties. In his study of rational central planning by imperial state bureaucracies from 580 B.C. to A.D. 1920, Pitirim Sorokin found some important variations in the rationales used and in the degrees of planning attempted, but the general practice was the same in "Ancient Egypt, Ancient Rome (beginning especially with Diocletian), Ancient Peru and Mexico, certainly Ancient China, and many others; and their planning was on a vast scale; it was even centralized and 'rationalized' in accordance with the science and wisdom of their time...Some of these plans are remarkably like, indeed one may say almost identical with, the government planning of the present time."[4]

So inherent in the "mature" bureaucracy is the drift toward rationalistic central planning that remarkably few empires have acquiesced in the inherent efficiencies of decentralization. Ancient Persia is the only clear example I know of. Instead, almost all strove eventually, as their bureaucracies became more institutionalized, to impose their plans rigidly (absolutely), up to the point of effective resistance, corruption, or escape from The Plan by the immiserated masses. Cyril Mango, for example, has described the rapid erosion of the economy and tax revenues that quickly followed in the wake of Diocletian's plan for the Great Roman Society and the "tempering" of this catastrophe by escape and corruption both in the Western and Eastern (Byzantine) empires that allowed them to limp on:

> A planned economy made possible something that had not existed earlier, namely a State budget. How else could one meet the vastly increased, yet variable, cost of the army? A budget meant a rationalized system of taxation, which meant a census, which meant an expanded bureaucracy. As a result of Diocletian's reforms, the Roman world was filled with officialdom, and it could already be said in the fourth century (no doubt with considerable exaggeration) that the number of beneficiaries exceeded that of taxpayers. As we all know, however, a bureaucracy generates its own momentum, and taxes have a tendency of going up rather than coming down. It is an undeniable fact that from the fourth century onwards more and more land was going out of cultivation, and it is highly likely that the main cause of this was taxation. As the tax yield diminished, the officials, armed with their registers, had no choice but to apply more repressive measures: everyone, from the lowly *colonus* to the decurion, had to be kept in his place. But the wheels of government ground slowly, distances were great, and there was plenty of scope for fraud and evasion. The figure of the patron, the "fixer," the man of influence thus came to stand at the centre of the state, so much so that even the cult of Christian saints was visualized in terms of patronage...The rigidity of the Early Byzantine social and economic structure could always be circumvented by devious means. Whatever the laws prescribed (and there is no reason to think that they were systematically applied), a

resourceful man usually found a way of getting on in life. . .Rigidity tempered by evasion may thus be a suitable description of the Early Byzantine social structure. Perhaps it applies to other planned economies as well.[5]

Centralized, rationalized planning was precisely the way kings and their ministers tried (generally very unsuccessfully) to run their societies in the great age of mercantilism when Western societies were complicated enough and international enough, and governments powerful enough, to demand society-wide policies, but still primitive enough and feudal enough by our standards to allow the central planners to have some sense, even if it was largely an illusion, that they could know and determine what was going on throughout the entire society.[6] It was precisely the simplicity and the lingering communalism of these societies, combined with massive evasions, which allowed central planning to be used for many decades before producing terrible stagnation and economic and political catastrophe. And, of course, if enforcement were weak enough and, consequently, escape into a free-market underground pervasive enough, the society could limp along with its low level state of stagnation or even a low rate of growth for centuries.

In such societies the most inventive and courageous create a system of corruption which runs parallel to and is integrated with the official planning bureaucracy through the bribing of officials. In general, the underground economy and the dual system corrupting the official system vary directly in both scope and form with the official system. The Spanish, laboring under the immense weight of one of the most gargantuan bureaucracies since the sixteenth century, have created a massive system of "patrons" whose ties of patronage are commonly even hereditary, *and* a dual private bureaucracy to "lubricate" the otherwise immobile monster. The low growth rate of even the most lubricated bureaucratically planned society is abysmal simply because the transaction costs," including bribes, time lost, endless dickering, and risks of police action, are so vast.

All rational central planning assumes a high degree of knowledge of all the parts of the system one is planning and a high degree of predictability in the aggregate decision making within that system. The simpler, more unchanging, homogeneous, and moralized a society, the more these conditions hold. The more free, individualistic, changing, conflictfully demoralized, and complex a society, the less they hold. Individual freedom, social complexity, change, and conflict are necessary (but not sufficient) for creativity, thus for efficiency and growth; but they are the most terrible enemies of central state planning and they inevitably destroy its effectiveness—or the state destroys them, or drives them into the underground, out of the officially taxed economy. This was clear in general to the classical liberal thinkers in Western history. This is why they wanted to stop state centralized planning of the economy and to make individuals, as much as possible, the planners of their own lives, especially through the use of the democratic free-market system in which the prices are a vastly complex, approximate tabulation of the demands and supplies of all goods by all the people. Individual freedom, social diversity, and creative change were the goals of all the John Lockes, Adam Smiths, Thomas Jeffersons, and their successors, so they rightly opposed the medieval forms of thought involved in state centralized planning.

The one basic difference between the ancient and medieval ideas of social planning and those dominant today is the synthesizing of rationalism-scientism (especially social scientism) with modernism and millennialism in planning today. In the ancient and medieval world, the ideas of planning of the imperial state bureaucrats were normally constrained by an implicit understanding of the irrational—impassioned—and even "evil," "selfish" nature of human beings. It is the synthesis of rationalism-scientism, modernism, and millennialism with the ancient ideas of planning that leads to the immense central planning in our modernist states and, thence, to their eventual catastrophes.

Human Nature and Planning

Humans are by far the most rational of animals, as we have always known. The difference between rationalistic views of humanity as denatured beings using reason to guide their lives and that of a human-naturist view of humanity is that both the Christian and scientific believer in a psychosocial, biosocial, genetic nature of humanity sees rationality as ultimately serving as the guide to the inherited passions or emotions. (Christians, of course, oppose this, but they do not deny the obvious.) This view, first so clearly and systematically presented by David Hume, in no way belittles the importance of reason or moral conscience in human life. Just as we human beings are genetically programmed to fulfill and enhance our emotions, over the long run and in accord with the hierarchy of motives, so are we also genetically programmed to use our memory, cognitive categories (including those sedimented in language over the eons), our reason, our grasp of ourselves (our basic "sense of self"[7] which relates our basic values, emotions, and will to all major aspects of our past, present, and future), and our will power to temporarily inhibit our emotions (except in situations in which the emotional costs are so great as to override or take control of our will power and force us to act to fulfill themselves) and then to plan ("feed-forward") how best to enhance and fullfill them in concrete situations over time.

Everyday, commonsensical rationality is our vastly complex set of *heuristic* programs for cognitively, consciously relating all of these internal and external states of affairs to each other to provide some optimum enhancements and fulfillments of the emotions and morals. Heuristic programs are flexible, open to situations for creative changes. *Hard* programs are not. Planning is our most systematic, consciously controlled form of rational thinking and programming. Most of our everyday lives do not require any significant new planning because we live by customs or experiential traditions that work, that is, allow us to feel that our emotions and our entire senses of self are being optimally enhanced and fulfilled, at least within the practical limits we believe exist within the everyday situational constraints we face. In fact, planning, even at the individual level and even when done by the most knowledgeable and rational human being, is an extremely inefficient way to achieve goals in any situation other than one that is new, that is, that involves significant uncertainties for the actor. But when there are significant uncertainties facing us that cannot be resolved by observational learning and doing, then planning is the most efficient way to manage our responses. This allows for the use of planned nonplanning, such as tossing a coin in situations that involve so much uncertainty that we do not see any rational way of planning other than by nonplanning, or chance. We should note that "playing it by ear," "flying by the seat of your pants," and so on, are not instances of nonplanning. They are planned forms of responding only in the most immediate situation because we believe that crucial bits of information will become available, such as the "vibes" or body language of negotiators, which will indicate to our rational calculations how we should respond in the evolving situation to achieve our goals.

While behavioristic psychologists are apt to commit the sin of seeing human beings as never planning, neoclassical and Keynesian economists are apt to see them as continually planning to minimize, maximize, or optimize everything. But a continual state of planning would guarantee the maximization of anxiety and exhaustion and the minimization of success in achieving our goals, and thus a minimization of happiness. To optimize life satisfaction, we relegate planning to those situations that are new or uncertain. The reason is that planning involves a massive amount of information processing and, thus, is tremendously time-consuming and costly to the organism. The brain and the peripheral nervous system are programmed to minimize all such rational planning. Reflexes are the most obvious instance of an extreme degree of decentralized responding: we allow our reflexes to respond automatically, unless we fear that some new situation threatens us with harm when we go along with our reflexes. Only then do we inhibit our reflexes and plan out a higher response. Tremendously important subsystems of life, without which we could not live more than a few minutes, are automated almost to this same degree. Vastly complex, little understood neuroendocrinological and sympathetic-parasympathetic nervous sub-systems operate in this way to start, speed up, slow down, and stop very large numbers of habituated reactions to standardized environmental stimuli. Heart and lung functioning are examples of this. They work very well on their own by hierarchicalized feedback systems. As most of us are aware, we can easily control our breathing by conscious, planned activity. Heart functioning can also be controlled this way but it takes systematic effort, such as is done in yoga and biofeedback learning. As we are also aware, consciously planning our breathing from moment to moment is unnecessary except when we face a new breathing problem, in which case it can become very valuable, which is no doubt why we evolved the ability. Consciously, planned, controlled breathing is in all other situations very counterproductive because it makes it hard to get the right amount of oxygen since we do not consciously know how rapidly and deeply we need to breathe to get the amount of oxygen our body needs in a given environment and state of activity, whereas centers in the hypothalamus can tell automatically by testing the amount of carbon dioxide in the blood, and it takes up conscious effort that we could be putting to planning in areas of life that are uncertain.

As everyone says, tying your shoestrings is easy until you think about it consciously. This same principle is at work in most of life. The cerebellum stores up programs of vastly complex habituated patterns of physical activity which allow us to walk, run, pass footballs, fight with swords, and so on—all without any significant planning, once we have habituated them by lengthy conscious learning. As the Zen masters have said for many centuries, the great swordsman is the one who learns his skills from observation and practice so well that he fights without consciously thinking about it. As Wilder Penfield has shown from studies of epileptic seizures (in which the individual is made unconscious by the too-rapid neural firing, but is left fully capable of following out programs of physical behavior), the adult human computer (the Automata) contains programs of habituated behavior of such vast complexity that, if the individual has planned and willed to drive across town in a habitual manner before the seizure and unconsciousness, he can do so normally without major mishap (though he may run a red light or two).

Though most of us do not operate completely as automata even in the very short run, we all carry out most of our life processes, our thinking, our social interaction, and our economic activity without significant planning. Nonplanning is the only workable genetic program for most of the life processes. More specifically, we are apparently genetically programmed to deal with every habitual environmental input in a nonplanned, habituated, decentralized way because that is by far the most efficient way of acting—automatic programming for habitual experiences maximizes the efficient response to the environment, minimizes the costs to us emotionally, and frees us to plan how to deal with new problems or how to plan a better overall life for ourselves. Are practitioners of yoga really happier, healthier, or morally superior because they have learned through years of strenuous effort how to spend most of their waking hours planning the movements of the individual muscles and other parts of the body, which everyone else does unthinkingly, while they go about creating great works of art, tending the sick, or videotaping these feats of planned contortions? If this were true, would these ancient practitioners of body planning be such rare specimens of human endeavors?[8]

Just as the body as a whole operates almost entirely independently of conscious planning and control, so does the mind in general and so does even the most creative situated planning. The nervous system is built from the bottom to the top to recognize and respond to patterns of crucial importance to our basic emotions. Even a seemingly discrete phenomena such as the tactile perception of pain is actually a patterned recognition and response to the varying stimulation of a number of pain receptors. This does not mean that we are the prisoners of our preconceived patterns, as some cognitive theorists seem to think. We are able to perceptually and cognitively override our pattern recognition and search out the unique in experience. Most perception and cognition involves both recognition of the patterns and of the unique, as when we see a specific human face—we see its humanness and this becomes a vital grounding or context for our recognition of the unique individual. The reliance of the brain on pattern recognition is once again a matter of efficiency and effectiveness. The subconscious recognition of important, already-known patterns can take place almost instantaneously, whereas thinking consciously about what the pattern is would take a long time, and responding quickly is often the difference between life and death, as can be seen in the almost reflexive and instantaneous startle movement away from something we are programmed to perceive as threatening. Individuals with great experience in a realm of life develop a grasp, sense, feel, gut feeling or intuition for the patterns of crucial importance in that realm which is both very quick in coming and very effective in spotting the important things going on. A mother will sense from an unusual silence that something is wrong with her child in the next room and a businessman will sense from his vast experience that something is wrong with the figures or that an opportunity is better than the figures suggest. Even in the most rational forms of creative work, the crucial creative leap apparently comes after long concentration has allowed the subconscious mind to recognize and evaluate new patterns in the old, already-known patterns. These are crucial reasons why efficient actions are so highly situated.

Like almost all of our mythological thinking about individual and social life, the rationalistic-scientistic, technicist social planners have seized upon one important part of life and treated it as if it were the only part. It is because the rationalist has seized upon a vital part of life, especially one part that is very important in a rapidly changing and creative society such as our scientific and technological society is, that their argument seems plausible to so many people. The rationalistic planner has seized upon the important truth of our need for more situated (decentralized) planning in a more rapidly changing and creative society but, by extrapolating it—through the media of the myths of rationalism and modernism—to everything and asserting that some centralized experts can plan effectively for everyone, has turned it into a monstrously self-destructive myth. Of course, this would be true only of totally consistent rationalistic planners, perhaps reincarnated Condorcets with some unbelievably complex set of differential equations. Even the most extreme planning mythologizers within the inner sanctum of the Kremlin would not imagine doing that yet (let us hope!). Almost all serious proponents of state planning fall somewhere short of its extreme in their proposals.

Social Planning

There are at least four continuous, independent dimensions of planning. These are schematized in Table 1.

Table 1.
The Four Continua of Planning

Conservative Planning	Democratic Welfare State Planning	Totalitarian Planning
I. Situated/Decentralized ....Abstract/Centralized		
II. Flexible/Open to change ....Inflexible/Closed to ("Heuristic") Change ("Hard")		
III. Step-by-Step (Marginal or Iterative)..Rationalistic/Radical (General)		
IV. Short-Run ....Long-Run		

Almost all the discussions of state planning fail to note the existence of these continua of planning.[9] As a result, they often sound the same but mean very different things. Social planners such as W. Arthur Lewis[10] can propose the planning of international development and sound, in general, as if they are calling for the same sort of macro-economic, national accounts, computer-simulated, model-based planning as Jan Tinbergen[11] and others have used to try to plan the economy of Holland, yet really mean they are in favor of a far more flexible and decentralized (if still reasonably general and long-run) plan than Tinbergen, and others, have in mind.

It is precisely the failure to see that planning falls along these independent continua and that, therefore, there are vastly different kinds of planning, that has led to the frequent confusion of the planning of individual lives and businesses with the state planning of the rationalistic-scientistic planners. It is extremely common for the rationalistic planners to argue, with an air of plausibility that easily takes in people who do not make these distinctions, that businesspeople plan all the time and, therefore, it is really hypocritical of them to oppose the rationalist's state planning.[12] There is nothing rational at all to the either/or argument over planning.

We all necessarily plans some of our lives, especially our economic lives in a market economy. A market economy is a rapidly changing and conflictful competitive one in which decentralized, flexible, marginal, and short-run planning is efficient because the crucial information used in such planning, that is, pricing information, is a relatively reliable, quantitative measure of vastly complex society-wide states of relative demand and supply. (The reason will become clearer in the next chapter.) Medieval peasants did not do much economic planning, even for the small part of their produce that they sold in the local market. Instead, they behaved largely by custom (though not by as much custom as historians once thought) because the common land system dominant in much of Europe largely prevented their affecting their fate, and because things were pretty much the same from year to year—or beyond their control, as was true of weather. The more pricing information used in economic planning is determined by market forces, and the more complex, changing, and competitive the market, the more planning individuals do to achieve their economic goals efficiently. Thus, modern businesspeople place a great emphasis on planning. But their planning is normally at the opposite end of the four continua from what the rationalistic state planner calls planning. (For exceptions, see below.) In fact, it is precisely when the state planners begin to destroy the free market, and especially when they begin to destroy the validity and reliability of the pricing information (thus increasing uncertainty) by manipulating the currency and controlling prices, that businesspeople move further toward the left end of the continua in planning, further away than ever from the state planner. I am not calling them leftists because of this. It is a tradition in Western writing to go from the less on the left to the more on the right. State planners are rightists only on paper.

There are, of course, businesses, especially big businesses, that try to plan abstractly, "strategically", from headquarters and that do so with relative inflexibility, with a high degree of generality (not taking into consideration much about the different situations faced by the far-flung parts of their enterprises), and do so over the very long run (even thirty to forty years in the case of some utilities or commodity firms, including those that grow trees). But these are corporations that are now planning the way rationalistic states do. There is every reason to believe that, especially as the uncertainties grow in the economy because of the activities of our megastates, those corporations will go bankrupt—or go back to highly situated planning. Of course, the nature of a product, the technology involved in producing it, and its markets all affect the efficiency of planning along the four continua.

A classic statement of such relatively abstract planning by big business can be found in a *Harvard Business Review* article by F. F. Gilmore and R. G. Brandenburg.[13] Their model of business planning is full of the massively complex flowcharts and computer simulation models later to be immortalized in the McNamara strategy for winning the Vietnam War (and still later to be installed in various grand schemes at the World Bank for winning the international war on poverty from the top down). Gilmore and Brandenburg described their final step, their "program of action," in these terms:

> The purpose of the program of action phase is to specify, sequence, and schedule the major activities and events necessary to accomplish efficiently the strategy agreed on in the previous step. In this phase, operations research is beginning to offer increasingly useful techniques for top management. Critical path planning and scheduling, mathematical programming for resource allocation and capacity planning, capital budgeting models, and simulation, all can be of value in comparing alternatives.[14]

Since this is only step 42 of a 43-step Top-Management Planning Framework, and must, presumably, be integrated in some vastly complex ways with more specific lower-management planning frameworks, it is hard to believe that management would ever have the time to get to step 43, which is called Operations and, hopefully, finally brings them into contact with the consuming environment in which the effects of all their planning will finally be tested. In fact, in this particular instance, the managers may never have made that contact with reality, since the authors reveal that they developed the program by first making an "intensive study of the military decision-making process at the U.S. Army Command and General Staff College at Fort Leavenworth" (just before the model was tested out in Vietnam) and then by modifying their model to fit the planning processes of a really big business:

> The final step was to compare and modify our model in light of the top-management planning process employed over the past five years by the Lockheed Aircraft Corporation, which has been carrying out a major diversification program.[15]

One of the unexpected and clearly unintended consequences of this plan might well have been the federal de facto receivership that Lockheed soon achieved without much general planning for it.

While no one has yet done a systematic study of the nature and effects of business planning, such a study will most likely find that any big-business planning that falls far to the right on our continua will meet a similar fate, with a time lag directly proportional to the net assets of the company at the time the real operational application of the planning starts. Certainly this is the implication of the in-depth studies of the most and least successful firms. Receivership appears to be one of the long-run externalities of abstract, rationalist-modernist planning. The attempt to rely on such planning, rather than upon the highly situated planning of the entrepreneur who built the company, might well account in large part for the low life expectancy of big corporations after the founder moves on and for the decline of so many multinational corporations today, especially those run by the American business-school trained planners rather than those run by the "old boy" nonsystem of Japan.

Abstract, inflexible, general, long-run planning works only when four conditions are met: (1) the situation is highly standardized and unchanging; (2) the information about it is extremely valid and reliable; (3) the causal relations among the variables exist and are known by the planners, so they can predict social trends and outcomes of plans; and (4) the planners have effective power to enforce their plans. It should be obvious from our discussion above that this situation at the extreme is one in which planning would actually be very close to being no planning at all. When those four conditions are met, we can use highly habituated responses to the standardized situations. Such planning might demand massive amounts of work in the beginning, but then it would operate pretty automatically over the long run, with little planning.

It is at the left end of the continua that we find maximized planning, or the maximum amount of consciously fitting our situational strivings to our goals, consciously creating ways to get what we want. It is precisely this kind of situated planning for our own lives that the human brain is built to handle with an efficiency that vastly exceeds that of any computer. And it is this kind of planning that successful businesspeople do. The entrepreneurs, or business creators, are no doubt to the left compared to the successful administrators who succeed in maintaining and developing what the entrepreneurs create, but the difference does not appear to be great. Not all big businesses are as decentralized, fluid, project oriented, internally competitive, and entrepreneurial as (to varying degrees) Arthur D. Little, DEC, IBM, Mitsubishi, and 3M. But this has been the real general, if bumpy, trend almost from the beginning of really big-business administration, with the original General Motors revolution setting the model. This fact has been obscured by two developments, at least to politicians and members of the public not involved in business, such as most academic theorists.

When theorists first began studying big businesses, they looked at them very largely through their strong preconception of the theory of bureaucracy formulated by Max Weber. Weber's theory was based on little significant empirical evidence and was concerned predominantly with the "ideal type" of centralized state bureaucracies found in welfare-statist Prussia (see the next chapter). Weber saw bureaucracy as the rationalized way of organizing human activity and predicted that this formal rationalization of human activity would sweep all before it, eventually imprisoning all of us in an "iron cage of bureaucracy." Because Franz Kafka provided an even more grim, actually a terrifying, psychotic, image of bureaucracy which the literati in general accepted, the idea of the inevitable triumph of the impersonal, totally rationalized bureaucracy took firm hold among academic theorists and intellectuals. It then trickled down to the educated and less educated public through the mass media, especially mass entertainment.

In World War I and, far more, World War II this entrenched preconception of rationalized, planned bureaucratic functioning was synthesized with the general idea of socialist state planning, very largely as a result of the supposed success of the war planning boards in planning the massive effort needed to win the war. It then became almost an article of faith among intellectuals, including many academic economists, that big business had shown the way to rationalized, centralized planning, created and administered by bureaucracies, which actually led to sustained economic growth, eliminating the supposed "anarchy" of the marketplace and ending for all time the disruptions of business cycles. Most economists, perhaps made cautious by over awareness of the facts about business operations, went no further than arguing that all of this could be achieved by centralized planning of a minimal bundle of national economic aggregates. But many went beyond this Keynesian middle-range, democratic welfare state planning. Even Joseph Schumpeter, in spite of his deep preference for entrepreneurship, became a foremost advocate of the inevitability of socialistic, bureaucratic planning, supposedly because big business had been so successful in showing the way to that rationalistic Valhalla.[16] John Kenneth Galbraith, ecstatic over his supposed success as bureaucratic czar planning and supposedly controlling all prices in the American economy during the war, became the cheerleader of rationalized, centralized state planning for the economic happiness of everyone. His best sellers proclaimed over and over again that big businesses planned their activities rationally from central headquarters and carried out these plans by the aid of such miracles as mass persuasive advertising.[17] If big business could do it successfully, why couldn't government do it better?

The entire myth of rationalistic business planning was unintentionally aided and abetted by big business itself. In an age of science and technology, what sounds scientifically and technically rational is seen by the general public as being more legitimate and more of a likely winner in any competitive struggle. So big business presented itself as rational in scientific and technological terms, partly with the "help" of academic theorists. They did so first of all by constructing their formalized, rationalized organizational charts (bureaucracy) showing how they supposedly worked. This was succeeded by the far more complex flowcharts of operations, then by the far more rationalized (scientific and technological) models of operations analysis, input-output analysis, computer simulations, etc. These finally were all put together and became highly rationalized big plans of the Lockheed and Pentagon ideal type.

Meanwhile, *successful* big businesses were not actually being run in this way at all. When social scientists began studying big businesses, they did so almost entirely from the outside, so they saw little more than the public image of the rationalistically planned corporation, the totally modern bureaucracy at work planning its future and carrying out the central plan by all the abstract rules of science and technology. These studies were enshrined in a field of study still commonly called "formal organizations"; but it could even better have been called "rationally planned, bureaucratic organizations." As the social scientists got more and more into the businesses so that they could see beyond their public presentations, they began to discover that the formal organization chart gave an idealized image of how the organization actually operated. They discovered that informal organization was necessary to succeed in reality. And what was informal organization? Unrationalizable, personal relations and situated decision making that, hopefully, were rationally planned but always were done in the light of the immediate, concrete situation and continually revised to meet the situation as it emerged and as information about the success and failure of the expectations and plans ("feedback") became available. The social scientists found more and more informal, unrationalizable activity, more and more conservative or situated planning.

Relying on his own inside experience in three industrial chemical plants (which, as highly technological and capitalized industries, do more planning than most firms), Melville Dalton wrote the classic work *Men Who Manage*,[18] which showed in minute detail how "existential" (situated, individually free, and emotionally intuitive) their decision making actually was. He subtitled his work *Fusions of Thought and Feeling*. In management, reason and emotion were necessarily interdependent and the emotions served as the guides for reason.[19] At roughly the same time, economists and even public administration experts were discovering the same realities of situated, conservative planning lurking behind the public rhetorics of abstract, rationalized planning of big business. Warren Bennis,[20] Herbert Simon and J. C. March,[21] C. E. Lindblom,[22] and others discovered the same realities behind the rhetoric. In general, they concluded that rational model building could help to clarify and systematize actual operations of limited types of activities, basically those that fit the four assumptions of rationalized planning presented above, but that such planning has little relevance to successful real-world planning of complex activities such as big business and almost no relevance whatsoever to activities that are so complex, changing, and inherently uncertain as foreign relations.

Lindblom, presenting a model of planning and execution by what he called successive limited comparisons, contrasted this situated kind of planning with the ideal type of rationalistic planning so common in the social science literature, and quoted Charles Hitch, one of the foremost advocates of rational planning:

> I would make the empirical generalization from my experience at Rand and elsewhere that operations research is the art of sub-optimizing, that is, of solving some lower-level problems, and that difficulties increase and our special competence diminishes by an order of magnitude with every level of decision-making we attempt to ascend. The sort of simple explicit model which operations researchers are so proficient in using can certainly reflect most of the significant factors influencing traffic conrol on the George Washington Bridge, but the proportion of the relevant reality which we can represent by any such model or models in studying, say, a major foreign-policy decision, appears to be almost trivial.[23]

Succeeding generations of empirical analysts were to conclude that even traffic planning in this rationalistic way could be done only so long as the basic parameters remained unchanged, which is to say, only so long as the need for creative planning to deal with emerging uncertainties remained nil. By the late 1970s even businesspeople were ready to rediscover, or admit, the vital importance in business planning and operations of gut feelings, intuition, and hunches, the vital form of preconscious, rational recognition of pattern and analysis that the human brain does so immensely well in dealing with our world of uncertainty and which no computer could dream of doing, even if computers could dream.

The Debureaucratization of Planning in Business

We Americans have always cherished the spirit of the independent yeoman or freeholder as the embodiment of our value on economic freedom. As the typical American would put it today, "I don't take orders from anyone. I want to be my own boss." The independent farmer ("freeholder") was both the ideal and the overwhelming economic reality in American life until late in the nineteenth century. After the invention of the cotton gin in 1793, much of the land of the South became large plantations worked by slaves. But Southerners were far outnumbered by Northern freeholders. These independent farmers were the backbone of the Jeffersonian-Jacksonian "empire of liberty." Being dependent on no one for their livelihood, as Jefferson argued, they could be counted on to assert their real interests and, thus, to maintain the republican freedoms enshrined in the Bill of Rights.

Jefferson and his successors feared that this republic could not long endure if the freeholder vanished and workers became dependent on others. The corporate concentrations of capital and employment that developed over the century, fueled largely by changes in government laws, especially the introduction of high tariffs after the 1830s, limited liability for corporations and huge land grants to the railroads, and partly by new capital-intensive technologies demanding many workers (as in steel), was a severe challenge to this entire System of Natural Liberty.[24] It looked to an increasing number of Americans as if the economic freedom of a few big businesspeople was destroying the economic freedom of the many, turning them from independent freeholders into dependent wage earners, thus threatening liberty in general.[25] While few Americans heeded the prophesies of people like Marx, who believed monopoly and its immiserization of workers would be the inevitable outcome of capitalism, ever more of them turned against business because of this bigness. They turned to government and unions to protect them by regulating big business. This growing antibusiness ethos greatly potentiated the renaissance of statist myths.

By the early part of this century social thinkers, especially those influenced by the institutional economists of Germany and socialistic thinkers everywhere, began to see business in general in the form of big-corporate-bureaucratic business. Progressives, including such diverse thinkers as the young Walter Lippmann[26] and Herbert Hoover,[27] called for added restraint on business and increased planning by government. In the 1930s the great upsurge in antibusiness and prostatist sentiment triggered by the Great Depression combined with the argument of famous social scientists that big business was now thoroughly bureaucratized and divorced from ownership to convince ever more people that government bureaucracies could just as well own and manage them efficiently. Joseph Schumpeter, one of the extremely free-market oriented Austrian economists, argued in his famous book *Capitalism, Socialism and Democracy* that big business was successful because it minimized risks (especially those from recessions) and its success through bureaucratization was preparing the way for government bureaucracies to take them over. Big business, then, had prepared the way for statist bureaucratic planning.

This kind of argument was most successful in the 1930s in Britain, Sweden, Fascist Italy, and Nazi Germany. In Britain the government started intentionally encouraging the so-called "rationalization" of business, that is, concentration into big bureaucracies. In the 1940s the British government then started nationalizing big business, completing the Schumpeter scenario. By the 1960s, and continuing up to today, our college students, including many of our graduate students of business administration being groomed for big business, were looking at business through the collectivist-tinted spectacles of John Kenneth Galbraith, who proclaimed in *The New Industrial State* that big bureaucratic planning was inevitable. "By all but the pathologically romantic, it is now recognized that this is not the age of the small man."[28] Given his personal preconceptions and wishes, and living in the great period of corporate conglomeration of the 1960s, Galbraith failed completely to see that the Age of Big Business was already dying.

The Revolution of Littleness had already begun in business around the world, and especially in the United States. But its realities were still largely unnoticed until the 1980s. The early realities of even the most sweeping revolutions are normally unseen. Even the scientific and industrial revolutions were a hundred years old or more before many people began to realize that something of profound significance was happening. Our traditional preconceptions and our situationally limited views of the broader developments in society conspire to hide the newness and scope of such changes until they are so advanced that they become suddenly obvious.

Our Revolution of Littleness has gone unnoticed by most people both for these usual reasons and because our headlines and network stories paint the opposite picture. Most experts and politicians providing these stories are too committed to the myths of collectivism and too well versed in and rewarded for the traditional ideas about the Age of Big Business to see how rapidly the tide is now running against bigness. So are many of our big businesspeople, but they learn very quickly when the tide starts sweeping them away.

The great increase in mergers in the late 1970s and early 1980s has had the most misleading appearance, just as the much ballyhooed great era of mergers in the late nineteenth century led most people to fear the socialists were right that capitalism inevitably leads to monopoly.[29] Businesses in 1982, for example, put up approximately $80 billion for mergers. Many of these were very big mergers indeed in which very big businesses bought up much smaller ones. U.S. Steel's $6 billion takeover of Marathon Oil was the big headline of business news for weeks. On the surface this certainly shows big steel getting much bigger. But look beneath the surface. This move itself shows that, just as the United Steel Workers have claimed angrily, U.S. Steel is trying *desperately* to diversify away from the steel industry. The really big story in the steel industry is diversification away from steel and the rapid rise in profitability and growth of the smaller steel companies. The most efficient and rapidly growing steel producers in the U.S. (and in some other countries, like Italy) are generally small, slim-and-trim, with low debt-to-equity ratios and small, highly skilled, highly productive and nonunionized work forces. Over the five years leading up to its massive merger away from steel, U.S. Steel ranked eighteenth in growth and twenty-first in return on equity in the U.S. steel industry. In the same vein, once huge Kaiser decided to quit steel entirely. Some governments, notably Mexico, poured billions into huge, centralized steel mills, but these mills will almost certainly be uncompetitive white elephants kept alive, if at all, by vast subsidies.

This might still mean that, even if steel is decentralizing, U.S. Steel will get bigger. But that was not even the plan. U.S. Steel hoped Marathon, with its vast oil reserves, would provide 51 percent of its corporate sales and 83 percent of profits. Marathon, they hoped, would make up for their overall shrinkage in steel sales. Those of us who believe the market forces unleashed by the deregulation of oil and natural gas will destroy OPEC's monopolistic pricing suspect this merger will eventually prove as disastrous as most mergers do.

Of course, we must be careful about generalizing from steel to our whole economy. Those still mesmerized by bigness might insist that steel, tires, and autos are "dying" because of foreign competition, so they are symptoms of the deindustrialization of the U.S. which, of course, they use to proclaim the need for a collectivist salvation, "reindustrialization by America-Inc." Actually, there is no deindustrialization going on, not even in the steel industry. There is only change, above all a shift to smaller, more specialized producers, to mills processing the vast quantities of scrap steel, and to new products that function better than steel. Other industries, such as textiles and watches, went through this general process in the 1960s and 1970s.

But the skeptics have a serious point. So let's look at the other extreme, that of the very new, high technology world of computers. Here there is indeed a giant to fixate the glare of the believers in bigness. IBM remains huge and formidably creative, efficient, and profitable. It is probably the best example one could find in the world today to support—by appearances—the nineteenth-century argument that the economies of scale (of bigness) give the big an inherent advantage over the little and doom a free economy to ever-greater concentration.

But even IBM is largely a mirage of bigness power. Though in the early 1980s it ranked third in return on equity, probably because of its great backlog of successes, it ranked only ninth in growth over the five years from 1977 to 1982 in the U.S. computer industry. By 1988 IBM's market share and profitability were declining across the board. Even in huge and very fast computers, where bigness gives its greatest advantages because of the vast capitalization and many specialities demanded, companies like Amdahl (seventh in growth during the same period) and Cray were very successful competitors. Today Digital Equipment Corporation is challenging IBM's core market, that of mainframes. In the beginning IBM was badly beaten in the most rapidly growing new realm of computers, that of personal computers, by total upstarts like Apple. Apple was created by two "whiz kids" with a bright idea and no bureaucratic planning and budget-allocation committees. Though IBM is one of the most creative big corporations in history, it did not even see the personal computer as worthwhile until a small company created it and made it a massive success. IBM managed to capture about half of the personal computer market in the early 1980s, but this share has declined rapidly and steadily since then.

Studies show that in general small firms produce as many as four times more major innovations than medium-sized firms and twenty-four times more than big firms. Big firms use their largely government-mandated advantages (see below) to buy into innovators who succeed, but they rarely produce major innovations themselves.[30] Because of the long-standing obsession with and dread of bigness, conglomeration and the takeovers of little companies by big ones get the headlines and airwaves. But deconglomeration and divestiture (selling off parts of a company) go unnoticed by almost everyone except investment bankers. Who noticed when Bendix sold its forest products subsidiary for $425 million? Or its holdings in Asarco for $340 million? Or Skagit? Or United Geophysical Corporation? Almost certainly not senators or journalists. Partly because of this lack of concern, and even more because most decentralization ("re-littling") of business is not reported outside of the companies, we don't know exactly how much is going on. But we do know a great deal about the trends.

Very importantly, the recent "mega-acquisitions" are not the result of any economies of scale that doom us to more bigness. As economists have long argued, there has been no net increase in market concentration, or control of markets by big companies, in the United States over the past century.[31] The conglomerations that increase concentrations in some industries and temporarily affect a broader spectrum of the economy at times, have been due very largely to our tax laws, inflation, unions, and other massive government controls in some segments of the economy (railroads, trucking, airlines) which have severely penalized new and small firms. One of these many incentives, the double taxation of corporate dividends (first as corporate income and then as individual income), has been very important as an incentive for individuals to let corporations reinvest profits *within* the company, even when higher rates of pretax return could be gotten elsewhere (say in money funds). This way only corporate taxes are paid until much later (perhaps after retirement). When individuals do receive the dividends or sell the stock, they pay the lower tax on capital gains. Even some of the provisions of the Reagan "economic renewal tax" changes compounded this government incentive to bigness. Worst of all, the "leaseback provision" subsidized the dying dinosaurs.

The recent surge in mergers is predominantly a result of high inflation and other investment uncertainties that make it less risky (or make it seem less risky to those who believe inflation, OPEC, and all the other effects of collectivism will continue) to buy already-established businesses or proven reserves than start new ones or expand old ones. Royal Little, who as chairman in the 1950s made Textron the first of the famous modern conglomerates, and in the late 1970s was part owner of a venture capital firm helping companies to deconglomerate, noted, "This [upsurge in mergers] is one of the results of double-digit inflation, which makes it so costly today to go out and buy something new."[32]

But note that, in spite of these government generated incentives to bigness, even today outright deconglomeration and divestiture are probably not too far behind the mergers in money terms. The fact is that most mergers do not make good economic sense and are far more the result of vanity or proud arrogance than profit motives.[33] Even with the government generated incentives, most mergers fail and are followed by outright divestitures, by partial spin-offs, by radical restructuring that decentralizes decision making, or by bankruptcy. In an unusual study of the outcomes of mergers, Arthur Lewis found that the ten largest mergers among *Fortune* 500's largest corporations in one year were overwhelmingly failures over ten years:

> Most of the acquisitions produced appallingly low returns during 1981. In three cases...the estimated return on investment was less than 5 percent. In three more cases...the return was between 5 percent and 10 percent...and none of them matched the 13.8 percent median return for all the companies in this year's *Fortune* 500. If we go beyond the statistics and consider the paths of some of these corporate marriages, the case for conglomeration looks even bleaker...[Our study] strongly supports the notion that investing in unfamiliar businesses is unduly perilous—just as the critics maintain. Most of the acquirers evidently were lured into buying unstable companies, or into committing foolish mistakes that harmed stable ones. Only two mergers remained trouble-free from beginning to end of the decade.[34]

The trend to littleness is equally clear even in companies that are growing in the shares of their markets. The old stereotypic view of big business as a monolith run by rigidly centralized, top-down command the way an army is thought to be run (but actually is only by the losers) has never been true for many. The dominant form has been the Sloan model of decentralization of most decisions, with centralization only of those required to keep control (such as auditing and financing). Contrary to some of the popular soul-searching going on in the aftermath of the Japanese challenge, a high degree of decentralization and its concomitant of individual decision making has probably always been the dominant form of management in American business, but the degree has varied vastly from one segment to another and over time. This variation in decentralized decision making has probably been due mostly to differences in technology and markets. *In general, the more complex and changing a technology, and the more competitive and changing a market, the more the incentives are for decentralized planning and execution.* American industries, faced with little European or Japanese competition, dominated their markets until the 1960s or, in some cases (like autos), the 1970s. In addition, in some industries, notably steel and autos, technology changed little. When the technology did change in steel manufacturing, dominance in the domestic market was partially maintained by the union wage at the big firms (which eliminated much competition) and then by protectionism—both the result of government. These conditions combined with other government-generated inducements to bigness, especially in taxation and regulations, to produce growing bigness in some segments, especially in autos and steel. But even in that period competition was so great and technological development so rapid that in general there was no increase in concentration in our overall industry, regardless of the conglomeration headlines and the pronouncements of antibusiness ideologues.[35] At the same time autos and some other segments got more concentrated, the more technical and competitive segments, like electronics and cameras, fragmented and littleness was rampant. Within companies like IBM and Polaroid, the growing proportion of technical specialists were increasingly free to create their own jobs and work in small teams, often in nearly independent "special business units." Today, even with those government-generated incentives, all really big corporations are severely threatened by the more slim-and-trim ones, especially the new ones. Even General Motors, which a few years ago seemed a secure Goliath, is severely threatened by the much smaller, highly decentralized and automated automakers of Japan—ten of them, not one. Without the government's "orderly trade agreements" with Japan, who would bet on this Goliath surviving David's onslaught?

The big businesses that are meeting the challenge are doing so by systematic decentralization, partial spin-offs, and subcontracting to small teams both within and outside the company. One of the most efficient and rapidly growing big companies, 3M, continually decentralizes even its manufacturing plants to keep employees down to a few hundred at each plant, and increases its incentives for individual initiative creativity. Gordon Engdahl, 3M's Vice President for Human Resources, summed up their view: "We are keenly aware of the disadvantages of large size. We make a conscious effort to keep our units as small as possible because we think it helps keep them flexible and vital. When one gets too large we break it apart. We like to say that our success in recent years is due to multiplication by division."[36]

In his study of Digital Equipment, Geoffrey Colvin noted the general principle of diminishing returns—and eventual death—from growing size: "In business, as in nature, there seems to be a law that things slow down as they grow toward the elephantine." How has Digital maintained its dazzling growth rate this long? First, it is still reasonably young and a pioneer in the most rapidly growing major segment of the world economy. Beyond those factors, the systematic pursuit of littleness—decentralized decision making—is crucial. They've never acquired *any* company. The corporation is broken down into eighteen largely autonomous units. Says security analyst Stephan Dube, "It's not one big business—it's eighteen small ones." The heart of any high technology firm is its engineers. Digital keeps them efficient and creative by decentralizing its 5,000 into quality teams of about thirty, by avoiding almost all bureaucratic rules and forms, and by keeping them in direct contact with the equipment in use and with customers. In the mid-1980s DEC's chief executive officer, Ken Olsen, recentralized control of major financial decisions, but insisted that "a good manager never has to make any decisions at all," by which he meant giving bureaucratic orders.[37]

Subcontracting to outsiders is not only the now-famous "secret" of much of the success of Japanese auto makers, but is also growing rapidly in businesses around the world. Much of the programming for computers, especially the new personal ones, is being created by Lone Ranger entrepreneurs in their home studies, and then marketed by the computer firms or retail outlets. Even once arrogant IBM has moved more to use these outsiders and make its products compatible with those of other firms. And in 1983 IBM signed its first contracts for joint ventures with much smaller and highly efficient Japanese manufacturers. Today almost all office work could be done at home—or anywhere in the world where a computer console can be plugged into the Worldwide Electronic Net—and thus subcontracted out to the most efficient.

The Electronic Revolution is now rapidly transforming business in all economically advanced societies, and most rapidly in the United States. Computers wed to robots are rapidly making it possible for minifactories to efficiently manufacture products with far greater flexibility than was previously possible, thus allowing a far greater variety in the end products. It is also more efficient now for companies that once needed to be centralized because of their specialized products to decentralize. The Electronic Revolution makes decentralization even more efficient and this will quickly eliminate our ancient bureaucratic dinosaurs. This is one major reason why companies have been moving from more expensive cities like New York to less expensive smaller ones, especially in the South and West, and even to nonurban areas. For years Harcourt Brace Jovanovich, a major publisher, has been decentralizing its corporate headquarters from New York City to San Diego, Orlando, Paris, Canada, and elsewhere. By 1982 only 2,000 of its 8,300 employees were still in New York. In February of that year William Jovanovich, the chairman and chief executive officer, announced that almost all the remaining 2,000 would leave the City, thus saving an estimated $20 million a year just by moving all publishing functions to San Diego.[38]

These subcontractors of bigger businesses are predominantly service workers, by far the most rapidly growing segment of our economy. The Secretariat of the General Agreement on Tariffs and Trade found that between 1970 and 1980 there was a net increase of 19 million jobs in the U.S., or 24 percent. Roughly 87 percent of these were service jobs and the great majority of these were in small firms—some of one person. One study of data on 5.6 million firms by an MIT group found that, between 1969 and 1976, 66 percent of new jobs in the U.S. were in firms with fewer than twenty employees.[39] Since the underground economy has been growing extremely rapidly, and since almost all of these consist of one or only a few individuals, far more than two-thirds of all new jobs are in very small firms. By contrast, the U.S. Census Bureau's "County Business Patterns" surveys show that the proportion of Americans working for companies with over 500 employees was 27.6 percent in 1967 and shrank to 22.4 percent in 1979—a decrease of one-fifth in a mere twelve years. In the 1970s, for example, the number of employees at U.S. Steel shrank by one-fourth, from 531,000 to 399,000. The explosive growth in venture capital companies, which are so vital in the start-up of these new companies, has been overwhelmingly in about 200 very small limited partnerships (of four members on average) and 100 larger but still small spin-offs from large companies (like Xerox and Citicorp), most very independent from their parents. The same thing is happening in the other industrialized nations. In Japan one Japanese worker out of six has his own business and some of these are one-person robot-run factories. Even in the big companies the emphasis is strongly against top-down, bureaucratic decision making and very much on individual and team decision making. As Ezra Vogel notes, "The essential building block of a Japanese company is not a man with a particular role assignment and his secretary and assistants, as might be the case in an American company. The essential building block of the organization is the section. A section might have perhaps eight or ten people. Within the section there is not as sharp a division of labor as in an American company. To some extent, each person in the same section shares the same overall responsibility."[40]

Vogel errs only in failing to realize that the most creative, efficient, profitable, and growing American companies in high technology and with highly competitive markets have been doing this for decades. Thomas Edison, who created the first modern research lab early in this century, ran it entirely on the principles of team spirit and individual initiative. He was continually quoted for his satirically apocalyptic, antibureaucratic pronouncements: "Organization! Hell! I'm the organization! . . . Hell! There ain't no rules around here! We are tryin' to accomplish somep'n'"[41] They did and later high technology firms like IBM followed in their path. The Japanese borrowed these ideas and sometimes improved on them. Big bureaucratized business in America was always partly a figment of the imaginations of socialistic critics, partly rationalistic-scientistic rhetoric, and the rest was overwhelmingly due to government mandates on union powers, taxes, inflation, regulation, and even direct procurement policies by the Defense Department.

In a recent update on his earlier prophecy, Norman Macrae finds that the Revolution of Littleness is rapidly gaining momentum.[42] In addition to the accelerating rate of decline of the big and creation of the little, he finds the remaining big are seeing the handwriting on the wall and are rapidly introducing "intrapreneurial practices": that is, more and more firms are breaking themselves up into largely autonomous teams that compete with each other in bidding for company projects.

The general point is to internalize losses and profits into the smallest idea-creation and product-manufacturing team possible—bring the market incentive to each individual as directly and immediately as possible, while at the same time optimizing all the powerful motivating forces of teamwork ("fellow feeling"). Macrae is well aware that this idea has long been used by very successful American companies. But what is new is the rapid spread of the practices and—even shocking—the spread of the message. There are now consultants in Sweden and the U.S. (such as Mr. Bob Schwartz's Tarrytown School for Entrepreneurs outside New York) and even professors (such as Reg Revans at Manchester College of Science and Technology) who are propagating the message. By the early 1980s best selling books like *In Search of Excellence*, *Theory Z*, *Megatrends*, and *Managing Chaos* were trumpeting the rediscovery of decentralized planning and littleness in general by the most successful businesses in the United States, Japan, and everywhere—and showing that the "rediscovery" has been even more needed by "experts" and journalists.[43]

As technology and competition increase, what is now an early but powerful trend will become a tidal rush. In a study by Arthur D. Little of twelve major corporations during the 1981–1983 recession, Robert Tomasko found that most of them were cutting back their strategic planning staffs, two drastically, and were decentralizing the remaining strategic planning.[44] They were seeing the handwriting on the wall writ large and were rushing to plan decentralized freedom to plan. They had learned the hard way the truth of Moltke's old adage, "No plan survives contact with the enemy," and of his general strategy for dealing with that truth, planned decentralization of planning. If the government ever stops mandating inflation and punishing small business with regulations and taxes, the Revolution of Littleness will sweep all before it. And the Second Age of Little Business will be an age of greater economic freedom, thus of ever greater creativity, efficiency, and growth for all of us.

The Myth of the Success of Centralized State Planning

Parallel to these discoveries about the planning of big business, political analysts and comparative economists were slowly discovering that the same thing was true, only more so, for the centralized planning by states.[45] First, those who followed the massive planning efforts of the Soviet Union and the communist nations of Eastern Europe discovered that their initial efforts to plan their economies went totally awry in the early years after the Russian Revolution (unless they actually planned to cut their production in half, murder many millions of their own citizens, and cripple their army by purges just before the Germans invaded); were never actually constructed or enforced as they were presented even in their heyday immediately after World War II, when soaring morale temporarily helped overcome the stagnation of bureaucratic planning; had to be continually revised in planning procedures and applications to meet the unexpected situations they helped to create; produced such extreme pathologies of information (such as overestimates of costs and materials needed, hidden inflation, lies about actual production, and a total absence in the early days of comparative opportunity costs of capital investment because of a lack of interest charges for capital) which they relied on to produce and carry out the plans that they could never know how their plans were related to realities, either before planning or after planning; consistently failed to achieve their goals even in the sectors they emphasized above all others (such as agricultural production), as seen whenever good evidence could be gotten; and in general were maintained as an ideological ideal to hide the fact that the societies were actually moving toward unplanned, largely underground, free markets to prevent complete stagnation.

It was commonly predicted by economists in the early 1980s that the supposedly planned economy of the Soviets will stagnate in the very near future.[46] Considering how much lying is done by production bureaucrats and government bureaucrats (as seen in all the official denunciations of such "crimes" and as seen in the official admissions in recent years by the Chinese government that they had lied consistently to hide the stagnation and decline of the Chinese economy years ago), and considering the fact that in recent years they have been living increasingly on stolen Western technology and on "loans" from Western banks, it seems very likely they have already stagnated and begun to decline in everything but military equipment. That certainly seems to have been Gorbachev's rationale for proclaiming massive "restructuring" to decentralize the whole Soviet economy. At the very least, it is obvious that state-planned agriculture long ago began to decline rapidly, in spite of massive increases in investment. The tiny individual plots of land which are totally unplanned by the rationalistic bureaucracies, but which are no doubt planned by the individual farmers, have rapidly expanded their percentage of total agricultural production and now are estimated to produce 30 to 40 percent of total food from roughly 3 to 10 percent of the land. Without that bit of individualized planning, their imports of grain and other foodstuffs would have been even more massive and would probably have drained all other investments. But, in addition to this vital sector of situated, individual planning, there is the huge and growing underground economy. Hedrick Smith and others estimate that the underground, free-market economy in the Soviet Union now constitutes 25 percent or more of total production. If things continue the way they have been going for the past several decades, such "communist" nations will wind up being the only free market economies in the world; they will be operating without rationalistic state planning but under the aegis of the total Scientific Plan. Of course, simple extrapolations never work for long, so we need not fear this outcome. For one thing, the real Western economies are also increasingly going underground.[47]

Because the Western nations got into rationalistic state planning later, more slowly, and generally in the more limited forms of monetary planning and Keynesian planning of a few economic aggregates, social scientists have been slower to recognize that the state planning of our nations has actually gone the same route as that of the communist nations. Compared to the massive amount that has been written about why and how we should do rationalistic planning (now commonly done in the guise of "cost-benefit analysis of policies"), the study of how planning is actually done and what its actual effects are is still in its infancy. But the overall outline seems startlingly clear. From their very beginnings in wartime planning, the centralized plans of Western states (other than monetary plans—see below) have been little more than rhetoric and the little more has been almost entirely a rationalistic idealization of political decisions that were the outcomes of conflicts among competing interest groups. During the war, the planning was very rough-and-ready, was changed rapidly to deal with its failures, and was done overwhelmingly by a few individuals, such as Alfred C. Marshall, who worked ferociously to keep in touch with the far-flung realities of wartime production and who made their decisions on the basis of highly situated, marginal individual planning, the same way typical individuals plan their small business or their everyday life. Lionel Robbins[48] has argued that this is actually how the Russians have "planned" their heavy industry from the beginning, thus forestalling the chaos Mises[49] predicted on the assumption they would act in accord with their planning rhetoric. The gap between the facade of planning appearances and reality is probably not as yawning in Russia as it was in fascist Italy,[50] but it is still huge. These planning decisions were gravely hampered by the informational pathologies resulting from programs planned rationally to help make them work, especially by the pathologies of pricing information produced by the price controls of Galbraith and his other rationalistic bureaucrats. Fortunately, the grave mistakes in the allocation of materials which would have resulted from these information pathologies were largely overcome by creating a massive underground economy with free-market prices in everything from meat and sugar for consumers to rubber and steel needed to make war machines.

In a less hectic day, C. Jackson Greyson was to reveal the deep, dark secret of the rationalistic planning of prices under the Nixon administration:

> Running a [price] Control System, it was found, was not calm, orderly application of economic theories, but an eclectic mixture of economics, power, pressure, and politics. It was a drain of trivial and major events, a clash of personalities, brinkmanship, day-to-day craziness, improvisations, and squabble. It involved all the problems, challenges, and pitfalls of creating and operating a large, new organization—whether in the public sector or in private industry—in a volatile, high-pressure situation. It included recruiting and organizing staff, setting goals, building morale, planning and participating in meaningful production meetings, establishing and maintaining internal communication and public information. . .[51]

In brief, the fact is that the price planners never had any consistent, systematic idea of what they were doing and they certainly never constructed any empirical, rational plan that they could effectively enforce. The whole scheme was largely a media event intended to show that they were doing something rational (scientific!) to solve the problem of inflation. Media releases were used to threaten businesspeople to try to hold back price increases. They may have done so in the short run, but the explosion in prices after they were removed probably more than made up for them. The later "price stabilization" or wage and price controls programs promulgated by Alfred Kahn during the Carter administration rarely amounted to anything more than a media con game. Kahn actually proved to be a wonderful master of ceremonies setting exactly the right tone of satire, self-deprecation, and slapstick for this foray into the higher mysteries of centrally planning how to "control" the trillions of pricing decisions in our economy.

When we look at the more general economic planning that Western nations have supposedly done, we find that in almost all (nonmonetary) cases, with the likely exceptions of the very small, homogeneous, centralized, and bureaucratized state such as Sweden and the Netherlands, these general economic plans have actually been either direct carryovers from wartime planning, as was true in Britain from about 1945 to 1951, or have functioned in the same ways. Britain has been subjected to the greatest amount of political rhetoric about general economic planning, by both the Labourites and the Conservatives. Detailed case studies of their planning, such as the four done by Jock Bruce-Gardyne and Nigel Lawson for the 1960s, shows that chance factors, such as the situation, time pressures, and persons involved, were in fact far more important than abstract reasoning, planning ideology, and so on, in determining what was actually done politically.[52] By the 1970s and 1980s, this was obvious because the general plans were being continually, often radically revised by minibudgets of the Exchequer, U-Turns by prime ministers, and an almost universal failure to meet the targets of any general plan.[53] A. A. Shenfield's early conclusion seemed even more warranted as the years wore on:

> The Labour Party has for many years proclaimed itself to be the party of economic planning. In fact, not merely has it never produced a blueprint for planning, but even when it was in power and believed itself to be planning the economy, it never produced anything more than a succession of expedients which resembled one another only in that they all confined, hobbled and undermined the processes of the market. . .in truth, neither of the two great political parties wants such "real" planning. Both seek the pretense of planning, not the reality. . .planning in the half-free economy is a species of magic. It has the power of magic over men's minds; and it has the inability of magic to master men's problems.[54]

Studies that have been done, even of the narrow realms of government planning, find that the rationalism of the plans is largely a rhetorical front intended to make whatever the bureaucrats are doing or want to do to look good—rational. William G. McDonald, administrator in the Office of Management and Budget and the Atomic Energy Commission, and from 1977 to 1980 executive director of the Federal Energy Regulatory Commission, and thus involved in the massive attempt to plan the entire energy future of American society, gave his conclusion concerning top-level planning in federal agencies. In his advice to incoming Reagan administrators, he advised them not to bother trying to plan:

> After resolving budget issues, you turn to the future. What plans does your agency have, you wonder? For an answer, you search out the members of your agency's long-range analysis division. When you figure out who they are, they're apt to be attending seminars sponsored by Brookings or the American Enterprise Institute on subjects like "How to Convert Performance Budgeting to Program Budgeting to Planning Programming to Budgeting to Management by Objective to Zero-Based Budgeting." You realize that you'll be long gone before any planning efforts reach fruition.[55]

The crucial immediate reason McDonald believed all attempts at systematic planning are irrelevant is that the actual plans adopted, the real plans as opposed to nominal plans by the administrators, are overwhelmingly the outcome of the conflicts between *micromanagers*, who could better be called *microplanners*, or simply the usual form of highly situated individual planners. Regardless of how much idealized rhetoric the administrators may give forth concerning rational planning, McDonald concluded:

> In short, you are about to become a fulltime budget examiner, personnel analyst, and EEO (Equal Employment Opportunity] adjudicator. You are not really going to be a manager. Federal executives have long since been deprived of the time to think through problems, plan, give policy direction, and control their agencies.[56]

At precisely the time welfare-state planning has grown massively, McDonald believes that federal bureaucracies have become less and less efficient at achieving anything:

> Productivity and efficiency slowly dwindle, and dwindle, and budget overruns and inability to manage critical programs are coming to typify the federal bureaucracy.[57]

The same kind of evidence is found over and over again wherever (nonmonetary) planning and its outcomes have been studied. The studies by Jane Jacobs[58] and Martin Anderson[59] are only the best known of the whole literature showing the vast differences between the plans for rational urban renewal, the actual operations of them, and, above all, the dreadful, unintended consequences. Daniel Patrick Moynihan's[60] classic study of the actual ways in which a crucial part of the famous war on poverty was "planned"— that is, by the compromising of conflicting individual political planning— needs hardly be supplemented with evidence showing how intended consequences, the elimination of poverty, did not materialize in official figures while unintended and dreaded consequences like dependency and urban unemployment blossomed. Edward Banfield,[61] Aaron Wildavsky,[62] and many others have shown that the supposedly rational planning of cities and congressional budgets are actually planned by the same log-rolling process, probably cannot be planned in any other way in our vastly pluralistic and conflictful democracy, and produce autocatalytic drifts toward economic catastrophe when the shared controls like gold standards and moral bans on deficits are eliminated.

The Central Planning of Money

No evidence concerning rationalistic state planning is more stunning than that concerning the planning of the money supplies, which was the earliest and has remained the most sweeping form of centralized planning in our democratic welfare states. In the United States at least, no state planning has been more independent of the daily conflicts of politics, and, thus, potentially more rationalizable, than that of the Federal Reserve. No sources of information for state planning are more valid and reliable. No goals could be easier to define and measure. No outcome could be easier to define and measure. But, again and again, regardless of the particular goal chosen, and regardless of the people doing the planning and implementing the plans, the plans have gone awry. Recessions have been exacerbated by intended and unintended swings downward in the monetary aggregates at just the wrong times; and inflation has been created in the same way. There may be disagreements over Milton Friedman and Anna Schwartz's argument that the Great Depression was the greatest modern calamity of state planning and managing of monetary aggregates,[63] but few historians of money would argue that the Federal Reserve has managed to achieve its simple, stated goals with anything much more than chance. The plans become more extensive, more rational. When the old plans fail, new ones are made and carried out. But the monetary swings grow wilder, the differences between plans and outcomes wider, threatening to go completely out of control some day, if indeed, they are not already completely out of the control of the Federal Reserve planners.

The plan for state monetary creation and control of its supply was, of course, justified "rationally" by the usual argument against free-market ordering, that is, that a rational planning of the money supply by central, state authorities would eliminate the "imperfections" (chaos in the money markets, inflexibilities, the "drag" of undersupplies, etc.) resulting from the individual planning that reigned under the gold standard. These arguments and many others were advanced from the very beginning by Federalists, especially Alexander Hamilton, to justify the establishment of a central bank of the United States to help develop and regulate business. At the Constitutional Convention Hamilton had proposed a constitution that would have almost eliminated the states and granted the president lifetime tenure. The plan no doubt seemed preposterous and outrageous to most of the constitutionalists, but Hamilton never really gave up on it. He "joined the system," as modernist radicals put it, and worked in every way possible as a "loose constructionist" of the meaning of the Constitution to centralize the powers of government and give them as much "energy" (his own term) as possible. As first secretary of the treasury, he immediately proposed the federal assumption of state war debts, which he admitted was intended to decrease the fiscal power of the states and to bond the allegiance of the rich creditors to the federal government. This idea was well supported by historical precedent. In Florence the public debt owned by its citizens was a primary reason they were willing to accept a veiled tyranny by the largest bankers, the Medici, when the debt became so huge that default loomed. The bank was his second proposal and was intended to allow the mobilization of greater credit for commercial expansion than seemed possible under the fragmented state banks, to regulate credit and, obviously enough, increase the forces of centralization. Probably the most appealing aspect of the plan to businesspeople was the mobilization of credit.

But why could private banks not expand their deposits sufficiently without a federal bank to provide the growing credit demands of growing businesses? Actually, they could have, just as they did after the Jacksonians "killed" the "monopoly" bank in 1832. But Hamilton was probably right that there were serious "market imperfections" (as the neoclassical economists eventually called them) in the banking mobilization of credit in the U.S. There still are. These are the massive state regulations (and eventually federal regulations) of banking explicitly aimed at, and actually producing, a massive decentralization of banking, great impediments to interstate banking, and severe constraints on what banks can do, thus largely preventing the development of investment banking along the lines found so massively in Germany and Japan. These severe regulations have been maintained for centuries primarily because of the pleas for protection against competition by local banks wishing to monopolize (or oligopolize) their local markets and by the pervasive, myth-inspired fears of banking monopoly felt by the very people being monopolized by their local banks. Banking, money, and credit are very important and very emotional. They also inspire vast uncertainties and, thus, myths, in the vast majority of people. Probably nothing, not even race or Catholicism, has inspired more populist mythmaking in America than these "mysteries" of money. Someday educators will discover that a knowledge of money is vastly more important to the average student than a knowledge of how to "diagram" sentences or even of Bernoulli's principle, which 99.99 percent will never use again. In short, government regulations produced market imperfections that rationally justified a massive ratchet-up in government powers. Hamilton had discovered the most important enabling rationalization for government powers in our modernist era.

From the time Jackson allowed the bank to die up to 1863, the United States had no central bank or legal federal regulation of banking. This is the bulk of the era that Page Smith has so rightly called the "most remarkable. . .in the history of the world" in his great work, *The Nation Comes of Age*:

> The period covered by this volume—1826 to 1861—is the most remarkable era in American history, or even, it might be argued, in the history of the world. It extends from the deaths of Thomas Jefferson and John Adams on July 4, 1826, to the fall of Fort Sumter, a period of thirty-five years. The simple statistics are awesome. The population of the United States in 1826 is estimated to have been in the neighborhood of 11,000,000. On the eve of the Civil War it was nearly 33,000,000. The country had grown at the rate of more than 33 percent per decade and the

population had tripled. Eight new states were added to the Union, carrying the stars and stripes to the Pacific Coast. The land area over which the federal government exercised control, including the territories of New Mexico, Utah, and Nebraska, almost doubled, from 1,749,000 square miles to 2,969,000.

There were no railroads in 1826; by the end of the era there were 31,000 miles of rails tying the country together. The value of farm produce increased from some four hundred million dollars at the beginning of the period to more than two billion at its end, a sixfold increase. Immigration, estimated to have been 13,908 in 1826, was 180,000 in 1861—a sharp decline from the peak year of 1851, when 474,398 immigrants entered American ports. Cumulative immigration for the period was in excess of 8,000,000.

But statistics only hint at a story of remarkable drama and complexity. . .[64]

This, of course, is the Golden Age of Constitutional America, the age of the vast explosion of economic freedom and political freedom that proved to all the world that the great American experiment in freedom ushered in by the Glorious Revolution was a success. The faith that "Freedom Works!" was stunningly confirmed by American experience. There were bank panics and recessions, especially the prolonged one of 1837 (coinciding with severe recessions in Europe, as has been true from the beginning of our nation) and the lesser but major ones in the 1840s and 1850s; but banks and the nation sprang back from these and surged forward to ever new heights. However, one crucial and fateful aspect of this explosion of freedom was the explosion of moral outrage over slavery, especially its extension to new territories and states. As we saw in chapter 4, with the coming of the Civil War came the beginning of the major ratchets-up in the business welfare state. Railroads were being built everywhere profits beckoned rational business planners, but the thirty-seventh Congress in 1862 saw an urgent necessity for an immense "giveaway" of public lands to the biggest oligopolists. Agriculture was exploding, so an Agriculture Department was necessary. And, obviously, the nation with the highest per capita education in the world needed land-grant colleges. One of the first major initiatives was the establishment of federal regulations of banks by the National Banking Act of 1863 and the passage of a 10 percent tax on notes issued by state-chartered banks, to force almost all banks to become federally regulated. The immediate rationale for the act was the pressing need to mobilize credit to buy government bonds, probably because state regulations impeded this. But the same general enabling rationalization was there as well. Daniel Elazar, an important liberal revisionist historian, has given us a remarkable illustration of how the fixed idea of the need for a central bank to rationally plan away banking problems can surmount any mountain of evidence:

After a decade of readjustment in the 1840s, during which the machinery of American government began its reorientation to serve a free enterprise, rather than a mercantilist, economic order and an expanding urban-industrial society, American governments entered a period of expansion that continued without interruption for two generations. Between 1837 and 1847, the previous course of governmental expansion was halted and even reversed. After the end of the Mexican War, new governmental vistas were opened, slowly at first, but with the impetus of the Civil War, rapidly enlarging in scope until World War I. . . .

The Civil War brought the next major change in American banking. The last vestiges of the earlier forms of federal-state collaboration in the field had disappeared by 1850, and a chaotic, unstable "system" of wild-cat banking had become the norm in most of the states. The Panic of 1857 demonstrated the need for some type of nationwide banking and currency system.[65]

The explosion of economic growth in the 1850s was *not* blamed on private banking. But the ordinary recession of 1857, such as always follows any vast exertion, be it in sports or economic life, was blamed on free enterprise. And did the new federal regulations end all of this "irrationalism" and "instability" of free markets? Elazar does not directly address the question, but allows the reader to assume it did. Actually, a great depression struck in 1867, a mere two years after the rational central plans were firmly in place. (With the passage of the 10 percent tax in 1865, state-chartered banks sank to about 300 and federal-chartered ones soared to about 1600.) Unlike Elazar, I will not leave you to assume that selective correlation proves universal causation, that this plan caused this great bank panic and depression. Actually, this great depression started in Europe and spread to the U.S. The Kreditanstalt bank in Vienna collapsed when loans to Eastern Europe went into default, the same scenario that signaled banks' instability before the Great Depression over 60 years later. My point is merely that government plans and controls did not stop it and may have exacerbated it. During this same period and throughout the century, the only banking system that was totally unregulated was that of Scotland; and the Scottish system was the only one that did *not* suffer great panics. This astounding fact, however, was unnoted by minds increasingly focused on the hopes inspired by the soaring myths of planning, of rationalism-scientism and modernism.

American bankers in the late nineteenth century found ways to escape the federal charters (just as they are doing today). National banks decreased from 2,700 in 1885 to 2,500 in 1890, while state banks increased from 975 to 2,100. The growth of the great New York banks helped to fan the dread of monopoly, already burning brightly because of the mergers craze of the 1890s and the antitrust controversy, but their growth also made it possible to mobilize credit and coordinate actions in meeting any panics. This is what Morgan did, along with cooperation from the Treasury, to prevent a collapse of the system in 1907. But did this stunning demonstration of the vast flexibility, efficiency, and rationality of free banking prove that banking freedom works? It did the opposite, of course. It proved the dangers of a banking monopoly and the vital need for a rationally planned government monopoly bank to solve the problems of irrationality, inflexibility, and inefficiency inherent in mature banking freedom. From then on it was only a short and rationalistic slide into a great central plan to end all monetary problems. It did not even take an economic crisis looming on the horizon to enact the Federal Reserve Act of 1913. Hope for rationalistic central planning was the dominant theme, as banking historian R. S. Sayres has emphasized:

> The development of the Bank of England's functions in the pre-1914 period had some influence on the American discussions leading up to the establishment of the Federal Reserve System in 1913–1914; but a more powerful influence was the desire to provide directly for avoidance of the supposed (and perhaps real) disadvantages of the existing monetary system under the National Bank Acts. The new system was to operate as lender of last resort, and so save the United States from the periodic breakdowns that had characterized the banking history of previous decades; but it was to go further, and provide an elastic system responsive to the "needs of trade" as manifested in the supply of good commercial paper in the commercial banks. It was also—in further protection against periodic breakdown, and to reduce the need to adjust internally in the face of an international disequilibrium—to pool the reserves.[66]

The severe inflation in the years immediately ahead and the deep recession of 1922 only proved the necessity of more rational planning:

> With its strong balance of payments and excessive gold reserve, the Federal Reserve System was then able to develop its open-market operations, *with discount rate policy in support*, for the purpose of stabilizing the price level, this being regarded as the most effective way of averting cyclical fluctuations in output and employment. From some points of view, this radical development of American monetary policy, dating from about 1923, can be considered the beginning of genuine central banking. In the sense of there being avowed recognition of a complex of public (noncommercial) objectives, and a final break from reliance on semiautomatic indicators within the central bank's asset structure, this is indeed the beginning of the self-conscious, discretionary central banking we know today.[67]

So began the rational planning of discount rates and open market operations that would feed the greatest inflationary bubble in securities in history and the most catastrophic deflation and banking panic in history. Once the inevitable bust of the bubble came and deflation spread, the Federal Reserve did nothing to stop it. In 1931 it did the opposite by raising the discount rate. The Friedmans argue that the system rejected the obvious solution, open-market purchases of government bonds, because of the usual dominance struggle:

> The System not only had the power to prevent the monetary collapse, it also knew how to use that power. In 1929, 1930, 1931, the New York Federal Reserve Bank

repeatedly urged the System to engage in large-scale open market purchases, the key action the System should have taken but did not. New York was overruled not because its proposals were demonstrated to be misdirected or not feasible but because of the struggle for power within the System, which made both other Federal Reserve Banks and the Board in Washington unwilling to accept New York's leadership.

One ironic result of the perverse monetary policy of the Federal Reserve Board, despite the good advice of the New York Federal Reserve Bank, was a complete victory for the Board against both New York and other Federal Reserve Banks in the struggle for power. The myth that private enterprise, including the private banking system, had failed and that government needed more power to counteract the alleged inherent instability of the free market, meant that the System's failure produced a political environment favorable to giving the Board greater control over the regional banks.[68]

When the panic reached a crescendo on the very day of the inauguration of Franklin Delano Roosevelt, had the people seen enough proof of the folly of rationalistic government planning? Of course not. Just as each burning of little old ladies fed the witch craze for almost two centuries, so the greatest crash fed the modernist craze for the central planning of money. The rationalistic banking plans of the New Deal were quickly followed by the rationalistic plan for a fixed-rate exchange system (pegged to a planned value for gold) established by the agreement at Bretton Woods in 1944. By the 1960s that rationalistic plan, combined with rationalistic planning of budgets and deficits by the Johnson administration, was producing wild gyrations in the international money markets, runs on the dollar, raids on the American gold reserves (especially by Gaullist France) because the planned value of American gold was far below the demand value based on relative rates of inflation (money supplies) and exchange, and threats of international monetary collapse.

It should be noted that there are major theorists who argue that the Federal Reserve is not actually very independent of longer-run political pressures and that its consistent record of failing to meet its stated plans to restrict monetary growth are a direct result of its political willingness to go along with the fiscally inflationary policies of the politicians by monetizing their deficits. Though I believe this is true of many of the failures of the Federal Reserve to meet its plans, I suspect many of its failures have also been unintentional. Because economists often implicitly believe too strongly in the power of planning to achieve its goals, they too easily see the failure of state plans as the result of some more effective hidden plan of individual politicians and fall into an overconspiratorialized view of politics.[69]

There can be little disagreement with their analysis of what the Fed has delivered, yet the fact is that chairman Volcker had consistently proclaimed that the Fed's goal was precisely that slow and sustained reduction in the rate of monetary growth, and economists like Martin Feldstein accepted this as fact. Volcker also consistently maintained, and very rightly I believe, that the rapidly changing and increasingly complex, worldwide money markets were producing growing uncertainties in monetary information. There is no reason to think Fed officials have been masters of deceit for the seventy years of their central planning, but there is every reason to believe central planning does not work. Political lies, conspiracies and, above all, self-deception under the powerful sway of the soaring drive for dominance are very important in politics; but when it comes to rationalistic state planning, the politicians are often the victims of their own best-laid plans because of the inherent failures of such planning. The more catastrophic the results of their monetary planning, the more their dominance striving is threatened, so the more they deceive themselves and others by blaming the catastrophes on economic freedom and plead for more power to solve the catastrophes. As the Friedmans concluded in their survey of the Federal Reserve's history, "In one respect the System has remained completely consistent throughout. It blames all problems on external influences beyond its control and takes credit for any and all favorable occurrences. It thereby continues to promote the myth that the private economy is unstable, while its behavior continues to document the reality that government is today the major source of economic instability."[70]

Milton Gilbert has revealed in his book *Quest for World Monetary Order*[71] how he progressively and reluctantly came to see that the earlier general plans had failed and were actually producing the exact opposite of what they were suppose to produce. He had been a firm believer in the Bretton Woods plan until he went to work as an economist with the Bank for International Settlements. It was only then that he could see in concrete detail the real effects of that plan in the real world of government-planned or -allowed dollar inflation. He then became progressively terrified of the possibilities of monetary chaos the plan was unintentionally producing. He argued strongly that the U.S. must double the official price of gold to bring it into line with the politically mandated and Fed-accommodated inflationary realities of the dollar. The politicians steadfastly refused. American monetary officials refused to support that proposal even when they agreed with the reasoning. Gilbert concluded that the dominance drive was the real reason for this bit of government planning:

> France advocated a policy that gave the U.S. an escape route, and the U.S. chose to forego this option rather than lose face to de Gaulle. . .the door closed on any reasoned discussion of the problem. . .Pride goeth before a fall, the Bible tells us. Pride was certainly involved in this case, but in order to pretend it was not the fall has been called a reform of the international monetary system.[72]

The "reform" was a return to the supposedly more chaotic free pricing of international currencies, or, rather, a partial return to a mixed free-and-managed currency—the so called "dirty float".

Many economists hoped that the free market in exchange rates would produce more discipline, hence stability, in the world's money markets. The idea was simple enough and right enough on the surface: any nation that inflated its money supplies would find, after some undeterminable lag period (which actually proved undeterminable enough to allow wild gyrations), that its exchange rate was sinking, thus raising the cost of its imports, thus raising its inflation rate, and so on until they got the message to decrease their money supplies to reverse this whole drift toward hyperinflation. Unfortunately, in an age of pop-Keynesianism, in which many economists and far more politicians were convinced that inflated money supplies, and even declining exchange rates, are necessary for economic growth, the float allowed money planners around the world to inflate without facing the consequences (depreciation of the currency in international exchange) for as much as a few years (with enough "currency support" operations), thus inspiring hopes among politicians of "flying up and out" to higher office (or retirement to the "out years" of history) before the inflationary pigeons came home to roost. Under the Carter administration, these hopes were so exuberant at first that the monetary officials in charge of the primary international reserve currency actually talked down the dollar around the world. Only when inflation soared, the dollar plummeted, and a panic in the security and money markets loomed did they suffer a rude awakening and begin to reign in the money presses, but not before interest rates had soared on the wings of "inflationary premiums" to levels that caused investment to plummet.

These hopes were also dashed by a more fundamental weakness of the international float. With no long-run constraint on the money planners, such as a gold standard or some other commodity standard would provide, there proved to be even longer time lags, and far less political accountability, associated with the expansion of international reserves. The stage, then, was set for the vast and unprecedented explosion of international loans from roughly 1973 to 1981, largely through the Eurodollar market. In less than a decade roughly one-half trillion dollars was loaned to huge bureaucratic governments of vastly variegated stripes and degrees around the world which were lavishly planning their economies, exchange rates, and anything else they hoped they could get control of.

Much of this money was even poured by nations like Mexico year after year into propping up their exchange rates to ward off the inflationary effects of their policies, thus preventing dissatisfaction at home. When the Western money planners finally recognized how rapidly the whole world was drifting toward financial catastrophe—hyperinflation followed by hyperdeflation—and finally began curtailing money growth, these huge loans could not be repaid in the short run because of the worldwide recession caused by the high interest rates and curtailed money supplies or even, most likely, in the long run because collectivist planning produces highly inefficient production that cannot compete in the world market against free market producers. By 1983 even the Reagan administration had exuberantly embraced the next ratchet-up in international money supplies, the doubling of the reserves of the International Monetary Fund, which were being used to bail out the de facto defaults by bureaucratic planners around the world, and which would lead to a further bout of inflation down the road unless the stagflation was already so severe that the newly printed money could only exacerbate it.[73]

The only real safety from the chaos of rationalistic state planning of the money supplies will be a return to free banking and some kind of money based on some basket of commodities. Regardless of the solution, there is simply no doubt that, since the seventeenth century, the Western world has experienced relatively ordered, stable, slowly changing and thus rationally anticipatable—within margins set by inherent uncertainties—money values and trends in worldwide financial markets, as long as it relied exclusively on the individually planned exchanges of gold for its monetary values; and that every prolonged, chaotic, unintended period of monetary values has been associated with government plans and operations to go off the gold standard or to return to it (as Britain did in 1818 and 1926) when the effects of those paper plans proved too chaotic. However, as in most other aspects of the modernist welfare state, this one should not surprise us: it is, after all, merely a repetition of the experience of all earlier state planning of money supplies.[74]

The Necessary Failure of Central Planning

The overwhelming record of rationalistic state planning shows that (1) the planning is almost always largely rhetoric that is not rationally constructed or seriously applied for long (if at all) in the extreme forms claimed by totalitarian welfare states; (2) in Western democracies the rhetoric of rationalism is an ex post facto cleaning up given to politically ad hoc'ed decisions that are the outcome of competing interest-group planning more like the individually situated kind than the officials realize; (3) the plans have to be continually "updated" merely to keep them some months or years behind rapidly changing events (seen, for example, in plans to "control" expenditures and achieve balanced budgets); (4) when actually enforced, as in the central planning of money, the plans generally produce information pathologies (see more on this in chapter 9) that make rational planning and monitoring of actual operations and outcomes impossible or "guessy" at best over the years; (5) and, above all, enforced rationalistic planning has far more externalities, or unintended and unwanted outcomes, than the aggregate of individual planning ever had. The overwhelming record of rationalistic state planning is an example of what Kenneth Boulding has called the Law of Political Irony: "...a great deal of what we do to help people actually hurts them, and a great deal of what we do to hurt them actually helps them."[75] Boulding seems to think there are many exceptions to this. In the case of rationalistic state planning, it would be difficult to find any desirable outcomes over the long run, though some must pop up by chance, especially in the short run.

Why is the record of rationalistic state planning such a dismal one? The obvious general answer from our argument is that the four assumptions of effective planning outlined above cannot be met by state planners with a minimal degree of success, especially not in societies with a considerable amount of individual freedom that allows the individuals to opt out of the state plans. Let us look briefly at the major failures of planning to meet these assumptions, in a slightly different order from that given above.

First, human actions are only partially patterned and, thus, are only partially predictable. When it comes to predicting the efficiency of individual production and individual satisfaction, the individuals are on average far more able to predict these successfully than anyone else because of human nature. The principle of situated rationality and efficiency guarantees us that, the further removed we are from the individuals, the less efficient we will be in planning their production and satisfaction; and, conversely, the closer we are to the individuals, the more successful we will be in planning efficiently their production and satisfaction. This general conclusion is, of course, completely contrary to all of the mythical and fraudulent claims made by the structural-functional social scientists that, since society is a separate level of order or reality, we can statistically predict aggregate or mass social phenomena more successfully than we can individual phenomena. All such grandiose schemes of structural, or collectivistic, social science have proven illusory, from the thousands of mechanistic theories over the centuries to Keynesian planning of aggregate demand. Such statistical "predictions" are always successful only to the degree that they describe, not predict, observed phenomena and simply extrapolate them into the future. Simple extrapolations work only as long as the parameters (the properties of situations) of individual choices remain the same, so extrapolations always fail rather quickly, even for what might seem to be simple predictions, such as the changes in population. As Sorokin showed in the 1930s, even individuals cannot predict their own behavior with the precision one might expect, especially when they are not tied down most of their waking hours to a job. But individuals can certainly predict far more with far greater reliability than anyone else could do.

Because of this great difficulty in predicting what people will do and what will satisfy them, planning that allows for a maximum of flexibility and quickness of change to meet changes in situations and in individual desires and abilities will produce maximum efficiency of production and satisfaction; and, of course, conversely. This principle of flexibility of planning is enshrined in all great military planning from Herodotus to Liddell Hart. At least three of Liddell Hart's six positive principles of strategy and tactics, and both of his negative ones, include implicit use of this principal of flexibility—such as "adapting your plan to circumstances".[76] Herodotus argued that the Greeks beat the vastly more numerous Persians because the Greeks had far more individual initiative. The same argument has been made for the superiority of Western armies over the Russian army, which largely paralyzes individual planning by holding every individual totally responsible for carrying out the commands of central headquarters. And what form of decision making gives us the maximum of such flexibility in planning? The sum of all individual planning, of course. What gives us the minimum of flexibility? The maximum of rationalistic planning for everyone by the most distant central planners.

Very importantly, individual planning is heuristic planning, or planning of general goals in vaguely hierarchicalized form that allows individuals to choose their commitments and their means of trying to achieve them in terms of the situations they face at any give time. Rationalistic planning, especially bureaucratized state planning, cannot be nearly so heuristic because of the requirements for legal, detailed bureaucratic action. A plan for millions, or even hundreds, of people must be highly stable and spelled out in order to coordinate their activities. Such plans cannot be changed overnight without producing general chaos. Individuals generally lead stable lives, but they also make sudden turns to take advantage of unpredicted situations to become more efficient in production or life satisfaction. They sometimes throw their own lives and those of people immediately dependent on them into chaos, but this does not disrupt everyone's life and lead to the general disruptions of institutional life that erratic state planning can produce. (Friedman and Schwartz contrast the flexibility of individual monetary planning by Morgan to meet the crisis of 1907 with the inflexibility of the Federal Reserve's planning to meet the crisis of 1928–29.[77])

Second, planning for other individuals is always coercive to some degree. As Murray Rothbard[78] has argued, planning for people is always partly a planning of prohibitions for them, a plan that they cannot do what they would otherwise do without the plan. Individuals can and do accept the planning of others for their lives in the limited degree that they see that planning authority as legitimate. They tend to see the planning authority to be legitimate in direct proportion to which they see the planner as personally committed to themselves, thus to their self-interests. Parents and other loved ones are the most legitimate planners for individuals, since they are genetically bonded to us. Distant, central, impersonal, bureaucratic planners are legitimate only to the degree we identify ourselves with the statist common interest and the rulers we believe represent it. But, as we expect from the theory of reciprocal altruism and exchange, planning is accepted to the degree that it *successfully* coincides with people's plans and self-interest, and allows them to satisfy their plans. As central state plans progressively take goods away from individuals and as they progressively fail to produce the promised goods, they progressively undermine the legitimacy of the state planners. This is the reason why democratic states must quickly change their plans and allow massive evasion of their plans—or merely pretend to plan, or move to the use of tyrannical force. Tyrannical governments can obviously do the most central planning and implementing of their plans, but even they find that the people eventually find ways to circumvent their coercive and failing plans—including the use of revolution. In order to avoid revolution, they must either abandon their plans or allow these evasions to a large degree, but, hopefully for them, not to the degree that the planners become totally irrelevant.

Finally, it has long been the hope of the more technocratic planners that they would overcome these general failings of state planning by producing scientific theories of human action that would allow them to predict what will make individual action most efficient and provide the most efficient satisfaction of individual desires. We have already seen that human beings are condemned to be partially free because of human nature. Precisely because we cannot predict our own actions totally, because we are programmed genetically to respond in good part to the situation at hand, no one else can predict scientifically how we will feel and respond to the emergent, partially unpredictable, situations.

For all of these basic reasons, rationalistic state planning has always failed. As we noted earlier, all imperial state bureaucracies have tried to rationally plan much of the lives of their subjects. Even the otherwise unrationalistic Chinese mandarins (neo-Confucians) came in time to develop highly rationalistic ideas about their bureaucratic rule. Imperial bureaucrats do this planning to increase their own dominance over the lives of the people, regardless of whether they call it the king's central plan, Comecon, or Planning for Freedom. And they make it rationalistic, to widely varying degrees, because that is the only form of planning that is really consistent with bureaucratic, legalistic rule. As the plans fail, the bureaucratic planners often denounce the specific plans, though they always try first to blame the failure of their plans on the "subversive" plans of individuals or small groups (such as administered prices of the steel industry, Genoese price fixers, etc.). But they cannot give up on their bureaucratic plans without giving up on bureaucratic rule, so they always come up with a New Plan. Bureaucratic planners are the world's greatest reformers of plans. The central plan has failed, but the reason is only that it was not a really true plan—long live central planning! The

Ptolemaic planners were great reformers, especially as the economy spiraled downward; the "arbitristas" were great reformers of Hapsburg and Bourbon schemes to plan the revival of the once individualistic, wealthy, and powerful Spanish nation; and our modern imperial state bureaucracies come up with endless plans to reform their plans. After carefully detailing the colossal costs of the Federal Reserve's planning of our money, William Greider concludes that we must have some undisclosed form of monetary planning by our politicians, whose ignorance of money he has also detailed.[79] The one thing they cannot admit is that rationalistic planning by the bureaucrats is itself the cause of the failures and that the one solution—the perfectly obvious solution—is to progressively eliminate such planning. Instead, they try to ratchet-up to a new level of state planning and, thus, a new level of bureaucratic and political power. And so we get the well-known spiral upward, the ratchet upward, in state powers and planning now so familiar in our modernist megastates.

But this does not mean that there is an iron cage of bureaucratic planning in our future. We have already seen that such plans inevitably fail in the long run and that people create massive ways of escaping and subverting them. The dangers is not that we shall end up in an eternal, bureaucratic iron cage. All such imperial bureaucracies have eventually been destroyed, very largely because of the social stagnation they cause and, often, the inflationary policies they then use to try to overcome the effects of stagnation. The danger, rather, is that our own bureaucratic planners will continue to ratchet-up their planning at a faster rate than people can escape or subvert them, thus producing the catastrophe of international economic chaos and political revolution which are the least intended, the worst externalities of scientistic, modernistic, and millennial state planning.

Statist Planning versus Spontaneous Natural Orders

All significant, general decisions of government economic policies involve a choice of basic theoretical positions, whether the policymaker realizes it or not. The theoretical choice is relatively simple for those who understand the issues involved. Unfortunately, the choice is so fundamental, that is, it concerns so many of the vast complexities of our national economies and our international economy, and it seems to involve so many inherent uncertainties, that it is very difficult to make on the basis of ordinary rules of rationality. Instead, in our Western democracies, politicians choose one of the major perspectives on political economics.

First, there is the slightly more complex version of the neoclassical general equilibrium theory, commonly known as the *conservative theory*, most systematically developed by Friedrich Hayek in *Law, Legislation and Liberty* but shared in slightly variable forms by all conservative economists. The vastly complex social order we know as the economy is the result of a centuries-long natural process of growth or evolution. The order is a spontaneous or natural system, not one purposefully devised by anyone. In fact, the natural system came about in spite of or in opposition to the dictates of government and church officials. The natural economic order came about as a result of millions of individuals pursuing the concrete goals dictated by human nature, culture, and individual decision making, which often meant violating the laws. Adam Smith, for example, saw the smuggling of scotch as one massive form of this. In fact, Jacob Viner noted what a large part Smith himself played in creating this system of natural liberty: "When Adam Smith, in 1778, entered into his duties as a commissioner of customs, he was astonished to find, expert though he already was, how much of his own personal effects consisted of articles of foreign manufacture which it was illegal not only to import but also to possess. . ."[80]

Our modern economies are so vastly complex and so intricately interdependent that they could not possibly have come about as the result of any form of purposeful, planned human activity. Just as no one could possibly build a human body, so no one could possibly build a national or international economy. This is what Adam Smith meant when he said that the market system came about as if it had been produced by an "invisible hand"—it is ordered in the same way the parts of a human body are, but no one can see or fully understand how it was done. More modern thinkers would add that the interdependencies of the vast multitude of parts of the natural order may well prove to be impossible to ever determine because when you intervene to study one part, this changes other parts, which later change the part you studied. In other words, there may be what scientists call *uncertainty effects* so that we can never attain a high degree of precise scientific knowledge about the total interdependencies of the system.

. This entire natural system developed in such a way that it has a built-in tendency to counteract changes and to approach or move toward a general equilibrium. Whenever some significant part of the system is changed by any force, the rest of the system changes, with time lags, in such ways as to adjust to the changed part of the system. Just as an increase in body temperature leads to increased sweating to decrease the body temperature, so an increased interest rate leads to decreased borrowing, decreased consumption, and many other changes that tend to produce a decreased demand for the accumulated savings, and these tend to counteract the increased interest rate. Thus, interest rates may vary considerably in the short run but over the long run tend toward oscillations around a mean, a quasi "steady state", in any free, natural economic order. If the short-run change is great, the overall effects on the system are great. In the natural state almost all great changes come about only over many years, so that innumerable adjustments are made and the overall effect on the system at one time is small and generally not noticeable to the people undergoing the drift so that people normally learn about systemic drifts by historians "discovering" them. For example, the Western world economies have adjusted in such piecemeal fashion to vast changes in basic technology such as no other period of human history has ever known, all without any catastrophic effects on the oscillating equilibrium of the natural economic order. Each time basic new technologies are introduced, such as the vast leap into the computer and automation technology we are now undergoing, there are profound effects on most of the economic order; but they take place over many years and innumerable small adjustments. Joseph Schumpeter, who accepted this general theory, believed that there were some technological changes that were so profound that they did have effects on such things as general growth rates over a number of decades, but he did not believe these were great enough at any one time to really detect them at the time they were occurring. Moreover, the existence of such Kondratief cycles now seems unlikely.

This theory was progressively modified to include consideration of changes, which can drastically affect the natural economic order so as to produce violent shifts and disorder in the short run. These changes are like violent shocks. If any such shock changes any of the basic factors involved in the order, there will be sudden or catastrophic shifts, sometimes in almost random or unordered form, in the drift toward a general equilibrium. Such short-run movements may be quite predictable, if they are not too great, but the long-run effects tend to be highly uncertain, or chaotic, because of our limited knowledge of the vastly complex natural order. For example, we may shift the general equilibrium upward for employment by introducing short-run fiscal stimulus, unless consumers and investors come to anticipate adverse long-run effects, as now seems to be true, in which case even the short-run effects may shift downward; but this dislocation of the drift toward a general equilibrium is adjusted to over the long run in vastly complex ways that tend to counteract it and with some very uncertain possibilities. For example, Friedrich Hayek long ago argued that in 1925 the American Federal Reserve shifted to an easy-money policy to stop a decline in production and employment, a recession that was coming about as a natural adjustment of the economy to earlier changes. This easy-money policy did reverse the decrease for three years, but it had the woefully unanticipated consequence of making the decrease much worse when it did come. In fact, the shift downward was so sharp it was of the nature of a *catastrophe*—major structural changes in credit and other factors occurred, which triggered a panic, thus producing a very great and progressive shift downward.[81] Milton Friedman and Anna Schwartz have argued that the Federal Reserve's adoption of a tight money policy after the shift downward had started was crucial in making a sharp shift into a catastrophe.

This theory leads to what is rightly called the *conservative strategy*, though in economics it was first espoused by the classical liberals of the eighteenth century. It is conservative not only because it is the same strategy espoused in politics by Edmund Burke, the father of modern conservatism (the Whig theory we might call *adjustments* or *reform conservatism*), but because it is based on the idea of conserving the natural forces of the natural order. Its key idea is relatively simple. In a world of vast complexity in which things work and in which we do not yet have much certain knowledge about how they work, the wise policymaker constrains himself to making only small adjustments in the system which his knowledge has shown him with minimal uncertainty do allow the natural system to work slightly better. Knowledge is thus far sufficient only to allow us to help the system work naturally, not to recreate any important parts of it. The crucial point is that when one is basically ignorant of the overall system most changes will have unknown consequences and, thus, create unknown risks. It was this same conservative strategy that led the great physiologist Cannon to rely on the natural wisdom of the human body, which has developed successfully out of inanimate matter over a few billion years, and to intervene only where his knowledge was certain—and then only to aid the natural processes.

The second theory, Keynesianism, differs from this classical one only in two major respects. It accepts the general idea of the moving equilibrium. But it insists that some movements (the drift toward equilibrium) can be catastrophic in nature, such that there is a general and protracted shift downward or upward. Keynesians argue that the Great Depression was such a catastrophic shift downward (with which the conservatives agree, as we have seen) and that a shift upward is only possible by purposeful intervention. It is only this second point with which the conservatives disagree. Some Keynesians believe the new equilibrium can be permanent, and only purposeful policies to shift it upward will get it up. The conservatives agree that this could be true, if policy choices have been made that introduce permanent, government made rigidities, or ratchets, into the natural order; but then all one has to do is remove the rigidities or find a way around them and the quasi-equilibrium will shift toward its long-run trend state over time, the length of time depending on how great the man-made shock has been. The more intervention, and, thus, the greater the shock, the more time required. Moreover, they argue, individuals will act to counteract these short-run interventions so that over the long run the net effect will either be nothing or worse. Hayek, for example, argued in the 1930s that each Keynesian shift upward would eventually be counteracted, a shift downward would take place, and consumer-producer anticipations would change so that the next attempt to shift the equilibrium upward would require more fiscal deficit spending than the time before, and so on into spiraling inflation.[82] This kind of argument has become basic to the *rational expectations theory* in economics today. Most conservatives do not generally believe our knowledge is adequate to be as certain as Hayek has generally sounded, but his predictions have come true and conservatives, while unwilling to cede the point, take experience as crucial.

It is the second point of difference which is really crucial. The Keynesians believe that we already have the certain knowledge needed to introduce these changes into the natural order to make it work better, to shift it upward. They thus believe that our interventions do not pose any significant risks of producing catastrophes. It is this point that is factually wrong. Anyone who has observed the vast disagreements over major economic issues among scholarly and brilliant economists would be apt to expect this. But there is a more basic reason. Any highly complex and changing natural system is so inherently difficult to study and scientifically understand that our knowledge of it necessarily has a high degree of uncertainty. This means that intervening in basic ways in such a vastly complex system will always involve some risks of producing violent and catastrophic shifts. (In medicine there are certain catastrophic risks involved in any major medical care. General anesthesia involves certain necessary risks of death. The probabilities are small, but the risks are great because of the huge consequences.) Anyone who carefully compares the predictions of these interventionist economists with the outcomes will find that the predictions are commonly wrong, sometimes by a huge margin. No honest man can really survey such facts and conclude that there are not major risks, including catastrophes, involved in such attempts to produce major changes in the great systemic drift.

Keynesians sometimes chide the conservative economists with lacking trust in the rationality of common people. The reason for this distrust should be obvious. The average voter and politician cannot be presumed, even by the wildest populist, to have more knowledge and wisdom about the vastly complex natural economic order than the economists. Nevertheless, the view of conservative economists is that, in relation to the vast complexity of that natural system, we are all necessarily partially ignorant. Their opposition to "expert planning" is based on their humility, not contempt for common people. Because of the principle of situated rationality, they believe common people are on the average quite rational in handling their own lives, or, at least, more rational than any outsider, such as an expert planner, could be. This is why they believe individuals should insist on almost unlimited freedom in making decisions over their own lives. Many will make mistakes, including some personally catastrophic ones, but these will be fewer than those produced by government experts, and they will be localized and counteracted by the vast natural economic system so that they rarely add up to a shock to the general equilibrium. When a president makes a wrong decision on how to intervene in the economy, we can all suffer vastly. When you or I make a mistake in the vastly complex natural system, it is only we who suffer, not everyone. That gives us vast personal motivation not to make a mistake, which combines with our greater knowledge of our own personal situations and our vastly complex and semiconscious desires to make a minimum number of mistakes. Pitirim Sorokin noted in 1937 that it is the planners who presume to be able to predict the reactions of millions who suffer from hubris: "To foresee accurately how every one of these millions would behave and what the results of such a complex of behaviors would be, under, let us say, the condition of the annihilation of private property, or under the NRA or AAA or the 'Soak the Rich' taxes or with the elimination of the gold standard, is a task for a Super-Genius or a Divine Mind, not for the mind of mortals."[83] It is precisely our greater knowledge of our own selves and situations which makes individual freedom both a wonderful goal in itself and a tremendously efficient way of doing things. And it is precisely the relative ignorance, probably the necessary, partial ignorance, of everyone in the face of the vastly complex natural order that makes everyone inefficient in intervening in its basic workings.

The Keynesians, especially those dedicated as well to so-called "welfare economics," like to insist that, in spite of all this, there is still a basic difference of values or morality. They insist that they are true egalitarians, in spite of their distrust of the rationality of common people in running their own personal production and consumption that leads Keynesians to insist the government should control ever more of their decisions for them, while the conservative economists are against equality. In pursuit of that equality, the modernists want the government to intervene to make more equality whereas the free operation of the natural system we now have produces inequality. Here there is some of the usual factual disagreement. Actually, almost every economic historian knows that the trend for over a hundred years has been toward greater economic equality, especially in consumption, so that in some way the system was leading to more and more economic equality. No serious historian of American and British life over the past few centuries doubts that the middle class has grown vastly. Our free societies led to the greatest explosion in political, economic, and status equality in the history of civilization. Not since the hunting and gathering societies have we human beings been so equal. The inherent tendency toward inequality in a free society, like that toward business concentration, is a minimyth springing from the myth of immiserization, the darker side of our great myth of secular millennialism. Our desires and our envy are so boundless that the slightest imperfection is intolerable. Whig conservatives do not argue in favor of inequality as a value position. They argue that unequal outcomes in a free-market situation are the result of unequal abilities, motives, work, and luck. Inequality is really a result of human nature—including wide differences in motives and abilities—acting in conjunction with the human condition.

There is one profound difference in the values inherent in the different theories. Given the inherent risks of intervening in the natural order, the real value disagreement is over how much risk we *should* take with the social world of us all. Modernists insist that we should be willing to take very great risks with everyone's economic and political life in order to produce somewhat greater economic equality for a minority. Conservatives argue, at least implicitly, that no goal they know of is worth taking such big risks of impoverishing everyone and destroying democracy (i.e., making us all equal in our poverty and submission). It is really the same value difference that exists between those who gamble to strike it rich and those who work and save to get ahead slowly but steadily. If you place a high value on gambling to get rich quick, but accept the great risk of winding up poor in the process, then the modernist policy makes sense. As Sorokin said during the days of the paltry planning of the New Deal, long before the Great Society's vault into the ninth heaven, "We live indeed in an age of the most reckless planning, in an age of adventurous gambling with the life and values of millions of human beings."[84] If you are not a high-roller type, or believe that you should restrict your high-rolling to yourself, rather than risking everyone's neck, then you should reject the modernist megastate gamble.

The Quick-Fix and Addictive Effects of Planned Inflation

Most educated people today are aware of the dangers of the quick-fix effects of many psychoactive drugs. Alcohol and barbiturates, which have basically similar psychoactive and physiological effects, make you feel very good and have relatively little adverse effect in the short run—unless you take very large doses. The pleasure creates its own desire for more of the same. But getting the same pleasure requires taking increasing doses because the central nervous system adapts to each level (builds tolerance) to maintain its "general equilibrium" (oscillations around a mean). In some people it seems impossible to stop this accelerating spiral upward and they wind up as addicts. Even at that, it takes years of the steady acceleration of abusive levels to produce liver, kidney, and brain damage. But people who start the small doses run some dangers of eventually accelerating their doses to suicidal levels; and those who get into a prolonged period of accelerating their doses face a growing risk of eventual catastrophe. The quick fix of emotional problems in the short run is tremendously tempting precisely because the universally recognized dangers are so far off in the long run. And once one is addicted, it is tremendously difficult to get off the path to catastrophe. That is why millions of Americans alive and well today will eventually die early deaths from drug use and why even more millions will die early deaths from lung cancer and heart disease caused by cigarette smoking. They know the dangers and as they become manifest many years from now most of them will make valiant efforts to get off the path to catastrophe. Millions of them will fail and will eventually pay for their quick-fix behavior.

The same kind of lag effects are even more common in the realm of economic relations. In the same way that short-run feelings of euphoria from drugs can lead eventually to unintended long-run catastrophes, so do some of the most pleasant and appealing short-run economic activities lead to long-run individual and social catastrophes in economic life. Perhaps it is worst of all that these lag effects are more common and more pronounced in aggregate economic relations than in individual ones. The fundamental reason government-spending programs have been so productive of votes in Western societies today is precisely that their complex lag effects were either not seen or were heavily discounted by voters or by most politicians. The importance of Keynesian economics in the development of these programs was that it seemed to the slightly more educated public to offer a way of breaking these lag effects. That mistaken belief led to a generation of quick-fix policies whose lag effects hit with great severity in the 1970s and early 1980s.

The addiction process of inflation is a reasonably simple result of building inflationary expectations into the whole economy. Many Keynesians now propose to institutionalize these inflationary expectations by "indexing" all wages. As we have seen, a basic reason for opting for the inflationary process was to provide a quick fix for unemployment resulting from the shocks of wartime dislocations, the Depression, OPEC, the sudden influx of women or young into the work force, and various other things. The unemployment is prevented in the pop-Keynesian scenario by lifting consumption to higher levels by printing money and distributing it to masses of voters. This increased consumption feeds price signals in the forms of continued sales and, thus, continued profits, throughout the economy which tell producers not to adjust to whatever has caused the earlier unemployment and, instead, to expect continued sales and profit increases along the same lines of production. The result is that they do not adjust to the changed market situation, or, at least, not in proportion to the earlier disturbance in sales. As any recurrence of the disturbance comes along, or as new ones come along, the whole economy must be inflated more to prevent adjustments that would cause temporary unemployment. This is all very much like drug addicts moving to higher and higher levels of drug use because each time they try to level off they feel let down, no high, and each time they try to go down they feel real pain. It is also like phobic people who constrict more and more of their lives to avoid the feared object. More and more of their lives come to arouse the fear, so the process can eventually lead to an anxiety neurosis in which there is no escape except by almost total constriction of life.

Over time, of course, the investors begin to consider the inflationary policies, monetary expansion, in their investment decisions. As more and more investors do this, the time lag between increased monetary expansion and full discounting of the effects of expansion decreases. That is, the printing of money comes to have less and less effect in producing increased investment along the same lines of activity. At the extreme, investors enter a state of inflationary panic in which they have so much fear of the inflation and the recession it will almost certainly produce at some point that they overreact by insisting on interest rates ("risk premiums") higher than the money expansion would otherwise call for. When that happens, if the government continues to pursue inflationary policies, a state of real stagflation would set in and the time of the Götterdämmerung of the Keynesian policies would be at hand. Drug addicts would say they are "burned out," that is, the drug no longer provides that blissful escape from grim realities; yet one still cannot come down without a crash, a very severe crash because one has gone so high in drug use. The United States pulled back from the escalator to hyperinflation in the mid-1980s and went through a severe recession to "wring out" those inflationary expectations. We have not even begun the long trek down the via doloroso of de-ratcheting our megastate.

There is a decisive objection to the issue of paper currency by governments, upon whatever principle it may be founded. The experience of all nations where this expedient has been adopted demonstrates that this is a prerogative which will always be abused. It gives almost unlimited facilities for raising money and has everywhere led to extravagant expenditures, public debt, and heavy burdens, always increasing and never diminished. Where extravagant appropriations can be met by a mere vote of Congress and without an immediate resort to the pockets of the people, there will be found no sufficient check to boundless prodigality, except when the government finally loses its credit by pushing it to excess. It is then that it reacts upon the people; for this great resource being exhausted, the whole super-structure of credit falls on their hands and they must bear it as best they can.

Martin Van Buren

Money is more than an economic artifact; it is an idea, a central feature of civilization, the health of which depends, in a liberal society, on not only today but on the distant future. Money is, as Keynes said, a link between the past, present and future, in order that long-term commitments and contracts can be made and kept at interest rates that express the real scarcity of capital and the urgency of time, with as little chance of forecasting error as humanly possible.

Robert Mundell

Notes

1. Italy still is the most communal of major European societies. Its localism and corporatism greatly weaken centralized powers, thereby allowing the underground, free economy to thrive more than in any other European country. The official figures often make Italy look like a catastrophe, but the everyday realities belie the statistics. See Dennis Mack Smith's *Mussolini* (New York: Knopf, 1982) for the facts about his early lust for power and his impassioned pronouncements about the need for rationalistic state planning by buffoons.

2. M. Rostovtzeff, *Social and Economic History of the Hellenistic World* (Oxford: Clarendon Press, 1941).

3. Pierre Leveque, *The Greek Adventure* (London: Weidenfeld and Nicolson, 1968).

4. Pitirim A. Sorokin, "Is Accurate Social Planning Possible?" *American Sociological Review*, vol. 1 (February 1936), pp. 12–25. Like other analysts who have addressed the question of the ancient origins of bureaucratic planning, Sorokin gave little consideration to planning by the imperial bureaucrats of China. As far as I know, no one has yet analyzed the fascinating and vastly complex history of Chinese imperial bureaucratic planning. The subject deserves a major work by a sinologist because it has been a crucial issue throughout much of Chinese history and China is almost an extreme test case of the inherent tendency of bureaucracies to move toward rationalistic planning. Strong traditions of Taoism and Buddhism in China have been explicitly counterposed to the rationalism, centralism, and control inherent in the idea of bureaucratic planning of life; yet the bureaucratic planners have risen to power over and over again since the legalists of ancient Ch'in. The bureaucratic planners and their stern opponents have waxed and waned over the eons, like some great tidal waves of political Yin and Yang, and dynasties have waxed and waned with them in complex ways not normally seen by historians (because of the complexly interdependent lag effects). Michael Loewe has shown how explicit and fierce the conflict was between the neo-Confucian bureaucratic planners, whom he appropriately calls the "modernists," and the "reformers" who wanted to return to the decentralized and unrationalized ways of the original Confucians. Though there are certainly important cultural differences, especially the relative lack of millennialism among the Chinese, there is a remarkable similarily in the rhetoric of the Chinese "modernists" and our modernists today. The biggest difference is that they propounded their theories of the necessity for bureaucratic central planning in the first century B.C. See Michael Lowe, *Crisis and Conflict in Han China* (London: George Allen & Unwin, 1974); and chapter 7.

5. Cyril Mango, *Byzantium: The Empire of New Rome* (New York: Charles Scribner's Sons, 1980), pp. 44–45.

6. Colbert, the most famous of the mercantilists (see chapter 4), was endlessly besieged by businesspeople trying to inform him of their local realities and of how absurd these made his new-industries plans (such as that for growing mulberries and silkworms to substitute for Japanese imports). Colbert, of course, "knew better" than these irrationalists, only the rationalistic plans did not work.

7. The sense of self is the highest-order, central integrating aspect of human nature. I have not taken the space to deal with it in the last or present chapter, but it underlies much of what I say in both. See my essay on "The Emergence, Security and Growth of the Sense of Self," in Andrea Fontana and Joseph Kotarba, eds., *The Existential Self in Society* (Chicago: University of Chicago Press, 1984).

8. Commonsense observation indicates that the most important factor in curing the mass of hypochondriacal illnesses that afflict our modernist society is getting the victims to focus their attention on something other than their bodies.

9. See, for example, Vera Lutz, *Central Planning for the Market Economy* (London: Longman, 1969); and Herbert Stein, in Lawrence Chickering, ed., *The Politics of Planning* (San Francisco: Institute for Contemporary Studies, 1976).

10. W. Arthur Lewis, "Development Planning," in David Sills, ed., *International Encyclopedia of the Social Sciences* (New York: Free Press, 1968), vol. 12, pp. 118–25.

11. Jan Tinbergen, *Central Planning* (New Haven: Yale University Press, 1964); and "Western European Economic Planning," in David Sills, ed., *International Encyclopedia of the Social Sciences* (New York: Free Press, 1968), vol. 12, pp. 102–10.

12. This point has been made by D. Elton Trueblood, "Logical and Ethical Planning," and James W. Wiggins, "The Contagion of Planning and the Total State," both in Helmut Schoeck and James W. Wiggins, *Central Planning and Neomercantilism* (Princeton, NJ: D. Van Nostrand, 1964).

13. F. F. Gilmore and R. G. Brandenburg, "Anatomy of Corporate Planning," *Harvard Business Review*, vol. 40, no. 6 (November–December 1962), pp. 61–69.

14. Ibid.

15. Ibid.

16. See Joseph Schumpeter, *Capitalism, Socialism and Democracy* (New York: Harper and Bros., 1942).

17. See, especially, John Kenneth Galbraith, *The New Industrial State* (Boston: Houghton Mifflin, 1967). In fact, the central planning of economies in both world wars was a political sham and produced chaos that was overcome only by economic dictators (called "czars") and massive underground free markets. The great mass of evidence is still unanalyzed, but Robert Higgs has begun to analyze it in "Military Scandal, Again," *The Wall Street Journal*, June 27, 1988.

18. Melville Dalton, *Men Who Manage* (New York: Wiley, 1955). Thomas Peters and Robert Waterman, *In Search Of Excellence* (New York: Harper and Row, 1982) are very aware of the other works in this development of thought (discussed below), but somehow failed to see the great importance of Dalton's far more empirical and creative work done a whole generation earlier.

19. I have analyzed the fundamental significance of this in *Existential Sociology* (Cambridge: Cambridge University Press, 1977). David Wessel ("Fickle Forecasters," *The Wall Street Journal*, December 31, 1987) has shown how economic analysts "adjusted" their mathematical models of prediction to fit their commonsense wisdom, market experience, and gut-level feelings.

20. Warren Bennis, *The Unconscious Conspiracy* (New York: AMACOM, 1976).

21. J. G. Marsh and Herbert Simon, *Organizations* (New York: Wiley, 1958).

22. C. E. Lindbloom, "The Science of 'Muddling Through'," in H. Igor Ansoff, *Business Strategy* (Harmondsworth, England: Penguin Books, 1969), pp. 41–60.

23. Quoted in ibid., pp. 43–44.

24. Almost everyone has been aware of the importance of technology in determining the degree of concentration of business, at least since Adam Smith's discussion of the specialization, or division, of labor. But this obvious correlation has hidden from most analysts the greater importance of government actions in producing concentration (or preventing it, as in banking in the U.S.). See,

especially, Dominick Armentano, *Antitrust and Monopoly* (New York: John Wiley, 1982).

25. An excellent example of this whole way of thinking can be seen in the recent work by Wyn Wachhorst on *Thomas Alva Edison: An American Myth* (Cambridge, MA: The MIT Press, 1981).

26. See Ronald Steel, *Walter Lippmann and the American Century* (Boston: Little, Brown, 1980).

27. Martin L. Fausold, Ed., *The Hoover Presidency* (Albany, NY: State University of New York Press, 1974), and David Burner, *Herbert Hoover* (New York: Alfred A. Knopf, 1978).

28. Galbraith, *The New Industrial State*, p. 32.

29. The evidence that concentration has not increased significantly in the past century in the U.S. is overwhelming. See Dominick Armentano, *Antitrust and Monopoly*, and Yale Brozen, *Mergers and Public Policy* (New York: Macmillan, 1983).

30. This has been shown in all studies I know of. The evidence has been reviewed in Thomas Peters and Robert Waterman, *In Search of Excellence*; and David L. Birch, *Job Creation in America* (New York: The Free Press, 1987).

31. See Armentano, *Antitrust and Monopoly*, and Brozen, *Mergers and Public Policy*.

32. Quoted in Arthur M. Louis, "The Bottom Line on Ten Big Mergers," *Fortune*, May 3, 1982, pp. 84–89.

33. The difference between "vanity" and "hubris" is merely one of degree.

34. Louis, "The Bottom Line on Ten Big Mergers."

35. See Armentano and Broazen.

36. *The Wall Street Journal*, Feb. 5, 1982. And see "Keeping the Fires Lit under the Innovators," *Fortune*, March 28, 1988.

37. Geoffrey Colvin, "The Astonishing Growth of DEC," *Fortune*, May 3, 1982.

38. Obviously, decentralization is easiest in "information" businesses, but CAD-CAM is rapidly spreading it to manufacturing on a worldwide basis.

39. This kind of evidence is reviewed in Thomas Peters and Robert Waterman, *In Search of Excellence*.

40. See, for example, Ezra Vogel's study of the Japanese economy, *Japan As Number One* (New York: Harper Colophon, 1979).

41. Wachhorst, *Thomas Alva Edison*, p. 183, p. 180.

42. Norman Macrae, "Intrapreneurial Now," *The Economist*, April 17, 1982, pp. 67–71.

43. Ibid.

44. Robert M. Tomasko, "Subbing Division Linework for Corporate Staff," *The Wall Street Journal*, March 28, 1983.

45. See Lawrence Chickering, ed., *The Politics of Planning*. Edward Tufte has shown that the "rational" planning of money supplies and expenditure timetables has really been a form of legalized graft, that of "gunning" the economy before elections so the incumbents will win. See his book *Political Control of the Economy* (Princeton, NJ: Princeton University Press, 1978).

46. See, especially, Marshall Goldman, *USSR in Crisis* (New York: W. W. Norton, 1983). His later works have shown that the Soviet economy has indeed stagnated. See *The Gorbachev Challenge* (W. W. Norton, 1987). In an interview on the MacNeil-Lehrer "NewsHour" on June 29, 1988, he reported that his recent trip to Russia had revealed even worse problems than he had expected, including economic scarcities.

In *Russia* (New York: Pocket Books, 1976), Robert Kaiser has described the Russian economy as "Inefficiency According to Plan."

47. There are no reliable studies of the size of underground economies in Western nations, but it is obvious to everyone that they have grown rapidly in recent years. Economists generally guesstimate the American underground at 10 percent to 20 percent of the visible economy. I guesstimate it to be larger (one-third) because of reports by financial analysts and the pervasive hatred of government among businesspeople.

48. Lionel Robbins, *Political Economy: Past and Present* (New York: Columbia University Press, 1976), pp. 143–45.

49. Ludwig Mises, *Socialism* (New Haven: Yale University Press, 1956).

50. See Dennis Mack Smith, *Mussolini*.

51. C. Jackson Grayson, *Confessions of a Price Controller* (Homewood, IL: Dow Jones-Irwin, Inc., 1974), p. ix.

52. Jock Bruce-Gardyne and Nigel Lawson, *The Power Game: An Examination of Decision-Making in Government* (London: Macmillan, 1976).

53. When "general" plans are endlessly revised by very situational, short-run plans, they are not general at all.

54. Arthur A. Shenfield, "Economic Planning in Great Britain: Pretense and Reality," in Schoeck and Wiggins, *Central Planning and Neomercantilism*.

55. "Welcome to Washington, Reagan Man," William G. McDonald, *Fortune* 102 (December 15, 1980), pp. 100–1.

56. Ibid., p. 104.

57. Ibid.

58. Jane Jacobs, *The Death and Life of Great American Cities* (New York: Vintage Books, 1961).

59. Martin Anderson, *The Federal Bulldozer* (Cambridge, MA: M.I.T. Press, 1964).

60. Daniel Patrick Moynihan, *Maximum Feasible Misunderstanding* (New York: Free Press, 1970).

61. Edward C. Banfield, *The Unheavenly City* (Boston: Little, Brown, 1968, 1970 [paper]).

62. Aaron B. Wildavsky, *The Politics of the Budgetary Process* (Boston: Little, Brown, 1979) and *Budgeting* (Boston: Little, Brown, 1975).

63. Milton Friedman and Anna Schwartz, *A Monetary History of the United States* (Princeton, NJ: Princeton University Press, 1963).

64. Page Smith, *The Nation Comes of Age* (New York: McGraw-Hill, 1981), p. xi.

65. Daniel Elazar, *The American Partnership* (Chicago: University of Chicago Press, 1962), pp. 238–39.

66. R. S. Sayres, "Central Banking," *Encyclopedia of the Social Sciences*, vol. 2, p. 4.

67. Ibid.

68. Milton and Rose Friedman, *Free to Choose* (New York: Harcourt, Brace, Jovanovich, 1980), pp. 85–86; 88–89.

69. Though I believe he has documented lying by Federal Reserve officials, William Greider (*Secrets of the Temple: How the Federal Reserve Runs the Country* [New York: Simon and Schuster, 1987]) seems to overdo the interpretation of conspiracy.

70. Friedman and Friedman, *Free to Choose*, p. 90. As noted earlier, William Greider has recently argued (in *Secrets of the Temple*) that the Federal Reserve officials have lied systematically.

71. Milton Gilbert, *Quest for World Monetary Order* (New York: Wiley, 1980).
72. Ibid.
73. It is not possible to *predict* such specific details as inflation, because of the inherent uncertainties in human life.
74. This fact was known to everyone with a classical education and was routinely pointed out by early American leaders.
75. Kenneth Boulding, *Ecodynamics* (Beverly Hills, CA: Sage Publications, 1978), p. 195.
76. B. H. Liddell Hart, *Strategy*, pp. 348–49.
77. Friedman and Anna Schwartz, *A Monetary History of the United States*.
78. Murray Rothbard, *Man, Economy, and State* (Los Angeles: Nash Publishing, 1970).
79. Greider, *Secrets of the Temple*.
80. Jacob Viner, "Mercantilist Thought," *Encyclopedia of the Social Sciences*, vol. 4, p. 440.
81. See Friedrich Hayek, *A Tiger by the Tail* (London: The Institute of Economic Affairs, 1972).
82. Ibid.
83. Sorokin, "Is Accurate Social Planning Possible?"
84. Ibid.

9

The Informational Pathologies
Inherent in Bureaucracy

The production targets set [by Communist China] for 1958 during the "great leap forward" were extremely ambitious and completely unrealistic. The statistical reporting system gradually developed since 1952 was cast aside, and the local cadres dutifully reported unprecedented but impossible achievements. In April 1959 the regime announced 100 percent increases in the output of food crops, cotton, and steel in 1958 alone.

Ta-Chung Liu

The government's struggle to reform itself has been the continuing political story of the 1970s, but often the story has a familiar ending. No sooner has an agency been set up to save the environment, deliver the mails, cure the sick or discover new sources of energy than it begins to behave like the many other government agencies, which were created years ago in similar bursts of enthusiasm but quickly crossed the threshhold into bureaucratic ossification.

Charles Peters and James Fallows

I once suggested to the officials at the Department of Health, Education and Welfare that they devote some hours a week to reflecting on the basic nature of the department, asking themselves questions like...What has HEW ever done that was effective? We decided, after a little thought, that the department's most far-reaching effects were unintended, as when its welfare program triggered the wholesale migration of poor Black people to the Northern cities...Had the department tried to do this deliberately, with some federal "New Start" program, it would almost surely have failed.

Richard Cornuelle

393

James MacGregor Burns, one of the foremost observers and analysts of power, has echoed the nearly universal dismay of intellectuals over the "crisis of leadership today," the simultaneous rise of the cult of celebrity and the decline of really effective leadership in all of our major modern nations. Almost all presidents and prime ministers in our democracies have quickly been branded failures, first by our journalists and then by large majorities of the public, almost regardless of how massive the electoral majorities that launched their administrations.

One parliamentary government after another has fallen in Europe as coalition and voter defections have spread, and most of those who have weathered the storm from one regular election to the next have then been swamped by tidal waves of voter outrage. In the middle and late 1970s voters turned out one socialist administration after another, even in Sweden, the most thoroughgoing welfare state of all and the only one in which the Socialist party had ruled uninterruptedly since the early 1930s. Editors of *The Economist* and many others aware of the dire threats to democracy posed by the welfare state hailed this supposed "tidal shift" toward economic liberty. But it soon became apparent these new administrations were either incapable of changing things much or lacked the courage to try. Then in the early 1980s the tide seemed to shift the other way. Even the most entrenched conservative party, that in highly centralized France, was turned out by a massive turn toward the freewheeling collectivist policies of Francois Mitterrand. Though the complete returns of history are not yet in on Mitterrand's record, to succeed his program of economic centralization would have had to repeal all the historical failings of the collectivist welfare states stretching from the ancient pharaohs to Giscard D'Estaing. The partial return in by early 1988 reveals that thus far he has found no new miracle policy for these ancient failures.

In the United States one presidential administration after another has been savaged by the newspeople, with the acquiescence of their viewers and readers, then voted out or resigned in disgrace, or departed in disarray. Even the love of journalists and the adroit management of the resurrected myth of Camelot could not save the Kennedy administration from retrospective news savagery. By the 1970s more and more Americans were becoming aroused over the threat of big government.

The public, according to recent public opinion polls, shows a splendidly nonpartisan skepticism about government operation and government spending. The Gallup Poll in October 1978 asked: "In your opinion, which of the following do you think will be the biggest threat to the country in the future—big business, big labor or big government?" By far the most common response was "big government." Of all respondents, 47% identified government, as did 52% of Republic respondents, 43% of Democratic respondents, and 51% of independents. (In comparison, 19% of the sample said big business, and another 19% said big labor, with the rest giving no opinion.) When the same question was asked in 1959, only 14% of the respondents had identified big government as the major threat. The October 1978 Gallup Poll asked: "Of every tax dollar that goes to the federal government in Washington, D.C., how many cents of each would you say are wasted?" The median of all responses was 48 cents; for Democrats, it was 49 cents, for Republicans 48 cents, and for independents 48 cents.[1]

In 1976 they elected Jimmy Carter after he attacked big government throughout his campaign. When he expanded government massively they threw him out and elected Ronald Reagan, a far sterner critic of big government. When Ronald Reagan began to waffle on cutting back government powers, his popular approval ratings in the polls sagged. When his administration usurped powers to carry on secret warfare policies in Nicaragua, they plummeted.

Marxists everywhere were thrilled to see one democratic administration after another destroyed by their own failures to manage our welfare states and by internal dissention. The true ideologues once again began the drumbeats of exultant prophesies about "the inherent contradictions of late capitalism." Eric Hobsbawm, the premier Marxist historian, proclaimed the death of the bourgeois era and the beginning of *The Age of Empire*, supposedly produced by the internal contradictions of late capitalism. The millennium was once again just around the corner. Not since the Great Depression had freedom seemed more endangered or "the ultimate solution" so near.

But the same crisis of leadership seemed to afflict the totalitarian "alternatives" even more. The Russian dictators failed one after another to slow the descent into stagnation of their whole economy and the ratchet-down of agricultural production, in spite of massive infusions of Western capital and technology. The Chinese Communist dictatorship declared their latest revolution dead and began introducing "revolutionary" ideas of economic freedom. Poland's workers forced one dictator out, then overthrew the next by using the old socialist tactic of the general strike, but this new semidictatorship of the proletariat seemed even less able to manage the huge Polish state bureaucracies than their neo-czarist regimes had been able to do. When the Jaruzelski junta imposed martial law to "get the economy moving," production spiraled downward at a dizzying pace, except in the coal mines where the junta imposed a lucrative system of wage incentives. Massive payoffs of the Iranian masses with OPEC booty did not save the shah's bloated regime from their wrath. And one military junta after another proved incapable of effectively managing the massive state bureaucracies developed by welfare statists in Latin America. The agrarian socialist junta of Peru even expressed dismay over the results of their Great Experiment in social planning—and gave up, allowing an elected government to inherit the remains in 1981. Gorbachev proclaimed bureaucratic communist central planning to be in a "precrisis" stage and vowed to transcend this betrayal of the historical process with "restructuring."

The persistent failures of all these different kinds of regimes to effectively manage their massive state apparatuses and thus to satisfy their electorates or subjects was enough to inspire a devoted anarchist with the hope that every form of state power had suddenly become inherently self-contradictory and was thus doomed. But this hope seems almost as doomed to frustration as the Marxists' hope. There are some very modern societies that are growing rapidly and seem still to be granted general legitimacy by their electors and subjects. Just as with the far more numerous failures, these successes show considerable variation in their political regimes. Switzerland, by far the most economically successful and politically stable nation in the world, is extremely democratic, even relying heavily on voter initiatives by which one welfare state panacea after another has been defeated. At the moment a few tiny OPEC states have greater per capita wealth. But this is due to OPEC monopoly power, which was far more the result of the failures of the U.S. government than anything else, and is now crumbling with the partial deregulation of energy in the U.S. Other democratic and semi-democratic states, especially Japan, Singapore, and Malaysia are also doing extremely well, and the democratic British crown colony of Hong Kong is doing very well. But the far less democratic state of Taiwan is also doing extremely well, and even the fascist but not very bureaucratized state of South Korea (now being democratized) did quite well, while the more totalitarian Communist state of North Korea has been such an economic disaster that at times its diplomats have caused their dictators considerable embarrassment abroad by using their diplomatic immunity to engage in petty smuggling. Some of these states have severe racial problems; some have the severe "social problems" of massive immigration, low literacy, and starting with excruciatingly low per capita incomes.

What makes the crucial difference? At first, just looking at the surface of things, one might be tempted to argue that all of the economic and political success stories have one thing in common—a relative lack of natural resources. Most of the governments rich in natural resources are doing miserably. Though obviously an exception in the short run, OPEC nations are rapidly eroding their political legitimacy at home. I for one will be surprised if most others do not follow the ill-fated path of Iran to civil war or to coups—unless they lose their monopolistic powers soon. Some, like Argentina, which has vast natural resources, and which in 1930 ranked in the top ten nations in per capita wealth, have plummeted downward economically and into civil war. Russia, with by far the richest natural resources of any nation or empire in history, has stagnated all of its economy, except armaments, at the level of the barely developed societies. As George

Champion has rightly observed, "The strength of a nation is a multiple of the character, energy and ability of its people, not its natural resources."[2]
All of the nations growing the most rapidly today started with almost nothing in natural resources, all had very low per capita incomes, and most were so overpopulated that American environmentalists and development economists would have declared them unlivable and beyond all help. But it turned out they were not beyond self-help and most of their inhabitants find them quite livable. Rather than fleeing, as millions are doing from the communist states, these states are desperately trying to stem the flood of refugees from the communist Edens. Are we, then, presented with some universal Galbraithian paradox, or a Marxist transformation myth come true—only extreme poverty produces rapid economic growth and political legitimacy? Unfortunately, poverty is no more a panacea for itself than sudden infusions of wealth are for poverty. Some of the poorest nations, like Egypt, Ghana, and Nicaragua, are remaining stagnant or getting poorer. General social trends are never the outcomes of humorous paradoxes and rarely are they outcomes of single factors.

Certainly there are a number of major factors at work in these international economic and political trends, all of which we shall be considering at various points in this book. The degree of homogeneity, versus heterogeneity, makes a tremendous difference in the trends of different nations. (I shall deal with this below.) One factor at work in all of them seems to be a growing international ethos of democratic humanitarianism—a direct product of the great Age of Democratic Revolutions—which makes it extremely costly, in an age of interdependent economies and of growing free speech, for any government to use the barbarities of Hitler and Stalin to force people to work. Even *command economies* use less stick today than Hitler and Stalin did.

Again, many social analysts argue that "the revolution of rising expectations" has affected our democratic welfare states and the totalitarian states at the same time, making it difficult for all of them to maintain their legitimacy and prompting voters and subjects to turn against any of them for even temporary failures to deliver on their promises. As Ronald Reagan discovered in the fall of 1981, journalists often start blaming politicians *before* their programs start. This "revolution" is one very important result of the more general myths of modernism, rationalism, and millennialism that have long been sweeping our Western democracies and are now spreading to other societies. We have our Keynesian myth of welfare state utopia; the totalitarians are stuck with their far more sweeping Marxist myth of scientific-determinist planning for Utopia. And there are variations in the degrees to which members of different cultures have accepted these myths. There is something in general more traditional, less utopian, more "stodgy" about the current populations of Switzerland and Japan; and something more millennial, more sweepingly impatient in many of the people in Britain, the U.S., France, and other nations. But, equally clearly, this is only one part of an adequate explanation. The one general factor that seems more than anything else to underlie the economic stagnation and political delegitimatization of states around the world is their relatively high degree of centralized bureaucratic power. By the same token, the one factor that all the relatively successful states have in common is a relatively low degree of real centralized, bureaucratic power.

The Footprints of the Imperial State Bureaucracy

There was a rapid increase in agricultural productivity. (Grain cultivation. . .benefitted from improved techniques of irrigation and a greater use of treadle pumps. . .Much more fertilizer was used. A wider range of seeds was used, permitting a variety of multiple cropping patterns. Iron farm tools became almost universal and several new tools were invented. Advanced practices. . .were disseminated through printed books, official proclamations, and the circulation of a concerned and informed bureaucratic elite. . .

Water transport witnessed a number of small but cumulatively critical improvements. . .

The construction of corrals and lockgates became more skillful. . .

The amount of money in circulation rose at least ten times in these. . .centuries. Paper money was invented, and so were many types of credit instrument. . .

A national market was established. . .there appeared a measure of regular regional interdependence in food-grains. . .many peasants took up commercially oriented handicrafts, forestry, pisciculture, and mining on a full or part-time basis. . .there were specialists in collection, transportation, warehousing, brokerage, wholesaling, retailing. . .the swelling volume of trade made it for the first time worthwhile for the government to set up a regular network of internal custom offices. . .

The greater productivity of agriculture, the reduced costs of transport, and the enhanced importance of commerce combined to create. . .many more large cities. . .even. . .(of) a predominantly industrial character. . .

Ferrous metallurgy took great strides forward with the general use of coal. . .and per-capita production rose rapidly. . .Large-scale government and private enterprises which, with their hundreds of furnace workers and thousands of ancillary workers, were not to be surpassed in size anywhere in the world until the creation of the Urals iron industry in the eighteenth century. . .

In his famous *Treatise on Agriculture*. . .(the author) described a machine for spinning hemp thread, the motive power for which could be provided by a man, an animal, or a water wheel. . .Its thirty-two spindles, he said, could spin approximately 130 pounds. . .of thread in twenty-four hours. . .

(The nation) produced an astonishing series of discoveries in mathematics and natural science. . .she was the most literate and the most numerate nation in the world.[3]

What have we here? Obviously a vastly enterprising, creative, inventive, and investing people in the early throes of an "industrial revolution," a nation in the takeoff phase of development. Could it be thirteenth- or fourteenth-century Northern Italy? Perhaps the massive iron works and the newly invented spinning machine mean it's late-eighteenth-century England about to launch the Industrial Revolution that would transform the entire world? Not at all. It's Mark Elvin's description of China in the eleventh to fourteenth centuries, hundreds of years before England launched the Second Western Industrial Revolution. It's the Medieval Chinese Economic Revolution.

But, of course, China today is a basically nonindustrialized and impoverished—underdeveloped—nation. Its "takeoff" was aborted into an appalling crash by the fifteenth and sixteenth century, by which time even the wondrous spinning machine had completely disappeared and apparently been forgotten. This was followed by foreign conquest, then by slow recovery over the next few centuries and then descent into new foreign conquest, terrible civil wars, and Maoistic totalitarian immiserization.

What aborted this soaring takeoff? Well, it obviously wasn't the result of "the inherent self-contradictions of late capitalism" or of some ineluctable Keynesian tendency of mature capitalism to oversave. It was a wonderfully robust and pervasive revolution, but it never got beyond the adolescent stage of the economic takeoff. What caused this Great Chinese Depression and the deindustrialization of China?

Elvin tries to explain it in terms of a neo-Malthusian High-Level Equilibrium Trap.[4] Essentially, he argues that in the eighteenth and nineteenth centuries the Chinese population grew massively and pressed agricultural production to a point at which there was little room for further increases, and thus little for savings to invest. He fails to see that Malthus was wrong, in general, but, even if he were right, Elvin can't explain a fifteenth- and sixteenth-century crash in terms of what happened one to two centuries later. He himself notes that plagues in the sixteenth and seventeenth century "may" have killed 40 percent of the population after the crash, certainly leaving plenty of resource room for savings and investment to develop a new industrial revolution.

When I read his account of the crash, I was not surprised at all and immediately guessed the many little proximate causes and the one prime mover of them all. When you know how the imperial state bureaucracies have unintentionally strangled to death flourishing economies since the dawn of civilization, it's easy to spot even the slimmest traces of their massive footprints. In the quote from Elvin, you'll note that the state started building custom (tariff) houses within the nation, that it had built massive ironworks, and that it was printing paper money. That meant it must have ruled by a powerful bureaucracy and the inherent autocatalytic pathologies of imperial bureaucracy would ineleuctably run their course, crushing the once-vigorous economy beneath it. Almost certainly the rulers and bureaucrats had finally planned production, imposed massive regulations, imposed massive taxation, and drowned the economy in a flood of papered inflation. And it seemed very likely they also fostered an antibusiness, probureaucracy philosophy and snobbery. Perhaps they even got control of education to homogenize this marvelously hybrid society.

I then got Elvin's own book, *The Pattern of the Chinese Past*,[5] which surveys China's entire past. I thought I'd become inured to the cataclysmic follies of rulers and imperial bureaucracies by seeing how they have ravaged so many other societies—and by having lived through the takeoff phase of the American Imperial Bureaucracy. But even I was appalled to see what the Ming dynasty had done. The Ming dynasty (1368–1644) inherited this economic revolution from the defeated Yüan (Mongol) dynasty (1279–1368). The Ming was probably the most powerful, most totalitarian, and for long the most secure of all Chinese dynasties. The first three emperors (1368–1424) were extremely despotic, and two of them were extremely active in building the massive imperial bureaucracy that was to last until the overthrow of the Ming by the conquering Manchus (Ch'ing) in 1644.

The initial impact was quite favorable. In fact, I expect a careful examination of this early phase of the Ming would reveal an excellent example of the spring flowers of state powers and inflation. The beginning of a great increase in legitimate state powers is generally felt to be quite beneficial by most people. Obviously, an increase in state powers by conquest or tyrannical coup may have the opposite effect. But even a new tyrannical state that increases domestic tranquillity, by, for example, ending civil war, or effectively reorganizes in other ways, such as by averting state bankruptcy, can propagate the spring flowers of imperial bureaucratic powers and, thereby, gain widespread, if grudging, legitimacy. As noted earlier, this is what Augustus, Cosimo de Medici, Lenin, Il Duce, and other successful totalitarian tyrants did. It is precisely the many spring flowers of such state powers that tempt so many people to mythically discount—or not see at all—the canker blooms they will inevitably produce in the fall—the much-derided long run that inevitably comes. Governments have thus been able to tempt a strong coalition of groups, especially when a central government can show them how support of the central government will give the coalition greater freedom from or superiority over some more local powers—either local government, or business, or labor, or someone. The kings of Europe generally got great support from the businesspeople of the free cities by promising and delivering an end to local tariffs and all kinds of feudal regulations and taxations. The Tudors of England were especially adept at this. Once they got rid of the feudal barriers, investment, production, and trade grew, thus enriching the people and the tax collectors in precisely the same way tariff unions do, such as that produced by the American Constitution, the German Verein in the nineteenth century, the EEC and Gatt since the 1950s. But now, as there were no feudal lords to counterbalance the growth of the kings' powers, central taxations and regulations grew rapidly and soon became the mercantilist monster known today as absolute monarchy, but called "benevolent absolutism" by intellectuals of that day supported by grants from the monarchs. It was precisely this process that led Montesquieu, Burke, and the American constitutionalists to see decentralized vested interests as a necessary check and balance to absolutist centralization. And this led recent theorists to argue that the *massification* of society—that is, the destruction of local ties—leads to totalitarianism and is supported by would-be totalitarians.

Though the Yüan (Mongol) dynasty had allowed this great commercial and industrial expansion to take off, the decline of the dynasty was accompanied by the usual breakdown of public order and thus the partial disruption of production and trade. The government issued huge quantities of paper money. As a contemporary source soon wailed, "In order to pay the army, countless notes were printed every day. They were loaded onto an endless line of boats and carts...At the capitol, paper money worth ten ingots [in face value] would not buy one-tenth of a picul of grain."[6] The despotism of the new Ming dynasty restored order and thus allowed business to resume. Also, the government soon started inflating the economy (no doubt in new currency promised to be "hard") to build public works and the bureaucracy. The early stages of a slowly increasing inflation, at least when hidden by a money illusion (as it would easily be in a society without recent experience of inflation), stimulates consumption, investment, production, and general optimism. These were the halcyon spring days of the Ming, but they proved to be an Indian summer for the Yüan industrial revolution.

Toward the end of their reign, the Mongols had forbidden private citizens to trade abroad. The Ming, with far more real powers of enforcement, soon began to try to close the entire society to *all* foreign trade. In 1394 private citizens were forbidden to use foreign goods. Only the state was to indulge in foreign trade. In 1397 only foreign ships bringing tribute were allowed to enter Chinese waters.[7] "New maritime edicts, with increasingly savage penalties for disobedience, were issued in 1433, 1449, and 1452. At some point...the ban was extended to coastal shipping, so that, in the famous phrase, 'there was not an inch of planking on the seas.'"[8] The supply-siders, as in all ages, argued that more taxes by far would be gotten by allowing trade and taxing it, but, as usual, they were overruled.[9] Not until 1567 was the ban partially rescinded.[10] Certainly there was smuggling, but the ban was no doubt devastating to the economy. The local gentry became the dominant smugglers, so they, like most of our regulated big businesses, supported the ban on foreign trade.

Since the Yüan inflation led to a flight of silver, Ming had little silver. The siege-economic policy prevented getting any, so silver was outlawed in 1428, paper money was "necessary," and in 1400 private people were forbidden to use anything but paper.[11] "A pical of rice cost two-and-a-half 'strings of cash' (paper) in 1385; by 1426 it cost fifty 'strings,' and by 1457 from 200 to 250."[12] In short, inflation increased, from almost nothing at the beginning of the dynasty, by about one hundred times in about seventy-five years.

A "bureaucratic monstrosity"[13] produced a prolonged economic depression. State bureaucratized education grew. The bureaucrats revived Confucianism and looked back to the ancient kingdom as a golden age. (Arnold Toynbee argues that the Ming dynasty "petrified" Chinese civilization.) Soon, the earlier optimism and realism in art and literature gave way to sixteenth-century pessimism and sophistic subjectivism.[14] No new inventions are known of after 1400 and some of the old ones disappeared. Very importantly, the initial activism of the rulers gave way to weakness; and the bloated bureaucracy became both inefficient and largely paralyzed by the internal factionalism of bureaucratic enfeudation, especially between the Confucians and the eunuchs. The Ming, like the Mongols before them, were now ready for conquest by a more militaristic people. The Manchus conquered them and their Ch'ing dynasty repeated the cycle from spring flowers to fall canker blooms. Out of their final corruption and disorder eventually came the Maoist megastate. Mao imposed such an immense, totalitarian bureaucratic plan and real enforcements that the "spring of a thousand blooms" turned to drab canker blooms in a few decades.

The Bureaucratic Cycle

Chinese scholars have long recognized that, with all due regard for situational perturbations, there is a remarkable consistency in the basic pattern of the rise, growth, decline, and fall of Chinese dynasties. They call it The Dynastic Cycle.[15] They recognize very clearly such Ibn Khaldun patterns as the initial vigor of administration, the expansion of bureaucracy, the use of increasingly formal-rationalistic methods of bureaucratic recruitment and administration, the growing distance from the people (increasing status symbolism), the growing inefficiency, the growing subversion of state goods and powers to the bureaucracy (corruption and usurpations), the explosion of bureaucratic factionalism (bureaucratic enfeudation and feudal civil war), the fluorescence of reform movements, the decline of imperial controls, growing rebellion by the populace, and then successful rebellion by regional warlords or foreign conquest by barbarians who have learned how to do things the Chinese way and improved on them; then they repeat the whole cycle. The full cycle rarely takes more than three centuries, though really extravagant dynasts like the First Great Emperor and Mao (whose disciples literally compared him to Shih Huang-Ti) can contract the time roughly by a factor of ten.

This same cycle has been repeated, and observed by social analysts, around the world. The Middle Eastern world has seen the cycle repeated over and over again, generally far more rapidly or in truncated form because of all the militaristic competition. Almost never do imperial bureaucracies last for more than about three centuries. Even Egypt, with probably the most isolated, slow-changing, and homogeneous empires of all time, and with the least centralized and oppressive most of the time, seems to have had only one dynasty last about five centuries. The more decentralized a state is, and the more it is built-up by hybridization from the traditional societies under its sway, the more lasting it tends to be. The reasons for this will be made clear by this chapter. Ancient Egypt, Persia, and Rome were among the most decentralized and hybridized states of all the empires, but these slowly gave way to centralization and nontraditional policies, that is, growing collectivist-bureaucratic powers, for reasons also to be analyzed here. This latter phase, which Toynbee called the phase of Caesarism, is also commonly associated with ferocious military adventurism both because the massive power lures the most power-hungry and triggers their power lust and because they need tribute to sustain their eroding economies. Even theocratic bureaucracies, like the Roman Catholic Church, go through the same cycle and only survive by going through profound purgations and restructurings, generally by an external sword.

It was such cycles that led Ibn Khaldun in the late fourteenth century to formulate the most developed form of what social scientists now call the *theory of the circulation of elites* or of "the lions and foxes."[16] Having been an administrator and political insider, like Machiavelli in the fifteenth century, Ibn Khaldun was aware of many of the minute manifestations of the bureaucratic phenomenon. He was quite aware of the vigor of the new administrators, their tendency to grapple with real problems directly, simply, and successfully. He was aware that the bureaucracies grow and eventually become stifling with their regulations and taxes, but he focused most of his attention on the way the new administration gets great revenue with low tax rates while the declining administration is eroding its tax base so that it takes in lower absolute revenues with much higher tax rates. So-called supply-side economists rediscovered this Ibn Khaldun truth in the 1970s and 1980s. Khaldun was especially aware of the decline in the dedication to goals and their courageous pursuit. First the swift and effective lions give way to the more indirect and sophisticated machinations of the political foxes, then they in turn give way to the increasingly devious, ineffective, and corrupt little foxes. The stage is then set for death and rebirth.

This cycle of birth, expansion, decline, and death of the bureaucratic empires has led social philosophers in the last three centuries to propose hundreds of theories to explain it. Many have been historicists of the Hegelian and Marxist type purporting to see the "necessary, inevitable, ineleuctable, fated, iron-rule" at work. Many have seized on the organismic (life-process) similarities and spun out elaborate theories by analogy. Some, far more empirical and sometimes scientific, have contented themselves with trying to show that there are vast cycles of civilizational processes at work as well as minicycles within these colosso-cycles. Certainly one of the most empirical was Pitirim Sorokin's *Social and Cultural Dynamics*, which argues that cultures necessarily change through cycles of Ideationalism to Idealism and then to Sensatism.[17] The Sensate period, of which he believes we are entering the final phase (crisis), is a period of Caesarism, of colossal government bureaucracy, especially of ferocious war machines. In this period liberty, equality, fraternity, and prosperity are destroyed by growing tyranny masquerading as the benevolent force of "true" freedom. The last of these four volumes was originally published in 1941, but in 1982 anyone reading Sorokin's conclusion to it, in which he predicts what would happen in Western culture, must feel a certain chilled apprehension that Sorokin was inspired by The Great Scriptwriter. While recognizing the common pattern of the disintegration of the imperial bureaucratic stages of civilization, Sorokin offers no serious explanation and in the end literally calls it "the great socio-cultural mystery."[18] Though a little less colossal and apocalyptic, the great historian Henri Pirenne noted that over the past one thousand years of Western civilization there have been three great cycles of massive growth of centralized government powers and bureaucracies and two of decentralization and growth of freedom. He believed the third and greatest period of centralization had barely started when he made his prediction in 1919.[19] At that time there were bits and pieces of bureaucratic collectivism in all Western nations, but only in a few nations, notably Germany, was the megastate firmly ensconced in mass education and in business. Still, when you've surveyed the vast panorama of history's imperial state bureaucracies, it is easy to detect the merest traces of their footprints—and easier to predict the outcome.

Arnold Toynbee has provided the most massive and serious descriptions of and explanation for the disintegration of civilizations. Drawing on the insights of the ancient historians, he argues that the disintegration phase is always one of Caesarism in which tyrannical bureaucratic rule replaces legitimacy and consent. People try increasingly to escape into mythical utopias of the past or future. New and revived religions flourish. But what causes it all? Toynbee sees it as ultimately a failure of individuals, above all of the once-creative elites to respond with adequate creativity, to new challenges. Why? This is the weakest part, but he does suggest one possibility: "We can become demoralized by success. This may make us lazy or self-satisfied or conceited. We may be intoxicated with the pride that goes before a fall."[20] More importantly, he argues that both growth and disintegration are cumulative, or autocatalytic. In the disintegration phase, each attempted solution is actually a failure to deal with the one underlying, persistent problem, and each failed attempt seems to make it worse, presumably because the nominal "reform" merely adds one more burden to the Christmas tree of bureaucracy:

> In a series in which the outcome of each successive encounter is not victory but defeat, the unanswered challenge can never be disposed of and is therefore bound to present itself again and again until it either receives some tardy and imperfect answer or else brings about the destruction of a society which has shown itself inveterately incapable of responding to it effectively. Thus, in the disintegrations of civilizations, the perpetual variety which gives light and life to their growths is replaced by a merciless uniformity, and intensification, instead of diversification, is the form of change which now relieves the monotony of the series of performances. At each performance, now, the challenge is the same as it has been at every performance which witnessed the original breakdown; but, after each successive failure to respond to it, the old unanswered challenge presents itself ever more insistently and in an ever more formidable shape, until at last it quite dominates and obsesses and overwhelms the unhappy souls that are being progressively defeated by it.[21]

We, of course, are quite aware of this same general dynastic process at work in bigger businesses and certainly in our own modernist bureaucracies. Almost all students of business organizations recognize the crises that often quickly follow the rapid growth of a company (thus producing a great expansion of bureaucracy), the transition from an entrepreneurial style to a routine managerial one, and that few corporations last more than about forty years unless propped up by government grants of monopoly powers, generally through protective tariffs, or subsidies. We have seen over and over again how vigorous and effective a new bureaucracy *can* be. Though we've also seen how drastically ineffective some are from the very beginning, I suspect that on average, the trim, dedicated new bureaucrats can be effective at achieving their goals as long as their goals are simply and clearly defined, their resources sufficient, and their knowledge, intelligence, and political acumen of at least average levels. But we also know what almost always happens within a decade or so. The Ibn Khaldun fate befalls them: they become increasingly inefficient, self-serving, enfeudated and faction ridden, resistant to basic changes, and prone to fits of public-relations "reforms" that do little more than rationalize their appeals for more power, money, and personnel.

Entrepreneurial Bureaucracies

These early bureaucracies are bureaucracies by any of the classical definitions. They have a legally defined hierarchy of offices and internal rules specifying roles and modes of operation to achieve specified goals. But they have a minimum of these and a maximum of dedicated motivation by their members to their agreed-upon goal. In short, in spite of the legal definitions and bureaucratic forms of operations, they have a great deal of entrepreneurial spirit working through and bending the rationalistic, legalistic forms to achieve their goals. Their goals and success or failure are clearly enough defined for them, often because of a crisis situation, that the achievement of these external goals becomes a "profit" for them by which they can measure their success or failure. They use the bureaucratic forms flexibly to maximize their profits—the degree of profit provides them with a sense of individual feedback on the efficiency of their actions, and they adjust their actions to try to increase these profits, and so on. Let's take a look at an *entrepreneurial bureaucrat* of this sort at work on a colossal scale, under the immense time pressures of a great crisis, doing something totally new for him and all his staff, and let us take what might seem like an impossible case—that of a federal social welfare program:

> In October, 1933, with a desperate winter approaching, Roosevelt instructed Hopkins to act fast. Hopkins consulted both his own staff and outside contacts in the welfare and academic communities. The idea of federal work relief emerged from talks with two experts in public administration, Frank Bane, a professor of social welfare at the University of Chicago, and Louis Brownlow, Director of Public Administration Clearing House. They were among the men who supplied facts, figures, and precedents to persuade Roosevelt that a vast federal work relief plan not only was workable and salable but was also more desirable than a state-administered grant-in-aid program.

> With the continuing assistance of Bane and Brownlow, Hopkin's staff drafted the CWA program in about two weeks. They abolished the means test as undermining the self-respect of the unemployed. Within sixty days over four million unemployed had been put to work. All this was accomplished with a small staff of dedicated administrators who felt they were waging a holy war against want and were thus willing to put in killing hours. By the end of the first year Hopkins and his 121 civil servants, on a payroll of only $22,000 a month, had helped seventeen million work relief recipients. Total spending for the year was one and a half billion dollars, a sum which in 1966 dollars exceed the annual cost of the Great Society's entire anti-poverty program.[22]

Now, regardless of what one might think of the goals and actual long-run effects of WPA, I think there can be no denying that Harry Hopkins in this instance was working like a classic American entrepreneur. He was simply a public entrepreneurial bureaucrat. I strongly expect that close examination of the springtime of any very successful bureaucracy, whether private or state, will show such entrepreneurial bureaucrats feverishly and creatively at work maximizing whatever their goal is. These are the kind of people working the same way who made our semibureaucratized war planning and production work as well as they did. I believe the public has always failed to see how entrepreneurial their efforts were, how much the planning rhetoric was a front for individual planning fiats, how much their efforts were complemented by the free market and black market, how dedicated the public and the bureaucrats were to one clear and simple goal (increasing war production to win the war), how willing—moralized—people were to sacrifice for the general good, and how vast the waste was. But, regardless, entrepreneurial bureaucrats like this can make things go on a colossal scale. They are uplifted with ideals, with bounding confidence, with trust and belief in their master. Albert Speer and his dedicated team of wartime production staff in Nazi Germany was an excellent example. *Inside the Third Reich* shows how he circumvented all the traditional state bureaucracies and fought to prevent the extreme, rationalistic, bureaucratization of his team. Even today we can see some of these people at the highest level of our bureaucratic monstrosities. Joseph Califano was a good example under Jimmy Carter. In the springtime of imperial bureaucracies, these men and women produce the spring flowers of the bureaucratic rule which tempted people down this path to begin with. It is precisely because entrepreneurial bureaucracy appears to work in the beginning, at least in comparison with what went before, that people demand more and get hooked on it. Toynbee was right: it is an auto-catalytic process.

But, now, compare those beginnings by Harry Hopkins with Lyndon Johnson's War On Poverty and our welfare programs today, such as Aid to Families with Dependent Children. There is a huge literature on these programs, much of it produced or paid for by the bureaucrats themselves. The overwhelming impression of any outsider must be that there is almost no comparison. The bureaucracies have become immense, most of their resources go to the bureaucrats and their retainers (planners, consultants, "welfare whores," conferees, etc.), and there is remarkably little payoff for their expenditures that can be detected.[23] The payoff of such programs would presumably be recipients becoming independent of the dole. The actual result has been the opposite, that is, increased dependency, an increased demand for continuing and expanding the dole, even when the individual "clients" show a high turnover. The general conclusion is that much of their resources have gone to the bureaucrats and their retainers, not to the poor. And their general operation and effect is characterized by what Daniel Patrick Moynihan aptly called *maximum feasible misunderstanding*. Anyone who has watched them work knows that some of the bureaucrats are still dedicated, at least when they begin, but they soon burn out from the immensity of the rules, the relative inflexibility of the regulations, and the apparent uselessness and unprofitability of all their efforts. Most of them spend most of their working day consulting with each other, doing endless paperwork "dictation" (such as in AFDC) intended to justify their departmental budgets and "cover their asses," and "hiding out" in leisurely activities. The lower levels are highly alienated and have added another level of inflexible bureaucracy in the form of union rules. They are highly politicized and far more dedicated to lobbying for salary raises and keeping out less costly competitors by getting ever more "certification regulations" passed than to helping the poor. Careerism, alienation, factionalism, inefficiency, and displacement of goals are their most important products. Any competition would have bankrupted them long ago. Only government monopoly keeps them going.

The crucial point is that we must not see state bureaucratic systems of action and free-market systems of action as polar opposites: there is a continuum of totally unfree (inflexible) to totally free (flexible) action and a separate continuum of openness to information-feedback to closedness to information-feedback on the consequences of one's actions. Any individual or organized group actions can fall anywhere along these two continua, and where they fall on the two continua can be quite independent of each other. Now, the overwhelming finding about bureaucracies is that they fall to the right of center on both continua relative to where entrepreneurial action in a highly free-market situation falls; and, more importantly, they tend to move further to the right toward more inflexibility or less freedom of actors; and toward more closedness to information feedback on the consequences of their action. This has overwhelming consequences over the long run and it is this we want most to explain. But it only obscures our attempt to explain the phenomena when we talk in terms of polarized categories.

Although, as we shall see, I believe Ludwig Mises's[24] explanation of the dynamic process is basically correct, he has dealt too much with such polarized "ideal types." In the real world, as distinct from prescriptive models, there are government bureaucracies and business bureaucracies of many different degrees of freedom in action and openness-closedness to feedback about the consequences of their actions. It is quite true, as Mises argues, that without government bureaucratic controls firms in a free market will over the long run move toward greater freedom and openness—or be replaced by those that do. But in our world of massive government bureaucratic regulation, we can only rarely see that idealized process at work. On the other hand, they sometimes see some very rigid and closed industrial bureaucracies being prodded by new government bureaucracies to become more freely competitive and open. In his classical analysis of French business and government bureaucracies, Michel Crozier has even argued that the government bureaucracies first shielded the business bureaucracies from most free competition with each other, thus allowing French business to be far more family centered, paternalistic, concentrated, and centralized, thus less flexible and open, than in any other major Western nation. Then in fits and starts (especially during revolutionary eras of crisis) the government bureaucrats almost force the businesses to move to a new phase of flexibility and openness. The government bureaucracies are first the protection of relative inflexibility and closedness—and then when the people rebel or revolt the bureaucrats force more flexibility and openness.[25] Of course, Crozier, writing in 1963, did not expect that the long-run trend would lead to a gigantic jump in government bureaucratized industry under the Mitterrand regime. (Mises could have sighed, "I told you so.") But, still, in the short run Crozier saw some important fluctuations.

It is also important to recognize different degrees of unfreedom and closedness; that these greatly affect the pace of stagnation in collectivist states; and that reforms during crises can sometimes, if rarely, work over the short run. It is especially important to see the springtime phenomena to understand why people opt for the tortuous path of the bureaucratized life. Above all, we must see the general processes at work because, if we are ever going to debureaucratize our societies, we shall have to use entrepreneurial government bureaucracies to do so—or resort to violence.[26]

The General Principles of Information Systems and Bureaucracies

The earliest of the modern analysts of bureaucracy were concerned predominantly with the nineteenth-century Prussian model enshrined in theory by Max Weber.[27] In simplest terms, Weber and his successors saw bureaucracy as a "simple hierarchicalized centralized system" in which authorities at the top set up a general plan of rules of behavior for subordinates for rationally, thus, supposedly, efficiently, achieving their goals. This model was based largely on official information and, even worse, on official presentations to the public of their legality, rationality, efficiency, and benevolence. Nevertheless, this model roughly fit the behavior of state monopolistic bureaucracies in Northern Europe carrying out simple tasks like delivering the mail, for which there is a clear and valid set of information about output or payoff—the number of letters delivered, speed, and reliability. Especially in the Germanic nations, the state functionaries had a long history of relatively high social status going back to Frederick the Great, who declared, "I am the first servant of the state." Top officials were even at times of noble families. They shared a homogeneous subculture with high morale—dedication to duty. Since their tasks were very routinized, and they could never be compared to any kind of private-enterprise mail delivery, they got the job done and looked efficient.[28] Weber, and later Karl Mannheim, were taken in by appearances and overgeneralized. Weber thus feared the whole modern world would some day live in an iron cage of rigid, "rationally efficient," authoritarian bureaucratic rules. Lenin, relishing what they dreaded, exulted in the image of all Russia being run like the post office. And today much of it is. But the system and its effects fit Lenin's utopian dreams in only one respect—totalitarianism.

In recent decades all direct experience with and in-depth research on bureaucracies show the real world to be very different from the rationalistic model. Even the most traditional and authority-bound, with the simplest and most unchanging tasks to perform, like the post offices, must use a great deal of informal action to make the formal rules work,[29] and they generate a great deal of alienation—demoralization—both among their own workers and their clientele. Almost all serious students have at least tacitly agreed that the commonsense view of state bureaucracies handed down from the age of monarchical absolutism is right—they really are terribly inefficient and largely unresponsive to feedback from their clientele. In fact, even the best sociologists who do these studies have either decided Mises was right in arguing there is no way to determine their efficiency, or else they don't even seriously consider the question. Rarely do these analysts concern themselves with demoralization, responsibility, long run, historical trends, stagnation, usurpations, or corruption.[30] Their policy orientation seems to be implicitly based on the assumption "OK, sure, these bureaucratic Behemoths of the welfare state are generally pretty dreadful—but note we found one that might not be so today!—and you can trust us technocrats to figure out a way to solve all these problems." My general impression is that the technocrats are actually drowning in a sea of variables—environments, competition, technologies, numerous vertical structures, numerous horizontal structures, centralization-decentralization, recruitment practices, subcultures—and regression analyses. The complexity of all the waves and ripples hides the whirlpool from them, so we're all threatened with drowning while they try to predict what is probably unpredictable.

The best recent theorists recognize that bureaucracies become progressively unfree and closed to information feedback because something goes progressively wrong with the information they create and process. This is very clear historically and, indeed, has become obvious over our own lifetime. The crucial question is *why*? What are the basic processes at work? With some modifications to fit the evidence, the *information theory of bureaucracy* created by Mises, Hayek, and Sowell shows what they are.

The basic idea goes back to the argument of Edmund Burke that the collective social rules, or customs, of a society have a collective wisdom that goes beyond the conscious, rational knowledge of any individual or even of all individuals combined.[31] These rules "tell" members of the society how they can live together with roughly the same degree of happiness as others who lived by them did in the past. They tell individuals how to order their lives relative to everyone else, but they do this by a remarkably economical use of information. The potential relations among members of a society are unbelievably large, so large that no group of people could write out a program telling them how to do so. Social rules don't do so either. Rather, they provide us with a reasonably consistent set of interdependent rules that tell us how in general—heuristically—to relate to other people in everyday situations. Some of these rules also tell us how to reason and how to relate rules to each other and to situations. One subset of these rules about rules even tells us how to legislate new rules to deal with changes in our environment that make us less happy. Individuals must then make use of all these rules in the light of the concrete information they have about each situation and choose rationally and morally how to act. Since no one could possibly develop such an immensely complex set of interdependent, reasonably consistent rules (a system of rules), they had to evolve a bit at a time over vast periods of time, being adapted incrementally in each new situation to meet changes.

Burke, of course, was not as explicit about the process as this, but this is what he had in mind, and the whole theory was progressively developed later by Maitland, Mises, Hayek, Sowell,[32] and many others. Along the way, other thinkers discovered that vastly complex systems of all kinds must develop in this way because the direct production of the whole system in such a way as to make it internally ordered and ordered adaptively to a complex and changing environment would be possible only with near omniscience. Economists quickly saw that it must apply to the vastly complex order we call a free-market system. Biologists, especially Charles Darwin, saw it must apply as well to vastly complex living systems we call organisms. Eventually linguists saw that it describes the evolution and use of language. Ecologists discovered the same about vastly complex interdependent systems of living organisms and their environments. Entomologists discovered this *iterative programming* is the method by which termites build immensely complex structures (as I discussed in chapter 8). And, more recently, information theorists and cyberneticians have worked out the basic ideas for all such evolving systems. The only people who haven't discovered what is now common sense to scientists are the modernist millennialists who still try to make people believe the myth that they can play God and mandate heaven on earth with one wave of the wand of rationalistic-scientific general planning.

All these vastly complex systems develop by a process of incremental adaptation of the systems to their environments by an interchange of information. Individual human beings receive information from their situations and from their inner sense of self—their basic emotions, values, beliefs, and plans. They decide how to respond to the environment by comparing this internal information with the external information, then acting to increase their general satisfaction (utility) level. Actually, some comparisons are extremely specific rather than general. But these specific satisfaction levels are *roughly* hierarchicalized, as noted in chapter 7, so ultimately we do aim at increasing our general hierarchicalized happiness, which is all economists mean when they say we try to increase our "general utility function." Once we act, we get feedback information on the consequences of our actions and, thence, on our satisfaction level and once again decide what to do.

There is one difference between the human acting system and all other complex systems, though I suspect other higher animals are more like us in this way than is generally recognized. We have some degree of foresight and reason which allows us to see to some degree how we can creatively rearrange our external conditions and our internal conditions (not genetically programed) to try to increase our satisfaction level. We are able to even invest emotion (desire) in these plans for the future conditions and thus increase our satisfaction level now by anticipating future increases in satisfaction by foregoing some immediate satisfactions. We have *feedforward* as well as feedback. Feedforward is the expectation of greater satisfaction from future states which leads us to discount the feedback from our immediate situation—and thus put up with less satisfaction now to get more in the future. It is our ability to feedforward that leads us to plan and to invest now to reap rewards in the future—but only in direct proportion to the expected rewards (incentives). It is also feedforward which makes us willing to *loan* someone else our present assets, or utilities, without immediate rewards for us—but only in direct proportion to our expectations of greater future rewards for us (interest). But note that, the further into the future, the more we discount the reward, because future satisfaction gets more uncertain with each increase of time.

In planning for a more satisfying society all societies do some general feeding-forward. This general system planning is what we call *legislation*.[33] When we consistently find that present rules and laws produce dissatisfaction, we try to adjust our situation by passing new legislation that changes some of the rules. In this sense, *all human societies are partially open and changing systems*. Burke and all succeeding systems theorists have believed in legislated change: they merely insist that the only reasonable way to change the rules is by mimicking nature, that is, by planning incrementally and situationally to deal with the concrete situation at hand with as little effect on the general system as possible because we don't know how the whole general system works any more than we know how any individual's mind works. The ancient rule of medicine is "first do no harm"—that is, first minimize possible injury from intervention, then try to help by change. The best medicine of all is preventive medicine—doing what you know produces more health by the standard functioning of your body. Much of modern medicine is utopian medicine just as much of modern social thought is utopian.

This fundamental policy rule is the *conservative rule*. (See the discussion at the end of chapter 8.) It forbids interference except when necessary because we are generally ignorant of all the major effects of such intervention. The more positivistic conservatives generally hope we will know enough someday to intervene far more. The more existential conservatives, like Friedrich Hayek, see our ignorance as partly due to inherent uncertainties, so they have little hope of ever having enough knowledge to intervene successfully except incrementally, by trial and error, in ways that allow us to closely monitor the effects of specific interventions and at the same time to minimize the unexpected damages. In general, utopian intervention in the world consists of planning general system changes without complete knowledge of how the whole system works and will react to the changes. The immense ignorance of the utopians is hidden by myths, including exclusionary rules such as "Anything would be better than our present concentration camp" or "The rejection of our general plans is always due to greed."

This general systems and information theory was applied to the free-market economic system in the nineteenth century, then greatly clarified, generalized, and applied to such systems as bureaucracies by Mises, Hayek, and Sowell.[34] The crucial form of information and thus of feedback, in a free-market system is prices. In a free-market system prices are the ever-shifting outcome of all the buying and selling actions of all the individuals in the market. (There is, of course, much *noise* in all information systems. Noise varies inversely with the degree of freedom of action.) This system of buying and selling actions is the result of vastly complex decisions buyers and sellers make about how much they are willing to give up to achieve a given satisfaction. In making their decisions individuals in general compare the price of each possible item they might buy to all of their alternative satisfactions from spending money on some other items. (Behavior like impulse buying is "noise" that complicates the process and constitutes the well-known market imperfections.) Because all the buyers and sellers are doing this, the *system of prices* of all items becomes a vastly complex system of information, symbols, indicating the relative preferences for buying and selling of all the items by all the individuals at that time. Of course, no individual in the system needs to know that and, in fact, the whole system had evolved into an international system before anyone did recognize it. All that individuals have to be concerned with is the shifting set of prices that concern their own production and consumption activities. As an item increases in price, the system is signaling them that they must shift their purchase behavior, find an alternative supply at a lower price, or change their preferences, if they want to avoid a general decrease in their level of satisfaction. Sowell's very systematic argument shows just how much information is communicated in the system of pricing. For our purposes, it's enough to recognize that the changes in the system of prices are feedback signals telling people throughout the system to change their production and consumption behavior. The pricing system is the system of information that provides everyone in the system with the information necessary for the people to adapt to changes in the environment (such as decreasing supplies of oil that lead to increasing prices signaling people to produce more or consume less) or to changes within the system. Without the system of prices, the actors lack the feedback information telling them whether they are adapting successfully to changes, or catastrophically, in unadaptive ways that are producing drifts toward tremendous imbalances in supplies and demands. For instance, when our government regulated oil prices below market prices, people did not get the message to consume less and produce more, so we drifted toward no domestic supplies.

A crucial point of the argument is that any alternative source of information will, at least, be far less efficient and, at worst, be so inefficient as to grind to a halt—or produce so much dissatisfaction as to lead to revolution against it. The primary reason for this is that the system of prices represents the actual choices of all individuals—what they have really preferred when they confronted the concrete choice situation. Even a computerized referendum on all possible combinations of purchases and sales would not do as well because *we can predict our actual preferences only quite imperfectly. The choices we actually make in concrete situations when we get a maximum of situational evidence will on average be different from the choices we expect or plan to make.*[35] And such a system would be terribly costly. People vote the most validly and reliably and at the lowest cost through a free-market system. (This argument that all perceived information, emotional satisfactions, and choices will be partially situational is fundamentally different from the neoclassical theory, as found, for example, in expected utility theory, which *assumes* the existence of an abstract utility function independent of the situations the actor faces.)

Ludwig Mises took this basic model and applied it in a very simple way to bureaucracies and the socialist societies run by government bureaucracies.[36] He focused most of his attention on the profit information provided by the pricing system. Profit (the difference between revenues and costs) is calculated from prices of inputs and sales, and profit changes signal individuals to change their behavior. In general, if their profits go up, they're adapting to the market in the right direction so the message is "keep doing more of this and other buyers will be happier and so will you." If profit goes down, the signal is the opposite. Business organizations, Mises argued, are broken down into separate internal units for which costs and revenues, and thus profits, can be calculated.[37] In this way businesspeople can tell not only how well their whole organization is adapting, but how well each component is, so they have detailed feedback to guide them by incremental planning to greater profitability, thus adaptability. When this breaks down, or when they can't adapt adequately to changing signals, they go bankrupt (or are defeated in proxy battles, bought out, etc.). Somebody else takes up their unused resources and tries to be more adaptive.

The bureaucratic problem is that there are no market prices for the "sales" of the government bureaucracies, so there are no profit signals. You can see how much they cost, but not what you're getting in return relative to the price. In a free market you can tell not only costs and revenues, but competitors show you what is more profitable, thus signaling you to invest more in the more profitable to get more satisfaction—profit. Bureaucracies try to make up for this by providing records on such things as how many clients each bureaucrat "helps." The same is done for subdivisions. Clients generally get no choice, so there is no feedback on their satisfaction until they scream or revolt. None of this comes remotely near the efficiency made possible by incremental adjustments to profit figures and a competitive free market. The result is that such a bureaucracy drifts blindly and on average becomes more and more unadaptive—more and more costly relative to any satisfactions it might supply. The same is true, probably in a multiplied way, for any socialist society run by such bureaucracies. Mises predicted all the ghastly inefficiencies and dissatisfactions of the communist-planned economies and that they would either collapse or drift toward freer markets. As we saw, they have.

Of course, Mises's argument is very general and can not explain the wide variations in observed bureaucratic efficiency and clientele satisfaction, including variations in the very important dynastic cycle. We get some help on this from general information theory and from Sowell's elaborations of the theory of price information systems. Both consist of looking at the more detailed internal workings of bureaucracies. We can expect in general that the greater the distance information must be transmitted in a world in which there are always some imperfections in the transmission, the more noise or distortions of information there will be. Thus, the bigger a bureaucracy grows and the greater the distance from top to bottom, the more distortion in information and the greater the inefficiency and dissatisfaction in using it. We shall see specific evidence for this later when we consider Harold Wilensky's work.

Sowell has added another major element to understanding the dynastic cycle of bureaucracies. He argues that the incentives for the bureaucrats change over time. Very importantly, the bureaucracy provides very different rewards to founders from those it provides once it is operating routinely. From what I've said earlier, we know founders are far more entrepreneurial pioneers—the opposite of "stodgy bureaucrats." But over time people looking for more routine are the ones drawn by the changed incentives. (Seemingly paradoxically, Sowell also suggests that people are drawn to bureaucracies by a desire for dominance. I believe both points are true, but will return to this.) But here he is assuming, not explaining, the trend of bureaucracies to become inflexible—plagued with massive rules and "ritualistic" invocations of the rules. The question is *why* they do this.

And here the original Burkean theory of social order comes to our aid. *Bureaucracies are like any other social system. As they grow and expand their activities, they quickly reach a level of complexity in processing information that can only be managed by using a vastly complex system of interdependent rules that are adjusted to each other and to the environment by incremental changes.* Bureaucracies are conservative for the same reason all societies are. But they go beyond this into hyperinflexibility. The first reason is that all bureaucracies are subordinated by their rulers until their later stages, both to the ruler's desires (policies) and to the general laws of the land. The laws of the land always impose their own vastly complex system of rules that can only change incrementally. In our society today our vast bureaucracies have their own vast system of in-house rules, but they are also subject to our exploding system of general laws which can be used to sue them and prosecute them. The ancient foxhole strategy of bureaucracies ("Cover your ass before all") is soon in full operation.

Certainly these general principles of the operations of information systems give us much insight into the pathologies of bureaucracies. But we need more specific understandings of how these informational pathologies work in bureaucracies to understand the variations in their operations and the general bureaucratic cycle.

The Special Pathologies of Information and Control in Bureaucracies

Harold Wilensky begins his sweeping survey and analysis of *Organizational Intelligence*[38] by arguing that the vast growth of decision making by bureaucracy in our society makes action less and less efficient—at times catastrophically so—because the information is not processed efficiently and, more fateful, is often untrue. His analysis focuses more on inefficient processing, perhaps because these show even more dramatically what effects bureaucratization can have: even when they get a true picture of the world they can still produce catastrophes, as we see in the failure of American intelligence officers to get the specific implications of their information about the planned Japanese attack on Pearl Harbor to the military leaders on the scene. He begins with some general considerations of information-processing pathologies, such as sloganeering (rigid labeling) and preconceptions. Then he considers the inherent effects of bureaucratic structures on information pathologies:

> Intelligence failures are rooted in structural problems that cannot be fully solved; they express universal dilemmas of organizational life that can, however, be resolved in various ways at varying costs. In all complex social systems, hierarchy, specialization, and centralization are major sources of distortion and blockage of intelligence. The quality of intelligence is also shaped by the prevailing concepts of intelligence, the problems to be confronted, the stages of growth of the organization, and the economic, political, and cultural contexts of decision.[39]

Wilensky argues that any complex, formalized organization necessarily faces a series of at least six major *dilemmas of information processing*. The general idea is that there are six basic strategies that organizations can use to try to decrease their costs of information use and/or to try to increase their payoffs in achieving their goals (that is, to try to increase their *efficiency of information use*); but increasing the use of each of these strategies (past a threshold level?) increases the distortion of information and/or decreases the flow, processing, and use of information. These dilemmas all revolve around basic properties of all bureaucratic organizations ranked roughly in their order of importance. Since my purpose is not exegesis, I've taken some liberties in drawing out some of what seems merely implicit in Wilensky's argument and in formalizing it a bit:

(1) the degree of hierarchy;

(2) the degree of formalization-legalization;

(3) the degree of centralization of decision making;

(4) the degree of negative sanctions used to maintain centralized control;

(5) the degree of compression (and thus of homogenization) of information;

(6) the degree of secrecy in the construction and use of information.

In general, and other things remaining the same, *increasing any of these six factors in an organization tends to increase distortions of information and to decrease the flow, processing, and use of the information.*

The degree of hierarchy is roughly the degree of dominance of those at the top over the lower-downs and the sheer distance in levels between the top and the bottom. Hierarchy tends, of course, to be associated with the level of centralization, of the use of negative sanctions, the degree of compression (just because of the sheer amount of information), and sometimes even to secrecy. Hierarchy, then, is by far the most important factor, and Wilensky's analysis of its effects will show roughly how he deals with the effects of the others:

> Insofar as the problem of control—coordinating specialists, getting work done, securing compliance—is solved by rewards of status, power, and promotion, the problem of obtaining accurate, critical intelligence is intensified. For information is a resource that symbolizes status, enhanced authority, and shapes careers. In reporting at every level, hierarchy is conducive to concealment and misrepresentation. Subordinates are asked to transmit information that can be used to evaluate their performance. Their motive for "making it look good," for "playing it safe," is obvious. A study of 52 middle managers (mean age 37) found a correlation of +.41 (p is less than .01) between upward work-life mobility and holding back "problem" information from the boss;
>
> ...In addition to a motive for holding back and distorting, there must be a corresponding opportunity. Middle-level managers, and even lower-level employees, sometimes have a near monopoly of insight into feasible alternatives.
>
> ...Thus, if an organization has many ranks and if in its administrative style and symbolism it emphasizes rank, the greatest distortion and blockage will attend the upward flow of information.
>
> ...Without stable, comfortable, certified ways of talking and writing to one another, without observance of the rules of deference and demeanor, people of different rank or different function do not easily maintain harmony. But the harmony is achieved at the cost of lowering the quality of intelligence channeled to the top; and the symbolism tends to metastasize.
>
> ...Afraid that they are being deceived or kept in the dark, men at the top take action: they emphasize criteria for loyalty in recruitment and promotion, uniform indoctrination, and other efforts to create organization men. These "solutions" in turn complicate the intelligence problem: fewer fresh slants, new ideas, and critical questions will be lodged in the system or work their way to the top.
>
> ...Where the pyramid is tall and narrows sharply at the top, providing a long promotion ladder for a few, there are many time servers at lower ranks who have neither information nor the motive for acquiring it. In the middle, among the non-mobile, there are many defensive cliques who restrict information to prevent change, many mutual aid and comfort groups who restrict information because of their resentment of their more ambitious colleagues, and many coalitions of ambitious men who share information among themselves but pass on only the portion that furthers one or more of their careers.[40]

Bureaucrats create and adopt a vast (potentially infinite) number of countertactics to try to overcome the distortions, the blocks, and the non-use of information produced by increasing any of these six organizational strategies. Probably the most effective in general is the "end runs" around the bureaucracy, that is, the establishment by those higher up of friendly, informal, relations with "contact people" lower down, including the use of mobility cliques or teams, the use of outside spies, and even creating lines of action that go completely outside the organization, as Henry Kissinger did whenever he had to do anything important within the province of the State Department behemoth. These measures, however, either constitute a complete circumvention of bureaucracy or at least a diminution of hierarchy and formalization, so they are no solution to the dilemmas. The vast number of lesser "reforms," such as indexes of internal compliance and other audits, commonly produce some short-run improvements, or, more likely, appearances of improvements, followed by a rapid "decay to trend." For several years now top executives of many big companies, such as Westinghouse Electric Corporation and Northwest Industries Inc., have been using "executive information systems" that allow them to tap the computer data bases at any level of their companies. The purpose, of course, is to circumvent all of the lower bureaucratic filters and blocks of information and, thus, give the higher bureaucrats more control. Reports indicate this has happened so far but we can confidently predict, on the basis of 5,000 years of imperial evidence, that ingenious underlings are already secretly doctoring those data bases to "cover their asses" and, thereby, regain control.[41] It is an ancient pharaonic law that every bureaucratic offensive from the top down will soon be effectively countered by a bureaucratic defensive from below. In the well-enfeudated bureaucracy, power flows uphill and the erstwhile leader becomes a spokesperson for the erstwhile minions.

This, of course, means they merely follow the path of the *Hawthorne effect* in human behavior: almost any increase in attention to human beings changes their behavior in the short run, then they go back to their more traditional patterns. The original theory of Hawthorne effects argued that the increased attention leads to increased compliance with rules enforced by the observers. Actually, it often produces the opposite, especially increased deceit to hide deviance. (See below.) The Russian revolution of 1917 led to a burst of freedom and democratic government under the soviets (workers' councils) and the Kerensky government, then a slow return to oriental despotism (slavery) under Lenin and Stalin. The same thing happens to the ever-recurrent "reforms" of bureaucracies that do not involve permanent reductions in hierarchy, formalism, and legalism—the heart of bureaucracy itself.

Wilensky recognizes that there are other general factors that influence the use of these six strategies. The size of an organization is certainly the most important. It is, of course, the size of any working group, beyond a minimal scale, which forces anyone who wants to closely control the actions of the members to use feudal ties (chains of personal loyalty), kin ties, or bureaucratic ties. (I'm using "feudal" in the broadest sense here, not the specialized sense Western historians use. Feudal ties in the sense of non-kin chains of personal loyalty and succor are universal.) Feudal ties can be very powerful bases for coordination in situations of common peril, but in routine situations they tend to break down into warring segments—enfeudation—so they are not effective bases for coordinating large groups in routine situations. All rulers throughout history have found that bureaucratic organization using the six processes in various ways and degrees is necessary for routinely coordinating human action on a large scale and with tight control by the rulers. In general, the bigger the group and the more controlled the coordination desired, the more the rulers and top bureaucrats must increase these six basic strategies to maintain control; and, therefore, the more inefficient their use of information, the more distorted the information, the greater the internal blocks to information flow, the less the ratio of used to generated information, and the more purposeful distortions of information (information deviance) there will be. This is the general principle of the *inherent dilemma of bureaucracy.*

It is this inherent dilemma of bureaucracy which lies behind Wilensky's six basic dilemmas, and it is these in turn which more than anything else make all bureaucratic organizations inherently self-limiting: bureaucratic organization can only be extended so far before the six basic sources of information pathology generate unintended and intended (deviant) distortions, internal blocks, and such vast inefficiencies in information construction and use that the organization becomes dangerously unadaptive externally and increasingly enfeudated internally.

The only alternative form of coordination that can grow further is that of uncentralized ("spontaneous") chains of exchange known as free markets and based on reciprocal altruism. Free markets, however, do not allow anyone to control them centrally with much specificity. Even control of the means of exchange, the money, does not allow much specific control for long, though it gives the greatest degree of central control of otherwise free markets. It is precisely because rulers can partially control through bureaucracies but cannot control much through free markets that they build massive bureaucracies that try to control free markets as much as possible. And in doing so they set a long-run information and control trap for themselves. But we shall return to these crucial points.

Most systematic analysts recognize that there are several other general factors that influence the six basic dilemmas of bureaucracy. Very importantly, the more homogeneous the members of a bureaucracy, the slower the rates of growth of the information pathologies—that is, the lower the rate of increased pathologies with the increase in hierarchy, centralization, etc.

Consider, for example, the drastic informational effects of trying to use several languages in a bureaucracy—a *lingua franca* must always be developed. Also, the more homogeneous, the less changing, the more united and moralized by a common enthusiasm or threat (especially war), and the more the bureaucrats are committed to a homogeneous culture, the lower the rates of growth of the pathologies. It has often been noted that bureaucratic war planning of Western economies produced far fewer catastrophes than such planning generally does. While this was due largely to the massive evasions—black markets—it is an important truth. But note that shared prosperity has the opposite effect from that of shared threats. Internal fragmentation and conflict increase with increased prosperity because many motives higher on the hierarchy of motives are triggered—especially the fateful dominance motive.

Forest rangers in the U.S. are highly dedicated to environmentalism, which constitutes a homogeneous, if complex, subculture concerning their work goals and means. The service is relatively large and centralized but seems far more efficient and controlled than other federal bureaucracies.[42] Most analysts also recognize the dynastic cycle at work. New bureaucracies suffer far less from the pathologies. Most see this as due to greater dedication to their goals and subculture in the short run and a decay of this over time, with a resulting increase in informational pathologies. I shall return to this crucial point.

Most analysts, and certainly Wilensky, are aware of informational deviance as a source of informational pathologies. But few seem aware of how massive and important it is. In recent years a great deal of research has been done on official information, and David Altheide and John Johnson, who have studied the construction and use of this information in numerous settings, have analyzed it in *Bureaucratic Propaganda*.[43] They recognize that there are many different kinds of information within any bureaucracy and that some information, such as that concerning assets and debits, may generally be quite accountable and objective. This information is so vital that managers watch it intently. Nevertheless, the biggest frauds, such as Equity Funding,[44] are normally based on the conspiratorial production and use of totally false official misinformation, even that on assets and debits. For example, the conspirators at Equity Funding produced about two billion dollars of insurance policy contracts with nonexistent buyers which they then sold to reinsurers:

> What the conspirators did, in the main, was wait for the auditors to request certain policy files and then, at nighttime, "fraud parties" feverishly forged sets of files for delivery to the auditors. This involved filling out medical forms, policy applications, credit checks and other documentation for each policy issued. Later, when the bogus policies were created in huge numbers, a separate "mass marketing"

office staffed by young women would ship out forged documents in assembly-line fashion.[45]

Once they had sold these policies, they then began "murdering" their phantoms by filing phony death certificates and claims. At this point the conspirators began deceiving each other with bureaucratic misinformation and massive enfeudation set in:

> Banks was a principal architect and operator of the death-claim procedure, and before long he was diverting some of the proceeds into his own pocket. How could Banks, the company loyalist, do it? The atmosphere at EFLIC and the parent company was changing. A moral infection had become gangrenous, and Levin was removed from the day-to-day contact with his followers, spending most of his time above them on the twenty-eighth floor.

> That the underlings were risking their freedom for the men on that floor and getting little for it, became apparent at last. Morale plunged. Greed and fear took over. Gradually the company was riddled with subcells of conspirators and lone-wolf operators stealing everything they could while there was still something left to steal.[46]

Official information is systematically hidden and distorted in large organizations and even very small ones hide many billions in employee theft every year in government and in business. No one knows how much is lost by the government every year in phony claims made on all its bureaucracies and carefully hidden by misinformation, some of it constructed by officials "working the system" for clients or themselves. I have seen so much of this that I "guesstimate" the losses in government agencies vary from one-fifth to one-third of the total budgets, which is far beyond any official estimates. Yet financial losses and the misinformation intended to hide them are more carefully sought out than any other form of misinformation within organizations. Corruption and misinformation are also far less in our Western bureaucracies than in those of almost all other societies. In the communist nations the pressures to meet the central plan targets, combined with the near impossibility of doing so with centrally planned distributions of resources, leads to massive overestimations of production, far more on quality than quantity. As the official news has cried repeatedly, managers commonly produce massive oversupplies of anything they can produce successfully. As Khrushchev said, they wind up with vast supplies of the tacks no one wants and few nails everyone needs. All unbiased observers note that even recent buildings are crumbling. And to think one Russian shoe is equivalent to one Italian shoe in consumer satisfaction, as the champions of Russian "progress" imply, is ludicrous. Since even the Soviets now publicly admit that their GNP is increasing by only 2 percent to 3 percent a year, this consistent tendency to overestimate in a massive statistical con game indicates the public sector is actually stagnant or, more likely, declining into the Polish syndrome. Actually, even almost all the economic "growth" in the official Russian statistics in the past decade can be accounted for by the extremely rapid growth in the prices of oil, gas, and gold—its major exports—and to massive Western loans that paid for massive imports of machinery. Most of the roughly $80 billion in loans to the Russian block went to Eastern Europe directly, but much of that then went to pay for imports of oil and gas from Russia. Billions in Western loans also went to pay for Russian imports by other captive trade partners, like Cuba, and friends, like India. With the decline of OPEC and the slowing of Western tribute, the official figures will have to be doctored far more to "prove" that central planning works. Typically, when CIA bureaucrats study Russian statistics they fail to note such facts.[47] Gorbachev is silently appealing to apparatchiki who knew these facts from direct experience. He has also launched a massive buildup in Soviet loans from Western commercial banks. From 1985 to 1988 he borrowed roughly $15 billion. The underground economy is rampant in all societies with big regulatory bureaucracies. It is more affected by fear in the totalitarian societies, but the need is so great that one-fifth to one-third of the whole economy appears to be underground already.

All bureaucratic information is necessarily *decontextualized* to some extent: the meaning of the information to those who construct it is dependent in major ways on the bureaucratic context in which it is constructed and used. The people who use it within the organization normally take this for granted, but the further away they are from the context, the less they know just what the information means.[48] This, plus building personal contacts to build personal loyalty, is a basic reason effective business managers try to get wide experience ("working one's way up") and move around within the organization a lot. But certainly the bigger and more hierarchicalized the organization, the less they can do this. Rulers outside, or the general public, who are trying to use the official information to control the organization have far less sense of the bureaucratic contexts, since they have rarely experienced them. Consequently, they rarely understand the full intended meaning and it is easy for subordinates to evade accountability, insinuate falsehoods, and hide outright lies. The bigger the bureaucracy and the more bureaucrats there are to administer, the more this will be true. And the consequences can be devastating. Since Jack Kennedy had little experience with government bureaucracies, or any other practical activities, it is not hard to see how he could fail to recognize the tremendous uncertainties involved in intelligence guesstimates and thus fall into the Bay of Pigs. Few politicians have had more experience with bureaucratic information than Lyndon Johnson, yet he still apparently believed the intelligence estimates of enemy strength based, apparently, on outright lies and military estimates of enemy casualties based on insanely calculated "body counts." It is very likely that, if he had known what destroyer ensigns in Vietnam like John Johnson knew about body counts, he would not have jumped so confidently into this first fully computer-programmed and quantified national quagmire. After contemplating the official apocalypses already generated by 1967 by such intelligence pathologies, Wilensky concluded his book on a note of dread:

> To read the history of modern intelligence failures is to get the nagging feeling that men at the top are often out of touch, that good intelligence is difficult to come by and enormously difficult to listen to; that big decisions are very delicate but not necessarily deliberative; that sustained good judgment is rare. Bemoaning the decline of meaningful action, T.S. Eliot once spoke of a world that ends "not with a bang but a whimper." What we have to fear is that the bang will come, preceded by the contemporary equivalent of the whimper—a faint rustle of paper as some self-convinced chief of state, reviewing a secret memo full of comfortable rationalizations just repeated at the final conference, fails to muster the necessary intelligence and wit and miscalculates the power and the intent of his adversaries.[49]

The Growth of Bureaucracies and the Trap of the Dynastic Cycle

The more free a market system is from the constraints of the organized and legalized force we call politics, the more the market undermines these political concentrations of power. The reason for this is simple. All political concentrations of legalized power (as distinct from the feudal power of personal ties) are built on bureaucracies that redistribute justice, goods, and wage peace at home and both peace and war abroad. The more free a market system operates from political controls, the more it does the things for people that the political powers do but with far greater efficiency, thus producing far greater satisfaction. Many once-regulated American big corporations are discovering this today and not liking it one bit.

Since rulers want more power, not less, they tend to want more bureaucracies to preempt and control free markets, and the more they want power, the more they do this. A very important implication of this is that fascist systems, such as those in Mexico and South Korea today, tend to move either toward more freedom, when the rulers cannot stop the people, or, more commonly, toward greater central planning. This is the fatal flaw of fascism, without which political collectivists would be able to have power and growing wealth. Because of this fatal flaw, over the long run wealth and consumer satisfaction in politically collectivist societies can only increase beyond a basic, "subsistence" level by underground activity, by conquest, and by tribute. Contrary to the mass media images of the day, Mussolini never got much control of the Italian economy, so the escape into the underground, like today, doomed him to growing irrelevance. Hitler, on the other hand, steadily increased his controls, but did not last long enough to reach full-blown central planning. And here a crucial power-information system comes into play. Politicians may, and generally do, recognize these principles, but they can arrive at the same policy without realizing the general rationale. When a ruler first builds a bureaucracy, he expands his power beyond the power he can exert by personal ties. When the bureaucracy first begins, it is responsible to his will because it is not yet subject to all the general principles of complex information systems and the informational pathologies springing from the basic dilemmas of large, "mature" bureaucratic operations. Ruling over the bureaucrats alone increases his dominance and the bureaucracy extends his dominance to the rest of society. He gets feedback from the satisfied clientele who in this halcyon springtime of the imperial bureaucracy are more satisfied with their peace, justice, and welfare. He adjusts his policies incrementally to build the bureaucracies bigger to expand his own power.

The growth of the bureaucracies' power now is a signal to those who want more power. More nobles, more activist intellectual reformers, and so on, rush in to provide the rationales and the organizational energy and acumen to expand the bureaucracies. Here we get the great bureaucratic empire builders—the Sullys, Richlieus, Mazarins, Colberts, Hopkins, Califanos, and so on. These are truly heroic entrepreneurs who try to bureaucratize the whole world—they exult in their proud power just as their chiefs do. Like their chiefs, they are swept away by all the messages of power they see—the groveling clients, the office girls on the make for their share of dominance, and so on. Neither the rulers nor the bureaucrats (with the rare exceptions like William Simon) look at all the history of the rise, decline, and fall of bureaucracies. They are too good, to fall victims to the ancient fate of bureaucrats. Hubris soars and they plunge onward.

The rest is a tale of unintended consequences. The bureaucracies progressively stagnate and, if the people cannot escape underground, actually wither away the free-market economy. The free market is the source of all their assets, but they are responding far more to power signals than to the signals of declining production. Soon they reach a size of complexity at which they become progressively inflexible because of the necessary conservatism of any hierarchicalized system. The noise in the bureaucracy becomes greater: those at the top have a more and more distorted picture of what is going on inside and what the effects of the bureaucracy are on clients and on society more generally. The blind drift of the bureaucratic system begins. Clients and the rest of society generally become more dissatisfied and counterattack with shaming and stigmatization—"Bureaucrat!" becomes a term of contempt.

Before this, the fateful process of bureaucratic enfeudation has set in. As Eisenstadt[50] and his coresearchers found from the most thorough comparative study of imperial bureaucracies ever done, the most important bureaucrats come to see that their efforts are what maintain the power of the rulers. As I said, they were attracted by the power. Now they come to see the power and its products more and more as *their* property and the means to greater power for themselves. Usurpation and corruption always grow, precisely when the bureaucracy has become big and powerful. This was an incentive to join the bureaucratic "rat race" and all the wealth and power of the higher-ups still beckon. But as the years drag on, it becomes more and more obvious that all but a tiny percent of the ambitious crusaders have "plateaued," as big-business managers call it. The frustration of this midlife bureaucratic crisis is the worst precisely for those who joined the crusade for dominance, and least for lowly "time servers." The middle to upper-middle apparatchiks, who signed on for the dominance crusade, now become the most alienated and they are the most able to enfeudate the whole organization. They grab what they can. Now, of course, all the blocks to information flow and all the distortions of information they can create come to their defense. Misinformation grows to the rafters and steel beams of the pyramids and skyscrapers of power—and lies in wait over the centuries for naive scholars to rediscover.

And now, of course, comes the counterattack. The bureaucrats are now undermining the power of the ruler, who sees the informational signals of declining power—bankruptcy, angry mobs attacking the eunuchs, scathing congressional reports, etc. The time for "Reforms, reforms" has come.[51] First there is shining hope that reform will cleanse it all. The reformists spew forth a sea of proposals. When, for example, the Hapsburg welfare state went bankrupt repeatedly in sixteenth- and seventeenth-century Spain, the "arbitristas" produced libraries of reform treatises. I imagine they rediscovered every zero-base budget scheme and every sunset-law scheme ever invented by reformers in ancient Babylon or in Ming China. The reforms often consist of building mass civil-service exams and Mandarin universities. This only builds rationalistic legalism and, thus, inflexibilities. All reforms in the end throw the rulers on the horns of the inherent bureaucratic dilemma. Alienation, enfeudation, and disorder grow.

Great reforms are rarely even attempted until the perceived threats, both external and internal, are extreme, because great reforms threaten so many interests within and outside the bureaucracies that the would-be reformers are generally the first victims of the reforms. When they are attempted, the most successful are almost always "cleansing" movements that seek to return the prodigals to their original state (often a mythical Golden Age), as we see in the Great Reforms in the Catholic Church and in the Ottoman Empire under Sulton Murad IV and the Koprulu grand viziers in the seventeenth century. Most remarkably, even a prolonged series of disasters rarely produces a sufficient sense of threat to lead most bureaucrats to acquiesce in the great reforms. The Ottomans suffered one military catastrophe after another after the battle of Lepanto in 1571, but the army, especially the Janissaries, successfully resisted all serious reforms, overthrew the reforming Sultan Selim III and massacred reform leaders in 1807, until the sweeping reforms of the nineteenth century—and the destruction of the Janissaries in 1826.[52]

Except in cases, such as the Church, in which there are powerful external interests supporting them, great reforms may produce an Indian summer of the spring flowers but rarely, if ever, succeed in saving the imperial bureaucracies. Indeed their greatest successes probably come by "cleansing" the money supply of inflation, as Diocletian did for Rome. Deflating hyperinflation is the easiest of all great reforms because hyperinflation threatens almost everyone so immediately and severely and the returns of deflation have low lag times. After all, even a totally "cleansed" bureaucratic system would still face the ancient dilemma and would simply start over. But generally the prereform bureaucratic system has already so fragmented, alienated, demoralized, and infuriated the society before the reforms are dared or have a chance to be enforced that the fall of the empire soon follows this Indian summer. However, external powers may prop up the "shell empire" for their own reasons, as Europe long did for the Ottoman "sick man."

There is only one great reform that can possibly work: eliminate or greatly curtail the bureaucracies. Yet this is impossible for almost all rulers. The bureaucracies have eroded the rulers' earlier mythical legitimacy. The rulers' power, however shredded, now rests on them. As Sowell points out, the late emperors in Rome and in Ming China were now trapped by their own bureaucracies. At this point, the desperate rulers often turn to terror. The first step may be to build a smaller parallel system of bureaucratic power to check and make responsible the power of the big bureaucracy.[53] But these ombudsman systems build resentment, and the bureaucrats of the big system close ranks. Real terror may now be tried. Inspectors general, censorates, secret police, and "plumbers" now try to infiltrate and investigate the bureaucracy. At this point the rulers have either built a truly menacing bureaucratic threat of seizing their own power (as the KGB leaders may even now be doing in the Russian empire) or of producing civil wars. At the least, the rulers have fallen back on the personal ties of feudalism which will almost certainly produce further enfeudation. The dynastic cycle is now coming full circle.

Conclusion

Everywhere today people yearn for freedom, prosperity, and peace. But almost everywhere they have been drifting into a terrible bureaucratic oppression that enslaves them all to the will of the few, progressively produces material misery and an agonizing suffocation of the human spirit, and could eventually produce such terrible wars at home and Caesarism abroad that Vietnam will seem an idyllic quagmire. This drift has continued now for many decades, with ups and downs in its development and various plateau periods, like the Eisenhower era, during which the salespeople and cheerleaders of utopia urge the people on with promises of El Dorado to ratchet-up to a higher level of bureaucratic planning and control. Of course, even the most massive builders of our imperial bureaucracies do not support bureaucracy. They have all known, at least since John F. Kennedy, that the bureaucracies are usurpers of the power they believe they alone wield by right. They have all denounced the bureaucracies, fought them ferociously, and created extraconstitutional, sometimes illegal means to try to exercise their own powers and to circumvent the powers of the bureaucrats.[54] Some of them have even eliminated a few bureaucracies. But they have all built the powers of the bureaucracies in general to "solve" the innumerable enabling crises they have proclaimed, most of which they or the bureaucracies have themselves created. They themselves are the victims of the dilemma of government power in a free society: power is centralized to solve problems, but thereby becomes the biggest problem of all because it necessarily curtails more individual freedom and produces more inequality than it can ever undo by curtailing concentrations of power in other segments of society. The great myth of the modernist welfare state is used to hide this dilemma, to deceive the people into believing that this vast increase in centralized power *means* more freedom and equality. And so we see the tragic spectacle of those (our "liberals") who are most committed publicly to freedom and equality, yet, believing in this myth, working furiously to build our imperial bureaucracies in the very names of freedom and equality. The truth is so obvious to them when they are in office that they are driven to desperate outrage and to tyrannical usurpations of their own to try to undo what they are themselves creating.

Anyone who believes that human beings can only respond to the messages of their immediate situations and that systemic phenomena thus operate independently of individual ideas of the whole system, as Sowell comes dangerously close to at times,[55] might well believe we will necessarily continue on this path into the catastrophic stages of the dynastic cycle when the feedback of runaway inflation, deflation, and oppression breed despair, fury, and violence. People in earlier ages who have gone as far into bureaucratic tyranny as we have, have almost always done just that. But we human beings do have a limited capacity to take a broader view, to use reason and foresight when crises loom to see where our system is drifting, and to choose to avoid calamity by adjusting that system incrementally through new legislation.

There is only one different path that works: systematically cutting back political and bureaucratic powers. So far even the so-called "radical turn" of the Reagan Plan does little more than shift money and power from the civil bureaucracies to the military bureaucracies. Certainly, if carried through, this would at least return the nonmilitary segments of the economy to a considerably more free and, thus, efficient market system. But vast military buildups, even for strictly defensive purposes, are no cure for the dynastic cycle. Rather, they are temptations to Caesarism, and they decrease the general economic efficiency of the society. The Reagan "Revolution" and the Gorbachev "Perestroika" have been the latest instances of the ancient rhetoric of "Reforms, reforms" which have little effect on real events. The gigantic bureaucracies of our modernist megastates roll on like the ancient Juggurnauts toward economic and political catastrophies, crushing our lives beneath their immense pall of "rational" regulations and plans.

Chinese merchants and manufacturers themselves subscribed to the value system that limited their roles in society to comparatively modest proportions. They proved this by investing in land and in education for their sons, who thus joined the dominant landowning class and could compete for a place in the ranks of officialdom.

As a result, the traditional ordering of Chinese society was never really challenged. The governmental command structure, balanced (sometimes perhaps precariously) atop a pullulating market economy, never lost ultimate control. Ironmasters and shipbuilders, along with everybody else in Chinese society, were never autonomous. Where officials allowed it, technical advances and increase in the scale of activity could occur in dazzlingly rapid fashion. But, correspondingly, when official policy changed, reallocation of resources in accordance with changed priorities took place with the same rapidity that had allowed the upthrust of iron and steel production in the eleventh century and of shipbuilding in the twelfth to the fifteenth centuries.

The advantages of an economy sustained by complex market exchanges yet responding to politically inspired commands were well illustrated by these episodes. Chinese resources could be channeled toward the accomplishment of some public purpose—whether building a fleet, improving the Grand Canal, defending the frontier against the nomads, or building a new capital—on a grand, truly imperial scale. The vigorous market exchange system operating underneath the official command structure enhanced the flexibility of the economy. It also increased wealth and greatly expanded the resources of the country at large. But it did not displace officialdom from its controlling position. . . .Market behavior and private pursuit of wealth could only function within limits defined by the political authorities.

For this reason the autocatalytic character that European commercial and industrial expansion exhibited between the eleventh and the nineteenth centuries never got started in China. Capitalists in China were never free for long to reinvest their profits at will. Anyone who accumulated a fortune attracted official attention. . . .In every encounter the private entrepreneur was at a disadvantage, while officials had the whip hand.

William McNeill

Notes

1. Carol H. Weiss, "Efforts at Bureaucratic Reform," in Carol H. Weiss and Allen H. Barton, eds., *Making Bureaucracies Work* (Beverly Hills, CA: Sage Publications, 1980), p. 10. In a national poll by *The Wall Street Journal* and NBC News in July 1988, 72 percent of the respondents said they believed the leaking of confidential information by the Pentagon was common, not isolated. Barry Sussman's analysis of a mass of polls, *What Americans Really Think* (New York: Pantheon, 1988), shows us to be extremely "cynical" about government. (See *The Wall Street Journal*, July 15, 1988.) Herbert Gans' field research on *Middle American Individualism* (New York: Free Press, 1988) found "organizational avoidance" to be pervasive in our lives. Americans are "cynical" toward all bureaucracies and are fleeing all big, bureaucratic organizations.
2. George Champion, "Foreign Debts," *The Wall Street Journal*, January 11, 1983.
3. Mark Elvin, "The High-Level Equilibrium Trap," in W. E. Willmott, ed., *Economic Organization in Chinese Society* (Stanford, CA: Stanford University Press, 1962), pp. 137–72.
4. Ibid.
5. Mark Elvin, *The Pattern of the Chinese Past* (Stanford, CA: Stanford University Press, 1973). See, also, Charles O. Hucker, *China's Imperial Past* (Stanford, CA: Stanford University Press, 1975). For evidence of similar bureaucratic trends and economic consequences in China in earlier centuries, see Michael Loewe, *Crisis and Conflict in Han China* (London: George Allen & Unwin, 1947).
6. Mark Elvin, *The Pattern of the Chinese Past*, p. 161.
7. Ibid., p. 217.
8. Ibid., p. 218.
9. Ibid., p. 219.
10. Ibid., p. 218.
11. Ibid., p. 222.
12. Ibid., pp. 221–22.
13. Ibid., p. 161.
14. Ibid., pp. 225–27.
15. For an abbreviated statement of the ideas see Hucker, *China's Imperial Past*, pp. 16–17.
16. Ibn Khaldun, *The Muqaddimah: An Introduction to History*, 3 vols. (New York: Pantheon, 1958).
17. Pitirim Sorokin, *Social and Cultural Dynamics*, 4 vols. (New York: Bedminster Press, 1937–1941).
18. Ibid., vol. 4, p. 779.
19. Henri Pirenne, "The Stages in the Social History of Capitalism," *American Historical Review* (1914), pp. 494–515.
20. Arnold J. Toynbee, *A Study of History* (New York: Oxford University Press, 1962), vol. 5, frontispiece quote. For a survey and critique of such theories, see P. A. Sorokin, *Social Philosophies in an Age of Crisis* (Boston: Beacon Press, 1951).
21. Toynbee, *A Study of History*, pp. 12–13.
22. Harold Wilensky, *Organizational Intelligence* (New York: Basic Books, 1967), p. 52.

23. The literature on this is immense and convoluted. The best recent summations of findings, from different perspectives, seems to be Robert Goodwin, *Not Only the Poor* (London: Allen and Unwin, 1987); S. Butler and A. Kondratus, *Out of the Poverty Trap* (New York: The Free Press, 1987); and William O'Hare, "Separating Welfare Fact from Fiction," *The Wall Street Journal*, December 14, 1987.

24. Ludwig Mises, *Bureaucracy* (New Haven: Yale University Press, 1944, 1962).

25. Michel Crozier, *The Bureaucratic Phenomenon* (Chicago: University of Chicago Press, 1964).

26. Students of bureaucracy will recognize that my emphasis on the degrees of basic processes at work in bureaucracies, and on comparing different combinations of processes (such as in most government bureaucracies with most profit-oriented bureaucracies), is more in agreement with the theories of William Niskanen, Thomas Sowell, and their co-workers. But my theory is in fundamental disagreement with theirs about what the basic variables and processes are. In simplest terms, my theory disagrees on two points. First, their argument, which is not based on any *explicit* model of human nature, sees "budget size" as the thing bureaucrats are trying to maximize (their "maximand"). I believe that in our society the leaders (not their underlings) are normally (but certainly not always) trying to marginally increase their personal dominance. This very often leads them to try to increase budget size, because of the situation they face, but when the external situation they face is changed (by their government sponsors, by media coverage, etc.), they may even try to reduce their budget size if this increases their dominance. We see this, for example, in some department heads in the Reagan administration. (Some appointees in the departments of education and energy actively tried to dismantle their departments or major subsections—at least in the first few years.) Niskanen is right in his analysis of the internal pressures from his own staff and "clients" to expand the budget size, but these can be overcome by external incentives to his dominance drive (e.g., his hope for future appointments or elections to higher office because of his antibureaucratic actions). Second, they see the "structure" of decision making combined with the incentives mediated by this maximand of budget size as the crucial variables. They tend then to discount the importance of information and flexibility. In one instance Niskanen explicitly and rightly argues that "the superior performance of market institutions is not due to their use of better or more analysis," but he means information by expert social scientists. The greater validity of information communicated by market prices *is* crucial. Of course, this information must then be coupled with individual motivation ("incentives"), a crucial point Niskanen makes (and one sometimes overlooked in the Hayek-Sowell analysis I shall shortly be considering). In brief, Niskanen is right about the importance of incentives, but fails to see the crucial importance of dominance incentives and, most importantly, fails to see that the information produced and communicated by the "structures" is crucial. (The best intentions and greatest incentives will go awry if the information being used is false—or simply too gross!) Niskanen deals with inflexibility-flexibility almost entirely in terms of the ability to separate factors, costs, outputs, etc. This is one important dimension of flexibility, but there are also others. My two variables of information-feedback (which takes incentives into consideration) and flexibility are *proximate variables* that may be affected by many *ultimate variables* such as political

"structures" of communication. Note also that all kinds of "structures" are circumvented by informal processes—even very illegal ones *if* the actors have reason—information—to think their goals are best served by doing so. See William Niskanen, *Bureaucracy and Representative Government* (Chicago: Aldine, Atherton, 1971); and Thomas Sowell, *Knowledge and Decisions* (New York: Basic Books, 1980).

27. Max Weber, "Bureaucracy," in H. H. Gerth and C. Wright Mills, eds. and trans., *From Max Weber* (New York: Oxford University Press, 1946). Niskanen was quite right in his critique of this whole Weberian tradition.

28. For a classic study and defense of such bureaucrats at work, see Carl Friedrich and Taylor Cole, *Responsible Bureaucracy* (New York: Russell and Russell, 1932). Mises (*Bureaucracy*, p. 78) satirizes this popular view of the "altruistic" *Staatsbeamte.*

29. The classic work leading to most recent work of this sort is by Melville Dalton, *Men Who Manage* (New York: Wiley, 1955). (John Bradford's study of American postal workers reveals some hilarious—and illegal—informal processes at work. See "A General Perspective on Job Satisfaction: Relationship Between Job Satisfaction and Sociological and Psychological Variables," Ph.D. dissertation, University of California, San Diego, Dec. 1976.)

30. Niskanen (*Bureaucracy and Representative Government*) almost totally overlooks corruption of all types and shades. Thus, he totally fails to see how his proposed "reforms" of competing bureaucracies can produce massive corruptional usurpations. Colbert was a good example of an efficient but vastly corrupt competitive bureaucrat. For general analyses of such phenomena, see the book I edited with John M. Johnson, *Official Deviance* (New York: J. B. Lippincott, 1977). One of the best studies done, but showing most of these weaknesses, is Marshall Meyer, *Bureaucratic Structure and Authority* (New York: Harper and Row, 1972).

31. This entire theory has been synthesized and developed in its most sophisticated form by F. A. Hayek, *Law, Legislation and Liberty* (Chicago: University of Chicago Press, 1973), vol. 1.

32. Thomas Sowell, *Knowledge and Decisions* (New York: Basic Books, 1980).

33. This is basically the meaning of "legislation" in F. A. Hayek, *Law, Legislation and Liberty.*

34. This information theory of prices and markets has been most systematically developed by Thomas Sowell, in *Knowledge and Decisions.* George Soros has given us a brilliant analysis of how much more inherently problematic the decision making becomes when investors are predicting the future prices. See *The Alchemy of Finance* (New York: Simon and Schuster, 1987).

35. This might well be called the *principle of greater uncertainty inherent in all abstractions.* It is of overwhelming importance in understanding all human action. See J. D. Douglas, et al., *Introduction to the Sociologies of Everyday Life* (Boston: Allyn and Bacon, 1980).

36. See Mises, *Bureaucracy* and *Socialism* (New Haven: Yale University Press, 1951).

37. Marshall Meyer (*Bureaucratic Structure and Authority*) gives some details on how this is done, but also gives evidence of how strong the tendency to centralization to maintain control is even in businesses operating in this way (see especially, pp. 104–11).

38. Wilensky, *Organizational Intelligence*.
39. Ibid., p. 42.
40. Ibid., pp. 42–45.
41. All experienced academics are well aware today of how this "doctoring" of data is done.
42. See Harold Wilensky, *Organizational Intelligence*, p. 59.
43. David L. Altheide and John M. Johnson, *Bureaucratic Propaganda* (Boston: Allyn and Bacon, 1980). See also, Jack D. Douglas, *The Social Meanings of Suicide* (Princeton: Princeton University Press, 1967); and *American Social Order* (New York: Free Press, 1971).
44. William E. Blundell, "Equity Funding," in Donald Moffitt, ed., *Swindled!* (Princeton: Dow Jones Books, 1976), pp. 67–68.
45. Ibid., pp. 67-68
46. Ibid., p. 72.
47. See, for example, Lev Navrozov, "Why the CIA Undershoots Soviet Arms Spending," *The Wall Street Journal*, Nov. 6, 1983.
48. These are vital parts of the argument by Altheide and Johnson in *Bureaucratic Propaganda*.
49. Harold Wilensky, *Organizational Intelligence*, p. 191. See also, the massive evidence of "intelligence" misinformation and "snafus" analyzed by John Prados in *The Soviet Estimate* (New York: The Dial Press, 1982).
50. S. N. Eisenstadt, *The Political Systems of Empires* (New York: Free Press, 1963), especially pp. 159–60 ff.
51. Ibid., especially pp. 161–5.
52. See William McNeill, *The Pursuit of Power* (Chicago, University of Chicago Press, 1982), p. 135.
53. Ibid., p. 162.
54. For good surveys of these struggles see Garry Wills, "The Kennedy Imprisonment," *The Atlantic Monthly*, January 1982, pp. 27–38; and Charles Peters and James Fallows, *Inside the System* (New York: Praeger Books, 1976).
55. Thomas Sowell, *Knowledge and Decisions*, pp. 379–82.

10

"Freedom Works!"

Happiness is not the supreme value. . . .The idea that happiness is the supreme good and the final end has been instilled into man in order to keep him in slavery. Human freedom and dignity forbid us to regard happiness and satisfaction in this light. . . .Man is a free, spiritual and creative being. . . .No law can make him into a creature that prefers happiness to freedom, rest and satisfaction to creativeness.

Nicholas Berdayev

Hubris—self-righteous arrogance—was the most common tragic flaw in ancient Greece, as attested by her greatest dramatists. And the Bible tells us Eve was tempted to "the mortal sin original" by Satan's promise that eating the apple would make her a goddess, indicating that pride is a tragic flaw not limited to one culture. The hubris of modernism has now been the most important tragic flaw of Western peoples for at least two centuries and has increasingly pervaded mass politics in all nations, in widely varying degrees and times, for the past century. Hubris was triggered in Greece by the vast explosion of creative science and economic wealth during the great era of Athenian democracy lasting over a century. Modernism was triggered in the West over the past two centuries of our great era of freedom by our vast strengths in science-technology and in individual rational planning in economic life. Once triggered, modernism progressively blinded us to the limitations of these very real strengths, and this blindness allowed first our soaring greed and then our power-lusting politicians to tempt us into believing we could vault into a heaven on earth, even into Mao's ninth heaven— "Nothing is hard in this world if you dare to scale the heights!" The most primitive cargo-cult mentality and the most preposterous whims of the "tooth fairy" cult swept away reason, common sense, and the science of grim economic and political realities.

Wealth, leisure, security, justice—an end to all worldly cares and woes—all the things of the good life, right now! There is nothing new in these goals, for they spring from our genetic drives and from conflicts and insecurities inherent in civilization in proportion to the degree of repression of individuals by political power. They have been the dreams of the multitude of humanity since the statist forces dominating civilization imposed such powerful external constraints and shameful subordination upon almost all of us. It is not such dreams, such yearnings, such ideals and values that make us different—they and many other desires are what make us the same as almost all earlier civilized human beings. These yearnings and temptations are not really subject to dispute, though we may seriously argue this way or that about their relative importance, because they are constants of civilized human life, the same general goals presented and used in different symbolic forms as fatal lures into collectivist tyranny by Hammurabi, Narmer, Shih Huang Ti, Lenin and Stalin, Hitler, Mao, Castro, James Callaghan, Helmut Schmidt, Franklin Delano Roosevelt, Jimmy Carter, and François Mitterrand.

What separates our age from earlier ones, especially our American past, and what bitterly divides our most serious intellectuals, are the questions of reason and science, above all the ultimate questions of all reason and science—those of practicality. Do we and our political leaders really have such greater knowledge, wisdom, and moral transcendence of our animal lust for dominance that we can continually plan and attain that heavenly city on earth—now? Or are our politicians today misled by their own so-obvious ignorance and by their human lust for dominance, tempting us with mythical thought to believe the impossible and follow them down the road to a new promised land, but one which, in fact, produces economic catastrophe and eventually a tyranny made more terrible than any yet seen by the "rational" marvels of police terrorism in an age of technology and immense agitprop?

I have little doubt that most intellectuals and most social scientists trained in our collectivist universities of modernist Newthink, in spite of all the ominous evidence we have seen in recent decades, will continue to be sorely tempted by the lure of statist powers and largesse to assert that we do know too much, are too rational and morally transcendent to fall victim to such irrationalism. But there are some of us who believe we already see all too clearly the beginnings of our future and that what we see shows us that our path leads not to the promised land of milk and honey for all, but through the portals of grim realities to economic and political catastrophe. Those of us who have not yet forgotten human history and believe from those memories that there is a human nature that has changed little since the creation and imposition of civilization, have begun to fear that we are seeing another great loss of nerve, a failure of courage to face grim realities, which played such an important part in the triumph of myth and magic over science and economic and political freedom in the ancient world. We have not forgotten the great strength and creativity of Greek philosophy and science in the sixth to fourth centuries B.C.. There are even those of us who believe that Thucydides and Aristotle were generally more empirical and certainly more wise in interpreting individuals and societies than the majority of our social scientists today. Nor have we forgotten that their science and philosophy were overwhelmed in succeeding centuries by the magicians and mythologists who tempted the people with the promises of instant knowledge and power[1] —of vast wealth through the miracles of prestidigitation which created something from nothing, of total wealth through the miracles of alchemy, of security, knowledge, and power through the miracles of astrology, of love and erotic pleasure through the miracles of love potions, of health and eternal life through the miracles of religious faith and righteousness administered by an absolutist church bureaucracy.

Then as now science offered no real hope of instantaneously changing the grim realities of human life. It could not honestly promise to produce instant wealth, happiness, the security of foreknowledge of one's future, freedom from the pains of unrequited love, the ecstasies of erotic triumphs and Bacchanalian highs, health and eternal life, absolute justice, and all the other things we civilized human beings crave. Magic and myth promised all of that and more to anyone who would merely submit to the dominance of the magicians and priests who jealously guarded their secrets. The magicians and mythmakers gained control of the standardized institutions of imperial state education and of public opinion. They did so in part by using the prestigious symbolic forms of science and philosophy to convince educated people they could deliver on their promises. The tyrants, beginning with Constantine, found some of these very conducive to their own ends and so they joined forces. Myths wrapped in philosophical and scientific forms by the sacred statists of the Church and myths wrapped in scientific forms by astrologers and others became cornerstones of official power, and that power then enforced belief in all the myths as the absolute truths of life.

Millennial socialists in the eighteenth and nineteenth century commonly promised to really do what Christianity promised to do in heaven but could not do in this world. They promised the same goals—heaven—but now, here on earth. Only the means, political action, was different. Christian socialism, while inspiring desire, could not tempt many people, especially among the educated, because it could not be convincing in an age of science and technology. The mythmakers could only convince people by wrapping the myth in the symbolic forms of science. And thus we got the same kind of explosion of myths wrapped in science that had happened in Greece and Rome—Christian Science, scientology, positivism, Marxism, astrology, and many more. Marxism, which wrapped the promises of revenge against the

envied rich along with all the usual Christian goals within the forms of absolutely true scientism, became the most powerful religion in the history of the
world, the first scientistic religion of almost universal, cross-cultural appeal.
Christianity had promised revenge for the envious in the afterlife, but that
was too far off. Islam had tapped far more of that power of blood lust, but
Marxism was the first of the so-called great religions to justify *and* promise
absolute revenge for the masses of the envious around the world, and it did so
in a Holy Book (*Capital*) written by a suffering prophet and wrapped in all
the symbolic forms of sacred science. It so thoroughly taps the blood lust of
the dominated that its total failure at scientific predictions did not matter with
the masses, who hardly know that anyway, or with the most envy-wracked
and power-lusting intellectuals.

During times of great anxiety like the Great Depression, intellectuals, like
all human beings, are greatly tempted to believe such a myth, especially one
that combines the powerful appeals of community (justice, altruism) and
heaven on earth with those of envious blood lust. It is not surprising that earlier crises and the depression tempted even intellectuals to believe Marxism,
fascism, Nazism, and related myths. Nazism promised all the same things as
Marxism, and it too, if belatedly, wrapped itself in the mantle of science. But
in allying itself so closely with the myths of the German race and state, it
created a powerful emotional appeal within Germany, but dread of submission outside. The Russians and Chinese have carefully and wisely hidden
their myths of race and the state from the outside. But most social scientists,
especially economists, who knew the obvious failures of Marxist economics,
did not give in to the emotional temptation to believe. Moreover, the terrible
realities of Marxist tyranny began to leak out of Russia in the 1930s, and
even some intellectuals who had become true believers in Marxism began to
turn against the Lenin-Stalinist church. With the development of the Maoist
sect, the bitter sectarian struggles for dominance which have always torn any
absolutist political or religious party made even more intellectuals wary.

The modernist welfare state myth appealed to the same emotions as Christianity, socialism, Islam, and Marxism and it did so in a manner less immediately threatening to dominant groups than Marxism or Nazism, in very much
the same way Roman Christianity appealed to the slaves by promising, "The
meek shall inherit the earth," while appeasing the rulers by "rendering unto
Caesar." But among the educated it had the same problems as earlier
socialism—impracticality. The Keynesian myth of rationalistic economic
planning for eternal economic growth became the vital mantle of science
which could be wrapped around the modernist myth of the welfare state. It
was created in a time of anxiety to solve the dreaded problem of unemployment, was buttressed by a very narrow and selective appeal to interwar
British experience, presented in very "scientific" forms as an analysis of

inherent and necessary tendencies of "mature capitalism" to immiserate the masses (almost exactly like Marxism), was presented by a man of great scientific prestige in a holy book, and, like a bolt of God-launched lightning, converted many intellectuals around the world.

While the Keynesian and welfare-state myths tap the same emotions as Marxism, they obviously do so to a much lower degree. They tap the blood lust of the profoundly envious only slightly, leaving the field of deep hatred and lust for revenge to Marxism, Nazism, and similar hate-filled myths. Keynesianism and the modernist welfare state myth are thus already becoming victims of the far greater crises and resulting anxiety and dread they produce. The dilemma we now face is that the only real solution to our economic problems within the framework of individual freedoms we in the West have created in recent centuries is to return to the fundamental ideas and practices in the realms of economics and society abandoned and denounced by the mythmakers, while the intervening years of denunciation, the massive training of our young in the myths through agitprop, the partial unleashing of envy and lust for revenge by the myths, and, above all, the anxiety and dread increasingly triggered by the growing recognition of the collectist crises we face enflame both old and new myths, gravely complicating the task.

The Urgent Need to Rediscover the Vast Moral Strength of Freedom

"Popular revolt against a ruthless, experienced modern dictatorship, which enjoys a monopoly over weapons and communications, which has its own armed forces under tight control, and which retains its unity and its will to power, is simply not a possibility in the modern age."[2] Here George Kennan has unknowingly presented us with an avowal of the ancient myth of the inherent superiority in strength of totalitarianism over democracy and, far more ominously, an example of the grave moral crisis that today afflicts so much of the Western world. Where the founders of our democracy avowed an inherent and fatal flaw in all forms of despotism because they violate the passion for freedom of the human spirit, one of our foremost diplomats now avows the inherent stability of modern dictatorship, in spite of all the massive evidence of history.

Our American democracy was born in the fiery cauldron of popular revolution against the tyrannical repressions of individual freedoms by a mercantilistic monarch asserting his powers to plan the lives of all his "subjects"—for the common welfare, of course. Our glorious revolution inspired soaring hope and deepening conviction around the world that the ancient shackles of despotic statism, veiled in that day by the myth of mercantilistic benevolent absolutism, would at last be cast off and the spirit of every individual would fly free to recreate a world of justice, of plenty—and, above all, of "sweet liberty" for all. Our glorious revolution lit the fires of the succeeding mass revolutions in this great Age of Democratic Revolutions. So powerful is the lure of the torch of freedom in the modern world that all of the counterrevolutions against individual freedom are inspired by the promises of greater freedoms—absolute "liberation." Even today, when so many of our own misguided and deceived fellow citizens have begun to despair of the values of liberty, the most terrible slave states in human memory wrap themselves tightly in the mantle of the names of democratic freedoms and hide their brutal oppressions behind the external forms of republican constitutionalism.

"Freedom Works!" Freedom works for all human beings by allowing them to creatively adapt all of their own strengths and weaknesses to the evolving situations of their lives, to produce and consume to fit all of their vastly complex and changing desires, to forge an optimum of justice through their inherently problematic moral decisions, and to peacefully adapt all of their own strivings to the complementary strivings of their fellow citizens through the institutions of the free market, the common law, and representative democracy. The great System of Natural Liberty—political freedom, economic freedom, and cultural freedom exercised through the rules of moral consensus and common law—works by allowing all individuals to be more creative, productive, just, equal, peaceful, reciprocally altruistic, satisfied, and yet also more aspiring than any other possible arrangements of human life. "Freedom Works!" was then and remains today the fierce conviction, the fiery faith born of free reason severely tempered by practical experience, on which was built our entire American System of Natural Liberty.

The great majority of Americans have always shared this fiery faith in freedom. However inconsistent some of our lesser values and, worse, some of our actions have been with it, our faith in freedom has eventually inspired us to strive to overcome these failures. But there have always been small minorities of us who secretly revile the faith in freedom and far more of us who are deceived into violating the implications of our own faith. The mythical deceits of would-be collectivist rulers of all types have been mightily aided by the self-deceits of many more who are lured by utopian hopes of easy wealth and arrogant pride and driven by great anxieties in times of crises.

For the first hundred years, the counterrevolution against the Revolution of Freedom was inspired predominantly by the ancient ideas of monarchic legitimacy, especially in their Hobbesian and other Tory formulations of the theory of the necessity of absolute sovereignty to suppress chaos. But who could believe these ancient myths of monarchic despotism when the American and British systems of Natural Liberty and similar systems in other

Western nations were unleashing a vast explosion of scientific-technological creativity, wealth, philanthropic altruism, justice, equality, and political stability (marred only by our Civil War) such as the world had not seen since the creative effulgence of Athenian and early-Renaissance republics. The counterrevolutionaries then launched a moral offensive against the Systems of Natural Liberty in the very name of freedom, which would supposedly achieve everything everybody wanted at little or no cost. And how was all of this absolute freedom, absolute justice, absolute wealth, and absolute protection to be gained? Modernist statism and bureaucratic powers, in one form or another, by any name and under any pseudo-constitutional guise that appealed to the ignorant and deceived, became the fiery faith of the counterrevolution against the Systems of Natural Liberty.

For over a hundred years now, all civilized societies have been progressively swept up by this counterrevolution of the modernist megastates. The names, the institutional forms, the sacred symbols, the pseudo-scientific theories and the degrees of bureaucratic repression have varied greatly. Socialism, Marxism, communism, fascism, Nazism, anarchosyndicalism, Peronísmo, social-democratism, liberal-unionism, liberal welfare-statism, corporate-statism, state-capitalism, Maoism, Castroism, progressive-laborism, liberalism, state-planned reindustrialism, Japan-Inc., American-Inc.—on and on roll the sonorous litanies of statism. Each wave of millennial statism has been launched, has swept across our many lands toppling institutions and destroying lives, and then receded, leaving in its wake a rising chorus of agony—and the next wave of renamed millennial statism.

In the 1920s and 1930s the Nazi-fascists and Marxist-communists fought each other in the streets throughout Europe and Latin America. Masses of ignorant youths and envious people of all ages flocked to the Nazi-fascists, and the bright banners proclaiming their "radiant future" streamed by the millions down the wide boulevards of Germany, Italy, Hungary, France, Mexico, Brazil, Uruguay, Paraguay, Argentina—on and on strutted the jubilant millions toward the radiant utopia. Almost all their bright banners are gone now, burned in the flames of terrible wars they ignited or cast aside by the millions impoverished by the economic catastrophes they precipitated. But from their ashes have sprung the polychromatic phoenix of statism. The bright red banners of the Marxist-communist totalitarianism now proudly proclaim the terrifying enslavement and economic immiserization of one-third of humanity. The more subdued and motly-hued banners of the other forms of modernist welfare statism stream above almost all the other peoples of the world as they rush toward the economic abyss of a catastrophic world-wide deflation. Even as the abyss looms, the true believers in statism are quickly forging new banners—"autarchy" in Britain, "America-Inc." in America, Mitterrandisme in France, democratic socialism and Greenery in

Germany and Austria. Once again even the banners of the fascistic corporate statism are unfurled, but in a bright new color and in the new guise of "restructured" communism. The phoenix of millennial statism rises anew.

All of these mass political movements share one basic idea, the core enabling myth of modernist statism: government power to scientifically plan society is necessary to make individuals safe, rich, happy, just, and free. "Statism Works!" That is the statist faith. Since all statists strive mightily to wrap themselves in the sacred mantle of the System of Natural Liberty, none proclaims "Freedom fails!" Instead, they all proclaim, to the strains of their various marching tunes, "Only statism is *real* freedom!" In short, if you would be free from the diffused power of millions of owners of capital, you must support massive increases in monopolistic state power. So it was that Lenin lured the Russian peasants and workers into the dictatorship of the party by proclaiming the dictatorship of the proletariat; and welfare statists lured the American "masses" into bureaucratic oppression by proclaiming the Square Deal, the New Deal, the Fair Deal, the Great Society, and many other statist programs to "save" free enterprise. State slavery becomes the necessary foundation for political freedom, and government bureaucratic dictates become the necessary foundation for economic freedom. Such are the absurdities of political doublethink and newspeak agitprop in our age of modernist statism.

The greatest tragedy, the most fatal flaw of our megastatism is that it feeds upon itself—it is an autocatalytic process. The truth is precisely as the founders of the American System of Natural Liberty proclaimed: "Freedom works!" and, conversely, "Statism fails!" Freedom works because it allows the fullest possible expression and satisfaction of human nature and because the free markets and free forms of politics produce the optimal degree of information feedback on failures and successes, thus producing optimal adaptation to our ever-changing world and a systemic drift toward creative efficiency in all affected spheres. Conversely, the bureaucratic centralization of decision making (by any name and any form) fails in direct proportion to its degree because it suppresses human nature and produces misinformation and disinformation on failures and successes, thus preventing successful adaptation to our ever-changing world and a systemic drift toward inefficiency, entropy, and misery in all affected spheres of life. As the systemic drift reaches higher levels, the rulers always begin to use ad hoc measures of arbitrary rule—dictates, ukasi, fiats, etc.—to try to correct for the growing misinformation. That is, they use the censorate, Gestapo, KGB, and plumbers, to try to control the system. These arbitrary measures drift toward maximum uncertainty—secrecy and arbitrariness—to uncover the truth the people are hiding from them and to force them to work harder. This is the very nature of terrorism. Megastatism, then, always drifts toward terrorist methods to try to overcome its own tragic flaws. But terrorism, while commonly temporarily successful, eventually produces further ratchets-up in misinformation and disinformation to hide from the terrorists and in desperate attempts to escape the entire system. At the extreme, in the predatory states, the system then spins out of control at an accelerating rate as the terrorist "state within a state"—such as the SS or KGB—takes ever more direct control. Bonapartism and Stalinism are inherent tendencies in *late statism*. However seemingly successful their reforms in the short run, they are the death knell of that particular statist system.

Consequently, every ratchet-up in statism, intended to solve some problem not yet solved by free people, may do so in the short run (spring flowers) but eventually produces greater unintended problems (fall canker blooms) than the problems it ever solves; and these new problems then become the enabling crisis legitimizing the next ratchet-up in statist powers. Once statism has ratcheted-up to very high levels, the corruption resorted to in desperate attempts to escape destruction by bureaucratic planning and the envious rancour triggered by the greedy struggle to control the body politic produce pervasive demoralization, distrust, and conflict. Despair and anxiety soar as the primordial specter of chaos is unleashed. And these passions produce a powerful yearning for law and order that can only be slaked by the mythical purification rituals administered by a new messiah.

Napoleon, Lenin, Hitler—the tyrant always comes as the great friend of the people and the hero of law and order who will first purify the people of evil and, thereby, return them to the path of righteousness and heaven. The rise of the Greens in Europe today, with all their alienated moralism and utopian romanticism, sends shivers of fear through those who remember how their soulmates, the youth movements, especially the Wandervögel, presaged the coming of the mighty hordes of Hitler Youth. I happened to be in Metz, France, in the industrialized Lorraine Valley the day François Mitterrand's socialism swept to its "historic victory." All night the streets were thronged with exultant crowds proclaiming this historic victory by beeping horns. How deeply depressing it was to those of us who recognized León Blum in his new disguise, the beaming "papa" come to tempt the people with all the same romantic promises of benevolent collectivism—and to lead them into a deeper demoralization and rancor that might help prepare them for a more complete surrender to a far sterner "deliverance." In America today most of those filled with despair and dread by the rising tide of disorder and distrust have returned to fundamentalist religion, but the yearning for a more secular hero to turn back the tide is clear in the monomyth of the self-righteous hero of science now pervading our mass media, in our own puritanical and antinomian hippie-environmentalist variants of the Greens, and still more in the preposterous myth of the second coming of Camelot.

For the past one hundred years modernist megastatism, wrapped in the resplendent garb of pseudo-scientific theories, has swept across the entire civilized world in many different guises and to widely varying degrees. Our American System of Natural Liberty has been progressively eroded by ratchets-up in statist powers over an entire century now. Statist thinking now pervades much of our entire lives, from the planning of family lives and whole populations to national defense. It is pseudo-scientific statist thinking that tempts our diplomats to believe in the myth of totalitarianism, the myth that totalitarian regimes cannot be overthrown from within by popular revolt. Anyone who has eyes unclouded by collectivist agitprop can see the truth is the exact opposite. Every monarchic totalitarian system has now been obliterated or is tottering, as we see in Saudi Arabia today. Every fascist regime is gone or is under severe attack, as we see in South Korea, Iran, Taiwan, Iraq, and Mexico. Every communist totalitarian system is firmly ensconced on a powder keg of endemic revolution by the so-called proletariat, by would-be consumers, by tortured intellectuals, by terrified but embittered conscript-labor—military slaves—and by national minorities hungry for the spiritual food of cultural identity. They only appear stable to outsiders precisely because their terrorist methods lead to a massive hiding of the growing hatred of the rulers, right up to the day of explosion.

Everywhere totalitarians rule today, they do so only by an unrelenting war of mythical agitprop and terrorism against truth and the human spirit; and everywhere the wisest, most courageous and most decent human beings wage an unrelenting guerrilla war against them and seize even the slightest chance to escape or to launch desperate attacks on them. Roman terror could not forestall the desperate guerrilla attacks and escapes of Spartacus and the Christians, nor forever stem the tides of national liberation in Dacia, Parthia, Gaul, Germany—and, finally, everywhere. Every communist regime today is torn by desperate, bitter, and vengeful internal struggles. Most of the once-Marxist regimes of Africa, like that of Allende in Chile, have now been swept into the dustbin of history or, like China, are scuttling desperately to find shelter behind the fronts of "liberal reforms," new pseudo-constitutions and loan-subsidies from Western capitalists. Latin America has almost always been ruled by statists, generally by oligarchic fascists garbed as agrarian reformists, Catholic conservatives, or loyal subjects of the one-party, political machine "democracy" of the PRI in Mexico. As a result, the mass of people remain ignorant, repressed, and poor. Yet even there the immiserization of the people produced by Castroist communism is only partly hidden by the fig leaf of billions in Russian and Western alms and loans (now totaling roughly $4 billion a year from Russia alone). Every major communist regime of Eastern Europe has been battered by desperate revolutions that only external Russian force has been able to temporarily quell. The Russian empire itself has had many revolts by nationality groups, by workers, and even at least one mutiny by army slaves in the past twenty years. Where would the communist regimes now be if they had not been continually propped up by huge Western and Japanese loans of approximately $100 billion (counting Yugoslavia and China) in the past decade, by massive exports and thefts of technology, and, above all, by the unilateral moral disarmament of the West which has led our governments to tacitly accept the communist regimes as inevitable, as inherently stable, and even as if they were legitimate?

The entire world today is caught in a great crisis of collectivism that grows in direct proportion to the growth of statism. Of course, even the most statist nations, the communist regimes, have never been nearly as bureaucratically collectivized as they try to appear. Central planning in Russia, China, Poland, and everywhere else has always been massively supplemented by a parallel system of free enterprise—"corruption" and all black markets, without which extreme statist planning would have totally stagnated and then eroded their economies very quickly. Hungary is still called "communist" but is little more collectivized than Sweden except in politics and the mass media. But they are collectivized enough to have made life miserable (even with over $18 billion in Western loan subsidies) and to have produced a state of continual readiness for revolution.

At the same time, the Western nations have become collectivized enough to produce lengthening and deepening periods of stagflation and, someday, possibly even a fine-tuned catastrophe of centrally planned money and credit—a worldwide depression. Nevertheless, we have remained free enough, both officially and through massive, growing evasions and black markets, that no major Western democracy has had a single significant attempted revolution during the period the communist and other collectivist regimes have been rocked by revolutions. The dangers from within to our remaining freedoms are growing perilously as our collectivization grows, but the dangers to our lives and freedoms still come initially from outside, from all highly statist powers with the military strength to menace us.

The Russian threat to us has grown perilously in recent years primarily because of the rapid growth of statist collectivization in our own society.[3] The Russians have focused their economy and entire society on the production of weapons since Stalin ended Lenin's New Economic Policy. Their so-called "greatest military buildup in history" in the last fifteen to twenty years has merely been standard operating procedure for this military, predatory state with a "garrison-state" mentality. What changed was the beliefs and actions of Western nations. We embarked upon the most massive program of unilateral moral and material disarmament in the history of the world. While they continued to build weapons massively, we built the massive bureaucracies, legalistic regulations, and inflation of the modernist welfare state at an astounding pace. It was we who betrayed the American faith in freedom and thereby progressively stagnated our economy. It was we who redirected ever more of our economy away from defense against statists and toward breeding statist dependency and collectivist thinking at home and abroad.

If we had merely continued the degree of economic freedom we had in 1960 (already gravely curtailed by the collectivism of Square, New, and Fair Dealism) and the level of military expenditures, we would by now have vastly outdistanced the Russians in military power, just as we have in almost every other way. Had we not believed in the "inherent superiority" of statist bureaucracies and pseudo-science theories over individual creativity and incentive, we would not have suffocated our armed forces with layer upon layer of bureaucratic forms, of top-down discipline, of noncompetitive pro-curement policies, and of managerial scientism that destroys the morale of soldiers far more quickly than of civilians, for the lives of the soldiers are put immediately at risk by this gargantuan bureaucratization. Had Western bank-ers not started to subsidize communists with almost $10 billion in tribute a year, supplemented by massive transfers of technology, the Russians and their allies would most likely have had to greatly curtail their own military buildup to prevent revolution as their economies stagnated and then ran downhill at astounding rates. Had we not deceived ourselves into believing we could trust totalitarians enough to build effective arms limitations (detente), in spite of the failure of all such treaties throughout history, we would now be building massive defenses against any nuclear attacks. Had we been aware of the inherent failures and evils of all collectivism, in direct proportion to its actual implementation, we might not have deceived our-selves into believing we could stop Vietnamese communism by fighting for Vietnamese oligarchic fascism—or into believing in the first place that it mattered that much which of these systems of collectivism prevailed.

Why did we do all of these things that have brought us to our present peri-lous state? No doubt there were many situational factors, as there always are in the systemic drifts of great civilizations, but the one overriding, common, predisposing factor has been the growing modernist myth "Statism Works!" and, thus, "freedom fails!"

It is this core-enabling myth of modernist megastatism which led our bank-ers to believe that immense loans to Russian and Polish commisars, to Argen-tinian and Brazilian bureaucrats in uniform, and to Mexican oligarchic bu-reaucrats in disguise as peasant revolutionaries would produce creative and efficient enterprises behind their walls of tariff protections. It was this belief in statism which led our political leaders to believe that the Russian megastat-ists have the same basic interests and understandings of the world we do, that they can be counted on to be reasonable and decent—that Stalinist terrorism was a personal aberration rather than an inherent tendency in totalitarian statism, and that, therefore, we can trust them not to hide fifteen-foot cruise missiles in warehouses, not to build extra ICBM's for their cold-launch silos, not to really act in accord with the Lenin-Brezhnev Doctrine, and not to plan a decapitation nuclear first strike. It was this belief in the myth of totalitarian power that led our diplomats to see internal subversion as hopeless in communist nations, that led our leaders to speak so softly about communism over the Voice of America that brave men like Alexandr Solzhenitzyn were driven almost to despair of American sanity, and to believe nuclear defense is useless against such "mighty" foes.

Our growing myth of modernist megastatism and our belief in the pseudo-scientific theories that saw statist bureaucracies as inherently more successful and morally superior progressively eroded our moral case against communism, led us to retreat steadily even to the point of terrorizing the world with the pseudo-rationalistic policies of MAD (mutual assured destruction) and "flexible first use of nuclear weapons," and become ever more defensive morally. And our growing myth of modernist megastatism increasingly paralyzed us in the great moral conflict with the communist totalitarians. It is only by rediscovering and exercising our own fierce faith in freedom that we can reverse this perilous drift and launch successful moral offensives against the communists. By practicing freedom at home and abroad, we will revitalize our entire society, especially our economy and military forces, and we will show by example how all people can best fulfill their desires for freedom, justice, plenty, equality, community, and charity.

A Rebirth of Freedom

But have we gone too far to turn back? Have too many Americans forgotten the joys and foresworn the moral principles of freedom? Have too many of us become too dependent on the statist bureaucrats to ever relinquish their payoffs? Today these and similar questions haunt many of us most committed to freedom. Only the mythmakers can offer us answers to them with the certainty born of anxiety, ignorance, and deception. The issues, as we have seen, are vastly complex and, therefore, there are always irreducible residues of uncertainty.

We who have endured the twentieth century have lived through an age of anxiety only to enter an age of peril and dread. The peril of depression faced by our great worldwide economy, and of the vast suffering and political upheavals contingent upon that peril, is exceeded only by the peril of nuclear war wrought by our modernist megastatism. For fifty years now we have been climbing an ever steeper and more slippery pinnacle. The higher we go, the greater the danger of slipping into the abyss and the worse our crash will be. Even as I write these concluding words, bankers and politicians are scurrying furiously around the world to prevent the massive bankruptcies of statist regimes that *might* trigger the catastrophic deflation that would catapult us into the abyss. And they are tying to do so by ratcheting us up to an even higher, steeper, and more slippery point on the megastatist pinnacle. They are now spewing forth currency through the international banks to create one gigantic interlocking of the statist regimes of all stripes around the world. They are building a modernist international welfare system of truly colossal proportions.

But, as my analogy of the pinnacle of megastatism suggests, there is no safe flatland at the top. Our modernist megastatists cannot save themselves by infinite and eternal expansions of the money supplies. No one can predict whether the current inflationary rescue effort will work, or even whether an unlikely total default of $300 billion or so would actually precipitate a catastrophic deflation in a world economy many times larger (in which international trade alone is $2 trillion a year). It is my guess that it will work this time because OPEC was the major incentive for the explosion of inflation in the late 1970s and because, since that shock, politicians have grudgingly allowed enough freedom in the energy markets to undermine OPEC. Statists, after all, are not fated to be stupid, and only a truly stupid politician would continue the explosive ratchets-up of regulation and inflation toward the hyperinflation and stagnation that would surely burst and cast us into the abyss. If the immediate peril is overcome, with a modicum of intelligence statists may be able to continue their stop-go inflationary-deflationary policies for many years, *slowly* ratcheting-up the pinnacle.

Eventually, however, the day of reckoning will come, if we continue our perilous climb. The longer it is put off, the higher we go on the collectivist pinnacle, the greater the peril grows. What then? Such a worldwide collapse is so unprecedented that our only certainty in such speculations is uncertainty. However, we do know that freedoms are normally the first victims of great economic and political crises. In the grip of dread we human beings normally revert to the simple, absolute patterns of panic—fierce attacks on those stigmatized as the causers of the crises, expiations of the gods, and other magical flights from the grim realities. The everyday practices and the institutions that have grown over centuries to form the foundations for freedom could probably not long withstand these panicky reversions to absolutist defense mechanisms. Even the powerful traditions and institutions of the Roman Republic in a far simpler age could not withstand the panic to escape the terrors of the civil wars. Only their outer forms were left standing to help shield the once-proud freemen from the shame of their submission to imperial collectivism.

We cannot really plan for such a great crisis, for, if it does come, the immediate situation and the powerful emotions and defense mechanisms it triggers will most likely win the day. Fortunately, the actions we should take to ratchet-down the megastatist pinnacle are the ones that will do most to prevent that great crisis from ever coming and the ones that will best prepare us to make the "softest landing"—with the least panic—possible if it does come, thereby giving us the best chance of preserving freedom.

Our one great need, on the achievement of which all else depends, is for a revival of the spirit of freedom, a rediscovery of the joys of living righteously—of living in accord with that fierce faith in freedom that still burns or smolders in most of us. We Americans have not expunged or forsaken our values on freedom, on initiative, on creativity, on nonconformity, on work, on individual responsibility, on love, and on charity. Yes, the fires of liberty burn less fiercely in many breasts today than a century ago. Some Americans have acquiesced in the deadening and deceiving sense of peacefulness and security the rationalistic forms of statist bureaucracy give them. But to the majority of us these are a contemptible minority—the dehumanizing purveyors of misinformation and myths at whom the great majority of us still hurl the hated epithets "Bureaucrat!" and "Politician!"

We have not drifted into this deadly thicket of the modernist welfare megastate in a rational attempt to escape freedom—or even in a rational attempt to defraud our neighbors through special-interest payoffs. We have strayed from the paths of freedom because we have been blinded by our modernist myths, by giving in to the temptations used by politicians who are self-deceivers, other-deceivers, and defrauders luring us into giving them ever more power. The great myth of a modernist millennium and the lesser myths of rationalism and scientism have been the most important, and they have been used by others and by ourselves to deceive us into believing we can have a heaven on earth—including absolute freedom.

It is precisely because freedom is still such a fiery faith for most Americans that such deceitful and mythical lures can be fashioned to tempt us into giving up political freedom in the pursuit of impossible and self-destructive freedom. (And, of course, the Tory conservatives who react repressively, out of a panicky fear that the foundations of all social life—love and family—will be dissolved by this myth of libertinism, drive many of the young into the already-enticing arms of the mythical deceivers. If left alone, even the most prodigal soon find themselves deeply depressed and readily embrace the ancient natural limits imposed by the vastly complex, delicate balancing of conflicting human passions and social values.) No, we Americans have not lost our fiery faith in freedom. We have been led down the path toward totalitarian megastatism in part by mythical appeals to our very passion for freedom. Since that passion still burns brightly, we can still regain our freedom and reverse this terrible drift by dispelling the myths. All individuals and all peoples are tempted at times to stray from and even to betray their own deepest values by mythical deceptions that tempt them. But the further they stray, the more they betray their moral convictions, the more likely their recognition of their own betrayal becomes. The more extreme their prodigality, the more extreme will be their sufferings the "morning after" when they can no longer deny the increasingly obvious truth of self-betrayal. Then come the pangs of guilt and remorse and the desperate attempts to regain the path of virtue and make amends. In time comes the joyous reawakening of the feeling of self-rediscovery and of righteousness, of living in accord with their deepest sense of self, including their most fiery moral convictions.

The greatest and most Christian hearts and minds surveying the condition of the Church and of society more generally in the fifteenth century were driven almost to despair. Everywhere the Antichrist seemed to reign supreme, but nowhere more supreme than in the citadels of the colossal Church bureaucracy itself. The mighty princes of the Renaissance welfare states strutted proudly in their convictions of a divine right to plan the lives of their far-flung subjects, but none strutted more proudly than the Church leaders who sold the very grace of their God (through "indulgences" and "immunities") to feed the insatiable maw of their own Church welfare state and of their own debauched passions.

We must, of course, be cautious in accepting the most livid portrayals of Church libertinism painted by the rising chorus of those who hated this new Babylon, but there is no doubt the Church was ruled by devotees of libertinism (for themselves at least—much like our liberal politicians who enforce stern rules of probity on businesspeople and bind themselves with the soft rules of laxity). Even Machiavelli, no stranger to the wayward ways of worldliness, looked with shock upon this gross corruption of all the letters and spirit of Christianity. As the sixteenth century approached, he could see the storm of protest growing beneath the iron rules of Inquisitorial repression and he prophesized the downfall of this Church of corruption, this Church of Antichrists ruling by appealing to the very Christian convictions and passions of the mass of Europeans which the Church had fostered in earlier centuries and even then preached as a front to hide its real betrayals. And, of course, the people did rise up, cleansed the corrupt Church and eventually overthrew the strutting courtiers and princes. It took centuries of terrible warfare to do so, but the people were inspired by the Christian convictions the Church could not effectively corrupt. The Puritans were inspired by their hatred of the worldly church to try to fly to the opposite extreme of a Christian utopia that would transcend the "evils" of human nature (much as anarchists today are driven out of hatred of the modernist welfare state to dream of a utopia of no government). Like all utopians in power long enough, they became totalitarian statists. But these extremists too were merely the most extreme evidence that the faith that so long seemed to have been murdered by corrupters was only repressed, lying dormant but being reawakened by each more wayward drift into the world of Antichrist.

We too have drifted so far in betraying our fiery faith that the truth of betrayal is becoming apparent to ever more Americans. Many of us are still tempted by this myth and the promised payoffs triggering our passions, but ever more of us look with real dread upon the colossal statist betrayal. All of our presidents since Lyndon Johnson have been elected on platforms and rhetorics that denounced state powers. There is a rising tide of grim reality—of modernist-induced stagnation—and, thus, of reaction against the modernist welfare state.

The more the myths are exposed by the emerging realities and by those who speak the truth, the more the spirit of freedom will be reawakened from its long slumber. The three greatest enemies of this rising tide of reality and truth telling are statist education, the regulated oligopolies of the mass media, and all bureaucratic secrecy beyond the minimum necessary in military matters. All statists know they can control public discourse in direct proportion to their control of education, the mass media, and public access to information about government. If the statists can continue to gain ever greater control over public discourse, whether under the guise of "improving" education, the guise of "truth in advertising," the guise of "executive privilege," or any of the multifarious guises they will surely create, then we will continue to accelerate our drift toward the great crisis and the plummet into the unknown. If these powers can be wrested from them, the rising tide of truth will further stir the reawakening of the spirit of freedom and we shall see what wonders our second great American experiment in the System of Natural Liberty will allow individuals to achieve.

Americans everywhere are yearning desperately to break free from the deadening weight of bureaucracy and to recreate a world of liberty. There is a vast, suppressed energy throughout our land today. Someday we will free that vast energy and there will be a great explosion of work, of creativity, of justice, and of loving charity such as earlier Americans achieved in our first great experiment in freedom.

> It was answered, that all great, and honourable actions are accompanied with great difficulties, and must be both enterprised and overcome with answerable courages. It was granted the dangers were great, but not desperate; the difficulties were many, but not invincible. For though their were many of them likly, yet they were not cartaine; it might be sundrie of the things feared might never befale; others by providente care and the use of good means, might in a great measure be prevented; and all of them, through the help of God, by fortitude and patience, might either be borne, or overcome.

True it was, that such atempts were not to be made and undertaken without good ground and reason; not rashly or lightly as many have done for curiositie or hope of gaine, etc. But their condition was not ordinarie; their ends were good and honourable; their calling lawfull, and urgente; and therfore they might expecte the blessing of God in their proceding. Yea, though they should loose their lives in this action, yet might they have comforte in the same, and their endeavors would be honourable. . . .

William Bradford

Notes

1. See E. R. Dodds, *The Greeks and the Irrational* (Boston: Beacon Press, 1957).
2. George Kennan, *On Dealing With the Communist World* (New York: Harper & Row, 1964), p. 11.
3. I have presented the details of this argument about the Russian threat in "A Grand Moral Strategy for Waging Peace and War," in Robert Poole, ed., *Defending a Free Society* (Lexington, MA: D. C. Heath, 1984).
4. Dodds, *The Greeks and the Irrational*, pp. 246 and 262.

Appendix I

The Ancient Model of Tyranny

Peisistratus of Athens became the most famous of the ancient Greek tyrants. Solon rightly described Peisistratus in his youth: "There is no better disposed man in Athens, save for his ambition." He radiated benevolence for all Athenians, except, of course, those who dared to oppose him. Although we have no reports by a contemporary Machiavelli or Guicciardini on his thinking, he obviously recognized a basic fact of politics in a society in which internal divisions prevent any one group from dominating all of the others: the successful politician must pursue a coalition strategy. That means he must indeed be benevolent in the beginning toward a majority, which means he must transcend narrow sectional, class, or ideological interests. American politicians today face the same situation, so the label of "ideologue" or "extremist" is the kiss of political death to anyone on the national level. Those who successfully ride the ideological tiger at the local level where one group dominates, such as a Goldwater from Arizona or a McGovern from North Dakota, must work furiously at transcending that narrow base, and become "benevolent" toward a majority coalition, or they are easily overwhelmed.

Peisistratus first became a media star in the classic manner, that is, by becoming a successful military leader. Like most modern media politicians, he was very attractive, highly charming, and more or less witty. Though we do not know of his early associations with the new class of Athenian literati, who were rapidly becoming a major force in Athenian public opinion in this early period (around 600 B.C.), he probably carefully cultivated the most popular of the poets, dramatists, philosophers, and other teachers. We do know that once he became tyrant he always assiduously cultivated close and excellent relations with these gatekeepers of the mass media. Modern social scientists who believe that the mass media came into existence only in the nineteenth century with the introduction of the new technology of high-speed printing presses have simply not assessed opinion making in earlier societies. In ancient Athens the dramatic performances were attended by far higher percentages of the citizens, especially those of influence, and were taken far more seriously than any single modern media event. One Sophocles or Aristophanes was worth two dozen Cronkites, roughly speaking. Those close and excellent relations served Peisistratus well both in his period of reign and in transmitting his fame down through all of these centuries. His major opponents, the aristocrats led first by Miltiades and later by Megacles, got an extremely bad press, so bad in fact that modern historians who do not understand economics almost always assert blandly that the aristocrats "oppressed the poor." Who now reads about these presumed oppressors, Megacles and Miltiades? Only those who are interested in Peisistratus and thus in his "evil enemies." All historical victory goes to the media victor. And the media victor is the one who best bribes and flatters (with grants and favors) the media workers, the newspeople, and intellectuals.

No amount of charm, media fame, or payoffs to the intellectuals by themselves would have allowed Peisistratus to become tyrant in a society with a long tradition of legitimate, consitutional political life. Augustus, the Medicis, Cromwell, Napoleon, Bismarck, Lenin, Hitler, and almost all similar tyrants must wait and pray for their *enabling crises*, those crises that do not appear to be managed by the creative use of traditional, legitimate forms of political life. Those crises are at times dominated by foreign military problems, but those produced internally are almost always dominated by some economic problems that have severe effects on the everyday lives of a large part of the population. Ordinary citizens normally pursue their daily life with little direct concern for politics, simply because there is in fact little they can do about politics, until their lives, livelihoods, or status (dominance position) is threatened. Economic crises affect all of these, while few other forms of crisis do; or else, as in the case of plagues, there is little that can be done about them by political action.

Historians generally give a very garbled account of the economic crisis faced by Athens which enabled Peisistratus to satisfy his political ambitions. Almost all of them fail to understand the economic or demographic situation Athens apparently faced. As a result, they almost always see the economic problem as a result of the political system: the aristocrats oppressed the poor, who thus became revolutionaries.

Even the historians who have understood that the population and economic changes were obviously of vital importance have generally given garbled analyses of the whole situation. For example, one early *Encyclopedia Britannica* account waxes moralistic about the economic factors: "(New measures) were necessary owing mainly to the tyrannical attitude of the rich to the poorer classes. Of these many had become slaves in lieu of payment of rent and loans, and thus the land had fallen gradually into the hands of capitalists. It was necessary to readjust the economic balance and to provide against the evil of aristocratic and capitalistic predominance."[1] All contemporary accounts saw the aristocrats as the ones involved in the land problem. This author obviously assumed that, since they were evil, they must have been capitalists. This is another of those mythical tricks of symbolic identity a powerful emotion like hate can play on the mind. In fact, the "capitalists" wound up joining the coalition Peisistratus eventually put together in opposition to most of the aristocrats, so this explanation lacks any value other than that of intellectual piety. Even the otherwise admirable account of Stringfellow Barr in his lovely work *The Will of Zeus* oversimplifies the situation to the point of absurdity by seeing it as all due to the introduction of coinage to Greece.[2]

Such oversimplifications are abetted by the grave lack of information that we would need to fully understand what happened. The Greeks themselves clearly did not have any full understanding of what was happening, any more than most people today can understand what is happening economically. That is probably the reason they gave no full account of it or full explanation of why they did what they did. But the few historians who have known economics and economic history, especially H. Michell,[3] R. J. Hopper,[4] and Chester Starr,[5] have pieced together a convincing picture of what was happening.

Athens had long since become an oligarchic state dominated religiously, judicially and, to a less extent, economically by a set of semiaristocratic families. But it was an individualistic society with strong government support through the judicial system for private property rights. Moreover, the pursuit of wealth through foreign trade was an honorable occupation even for those of noble family. Solon himself was a successful international merchant born of a poor but respectable noble family. The population of the tiny land area of Attica (of approximately 1,000 square miles) was clearly increasing. This was leading to colonization around the Mediterranean, but the population pressure on the land was still growing. The developing economy of the city allowed many of those remaining to take on jobs as artisans, merchants, and service workers (such as the media experts). As all of this was happening, agriculture seems to have been undergoing commercialization, probably in good part in response to competition from more efficient foreign producers. Olive farms were increasingly oriented to export trade and, very importantly, the average farm size was growing, probably to make farming more efficient to keep up with the competition. We know very well from massive experience in Western societies in recent centuries what that process does. It makes farming far more productive and lowers prices. But it also creates a large class of very disgruntled "subsistence-level farmers" who were once proud, successful independent farmers, but who can now remain in their ancestral homes only by becoming submissive retainers of large landholders who tell them what to do to produce efficiently. More and more of the farmers became sharecroppers (hectemoroi) who had to pay a sixth of their produce to the landlords.

Athens was already becoming an important center of international trade and Greece in general was developing rapidly economically, as was much of the nearby mainland. As the international economy expanded in the seventh century, financial institutions developed rapidly. Somewhere around 650 B.C., coins were minted for the first time (possibly in Lydia) and spread rapidly throughout the Greek World. By 600 B.C. silver coins had probably replaced the earlier iron ingots in Athens as the measure of value. Gold was scarce, so was little used. Chester Starr, author of *The Economic and Social Growth of Early Greece*,[6] and other recent analysts of this crisis believe coins were not significant because they were not in general use. They fail to see that societies can easily use coin values without actually having coins. This is done primarily when coins are scarce because they are new. Ancient Egyptians apparently used a *symbolic money* before they used any actual coins. Medieval Europeans developed a highly complex symbolic money without material form that gave a universal measure of the different values of all the coins in use in a given regional market. They were able to use this symbolic monetary equivalent with great dexterity, but it was so complex they did not adequately describe it in words. The European Economic Community has created a formal monetary measure of the same sort. Ancient Greeks almost certainly switched to coin values before coins were in widespread use.

So, by 600 B.C. financial contracts were made in terms of these silver coins. Credit institutions also developed rapidly in the seventh century and by 600 B.C. it was common to borrow money at interest, with the terms almost certainly being specified in coins. The ancient rules, made for a society in which loans were rare, coins nonexistent and the economy more or less stable, allowed creditors to force defaulting debtors into slavery. (We should remember that in our own far more economically advanced society of the nineteenth century it was still possible to send defaulters to debtors' prisons.) The increase of population pressure on the land and competitive struggle would probably have been sufficient in themselves to force a growing number of marginal farmers into slavery. But there was almost certainly a far greater social problem at work as well: deflation.

Since the Athenian economy was expanding its transactions, it required an expanding coinage to prevent deflation (increasing real value of the coinage). But Athens at this time had no source of silver itself and had to import its coinage. (Under Peisistatus they discovered a major silver lode and this greatly helped their expanding economy.) Yet at this time they were probably suffering a bad balance of trade as well. This would lead to the export of what little foreign coinage they managed to get. The result was deflation, which would tend to stagnate the economy, that is, decrease investment in the young industries and increase urban unemployment. Very importantly, deflation made the interest and principle owed on loans worth more in real terms. The overall effect was to make it increasingly difficult for the small, marginal farmers to pay their debts or to find alternative employment. The number of bankruptcies grew, thus casting more and more families into slavery. As usual, the growing urban unemployment, risk of bankruptcy, and actual enslavement increased the anger of the poor and decreased the legitimacy of the traditional order headed by the aristocrats, and the willingness to revolt grew.

These "mysterious powers" of money are not mysterious to anyone knowledgeable about economics today, yet precisely the same sorts of social problems resulting from variations in the real values of money have been almost universal. The process since the medieval era has generally been the opposite of that faced by Athens. Ever since officials discovered that they could deceive the people into transferring more real value to themselves by inflating the coinage, they have done so whenever they thought they could get away with it. Most periods have thus been periods of inflation, so that the money terms of contracts have worked against the traditional order of landed aristocrats. This very process probably did more than anything else to bring the bourgeoisie to power in Europe, Japan, and elsewhere, because they learned how to use money rates to advance their interests faster than did the aristocrats. Adam Smith spent much of chapter 5 in *The Wealth of Nations* explaining the way in which inflation destroyed the landed aristocrats whose contracts specified rents in money terms during an era of inflation. But it was already too late for the European aristocrats and for their kings who had thought themselves so smart in outwitting the people through inflation. How ironic it is that the twentieth-century politicians representing the coalition of lower classes and the new welfare-state classes should use the same "mysterious weapon" of inflation to attack the bourgeoisie investors locked into fixed-rate contracts.

The major groups of Athenian politics (the aristocratic "plains" group, the poor "hill" people, and the new commercial and industrial businessmen and artisans) finally recognized that the crisis called for extraordinary measures. Using an ancient custom, they appointed Solon constitutional dictator, a leader with extraordinary powers, to reorder their economy to prevent further conflicts. Having been a successful merchant involved in international trade, Solon apparently recognized the deflation to be the ultimate source of the political problems and set about trying to undo its effects. He clearly freed most or all of those enslaved and tried to prevent further enslavement for debt. It is not really known whether he tried to decrease the interest rates, but he apparently debased the coinage to try to counteract the deflation, and he probably began the active state encouragement of commerce which would do most of all to reverse the trade deficit producing so much of the deflation. Whatever his mix of reforms, they did not effectively solve either the economic problem or the resulting political problem. The conflicts resumed after a short lull and seemed to grow even worse.

It was this growing crisis that gave Peisistratus his chance. But it was a split within the ranks of the aristocrats that made it possible for him to build the short-run coalition necessary to get longer-run power. Peisistratus used his personal relations, his great personal charm, and his eloquence to build a temporary coalition of one segment of the aristocrats, the poor hill people and the urban merchant industrial interests. The aristocrats had suffered some failure of nerve and had split their forces, with a major segment deciding that a tyranny by such a seemingly benevolent person as Peisistratus would not be all that bad. After all, he proposed only reforms, not an end to their rule, so a few extra legal means hardly seemed important in the crisis situation. Probably because they became more aware of where he was headed, this segment later deserted him and drove him out.

But while in power he had been able to build a powerful base of support. He did this in good part by being genuinely benevolent to the widest possible coalition of interests. In fact, he was generally so benevolent that Pierre Levêque has called him "a good-humored tyrant." He moved quickly to build public-works projects to alleviate unemployment; and he actively encouraged commerce and industry. Very importantly, during this transition period, he did not directly challenge any more of the traditional forms of legitimacy than seemed absolutely necessary. The historical records contain severe denunciations of the tyrants in all the Greek city-states, but those were later denunciations by the educated aristocrats who had learned how severe the oppression of themselves could be in the service of paying off the business and worker interests. Pierre Levêque has put the case well:

> The tyrant did not change the established constitution. The old magistratures continued to be served, primarily by men devoted to him. The council and the assembly (where it existed) ratified the new policy. But this was only a facade: all power was in the hands of the tyrant, who generally lived in the citadel and was accompanied by a bodyguard. To the thinkers of the fourth century, this seemed the most striking external manifestation of tyranny. Numerous anecdotes stress the arbitrariness and violence of the tyrants: for example, Periander, who involuntarily caused the death of his wife and was at odds with his mother and his sons, provided moralists with a good illustration of the misfortunes engendered by excess. A critical approach to all this material is necessary. Most of these tyrants were too mindful

of their own interests to indulge in useless excesses which would have made their positions even more dangerous.[7]

Peisistratus had also begun to undermine the old sources of legitimacy and to build new ones. He strongly supported new religious practices and cults that were identified with his interests and opposed to the ancient religious institutions supporting the aristocrats. He soon returned as Athens' first successful tyrant. He wisely chose to follow Solon's basic program and succeeded greatly in building up industry and trade, which in time decreased the problem of deflation and unemployment. He wisely gave grants to his intellectual media supporters and to his new cult groups. As Levêque has said of all the major tyrants who succeeded, "They also liked to gather artists and poets around them. Cleistheses summoned two famous sculptors, Dipoenus and Scyllis, from Crete. The link between the ultimate development of lyricism and tyranny is not fortuitous. Their courts readily became coteries where poets were welcomed provided they sung of their glory."[8] His tyranny flourished and on the whole seems to have been a benevolent tyranny for the growing city. Only under his two succeeding sons did benevolent means drift into increasingly cruel and totalitarian methods. But the family policies had built a strong new class of free businessmen, merchants, and artisans. They revolted against the tyranny, but extended the basic policies and thus built the Athenian democracy of the fifth century.

Notes

1. "Solon," *Encyclopedia Britannica* (Chicago: University of Chicago Press, 1947), vol. 20, pp. 954–56.
2. Stringfellow Barr, *The Will of Zeus* (Philadelphia: Lippincott, 1961).
3. H. Michell, *The Economics of Ancient Greece*, 2d ed. (Cambridge: Cambridge University Press, 1957).
4. R. J. Hopper, *The Early Greeks* (New York: Harper and Row, 1977), especially pp. 188–215.
5. Chester Starr, *The Economic and Social Growth of Early Greece* (New York: Oxford University Press, 1977), especially, pp. 181–93.
6. Ibid.
7. Pierre Lévêque, *The Greek Adventure* (London: Weidenfeld and Nicolson, 1968), p. 124.
8. Ibid.

Appendix II

American Political Labels

Political "labels" are such potent political weapons in our age of the megamedia, and are thus so corrupted, that they must be used only with greatest caution in any objective work. I shall use them only as shorthand for ideas systematically presented in the work. I use them only as *ideal types* to refer to sets of ideas and practices which have a high probability of hanging together but which in any particular individual or situation may overlap significantly. I myself do not reify political labels, so I am not impassioned over them. I personally agree with some ideas from every persuasion. No successful political idea is completely contrary to human nature, so, being a human being, none of these political ideas is completely foreign to me now. The "big" labels—such as fascism, and communism—are dealt with in detail in the body of the work and noted in the index. The labels that are more "hashed" and "treacherous" in political discourse today are the common ones referring to our domestic politics. It will be most helpful to keep these major distinctions in mind.

The proponents of individual liberty from most government regulation were originally called *liberals;* they are now called *classical liberals,* or more commonly, *libertarians.* These theorists differed with each other over how much and what types of liberty are compatible with social order. Those who advocated extreme liberty within a government federation were called *radicals,* whereas that generally refers now to advocating extreme action, even revolution at first, to achieve economic equality through massive government power. Extreme classical liberals are now called *minimal government libertarians* and the ultimate extreme, those who are against all government, are *anarchists.* Those who oppose moral rules in general are *libertines,* not libertarians. Unfortunately, as usual, there is much confusion over this, so some people think libertine "hippies" are libertarians.

Conservatives of all types have always been more suspicious of individual liberties and believed more in the need to restrain these by social rules and enforcements; and they have believed that, in general, there is more value in traditional cultural rules and beliefs, especially those of the family and religion. But there is great variation in the degrees of these and especially in the degrees of government power and inequality they support. *Tories* generally believe in a high degree of state power and inequality. They like aristocracy and generally prefer it to be inherited. But almost all modern American conservatives are *Burkean conservatives,* or *Whigs,* who oppose the Tories. They believe to varying degrees in Aristotle's "natural aristocracy," which achieves social dominance rather than inherits it. They are more in favor of the authority of family, religion, and local government than most libertarians. They are against the Tory's very strong central government; but they support the state powers more than libertarians, and are especially apt to favor interventionism in foreign policy. This is why Whig neoconservatives accept more big-government programs, especially in foreign affairs, than almost any libertarian would. Modern British conservatives are often Tories who accept the very big government of socialist Labourites as long as it does not attack aristocratic inequality. *Thatcherism* is an intraparty coup by Whigs and is much resented by the real Tories. So-called conservatives in France and Germany, such as the Gaullists, are descendants of more absolutist monarchists and theocrats, like Bonald and de Maistre, who support far more collectivism. Conservatives, especially Burkeans, are certainly in favor of using reason to produce change, but they emphasize local group change and expect it to be slow.

Modern liberals, now called *liberals,* or *New Deal liberals,* believe in taking strong government action to "help" the "worse-off," but within some vague limits that stop short of government control of most of the economy, of most of individual lives, or of most equality. Liberals vary widely in how much emphasis they place on moral improvement through education and regulation, economic controls, equality, and so on. *Socialists* are those who insist the mix must fall far on the side of government controls, and involve considerable social planning, but must fall short of the more totalitarian extremes such as fascism or communism. Almost all American socialists are *democratic socialists* who stress democratic participation. They overlap greatly today with *populists,* who emphasize socialism more at the local level than that of socialist central planning and emphasize equality more than government controls. Socialists generally want the state to nationalize or run the big corporate bureaucracies in other ways, whereas populists want to break them up to reduce control to the more local level.

Neoliberals share the goals of other modern liberals, but want to use more indirect means. They commonly favor using taxes, for example, to provide incentives for individuals and corporations to move in the direction of their goals (such as clean air and water), rather than using bureaucratic regulatory agencies. *Industrial-policy neoliberals* believe in using the same indirect means, but place great emphasis on generalized, central planning of the incentives to achieve the economic goals, especially of industrial growth. They believe in indicative central planning—pointing the way with incentives.

Appendix III

Theories of the Origins of the Democratic Welfare State

The specific political processes by which our modernist welfare states have arisen are remarkably diverse and vastly complex. As already noted, some of them, notably those in Germany and France, are merely revisions and expansions of the massive bureaucracies of sixteenth to eighteenth century absolutist monarchies. Others, especially those in most of the Anglo-Saxon nations, with their many centuries of liberal philosophy and of liberty and decentralization, have grown only very slowly against ferocious resistance over the past century and a half; and these have grown by many different paths. Others, such as those of Uruguay, Argentina, and Chile, grew very rapidly, sometimes running through the entire dynastic cycle from "rich land of liberty" to "impoverished tyranny" in one astounded generation or less.

Harold Wilensky[1] and others who have studied this vast diversity of paths and rates of growth have been struck by the equally vast diversity of political values, tactics, goals and, above all, rhetoric used to get public support for each ratchet-up to a greater level of state power. Perhaps most striking is the diversity of political shibboleths under which the builders of our welfare states have marched—Labour, Socialist, Conservative, Liberal, Social Democrat, and so on. Most people have been quite confused by this lack of fit between labels and programs and, combined with their ignorance about the many different policies being pursued, this has obscured both the causes of their rise and their various effects. When supposed conservatives like Edward Heath in Britain and Richard Nixon in the United States pursue policies that are more socialist than those pursued by some leaders in other nations who pursue far more free-market policies but are called Socialists, like Helmut Schmidt in West Germany, it is not hard for people to be confused or misled.

This confusion is further multiplied by the often great difference between political rhetoric, including laws actually passed, and everyday realities. Mexican presidents make a great show at home of being Castro sympathizers and revolutionary redistributors, but in reality they run a state capitalist, one-party machine system that controls most of the economy, dispenses poverty to the masses and plutocracy to the few, and controls the mass media by ownership and massive corruption to hide all of this. Since the 1930s, Swedish Labor prime ministers and their laws have often sounded far more socialistic than their British or French nominal counterparts, but in fact their laws have been administered far more to support business investment, especially in new technology, than in Britain, and Swedish industries were not nearly as nationalized as those of Britain or "conservative" Gaullist France. You have to watch the political shell game very closely to tell under which cup the political peas are really hidden.

But all of this vast diversity has led to one general situation: our bureaucratically controlled economies are run by multifarious forms of central planning and redistributive policies; and one general outcome: creeping (and sometimes galloping) stagnation. Certainly there are important differences in the policies pursued, the administrative means used, and the effects of these in societies with widely varying mixes of bureaucratic centralism, cultural homogenization, and morale; and certainly these produce considerable variations in the rates at which the ultimate stagnation grows. We shall see many instances of these different policies and their effects throughout this book. But, for all of this remarkable diversity of policies and means, the proximate result has been roughly the same modernist megastate, and the ultimate result for all who continue along the path very long, regardless of the mix of policies, is stagnation.

How can we explain so many different kinds of societies following so many different paths to the same general outcome? Many different explanations have been given. Most of them are of no use because they focus on only one nation at a time and see only what is different about that nation, not the underlying factors at work leading them all in the same direction. As Hugh Trevor-Roper said about the revolutions that swept away most of the seventeenth-century Renaissance welfare states, "A wholesale coincidence of special causes is never plausible as the explanation of a general rule."[2] Many others have focused on the Great Depression, especially in explaining the birth of the American welfare state. There is no doubt that this was a crucial factor in producing ratchets-up in many nations, and certainly in the United States. But the basic patterns of feelings and thoughts were already highly developed in the United States (as we saw in chapter 4) in the Progressives, including Walter Lippmann and Herbert Hoover, and were this not so, the Great Depression probably would not have happened and, if it had, it would not have been so drastically protracted had the state not adopted policies that prevented economic adjustments to the deflation. Moreover, Britain was already well on its way, the depression was not so severe there, and the British government did not make its most fateful ratchet-up until the end of World War II. It has also often been argued that the great ratchets-up in tax rates, deficit financing, and regulations of World Wars I and II prepared the way. Certainly these were important factors, yet, while our tax rates remained at roughly those levels (with slight waxings and wanings), the Truman and Eisenhower administrations did eliminate most wartime planning, almost all wartime controls, and most deficit financing (from roughly 120 percent of GNP in 1952 to roughly 35 percent today). War set dangerous precedents of seeming success with great state powers (spring flowers), but it was only one of the important factors, as Robert Higgs demonstrates.[3]

Many more systematic commonsensical and ideological theories have been proposed. Most of the commonsensical theories are quite moralistic. Those against the welfare state focus on the presumed evil conspiracy of a few politicians, such as Franklin Delano Roosevelt, Juan Peron, or Francois Mitterrand. Some have even seen Dwight D. Eisenhower as a communist conspirator because he did not completely dismantle the welfare state. Such a sweeping systemic drift of an entire worldwide civilization is hardly due to the wills of a few evil people, especially when those people were elected by hundreds of millions. Those moralists in favor of the welfare state see it as "the necessary correction to the terrible abuses of capitalism" and so on. This supporting moralism is so tied up with all of the great myths of the modernist welfare state and the plethora of submyths (such as the "immiserization of the masses") that I have been showing what is wrong with it throughout this book.

Probably the ideological explanation most commonly accepted by intellectuals is the Marxist one. The Marxist argument is somewhat complex, especially in the many neomarxist variants now proposed, but basically Marx and his followers believed "late" (or "mature") capitalism would inevitably, necessarily stagnate and immiserate the masses because in his historicist evolutionary scheme the relations among the basic variables of investment and consumption change during evolution. He was simply wrong in his specific argument and some of his brighter successors have changed the argument to try to show that the welfare state—and, especially, its fascist forms—is a desperate attempt to forestall the inevitable.[4] Actually, as noted in chapter 4, the basic policies of the modernist welfare state in nations like Germany and Britain began in the exuberant youth of their capitalism in the nineteenth century. And, of course, anyone with economic common sense can see that capitalists who would support our immense taxes on income, our immense regulatory bureaucracies, our immense subsidies for not working, and our antisavings policies in general in order to save capitalism would be like a drowning man who strangles himself in his panicky attempt to get air. As Sven Rydenfelt has said about Sweden:

> By means of straitjackets woven from thousands of state regulations supplemented with tax confiscation of resources, parties in power have gradually deprived Sweden's entrepreneurs of that freedom and operating space they need in order to function. As a consequence, the entrepreneurs have lost much of their will to work and invest. Economic stagnation, unemployment and crisis is the result. From this the enemies of free enterprise conclude that the capitalistic system has proved its incompetence and therefore must be replaced by a socialist system.
>
> The roots of the crisis are to be found in the oppression and exploitation of the entrepreneurs. The Socialist parties of Sweden have promised to cure all evils with a miracle medicine implying more oppression and more exploitation of the entrepreneurs.[5]

The Marxists have been misled by the obvious fact that many business-people have indeed worked assiduously to get payoffs from the state. But this was always the case with businesspeople and with the poor and with rich Marxist academics and intellectuals. Businesspeople were often more insistent and successful in getting state payoffs under the sixteenth- to eighteenth-century mercantilist regimes than today. Classical liberals from Adam Smith on have always denounced these hypocritical free marketeers and argued that failure—including bankruptcy—is a vital part of the system of natural liberty, necessary to its progress and, over the long run, its very existence. The reason for this will become clear later, but it is fundamentally simple. Life is inherently partially unpredictable. A vital part of all learning and success is, therefore, by trial and error. There will, then, be errors in any attempt to succeed. The goal of reason, then, is to minimize the errors by making the decisions as much as possible in the light of the immediate, concrete situation and their costs by keeping the failures as small as possible and allowing their resources to be redirected to new endeavors as efficiently as possible. Contrary to what Marxists think, the failures of some businesses are not signs of the "inevitable" collapse of "mature" capitalism, but vital to the continued health of the entire system of liberty. Welfare statists who tax the successes to "save" the failures weaken and endanger the entire system and undermine it morally. As usual, the Marxists have turned reality and truth on their head.

Many social scientist have come up with similar evolutionary theories of the origin of our modernist welfare states. All of them argue that there is some kind of "inherent contradiction" in the working of the System of Natural Liberty, but they do so in phantasmagoric ways and all use evidence from our highly collectivized societies as if they were still classical liberal societies. Most argue that there is some inherent weakness that either gets worse as the system develops or begins only in the mature stages. John Maynard Keynes's neomarxist theory is built on such an assumption.[6] All of these works have been based on some denial of the ability of the entire free-market system to adjust to changes within some part of the system, and all of them have failed to see that such failures to adjust are caused by state intervention, not by some inherent weakness that can be solved by the state. Great, sudden success of economic freedom does tend to trigger modernist millennialism (see chapter 6) but political intervention has exacerbated it terribly and greatly protracted the adjustments to the busts that always eventually follow "booms."

One of the worst results of the narrow perspectives—the loss of the general context—resulting from the professional specialization of social thought has been that our experts cannot see the whole system working over time. Keynes could not see how unique the British unemployment situation was in the 1920s and how much it and the prolongation of the Depression were a direct result of state intervention. It was especially important that the state mandated monopoly union powers that prevented wages from deflating proportionately when the rest of the system was deflated by monetary shocks (such as Britain's going back on the gold standard in 1926 at prewar parity values). Since wages were then proportionately too high in real terms and were kept too high by monopoly union powers, unemployment increased. The great Keynesian John Hicks came eventually to see this in general, but only after a quarter century of Keynesian-induced "inherent contradictions" had wreaked far greater havoc.[7]

Another variant on this idea has been Joseph Schumpeter's idea in his famous book on *Socialism, Capitalism and Democracy*[8] that capitalism will eventually be superceded by socialism because big, bureaucratized capitalist firms are so successful. Schumpeter believed that the success of great entrepreneurial firms made it possible for government bureaucrats to simply take them over and continue running them as they had been run. He rightly recognized that this government takeover would result in an end to creative, entrepreneurial production and, thus, an end to growth; but he believed the bureaucrats could maintain a stable equilibrium. He failed to see the growing informational pathologies inherent in bureaucracy (see chapter 9). Success, then was the inherent contradiction of mature (bureaucratized) capitalism— the exact opposite of Marxist ideas, but equally dooming in its praise. In the light of all the catastrophes of the most bureaucratized corporations (see chapter 9) and of nationalized and government-regulated industries since publication of that prognosis, few serious thinkers now even consider it. They concentrate, instead, on his correct prediction that growth would produce a vast growth in intellectuals and academic bureaucrats who oppose economic freedom. But John Kenneth Galbraith's *New Industrial State*[9] gave it one last mass-mediated gasp in the 1960s. All of these works suffer mortally from believing that big-and-bureaucratic can be more efficient than little-and-decentralized (an idea I carefully dissect factually and theoretically in chapter 9).

Other social scientists have proposed many single-factor, monocausal, nonevolutionary explanations. Most of these have focused on political processes, especially on the great ratchet-up of the American modernist welfare state under Lyndon Johnson and Richard Nixon in the 1960s and 1970s. Each of these normally focuses on some factor that the social scientist has studied previously in detail. For example, in *How to Limit Government Spending*[10] Aaron Wildavsky, whose specialty is government budgetary processes, argues that the most important factor in the 1960s was the abandonment of the idea of a balanced budget. But, as David Friedman pointed out in his review of the book, "He somehow neglects to mention that by 1960 the federal government was already spending 18.5 percent of GNP, up from 2.5 percent in 1890; it is currently [1982] spending about 22.5 percent. Causes usually precede their effects."[11] By the 1960s most of the foundations of our modernist welfare states were firmly in place everywhere. Congress merely expanded these foundations by shifting federal spending from the military to the civilian spheres, by mandating entitlement programs for state and local areas, and, most of all, by building massive regulations. Regulations always impose costs on someone and benefits on others. They are, of course, *presented* as "for the common welfare," but, if they really were without major cost for many people, no one would resist them and, if they really benefited everyone, almost everyone who is rational would already comply. After all, we don't need regulations ordering people to live, try to be happy, try to get richer, breathe, drink water, eat, eliminate, copulate, procreate, and so on. A vastly greater percentage of people do these every day with no regulation than the percentage who comply with any regulations, in spite of the often-severe penalties for violating regulations.

Again, Harold Wilensky[12] has done one of the most extensive statistical comparisons of our modernist welfare states and found that there is a very strong positive correlation between the per capita incomes of our Western nations and their levels of general support for welfare-state policies. He notes, for example, that a nation like Britain has one of the lowest per capita welfare expenditure levels and tries to "explain" this by noting that they also have one of the lowest per capita income levels. Unfortunately, all such statistical studies are treacherous in such a vastly complex realm so wrapped in layers of political deceit, as Wilensky is quite aware this one is. I think he is right in a general way that richer (per capita) nations find their citizens less revolutionary when they are taxed heavily than citizens closer to the elusive margins of subsistence are. As economists say, even income has diminishing rates of satisfaction or utility: starving people will work desperately for a cup of rice, while a rich man would not find it worth his accountants' time to list it under his assets. But that doesn't help us very much. After all, Prussia had the foundations of many of the modernist welfare programs in 1800 and almost all of them by the 1880s, before they had reached the British level of wealth. Britain started their basic programs when they were the richest nation, but when they were several times poorer than now, and it was in good part because of the welfare-state drain on incentives and efficiency that they have sunk to the position of "sickest big man of Europe." The fact is that some nations that are quite rich still have relatively small welfare-state bureaucracies. The fastest growing economy in the world, Hong Kong, is rich by Third World standards but it still has almost no modernist welfare state. (Probably because of its peculiar situation, it does have public housing.) Switzerland is the richest nation outside of OPEC and has by far the lowest rate of government expenditures in Europe (but it has some stringent regulations in areas such as land use). The same argument holds for Japan today. The United States was far richer than Britain before the 1960s and had far fewer modernist programs. Many poor countries, especially those in Africa, launched modernist welfare states, commonly under the aegis of Marxism, in the 1960s large enough to stagnate and actually erode their economies terribly, thus becoming desperately poor and eventually cutting back some of their welfare programs.

Melvin Krauss has shown that the crucial factors are things like the tax rates, especially on investment. If a society keeps tax rates (and other factors destructive to investment and efficiency) low, it is possible to grow even if one is also increasing modernist welfare programs, as long as the economic growth is normally faster than the growth in the welfare (and, I would add, is not paid for with inflation or foreign borrowing untied to efficient investments and is not complemented with bureaucratic regulation). This in fact is what Western nations did at first. The early welfare-state developments can actually use inflation to increase growth in the short run. Only when investors become aware of the inflation and of "monetary illusions of profits" does it decrease the rate of growth, and it is only when these states have ratcheted-up to higher levels that they erode the economy, produce stagflation and finally Peronist immiserization. Krauss has applied this to the Third World and found some striking differences:

> All of the low-tax, high-growth economies in the Pacific Rim had impressive public consumption growth from 1960 to 1977. After Singapore at an average per year increase of 9.8% come Hong Kong at 8.6% (Hong Kong is the low-tax champion of the Third World with a top marginal rate of 15% at $20,000), Korea at 6.9% and Taiwan at 4.5%. These figures indicate that the benefits from low-tax, high-growth policies do more than trickle down to the poor—they gush down upon them. High tax rates, on the other hand, yield the poor little public consumption benefit.[13]

Krauss presents a vast number of further detailed comparisons showing the same thing. He may not have recognized that some of these nations, notable Singapore, now seem in the early stages of building modernist welfare states and have already begun to reap the bitter harvest that grows from the seeds of all forms of collectivism. Australia is a land blessed with vast natural resources and few people. In 1900 Australia had the highest GNP per head in the world, but they also had the most advanced welfare state. They now rank fifteenth in the GNP sweepstakes and are sinking steadily.

One of the most common explanations of the sweeping growth of our welfare states, more frequently proposed by people with direct experience with the politicians passing the enabling legislation than by intellectuals and social scientists, is that politicians are systematically deceiving people with a cloud of incandescent and obscurantistic rhetoric about "crises" and good intentions to get more power for themselves. Certainly the soaring drive for dominance and the growing use of political deceit in our welfare states are of crucial importance in understanding how this has happened to us. We have seen (in chapters 8 and 9) how and why they are especially important after our governments and bureaucracies have become extremely powerful. We have also seen that they are important in understanding the importance of interest-group politics in the ratchet-up of welfare-state powers today, but they were not very important in the beginning (see chapter 4). We have also seen that, just as our American constitutionalist knew so well, the powerful drive for dominance is universal in human beings: though varying considerably from one individual to another, it is always there ready to be triggered by certain situations and will grow and lead to ever greater dominance until it is counterbalanced (checked) or outdone by the resistance of other human beings. Given this fact of human nature, we must explain how the politicians were able to overcome such intense resistance to their dominance, especially in America. Many of the politicians, especially in the early years, were themselves deceived as much as and often far more by mythical thinking than their electors.

The Rational Interest-Group Theory

The best monocausal theory proposed so far is the rational, democratic interest-group theory. This theory is built on the very old commonsense idea that, if given the political power to control the police powers of the state through the extension of the vote, the poorer voters will elect politicians who will take from the rich and give to the poor. This was, in fact, exactly what Tories in America, Britain, and everywhere feared would happen as suffrage was progressively extended in the nineteenth century. This ancient idea, which was based firmly on the evidence from Ancient Athens and Rome, sounds so reasonable to many people that it has become the (hidden) foundation for most of the rationalistic explanations of the rise of the modernist welfare states. The best refinement of it is found in the idea of many economists that any potential recipients of government favor have a greater incentive to seek it than the average citizens have to resist it. The cost to the potential recipients is small compared to the hoped-for gain; whereas the potential opponents would bear a roughly equal cost to stop them, with no gain in sight (unless they hope to get it instead, in which case their costs are minimized and expected gains maximized by cooperating with the other supplicants, that is, forming or joining an interest group). Gordon Tullock, who has given one of the finest expositions of the rational interest-group theory, quotes approvingly the classical statement of it almost a century ago by Vilfredo Pareto. (See chapter 4 for the quote and further evidence against the theory.)

The most telling argument against Pareto's theory is that as a simple matter of fact it did not work. For example, the Bank of the U.S., a rare success, was sold to the politicians initially as something good for everyone because it would end the inflation so endemic to state banking, but the people became aroused over its monopolistic privileges and cancelled it, in spite of the success the first bank had in stabilizing the currency, in spite of the immense vested interests its owners and other beneficiaries had in continuing it, and in spite of the immense effort they put into trying "day and night" to save it. Only on extremely rare instances, specifically those of government subsidies for land purchases, roads, mails, and the tariffs, could the people be convinced to grant interest-group privileges. In those instances they were convinced because they could see the real gains to most of them of mails, roads, and land subsidies and, apparently, failed to see the real (but hidden) losses to most of them incurred by the violation of consumer freedom ("consumer sovereignty"). Moreover, even these rare instances were administered in ways to avoid establishing huge government bureaucracies (the mails probably being the biggest exception) so the direct, visible costs were roughly minimized and the ancient specter of bureaucratic tyranny was exorcised.

The average educated American of that era knew that for hundreds of years the mercantilist welfare states had proclaimed they were serving the common interest by mandating and subsidizing monopolies. They knew the fact was that government programs "for the common interest" wound up drifting to the interest only of the most powerful—the rich special interests, the monopolies, and the politicians who milked them. It wouldn't surprise the most knowledgeable of them to learn that our "regulatory" agencies, supposedly intended to serve the public interest, drifted into regulating— "rigging"—the market monopolistically for the benefit of the biggest railroads, trucking firms, airlines, and so on; or that social security, which was sold politically as insurance for the poor, wound up being a very regressive tax, transferring many billions from the poor to the middle-income people; or that our War on Poverty in fact wound up being a secret war on the poor in which the poor were largely statistical phantoms serving as the pawns of a vast poverty industry who milked off much of the money targeted for the poor, used the poor as a moralistic shibboleth to attack the moral susceptibilities of caring Americans, put the poor in a state of permanent dependency on themselves through a mass of regulations ranging from minimum-wage laws to certification laws, and used part of their "poverty profits" to reelect the politicians who made all of this possible.

As Jefferson and Jackson knew so well, and proclaimed so stingingly, when governments become "caring" they wind up supporting monopolies and oppressing the common people. In their own day the Federalists' Bank of the United States had repeated this ancient scenario (though only in miniature), giving the people a striking reminder of all the evils of government "caring." What they and the voters demanded was an end to *all* privilege, or "equal opportunity." Jackson abolished this "development" bank with overwhelmingly popular support—and against immense political pressures from the special interests. It might be even more shocking to modern Keynesians to learn that, as noted in chapter 4, it was also Jackson's working supporters who demanded and got a gold-based currency because they believed the paper money of the Hamiltonians did not produce real "increases in capital," as Hamilton claimed, but did produce roaring inflation. Even much later, the poorest immigrant groups, such as the Chinese and Japanese, often made specific political decisions not to seek government welfare or other political favors.[14] They saw, very rationally, what business supplicants and our most recent, internal, immigrant group, the blacks, would have seen had they really been rational: government favors might help a special interest in the short run, but also have some serious short-run costs, especially the resentment and hatred from other groups, and some severe long-run costs, especially dependency and the lack of self-confidence and skills dependency breeds.

This rationalist explanation of the explosion of our welfare states also fails to note that there has always been strong opposition to each major ratchet-up, including growing opposition from interest groups representing far larger percentages of the people, such as taxpayers' unions and employer federations, which have grown rapidly to oppose those demanding privileges. There have always been powerful legions of intellectual and political Cassandras—stretching from Adam Smith, Thomas Jefferson, Ludwig Mises, Friederich Hayek, Lionel Robbins, Robert Taft, and Milton Friedman to all those today warning about the long-run catastrophes and, thus, opposing all interest groups trying to gain privileges. They were a minority and commonly suffered terrible losses for their opposition to each ripple of the tidal drift toward catastrophe. But there was nothing irrational in their calculations of the expected gains and losses for themselves and the general welfare. It always was rational over the long run for almost everyone to oppose the special interests.

Many statistical studies have been done recently by James Payne, Robert Bernstein, and others showing that there is no significant general correlation between votes for expenditures in Congress and reelection.[15] The belief in the rational interest-group theory is now so pervasive even among members of Congress that many of them, and certainly some noncongressional devotees of the theory, were shocked to see Congress cut individual taxes in 1987.[16] Raw statistical studies and votes on single issues, however, are quite misleading. Few members of Congress vote for expenditures across the board. On the contrary, they tend to be very select in pinpointing their "payoffs" at crucial voting blocks in crucial situations. The mere fact that they vote for one payoff increases the likelihood they will vote against others opposed by their crucial blocks. This also covers their tracks so they don't look like they're voting payoffs. When statisticians aggregate these crosscutting votes they largely cancel each other. Even more importantly, most payoffs are kept very indirect to hide them from the public. Most, for example, come in the form of regulatory payoffs that aid the pay-offees and hurt their enemies. Huge payoffs also come in the form of appointments of feminists, ethnics, etc., to courts and regulatory bodies. Billions in pin-point payoffs are also literally hidden in omnibus expenditure bills passed under the cloak of panic legislation the day of adjournment, as in the now infamous Great Christmas Recess Robbery of 1987. The rational-interest-group theorists are quite wrong about how the tidal drift started, and in failing to see the great myths that still undergird the whole drift process, but they are right that there are massive payoffs going on now. The obvious is still obvious, but it is only part of the whole truth and harder to demonstrate than statisticians assume.

There is, however, a further great embarrassment for the rational special-interest group theory, at least at the higher levels of our modernist welfare states: *people cannot rationally calculate the balance of their losses and gains from modernist welfare-state policies.* Economically knowledgeable people might well calculate their past gains or losses from the now-defunct Regulation-Q, which limited the interest rate banks could pay on their savings accounts, but how do they estimate the greater risk of systemic collapse produced by such regulations? They might calculate the benefits they got from Regulation-Q in subsidized mortgage rates, but how did they calculate the amount of their wealth lost by the decreased incentive for saving (thus decreased investment, productivity, and growth)? Even if they could do all of that, how could they calculate all their pluses and minuses from public education and the taxes and bureaucratic inefficiency these entail? Or the pluses and minuses from regulated oil and gas prices? And the many thousands of other ways they are entangled in our octopal bureaucratic mega-state? I know I cannot do this even for myself, though my guess is that I would be well-off in the short run (if I were willing to be an academic grants-man "milking the welfare state"), but I know that the whole system drifts toward long-run catastrophe. And for the truly rational people, that long-run "bottom line" overwhelms short-run costs and gains, especially when they recognize their inherent uncertainties about their current balance sheet. Morris Janowitz[17] has actually argued that these uncertainties about the costs and benefits of our welfare states are now so great for most people that it is causing a pervasive sense of disorientation, irrationality, and disorder.

Samuel Beer has proposed an explanation of the rise of the British mod-ernist welfare state which sees special-interest-group conflicts and the politi-cal payoffs system as of vital importance in the later stages of its growth, the explosive stage of the full-blown modernist welfare state. He argues that the British welfare state grew first out of two basic changes in the political cul-ture. The custom of deference, presumably based on the high degree of tradi-tional legitimacy found in Britain (and very weak in the United States), declined and distrust grew. Second, a new ethos of instrumentalism grew, which involves a growing assertion of one's interests. (This second factor is a part of the soaring greed that is so important in unleashing millennial modernism—see chapter 6—but that is only part of it.) Once these basic changes were well underway, the *prisoner's dilemma* game plan came into play. A reviewer for *The Economist* has given an excellent summary of Beer's theory of the prisoner's dilemma:

> Structurally, in the author's view, Britain has suffered from the working out in real-ity of the logic of the mathematician's "prisoner's dilemma." Each actor in the sys-tem knows that his interests will best be served if he and all other actors in the sys-tem can agree on, say, a policy of restraining wages or closing down inefficient fac-tories. But each actor in the system also knows that he can make substantial gains in the short term if, while everyone else is exercising restraint, he succeeds in win-ning an extra-large pay rise or securing a government subsidy for his factory. Each actor also knows that every other actor in the system is in the same position—that is, tempted to try to maximize his short-term gains. In the absence of mutual trust, and in the absence also of a credible overriding authority, the result is a Hobbesian struggle of all against all, "a paralysis of public choice." In recent British politics, Professor Beer identifies not only a pay scramble, but a benefits scramble and a subsidy scramble.[18]

This sophisticated version of the rational group theory rightly sees that *fun-damental changes in the perceived situation were necessary before the explo-sion of interest-group payoffs could happen.* It fails to note that a crucial condition of the prisoner's dilemma is that each prisoner is isolated from the other and, thus, can neither negotiate a cooperative strategy nor reestablish trust by acting in a trustworthy manner (thus signaling a willingness to act on the basis of the silver rule of reciprocal altruism). We, on the contrary, can negotiate an end to this irrational "swamp of stagnation" once people see that it is the welfare state causing the stagnation. Otherwise, we would necessarily plummet onward into an iron cage of totalitarian immiserization. Beer rightly sees that some crucial change occurred to unleash a ratchet-up toward a most irrational outcome. He is wrong only in implicitly assuming this change prevented our negotiating an end to the crazy spiral. We are perfectly capable of negotiating—and are doing so at maddening length. The problem is that a large part of our population, especially the most educated, mass-mediated and politically mobilized, does not yet *see* that it is the ratchet-up in state powers that is causing the growing stagnation and soaring political distrust and conflicts we all abhor. As we shall see, they are blinded to these causal realities by the great myths and the plethora of minimyths that have become their political dogmas.

Most economists (the so-called neoclassical economists) are committed to some version of the rationalist (nineteenth-century positivist) doctrine known as "homo economicus" which presupposes that human actors see the world of economic choice, present and future, as it really is and act rationally to optimize their satisfactions on returns. They believe, then, that there is a direct, one-to-one correspondence between the external, real structures of economic choice and the actors' ideas about it. Understanding, therefore, is dependent on the structures; only the structures are independent variables. As a result, economists do not even bother to actually observe the thoughts and feelings of the actors. In fact, though they give it somewhat more attention, they barely observe the structures. They are so convinced of their rationalist theories that they look at the outcome (say our modernist megastatists paying-off voters) and then infer backward to the structure what their preconceived theory would predict would cause this outcome of presumed rational calculations within the structure. Nick Eberstadt has shown how this approach led Mancur Olson to see *The Rise And Decline of Nations*[19] entirely in terms of the structure of *distributional coalitions*, that is, the structure of interest groups and, thereby, to fail to see that the crucial, real independent variable at work has been *attitudinal differences*:

> For example, think of a society in which nearly two-fifths of the labor force is unionized—about twice as much as in the United States today. Imagine further that these unions negotiate new contracts with employers every spring, and that negotiations take place on a company by company basis, so that any of a number of unions could bring a given firm to its knees while sparing rival businesses. Imagine next that industry in the leading sectors of this nations's economy is heavily cartelized, with a few major firms in each of these areas not only setting prices, but also augmenting their profits through preferential access to cheap credit. In these favored

firms it is extremely difficult for salaried employees to be fired; even if their performance is deemed inferior by their peers and superiors they can expect a lifetime of raises and promotions. Finally, imagine that government collaborates with these favored companies by erecting elaborate non-tariff barriers against foreign competitors in certain key markets, and allocates contracts among bidders in such a way that projects do not always go to the firm with the lowest price.

If I read Olson correctly, such a society would be a prime candidate for stagflation. Yet the country I have just described is not Britain. It is, of course, postwar Japan, the industrialized nation with the highest growth rate since the 1950s, and one of the very best records on inflation and unemployment since the early 1970s. . .

Nevertheless, it would be difficult to marshall the Japanese experience behind an argument that powerful special interest groups bring on economic paralysis. Japan's postwar success is more easily explained by the attitudes that animate its special interest groups than by the structure of those groups or the personal interests these would "logically" generate. Visitors and observers returning from Japan are consistently struck by the fact that workers, managers, industrial leaders, and government officials by and large act as if they were living in an environment in which it was necessary to minimize costs and maximize productivity to survive. That is, they seem to disregard the ostensible protection they would enjoy against economic competition. Olson would like to explain Japan's postwar drive for efficiency as a consequence of weak "distributional coalitions" and "encompassing alliances," but his command of modern Japanese history is less than complete. (He believes, for example, that Japan was a totalitarian nation before the American occupation.)[20]

While economists such as Gordon Tullock and Mancur Olson escape the gravest problems of the more simplistic interest-group theorists, they commonly start with the rationalistic assumption that actors will always on average act rationally. From there on the evidence is selected to fit the model. Anyone who starts with the evidence, not with an assumption of rationality and a predictive model that follows rationality from that, almost always winds up with a very different theory. In fact, starting with the evidence led the first general theorist of the concentration of powers in democracies, Alexis de Tocqueville, to an exactly opposite explanation from that of the economic interest-group theory.[21] Tocqueville argued that it was precisely the lack of interest-group coalitions in some egalitarian democracies which made each isolated, weak individual turn in time of need to the central power for help. This became the basic idea of the so-called *mass society theory* of the rise of modern collectivism, a theory always unconsidered by the interest-group theorists. Since the Anglo-Saxon societies, above all American society, with their vast plethora of free associations, every one of which is in some way an interest-group coalition, have been generally far more resistant to collectivism in the beginning in any form, Tocqueville and his successors are clearly more right. But, by starting with the vastly complex evidence and working up toward a theory, they have also seen that there are many other factors at work and subsequent history has revealed that they were remarkably prescient. (I have incorporated most of their ideas into my more general model.) Tocqueville, for example, saw how important the power of envy for one's *near equals* is in generating support for government "redistribution," how important "mores" are in determining the support for and opposition to collectivism, regardless of economic interests, how important education is in leading individuals to see the dangers of collectivism—or in not seeing them when the rulers can dictate what is learned, how important foreign threats and wars are in leading individuals to support centralization, and how the lust for power plays its important part. Though Tocqueville did not see completely how important the great myths have been, or how important the passions unleashed by the vast progress produced by freedom have been in inducing such mythical thought,[22] he saw the trends at work better than those who came after and neglected to start with the evidence—or at least with a serious reading of Tocqueville.

There are many proponents of the opposite extreme from the positivistic rationalists. These are the subjectivist historians of ideas who see the actors' ideas as the only independent variable. Even theorists such as Jacob Talmon, for example, seem to be arguing that the ideas of totalitarian democracy in the eighteenth century have caused the growth of our megastates in the twentieth century. It is my purpose in this book to show that there is a far more complex interaction among external and internal factors. Situations have great effects on human constructions of the meanings of the situations, but these constructions of meanings, including the crucial emotional reactions to them, are partially independent of the situation.[23] However, the most important (especially early) situational effects are not what the neoclassical economists have thought, and the most important internal variables are not rational calculations.

The modernist welfare state grew not because of some contradiction in rational calculations inherent in all democracy, or in our changed Western democracies, but first and primarily because a majority of people, especially a majority of politicians and influential educated people, began calculating irrationally. It is this irrationality, this loss of the truly rational understanding of their long-run general welfare that must be explained. Were this not so, even the remnants of our System of Natural Liberty which remain in place would be doomed by "rational calculations" (and the writing of this book would be monumentally irrational). It is quite true that there is always a temptation to pay off voters with the public treasury in any mass democracy, as we see in ancient Athens and Rome and in our own societies today. And this has been *one* important factor in our ratchet-up processes, at least in the later stages, but before outrage over the payoffs and their effects gets very strong. But that was probably even more important in the development of our business welfare state before the New Deal than in the development of our more modernist welfare state since then. It is also quite true, as the rationalistic models of economists commonly assume, that human beings progressively discount the future (see chapters 7 and 8) and that this leads to a weighting of their decisions in favor of the short run and against the long run, so that what is rational for the short run, considered independently of the long run, may be catastrophic for the long run.[24] But this was always the case and, in fact, was far more true in earlier periods when economic uncertainty and risk in the future were greater, which is precisely why progress led interest rates to decline almost steadily until the coming of the modernist welfare state. Even children's tales, such as those lauding the virtues of squirrels and bees, have always assumed that only strategies of action which combine short-run actions and outcomes with the long-run outcomes can be rational. And the prudence of "caring for the morrow"—of looking constantly at how short-run actions affect your long-run outcomes—was pervasive in the homilies of Americans. In fact, the values and practices of all Western nations strongly emphasized saving for the long-run until the welfare states began progressively taxing saving, subsidizing consumption, and increasing long-run uncertainties. The *consumer society* was produced by growing government power. It is only because most economists (as Jacob Viner noted as early as 1939)[25] have themselves been affected by the great myths that they do not see it as a problem to explain how American interest groups could come to "rationally" calculate their welfare in terms of short-run government pay-offs with no discounting of those pay-offs in terms of the fearsome long-run outcomes. Our goal is to explain how such a drastic transformation in supposedly "rational" calculations came about, not to assume away the problem.

We saw in chapters 5 and 6 that the crucial general factor underlying and making possible such limited factors as interest group payoffs in the modernist welfare states was the power of mythical thought which led people to believe that the government could create real value by political, rational-scientific, and bureaucratic action and, thus, that everyone could gain something for little (or nothing) from the modernist megastate. Out of nothing would come everything. By rationalistic schemes, such as the central planning of paper-money expenditures, would come the "free lunch." From the electronic blips of the Federal Reserve creating money would come unlimited new reserves that would ban recessions, multiply consumption, and endlessly multiply the justice for all—the "common welfare."

Most of the trends and policies of our modernist welfare state are not rational by objective standards for anyone but those who use the payoffs of massive swing-voting groups to gain power and get-up-and-out before the too-real Economic Gotterdammerung descends. Normally, the ideal goals these politicians brandish, such as liberty, equality, fraternity, justice, caring and, withal, security, are obviously goals almost everyone seeks, at least within bounds. That is why they are so politically appealing. Sometimes, though it is remarkable how rarely, the general idea of the policy enacted is objectively right, though in these instances the idea is almost always very old rather than some bright discovery by the scientistic experts. But even the best of these general ideas has almost always become a basis for expanding government regulatory bureaucracies that in the long run involve such vast costs—such as risks of systemic catastrophe—as to totally overwhelm any benefits.

A good example is bank deposit insurance. Any monetary and banking system involving credit expansion (fractional reserves) faces a risk of catastrophic deflations caused by panicky runs on the banks. Before the Federal Reserve Act of 1913, American banks commonly stopped these catastrophic deflations by suspending specie payments, refusing to pay gold to the bearers of paper—or even by taking informal bank holidays until the panics stopped. They did this successfully, for example, in 1837 and 1907. But doing so always involved some deflation and, since it was considered immoral and illegal—indeed, a violation of contract law—it made people who could not get their money immediately very angry at banks. Depositor insurance can easily prevent any but the most severe panic. This was obvious to many monetary experts and by 1878, after a depression, was recommended to a House select committee investigating the causes of the depression. It was not enacted until the Great Depression, which, as Milton Friedman and Anna Schwartz argue, was not stopped in time because the Federal Reserve was more bound by law, so could not suspend payment until Roosevelt proclaimed a bank holiday.

This was one of the best laws enacted during the New Deal era. In the 1920s roughly 600 banks failed each year. Since the beginning of the Federal Deposit Insurance Company in 1933, bank failures have averaged only twelve a year until the near catastrophe of 1982. But, instead of merely making banks contractually liable for deposits, or, somewhat worse, making deposit insurance a requirement for incorporating a bank, and letting private insurance firms do the job with optimum efficiency and system-wide security, the FDIC was made part of what became a massive quasi-system of interlocking and overlapping banking regulatory bureaucracies. As usual, the regulators drifted to an undeclared policy of protecting and advancing the interests of those they were supposed to regulate. The now-infamous Regulation-Q milked the savers, subsidized mortgage borrowers and the banks (especially "thrifts"), and decreased incentives to save. When this limit and inflation led in recent years to the massive flight of savers from "thrifts" to higher interest rates ("disintermediation"), the FDIC, other regulators, and finally Congress and the president bailed out the banks. In general, this policy of protecting banks from the consequences of regulation and their own mistakes encouraged them to make more risky loans. As more and more of these went into default, the entire system drifted toward bankruptcy, thus raising the specter of systemic panic which, if it ever comes, might only be prevented by another bank holiday and, possibly, massive infusions of Federal Reserve money, which would then fuel inflation. A system of total security—no risk of failure—in the short run encourages precisely those actions that move the entire system toward bankruptcy. (As noted above, failures are a necessary part of any self-adapting system, thus of the System of Natural Liberty.) In this sense even the FDIC success story becomes in the long run a morality play of the drift of the entire modernist welfare state toward catastrophe. (I examine the fundamental reasons why this happens in chapter 9.) Private insurance companies that provided all the usual rewards (gains) and punishments (costs) for lower risks and higher risks would in the short run and on average have imposed more losses on the bankers making risky loans, thus discouraging the actions that over the long run have endangered all depositors (or all taxpayers and consumers if the Federal government must eventually bail out the entire system with the printing presses). By the 1970s bankers had become so convinced that governments would not allow them to fail that they felt arrogantly safe to lend $300 to $500 billion to shaky collectivist regimes around the world. By 1983 the governments began bailing them out by massive increases in paper reserves, especially those of the International Monetary Fund, which allowed the IMF to loan more money to the de facto bankrupts so they could pay the interest to the banks, thereby allowing the banks to carry those bad loans in their books as assets. By 1988 around 200 American banks were already in various stages of de facto bankruptcy.

While most people do not generally know the details well enough to see the specific forms of these programs as irrational, they do almost always know that some of the basic policies of our welfare states are irrational. They have always known, for example, what it took decades for most experts to "discover," and what many still have not: most welfare in the form of the dole (such as Aid to Families with Dependent Children) breeds dependency, sloth, unemployment, corruption, a huge poverty industry, and ever greater demands. No one has said it better or more sternly denounced the "narcotic" of "relief" than Franklin Delano Roosevelt. How did he know this before the massive studies were done by experts? He used his common sense and recognized the obvious. In his lectures Milton Friedman appeals to this sense of the obvious, rather than to the endless, convoluted, and often misled studies based on official misinformation, by pointing out such things as, "If you teach people to be lazy and you then reward them for being lazy, they will be lazy." And the average citizen guffaws, "Obviously!"

The Mythical Exorcism of Costs and the
Drift into the Modernist Welfare State

Rational calculations by themselves are not the explanation of very much in the growth of the modernist welfare state until its later stages. As we shall see, the crucial change was the decrease in the degree of resistance to the growth of state powers. The crucial question is, what factors led to this decreased resistance? The general answer is that the rise of the general enabling myths of the modernist welfare states, of the three great myths that inflame them in modern societies, and of their many submyths (encouraged by the great myths) led ever more people to see the costs and benefits differently. Once the myths had changed these conceptions of costs and benefits—so that people did not see all of the objective costs and imagined many benefits—then pseudo-"rational" calculations produced very different implications.

But we must remember that there is nothing inherent in the reality of democracies that leads to modernist welfare states. There are certain broadly patterned similarities in most democracies, as in the use of the state treasury to pay off voters, but these can only develop in certain situations, especially those that make it look as if the payoffs are really "free" (that is, have no, or fewer, costs for the taxpayers). This is where the great myths of modernism, rationalism, and millennialism and the many lesser myths springing from or supported by them—such as the "money illusions" of inflationary policies and Keynesian myths and political deception—all become so important.[26] They inflame greed and encourage mythical, utopian expectations that greatly reduce the general resistance to the growth of state powers even when the individual knows in general that the growth in state powers is dangerous. In the ancient world inflation was also commonly used, but the Athenian welfare state exploded only when Pericles used the money paid to Athens by the Delian League to pay off his voters; and the Roman welfare state exploded only when foreign conquests gave the rulers foreign wealth to pay off the plebeians. The normal connection between benefits and costs was literally severed in the beginning. By the time the costs were directly borne by citizens, dependency was so great the rulers feared revolt if they tried to de-ratchet the state payoffs.

Most people do not normally rationally relate the many specific (situational) policies of our welfare states to the general idea of the welfare state; nor do they normally go rationally from their general ideas to the specific programs. We saw in chapter 4 that even the most flaming laissez-faire idealists in the nineteenth century often voted for specific, limited programs ("special cases" or "exceptions") that taken together over the long run undermined the very foundations of the libertarian welfare federation. *The modernist* welfare state was above all an unrecognized and unintended—and increasingly hated—consequence of a social drift process produced by piecemeal decisions made under the influence of the increasingly powerful great myths. The goals, such as ending poverty or preventing the "exploitation" of child labor, and so on, almost always sound good in themselves to most people. They always have. In fact, since early Americans were more staunchly Christian, more antimaterialistic, and more caring, and even commonly tithed themselves voluntarily for local poor relief programs, most of those programs sounded even better to them than to us. But what did not sound good were all of the long-run costs—especially all the grave dangers of government power the programs would entail and the immorality of the infringements on others' liberty they would entail.

As the great myths replaced these earlier commonsense ideas and morals, resistance to the adoption of the programs declined in direct proportion. *The myths hid the costs, so what always seemed good in itself became an unalloyed good, a good with no (or far less) cost.* The average mechanic voting for Andrew Jackson liked the idea of having more money, but when he came to see the cost of inflation—a decreasing loaf—he was against paper money unsecured by gold or silver. If you believe, as popular interpretations of Keynes put it, that you can have more and more of a loaf by "pumping up consumption" with the money-printing presses, without ever producing inflation (because that is supposedly due to businesspeople rigging prices) or a decreased loaf, then the only rational thing is to get the biggest and fastest money presses possible. Keynes, of course, did not believe in the *pop-Keynesianism* that came to dominate mass-mediated economics and economic politics. He only provided the mantle of scientific respectability for deficit "stimuli" which inflamed pop-Keynesians.

Carl Becker argued that "Locke. . .made it possible for the eighteenth century to believe what it wanted to believe,"[27] by which he meant that Locke provided a rationale, a system of largely mythical beliefs, but based on vital facts, which extended the powerful ideas of Newtonian mechanics to the political realm in such a way as to delegitimize monarchy and Church and to legitimize the growing dominance of the nonaristocratic but propertied and educated. His theory of "natural laws" and "natural rights" mythically exploded the myths of divine right and of Hobbes's Leviathan state. In the same way, Keynes and other scientistic and rationalistic experts crafted the myths which, by inspiring mythical blindness to long-run economic and political consequences, tempted people to believe what their growing millennial greed already tempted them to believe and, thereby, eroded the System of Natural Liberty. Unfortunately, the long-run costs were not myths.

Now that we have that modernist welfare state, even people who hate it passionately and see its dangers, but who are still affected by those myths, cannot normally see that the only way to have less of the state powers is to have less. Making the rational, systematic connections between the specifics and the general is a very difficult and creative task that is greatly hindered or prevented by the lingering, but declining conviction the myths are true. Once the myths are mistaken for reality, then and only then do pseudo-rational calculations of benefits from government programs lead to a massive demand for them.

Notes

1. Harold Wilensky, *The Welfare State and Equality* (Berkeley: University of California Press, 1975).
2. Hugh Trevor-Roper, *The European Witch Craze* (New York: Harper and Row, 1969), p. 3.
3. Robert Higgs, *Crisis and Leviathan* (New York: Oxford University Press, 1987).
4. See chapter 2 and following for treatment of the *contemporary versions* of this Marxist idea which have been incorporated into neoliberal theories.
5. Sven Rydenfelt, "Sweden's Meidner Plan for Industrial Takeover," *The Wall Street Journal*, editorial page, December 23, 1981. See also his book *A Pattern for Failure* (New York: Harcourt, Brace, 1985).
6. See chapter 2 and following.
7. John Hicks, *The Crisis in Keynesian Economics* (Oxford: Basil Blackwell, 1974).
8. Joseph Schumpeter, *Capitalism, Socialism and Democracy* (New York: Harper and Bros., 1942).
9. John Kenneth Galbraith, *The New Industrial State* (Boston: Houghton Mifflin, 1967).
10. Aaron Wildavsky, *How to Limit Government Spending* (Berkeley: University of California Press, 1980).
11. David Friedman, "Review of *How to Limit Government Spending*," *Reason Magazine*, February 1982, p. 45.
12. Wilensky, *The Welfare State and Equality*.
13. Melvyn B. Krauss, "Supply-Side Policies Benefit the Third World's Poor," *The Wall Street Journal*, December 23, 1981, editorial pages.
14. Thomas Sowell, *Ethnic America* (New York: Basic Books, 1981), especially pp. 81, 144, and 168.
15. James Payne, "Voters aren't so Greedy after All," *Fortune*, August 18, 1986, p. 91.
16. J. H. Birnbaum and A. S. Murray, *Showdown at Gucci Gulch: Lawmakers, Lobbyists, and the Unlikely Triumph of Tax Reform* (New York: Random House, 1987).
17. Morris Janowitz, *Social Control of the Welfare State* (New York: Elsevier, 1976).
18. Samuel H. Beer, *Britain against Itself: The Political Contradictions of Collectivism* (New York: W. W. Norton, 1982). The quote is from *The Economist*, October 9, 1982, p. 100.

19. Mancur Olson, *The Rise and Decline of Nations* (New Haven: Yale University Press, 1982).
20. Nick Eberstadt, "Economics and the 'Big Picture,'" *The Public Interest*, no. 71, Spring 1983, pp. 129–30.
21. Unfortunately, Tocqueville's ideas are complex, subtle, and not highly systematized. The main ideas are found in *Democracy in America* (Garden City, NY: Anchor Books, 1969), vol. 1, part II, chs. 7–9, and vol. 2, part IV, chs. 1–7.
22. As the body and references of this book show in many places, many economists, especially very empirical ones (like Friedrich Hayek, Ludwig Mises, Peter Drucker, and Milton Friedman), have certainly seen the general importance of mythical thought in this great systemic drift.
23. Most of my earlier works have dealt with the construction of social meanings. See, especially, *The Social Meanings of Suicide* (Princeton: Princeton University Press, 1967); *Deviance and Respectability* (New York: Basic Books, 1970); *American Social Order* (New York: Free Press, 1971); *Understanding Everyday Life* (Chicago: Aldine, 1970); and (edited with John M. Johnson) *Existential Sociology* (Cambridge: Cambridge University Press, 1977).
24. Jacob Viner, "The Short View and the Long in Economic Policy," in *The Long View and the Short* (Glencoe, IL: The Free Press, 1958).
25. Ibid.
26. James Buchanan and Richard Wagner, *Democracy in Deficit* (New York: Academic Press, 1977), have presented the evidence showing how Keynesianism decreased the recognition of the costs of welfare state programs. I agree, but am trying to show that Keynesian ideas always were rejected before in our federal (not state) policies and were accepted only because the Great Myths had already changed basic ways of thinking.
27. Carl Becker, *The Declaration of Independence* (New York: Knopf, 1942, rpr. 1960), p. 57.

Appendix IV

Emanationist Rationalism and the Rise of Secular Millennialism

Emanationist rationalism has its ancient roots in Egyptian sects, Zoroastrianism, gnosticism, the Wisdom literature, the Bible, the Jewish Kaballah, Manichaeism, Neoplatonist Rationalism, and Augustinianism. Since the Neoplatonic Augustinians, most Western secular emanationists have seen reason, especially as embodied in the abstract symbols of mathematics, as the Godhead, or at least the emanation—revelation—of the Godhead in the material world.[1] The basic idea of emanationism is that the world perceived by the senses is largely an illusion produced by the corruption of material or matter. The ultimate reality of all is the One (Prime Symbol) or Godhead that is the apex from which all being emanates, as a light emanates outward in an ever wider wave from a prime source, a single bright point, to light the world. Some of these rays emanated as far as the shores of the new American nation, most literally through the lodges of Rosicrucians and Freemasons. To this day the American dollar retains the Great Seal of the United States with its soaring hope, "E pluribus unum" ("Out of many, one,") and an Egyptian pyramid with one great eye—the Sun God?—from which emanates the light of the world, with the mottos, "Annuit Coeptis" ("He has favored our undertakings") above and "Novus ordo seclorum" ("A new order of the ages") below.[2] The natural order had godly and, to some, emanationist roots. This emanationism reached its zenith in transcendentalism. It has waned as an independent movement, but is still very alive in our myths of rationalism scientism.

There was always a dualistic strain in emanationist thought in the West. The One Godhead, the One Apex from which all the complex and confusing diversity of the world of senses emanated, was the totally pure. Everything else was less pure, more evil, and against the one God, in proportion to its distance away from this monolithic Apex. (The Great Chain of Being was totally Neoplatonic, descending from the One Good God to the lesser multitudes.) Augustine and the Church defeated the dualism of the Manichaens, but it always remained an inherent undercurrent (a Jungian "shadow") with great appeal to Christians to explain the obvious gradations of evil in the world. (Augustine himself had been a Manichaen for nine years before he found Plotinus's Neoplatonic emanationism as a way out.[3] That way out normally consists of seeing the emanations as "lesser goods," but what is a lesser good if not a greater evil?) Whenever the evils of the world seem great, the natural tendency of human beings is to purify themselves and the world to escape the evil. Purification rituals and expiation rituals are universal when human beings face great threats. In the West Christian dualism had greatly increased this tendency. Christians and Jews faced with great threats tend to revert to this dualism and try to eradicate, or purify, the evil many to let the pure light of the One Good shine forth and save the world.[4] The Albigensians and Cathari reverted to the Manichaen, dualistic emanationism with its millennial goal of purifying the world and, thereby, letting in the light of God. (They had a direct link through the Bogomils with the original Manichaeans.) The sources on these "heresies" were largely destroyed by the Church, so it is not clear whether any of them expected to create a heaven on earth by transforming the worldly order through a violent purging of evil. However, it is clear that this was the goal of some of the extreme Puritan revolutionaries at Munster and among the Diggers in the English Civil War. Even the less extreme Puritans showed an obvious willingness to use total methods to purify the world to let in the One Good of all Being, as we see in Cromwell. Whenever things have gone very well, Western people have the natural human tendency to be optimistic (and, thus, to feel pride), but multiplied by their millennial expectations of an imminent heaven on earth.

The wondrous medieval conquests of free economic activity, free technology, and free science unleashed a secular vertigo throughout Europe among intellectuals and those affected by them. As Jean Gimpel[5] has argued, the great economic and technological advances slowly gained momentum from the tenth to fourteenth centuries. These stalled in the fourteenth and fifteenth centuries (largely because of the tremendous growth of state and church bureaucracy[6]), then rapidly gained momentum and by the eighteenth ignited a soaring *psychological dynamism*. The ancient dream of "natural magic," that of penetrating the "secret of nature" and returning with the "light" of absolute knowledge that would give the discoverers the power to get anything they wished, now seemed within easy reach. George Boas[7] has shown that from at least the twelfth century the idea of an earthly paradise became popular. The first tales of the earthly paradise were primitivistic tales of long ago and away, but prophecies of a far-away, future paradise on earth began as early as the twelfth century with Joachim of Florus, who even preached that a saintly elite of common people would be necessary to overcome the evil forces of the Church hierarchy blocking the way to the earthly millennium. Over the centuries the dreams, tales, and prophecies came to seem more possible, more realistic, more immediate and, thus, far more compelling to action. There are traces of millennial communism even in the revolutionary proclamations of John Ball in fourteenth-century England. The great discoveries of the new world and of many new parts of the only vaguely known worlds of Africa and the East quickly led to ecstatic explosions of wondrous expectations, even of turning the next bend and discovering the earthly paradise itself.[8] (In an age when some scientists, such as Robert Oppenheimer, have dreaded their discoveries were opening the portals of mind onto the darkness of Satanic death, it may be hard to remember the vast excitement which Neoplatonic theological magicians, even Isaac Newton late in the seventeenth century, felt as they probed the tiniest and most distant crevices of nature in search of the light.) Sir Thomas More's *Utopia*, published only twenty four years after Columbus's first voyage, was directly inspired by the great discoveries. It was presented as an ideal, a "land nowhere," but it has the nearly real feel of all waking dreams—myths—and was only the first of a huge outpouring of "fictions" that have enflamed political imagination and movements ever since.[9] For several centuries Western peoples throbbed with the very real hopes of discovering El Dorado, the elixir of eternal life, and God, and set sail to do so, just as later utopians would set sail on political pilgrimages to Russia, China, and Cuba to make the dreams real.

The soaring optimism of the natural magicians united with the Christian millennial vision to give birth to the fiery vision of using the power of reason to sweep away the delusions of the world, to unlock the secret of nature, and by this act to *see* the ultimate One and usher in a heaven on this earth, a secular millennium. This rationalistic secularization of the fiery faith of the mystic was already partially revealed in the work of Nicholas of Cusa in the fifteenth century. Nicholas's Neoplatonic rationalism and his quest for the secrets of nature were restrained by his primary commitment to Christian faith and Churchly hierarchy. But in the next century his disciple, Giordano Bruno, cast aside all restraints on rationalism, the quest for the secret of nature, and the mystical ecstasy.[10] It is in Bruno that we first see the mystical ecstasy springing from the secularized rationalism (of natural magic) and revolutionary millennialism of our most extreme modernist collectivists. It was Bruno, inspired by the great discoveries of new worlds, who first dreamed of real new worlds beyond our earth. The growing explosion of wealth resulting from economic freedom and scientific-technological freedom turned millennialism increasingly toward soaring lust for a materialistic heaven on earth (a universal El Dorado) far more than Bruno envisioned, but Bruno is the first known truly modernist revolutionary. He was a direct source and inspiration for the seventeenth and eighteenth century rationalist-scientistic millennialists who in turn inspired Marx and all of the others.[11]

The revolutionary success of Newtonian mechanics and astronomy in overturning the ancient Aristotelian and Ptolemaic sciences ignited a far more widespread conflagration of soaring optimism in the power of reason. The literal apotheosis of reason and science reached its zenith in France, where even Voltaire worshipped figuratively at the shrine of Newton and where the Goddess of Reason was worshipped literally by millions during the Revolution. But the English-speaking world emphasized the empiricism of science, while the French emphasized the rational theorizing and moved increasingly toward rationalism (see chapter 4). When these new forms of thought were applied to the political realm, as Talmon says, the English-speaking theorists emphasized empiricism even more. Americans became the extreme pragmatists long before Charles Peirce codified this taken-for-granted American tendency into an epistemology.[12] This pragmatic attitude actually sprang from the synthesis of the new rationalism with the moderate conservative (Whig and Puritan) assumption that there are some grave limitations to our rational knowledge. One of the earliest and most important arguments in *The Federalist* is that the passions aroused by multifarious factions easily lead people to deceive themselves (in mythical thinking, as we shall see) about their own motives and, thereby, fall into wars, if they are not constrained by the common "umpire" of a federation.[13] Certainly the American constitutionalists were inspired with hope for their great experiment in natural liberty. But they offered no promises of a common millennium just around the corner (perhaps in part because they knew there was a vast, dark, and dangerous wilderness just around the corner). Above all, rather than creating an all-powerful government that could be the efficient tool of a godly man of reason who would rationally plan a millennium of common welfare, they did the exact opposite.

The French, on the other hand, were quickly swept away by the most impassioned millennial yearnings for a heaven on earth to be enjoyed equally by all. From the very beginning, the great tidal wave of enflamed theorizing that led to Rousseau and his revolutionary disciples embraced extremely rationalistic plans to unlock the "secret" of natural liberty and plan universal happiness in mathematical scientific ways that would ban all chance factors.[14] The French Enlightenment sprang overwhelmingly from the same common emotional source, the soaring hope born of the great triumphs of science, especially of Cartesian and Newtonian science, and from Locke's philosophy of the Natural System which swept away both the sacred ideas of the Church and the innate and immutable ideas of the conservatives. However, with some important exceptions (such as Diderot's antimathematical ideas and Voltaire's works on history[15]), the climate of opinion in France was increasingly pervaded by the dualistic and emanationist rationalism (see below) of Descartes, Malebranche, and Spinoza (and Leibnitz by the time of the revolution). Adam Smith's early work, including *The Moral Sentiments*, was pervaded by the deistic idea that there is a godly natural order, including a first principle that moves and orders the world of sense appearances toward an ultimate goal of goodness (progress), but by the time he wrote *The Wealth of Nations* the natural order (the "invisible hand") was partly transformed into the secular natural order that later economists called the shifting general equilibrium.[16] (Hume's devastating critique of natural religion[17] was worked out around the same time, though published only posthumously in 1779. This may well have influenced his friend, Adam Smith, but this secularization of social thought was a general trend in the English-speaking world.) The French social thinkers and growing legions of popularizers turned in the opposite direction toward the synthesis of the rationalist and deistic emanationism of Bruno, Descartes, Malebranche, and Spinoza.

Cartesian deistic rationalism was the prime source of French rationalism and long remained the great impetus away from the empiricism so obvious in such earlier French thinkers as Montaigne and, later, Montesquieu.[18] Though ostensibly in the service of empirical knowledge, Descartes's social thought and his general philosophy were not pervaded by any of the spirit of naturalistic observations which seeks to know and understand nature on its own terms. Even his method of systematic doubt was intended from the first to find that one ultimate truth, the apex of knowledge upon which his reason could found all certain knowledge and, thereby, turn the whole world. It comes as less than a surprise to find that the apex revealed to reason, and the one guarantor of the truth of reason, is God. It is more surprising that he reverted so completely to the pre-Augustinian dualistic emanationism, but not to find that mind, the godly substance, is independent of inferior (evil?) matter. Malebranche found no great difficulty in synthesizing Cartesian rationalism with the Augustinian and scholastic thought of the Church. Reason (logos) and God are identical: thus, extreme rationalism is canonized and is synthesized with the Neoplatonic emanationism of Augustine. At roughly the same time, Spinoza was extending Descartes's rationalism into a mathematically deductive, absolutely deterministic system of universal ethics and synthesizing this with the magical emanationism of the ancient Kaballah. Spinoza went beyond Descartes in his rationalistic emanationism to produce a universal mathematical plan for ethics and, thence, all practical political action to "perfect human nature" and usher in an age of godly perfection. In Spinoza's system absolute determinism, even in people's passions and thoughts, emanated from God as the primal cause of all; freedom consists only in acting out this universal plan of necessity. This idea had a profound and direct impact on the French philosophers and even more on later revolutionary totalitarians.[19]

The so-called Renaissance was an age of vast, centralized bureaucratic power and growing bureaucratic corruption. Though it is still popularly thought of as "the age of declining and corrupt feudalism," the feudal lords were thoroughly vanquished and co-opted by the increasingly "absolutist," "benevolent," and bureaucratic monarchs of these Renaissance Welfare States.[20] In addition, the vast and corrupt Church bureaucracy so loathed in the fourteenth and fifteenth centuries was reformed under the threat of the Reformation only to become the more efficiently repressive and Inquisitorial bureaucracy of the Counter-Reformation Church in the Catholic nations of the sixteenth to eighteenth centuries. In France the absolute monarchs and their vast, corrupt bureaucracy rationally planned the economy to produce the common welfare, but lurched, seemingly inevitably and against all reason, into ever-deeper debt and toward bankruptcy (see chapter 4). This benevolent absolutism was united with the even more benevolent absolutism of the Church to produce a vast and seemingly endless "infamy" that drove even moderate men like Voltaire to exasperated extremes. Commerce, agriculture, technology, and science were exploding in England and the Netherlands, and developing in France in spite of the deadening inertia and taxation of the bureaucracies, but France, by far the biggest, most populous, and richly endowed nation of Europe, was being greatly outdistanced and defeated by her small rivals around the world. It was this *pressure-cooker effect*, the threatening suffocation of the burgeoning hopes triggered by very real progress, that produced the soaring, ever more irrational rationalistic millennialism among the intellectuals and even many businesspeople. Descartes, a man of vast patience and detailed consideration of facts of natural observation in his scientific works, denounced the entire realm of historical facts about society and banished them to the flames. He proclaimed everyone capable of seeing the whole and simple truth about the social realm by the exercise of reason alone. He launched a crusade of "intellectual terrorism" against all the casuistry and sophistry of the bureaucratic absolutists which became a Holy War against all empirical evidence about society.[21] While the British and Americans were ransacking history and everyday observations to find evidence, precedents, dangers, and possibilities of economic and political life, the French intellectuals turned inward. Where the British and Americans found facts supporting hope, but hedged in by all the dangers of self-deceiving myths inspired by such passions as the proud lust for power, the French were finding their own millennial dreams of a heaven on earth ushered in by the fiery use of reason. The difference between the two streams of thought is at the extreme in their different ideas of the "general welfare" and the "common welfare."

The philosophes had a deep and sincere commitment to act for the common welfare. They longed for a heaven on earth for Everyman and the most idealistic of them, men such as Robespierre and Saint-Just, were ascetics willing to suffer terribly and even die to usher in that secular millennium for Everyman. Their early works, such as Morelly's *Code de la nature* in 1755, showed some of the dualistic perspective common to emanationism, but it was only in the polarizing centrifuge of civil and foreign war that their dualistic visions of Good and Evil reached the extreme incarnate in the Great Terror that would cleanse the world of Evil and usher in the millennium. Remarkably enough, it was the very monotheism of the earlier rationalistic emanationists (at the extreme in Malebranche and Spinoza) which encouraged the extreme dualism of the Terrorists. They believed the human mind emanates from God and can, by the exercise of pure reason, reveal the necessary and one Good, the system of natural law which man must obey in action to be free. The necessary and one Good was necessarily the common welfare of all humanity. They thought anyone *can* ascend to this rational grasp of God's natural law and the early presumption was that everyone *would* so ascend. But they were always at least vaguely aware that some people, perhaps many, might resist this necessary and one Good. These people were either willfully resisting what was obviously Good to any rational person or were deceived by their evil passions. (As the Jacobins of Limoges said, "Is it not to be in reality the friend of one's brothers to force them, in a manner of speaking, to accept the cup of salvation which is offered them in the name of reason and humanity?") Rousseau was even led to argue explicitly that a majority of voters could be completely wrong in grasping this common welfare (the "conscience collective").[22] When the Revolution came, enemies of the necessary, natural law arose on all sides and, most horrifying and incomprehensible of all, within the ranks of the rational diviners themselves. Sectarian factionalism grew rapidly, just as it does in all groups committed to absolutist forms of thought and action because all compromise is seen as evil. And with it the ancient Manichaean dualism grew: the erstwhile monotheists rediscovered the ancient powers of Satan and moved with absolutist conviction to "erase the infamy." Later revolutionaries made this Manichaean dualism a basic part of their myth of heroes serving the common welfare, from which sprang today's monolithic parties and totalitarian welfare states.

Notes

1. Eric Voegelin has dealt with this whole stream of thought under the name of gnosticism. See Eric Voegelin, *The New Science of Politics* (Chicago: University of Chicago Press, 1952).

2. See Forest MacDonald, *Novus Ordo Seclorum: The Intellectual Origins of the Constitution* (Lawrence, KS: University Press of Kansas, 1985).

3. See Peter Brown, *Augustine of Hippo* (New York: Dorset Press, 1986).

4. I have argued in *Deviance and Respectability* (New York: Basic Books, 1970) that dualism is inherent in the human moral sense. It is at an extreme in the stigmatization of evil.

5. Jean Gimpel, *The Medieval Machine* (Harmondsworth, England: Penguin Books, 1976).

6. My explanation of ultimate causes is quite different from Gimpel's. Ibid.

7. George Boas, *Essays on Primitivism and Related Ideas in the Middle Ages* (New York: Octagon Books, 1966).

8. The literature on the "earthly paradise" is immense. See, for example, G. Arciniegas, *America In Europe* (San Diego: Harcourt Brace, 1986).

9. See Frank E. Manuel and Fritzie Manuel, *Utopian Thought in the Western World* (Cambridge, MA: Harvard University Press, 1975).

10. See Dorothea Waley Singer, *Giordano Bruno* (New York: Henry Schuman, 1950).

11. The direct links between Giordano and nineteenth-century thinkers like Schiller and Hegal are presented in Singer, *Giordano Bruno*.

12. American empiricism and practicality in social thinking have been emphasized from Tocqueville (*Democracy in America* [Garden City, NY: Doubleday Anchor, 1969]) to Daniel Boorstin (*The Americans* [New York: Random House, 1965]).

13. *The Federalist* (New York: The Modern Library, no date).

14. See Jacob Talmon, *The Origins of Totalitarian Democracy* (London: Secker and Warburg, 1955).

15. Carl Becker has argued that these were not really exceptions, that they really *used* history and other seeming empiricism to illustrate their preconceptions, very much in the way Marxists and other "schoolmen" do today. See *The Heavenly City of the Eighteenth-Century Philosophers* (New Haven: Yale University Press, 1932), especially pp. 71–118.

16. See Jacob Viner, *The Long View and the Short* (Glencoe, IL: The Free Press, 1958).

17. David Hume, *Dialogues Concerning Natural Religion*, edited and introduced by Henry Aiken (New York: Hafner, 1948).

18. It is important to note that Montesquieu had the greatest effect on American constitutionalists. He was the most empirical of the philosophes, the least rationalistic, ideological, and millennial, a point accepted even by Becker (in *The Heavenly City of the Philosophers*).

19. While the works of Spinoza clearly had powerful direct impacts on the philosophes, I suspect they were even more important later through their impact on Germanic Romantic thought, which James Billington has shown entered France during the revolution through Strasbourg. (See his work *Fire in the Minds of Men* [New York: Basic Books, 1980].) He notes as well the striking fact that a remarkably high percentage of the most "idealistic"—dualistic emanationist—

leaders of the revolution came from Piccardy. It is possible Piccardy was one of those rural regions harboring a secret Manichaean tradition, which Hugh Trevor-Roper (*The European Witch Craze of the Sixteenth and Seventeenth Centuries* [New York: Harper Torchbooks, 1969]) has argued existed widely throughout Europe. Piccardy could be a test case for the arguments of both Trevor-Roper and Voegelin.

20. See Hugh Trevor-Roper's sweeping argument in "The Renaissance Welfare States" in *The European Witch Craze of the Sixteenth and Seventeenth Centuries*.

21. Robert Nisbet's strong portrait of the "two Descartes" (*History of the Idea of Progress* [New York: Basic Books, 1980], pp. 115–17) seems justified.

22. Talmon, *The Origins of Totalitarian Democracy*.

Index

504   Myth of the Welfare State